JUDAH AND TAMAR (GENESIS 38)
IN ANCIENT JEWISH EXEGESIS

SUPPLEMENTS

TO THE

JOURNAL FOR THE STUDY OF JUDAISM

Formerly Studia Post-Biblica

Editor

JOHN J. COLLINS

The Divinity School, University of Chicago

Associate Editor

FLORENTINO GARCÍA MARTÍNEZ

Qumran Institute, University of Groningen

VOLUME 51

JUDAH AND TAMAR (GENESIS 38) IN ANCIENT JEWISH EXEGESIS

Studies in Literary Form and Hermeneutics

BY

ESTHER MARIE MENN

BRILL
LEIDEN · NEW YORK · KÖLN
1997

This book is printed on acid-free paper.

Library of Congress Cataloging-in-Publication Data

Menn, Esther Marie.
   Judah and Tamar (Genesis 38) in ancient Jewish exegesis : studies
in literary form and hermeneutics / by Esther Marie Menn.
   p.   cm. — (Supplements to the journal for the study of
Judaism, ISSN 1384-1261 ; v. 51)
   Includes bibliographical references and index.
   ISBN 9004106308 (cloth : alk. paper)
   1. Bible.   O.T.   Genesis XXXVIII—Commentaries.   2. Judah
(Biblical figure)   3. Tamar (Biblical figure)   4. Bible.   O.T.
Genesis XXXVIII—Criticism, interpretation, etc., Jewish.
5. Testament of Judah—Criticism, interpretation, etc.   6. Bible.
O.T. Genesis XXXVIII.   Aramic—Versions—Targum Yerushalmi.
7. Midrash rabbah.   Genesis LXXXV—Criticism, interpretation, etc.
I. Title.   II. Series.
BS1235.3.M46   1997
222'.1106—dc21   97–5218
                                                            CIP
                                                            r97

Die Deutsche Bibliothek – CIP-Einheitsaufnahme

Menn, Esther Marie:
Judah and Tamar (Genesis 38) in ancient Jewish exegesis : studies in
literary form and hermeneutics / by Esther Marie Menn. - Leiden ;
New York ; Köln : Brill, 1997
   (Supplements to the journal for the study of judaism ; Vol. 51)
   Zugl.: Chicago, Univ., Diss.
   ISBN 90-04-10630-8 Gewebe
[Journal for the study of judaism / Supplements]
Supplements to the journal for the study of judaism. Supplements. -
Leiden ; New York ; Köln : Brill
   Früher Schriftenreihe
   Bis Vol. 48 (1995) u.d.T.: Studia post-biblica
Vol. 51. Menn, Esther Marie: Judah and Tamar (Genesis 38) in ancient
Jewish exegesis. - 1997

ISSN 1384-1261
ISBN 90 04 10630 8

PRINTED IN THE NETHERLANDS

FOR BRUCE

CONTENTS

viii CONTENTS

LIST OF ABBREVIATIONS

Abbreviations of the names of biblical books follow the conventions listed in "Instructions for Contributors," *JBL* 107 (1988) 584.

Ag.Ap.	Josephus, *Against Apion*
'Ag.Ber.	*'Aggadat Berešit*
'Abod.Zar.	*'Aboda Zara*
AJSL	*American Journal of Semitic Languages and Literature*
ANET	James B. Pritchard, ed., *Ancient Near Eastern Texts Relating to the Old Testament*
Ant.	Josephus, *Jewish Antiquities*
2 Apoc.Bar.	*2 (Syriac Apocalypse of) Baruch*
b.	Babylonian Talmud
B.Bat.	*Baba Batra*
B.Meṣ.	*Baba Meṣi'a*
B.Qam.	*Baba Qamma*
BASOR	*Bulletin of the American Schools of Oriental Research*
BDB	Francis Brown, S. R. Driver, and Charles A. Briggs, *Hebrew and English Lexicon of the Old Testament*
Ber.	*Berakot*
Bib.Ant.	Pseudo-Philo, *Biblical Antiquities*
BJRL	*Bulletin of the John Rylands University Library of Manchester*
BTB	*Biblical Theology Bulletin*
Cant.Rab.	*Song of Songs Rabba*
CBQ	*Catholic Biblical Quarterly*
Deut.Rab.	*Deuteronomy Rabba*
Eccl.Rab.	*Ecclesiastes Rabba*
Exod.Rab.	*Exodus Rabba*
FJB	*Frankfurter Judaistische Beiträge*
frg(s).	fragment(s)
Frg.Tg.	*Fragmentary Targum*
Gen.Rab.	*Genesis Rabba*
Gnz.Tgs.	Geniza Targums
HSCP	*Harvard Studies in Comparative Literature*

HTR	*Harvard Theological Review*
HUCA	*Hebrew Union College Annual*
IDB	G. A. Buttrick, ed., *The Interpreter's Dictionary of the Bible*
IDBSup	Supplementary Volume to *IDB*
JAAR	*Journal of the American Academy of Religion*
JAOS	*Journal of the American Oriental Society*
JBL	*Journal of Biblical Literature*
JJS	*Journal of Jewish Studies*
JQR	*Jewish Quarterly Review*
JR	*Journal of Religion*
JSJ	*Journal for the Study of Judaism in the Persian, Hellenistic and Roman Period*
JSOT	*Journal for the Study of the Old Testament*
Jub.	*Jubilees*
Ketub.	*Ketubot*
Lev.Rab.	*Leviticus Rabba*
LIMC	*Lexicon Iconographicum Mythologiae Classicae*
LXX	Septuagint
m.	Mishna
Mak.	*Makkot*
Meg.	*Megilla*
Mek.	*Mekilta de Rabbi Ishmael*
MGWJ	*Monatsschrift für Geschichte und Wissenschaft des Judentums*
Midr.	*Midraš*
MS	manuscript
MSS	manuscripts
MT	Masoretic Text
n(n).	note(s)
Ned.	*Nedarim*
NedTTs	*Nederlands theologisch tijdschrift*
NovTSup	Novum Testamentum, Supplements
NTS	*New Testament Studies*
Num.Rab.	*Numbers Rabba*
NV	New Version
Or	*Orientalia* (Rome)
Pesaḥ.	*Pesaḥim*
Pesiq.R.	*Pesiqta Rabbati*

Pesiq.Rab.Kah.	*Pesiqta de Rab Kahana*
Pirqe R.El.	*Pirqe Rabbi Eliezer*
Qidd.	*Qiddušin*
R.	Rabbi
RB	*Revue biblique*
RevQ	*Revue de Qumran*
Roš Haš.	*Roš Haššana*
Ruth Rab.	*Ruth Rabba*
Sanh.	Sanhedrin
SBL	Society of Biblical Literature
Šabb.	*Šabbat*
SJOT	*Scandinavian Journal of the Old Testament*
t.	Tosepta
Theodor/Albeck	J. Theodor and C. Albeck, *Midraš Berešit Rabba*
T.A.	*Testament of Asher*
Ta'an.	*Ta'anit*
Tanh.	*Tanhuma*
T.B.	*Testament of Benjamin*
T.D.	*Testament of Dan*
T.G.	*Testament of Gad*
Tg.Neof.	*Targum Neofiti 1*
Tg.Onq.	*Targum Onqelos*
Tg.Ps.-J.	*Targum Pseudo-Jonathan*
Testaments	*Testaments of the Twelve Patriarchs*
T.I.	*Testament of Issachar*
T.Jud.	*Testament of Judah*
T.Jos.	*Testament of Joseph*
T.L.	*Testament of Levi*
T.N.	*Testament of Naphtali*
T.R.	*Testament of Reuben*
T.S.	*Testament of Simeon*
T.Z.	*Testament of Zebulun*
Vg	Vulgate
VT	*Vetus Testamentum*
VTSup	Vetus Testamentum, Supplements
v(v).	verse(s)
WCJS	*World Congress of Jewish Studies*
y.	Jerusalem Talmud
Yad.	*Yadayim*

Yal.	*Yalquṭ*
Yebam.	*Yebamot*
ZAW	*Zeitschrift für die alttestamentliche Wissenschaft*
Zebaḥ.	*Zebaḥim*
ZNW	*Zeitschrift für die neutestamentliche Wissenschaft*

ACKNOWLEDGMENTS

This book is a revision of my doctoral dissertation, so primary thanks go to my advisor at The University of Chicago Divinity School, Michael Fishbane. Working with him during my final years as a graduate student decisively shaped my perspectives on biblical literature and midrash, and his good council and steady encouragement saw this particular project to completion. I also extend heartfelt thanks to the other members of my committee, John J. Collins and Wendy Doniger, for their careful reading and helpful suggestions. Many other people as well read chapters or smaller sections, including a dissertation reading group composed of Benjamin Sommer, Colleen Stamos, and Anthony Tomasino; Arthur J. Droge and Michael Wise, also at The University of Chicago; and Larry D. Bouchard, David P. Kovaks, Judith L. Kovaks, and Michael L. Satlow, at the University of Virginia. On two separate occasions, participants in The University of Chicago Jewish Studies Workshop responded to presentations of chapter drafts. Those listed above and the many others with whom I discussed this project more informally have my deepest gratitude. I also take this opportunity to recognize Jon D. Levenson, who served as my graduate advisor while I was doing course work at The University of Chicago, and to thank him for introducing me to rabbinic commentary on biblical texts.

Jennifer Geddes, Mari Schindele, and Lynn Tryggestad deserve special recognition for their conscientious and supportive editorial assistance at different stages in the emergence of the manuscript. Financial assistance from the University of Virginia Small Grants Committee, A. James Arnold and Marita P. McClymonds, Chairs, and from the University of Virginia Department of Religious Studies, Harry Y. Gamble, Jr., Chair, helped defray copy-editing expenses. I gratefully acknowledge John Collins yet a second time in his role as series editor, and I commend Hans van der Meij, Mattie Kuiper, Pim Rietbroek, and others at Brill for attending to the details of publication.

On a more personal level, I thank the Bertsche, Mulholland, and Erickson families for regularly welcoming our daughter Kaia into their homes, so that I could concentrate on research and writing. Kaia herself helped me maintain a proper attitude towards the academic world, and her contagious joy often refreshed me and inspired me to persist. I also thank my parents, Myrtle Vassberg and Robert Llewellyn Blevins, Jr., and my parents-in-law, Carol Jane and W. Robert Anderson, for their confidence in me. I owe most, though, to my husband, Bruce K. Tammen, who encouraged and supported me in every way imaginable. As an expression of appreciation, I dedicate this book to him.

ONE BIBLICAL NARRATIVE, MANY POST-BIBLICAL MEANINGS: JUDAH AND TAMAR (GENESIS 38) IN ANCIENT JEWISH EXEGESIS

> There is no reading worthy of being communicated to another unless
> it deviates to break form, twists the lines to find a shelter, and so
> makes a meaning through the shattering of belated vessels.[1]

Biblical narrative has a dynamic interpretive life. The authors of the
wonderful and often perplexing stories in the Bible no doubt had
their own intentions, but as these stories moved forward into new
historical and cultural settings they acquired additional layers of
significance. This book explores how new meanings emerge through
encounters between ancient texts and later communities by focusing
on one ambiguous biblical narrative, the story of Judah and Tamar
in Genesis 38, and three early Jewish interpretations of it. These
interpretations appear in the *Testament of Judah*, from a Hellenistic
cultural context, and in *Targum Neofiti* and *Genesis Rabba*, from Palestinian cultural contexts. While the narrative features, themes, and
canonical contexts of Genesis 38 guided early Jewish interpreters to
some natural conclusions, these interpreters also made hermeneutic
decisions at critical junctures in the biblical narrative and reconfigured
the story's plot and characters to correspond with their understanding
of its central message. Through bold and creative means, early Jewish
interpreters of Genesis 38 interjected contemporary ideals and values
into traditional writ, and, by doing so, ensured a vital function for
this passage of scripture within their own religious communities.

Genesis 38 provides an appropriate point of departure for this study
because it exemplifies the understated and provocative style that
characterizes biblical narrative. This style invites—even demands—
interpretation.[2] The story of Judah and Tamar is a strange one, and

---

[1] Harold Bloom, "The Breaking of Form," in *De-Construction and Criticism*, ed. Bloom,
Paul de Man, Jacques Derrida, Geoffrey H. Hartman, and J. Hillis Miller (New
York: Continuum, 1990) 22.

[2] Discussions of biblical narrative's elliptical style include Erich Auerbach, "Odysseus'

its narrator offers little assistance to interpreters. For example, even
the status of Genesis 38 as a story of royal origins must be deduced
from the position of Perez, one of the twins born in the final section,
in genealogies from other biblical books.[3] But once one has determined
that the story concerns David's lineage, its unseemly aspects become
even more disturbing. Tamar intentionally deceives her father-in-law
by impersonating a prostitute, and Judah engages a woman he considers to be a prostitute; moreover, he and his daughter-in-law commit what appears to be incest. This inappropriate behavior on the
part of the royal ancestors creates an intolerable tension within the
narrative that calls upon the reader for meaningful resolution.

Early Jewish interpreters responded to the challenges of the story
of Judah and Tamar with eagerness and creativity. The *Testament of
Judah* presents Genesis 38 as the story of a warrior king's tragic
weakness for women, which nearly results in his loss of royal status.
By contrast, *Targum Neofiti* develops the characters of Tamar and Judah
as positive exemplars of moral behavior under duress, who sanctify
God's Name through their principled acceptance of death and ultimately gain divine reprieve. Finally, *Genesis Rabba* depicts Genesis 38
as a series of providential and miraculous events leading to the origin of the royal and messianic lineage from the union of two worthy
ancestors.

This variety of interpretive trajectories arising from a single biblical
narrative becomes comprehensible only if one takes seriously the role
of interpreters situated within particular historical and cultural contexts.
Interpreters bring to Genesis 38 different expectations, associations,
and exegetical strategies, and therefore discover different resonances
within the same biblical narrative. They go even further, crossing
the line between interpreter and author, when they reshape that narrative so that it better expresses a particular meaning and incorporate
this revised narrative within a new literary composition. My central
purpose in this study is therefore to explore the intersection between
hermeneutics and literary form in three interpretations of a single

---

Scar," in *Mimesis: The Representation of Reality in Western Literature*, trans. Willard R.
Trask (Princeton: Princeton University Press, 1953) 3–23, and Meir Sternberg, "Gaps,
Ambiguity, and the Reading Process," in *The Poetics of Biblical Narrative: Ideological
Literature and the Drama of Reading*, Indiana Studies in Biblical Literature (Bloomington:
Indiana University Press, 1985) 186–229.

[3] Perez heads David's lineage in Ruth 4:18–22 and 1 Chr 2:3–15.

biblical narrative, to describe how early Jewish interpreters of Genesis 38 create religious "meaning through the shattering of belated vessels."

The emphasis on the interpreter's centrality connects this project with recent movements in literary criticism and philosophy that stress the contextual nature of interpretation. These movements include reader-response theory, represented by the writings of Stanley Fish, Wolfgang Iser, and others, as well as the dialogical hermeneutics of Hans-Georg Gadamer and philosophers from the same tradition.[4] Contemporary discussions about texts, readers, and the interpretive process are multifaceted, but two tenets that reader-response theory and dialogical hermeneutics share have special relevance here.

The first tenet is that the meaning of a text is not limited to the author's original intent, to the understanding of its original audience, nor to some "objective" meaning conveyed through its language, form, and style. Rather, the meanings of a text arise through creative encounters between various readers and the written material. The historical-critical methods of the last two centuries, with their focus on the moment of composition or initial reception of biblical passages, have furthered understanding of biblical literature in its original contexts. At the same time, these approaches miss something essential about how scripture functions for successive generations of believers. For traditional religious literature to retain its central place within religious communities, interpretation that transcends any original meaning is both inevitable and necessary.

Different theorists focus on different aspects of the dialogical interaction between text and readers through which meaning emerges. Iser, for example, emphasizes the "polysemantic nature" of the text itself, including its "gaps," "indeterminacies," and multiple "impulses," as a major factor contributing to the diversity of "realizations" of any given work by different readers. His attention to the "inexhaustibility"

---

[4] For an overview of reader-response theory and its relation to wider philosophical movements, see Terry Eagleton, "Phenomenology, Hermeneutics, Reception Theory," in *Literary Theory: An Introduction* (Minneapolis: University of Minnesota Press, 1983) 54–90. The essays collected in Jane P. Tompkins, ed., *Reader-Response Criticism: From Formalism to Post-Structuralism* (Baltimore: Johns Hopkins University Press, 1980), provide a good introduction to the range of issues and approaches articulated by leading critics in this school. For an overview of the thought of Gadamer, see Georgia Warnke, *Gadamer: Hermeneutics, Tradition and Reason* (Stanford: Stanford University Press, 1987).

of the text suggests that the participatory role of readers consists primarily of selecting among interpretive options in order to "concretize"
the text as a unified work.[5] By contrast, other theorists point to the
literary competencies, historical perspectives, and psychological motivations that readers bring to the text in order to explain their various
interpretations of it. Fish, for example, discusses the "framing process"
that shapes readers' perceptions of a written work. Readers apprehend
a text through prior mental grids consisting of literary expectations
and verbal associations that shape their experience of it.[6] Similarly,
Gadamer stresses the contextual nature of all interpretation when he
argues that the historical situations of readers constitute the "horizons," or perspectives, from which understanding of a text in specific
contexts becomes possible. In Gadamer's view, "perception includes
meaning" because perception involves projections of the concerns and
prejudices of historically situated interpreters onto the foreign "hori-
zon" of a literary work.[7] Harold Bloom posits a more conscious and
intentional relation of interpreters to a text, which he describes as an
aggressive will to poetic freedom and power. This stance is intended
to alleviate the "anxiety of influence" felt by all who stand within a
literary tradition.[8]

This diversity of emphasis within the contemporary discussion of
readers, texts, and interpretation fosters a sensitivity to the complex
dynamics operative in the early Jewish readings of Genesis 38. At
times, interpreters filled in actual gaps and resolved textual indeterminacies to further a coherent understanding of the biblical narrative.
At other times, particular historical and cultural contexts of interpretation and different expectations and strategies of reading motivated
exegetical trajectories. There may even be instances when interpreters consciously asserted their theological will to supplant the content

---

[5] Wolfgang Iser, "The Reading Process: A Phenomenological Approach," in *The
Implied Reader: Patterns of Communication in Prose Fiction from Bunyan to Beckett* (Baltimore:
Johns Hopkins University Press, 1974) 274–94.

[6] Stanley Fish, "What Is Stylistics?" in *Is There a Text in This Class?: The Authority
of Interpretive Communities* (Cambridge, MA: Harvard University Press, 1980) 109.

[7] Gadamer argues that the hermeneutic process involves a "fusion of horizons" in
which the gap between interpreter and text is mediated. See Hans-Georg Gadamer,
Truth and Method, 2d rev. ed., trans. Joel Weinsheimer and Donald G. Marshall
(New York: Continuum, 1993) 302–7.

[8] Bloom, "The Breaking of Form," 1–37. See also Harold Bloom, *The Anxiety of
Influence: A Theory of Poetry* (Oxford: Oxford University Press, 1973). Bloom speaks
primarily of later poets within a literary tradition, but suggests that the same applies
to all who specify the sense of a work of literature.

or implications of the biblical narrative, although discerning an interpreter's position on the continuum between conscious and unconscious manipulation of the narrative is difficult, if not impossible.

The second tenet of reader-response theory and hermeneutic philosophy important for this study concerns the traditional nature of all interpretation. The expectations, associations, and perspectives that readers bring to a text are never wholly subjective, but rather they stem also from larger traditions of interpretation and modes of making sense of literature and the world in general. Fish addresses this traditional dimension when he notes that the members of every "community of interpretation" share "strategies of interpretation." These common strategies explain the relative stability of interpretation among the "informed readers" of any given community.[9] In a similar vein, Jonathan Culler defines the idea of "literary competency" as the internalization by individuals of rules, conventions, and procedures of reading that render literature intelligible for a particular period.[10] Gadamer also emphasizes that the larger historical contexts of readers, or the "horizons" from which a text is viewed, include aesthetic standards and interpretive traditions. This recognition of the traditional nature of interpretation supports my contention that the three Jewish representations of Genesis 38 explored here are neither subjective nor insignificant. While they obviously do not reflect twentieth-century models of exegesis, these creative and often ingenious interpretations are nevertheless serious readings that incorporate traditional material and exemplify traditional hermeneutic maneuvers. These interpretations reveal much about the communities in which they made sense, including some of the central concerns and modes of self-definition, the moral values and aesthetic standards, and the traditions of reading and interpreting scripture characteristic of those communities.

Distinctive features mark early Jewish hermeneutics. The most fundamental characteristic shared by the three Jewish interpretations explored here is that each arises from the context of a religious community that regards Genesis 38 as part of a set of authoritative and revelatory written texts. As such, these interpretations attest to "the most characteristic feature of the Jewish imagination, the interpretation

---

[9] Stanley Fish, "Interpreting the *Variorum*," in *Reader-Response Criticism*, ed. Tompkins, 164–84.

[10] Jonathan Culler, "Literary Competence," in *Reader-Response Criticism*, ed. Tompkins, 101–17.

and rewriting of sacred texts."[11] The revisions of traditional material incorporated into the corpus of the Hebrew Bible itself illustrate this exegetical impulse,[12] which becomes even more pronounced in the extra-biblical writings of second temple and rabbinic Judaism.[13] Exegesis of a limited number of ancient, often obscure or even offensive, texts becomes the new site of revelation. Both conservative and innovative, scriptural interpretation simultaneously articulates a link with the traditions of the past and revitalizes these traditions for the present. The purpose of exegesis is therefore "to extend the divine voice into historical time while reasserting and reestablishing its hierarchical preeminence over all other cultural voices."[14]

The readers responsible for the interpretations of Genesis 38 explored here are therefore invested readers. They expect to discover in the ancient literature of the canon relevant and edifying scriptural truths, and they trust that their discussion of particular aspects of the biblical narrative will free the divine voice to speak for their generation. Through exegesis they recraft a morally ambiguous story in order to eliminate its problematic aspects or to exploit them ingeniously as object lessons for those who stand in the shadow of biblical tradition. In addition, they devise for this narrative positive and vital functions, including the articulation of cultural identity and the expression of religious and moral ideals. Through the medium of exegesis, the interpreters of Genesis 38 interpret themselves and their religious communities, even as they ostensibly interpret the biblical text.

Modern interpreters might accuse those responsible for the *Testament of Judah, Targum Neofiti,* and *Genesis Rabba* of violating the integrity of the biblical narrative. In actively working to extend scriptural revelation through exegesis, these early Jewish writings select episodes and other components of Genesis 38, or some altered form of it, and put them to use within different interpretive genres, including testament, para-

---

[11] Michael Fishbane, "Extra-Biblical Exegesis: The Sense of Not Reading in Rabbinic Midrash," in *The Garments of Torah* (Bloomington: Indiana University Press, 1989) 18.

[12] See Michael Fishbane, *Biblical Interpretation in Ancient Israel* (Oxford: Clarendon Press, 1988).

[13] The pesher commentary on Habakkuk found at Qumran and numerous "rewritten bibles," including *Jubilees* and the *Genesis Apocryphon,* provide good examples of this proclivity during second temple Judaism. For the concept of the rewritten bible, see Géza Vermès, *Scripture and Tradition in Judaism: Haggadic Studies,* 2d rev. ed. (Leiden: E. J. Brill, 1973).

[14] Michael Fishbane, "Inner-Biblical Exegesis: Types and Strategies of Interpretation in Ancient Israel," in *The Garments of Torah,* 8.

phrastic translation, and anthological commentary. Confident freedom to reshape and recontextualize the biblical narrative characterizes
these examples of "writing with scripture" for contemporary purposes.[15]
The alterations, suppressions, counter-readings, and repetitions of
features of Genesis 38 within new literary contexts flag aspects of the
text that engaged Jewish readers and indicate their creative responses.
The inner logic motivating the reconfigurations of the biblical text
can be reconstructed through close reading and sensitivity to the larger
thematic concerns of these later compositions.

Paradoxically, in light of their apparently free treatment of the
biblical text, the three interpretations discussed here are also traditional
in important respects. As noted above, all interpretation is traditional
in nature according to reader-response theory and modern hermeneutics; however, in the case of early Jewish biblical interpretation,
the traditional dimension of interpretation manifests itself in a very
concrete way. Interpretive motifs and traditions of exegesis virtually
become part of the larger text that later generations inherit and interpret. For example, at some point in the transmission of Genesis 38,
Judah's declaration concerning Tamar, "She is more righteous than
I" (צדקה ממני, Gen 38:26), came to be read as two separate utterances,
"She is righteous" (צדקה) and "It is from me" (ממני); moreover, the
second of these two utterances, "It is from me" (ממני), was attributed
to a divine voice. God's acceptance of responsibility for events in
Genesis 38 implied by this exegetical tradition became part of the
raw materials out of which later interpreters constructed their version of the narrative. This particular motif appears in all three of
the selected interpretations, although the specific divine purpose is
markedly different in each. Rather than the works of individuals or
even single generations, the three selected interpretations prove to be
compositions marked by the accumulation of exegetical traditions over
many generations.

At times, therefore, the latest stratum of interpretation may not
precisely line up with traditional material that has been nevertheless
dutifully incorporated. The challenge becomes to identify both what
is inherited, through a comparison with other sources, and what might
be original, judging from the absence of concurrence with other sources

---

[15] This expression comes from the title of Jacob Neusner's book, *Writing with Scripture: The Authority and Uses of the Hebrew Bible in the Torah of Formative Judaism* (Minneapolis: Fortress Press, 1989).

and from the fit with larger thematic and verbal configurations within the particular interpretive composition. There may be tensions within early Jewish interpretive works due to the common practice of including traditional material as well as designating innovative exegetical directions. These tensions between the exegetical voices within a single document constitute part of the complexity of the early Jewish interpretations of Genesis 38.

Finally, one of the most interesting features of these three interpretations lies in their implicit claim to articulate the true significance of the biblical narrative, rather than reshape it opportunistically according to the purposes of the contemporary generation. The rhetorical means through which various later readers argue for a particular valence of the biblical narrative therefore receives analysis in this study. Sometimes interpreters argue for their understanding of Genesis 38 through narrative developments artfully integrated into the biblical story, sometimes through repetition of particular themes which take on distinctive associations, and sometimes through verbal links and intertextual allusions to other scriptural passages. Through these various rhetorical means of linking creative interpretation to biblical text, later exegetes appropriate the truth and authority of scripture for their particular representations of the biblical narrative.

This study of several early Jewish interpretations of Genesis 38 has connections with a second, more circumscribed, academic field known as "comparative midrash." Comparative midrash is a field within Jewish studies that explores the origins of exegetical motifs and traditions, traces their development over time, and accounts for the different forms they assume in a variety of post-biblical documents. During this discipline's history, a number of different approaches have been employed. At the turn of the last century, scholars including M. Güdemann and Bernard Heller exhibited a keen interest in foreign influences on post-biblical elaborations of biblical narratives.[16] Perhaps in reaction to this early emphasis on foreign influence, other scholars

---

[16] For instance, M. Güdemann seeks to uncover the influence of the Egyptian myth about Osiris and Isis on Jewish traditions concerning Joseph's bones in "Joseph = Osiris," in *Religionsgeschichtliche Studien* (Leipzig: O. Leiner, 1876) 26–40. Bernard Heller, "Die Sage vom Sarge Josephs und der Bericht Benjamins von Tudela über Daniels schwebenden Sarg," *MGWJ* 70 (1926) 271–76, also explores the impact of Egyptian myth on Jewish legend, as well as the influence of an Arabic tradition concerning Daniel's grave. These examples and those listed in the following three notes treat the fate of Joseph's bones in Egypt and Moses' recovery of them before the exodus.

came to emphasize dynamics internal to biblical literature itself. For example, Jakob Horovitz stressed the crucial role that exegesis of difficult biblical passages played in the development of post-biblical traditions and noted the influence that the larger canon exerted in determining interpretive directions.[17] More recent scholars as well, such as James Kugel, emphasize the importance of internal, biblical factors in the generation of midrash, including the exegesis of specific difficulties (awkward grammar, word choice, and other surprising features) in the Hebrew consonantal text.[18] Other scholars, including Joseph Heinemann, highlight the literary creativity of those responsible for midrashic developments, maintaining that certain motifs arise out of the demands of good storytelling.[19] Each of these approaches to comparative midrash is valid, although none of them alone accounts for the complexity of the early Jewish biblical interpretations explored in this book. In my analysis, I try to remain sensitive to a variety of factors that may have motivated the emergence of individual exegetical traditions, including the influence of foreign literary patterns and larger historical realities, the impact of intertextual links with other canonical passages, the peculiar details of the Hebrew consonantal text itself, and the folkloric quality of the revised narratives.

Although I draw widely on earlier approaches to comparative midrash, I ultimately depart from them in an important way. The scholars mentioned above share a primarily diachronic thrust, in that they all chart the origins and historical development of single exegetical traditions. Renée Bloch articulates, perhaps most clearly, a method for this type of diachronic study in her article, "Methodological Note for the Study of Rabbinic Literature."[20] In it she calls for the application of form criticism and other methods commonly used in biblical scholarship to individual aggadic traditions. In the present study, I

---

[17] Jakob Horovitz, "Osiris im Midrasch? Die haggadischen Überlieferungen über das Grab Josephs," in *Die Josephserzählung* (Frankfurt am Main: Kaufmann, 1921) 120–46.

[18] James Kugel, "Inaccessible Bones," in *In Potiphar's House: The Interpretive Life of Biblical Texts* (San Francisco: HarperSanFrancisco, 1990) 125–55.

[19] Joseph Heinemann, ויקח משה את עצמות יוסף עמו [And Moses took Joseph's bones with him] in אגדות ותולדותיהן: עיונים בהשתלשלותן של מסורות [Aggadic traditions and their development: Studies on the evolution of traditions] (Jerusalem: Keter Publishing House, 1974) 49–63.

[20] Renée Bloch, "Methodological Note for the Study of Rabbinic Literature," trans. William Scott Green and William J. Sullivan, in *Approaches to Ancient Judaism: Theory and Practice*, ed. Green, Brown Judaic Studies 1 (Missoula, MT: Scholars Press, 1978) 521–75.

also explore the origins and development of particular exegetical traditions pertaining to Genesis 38, but I do not consider these diachronic
probes as an end in themselves. I fix my focus finally on clusters of
exegetical traditions working together as a system to make a comprehensive statement. The studies of individual traditions here merely
serve to illuminate the larger exegetical trajectories of Genesis 38 in
the interpretive writings. For example, knowing the hermeneutic pressures that led to a particular motif's emergence can help one define
the larger exegetical context of a given interpretive work, and understanding the history of an exegetical motif can highlight how its distinctive form within an interpretive work relates to that work's larger
purposes. Conversely, understanding a motif's origins and history may
lead to the conclusion that it stands in tension with a certain document's latest layer and that it has been recorded merely out of a
conservative tendency towards preservation of traditional material.

Analysis of individual motifs is only a preliminary step, however,
since my goal here is to view each interpretive treatment of Genesis 38
as a coherent system of parts. The analogy between language and
myth employed by structuralists proves helpful in this regard, because
it points out that each element of a system has meaning only within
the context of that system as a whole.[21] In this study, I hope to make
sense of the synchronic presentation of a complex web of motifs in
three interpretations of Genesis 38. To grasp the shape of these systems, I note broad changes in plot and character roles in the different
versions of Genesis 38 embedded in the interpretations. I then go on
to consider the thematic transpositions accomplished through these
alterations.

By attending to the interpretations of Genesis 38 as structural
systems of motifs, this study echoes Jacob Neusner's critique of Bloch
and others' diachronic, acontextual methods of comparative midrash.[22]
Neusner argues that it is meaningless to isolate motifs and exegetical
traditions from their larger contexts in written documents, since these

---

[21] In the field of folklore, Alan Dundes similarly calls for the examination of longer
complexes of motifs in traditional tales, and not merely isolated motifs as has been
customary in the past, in "From Etic to Emic Units in the Structural Study of
Folktales, *Journal of American Folklore* 75 (1962) 95–105.

[22] Jacob Neusner, *Comparative Midrash: The Plan and Program of "Genesis Rabbah" and
"Leviticus Rabbah,"* Brown Judaic Studies 111 (Atlanta: Scholars Press, 1986). He
presents the substance of his argument in "Toward a Theory of Comparison: The
Case of Comparative Midrash," *Religion* 16 (1986) 269–303.

components make sense only within these contexts. I agree with Neusner's emphasis on context, although I would stress that the context within which an interpretation makes sense is not limited to the written document in which it appears. It may also include larger cultural trends, literary patterns, and moral discussions. My unit of focus—the biblical narrative and its post-biblical versions—is intermediate, between Bloch's concentration on single traditions and Neusner's concentration on entire documents. My primary concern is to show how Genesis 38 made sense in three Jewish communities, based on the evidence of the interpretive writings.

Indeed, part of my purpose is to explore not just the content of these interpretations of Genesis 38, but also their poetics. When I refer to the poetics of interpretation, I mean the way in which interpreters implicitly argue for their understanding of scripture through literary and rhetorical means. For example, the literary genres of the *Testament of Judah, Targum Neofiti,* and *Genesis Rabba* themselves contribute to the overarching statements that these works make about the nature of scriptural interpretation. The three interpretations embed versions of the biblical narrative within the genres of testament, paraphrastic translation, and anthological commentary, thus allowing exploration of the interrelationship between a biblical text and its new literary contexts. Also important are the various means through which interpreters incorporate new exegetical material into the biblical narrative. These means of joining interpretation and received text reveal a range of attitudes towards scripture in early Jewish communities. Issues related to the poetics of interpretation such as these have not yet received sufficient attention in comparative midrash. With this study of Judah and Tamar in ancient Jewish exegesis I hope to partially redress this situation.

CHAPTER ONE

INVITATION TO INTERPRETATION:
NARRATIVE ART AND CANONICAL CONTEXTS

> She removed her widow's garments from upon her, covered herself
> with a veil, wrapped herself, and sat at the entrance of Enaim, which
> is on the way to Timnah, for she saw that Shelah had grown up,
> but she had not been given to him as a wife. (Gen 38:14)

To make sense of the story of Judah and Tamar, early Jewish
interpreters grappled with particular features of Genesis 38, including
its plot and characters, its narrative art and themes, and its numerous
points of contact with other canonical texts. Judging from the narrative's lively history of interpretation, these features can stimulate a
wide range of reactions when approached from different historical
and cultural perspectives. This chapter provides a close literary reading
of Genesis 38 within the canon, highlighting aspects of the biblical
narrative that in earlier times also elicited responses from the authors
and editors of the *Testament of Judah, Targum Neofiti,* and *Genesis Rabba.*
This preliminary discussion forms a backdrop for the selected interpretations, allowing them to stand in strong relief against the original—
or at least against one late twentieth-century understanding of the
original.

The first part of this chapter concentrates on the internal dynamics
and narrative art of Genesis 38 itself. Analysis of narrative structure
facilitates later comparisons between Genesis 38 and the variations
of this story embedded within the interpretative writings. Next, the
focus turns to the main characters of the biblical narrative and explores
the tension between the simple plot and its complex presentation
through shifting points of view—a tension which each of the interpretations attempts to resolve in one way or another. As part of this
discussion, the important themes of moral judgment and knowledge
receive extended attention, since they offer potential nuclei for exegetical developments.

The second part of this chapter concentrates on points of contact
between Genesis 38 and a variety of related biblical passages, which

pull the story of Judah and Tamar in a number of interpretive directions and thereby encourage the exegetical diversity evident in the early Jewish interpretations. The biblical narrative's problematic treatment of issues addressed in the pentateuchal laws (including laws concerning intermarriage with Canaanites, levirate marriage, incest, and prostitution) promotes one type of this productive intertextuality. Reading Genesis 38 within the context of the Joseph story at the end of the book of Genesis (Genesis 37–50) lends emphasis to very different aspects of the biblical narrative. The story's relation to the lineage of Davidic kings as depicted in biblical genealogies and its structural similarities with other biblical birth stories result in additional contextual resonances.

With its complex narrative art and suggestive interfaces with the canon, the biblical text itself provides a source of interpretive options for later readers. Although the biblical authors and editors no doubt had their own purposes when they composed the narrative in Genesis 38 and redacted the literature that came to be regarded as scripture, in the end the pieces don't fit together exactly. The loose play between plot and perspective, between characters and narrator, between narrative and law, and between isolated story and larger narrative context imparts a persisting instability. Only the hand of an intrepid hermeneut, one who does not shy from developing certain features and intertextual connections while slighting others, can steady the narrative to produce a consistent reading. Was this the intention of the biblical authors and editors? Did they desire to leave an ambiguous text to encourage a particularly active and creative type of exegetical engagement? Or did they assume that their understanding of the story of Judah and Tamar would show through its narrative features and strategic placement? Whatever the original intent, the narrative art and canonical contexts of Genesis 38 stimulated the creativity of early Jewish interpreters, who used biblical exegesis as a vehicle through which to express important religious ideals and cultural values.

NARRATIVE ART OF GENESIS 38

What is Genesis 38 about? Who emerges as the story's protagonist? Early Jewish interpreters give different answers to even these basic questions, depending on the parts of Genesis 38 that they emphasize, the other biblical passages they read in connection with this narrative, and the perspectives, concerns, and patterns of reading they bring to the text. In the following pages, I explore possible answers to these questions by charting the narrative's overarching movement from beginning to end, identifying major conflicts and their resolution, and establishing the contributions of the characters.

The emphasis on narrative structure and character function in this analysis attests to the general influence of Vladimir Propp's approach in *Morphology of the Folktale*,[1] although the specific results of his analysis of the Russian fairy tale have no bearing on the present study. Analysis of plot and character roles here simply serves as an effective means by which to discuss Genesis 38 as an organic whole and by which to throw the structural discrepancies of its interpretive versions into relief. To appropriate Propp's terminology, the analysis of Genesis 38 in terms of plot and character roles below serves as a "yardstick" against which to measure the variant versions of the narrative contained in the three selected interpretations.[2] The types of discrepancies between the biblical narrative and its post-biblical variants discernible through such comparative measurements include deletions, additions, substitutions, changes in the order of events and overall narrative shape, and transformations of the roles of characters that affect the internal grammar of the narrative. They also include alterations on the even more basic level of what constitutes the central issue driving the narrative and what constitutes the resolution that brings the narrative to closure. Despite the invariables of nomenclature, events, and details based on the biblical narrative, Genesis 38 and its later interpretive versions are actually dramatically different stories. Elements from the biblical narrative function quite differently in the interpretive writings than they do in Genesis 38 itself.

Detection of formal dissimilarities is only the first step, however, since the alterations in plot and character roles found in the three

---

[1] Vladimir Propp, *Morphology of the Folktale*, trans. Laurence Scott, 2d rev. ed., American Folklore Society Bibliographical and Special Series 9, Indiana University Research Center in Anthropology, Folklore, and Linguistics 10 (Austin: University of Texas Press, 1988). For a discussion of Propp's place within structuralism, see Anatoly Liberman, introduction to *Theory and History of Folklore*, by Vladimir Propp, ed. Liberman, trans. Ariadna Y. Martin and Richard P. Martin, Theory and History of Literature 5 (Minneapolis: University of Minnesota Press, 1984) ix–lxxxi. For a discussion of the continuing influence of Propp's work, see Alan Dundes, "From Etic to Emic Units in the Structural Study of Folktales," *Journal of American Folklore* 75 (1962) 95–105.

[2] Propp, *Morphology of the Folktale*, 65.

early Jewish interpretive writings are not due to carelessness. They reveal the frames of reading of later interpreters and correspond to their creative, revisionary intentions. Detection of revised plot structure and character roles therefore precedes exploration of the relation between literary form and hermeneutics, or, in other words, of how the shape of a narrative expresses meaning and cultural values.

Narrative Structure

Judging from the description of Judah's isolation from his own sibling group in the first verse of the chapter (Gen 38:1) and the account of the birth and naming of twin sons in the final verses (Gen 38:27–30), one may conclude that the central issue driving the biblical narrative consists of the transition from one generation of males to the next. Since the motifs of birth and naming appear earlier in the narrative as well (Gen 38:3–5), Genesis 38 may be viewed as a double tale of procreation, in which initial biological and social discontinuity is twice overcome, first in Gen 38:1–5 and next in Gen 38:6–30. Judah's explicit concern with the issue of "seed" or descendants for his eldest son in his instructions to Onan in Gen 38:8 confirms that the central movements of the plot involve generational transitions. This type of transition from father to sons is a fundamental and recurrent structure in biblical literature, undergirding both the extended birth narratives and the skeletal genealogies that mark the pages of scripture, especially the book of Genesis.[3]

Given the structural duplication in Genesis 38, the relationship between the two tales of procreation deserves further attention. Some modern commentators summarily dismiss the first five verses as merely setting the scene for the more interesting action of the rest of the narrative.[4] The simplicity and brevity of the initial account of reproduction indicates that it indeed does play an ancillary role to the more complicated procreative drama that follows; however, it provides much more than the minimal background information required for the ensuing story. A spare genealogical note that Judah fathered

---

[3] Naomi Steinberg goes so far as to argue that the basic plot of the book of Genesis concerns genealogy ("The Genealogical Framework of the Family Stories in Genesis," in *Narrative Research on the Hebrew Bible*, ed. Miri Amihai, George W. Coats, and Anne M. Solomon, Semeia 46 [Atlanta: Scholars Press, 1989] 41–50).

[4] In fact, Gerhard von Rad maintains that the real action of the story begins only with Gen 38:12 (*Genesis: A Commentary*, trans. John H. Marks, 9th rev. ed. [Philadelphia: Westminster Press, 1972] 357).

three sons would suffice to set the scene for the events beginning in
Gen 38:6.[5] Instead, the first section of Genesis 38 occupies an intermediate position between a fully developed birth narrative with its
complications and resolution, such as the one recounted in the rest
of the chapter, and a minimal genealogical list of fathers and sons.
The generosity of Gen 38:1–5 suggests that it contains clues for interpretation of the chapter as a whole:

> 1. At that time, Judah went down from his brothers and turned aside
> to an Adullamite man, whose name was Hirah. 2. Judah saw there the
> daughter of a Canaanite man, whose name was Shua, and he took her
> and went into her. 3. She conceived and gave birth to a son, and his
> name was called Er. 4. She conceived again, gave birth to a son, and
> called his name Onan. 5. She once again gave birth to a son and
> called his name Shelah. He[6] was in Kezib when she gave birth to him.

These introductory verses establish a basic sequence of male and
female actions leading swiftly to the emergence of the next generation.[7]
The sequence begins in the second verse with the report that Judah
"saw" (וירא) a certain woman, and it continues unceremoniously with
the notice that he "took her" (ויקחה) and "went into her" (ויבא אליה).[8]
The three verses that follow (Gen 38:3–5) depict the female procreative response to Judah's initiative of seeing, taking, and entering.
The first two of these verses explicitly record that Shua's daughter

---

[5] For purposes of comparison, see the brief genealogical note that "Noah had
three sons, Shem, Ham, and Japheth" (Gen 6:10), which sets the scene for the story
of the flood.

[6] The masculine singular verb at the beginning of this sentence in the MT (והיה
בכזיב בלדתה אתו) returns the narrative focus to Judah in preparation for his resumption of activity in Gen 38:6, and the masculine singular direct object at the end of
the sentence places a special emphasis on the birth of the third son, Shelah. The
LXX, by contrast, preserves an emphasis on the mother's role in the birth of all
three sons to the very end of Gen 38:5 in its reading, "She was in Chasbi when she
gave birth to them" (αὐτὴ δὲ ἦν ἐν Χασβι, ἡνίκα ἔτεκεν αὐτούς). The descendants of
Shelah are specifically associated with a place called Kozeba (כזבא) in 1 Chr 4:21–22,
suggesting that the MT reading may be preferable.

[7] Johanna W. H. Bos also notes the repetition of procreative verbs in Genesis 38,
although she does so in a larger discussion of verbal patterns within the narrative
("Out of the Shadows: Genesis 38; Judg 4:17–22; Ruth 3," in *Reasoning with the
Foxes: Female Wit in a World of Male Power*, ed. J. Cheryl Exum and Bos, Semeia 42
[Atlanta: Scholars Press, 1988] 40–49).

[8] "Taking" (לקח) is a term denoting marriage in the Hebrew Bible, as in Gen 24:3
and 25:1. "Entering" (בוא) is also used in connection with marriage, as in Deut 22:13,
although it is also used more generally to denote sexual intercourse with a woman,
inside or outside of marriage. In the Mishna, however, the verbal root "entering"
(בוא) is used specifically in connection with marriage, as in *m. Qidd.* 1.1.

"conceived" (ותהר), and the final verse implies conception as well.[9]
Each of these three verses also notes that she "gave birth" (ותלד) to
a son and ends with the naming of the newborn, and at least in the
last two cases the feminine form of the verb clearly specifies that it
was the mother who "named" (ותקרא) the child.[10] The list of procreative verbs in Gen 38:1–5, specifying the male initiatives of seeing
(ראה), taking (לקח), and going into (בוא אל), and the female responses
of conceiving (הרה), giving birth (ילד), and naming (קרא), constitutes
a schematic and normative plot pattern, from which the longer second part of Genesis 38 deviates and to which it finally returns. The
contrast between the two tales of reproduction accentuates the distinctive features of the more extended and interesting second tale
and highlights the identity of the heroic character responsible for
restoring its broken chain of events.

The first verse of Genesis 38 prefaces the opening reproductive
drama with three important details. It mentions that Judah took a
journey ("Judah went down from his brothers," וירד יהודה מאת אחיו),
veered aside ("and turned aside," ויט), and became allied with a local
man ("to an Adullamite man, whose name was Hirah," עד איש עדלמי
ושמו חירה). The motif of a journey made by a solitary male often
precedes marriage in biblical narratives,[11] but in Gen 38:1, Judah's
journey is supplemented with two other actions: his veering aside
and his association with Hirah. All three of these actions serve as
heralds of the simple plot of generation in the first part of Genesis
38. The same actions reappear in the second part of Genesis 38 as
well, although not immediately, since the second part opens with a
depiction of the next generation's thwarted attempts at procreation.

---

[9] The Hebrew verb "she conceived" (ותהר) is omitted in the final verse of this
section (Gen 38:5), although it is clearly implied by the verb "she continued" (ותסף)
which replaces it.

[10] The majority of Hebrew manuscripts indicate a masculine subject for the first
verb of naming in Gen 38:3 (ויקרא), and this reading is collaborated by *Targum
Onqelos* and the Peshitta. Some Hebrew manuscripts, however, attest to a feminine subject of the verb, thereby consistently representing the mother as the one who names
all three sons. The Samaritan Pentateuch and *Targums Pseudo-Jonathan* and *Neofiti*
also designate the mother as the subject of the verb in all three verses. See the discussion of this textual problem in J. A. Emerton, "Some Problems in Genesis 38,"
VT 25 (1975) 338–61. I have translated the verb in Gen 38:3 as an impersonal
expression, "his name was called Er," in keeping with a common usage of the third
masculine singular form of this verb in the Hebrew Bible.

[11] Jacob (Genesis 28–29), Moses (Exod 2:15–22), and Samson (Judges 14) under-
take journeys directly before their encounters with future wives.

Before turning to Gen 38:6–30, however, I want to indicate how the threefold recital of the Canaanite wife's actions in Gen 38:3–5 functions in the context of the larger narrative. Trebling is a common feature of folk literature, but in this specific context the triple account of conception, birth, and naming unites the two parts of Genesis 38. The repetition emphasizes that the goal of the first five verses is indeed the appearance of male descendants, and it establishes the expectation of an identical goal in the verses that follow. This triple account also introduces a thematic number of great significance for the structure of the second part of the narrative. Three times Tamar is paired with a sexual partner (Er, Onan, and Judah), the third of whom unwittingly succeeds in impregnating her.[12] There are three items in the pledge that identify Judah's responsibility for her condition and spare her life. Judah's culpability in withholding his son Shelah is emphasized by three different references to this behavior (Gen 38:11, 14, 26). Perhaps most importantly for the overall structure of the entire chapter, the emphasis on the birth of three sons made through the triple repetition of their conception, birth, and naming in the opening section facilitates a sense of closure when the birth of twins in the final verses restores the number of Judah's living sons to three. Finally, the dominant presence of the mother in the last three verses of the opening procreative tale, asserted through recurrent feminine verbs, foreshadows the dominance of another mother in the plot of the second procreative tale. The emphasis on the mediating role of a woman in the generational transition between father and sons in Gen 38:1–5 prepares the reader for the important mediating role of a different woman in Gen 38:6–30, although clearly Tamar's facilitation of the emergence of sons is not limited to her biological capacity for reproduction.

Gen 38:6–30 can be divided into brief episodes indicated either by the author's explicit transitional markers or by some other compelling shift in time frame or scene. Breaking the story in this manner aids comprehension of its kinetics, of how the narrative moves from

[12] Alternately, perhaps Er, Onan, and Shelah's failure and Judah's success conform to a pattern of three plus one that repeats itself in the Hebrew Bible. For example, this motif is expressed in Prov 30:15–16, 18–19, 21–23, 29–31, and by the prophet Amos in his opening prophecies against the nations in Amos 1:3, 6, 9, 11, 13; 2:1, 4, 6. For a discussion of this motif and other examples of it, see Yair Zakovitch, על שלשה ועל ארבעה [Upon three and upon four] (Jerusalem: Makor, 1979).

episode to episode, since the second part of Genesis 38 manifests an abundant surplus over the straightforward tale in the first five verses. For example, whereas Gen 38:1–5 focuses on the procreative actions of a couple from the same generation after briefly acknowledging the bride's father (Shua, Gen 38:2), the remainder of the chapter portrays a constant interplay between two generations of males in relation to a single female; moreover, this interplay ultimately results in the father's unwitting usurpation of his own son's reproductive role. In addition, Gen 38:6–30 interjects an explicit divine dimension lacking in the first five verses, by depicting two brief punitive intrusions. Besides these complications in narrative content, the second part of Genesis 38 presents a complication in structural form. There is an additional movement from tension to resolution, embedded within the larger movement towards the emergence of the next generation, that centers on Tamar's risk of her own life and involves mistaken identity, misjudgment, and last-minute reprieve from death. This additional crisis and resolution accounts for much of the chapter's dramatic interest and emphasizes the bravery of its female protagonist.

No introductory formula demarcates the opening episode of the second procreative story (Gen 38:6–11), but clearly the maturation of a male from the younger generation motivates an attempt to replicate the procreative pattern established earlier:

> 6. Judah took a wife for Er his first-born whose name was Tamar. 7. But Er, Judah's first-born, was evil in the eyes of the LORD, so the LORD killed him. 8. Judah said to Onan, "Go into your brother's wife, act as a levir for her, and raise up seed for your brother." 9. But Onan knew that the seed would not be his, and whenever he went into his brother's wife he would spill on the ground so as not to give seed to his brother. 10. What he did was evil in the eyes of the LORD, and he killed him also. 11. Judah said to Tamar, his daughter-in-law, "Remain a widow at your father's house until Shelah, my son, grows up." For he said, "Lest he die also like his brothers." Tamar went and remained at her father's house.

In this passage, for the first time in Genesis 38, third-person narrative and direct speech alternate. This alternation slows the pace of the story and emphasizes important details. Most strikingly, the quotations of Judah's instructions to his son and daughter-in-law stress his responsibility for the family's welfare and continuity.

The opening three words of this subsection ("Judah took a wife," ויקח יהודה אשה) suggest that the remainder of the chapter consists of

a variation on the initial procreative pattern in Gen 38:1–5. This
second notice of Judah's "taking" a woman triggers the expectation
that he is beginning the process leading to the birth and naming of
sons with another partner. This is indeed what eventually happens,
but the immediate clarification that he took the woman "for Er his
first-born" alters the reader's initial expectation and leads to an
ultimately erroneous conclusion that the task of procreation has been
transferred to the next generation.[13]

But whereas the biblical narrative portrays Er's father as an active
agent by describing his initial journey and his sexual engagement
with a woman who bears him sons, it never portrays Er himself as
an active agent. The text does not describe Er departing from his
family, seeing the woman who becomes his wife, nor taking her;
moreover, it remains mute on the question of whether Er had sexual
relations with Tamar. Instead of emerging as an active agent of
procreation like Judah, Er becomes the passive object of divine
evaluation in Gen 38:7. He is eliminated by God from the narrative's
cast of characters because of some unspecified evil. This subsection
thus introduces the motif of crisis concerning the continuity of an
important lineage, a motif common throughout the book of Genesis.[14]

Following Er's death, male reproductive responsibility returns briefly
to the older generation, as Judah arranges a levirate marriage between
Onan and Tamar, and then it shifts once again to another ineffectual
young male. Yet with Judah's charge to his second son and with
Onan's partial compliance, the normative masculine role established
in the first narrative comes closer to actualization. After Judah's instructions to Onan in Gen 38:8, which include the command, "Go into
your brother's wife" (בא אל אשת אחיך), Onan actually "goes into"
Tamar in Gen 38:9 ("and whenever he went into his brother's wife,"
והיה אם בא אל אשת אחיו). The report that he does so, however, appears
embedded in a longer sentence expressing his recognition that the
offspring born from their union would not be his and describing his
prophylactic technique. While having sexual relations with Tamar,
Onan intentionally fails to execute his father's design, and therefore
fails to initiate the female verbs of procreation emphasized in the

---

[13] For a father's role in choosing a wife for his son, see Gen 24:3; 28:1–2; 34:4;
Judg 14:1–7.
[14] See, for example, the stories concerning the matriarchs' barrenness in Gen
15:2–3; 16:1; 17:15–21; 18:10–14; 21:1–7; 25:21; 29:31, 35; 30:9, 17, 22–24.

first part of Genesis 38. Having declined to assume an effective procreative role, Onan, like his brother, is divinely eliminated from the
plot in Gen 38:10.

After two frustrated beginnings, there is a further retreat from the
point of generational transition in Gen 38:11. In this verse, Judah
sends Tamar back to her father's house, her former residence as an
unmarried daughter, and postpones Shelah's assumption of a mature
male role out of concern for his life. Tamar's compliance with Judah's
order ensures a delay in procreation. Although intended to prevent
the death of his last remaining son, Judah's solution prevents the
birth of all further sons as long as it remains in effect.

The opening episode of Gen 38:6–30 therefore presents two abor-
tive attempts to repeat the biological and social transitions portrayed
in the first five verses and concludes with a retreat from a possible
third attempt. In fact, the two actual attempts partially unravel the
first part's dénouement, since they end with the deaths of Judah's
sons. To prevent the total destruction of the family established early
in the chapter, Judah inhibits his youngest son from establishing his
own family. At the close of this initial subsection, it is not yet clear
that the life-denying stasis Judah imposes to preserve life is other
than temporary. The first subsection closes then with a delicate suspension of all procreative action. The two remaining couples in the
narrative, an older couple whose reproductive life together is accomplished and past, and a younger couple whose reproductive life
together is potential and future, express this suspension.

This tenuous equilibrium, however, cannot continue indefinitely.
The passage of time noted in the introduction to the second subsection (Gen 38:12–19) brings events that upset it and open the way for
reproductive progress through an unexpected alternate route:

> 12. Much time passed, and the daughter of Shua, Judah's wife, died.
> When Judah was comforted, he went up to Timnah to his sheep
> shearers, he and Hirah, his Adullamite friend. 13. It was reported to
> Tamar, "See, your father-in-law is going up to Timnah to shear his
> flock." 14. She removed her widow's garments from upon her, covered
> herself with a veil, wrapped herself, and sat at the entrance of Enaim,
> which is on the way to Timnah, for she saw that Shelah had grown
> up, but she had not been given to him as a wife. 15. Judah saw her
> and thought she was a prostitute because she covered her face. 16. He
> turned aside to her on the road and said, "Come, let me go into you,"
> for he did not know that she was his daughter-in-law. She said, "What
> will you give me so that you may go into me?" 17. He said, "I will

send a kid from the flock." She said, "If you give a pledge until you send [it]." 18. He said, "What is the pledge that I should give you?" She said, "Your seal, your cord, and your staff that is in your hand." He gave them to her and went into her, and she conceived by him. 19. She arose, went, removed the veil from upon her, and dressed in her widow's garments.

This episode focuses on Tamar's plan to end the reproductive impasse created in the preceding episode. The fragile stasis at the end of the first episode shatters with the death of the female member of the older couple. The continued unavailability of the male member of the younger couple, revealed in Gen 38:14, also negates the reproductive potential implicit in that stasis. The new configuration of remaining active characters, comprised of a widowed older man and a neglected younger woman, foreshadows the ensuing events. Since through either intentional design or careless oversight the older man has thwarted the progress of the narrative by denying his remaining son an active role, the younger woman emerges as the protagonist by facilitating the restoration of a broken pattern of procreation.

Even before Tamar herself acts in this subsection, however, the reappearance of two of the three introductory motifs from Gen 38:1 signals a resumption of movement towards the narrative's goal. In Gen 38:12, Judah once again takes a journey ("he went up to his sheep shearers," ויעל על גזזי צאנו) in the company of a familiar friend ("he and Hirah, his Adullamite friend," הוא וחירה רעהו העדלמי). In this second appearance of the motifs of journey and male companionship, additional details emphasize the potential for sexual activity, as well as the potential for deception. These details include the notice that Judah's period of mourning for his wife has passed and the allusion to the season of sheep shearing with its component of revelry— including the consumption of wine.[15]

After the reappearance of these introductory motifs, Tamar is informed of her father-in-law's journey in Gen 38:13. This information reveals an opportunity for action, which she immediately seizes in the next verse. Jumping ahead for comparative purposes, the anonymous report leading to Tamar's decisive action involving her father-in-law is echoed later by the anonymous report to Judah concerning

---

[15] The connection between sheep shearing and festivities, including wine drinking, is noted elsewhere in the biblical corpus, including 1 Samuel 25 and 2 Sam 13:23–29.

his daughter-in-law's behavior in Gen 38:24. This second report similarly leads to decisive action on Judah's part involving his affinal relative. The fact that the two remaining active characters learn of each other's behavior only through third-person notifications stresses the distance between them, despite Judah's promise to provide a sexual partner for his daughter-in-law. In addition, the different reactions to these parallel reports highlight a central and complex dynamic of the narrative. Whereas Tamar's deception of her father-in-law and conception outside of a legitimate social context leads ultimately to life for the next generation, Judah's concern for conventional propriety evident in his command that his daughter-in-law burn for illicit sexual activity might have prevented the emergence of an important lineage.

The list of actions at the beginning of Gen 38:14 ("she removed her widow's garments from upon her, covered herself with a veil, wrapped herself, and sat at the entrance of Enaim") presents Tamar as an active agent for the first time in the narrative. Since all conventional, socially sanctioned means for procreation have failed, only the clever, but scandalous and risky, initiative of Tamar depicted here guides the narrative towards its fortunate ending. Tamar's change of location in Gen 38:14 implies a solitary journey by this character to meet her targeted sexual partner. The motif of a journey by a female character preceding marriage or sexual union is relatively rare in biblical literature, in contrast to the more common portrayal of such journeys by male characters, noted above.[16] The assimilation of Tamar's behavior to that more typical of a male character stresses the absence of effective masculine initiative and underscores her unorthodox assumption of procreative responsibility. Following the success of Tamar's ruse, a second list of her actions in Gen 38:19 concludes this subsection ("she arose, went, removed the veil from upon her, and dressed in widow's garments"). Tamar's self-transformations thus frame the sexual encounter that her father-in-law ostensibly initiates, identifying her as the driving force behind the events on the road to Timnah.

While Tamar clearly controls this episode, her initial action at Enaim is not especially remarkable. Gen 38:14 simply reports that "she sat (וַתֵּשֶׁב) at the entrance of Enaim which is on the way to

---

[16] Other examples consist of Rebekah's journey to meet Isaac (Genesis 24) and Ruth's venture to the threshing floor to meet Boaz (Ruth 3).

Timnah." Tamar's sitting in this verse corresponds to her earlier sitting
at the end of Gen 38:11, which states that "she sat (וחשב) at her father's
house." In both instances, Tamar waits for her father-in-law to act.
In Gen 38:11 Tamar passively waits, at Judah's command, for Shelah
to mature. Once he has matured and Judah does nothing, however,
Tamar actively waits for her father-in-law in Gen 38:14 until he
directly, although unknowingly, performs the masculine procreative
behavior lacking to this point in the second part of the chapter.

Tamar's strategic waiting solicits from Judah two important masculine actions, replicating earlier behavior. Judah, who has already
"taken" Tamar in Gen 38:6, albeit for his eldest son, now "sees" her
in Gen 38:15 ("Judah saw her," ויראה יהודה) and mistakes her for a
prostitute. There is a brief pause before the final masculine verb of
the series appears, as the third introductory motif from Gen 38:1 reasserts itself with Judah's "veering aside" at the beginning of Gen 38:16
("He turned aside to her on the road," ויט אליה אל הדרך). Immediately following this third and final herald of the reproductive plot,
Judah unwittingly offers the male services earlier denied this woman
when he says, "Come, let me go into you" (הבה נא אבוא אליך) at the
end of Gen 38:16. His accomplishment of this final significant masculine action is postponed by the interjection of an extended dialogue between the two parties, however, until Gen 38:18, which notes
that "he went into her" (ויבא אליה).

Judah's discussion with the woman he assumes to be a prostitute
is the lengthiest dialogue in Genesis 38, indicating its importance.
This dialogue dramatizes Tamar's successful concealment of her identity, by portraying Judah's treatment of the exchange as a discussion
about a prostitute's fee. It also connects this encounter with earlier
events of the narrative through the wording of Tamar's first question
to her father-in-law. The woman who was not "given" seed by Onan
(לבלתי נתן, Gen 38:9) and who was not "given" to Shelah (לא נתנה,
Gen 38:14) now asks Judah what he himself will "give" her (מה תתן
לי, Gen 38:16). Her control over both the context of their discussion
and its course indicates that, unlike earlier in the story, it is she who
determines precisely what this male character will give her.

Ultimately, at the end of Gen 38:18, Judah "gives" her the personal items that she specifies (ויתן לה),[17] as well as the means for

---

[17] Herodotus *Histories* 1.195 mentions that every Babylonian owned his own distinctive seal and carved walking stick, which may be similar in nature and purpose
to Judah's seal, cord, and staff.

conception. Judah himself, however, recognizes only the transfer of the pledge as having any significance beyond the moment, and he considers it temporary until he sends a kid from the flock.[18] Through his double donation of pledge and semen following Tamar's prompting, Judah unwittingly contributes both to the development of the larger overarching movement towards reproduction and to the resolution of the secondary plot development introduced in this subsection, when Tamar risks her own life by manipulating the sexual double standard of a patriarchal society. Tamar's jeopardy remains implicit until the discovery of her pregnancy and Judah's order that she be burned in Gen 38:24, but the important function of the pledge in the resolution of this secondary crisis is foreshadowed through the attention it receives in the dialogue.

Tamar conceives at the end of Gen 38:18, immediately after her father-in-law gives her the identifying tokens and completes the masculine procreative action of entering her ("He gave them to her and went into her, and she conceived by him," ויתן לה ויבא אליה ותהר לו). The rapid progress from male to female procreative actions signals that Tamar has successfully facilitated progress towards generational transition.[19] But the verbs denoting birth and naming which always immediately follow the feminine action of conception in Gen 38:3–5 are once again delayed.

This delay is due to the discrepancy between Judah's perception of the nature of his sexual encounter with Tamar and its actual paternal implications, as well as to the threat to her life resulting from this discrepancy. At the end of this episode, therefore, although there has been substantial progress towards procreation, there is a concealment of this progress with Tamar's return to her father's house and her resumption of widow's dress.[20] What is needed is a reconciliation between the reality of the changed situation and Judah's perception of it.

---

[18] For an overview of the biblical concept of the pledge, see I. L. Seeligman, "Lending, Pledge, and Interest in Biblical Law and Biblical Thought" (in Hebrew), in vol. 1 of *Studies in Bible and the Ancient Near East Presented to S. E. Loewenstamm on His Seventieth Birthday*, ed. Y. Avishur and J. Blau (Jerusalem: E. Rubinstein, 1978) 183–205.

[19] Note that the use of verb lists to collapse narrative time is common in biblical narrative. See for example Gen 25:34, where Jacob gives Esau bread and lentil stew, and Esau "ate and drank and rose and went away and spurned" (ויאכל וישת ויקם וילך ויבז) his birthright.

[20] Tamar's secret measures to bring about conception contrast with Onan's secret measures to prevent conception in the previous section.

For another ruse achieved through the donning of widow's garb, see 2 Sam 14:2.

But this reconciliation does not occur immediately. The third episode of the complicated tale of reproduction, in fact, contributes little to Judah's enlightenment:

> 20. Judah sent the kid through his Adullamite friend to take the pledge from the woman's hand, but he didn't find her. 21. He asked the men of the place where she had been, "Where is the consecrated woman who was at Enaim beside the road?" They said, "There has been no consecrated woman here." 22. He returned to Judah and said, "I didn't find her, and also the men of the place said, 'There has been no consecrated woman here.'" 23. Judah said, "Let her take them, lest we be ridiculed. See, I sent this kid, and you didn't find her."

This humorous depiction of Judah's attempt to settle accounts with the woman he mistook as a prostitute appears to be a digression, since it does not forward the plot; nevertheless, it serves a number of important purposes. Judah's lack of awareness comments on the success of Tamar's deception and partially excuses his participation in incestuous sexual relations. The men's denial of the existence of a prostitute, or "consecrated woman" in local parlance, suggests that Tamar's disguised presence at Enaim was a singular occurrence and thereby substantiates her claims concerning Judah's paternity in the next episode. By maintaining the slower pace introduced in the previous subsection through the inclusion of dialogue, this episode prolongs the suspense concerning the outcome of Tamar's ruse and maintains the focus on the pledge that will eventually resolve the crisis to her life. It also introduces the motif of sending an object through an intermediary, repeated in the next subsection. But whereas Judah's transmission of a kid through Hirah remains unsuccessful because of the lack of correspondence between his perception and the reality of the situation, Tamar's transmission of the pledge through an unspecified agent in the next episode proves successful. Her success is due to the fact that she resolves the discrepancy between perception and reality that threatens to disrupt the movement from conception to birth and naming at the beginning of the fourth episode:

> 24. About three months later, it was reported to Judah, "Tamar, your daughter-in-law, has had illicit intercourse; moreover, she has also conceived through illicit sexual relations." Judah said, "Take her out and let her be burned!" 25. As she was being brought out, she sent to her father-in-law, "By the man to whom these belong I have conceived." She said, "Recognize! To whom do this seal, cord, and staff belong?" 26. Judah recognized and said, "She is more righteous than I, because I did not give her to Shelah my son." He never knew her again.

This episode is the dramatic climax of the narrative. It presents the crisis and resolution of the embedded plot tension, involving the jeopardy to Tamar's life. The anonymous report in Gen 38:24 informing Judah of Tamar's change of condition echoes his earlier assessment of this woman at the entrance to Enaim (Gen 38:15) with its charge of promiscuity. But Judah's reaction to a promiscuous woman within his own family is radically different from his reaction to the sexually available woman he meets in a public place, despite the fact that these two women are one and the same. His reaction to a family member, consisting of two imperatives ordering her death, makes explicit the danger Tamar accepted when she conceived through unconventional means.

But, for the second time in Genesis 38, Tamar overcomes a crisis threatening to suppress the emergence of the next generation. She sends the pledge and implicates Judah as the male participant in the crime for which he condemns her and as the father of her unborn children. Tamar's double utterance in Gen 38:25 concerning the significance of the pledge items attests to her earlier farsightedness when she bargained with Judah for them. The pledge's importance for resolving the crisis to Tamar's life is emphasized by the fact that she breaks her characteristic silence in the narrative only twice, once when she bargains for the pledge (Gen 38:16–18) and again when she produces it to identify Judah in this subsection (Gen 38:25).

The pledge forces Judah to reassess the situation and to acknowledge the comparative worthiness of Tamar's actions in light of his own failure to provide her with a suitable sexual partner in the person of his son Shelah. Implicit in his public recognition of Tamar's righteousness in Gen 38:26 is a revocation of the death sentence that he earlier imposed upon her in his role as paterfamilias, and indeed this reprieve due to extenuating circumstances is confirmed by the fact that she lives to give birth to twins in the final episode.

This fourth episode, ending as it does with Judah's recognition of the relative righteousness of Tamar's actions, his admission of guilt in withholding Shelah, and the notice that he refrained from further sexual relations with her, presents the appearance of a conclusion. But this appearance is belied by the fact that the narrative continues with yet another subsection. The sense of a double conclusion to the second part of Genesis 38 is due to the fact that it contains not one but two basic plot movements from crisis to resolution. This fourth episode presents the resolution of the embedded crisis involving the risk to Tamar's life inherent in her initiative to correct the procreative impasse. The fifth and concluding episode presents the resolution to the overarching crisis involving the biological and social emergence of the next generation:

> 27. At the time of her delivery, there were twins in her belly! 28. As she gave birth, one put out his hand, and the midwife took [it] and tied a red thread on his hand, saying "This one came out first." 29. When he drew back his hand, his brother came out! She said, "What a breach you have made for yourself!" And his name was called Perez. 30. Afterwards, his brother, upon whose hand was the red thread, came out. His name was called Zerah.

In this final episode, twin sons are born and named, thereby successfully completing the broken pattern of procreation established in the initial five verses of the narrative. This subsection elaborates the details of their birth, including a description of the reversed order of their emergence as witnessed by a midwife. It also augments the naming of at least one of the sons with an etiologic explanation (Gen 38:29).[21] The expansive description of this double event of birth and naming in comparison with the formulaic description of the three single births in the first birth narrative attests to the relative significance of the twins,[22] as does the tortuous route through which they were engendered and brought to life.

Character Roles and Narrative Perspectives

Tamar, the Marginal Protagonist

Although Tamar initially appears in the second part of Genesis 38 as a compliant, potential female partner in reproduction (similar to Shua's daughter in the first verses of the chapter), she ultimately emerges as the narrative's unconventional protagonist when the male characters fail to initiate progress towards procreation through conventional means. Her heroic ventures to overcome the childless stasis of the narrative include choosing for herself a sexual partner different

---

[21] Etiologies given in connection with the act of naming a newborn son are quite common as a conclusion to biblical birth narratives. See, for example, Gen 21:3–7; 25:25–26; 29:31–30:24; 35:18; 41:51–52.

[22] One might recall, however, the additional information about the location of Shelah's place of birth included in Gen 38:5, which singles him out as the significant brother of the initial sibling group. Shelah's survival after the deaths of his two older brothers constitutes a muted variation on the common biblical theme of the ascendancy of the youngest son, also evident in the birth of Perez and Zerah at the end of Genesis 38.

from the one designated for her, disguising herself and traveling on her own initiative to meet him, and deceiving him in order to elicit the male services earlier denied her. Her achievement of conception signals a resumption of the basic pattern of procreation established in the first five verses, but it simultaneously places her life and the life of her unborn children in grave danger. She overcomes this self-inflicted jeopardy by producing the pledge shrewdly obtained from her unsuspecting father-in-law, thus forcing him to reverse his earlier judgment. Following her resolution of the threat to her life, she successfully brings the narrative to closure by delivering twin sons, who receive names and therefore join the genealogical list of male generations. Twice, then, Tamar actively manipulates the plot, once on a biological level to facilitate conception and again on a social and legal level to save her own life and that of her unborn sons and to establish their paternity. Without the narrative control exerted by this female protagonist in her heroic restoration of a broken lineage, Genesis 38 would lack its fortunate ending.

In light of Tamar's centrality with respect to basic plot structure, the general opacity of the biblical text concerning her character becomes all the more striking. The narrator of Genesis 38 offers little information about this protagonist, few insights into her reactions to events and motives for action, and no mention of her fate after the birth of the twins. In addition, the events of the narrative are rarely viewed from her perspective, even when she herself is forcing its direction. This discrepancy between Tamar's important function in moving the plot forward and her marginal position within the narrative focus creates a dynamic tension, which each of the three early Jewish interpretations explored below attempts to resolve in one way or another.

A prime example of the narrator's reticence concerning Tamar is his introduction of this character in Gen 38:6, where he provides neither ethnic nor genealogical background for her as he did earlier for Judah's wife, the Canaanite daughter of Shua, who plays a much lesser role. Only Tamar's name is disclosed. Significantly, in the course of the narrative only the narrator (Gen 38:11, 13) and the anonymous voice of the report to Judah (Gen 38:24) continue to refer to Tamar by name after her introduction, thereby granting her at least a nominal personal identity. The other characters refer to her in their speech and their thoughts with a variety of relational and occupational terms.[23]

---

[23] See the discussion of the various relational terms applied to Tamar in Adele Berlin, *Poetics and Interpretation of Biblical Narrative* (Sheffield: Almond Press, 1983) 60–61.

In Gen 38:6 Judah regards her as "a wife for Er, his first-born"
(אשה לער בכורו). Later when he instructs Onan in Gen 38:8, Judah
refers to her as "the wife of your brother" (אשת אחיך). Similarly,
Onan thinks of her as "the wife of his brother" (אשת אחיו) in Gen
38:9. After the death of his sons, Judah orders her to remain a
"widow" (אלמנה) at her father's house in Gen 38:11, emphasizing
her relationship to her dead husband. In Gen 38:14, in the only
interior glimpse of the protagonist granted by the narrator, even Tamar
defines herself in terms of another character, as the "wife" that should
have been given to Shelah: "For she saw that Shelah had grown up,
but she had not been given to him as a wife" (לאשה). On the road
to Timnah in Gen 38:15, Judah considers her to be a sexually available woman or "prostitute" (זונה), an assessment echoed later in the
public charge against her in Gen 38:24. She becomes simply "the
woman" (האשה) to Judah and Hirah in Gen 38:20 when they attempt
to retrieve the pledge. Hirah calls her "the consecrated woman"
(הקדשה) in Gen 38:21 when he makes inquiries of the local men.
The narrator's depiction of Tamar through the changing perceptions
of the male characters creates a sense of distance from this protagonist and prevents the establishment of a stable identity for her, despite her central role in the plot.

Besides calling her by name, the narrator himself also refers to
Tamar as Judah's "daughter-in-law" (כלתו) in Gen 38:11 and 16. By
employing this term, which denotes a widely perceived relationship
judging from its appearance in the report to Judah in Gen 38:24,
the narrator joins the other characters in viewing Tamar in relational
terms. But the narrator also subtly passes judgment on Judah's
treatment of his daughter-in-law when he interjects this term, with
its connotations of familial responsibility, before the patriarch dis-
misses Tamar with the empty promise of his third son in Gen 38:11
and before he has sexual relations with her thinking she is a prostitute in Gen 38:16.[24] The narrator's employment of the relational

---

Berlin concludes from the employment of these different relational terms that Tamar
is a subordinate character in the narrative. Clearly, she fails to take into account
Tamar's role in the narrative plot. The indefinite nature of her character actually
helps her to overcome the reproductive impasse, in that she is able to shift identities
quickly from childless widow to prostitute and back, and ultimately to mother.

[24] Similarly, the appearance of the term "daughter-in-law" in the anonymous report
to Judah in Gen 38:24, directly before he condemns Tamar to death for an act in
which he participated, also implies a judgment on his character.

term "daughter-in-law" therefore has an additional evaluative function bearing on the character of Judah and is related to the ironic stance towards this character discussed further below. Even the narrator's use of this term to condemn Judah, however, directs the reader's attention away from the plot's protagonist and towards her morally deficient affinal relative.

The shifting perspectives in Genesis 38 also keep Tamar in the background for most of the narrative. Immediately following the narrator's cursory introduction of Tamar in Gen 38:6, he deflects the focus to Er's wickedness and God's punitive intervention in Gen 38:7. In Judah's instructions to his second son and in Onan's calculated partial compliance which follow in Gen 38:8–10, Tamar reappears merely as the silent object of their plans and actions. Finally after Onan's death, Judah speaks to her directly for the first time in Gen 38:11, thereby admitting her briefly to the narrative surface. The intention of his imperative ("Remain a widow at your father's house until Shelah my son grows up"), however, is to remove her physically from the central axis of the narrative to its periphery. Tamar's first actions in the story therefore occur in compliance with a command intended to deny her any further role in it ("Tamar went and remained at her father's house"). Then, instead of explicitly identifying with the twice-widowed woman by presenting her perspective on the events of the narrative, the narrator stylistically mimics Judah's neglect of his daughter-in-law. The objective record of Judah's wife's death and his engagement in routine seasonal activities in Gen 38:12 suggests the passage of time in a narrative world that has forgotten Tamar.

Tamar's lack of presence to this point in the narrative functions artistically to enhance the reader's surprise when she acts on her own initiative after being informed of Judah's journey. The narrator utilizes a series of verbs describing her unexpected and decisive actions in Gen 38:14, presenting Tamar at last as an independent agent who alters her appearance and moves herself to the geographical

---

It must also be noted that in depicting Tamar through the relational and occupational terms described in the previous paragraph, the author not only exercises an artistic option but also implicitly judges the male characters' treatment of this woman. The terms that Judah, Onan, and Hirah employ in their references to Tamar reveal that they always think of her as someone else's wife and therefore someone else's responsibility, or as a prostitute for whom no enduring responsibility is required. The male characters' attitudes towards Tamar suggest that she has no advocate and must act on her own initiative.

center of the narrative from its periphery. The narrator even offers
a motivation for her actions with the note that she perceived a lack
of honest intentions in her father-in-law's dealings with her: "for she
saw that Shelah had grown up, but she had not been given to him
as a wife." Significantly, the narrator is careful to portray Tamar as
compliant with the exact stipulations of Judah's command. Tamar
does indeed remain at her father's house until Shelah matures. Only
after she perceives Judah's lack of good faith does she temporarily
transform her appearance and change the location where she waits
for her father-in-law to act.

Although the direct revelation of Tamar's independent actions and
private thoughts momentarily strips away the layers of others' perceptions, she is immediately covered again in the opacity of the biblical
text's depiction of her. While the narrator permits us to know her
movements and her motivation, he leaves the reader ignorant concerning her plan of action. This can only be surmised if one assumes
that what happens after Judah turns aside to her on the road is what
she intended all along, for even the encounter that she contrives with
her father-in-law is viewed primarily through another's eyes.

It is Judah's perception of the woman he thinks is a prostitute to
which the reader is privy in Gen 38:15, not Tamar's perception of
her duped father-in-law. The narrator continues his open presentation of Judah's mental state with an explanation about why this
character fails to recognize his daughter-in-law in Gen 38:15 ("for
she covered her face") and with a reiteration of his ignorance concerning Tamar's identity in Gen 38:16 ("for he did not know that
she was his daughter-in-law"). Even the dialogue in Gen 38:16–18,
during which Tamar's voice emerges for the first time in the narrative, is initiated by her father-in-law and attests to his lack of perception of the real nature of their encounter. In keeping with his focus
on Judah's ignorance, the narrator leaves the reason Tamar insists
on procuring the pledge a mystery until these items become indis-
pensable for the resolution of the threat to her life.[25]

When the narrator depicts Tamar's retreat in Gen 38:19 in words
similar to those that precede her encounter with her father-in-law in

---

[25] For a remarkably different depiction of concealed identity, one only has to
compare Tamar's ruse with Joseph's first disguised encounter with his brothers in
Egypt in Gen 42:6–25. In this latter passage, the narrator provides information
concerning Joseph's thoughts and feelings as he deceives his brothers.

Gen 38:14, he confirms her control over the intervening events, but he also once again removes her from narrative view. She remains out of the narrative focus in the next subsection as well (Gen 38:20–23), which again concentrates on Judah's lack of perception, this time through its depiction of his unsuccessful attempts to find and pay the mysterious woman at Enaim. Despite her eclipse from view immediately following her encounter with her father-in-law, however, Tamar begins to structure the narrative temporally through the progress of her pregnancy beginning with Gen 38:24. But even at this point, she once again becomes the absent object of others' perceptions and discussions, first in the anonymous report to Judah and then in Judah's command that she be brought out and burned.

Precisely when she is passively being brought out in Gen 38:25, Tamar resurfaces from the background of the narrative and seizes control of the plot for the second and final time. She does so indirectly, however, by sending the pledge and a message from behind the scenes rather than appearing to confront her father-in-law herself. Through this oblique means, Tamar becomes the focus of Judah's attention for one final moment, when he positively compares her actions with his own in Gen 38:26. Then this subsection concludes with the note that Judah "never knew her again." Although this phrase refers primarily to the fact that Judah never again had sexual relations with his daughter-in-law, the wording seems especially appropriate given that the reader of the narrative too knows little about Tamar following her reprieve.

In fact, despite the final subsection's confirmation of Tamar's centrality for the plot through its depiction of the birth of twins from her womb, for the remainder of the narrative she herself is never again an active agent, nor even the focus of another's perceptions or attentions. Curiously and significantly, Tamar is not a central character in the birth scene, although she made this scene possible through great personal risk. Her presence in the scene that depicts her plan's fruition is apparent only through possessive pronouns. The scene takes place at the time of "her delivery" (לדתה) in Gen 38:27. It is then that the twins are found "in her womb" (בבטנה). Similarly, the twins emerge "during her delivery" (בלדתה) in Gen 38:28. But besides providing the time and the site of the birth, she is not an active participant in it as the narrator portrays it. She neither "gives birth" nor "names" her sons as did the Canaanite wife in the opening verses of the chapter.

Instead, other characters replace her as the active subjects in this final scene in Gen 38:27–30. Her two sons dominate the delivery through various actions: putting forth a hand, withdrawing it, breaking forth out of order, and emerging late from her body. In addition, the perspective on the birth is provided by another feminine charac-ter, the midwife. Unlike Tamar, this anonymous woman has an active role in the scene. She takes the first infant's hand, ties on the distinguishing thread, and comments on the reversal of birth order. Although the verbs of naming in Gen 38:29 and 30 are masculine singular in most manuscripts of the Masoretic Text, implying an impersonal statement of their names, a few Hebrew manuscripts, as well as the Samaritan Pentateuch, the Peshitta, and *Targum Pseudo-Jonathan*, indicate a feminine subject for these verbs. The feminine verbs in this variant version imply that the midwife names the twins after commenting on their unexpected order of birth, since these verbs appear within a passage where she is the only active female character. In light of the common depiction in biblical literature of mothers naming their children to reflect their experiences of childbirth,[26] this deflection to the midwife as the naming agent in these variant witnesses is striking. It signals that, although Tamar has an important role in the plot of the story, she is not necessarily the narrator's central interest. Genesis 38 cannot therefore be considered only in terms of this character's triumph over her recalcitrant father-in-law.[27]

The shifting perspectives described above are by no means unique to Genesis 38, but rather exemplify a characteristic feature of the poetics of biblical narrative.[28] In this narrative, however, the biblical poetics create a remarkable tension between Tamar's central role in the narrative plot and her marginal presence in much of the narrative surface. It is difficult to think of a comparable example of a biblical

[26] See for example Eve's naming of Cain in Gen 4:1 and of Seth in Gen 4:25; Leah and Rachel's naming of their sons in Gen 29:31–35; and Hannah's naming of Samuel in 1 Sam 1:20. Especially interesting is Rachel's naming of Benjamin in Gen 35:18, since in this delivery scene there is also a midwife who speaks, but leaves the naming of the son to the mother.

[27] This reading of Tamar as the moral victor in a fight against the injustice of patriarchy appears in some feminist interpretations of Genesis 38. See, for example, Sharon Pace Jeansonne, "Tamar: The Woman Who Demanded Justice," in *The Women of Genesis: From Sarah to Potiphar's Wife* (Minneapolis: Fortress Press, 1990) 98–106.

[28] See Berlin, *Poetics and Interpretation*, 83, and Meir Sternberg, "Viewpoints and Interpretations" and "The Play of Perspectives," in *The Poetics of Biblical Narrative: Ideological Literature and the Drama of Reading*, Indiana Studies in Biblical Literature (Bloomington: Indiana University Press, 1985) 129–85.

hero so lightly celebrated, emerging from nowhere and retreating to nowhere after shaping an important event in the history of Israel—in this case because of the narrative's genealogical connection with the Davidic kings.

Later readers of the biblical narrative find it difficult to leave the faint outline of such a strong character untouched and often take advantage of this tension and the spare portrayal of Tamar's character to recreate her in their own image, according to their own frames of reading. At times they positively enhance her character, as befits the central protagonist of an important story. At times they trim her role in moving the plot forward, in keeping with her marginal status in the narrative focus of the story. These widely divergent interpretive strategies are possible at least in part because of the gap between plot and perspective that characterizes Genesis 38.

Judah through Ironic Eyes

Judah's role in the procreative narrative depicted in Genesis 38 is extremely complex, vacillating between different forms of assistance and hindrance. In the first five verses of the chapter, he acts directly to initiate the movement of the simple plot by performing the necessary male reproductive actions. At the beginning of the second part of Genesis 38 as well, he attempts to facilitate the procreative drama of the next generation by selecting a wife for his eldest son and later by ordering a levirate arrangement between his middle son and his widowed daughter-in-law. Following the death of his second son, however, Judah's function in the narrative begins to shift, starting with his arrangement of an apparently temporary interruption in the progress of the narrative until his youngest son matures. But when he prolongs the delay past Shelah's maturation, Judah emerges as the fundamental obstacle to procreation. He thwarts the plot whether his failure to give Tamar to Shelah stems from neglect or intentional plan—two interpretations that the biblical text itself allows. Yet despite his status as the quasi-villain, it is Judah and not his mature third son whom the female protagonist of the narrative chooses to overcome the very impasse which he has perpetuated. Although unwittingly, Judah contributes positively to the restoration of the procreative progress of the narrative through a repetition of his earlier direct masculine reproductive role. Also unwittingly, he contributes positively to the resolution of the crisis brought about by his daughter-in-law's unorthodox conception by donating the pledge that

identifies him as the party responsible for her pregnancy. After learning of Tamar's pregnancy, Judah once again threatens to repress the
next generation, this time permanently and irrevocably with his order
that she be burned. But following his sudden recognition of his own
responsibility for the course of events, Judah's function oscillates one
final time from villain to champion. His acknowledgment of the righteousness of Tamar's actions in comparison with his own failure to
provide a legitimate avenue for procreation removes the threat to his
daughter-in-law's life and allows the completion of the narrative with
the birth and naming of twin sons.

Judah's actions and perspectives receive prominent coverage in
Genesis 38, and this expansive treatment contrasts with the narrator's
spare treatment of Tamar. The attention to Judah appears quite
appropriate in light of the importance of this character within both
the larger Joseph story and the even larger history of Israel. After
all, it is the name of this fourth son of Jacob that later becomes
synonymous with the Southern Kingdom, and eventually with the
Jewish people as a whole. Given the status of Judah and the tribe
associated with his name elsewhere in the Bible, however, the generally negative evaluation he receives in Genesis 38 is particularly
discordant. In addition, this negative evaluation of the character whose
actions and perspectives dominate the narrative foreground of Genesis 38 further complicates interpretation of the narrative, in that it
encourages readers to turn their sympathies away from Judah and
towards Tamar, despite the opacity of her character.

As a rule, the negative evaluation of Judah in Genesis 38 appears
in the subtle form of ironic understatement and implication.[29] For
example, interpreting Genesis 38 within its larger canonical context,
the reader detects ironic judgments in the dispassionate accounts of
Judah's behavior in violation of the law and spirit of other biblical
passages. His marriage with a Canaanite (Gen 38:2), his sexual engagement with a woman whom Hirah at least identifies as a type of
priestess (Gen 38:15–23), and his incestuous relations with his daughter-
in-law (Gen 38:15–18, 25–26) all reflect poorly on Judah in light of
biblical prohibitions against precisely such behavior, discussed further

---

[29] For a discussion of biblical irony and an analysis of a sustained instance of it
in the portrayal of Judah's distant descendant David, see Sternberg, "Gaps, Ambiguity, and the Reading Process," in *Poetics of Biblical Narrative*, 186–229. For a more
specific study of irony in Genesis 38, see Jean Louis Ska, "L'Ironie de Tamar (Gen
38)," *ZAW* 100 (1988) 261–63. See also Thomas Mann, *Joseph and His Brothers*, trans.
H. T. Lowe-Porter (New York: Knopf, 1948).

below. In addition, the narrator's choice of the verbal root "to turn aside" (נטה) to describe Judah's association with foreigners and his engagement of a prostitute is suggestive.[30] The basic meanings of this verbal root include "to stretch out" and "to incline," so this verb may simply denote Judah's settling near his Adullamite companion by alluding to the action of stretching out or pitching a tent in Gen 38:1,[31] and later it may simply denote his temporary detour from the road to Timnah in Gen 38:16. But since this verbal root in the causative stem can express the idea of leading someone astray,[32] its use may imply that Judah erred in his alliance with the foreign population and with a prostitute.

Judah also exhibits a certain hastiness and insensitivity in his perfunctory marriage with the daughter of Shua and in his unceremonious solicitation of the woman he takes for a prostitute. In both these instances, the absence of courtship behavior contrasts markedly with other, more extended, biblical encounters with future wives, typically at a well.[33] Judah's lack of deep feeling is also implied through the omission of any mention of mourning after the deaths of his two sons and through the placement of a brief notice that he was comforted, immediately following the report of his wife's death (Gen 38:12). The absence of portrayals of Judah's grief in Genesis 38 is especially striking in contrast to the extended depiction of Jacob's continuous mourning for his son Joseph in the preceding chapter (Gen 37:33–35).[34]

Even the first active verb of the chapter, contained in the sentence, "At that time, Judah went down (וירד) from his brothers," obliquely expresses an ironic stance towards Judah. While this verb may indicate a geographical direction of travel,[35] the report of Judah's

---

[30] After all, alliance with the local population was rejected just four chapters earlier in Genesis 34.

[31] The root נטה with this meaning appears in Gen 26:25 and 2 Sam 16:22.

[32] This meaning appears in Isa 44:20 and Job 36:18.

[33] Compare, for example, Gen 24:10–61; 29:1–30; and Exod 2:15–22. Robert Alter discusses variations on the convention of the betrothal scene at the well and comments on the significance of its absence in certain biblical narratives, although not specifically in Genesis 38 ("Biblical Type-Scenes and the Uses of Convention," in *The Art of Biblical Narrative* [New York: Basic Books, 1981] 47–62). There is actually a brief allusion to a source of water in Genesis 38, in the name of the location where Judah meets Tamar, "the entrance of Enaim" (פתח עינים), which may also be translated "opening of twin springs." This allusion points to Tamar's importance as a sexual partner and the mother of Judah's twin sons.

[34] Alter makes the same observation (*Art of Biblical Narrative*, 4–7).

[35] This notice that Judah "went down" may refer to a geographical descent from the hills in the vicinity of Hebron to the plains of Adullam, part of the territory associated with the tribe of Judah (Josh 15:35). Genesis 38 may therefore express the

descent follows his successful advocacy of the sale of Joseph, and so
these words take on an additional connotation. This sale distanced
Joseph from the murderous intents of his brothers, but it had other
less positive effects as well. Together with the brothers' subsequent
deception of their father, it brought about Jacob's forlorn claim that
he would "go down" (ארד) mourning to his son in Sheol (Gen 37:35).
Also as a result of this sale, Joseph was "brought down" (הורד) to
Egypt, where Potiphar purchased him from the Ishmaelites who "had
brought him down" (הורדהו, Gen 39:1).[36] Embedded between his
father's pathetic, imagined descent and his brother's forced, actual
descent, Judah's descent signifies more than an incidental direction
of travel. Within the extended play on the verb "to go down" (ירד)
that provides linguistic and thematic cohesion between Genesis 37,
38, and 39, the description of Judah's journey as a descent implies
a moral judgment on this character and hints at a loss of status due
to his flawed leadership of his brothers.

    The fact that two of Judah's sons are summarily slain by God be-
cause of their wickedness raises further questions about their father's
character. It is especially appropriate that Judah's son Onan should
refuse to act charitably toward his dead brother by providing him with
descendants, since Judah himself fails to act charitably toward his own
live brother when he advocates selling him into slavery (Gen 42:21).
Like his father before him, Onan acts to consign his brother to oblivion, and in both cases monetary gain appears to have been a consideration. In the case of Onan, the issue of inheritance rights may
have motivated his refusal to procreate for his brother (Gen 38:9),
and in the case of Judah, the issue of profit, along with the undesir-
ability of actually killing one's own flesh and blood, motivated his
advocacy of the sale of Joseph (Gen 37:26–27). Also like Judah before
him, who participated in the deception of Jacob (Gen 37:31–33),
Onan deceives his own father when he only partially complies with

---

memory of an early historical separation of this tribe (Judg 1:1–20), which is strikingly
absent in one of the oldest biblical poems referring to the tribes (Judges 5). Adullam
is also connected to the early career of David, Judah's distant relative (1 Sam 22:1).
For a discussion of possible interpretations of the notice that Judah "went down"
(וירד), see Emerton, "Some Problems in Genesis 38," 349–50.

[36] Although the specific verbal root "to go down" (ירד) is not employed in the
earlier report concerning Joseph's whereabouts in Gen 37:36, it is obvious that the
Midianites have successfully managed to bring Joseph down to Egypt, just as they
have managed "to bring down" (להוריד) their cargo of spices, balm, and ladanum
(Gen 37:25).

the levirate arrangement, by going into Tamar but taking precautions to prevent conception (Gen 38:9). Judah's evil sons, and especially Onan about whom more information is given, therefore cast a negative light on their father by mirroring his image.

Judah is also portrayed as an unreliable character in Genesis 38, in that twice he fails to follow through with his stated intentions. In the first instance, although Judah initially takes measures for the emergence of the next generation through his ordering of a levirate marriage between Onan and Tamar and later through his promise of a second levirate marriage between Shelah and his daughter-in-law, ultimately he fails to implement his plan, and he never actually gives Tamar to his youngest son once he has matured (Gen 38:14). In the second instance, despite a preliminary attempt, Judah ultimately fails to deliver his promise of a kid to the same woman, whom he mistakes for a prostitute (Gen 38:20–23). Paradoxically, while Judah's failure to keep his word concerning Shelah leads to the crisis of continuing childlessness, his failure to keep his word concerning the kid—or even to further investigate the mysterious circumstances of his encounter with the woman on the road—contributes to the resolution of this same crisis.

Judah's failure to follow through with his intentions in these two instances contributes to the more general portrayal of this character in Genesis 38 as ineffectual. Although Judah acts throughout the narrative in a commanding manner befitting the head of a household, his arrangements and imperatives never have the intended results. Judah's plan for marriage between Er and Tamar is thwarted by divine intervention (Gen 38:6–7); his arrangements for a levirate marriage between Onan and Tamar are subverted by Onan (Gen 38:8–10); and his promise of a levirate marriage between Shelah and Tamar remains unfulfilled. Although Tamar initially obeys Judah's command to return to her father's house until Shelah matures (Gen 38:11), once the young son has matured she ventures out without Judah's permission or even knowledge to accomplish her own plan (Gen 38:14). Finally, Judah's order that Tamar burn is never carried out because of the implicating evidence of the pledge and the reversal of judgment it brings (Gen 38:24–26). Through these repeated illustrations of Judah's unsuccessful efforts to control his family and to determine the course of events, the narrator ridicules this ineffectual paterfamilias who would, but cannot, rule.

Instead, Judah is ruled by Tamar, one of the subordinates of his household. Twice she effectively directs his actions, once to obtain his embrace and the pledge items and again to exact an admission of the justice of her actions in comparison with his own. In the first instance, Tamar's mere appearance in the right clothes at the right place leads Judah to perform in compliance with her will. He immediately offers to have sexual relations with her and follows her suggestion concerning the pledge items without question or hesitation. In the second instance, Tamar directly commands Judah to recognize the pledge items ("Recognize!" הכר נא, Gen 38:25), and he immediately complies ("Judah recognized," ויכר יהודה, Gen 38:26). Judah's obedience to his daughter-in-law's imperative contrasts with the instances of disobedience, unexpected predicament, and retraction that follow his own attempts to control the behavior of others. One of the strongest expressions of irony in Genesis 38 therefore consists of the depiction of Judah as the ineffective leader, effectively led by the woman whom he has misled. The repeated dramatization of Judah's ignorance of his daughter-in-law's identity and plan throughout the latter part of Genesis 38 further emphasizes his lack of effective control over the narrative events. In addition, it imparts an ironic undertone to the narrator's final note concerning Judah that "he never knew her again" (Gen 38:26), since even as he "knew" her at Enaim, he knew neither her identity nor her intention.

Implicit in the depiction of Judah as an unwitting pawn in his daughter-in-law's plan is an element of shame. The humiliation of this family head is also made explicit by the public revelation of his involvement in the very act for which he condemns Tamar and by his admission of responsibility for the extenuating circumstances that forced her hand. Significantly, it is Judah himself who introduces the theme of shame into this narrative, when he instructs Hirah to drop the search for the woman with the pledge to avoid becoming ridiculous ("lest we be ridiculed," פן נהיה לבוז, Gen 38:23). Ironically, Judah's attempt to conceal his involvement with this woman to avoid embarrassment ultimately facilitates the public disclosure of his involvement with her, since she consequently retains the pledge (Gen 38:25). Yet, it must be granted that Judah's willingness to let Tamar's unorthodox solution to the problem of his own making stand—despite the attendant public humiliation—ultimately redounds to his credit.

The presentation of Judah as a fallible human being in this narrative corresponds to the general tendency against idealizing ancestral figures in the Hebrew Bible. Within the specific context of the

Joseph story, Judah's loss of narrative control and his humiliation acquire additional resonances as well. They appear to be deserved punishments for mistreating his younger brother and for participating in the deception of his father in Genesis 37 and goads towards the formation of the much more responsible version of his character that resurfaces in the final chapters of Genesis. Be this as it may, the negative portrayal of an important Israelite ancestor in Genesis 38 proved problematic for early Jewish interpreters of this narrative. At least two of the interpretations of Genesis 38 examined below employ creative tactics to reform Judah's character into a more or less ideal ancestral hero, whose particular strengths correspond to the overarching orientation of each respective interpretation.

Divine Presence and Absence: Moral Judgments and the Limits of Knowledge
Intruding without introduction into the second procreative tale, God decisively influences the direction of Genesis 38 through his abrupt evaluation and elimination of Judah's two eldest sons. If one views the narrative simply in terms of the movement towards the emergence of the next generation, then God doubly thwarts this progress by eliminating potential fathers and may be described as a villain. But the story is more complex than its linear sequence of actions suggests, since the narrator specifies that the motivation for divine intervention is the moral defects of Er, who is "evil" (רע, Gen 38:7), and of Onan, whose deeds "are evil" (וירע, Gen 38:10). The remainder of the biblical narrative lacks an explicit divine presence; however, the punitive deaths of Er and Onan continue to affect the course of events, in that Judah prevents Shelah from assuming a mature masculine role to protect him from his brothers' fate.

God's relatively minimal role in Genesis 38 contrasts with his central role in the earlier chapters of Genesis and in the later books of the Pentateuch, which are replete with revelations of divine thought and speech, with self-disclosures to individuals and a chosen people, and with powerful displays of mercy and anger towards the created world, humanity, and Israel in particular. Even within the immediate context of the Joseph story, where an underlying divine guidance of the narrative is repeatedly noted indirectly by the narrator or by the characters themselves,[37] the direct, punitive interventions early in Genesis 38 and the subsequent divine silence stand out markedly.

---

[37] Repeatedly, the chapters at the end of Genesis that focus on Joseph in Egypt

A question arises in light of the striking presence and absence of
God in Genesis 38. What effect does the discrepancy between God's
early moral evaluations and direct punitive actions and his later silence
and apparent inaction have on a reader's attempt to evaluate the
narrative and its characters? Perhaps most immediately, because God's
double interventions are motivated by divine indignation at wickedness,
the reader becomes similarly predisposed to evaluate the rest of the
narrative in moral terms. A moral interpretation of the narrative
immediately raises objections to a whole array of problematic behavior by Judah and Tamar. Some of the objections arise from these
characters' apparent disregard for biblical laws, including those concerning marriage with Canaanite women, levirate marriage, incest,
and prostitution, discussed below. Others arise from these characters'
unkind, less than exemplary behavior, including Judah's offhand manner with women and his failure of responsibility towards his daughter-in-law, and Tamar's deception and public humiliation of her
father-in-law. But while reading Genesis 38 through the lens of morality raises serious questions about the appropriateness of Judah and
Tamar's actions, the biblical narrative itself does little to resolve these
questions. Additional divine, and therefore ultimately authoritative,
judgment is withheld for the remainder of the narrative, and Judah's
initial sentencing of Tamar demonstrates the qualified nature of human
judgment. Whereas God's evaluations of Er and Onan as evil lead
swiftly to their deaths, Judah's order for Tamar's death based on his
evaluation of her guilt is never carried out.

The final explicit moral evaluation in Genesis 38 also originates
with Judah, when he reverses his earlier evaluation of Tamar and
declares "She is more righteous than I" (צדקה ממני, Gen 38:26). Judah's
climactic acknowledgment of Tamar's righteousness provides an important focal point for interpretive transformations of the narrative, as
the following chapters show. Within Genesis 38 itself, the verb "to be
righteous" (צדק) contained in Judah's comparative evaluation of Tamar

---

(Genesis 37, 39–50) draw attention to God's controlling force behind the narrative.
Several times the narrator asserts that God was with Joseph and granted him success (Gen 39:2–3, 5, 21, 23). Joseph himself frequently points to the presence and
power of God (Gen 39:9; 40:8; 41:16, 25, 28, 32; 42:18; 43:29; 45:5, 7, 8, 9; 48:9;
50:19–20, 24, 25). Other characters as well acknowledge the divine presence, including Pharaoh (Gen 41:38, 39), the brothers (Gen 42:28; 50:17), Joseph's steward
(Gen 42:23), Judah (Gen 44:16), and Jacob (Gen 43:14; 46:1; 48:3–4, 15–16, 20,
21; 49:24–25). God himself appears once in a vision to reassure Jacob before his
descent into Egypt (Gen 46:2–4).

contrasts markedly with the adjective "evil" (רַע) and the denominative verb "to be evil" (רָעַע) contained in God's definitive evaluations of Er and Onan. The appearance of these opposite words suggests that the story's message includes a moral contrast between Judah's sons and his daughter-in-law. But significantly, it is not God who offers the final evaluation of Tamar, but a more limited character. Judah's limitations as a judge stem not only from his humanity, but also from his flawed character. Judah himself admits one of his own failures immediately after he positively evaluates Tamar, when he concedes that he neglected to give her to his son Shelah (Gen 38:26). This acknowledged failure, his role in the sale of Joseph, and the deception of his father in Genesis 37, along with all of his other questionable behavior in Genesis 38, cast doubt on Judah's trustworthiness as a commentator on issues of morality. Perhaps the reader is to accept Judah's moral judgment of Tamar as the words of a man chastened and reformed by experience. The narrator's statement that Judah "never knew [Tamar] again" at the end of Gen 38:26 and Judah's self-sacrificing performance later in the Joseph story (Gen 44:18–34) support such an interpretation. But even if this is the case, Judah's positive comparison of his daughter-in-law with himself is no ringing endorsement of her virtue, given the long list of his own foibles and faults. Indeed, lingering in the reader's memory are Tamar's own questionable acts of deception, impersonation of a prostitute, conception outside of sanctioned social contexts, incest, and public humiliation of her father-in-law.

Despite all these qualifications, there may be at least a partial concurrence of human and divine moral judgments when Judah applies the term "righteous" to Tamar and, obliquely through comparison, to himself. Unlike Er and Onan, both Tamar and Judah are left unscathed by divine punishment. This absence of divine intervention in a narrative that has twice dramatized its possibility suggests a measure of tacit divine approval. In addition, the emergence of twin sons in the final scene also imputes a positive valence to the narrative as a whole, both generally because the birth of male offspring brings positive closure to many biblical narratives and specifically because one of the sons is the ancestor of an important lineage. Perhaps, as in the larger Joseph story, God may be present despite his narrative absences in Genesis 38, working through the morally ambiguous matrix of human lives for more comprehensive purposes. Words similar to Joseph's in Gen 50:20, "As for you, you intended to do evil against me, but God intended it for good," could be loosely applied to the characters of Genesis 38.[38] But this conclusion is not stated explicitly, and the mixed signs pointing to it compose some of the data sifted and sorted by earlier interpreters, with varying results.

The two brief moments of divine omniscience early in a story that subsequently illustrates human misperception have the additional effect of highlighting the pervasive theme of knowledge, concealed and revealed, in Genesis 38. Biblical narrative, like other types of narrative, frequently illustrates a progression from partial and sometimes mistaken apprehensions of truth by individual human characters towards a more comprehensive and accurate assessment of reality.[39] In its particular depiction of this dynamic of human experience, biblical narrative points both to the educational aspects of experience and to the chasm that separates limited human perceptions from divine omniscience. Genesis 38, with its shifting perspectives holding various relations to the truth and its progression from deception and mistaken identity to recognition, typifies the thematic biblical movement from partial to more complete knowledge among human characters, while still positing a divine perspective that exceeds all other perspectives.

Genesis 38 underscores the theme of knowledge through repeated employment of verbs of perception, including "to know" (ידע, Gen 38:9, 16, 26), "to recognize" (נכר, Gen 38:25, 26), and "to see" (ראה, Gen 38:2, 14, 15). Further emphasis on the knowledge that visual perception allows is made through references to the "eyes of the LORD" (עיני יהוה, Gen 38:7, 11), through the place name Enaim (עינים, Gen 38:14, 21) which can mean "eyes," and through the repetition of an exclamatory particle (הנה, Gen 38:13, 23, 24, 29) generally associated with reactions to visual phenomena.[40] But whereas one assumes that the "eyes of the LORD" in Genesis 38 are clear-sighted, one discovers

---

[38] For a discussion of divine guidance over history in wisdom literature, see Gerhard von Rad, "The Joseph Narrative and Ancient Wisdom," in *The Problem of the Hexateuch and Other Essays*, trans. E. W. Trueman Dicken (Edinburgh and London: Oliver & Boyd, 1966) 292–300.

[39] For a discussion of various aspects of this dynamic, see Sternberg, *Poetics of Biblical Narrative*, 230–63.

[40] This relation to visual perception is captured by the King James Version's translation of this particle as "Behold!" In Genesis 38, this exclamatory particle appears in the anonymous report that reveals Judah's travels to Tamar (Gen 38:13), in Judah's discussion of the failed search for the woman with the pledge (Gen 38:23), in the anonymous report that reveals Tamar's pregnancy to Judah (Gen 38:24), and in the narrator's disclosure of the twins in Tamar's belly (Gen 38:27).

that the perceptions of the human characters are not as reliable. In particular, Judah illustrates both the limitations of human perception and the possibility of movement from partial to more complete knowledge. Judah's sight of a veiled woman leads to the erroneous conclusion that she is a prostitute, and his subsequent search for this woman ends without a sighting. But Judah also comes to appreciate the true state of affairs upon seeing the pledge that his daughter-in-law returns to him.[41] This climactic moment of visual recognition in Genesis 38 stimulates recognition of a more fundamental nature and leads to Judah's public admission of responsibility for the crisis that forced Tamar to act in an unorthodox, but effective, manner (Gen 38:26). The fact that Judah accuses himself in Genesis 38 emphasizes his personal progress from irresponsibility and ignorance to self-knowledge and responsibility.[42]

But Judah's didactic journey is by no means the only dynamic operative with respect to the theme of knowledge in Genesis 38. Relatively early in the story, Tamar becomes a responsible and decisive agent when she "sees" (ראתה) that Shelah has matured and that Judah has failed to keep his promise (Gen 38:14). Paradoxically, Tamar's clear vision motivates deceptive behavior that temporarily clouds Judah's perception,[43] until ultimately he himself acknowledges her superior insight (Gen 38:26).[44]

But Genesis 38 is not a simple didactic tale, since the multiple perspectives through which the narrative unfolds never ultimately coalesce into a unified and unambiguous point of view. Instead, when interpreting Genesis 38, the reader experiences limits of knowledge

---

[41] In Genesis 38, Judah's visual perception of articles of clothing and personal belongings lead either to concealment or revelation of truth, depending on Tamar's employment of them. Significantly, articles of clothing, specifically those belonging to Joseph, are also used deceptively in Genesis 37 and 39.

[42] Judah's descendant David similarly accuses himself of wrongdoing in 2 Sam 12:1–14 and 14:1–24, although in these cases the king accuses himself obliquely by reacting to a narrative with parallels to his own situation.

[43] By removing her widow's garb and covering herself with a veil (Gen 38:14), Tamar conceals her true identity from her father-in-law and leads him to conclude that she is a prostitute. By removing the veil and resuming her habitual widow's dress (Gen 38:19), she temporarily conceals the fact that anything of import has transpired.

[44] In addition to these two examples of individuals who gain knowledge through the course of the narrative, the general public (implied by the anonymous report to Judah and by his plural imperative, "Take her out!" [הוציאוה], in Gen 38:24, and by Tamar's employment of an intermediary, or intermediaries, in Gen 38:25) comes to a more accurate assessment of Tamar's behavior through the events in Gen 38:24–26.

similar to those that mark the perceptions, choices, and actions of the narrative's human characters. In particular, the flashes of omniscience early in the narrative stimulate reflection about the main human characters' awareness of the divine perspective. For example, Judah's instructions to his daughter-in-law to return to her father's house until Shelah matures (Gen 38:11) do not disclose his understanding of first Er's and then Onan's demise. Does Judah have the same knowledge that the reader has of God's thoughts and deeds in relation to Er and Onan? Judah's expression of concern for the life of his third son ("Lest he die also like his brothers," Gen 38:11) eliminates the possibility that he regards their deaths as mere accidents of chance. If Judah is privy to the divine perspective, perhaps he fears his third son will similarly fail to meet divine standards and hopes that the passage of time will allow a positive development of his character. Equally likely, however, is the supposition that Judah wrongly holds Tamar responsible for his sons' deaths, since in each instance they die after association with her. The motif of the bride who brings death upon her new husband appears in Jewish literature from later periods, for example in the second-century BCE story of Tobit, which features the often-widowed bride Sarai.[45] It may be that Judah's fear for his third son's life at the hands of a twice-widowed woman is an earlier expression of a similar superstition. In this second reading, Judah's dismissal of Tamar and his continued withholding of Shelah stem from a clear misplacement of blame on his daughter-in-law, due to his ignorance of God's judgment and intervention. In line with this reading, Judah's final words in Gen 38:11, "Lest he also die like his brothers," become a private aside, expressing his groundless suspicions of his daughter-in-law and hinting that his promise to give her to Shelah is from the beginning an empty deception.[46]

Tamar's understanding of the cause of Er and Onan's deaths and

---

[45] Tob 3:7–17; 6:9–8:21. For other examples, and for a discussion of Genesis 38 as a refutation of the "killer wife" superstition, see Mordechai A. Friedman, "Tamar, a Symbol of Life: The 'Killer Wife' Superstition in the Bible and Jewish Tradition," *Association for Jewish Studies Review* 15 (1990) 23–61.

[46] Interpreting Judah's treatment of Tamar as deceptive is facilitated by the numerous depictions of deception in the Joseph story. Specifically, the brothers deceive their father concerning the fate of Joseph in Genesis 37, Tamar deceives her father-in-law concerning her identity in Genesis 38, Potiphar's wife deceives her husband and the other members of the household concerning Joseph's behavior in Genesis 39, and Joseph deceives his brothers about his identity in Genesis 42–45.

of her father-in-law's intentions towards her remains similarly ambiguous. One might at least assume that Tamar knows more than her father-in-law about Onan's refusal to father children for his deceased brother. But it is unclear whether or not she is aware of the divine evaluation and dispatch of the brothers. Her remarkable and unexplained targeting of Judah rather than Shelah to be her unwitting partner does little to resolve this issue; indeed, it provides an opening for further speculation. Perhaps Tamar's choice of Judah indicates that she thinks his third son is no better than the first two. Alternatively, perhaps she chooses Judah as the means towards conception because it is he who thwarts conception by withholding Shelah. In this case, especially if she suspects that Judah has neglected her because he considers contact with her to be dangerous, the deception of her deceiver in order to engage him sexually has a special poetic justice. In this interpretation, the narrator's final note concerning Judah, that "He never knew her again" (Gen 38:26), conveys more than a concern with the morality of the patriarch. It also expresses Judah's continuing wariness of the woman he suspects in his sons' deaths and his resolve to distance himself from the dangers of her embrace.[47]

Nothing in the concluding verses of Genesis 38 resolves the issues concerning Judah and Tamar's cognizance of God's role in the narrative or of each other's motives and behavior. The narrative background remains opaque, and the reader is left with insoluble riddles involving the accuracy of these characters' perceptions, despite the general movement in Genesis 38 towards common, life-preserving knowledge. The reader may suppose that Judah and Tamar themselves never experience a full disclosure of each other's intentions and of the larger significance of the narrative. Indeed, in an important respect, the reader actually has an advantage in perspective over Judah and Tamar. By interpreting Genesis 38 within a larger canonical context that articulates its royal implications, the reader approaches a perspective of omniscience generally reserved for God in biblical narrative. Although an explicit divine perspective is lacking in Genesis 38 following the deaths of Er and Onan, the reader virtually assumes this

---

[47] Friedman, "Tamar, a Symbol of Life," 29, expresses this interpretation of Judah's permanent avoidance of Tamar. Judah's fear of Tamar as a "killer wife" whose sexuality dispenses death would be ironic, in that it is he himself who almost causes her death following their sexual relations, and not the other way around.

perspective due to his or her knowledge of the important consequences of this narrative. But in addition, an examination of this biblical narrative in terms of the theme of concealed and revealed knowledge gives rise to a compelling theological understanding of the human condition. Although people make decisions and follow courses of action in the half-light of partial human knowledge, there may be a greater purposefulness to their lives visible only to the divine gaze.[48] Each of the early Jewish interpretations examined below develops the prominent theme of concealed and revealed knowledge highlighted by the two instances of divine perspective in different ways.

CANONICAL CONTEXTS OF GENESIS 38

Interpreters of written texts draw upon their memory of other, related texts for the comparisons and contrasts that allow meaning to emerge.[49] This generalization holds true in a special and concrete way for biblical interpretation, which takes as its subject passages within a circumscribed textual corpus of sacred writings.[50] The three ancient Jewish interpretations of Genesis 38 analyzed below illustrate the intertextual nature of biblical hermeneutics, although certainly the guiding external referents in these examples may include wider literary and cultural influences as well as scriptural texts. These wider literary and cultural influences vary and must be identified in the course of analysis of each particular interpretation, but a study of some of the most obvious points of interface between Genesis 38 and other biblical passages provides a helpful common introduction to all three interpretations. Such a study highlights intertextual links within the canon readily available to all readers of scripture, including

---

[48] Significantly, the results of Judah's scandalous behavior in encouraging the sale of his brother (Genesis 37) and in buying the sexual services of a woman who turns out to be his daughter-in-law (Genesis 38) are ultimately positive. In the first case, Joseph's descent into Egypt ensures the survival of his family and of all Egypt during the great famine, and in the second, Tamar's conception signals the emergence of the royal lineage.

[49] For discussions of the intertextual nature of reading, see John Sturrock, ed., *Structuralism and Since* (Oxford: Oxford University Press, 1979); Jonathan Culler, *The Pursuit of Signs: Semiotics, Literature, and Deconstruction* (Ithaca: Cornell University Press, 1981); Ziva Ben-Porat, "Intertextuality, Rhetorical Intertextuality, Allusion, and Parody," *Ha-Sifrut* 34 (1985) 171–78; and Jay Clayton and Eric Rothstein, eds., *Influence and Intertextuality in Literary History* (Madison: University of Wisconsin Press, 1991).

[50] Brevard S. Childs, *Old Testament Theology in a Canonical Context* (Philadelphia: Fortress Press, 1986), takes seriously the special case of scriptural intertextuality with his emphasis on the canon as the primary context for biblical interpretation.

those responsible for the *Testament of Judah, Targum Neofiti,* and *Genesis Rabba*. Perhaps not surprisingly, these same intertextual junctures between Genesis 38 and other biblical texts also inform modern interpretations of the biblical narrative, as will become evident in the following discussion.

Legal Questions

One of the most perplexing and enduring issues in the study of the Pentateuch concerns the relationship between the narratives and the legal material. In addition to a basic difference in genre, these two types of biblical material frequently display a marked difference in their representation of normative, or even acceptable, behavior. This disturbing discordance, evident particularly in connection with the patriarchal narratives of Genesis, has stimulated various attempts throughout the ages to explain the apparently irregular behavior of the biblical ancestors.

Some of these attempts appeal to the concept of chronology. For example, one explanation offered in second temple and rabbinic literature for the obvious discrepancies between biblical narrative and biblical law emphasizes that the characters of Genesis lived before the revelation at Sinai. They were therefore neither knowledgeable of divine laws and commandments not yet given, nor accountable for their observance.[51] Modern historical criticism also relies on the concept of chronology in its very different explanation of the tensions and contradictions between biblical narratives and laws, and indeed between different versions of the biblical laws themselves. It maintains that these discrepancies simply point to the distinctive sources that make up the Pentateuch—sources stemming from different time periods, and perhaps from different social classes and geographical locations as well.[52] From a historical-critical perspective, a biblical

---

[51] For an example of this chronological explanation, see *Jub.* 33:16, which maintains that Reuben was spared execution for having sexual relations with his father's concubine only because "the ordinance and judgment and law had not been revealed till then [as] completed for everyone." Similarly, in *Gen.Rab.* 22.12 Cain is spared execution following his murder of Abel, since "he had none from whom to learn [the enormity of his crime]." A conflicting tradition appearing with much greater frequency in second temple and rabbinic literature, namely that the patriarchs and other biblical worthies were graced with a pre-Sinaitic revelation of the Tora, greatly weakens this position, however.

[52] For example, a modern chronological explanation of the discrepancies between the depictions of levirate marriage in Genesis 38 and in Deut 25:5–10 may be found in Eryl W. Davies, "Inheritance Rights and the Hebrew Levirate Marriage,"

narrative may predate certain laws and therefore express an earlier social and legal reality, or vice versa.[53]

The chronological theories of both early Judaism and historical criticism provide rational explanations for puzzling aspects of biblical texts, and the latter's presuppositions concerning the historical evolution of social and legal norms underlie the analysis below of the relation between Genesis 38 and the biblical laws. The fact remains, however, that the juxtaposition of discordant traditions within a single literary corpus has almost unavoidable hermeneutic consequences. At the very least, the presence of biblical laws related in one manner or another to a biblical narrative encourages exegetical concentration on the legal issues and situations that both describe. At times, reading biblical narrative in connection with biblical law has even more decisive effects. For example, it may raise questions about the morality of biblical characters or it may foster supplementation of a spare narrative with the contents of apparently related legal passages.

The following discussion revolves around some of the most obvious interfaces between Genesis 38 and the pentateuchal laws, including those concerning intermarriage with Canaanites, levirate marriage and incest, and prostitution and consecrated women.[54] Special attention is given to the exegetical potential inherent within the juxtapositions between Genesis 38 and these laws—a potential that comprised part of the hermeneutic matrix out of which later interpretations of the narrative arose.

VT 31 (1981) 138–44, 257–68. Davies maintains that Genesis 38 stems from an ancient narrative source and therefore portrays a primitive form of levirate marriage, whereas Deut 25:5–10 reflects a later development of the practice.

[53] This summary of one possible relationship between biblical narrative and biblical law is by no means the only one current in biblical scholarship. A distinctive, although not entirely convincing, approach is advocated by Calum Carmichael (*Law and Narrative in the Bible: The Evidence of the Deuteronomic Laws and the Decalogue* [Ithaca: Cornell University Press, 1985]). Unlike proponents of historical-critical methods, Carmichael maintains that the interface between narrative and law in the Pentateuch is not arbitrary. He argues, rather, that in some cases biblical laws are intended to comment on particular biblical narratives.

[54] Many other intertextual links between Genesis 38 and various Pentateuchal laws could have been explored as well, including those involving the use of pledges preceding payment (Exod 22:25–26; Deut 24:6, 10–13, 17); the punishments for sexual offenses (Lev 20:12, 14; 21:9; Deut 22:13–22, 23–24); and the procedure for trial, including the calling of witnesses, in capital cases (Num 35:29–34; Deut 19:15–21; 17:2–7).

Canaanite Wives

The Bible expresses a variety of attitudes towards non-Israelites and towards Israelite relations with them, particularly intermarriage.[55] Judging from the evidence of biblical narratives and genealogies, intermarriage was a common practice from the very beginning of Israelite history to the post-exilic period. In some instances, marriages and other forms of permanent sexual relationships between Israelite men and foreign women are simply noted objectively, without further evaluation.[56] In a few cases, such marriages receive either tacit or explicit approval.[57] At other times, the social reality of intermarriage is acknowledged, although it is portrayed as far from ideal.[58] In still other very important instances, the possibility of exogamous

---

[55] For an overview of the attitudes towards intermarriage expressed in biblical literature, see Athalya Brenner, אהבת רות: אשר היא טובה לך משבעה בנים [The love of Ruth: Who is better to you than seven sons] (Tel Aviv: Sifriat Poalim, 1988) 51–58.

[56] For example, Abraham takes a second, apparently foreign wife, Keturah, after Sarah's death (Gen 25:1, 4; 1 Chr 1:32–33). According to the genealogy in Gen 46:10, Simeon has sons by a Canaanite wife. Elimelech's Ephrathite sons, Mahlon and Chilion, take Moabite wives during the family's sojourn in Moab (Ruth 1:1–5). King David takes the wife of a Hittite, presumably herself also a Hittite, as his queen (2 Samuel 11), and although the biblical narrator comments that "the thing David had done was evil in the eyes of the LORD" (2 Sam 11:27), the divine displeasure lies in David's adultery and murder rather than in the ethnic identity of Bathsheba, as Nathan's parable makes clear (2 Sam 12:1–14). David also has a foreign wife from Geshur, namely Maacah, who bears him Absalom (2 Sam 3:3).

[57] For example, Joseph's marriage with the Egyptian woman Asenath, daughter of Potiphera, priest of On, is depicted as a sign of Pharaoh's favor (Gen 41:45), and the offspring of this marriage, Manasseh and Ephraim (Gen 41:50; 46:20), are featured prominently at the end of the Joseph story, when Jacob blesses them (Genesis 48). Similarly, Moses' marriage with Zipporah, daughter of the priest of Midian, produces important offspring and figures in his delivery from the mysterious divine attempt to take his life (Exod 2:15–22; 4:24–26; 18:2). After the exodus from Egypt, God takes Moses' side against Miriam and Aaron, who criticize his marriage with a Cushite woman (Numbers 12).

[58] So, for example, although Abraham has a son with the Egyptian slave Hagar (Gen 16:15; 25:12), this son, Ishmael, is not divinely designated as the descendant who will stand in a covenantal relationship with God in Abraham's stead (Gen 17:18–21). Isaac and Rebekah react negatively to Esau's marriages with local women (Gen 26:34–35; 27:46; 28:6–9), who are described in a genealogy as Canaanites (Gen 36:2–3). Similarly, Samson's parents object to his desire to marry a Philistine woman, and serious problems ensue from this marriage (Judges 14–15); however, the biblical narrative makes it clear that the events of Samson's life occur in accordance with a divine plan to release Israel from Philistine rule (Judg 14:4). Solomon's marriages with Egyptian, Moabite, Ammonite, Edomite, Sidonian, and Hittite wives are viewed by the deuteronomic historian as the cause of his fall into idolatry and the subsequent decline of the Davidic dynasty (1 Kgs 3:1; 7:8; 9:24; 11:1–13; 14:21), and Ahab's marriage with the Sidonian princess Jezebel is regarded as the reason for his worship of Baal, which provokes divine anger against him (1 Kgs 16:29–34).

marriage with local women is depicted as undesirable and problematic, and decisive measures are taken to avoid it.[59]

When one turns from biblical narrative and genealogy to biblical
law, the attitude towards intermarriage with foreigners—specifically
towards intermarriage with the indigenous populations of Canaan
following the conquest—is more consistently negative. Explicit warnings against marriage with Canaanites and other local peoples appear
in Exod 34:11–16 and Deut 7:1–5.[60] These warnings stress that intermarriage with native populations would lead to apostasy, since Israelites would naturally follow their foreign partners in worshipping
local gods. In the exilic and post-exilic periods, the prohibitions in
Exod 34:11–16 and Deut 7:1–5 against marriage with the autochtho-
nous peoples of Canaan following the conquest are further extended.
For example, Ezra 9–10 interprets the pentateuchal laws extremely
stringently, forbidding even marriages with foreign women not related
to the original inhabitants of Canaan and specifying divorce and
expulsion of foreign wives and their children as severe remedies for
the sin of intermarriage.[61] Similar broad strictures against intermarriage

---

[59] For example, Abraham and his servant take measures to prevent Isaac from
marrying a local Canaanite woman (Genesis 24), and Jacob travels to Paddan-aram
to find a wife among his relatives (Gen 27:46–28:5; 29:1–30). Genesis 34 also dramatizes the rejection of intermarriage, although the issue of rape must also be factored
into any interpretation of this narrative.

[60] For a discussion of the passage from Exodus, see F. Langlement, "Israël et
'l'habitant du pays:' vocabulaire et formules d'Ex. 34:11–16," *RB* 76 (1969) 321–50,
481–507. The indigenous peoples mentioned in both passages include the Amorites,
the Canaanites, the Hittites, the Perizzites, the Hivites, and the Jebusites. To this
list, Deut 7:1 adds the Girgashites, bringing their number to seven. Some of these
peoples (the Hittites, the Jebusites, the Amorites, the Girgashites, and the Hivites)
are considered descendants of Canaan in Gen 10:15–18, and therefore belong to
the larger ethnic category of the Canaanites. Josh 23:12–13 and Judg 3:5–6 express
similar negative evaluations of intermarriage with the indigenous peoples of Canaan.

[61] For example, Ezra 9:1 includes Ammonite, Moabite, and Egyptian women in
an expanded list of forbidden wives. For an analysis of Ezra 9–10 as an example of
inner-biblical exegesis of Deut 7:1–6 and 23:4–9, see Michael Fishbane, *Biblical
Interpretation in Ancient Israel* (Oxford: Clarendon Press, 1988) 114–23.
   Similar zeal for the eradication of intermarriage extending beyond the original
pentateuchal prohibitions may be found in 1 Kgs 11:1–13 and in Neh 10:29–31
and 13:23–27. 1 Kgs 11:1–13 applies a prohibition against intermarriage, paraphrasing
Deut 7:1–5, to Solomon's marriages with Egyptian, Moabite, Ammonite, Edomite,
Sidonian, and Hittite women; however, while there is a prohibition against intermarriage with Hittites in Deut 7:1, there is no prohibition against intermarriage with
the other ethnic groups listed in 1 Kgs 11:1. Neh 10:29–31 refers to separation, not
from the people of a specific land, namely the land of Canaan, but to a broader
separation "from the peoples of the lands" (מעמי הארצות, Neh 10:29). Neh 13:23–27
excludes marriages with women from Ashdod, Ammon, and Moab in its expansive

between Jews and non-Jews also appear in second temple and rabbinic literature.[62]

In Genesis 38 itself, Judah's marriage with the daughter of the Canaanite Shua receives no explicit evaluation (Gen 38:2).[63] Modern biblical commentators generally agree that this narrative's portrayal of intermarriage accurately reflects the mixed ethnic identity of the southern tribe of Judah.[64] According to this view, Genesis 38 expresses an early historical reality and therefore predates the prohibition against intermarriage with local populations found in Exod 34:11–16 and Deut 7:1–5, and even more so the later, broadened understanding of this prohibition found in Ezra and other post-exilic literature.

It is exceedingly difficult, however, to prevent the pentateuchal laws from negatively coloring one's perception of Judah's choice of spouse. His unceremonious selection of a Canaanite wife also contrasts sharply with the efforts earlier in the patriarchal narratives to insure that Isaac and Jacob did not marry local women.[65] Within

---

interpretation of the prohibition against intermarriage with the peoples of Canaan in Deut 7:1–5.

By contrast, other parties from the same period, including those responsible for the corpus known as 2 Isaiah and possibly those responsible for the book of Ruth, express more inclusive attitudes towards intermarriage and the offspring produced by such marriages.

[62] For example, in Tob 4:12 Tobit instructs his son Tobias to avoid immorality by rejecting marriage with a foreign woman and cites Noah, Abraham, Isaac, and Jacob as positive examples of endogamy.

See Géza Vermès, "Leviticus 18:21 in Ancient Jewish Bible Exegesis," in מחקרים באגדה תרגומים ותפלות ישראל לזכר יוסף היינימן [Studies in aggada, targum, and Jewish liturgy, in memory of Joseph Heinemann], ed. E. Fleischer and J. J. Petuchowski (Jerusalem: Magnes Press; Cincinnati: Hebrew Union College Press, 1981) 108–24, for a study of the aversion to intermarriage expressed in second temple and rabbinic exegesis of a scriptural passage not originally related to the subject.

A historical overview of the evolution of Jewish attitudes towards intermarriage evidenced in the Bible and rabbinic literature appears in Louis M. Epstein, *Marriage Laws in the Bible and the Talmud* (Cambridge, MA: Harvard University Press, 1942) 145–219.

[63] See also 1 Chr 2:3, which simply notes the ethnic identity of Judah's wife.

[64] For expressions of this view, see S. R. Driver, *The Book of Genesis*, 3d ed., Westminster Commentaries (London: Methuen and Co., 1904) 326; John Skinner, *A Critical and Exegetical Commentary on Genesis*, The International Critical Commentary (New York: Charles Scribner's Sons, 1910) 449, 451; von Rad, *Genesis*, 357; and E. A. Speiser, *Genesis*, The Anchor Bible (New York: Doubleday, 1962) 300.

[65] See Genesis 24; 28:1–5; and 29:1–30. Reading Judah's choice of a Canaanite wife in the narrative context of Genesis creates an implicit comparison between Judah and Esau. The latter married local women, lost the birthright and the blessing, and finally married one of Ishmael's daughters in an attempt to please his parents (Gen 25:29–34; 26:34–35; 27; 28:6–9).

Genesis 38 itself, the divine judgment of Judah's offspring with the Canaanite (Gen 38:7, 10) seems to confirm the external indications that this marriage was less than ideal.

In view of the pressures within the larger canon to read Judah's marriage with the Canaanite daughter of Shua as a serious misdeed, the unexpected silence in Genesis 38 concerning Tamar's ethnic identity becomes highly suggestive. Twentieth-century commentaries tend to transfer the Canaanite ethnic identity of Judah's first wife to Tamar as well.[66] The setting of the narrative in an area inhabited by Canaanites and Adullamites (Gen 38:1–2) and the lack of special measures to procure a non-Canaanite wife for Er support filling in the curious gap in the biblical text this way. But the assignment of a Canaanite background for Tamar also serves a further modern purpose: it bolsters the current consensus that one of the major purposes of Genesis 38 is to depict the mixed ethnic ancestry of the Judah tribe.[67] But if this were actually one of the major purposes of the narrative itself in its present form, one would expect at least a passing reference to the foreign ethnic identity of its most important female progenitor.

The absence of any such reference may actually reflect the narrator or redactor's attempt to shield Tamar and her relations with Judah from the pejorative force of the biblical laws and narratives condemning intermarriage with Canaanites. Building upon this biblical silence, however, some later Jewish interpreters view Tamar as an ethnic contrast to the Canaanite daughter of Shua, rather than as her parallel.[68] As pointed out in the following chapters, the three interpretive works develop Tamar's ethnic and genealogical background in a variety of ways, in harmony with their wider purposes. Without

---

[66] Tamar becomes a Canaanite in Driver, *Book of Genesis*, 326; Skinner, *Commentary on Genesis*, 449, 451; von Rad, *Genesis*, 357; and Speiser, *Genesis*, 300, as well as in S. Cohen, "Tamar," in vol. 4 of *IDB*, 515. J. A. Emerton furthermore argues that the story first circulated in its oral form among the Canaanite population, since its female protagonist (Tamar) is of Canaanite origin ("Judah and Tamar," *VT* 29 [1979] 409–13).

[67] A concise and clear expression of this modern understanding of the story appears in *The Westminster Study Edition of the Holy Bible*, King James Version (Philadelphia: Westminster Press, 1948) 70, which designates the entire chapter simply as, "Canaanite Blood in the Tribe of Judah."

[68] This same constructed contrast between Judah's first wife's foreign ethnic identity and Tamar's "pure-blooded" ethnic identity serves as one of the bases for Edmund Leach's structural reading of Genesis 38 ("The Legitimacy of Solomon," in *Genesis as Myth and Other Essays* [London: Jonathan Cape, 1969] 25–83, especially 59).

doubt, however, one dominant factor influencing early Jewish interpretations of Judah's relations with the two women of Genesis 38 consists of the textual interplay between this biblical narrative and the
biblical laws and narratives touching upon the issue of intermarriage.

Levirate Law and Incest

Following Er's death, Judah instructs his second son Onan to "Go
into your brother's wife, act as a levir for her (ויבם אתה), and raise
up (והקם) seed for your brother" (Gen 38:8). With these instructions,
Judah proposes a course of action to provide his eldest son with
descendants posthumously. Although Onan subverts his father's intentions (Gen 38:9), this episode attests to the practice of levirate marriage
in ancient Israel, which suspended normal prohibitions against incest
in order to produce a genetically related heir for a deceased man.
Other references to levirate marriage appear in the Hebrew Bible,
as well as in the laws and literature of other ancient Near Eastern
societies and of other even more distant cultures.[69] Within the Bible,
such references appear in Deut 25:5–10 and possibly Ruth 3–4.[70]
The similarities between the levirate arrangements in Genesis 38 and
the levirate law in Deut 25:5–10 are particularly strong, although
there are important differences as well:

> 5. When brothers dwell together, and one of them dies and has no
> son, the wife of the dead man shall not [go] outside to a strange man.
> Her brother-in-law (יבמה) shall go upon her and take her for himself as
> a wife and act as a levir for her (ויבמה). 6. The first-born whom she
> delivers will ascend (יקום) to the name of his dead brother, so that his
> name will not be erased from Israel. 7. But if the man does not want
> to take his sister-in-law (יבמתו), then his sister-in-law (יבמתו) shall go up

[69] For an overview of the issues involved in Hebrew levirate marriage of the biblical period and a survey of parallels in other Near Eastern cultures, see Ephraim
Neufeld, *Ancient Hebrew Marriage Laws with Special References to General Semitic Laws and
Customs* (London: Longmans, Green & Co., 1944) 26–55. For further discussion of
levirate marriage in the ancient Near East and in other cultures, see Millar Burrows,
"The Ancient Oriental Background of Hebrew Levirate Marriage," *BASOR* 77 (1940)
2–15.

[70] For a discussion of the complicated relation between levirate marriage, redemp-
tion of ancestral property and a childless widow, and inheritance in the book of Ruth,
see Millar Burrows, "The Marriage of Boaz and Ruth," *JBL* 59 (1940) 445–54;
Thomas Thompson and Dorothy Thompson, "Some Legal Problems in the Book of
Ruth," *VT* 8 (1968) 79–99; D. R. G. Beattie, "The Book of Ruth as Evidence for
Israelite Legal Practice," *VT* 24 (1974) 251–67; and Anthony Phillips, "The Book of
Ruth—Deception and Shame," *JJS* 37 (1986) 1–17.

to the gate to the elders, and she will say, "My brother-in-law (יבמי)
will not raise up (להקים) for his brother a name in Israel; he does not
desire to act as a levir for me (יבמי)." 8. Then the elders of his city shall
call him and speak to him, and he shall stand and say, "I do not desire
to take her." 9. Then his sister-in-law (יבמתו) shall approach him in the
sight of the elders, and she shall pull his sandal off his foot and spit in
his face; and she shall answer and say, "Thus shall it be done to the man
who will not build the house of his brother." 10. And his name shall
be called in Israel, "the house of the one with the sandal pulled off."

Both this deuteronomic law and Genesis 38 describe the death of a
married man before producing male offspring, indicate the presence
of surviving brothers, articulate the goal of establishing progeny for
the deceased through a legal fiction concerning paternity, and shift
the responsibility for procreation to the dead man's brothers. Additionally, both suggest through their portrayals of evasions (Gen 38:9;
Deut 25:7–10) that the role of levir was not a particularly desirable
one, probably because of the ensuing disadvantages in inheritance
rights.[71] But both also argue that refusal to assume levirate responsibility had dire consequences, ranging from loss of life (Gen 38:10) to
loss of reputation (Deut 25:7–10).

Specific linguistic correspondences between Deut 25:5–10 and
Genesis 38 reinforce these similarities in content. The most striking
of these is the appearance of words from the verbal root signifying
the levirate relationship (יבם) in both Genesis 38 and Deut 25:5–10.
This verbal root is not used elsewhere in the Hebrew Bible, and its
single appearance in Genesis 38 ("act as a levir," ויבם, Gen 38:8)
immediately directs the reader to the Deuteronomic law, which contains various usages of it ("her brother-in-law," יבמה, Deut 25:5; "my
brother-in-law," יבמי, Deut 25:7; "his sister-in-law," יבמתו, Deut 25:7
[twice], 9; "he shall act as a levir for her," ויבמה, Deut 25:5; "to act
as a levir for me," יבמי, Deut 25:7).[72] Another distinctive semantic
link is the usage in both passages of the verbal root "to arise" (קום) in

---

[71] For a discussion of the impact of levirate marriage on inheritance, see Davies,
"Inheritance Rights." In the book of Ruth, the next of kin refuses to produce a son
with Ruth specifically because of anticipated complications in his own inheritance
(Ruth 4:6). Curiously, there is not a single illustration of a straightforward execution
of levirate marriage in the entire Hebrew Bible. Each biblical passage alluding to
the levirate custom depicts a failure to implement the practice (Gen 38:26; Deut
25:7–10; Ruth 4:1–12).

[72] For a discussion of the significance of this verbal root and of its employment
in the epithet for the Canaanite goddess Anat (y-b-m-t limm), translated by William
F. Albright as "progenitress of the nations," see Burrows, "Ancient Oriental Background," 6–7.

connection with the levirate duty to provide offspring for the deceased brother ("raise up," וְהָקֵם, Gen 38:8; "to ascend," יָקוּם, Deut 25:6; "to raise up," לְהָקִים, Deut 25:7). A number of other common verbs and nouns appear in both places as well, although the coincidence in these cases may be attributed to the similarity in subject matter.[73]

There are also significant differences, however, between the depictions of levirate arrangements in Genesis 38 and in Deut 25:5–10. For one thing, the expressions indicating the desired results of the sexual relations between the widow and her brother-in-law vary in the two passages. In Gen 38:8, Judah specifies that "seed" or "offspring" (זֶרַע) for the dead brother is the object of the levirate union, and Onan's subversive act of spilling on the ground rather than giving "seed" (זֶרַע) to his brother in Gen 38:9 confirms that this is its intended goal. By contrast, the Deuteronomic law emphasizes the more abstract concept of preserving the "name" (שֵׁם) of the deceased (Deut 25:6, 7).[74] Concern for the dead man's name stresses additional issues such as reputation, inheritance, and continued existence through one's progeny.[75]

Another possible discrepancy between the levirate arrangements in Genesis 38 and Deut 25:5–10 may stem from this difference in stated goals. The emphasis on physical reproduction in Genesis 38 suggests that in this version of the levirate custom the sexual relationship between the widow and her brother-in-law may have been a temporary one, lasting only until a son was born. Supporting this view is the fact that Judah's address to Onan in Gen 38:8 lacks specific instructions that he take Tamar as his wife.[76] Also, once Tamar has conceived there is no further discussion of giving her in marriage to

---

[73] For example, both passages use such words as "brother" (אָח), "death" (מוּת), "wife" (אִשָּׁה), and "go into" (בּוֹא).

[74] Appropriately, in the biblical law the levir's refusal to preserve the "name" of the dead through levirate marriage results in the assignment of an unflattering "name" to him and his house (Deut 25:10).

[75] For a discussion of the additional issues suggested by the term "name" in Deut 25:5–10, see Millar Burrows, "Levirate Marriage in Israel," *JBL* 59 (1940) 32–33, and Davies, "Inheritance Rights," 139–42. These issues may be implicit in Genesis 38 as well. Thompson and Thompson ("Some Legal Problems") argue that since Perez and Zerah are listed as Judah's sons in the biblical genealogies, and not as Er's, the term "name" in the context of levirate practice refers primarily to inheritance. Note also that Obed is also listed as the son of Boaz, not Mahlon or Chilion (Ruth 4:21).

[76] But one should note that the biblical narrator employs terminology associated with permanent marriage when describing Tamar's view of her plight in Gen 38:14: "for she saw that Shelah had grown up, but she had not been given to him as a wife" (לְאִשָּׁה).

Shelah, and Judah himself avoids additional sexual relations with her
(Gen 38:26).[77] By contrast, Deut 25:5 specifically states that the levir
shall take his brother's widow as a wife, rather than allow her to
marry a man outside the family.[78] In addition, the stipulation in Deut
25:6 that the first-born should perpetuate the name of the dead implies
that other children might also be produced from the union between
a widowed woman and her brother-in-law. This passage in Deuteronomy thus suggests that their relationship is a permanent one,
rather than a temporary one for the sake of producing an heir. The
levirate practice depicted in the deuteronomic law therefore emphasizes the welfare of the widow by immediately securing her in a second
marriage.[79]

The most important discrepancy between Genesis 38 and Deut
25:5–10 for present purposes, however, consists of the prominent role
of the dead man's father in the biblical narrative. In Genesis 38,
Judah dictates the initial levirate arrangement between his middle
son, Onan, and Tamar (Gen 38:8) and promises a second levirate
arrangement between her and his youngest son, Shelah (Gen 38:11).
Although he fails to follow through with this promise (Gen 38:14),
he ultimately acknowledges that he should have done so (Gen 38:26).
By contrast, in the passage in Deuteronomy, there is no mention of

---

[77] The lack of specification of a permanent husband for Tamar has troubled some
modern commentators, including von Rad (*Genesis*, 361) who remarks that the narrative ends "without telling whose wife Tamar finally became. According to v. 26b,
in any case, she was not Judah's. Was she then Shelah's? Should that not have been
said?" For one solution to these questions, namely that the childless widow was
guaranteed a son, not permanent marriage, through the levirate custom in Israel,
see George W. Coats, "Widow's Rights: A Crux in the Structure of Genesis 38,"
CBQ 34 (1972) 461–65. Whether or not Judah's relations with Tamar constitute a
normative form of the levirate custom is far from certain, however.

[78] See also Deut 25:7 and 8, which mention the refusal of the brother-in-law "to
take" (לקחתה, לקחת) the widow. The verbal root "to take" (לקח) commonly denotes
marrying a woman in the Hebrew Bible, as in Gen 38:2 and 6. Similarly, in the
book of Ruth, Boaz states before the elders that he has acquired Ruth "as a wife"
(לאשה, Ruth 4:10); he subsequently "takes" her (ויקח, Ruth 4:13).

[79] Some, such as Neufeld (*Ancient Hebrew Marriage Laws*, 29–33) go so far as to
argue that the primary purpose of the levirate custom in Israelite society was to
provide for the childless widow through remarriage and further opportunity to bear
children. See also Susan Niditch's discussion of the levirate law as the resolution to
the anomalous social position of the childless widow in "The Wronged Woman
Righted: An Analysis of Genesis 38," *HTR* 72 (1972) 143–49. In all three biblical
depictions of levirate practice, it is the widows themselves, rather than their male
relatives entrusted with levirate responsibility, who emerge as the most invested and
active parties. This fact suggests that the levirate custom worked to their advantage.

the deceased's father. The surviving brothers themselves are responsible for executing the levirate law.[80]

Given Judah's active role in making levirate arrangements in Genesis 38, it is tempting to interpret his sexual relations with Tamar as merely a further extension of his commitment to secure a son for Er. Some modern commentators advance this very interpretation. They consider Genesis 38 as evidence for an early form of the Hebrew levirate custom, obligating not only the dead man's brothers as potential levirs as in Deut 25:5–10, but also his father. Laws from other ancient Near Eastern societies reveal that in surrounding cultures both brothers-in-law and fathers-in-law could fulfill the role of levir.[81] According to this contemporary reading of the narrative in light of Near Eastern parallels, Judah emerges as a successful and socially acceptable levir in Genesis 38, despite his initial ignorance as to the exact nature of his sexual relations with his widowed daughter-in-law.[82]

---

[80] Whether or not Deut 25:5–10 assumes the father is dead remains unclear, however. In his discussion of the levirate custom, Epstein (*Marriage Laws*, 77–92) contends that the father is still alive in the scenario presented in Deut 25:5–10, since the brothers have not yet divided the family property and are "dwelling together" (Deut 25:5). By contrast, David Daube ("Consortium in Roman and Hebrew Law," *Juridical Review* 62 [1950] 71–91) argues that since there is no mention of the father, he must be dead, and the fact that the brothers are "dwelling together" attests to the practice of consortium in Hebrew society, in which ancestral property is jointly owned by more than one heir.

The differences listed here between the depictions of the levirate custom in Genesis 38 and in Deut 25:5–10 are by no means exhaustive. For example, another difference lies in the fact that whereas Onan apparently had no socially sanctioned means through which to reject the role of levir (Gen 38:9), the bulk of the law in Deuteronomy describes a ritual designed to terminate the potential levirate relationship between a widow and her brother-in-law (Deut 25:7–10). In fact, Carmichael (*Law and Narrative in the Bible*, 291–99) argues that a basic thrust of the deuteronomic law is precisely to provide an alternative lacking in Onan's day—an alternative that would prevent the deaths of future reluctant levirs.

[81] Middle Assyrian law no. 33, *ANET*, 182, and Hittite law no. 193, *ANET*, 196, designate the widow's father-in-law as well as her brothers-in-law as levirs. For further evidence of the involvement of fathers-in-laws in levirate relations in other cultures, see Burrows, "Ancient Oriental Background," 8–9. Interestingly, Ruth 3–4 suggests that at some point in Israelite history the levirate relationship, or something akin to it, was not even limited to the immediate family of the deceased, but included more distant relatives as well.

[82] For typical expressions of the view that Judah's sexual relations with Tamar constitute a fulfillment of his duties as a levir, see Neufeld, *Ancient Hebrew Marriage Laws*, 34–39, and Harry A. Hoffner, Jr., "Incest, Sodomy, and Bestiality in the Ancient Near East," in *Orient and Occident: Essays Presented to Cyrus H. Gordon on the Occasion of His Sixty-Fifth Birthday*, ed. Hoffner, Alter Orient und Altes Testament 22 (Kevelaer: Butzon & Bercker; Neukirchen-Vluyn: Neukirchener Verlag, 1973) 81–90, especially 82.

The extent to which foreign laws illuminate the behavior of biblical characters is debatable, however. In any event, it seems imprudent to draw conclusions about the historical development of a social practice from a story that so clearly portrays a series of misadventures and aberrations.[83] The naming of both Perez and Zerah as Judah's (and not Er's) sons in genealogies elsewhere in the biblical corpus further suggests that the act of intercourse between father-in-law and daughter-in-law depicted in Genesis 38 was not commonly considered a levirate union to perpetuate the name of a dead man in Israel (Deut 25:7).[84]

Since Judah's sexual relations with his daughter-in-law do not fall comfortably under the rubric of levirate relations described in Deut 25:5–10, it remains to define them more accurately, or at least to explore the biblical passages which might be brought to bear on such a definition. The prohibition against incest between father-in-law and daughter-in-law (Lev 18:15) in the list of forbidden relations in Leviticus 18 is one such passage:

> The nakedness of your daughter-in-law (כלתך) you shall not uncover. She is the wife of your son. You shall not uncover her nakedness.

Lev 20:12 contains the same prohibition and stipulates that its violation constitutes a capital offense:

---

[83] Beattie also cautions against the use of Genesis 38 as evidence of levirate practice involving parties other than the widow's brothers-in-law ("Book of Ruth as Evidence," 260–61). Similarly, Burrows argues that Judah does not act as a levir in Genesis 38 ("Marriage of Boaz and Ruth," 445).

[84] The concluding genealogy in the book of Ruth (4:18–22) similarly portrays Obed as the son of his biological father Boaz rather than as the son of one of Elimelech's deceased sons; however, earlier in the narrative the women refer to Obed as Naomi's son (Ruth 4:17), implying that Ruth somehow acted as a surrogate for her mother-in-law. This idea was suggested by Wendy Doniger in a personal communication.

I have not come across an explicit interpretation of Tamar and Judah's union as levirate marriage in second temple or rabbinic literature. Generally their relations, if discussed at all, are considered incest. The one possible exception consists of a tradition depicting Judah's enduring marriage with Tamar, arising from an understanding of the biblical phrase "he [Judah] never knew her again" (Gen 38:26) as "he did not cease to know her." This interpretation, found in b. Soṭa 10b, equates the verb in the phrase "he did not continue" (ולא אסף) in Gen 38:26 with the verb from the root "to remove, withdraw" (אסף) in the phrase "a great voice which did not cease" (לא אסף) in Deut 5:22(19). In light of the emphasis on marriage of the levirate partners in Deut 25:5–10, it is possible that this tradition understands the continuing relationship between Judah and Tamar as a levirate marriage.

As for the man who lies with his daughter-in-law (כלתו), both of them shall surely be put to death. They have committed incest. Their blood is upon them.

The presence of these pentateuchal laws against incest between father-in-law and daughter-in-law promotes the interpretation of Judah and Tamar's sexual relations as a serious matter.[85] Strikingly, the involvement of too closely related sexual partners in the latter part of Genesis 38 contrasts with the involvement of too distantly related sexual partners from different ethnic backgrounds earlier in the same chapter. There is, however, at least some room for speculation concerning Judah's kinship with Tamar after the death of Er. Perhaps with the death of his son, Judah is no longer technically Tamar's father-in-law, and she in turn is no longer technically his daughter-in-law. If this is the case, then their intercourse would merely constitute an incidence of non-marital sex, which would carry far less onus than incest.[86]

---

[85] See also the prophetic castigation against sexual relations between father-in-law and daughter-in-law in Ezek 22:11.

There are also biblical prohibitions against incest between brother-in-law and sister-in-law in Lev 18:16 and 20:21. Some commentators view these laws as a polemic attack on the more ancient practice of levirate marriage. O. J. Baab ("Marriage," in vol. 3 of *IDB*, 282) expresses this view concisely: "A late priestly document indicates strong opposition to, or complete unawareness of, the levirate concept. Sexual relations (marriage) with one's brother's wife are forbidden (Lev 18:16; 20:21). These prohibitions may, of course, be interpreted to mean that they are in effect only while the brother is alive. Yet the language is emphatic and unqualified." The inclusion of a note in Lev 20:21 that the man who takes his brother's wife "shall be childless" is suggestive in this connection, in that it is precisely the purpose of levirate marriage between a man and his brother's wife to bear children. This note is doubly suggestive in that the adjective "childless" (ערירים) is reminiscent of the name of Judah's eldest son Er (ער) and therefore recalls the disastrous attempts in Genesis 38 to implement the levirate relationship.

But at least in the levirate law in Deut 25:5–10, the term "levir" (יבם), applied to the brother-in-law after the death of his brother, and the term "levirate wife" (יבמת), applied to his sister-in-law after the death of her husband, concretely express the suspension of the former prohibitions against incest and the establishment of a new, mandated relationship, signified by the verb "to act as a levir" (יבם). There are no corresponding terms in the Hebrew Bible expressing the transformation of the relationship between father-in-law and daughter-in-law from prohibition to responsibility.

[86] A rabbinic debate about this very question of the relationship between a widow and her husband's family resulted in the emergence of two opposite opinions. Hillel and his followers argued that the levirate marriage was actually a continuation of the widow's first marriage and that she therefore retained the status of a married woman while waiting for its implementation. In line with this position, one might reason that Judah and Tamar retained their relationship as father-in-law and daughter-in-law, despite the fact that she was not actually cohabiting with one of his sons at

But the repeated references to Judah as Tamar's "father-in-law"
(חָמִיךָ, Gen 38:13; חָמִיהָ, Gen 38:25) and to Tamar as Judah's "daughter-
in-law" (כַּלָּתוֹ, Gen 38:11, 16; כַּלָּתֶךָ, Gen 38:24) after the deaths of
Er and Onan make such a position untenable.[87] In addition, the
authority which Judah exercises over Tamar, apparent in his dismissal of her to her father's house until Shelah matures (Gen 38:11)[88]
and in his order for her death (Gen 38:24),[89] indicates that their
affinal relationship continues throughout the narrative. Tamar was,
after all, promised marriage to Shelah, and thus her status may have
resembled that of a betrothed woman.[90] The narrator himself indicates that he considers the sexual relations between Judah and Tamar
as a grave infraction of the incest taboo with the care he takes to
ameliorate Judah's behavior. Not once, but twice, he draws attention
to Judah's ignorance concerning his daughter-in-law's identity before
their sexual relations (Gen 38:15,16). He furthermore illustrates
Judah's lack of awareness concerning the nature of his sexual act
through a long digression depicting his search for a nonexistent prostitute (Gen 38:20–23) and through a portrayal of Judah's hasty misjudgment of Tamar and his equally hasty reversal upon attaining
more complete insight (Gen 38:24–26). The final note that Judah
"never knew her again" (Gen 38:26) similarly functions to assure the
reader that he did not intentionally transgress the prohibitions against

---

the time of their intercourse. On the other hand, Shammai and his followers argued
that levirate marriage had to be contracted separately, as a distinct, second marriage. In line with this dissenting position, one might reason that during the period
between her levirate marriages with Judah's sons, Tamar had no affinal relationship
with Judah. For a discussion of this difference of opinion between the houses of
Hillel and Shammai, see Samuel Belkin, "Levirate and Agnate Marriage in Rabbinic
and Cognate Literature," *JQR* 60 (1970) 275–329, especially 305–20. In light of the
evidence presented in the following paragraph, the position on the issue assumed in
Genesis 38 appears closer to that of Hillel than Shammai, in that Judah treats
Tamar as a woman convicted of adultery before he grasps the particulars of her
case. For a discussion of Judah's understanding of Tamar's apparent promiscuity as
adultery, see Neufeld, *Ancient Hebrew Marriage Laws*, 163, and Louis M. Epstein, *Sex
Laws and Customs in Judaism*, with an introduction by Ari Kiev (New York: Ktav
Publishing House, 1948) 199–204.

[87] 1 Chr 2:4 also describes Tamar as Judah's "daughter-in-law" (כַּלָּתוֹ) in a genealogy recording the parentage of Perez and Zerah.

[88] The custom of the childless widow's return to her father's home is attested to
also in Lev 22:13 (specifically concerning a priest's daughter) and Ruth 1:8.

[89] See the discussion in Anthony Phillips, "Some Aspects of Family Law in Pre-
Exilic Israel," *VT* 23 (1973) 350, concerning the unilateral authority of heads of
households over family members, particularly women who generally had no appeal
to legal courts in matters of family law.

[90] For biblical laws concerning violations of a betrothal, see Deut 22:23–27.

incest between father-in-law and daughter-in-law, although apparently such a transgression occurred.[91] Similar excuses of ignorance and lack of intentionality clearly do not apply to Tamar, however, who orchestrated the sexual encounter with her father-in-law.[92]

In light of these considerations, what should one make of this curious depiction of incest in Genesis 38, especially since it does not lead to the execution of the parties involved, but to the birth of twins? And what should one make of these twins, who might most accurately be considered bastards since they are the product of a prohibited degree of sexual relations,[93] but who come to head the genealogy leading to the Davidic kings? In the Bible, as well as cross-culturally in other literatures of the world, genealogies of important ethnic or social lines are often initiated through sexual relations between closely related couples.[94] It is debatable whether the central issue in this common

---

[91] For a cross-cultural discussion of ignorance as a defense in crime, see David Daube, "Error and Ignorance as Excuses in Crime," in *Ancient Jewish Law: Three Inaugural Lectures* (Leiden: E. J. Brill, 1981) 49–69.

[92] Both the prohibition against sexual relations between father-in-law and daughter-in-law in Lev 18:15 and the hypothetical case described in Lev 20:12 directly address men, not women, as the responsible agents in sexual matters, although Lev 20:12 specifies that both parties are guilty and liable to punishment.

[93] In the Bible, illegitimacy is never explicitly defined. In biblical law, a "bastard" (ממזר) is denied entrance to the congregation of Israel even to the tenth generation (Deut 23:3), but no definition of this term is provided. In the following, very similar verse (Deut 23:4), however, an Ammonite and a Moabite are denied entrance to the congregation of Israel even to the tenth generation. The specification of these two peoples, whose origins lie in the sexual relations between Lot and his daughters, suggests that Deut 23:4 may be a concrete illustration of the more general law in Deut 23:3. According to this line of reasoning, the definition of the "bastard" of Deut 23:3 therefore includes offspring of incestuous unions. Alternatively, the term "bastard" in Deut 23:3 may simply signify a person of uncertain foreign ancestry, parallel to the Ammonite and the Moabite of the following verse. In Zech 9:6 "bastard" apparently refers to a person of mixed ancestry living in Ashdod. It is not until the Mishna that a clear definition of the term "bastard" appears. Although several definitions are presented in *m. Yebam.* 4.13, for legal purposes a bastard is defined as any offspring of prohibited relations, including adultery and incest, for which the punishment is extirpation at the hands of heaven (Lev 18:29) or death. According to this definition, Judah and Tamar's children would be bastards, since they were the offspring of a union punishable by extirpation (Lev 18:15, 29) and death (Lev 20:12). It must be noted, however, that at least in rabbinic thought, although a bastard could not marry an Israelite, he was still eligible to inherit property and to hold public office, theoretically even that of king. For a discussion of the status of the bastard in post-biblical Judaism, see Ben Zion Schereschewsky, "Mamzer," in vol. 11 of *Encyclopaedia Judaica* (Jerusalem: Keter Publishing House, 1971) 840–42. For a reconstruction of the semantic history of the term ממזר, see Epstein, *Marriage Laws*, 279–90.

[94] In the Bible for example, Adam and Eve, who is formed from his own side (Gen 2:21–23), stand at the beginning of the human race, and Abraham and Sarah,

association of origins with acts of incest is purity of lineage arising
from the genetic similarity of related founding partners, or whether
there are other considerations, such as the need to demarcate new
beginnings clearly through violations of accepted social mores. Whatever the case, here in Genesis 38 the inception of Israel's royal lineage is portrayed as emerging from an act of incest. Indeed, the
motif of incest is present in other birth narratives associated with the
Davidic line. The most graphic example involves the emergence of
the Moabites, David's great-grandmother's people, from an act of
incest between Lot and his eldest daughter (Gen 19:30–38). By contrast, Genesis 38 finesses the motif of incest in a number of ways.[95]
Not only does the narrator protect Judah from the charge of intentional incest through the steps outlined above, but he also introduces
the concept of levirate marriage early in the narrative. The allusion
in Genesis 38 to levirate practice, which includes the suspension of
normal prohibitions against incest for a greater social good, may
therefore exert a mollifying force on the reader's evaluation of Judah
and Tamar's incestuous union, since it too had an ultimately beneficial
outcome. In any event, the deuteronomic law concerning levirate
marriage and the levitical laws prohibiting incest between father-in-
law and daughter-in-law factor into the complicated equations that
produce the distinctive interpretations of Genesis 38 examined below.

Prostitutes, Promiscuous Daughters, and Consecrated Women
Genesis 38 depicts an interaction between a man and a woman he
considers a "prostitute" (זונה, Gen 38:15).[96] The narrator himself

---

who is his paternal half-sister (Gen 20:12), are the ancestors of the Hebrews. Extra-
biblical examples on a divine level include the Egyptian sibling gods Osiris and Isis,
whose union produces Horus, the representative of earthly kingship, and the Hindu
god Prajapati and his daughter, whose union initiates cosmic creation. Similarly, in
one version of the story Dionysus was conceived through an act of incest between
Zeus and his daughter Persephone, and Adonis was conceived through incest between Theias and his daughter Smyrna. For other examples, see Otto Rank, *The
Myth of the Birth of the Hero: A Psychological Interpretation of Mythology*, trans. F. Robbins
and Smith Ely Jelliffe (New York: Robert Brunner, 1952). For a discussion of the
motif of incest in Israel's royal lineage, see Leach, "Legitimacy of Solomon," 25–83.

[95] For a discussion of the different articulations of the theme of incest in the
stories of Lot and his daughters, Judah and Tamar, and Boaz and Ruth, see Harold
Fisch, "Ruth and the Structure of Covenant History," *VT* 32 (1982) 425–37.

[96] As discussed further below, the verbal root זנה includes not only professional
prostitution, but also adultery and other forms of illicit sexual activity. In Gen 38:15–
18, however, Judah considers Tamar sexually available for a price, so the narrow
English translation "prostitute" is appropriate for the word זונה in this context.

provides no explicit moral evaluation, either of Judah's eagerness to consort with a prostitute or of the supposed profession of the woman who made herself available by sitting "at the entrance of Enaim which is on the road to Timnah."[97] This apparently nonjudgmental depiction of a casual sexual transaction—which is at least Judah's view of the affair—challenges biblical readers to search for other scriptural texts that might interpret this passage.

Judging from other biblical passages, prostitution was part of the social reality in the lands inhabited by Israel,[98] and some Israelite women also practiced the world's oldest profession.[99] Biblical law does not prohibit a man from associating with a female prostitute. Even the didactic advice for young men in Proverbs stresses not the immorality of consorting with prostitutes, but the dangers of adultery.[100] Nor are there any explicit strictures against a woman engaging in sexual activity for economic gain, as long as she is not under some form of male familial authority (as, for example, a daughter).[101] Indeed, the story of Solomon's judgment of the two prostitutes (1 Kgs 3:16–28) suggests that, far from being outlaws and criminals, prostitutes had recourse to legal arbitration in disputes.

Prostitutes nevertheless occupied marginal positions in society, and their profession was not a respectable one. Especially telling is the

---

[97] Other depictions of women making themselves sexually available by venturing into public places may be found in Prov 7:10–20; 9:13–18; Isa 23:16–17; Jer 3:2–3; Ezek 16:24–25. The targums translate the term זונה in Gen 38:15 and elsewhere as נפקת ברא (Targums Onqelos and Pseudo-Jonathan) or נפקת בר (Targum Neofiti), literally, "a woman who goes outside." Through this translation, the targums incorporate the positioning of prostitutes in public areas into their designation of them. Significantly, other biblical incidents of illicit sexual activity are also set outside, for example, at the "entrance" (פתח) of the tent of meeting (1 Sam 2:22; cf., Exod 38:8), which recalls the "entrance" (פתח) of Enaim (Gen 38:14) where Judah meets Tamar.

[98] See the matter-of-fact description of Rahab as the "prostitute" (זונה) who befriends the spies during their reconnaissance of Jericho in Josh 2:1 and 6:25. See also Samson's less auspicious association with a "prostitute" (אשה זונה) from Gaza in Judg 16:1.

[99] For example, Jephthah's mother was a harlot (זונה, Judg 11:1). See also Solomon's judgment of the two prostitutes (נשים זנות) in 1 Kgs 3:16–28.

[100] According to Proverbs, consorting with prostitutes wastes one's resources (Prov 29:3), but adultery is a far more serious matter. For example, Prov 6:26 states, "For the sake of a harlot, [one may forfeit] a loaf of bread, but another man's wife stalks one's very life." The dangerous woman in Prov 7:6–27, although dressed as a harlot (זונה, Prov 7:10), is clearly married (Prov 7:19–20). By contrast, the prophet Hosea unequivocally condemns men who keep company with prostitutes (Hos 4:14).

[101] This assertion depends on an understanding of the word קדשה in the prohibition in Deut 23:18 as a "consecrated woman" or a "cult functionary," not as an ordinary prostitute.

outrage Jacob's sons feel because Shechem treated their sister Dinah as a harlot (Gen 34:31). The depiction of King Ahab's disgrace after his death in 1 Kgs 22:38, when prostitutes washed in his blood at the pool of Samaria, also illustrates the dishonor of their profession. The law in Deut 23:19 rejecting "the prostitute's fee" (אֶתְנַן זוֹנָה) for payment of a religious vow simultaneously acknowledges the existence of prostitution in Israel and labels its profits as "an abomination to the LORD your God." Along the same lines, the law in Lev 21:7 prohibiting priests from marrying prostitutes suggests that other Israelites could marry them, but that these women were unworthy partners for those set apart for cultic service. Even Genesis 38 hints that Judah considers his own involvement with a prostitute unseemly, when he drops his search for the woman with the pledge rather than risk public ridicule (Gen 38:23).[102]

By contrast, biblical law prohibits prostitution by Israelite girls and women under the authority of their fathers in no uncertain terms. The law in Lev 19:29 addresses males with daughters under their protection:

> Do not profane your daughter by making her a prostitute (לְהַזְנוֹתָהּ), so that the land does not whore (תִזְנֶה) and the land is not filled with depravity.

This law apparently prevents fathers from making a living off their daughters' sexuality and from thereby encouraging licentiousness among their family members and neighbors. When read in juxtaposition with Genesis 38, however, this passage may emphasize Judah's mistreatment of Tamar. While Judah is Tamar's father-in-law and not her father, and while he does not deliberately lead her into prostitution for economic gain, he nevertheless forces her to take drastic measures at Enaim. In effect, Judah makes Tamar a prostitute, albeit a temporary one with an unusual purpose, both by failing to provide her with a legitimate sexual partner and by treating her as a harlot during their encounter.

---

[102] Alternatively, the ridicule Judah imagines might stem not from exposure of his consortion with a prostitute, but from his insistence, counter to local opinion, that there had been a prostitute in the area, and the scandalous implication that perhaps this woman was actually some other man's wife or daughter.

For further discussion of prostitutes in Israelite society and biblical literature, see Epstein, "Harlotry," in *Sex Laws and Customs*, 152–78, and Phyllis Bird, "The Harlot as Heroine: Narrative Art and Social Presupposition in Three Old Testament Texts," in *Narrative Research on the Hebrew Bible*, ed. Miri Amihai, George W. Coats, and Anne M. Solomon, Semeia 46 (Atlanta: Scholars Press, 1989) 119–39.

Two other biblical laws deal with wayward daughters under parental control (Lev 21:9 and Deut 22:20–21). In these laws the daughter, not the father, appears as the responsible party, and the prohibited sexual behavior is not necessarily limited to prostitution. The law found in Lev 21:9 addresses the specific case of a priest's promiscuous daughter:

> The daughter of a priest who defiles herself by having illicit intercourse (לִזְנוֹת) defiles her father. She shall be burned (תִּשָּׂרֵף) with fire.

The law found in Deut 22:20–21, on the other hand, deals more generally with the case of a bride discovered by her groom to be a nonvirgin:

> But if this charge is true, the tokens of virginity for the girl not being found, then they shall bring out the girl to the entrance of her father's house, and the men of her city shall stone her to death with stones. For she has committed folly in Israel, by having illicit intercourse (לִזְנוֹת) in her father's house, and you shall destroy the evil from your midst.

Both of the laws cited above employ the same verbal root (זנה) found in Gen 38:15 (לְזוֹנָה) and Lev 19:29 (לְהַזְנוֹתָהּ), but in Lev 21:9 and Deut 22:20–21 the broad semantic scope of this root becomes evident. In biblical Hebrew, the verbal root זנה encompasses much more than the exchange of sexual services for compensation indicated by the English phrase "to prostitute oneself." The root זנה includes the concepts of promiscuity and adultery, in addition to prostitution.[103] Lev 21:9 and Deut 22:20–21 prescribe the death penalty for daughters guilty of sexual misconduct and specify a means of execution. In the law concerning the priest's daughter (Lev 21:9), an unspecified type of illicit sexual behavior is punishable by burning. In the law concerning the new bride (Deut 22:20–21), premarital loss of virginity is punishable by stoning.

There are some general correspondences between these two laws and the events in Genesis 38. In the biblical narrative, an anonymous report (Gen 38:24) alerts Judah to his daughter-in-law's sexual activity, apparent from her pregnant condition: "About three months later, it was reported to Judah, 'Tamar, your daughter-in-law, has had illicit intercourse (זָנְתָה); moreover, she has also conceived through

---

[103] This wide range of negative meanings, perhaps captured best by the somewhat dated English term "fornication," made the verb זנה especially useful as a metaphor for Israel's apostasy. Some examples of this metaphorical usage include Num 25:1–2; Judg 2:17; 8:27, 33; Jer 2:20; 3:6; Ezek 6:9; Hos 4:12.

illicit sexual relations (לזנונים).'" The double use of the root זנה in this report does not necessarily indicate a general knowledge of Tamar's impersonation of a prostitute in Gen 38:12–19, although it certainly draws the reader's attention back to that earlier section. Rather, in this report the term זנה apparently denotes any sexual activity inappropriate for a widow awaiting an arranged levirate marriage. Judah immediately responds by calling for her death ("Judah said, 'Take her out and let her be burned! [ותשרף],'" Gen 38:24), as mandated in Lev 21:9 and Deut 22:20–21. The correspondence with the biblical laws superficially suggests that his harsh sentence is appropriate; however, this conclusion does not take into consideration the extenuating circumstances motivating Tamar's behavior, which Judah himself finally acknowledges. Curiously, the specific order that Tamar be burned most vividly recalls the law for the priest's daughter (Lev 21:9), although Genesis 38 nowhere indicates that she is a priest's daughter.

Yet another issue emerges from the curious wording of Hirah's question to the local men when he attempts to retrieve the pledge (Gen 38:21). He asks, "Where is the consecrated woman (קדשה) who was at Enaim beside the road?" The men use the same expression to describe the woman in their reply, "There has been no consecrated woman (קדשה) here," and Hirah employs this word again when he quotes them in his report to Judah (Gen 38:22). Perhaps the expression "consecrated woman" (קדשה), from the verbal root "to be set apart, consecrated, holy" (קדש), functions as a loosely synonymous term for female "prostitute" (זונה) in Genesis 38. There must be at least some semantic overlap between the two words, or Hirah's question would make no sense in his search for the woman Judah employed as a prostitute.[104] In any event, the substitution of the word "consecrated woman" (קדשה) in this interchange and report (Gen 38:21–22) for the word "prostitute" (זונה) in Judah's appraisal of the same woman (Gen 38:15) creates a verbal link between Genesis 38 and yet another biblical law, that found in Deut 23:18:

---

[104] The view that the two terms are synonymous in Genesis 38 was common in much earlier times, as the translations of the LXX and the Palestinian targums indicate. In both Gen 38:15 and Gen 38:21–22, the LXX uses the term "prostitute" (πόρνη). In both passages, *Targum Neofiti* uses the term "prostitute" (נפקת בר) as well, although *Targums Onqelos* and *Pseudo-Jonathan* preserve the distinction between the two terms in their translations. For a discussion of the translation of the term קדשה and its masculine equivalent in the LXX, see Paul E. Dion, "Did Cultic Prostitution Fall into Oblivion during the Post-Exilic Era? Some Evidence from Chronicles and the Septuagint," *CBQ* 43 (1981) 41–48.

There shall not be a consecrated woman (קְדֵשָׁה) among the daughters of Israel. Nor shall there be a consecrated man (קָדֵשׁ) among the sons of Israel.

This prohibition against the female Israelite "consecrated woman" and her masculine counterpart is unequivocal, but the exact significance of the term remains unclear in the context of this law, as it did in Gen 38:21–22. The understanding of "consecrated woman" (קְדֵשָׁה) and "prostitute" (זוֹנָה) as synonyms finds some support in the wording of the law in Deut 23:19, immediately following the law prohibiting the consecrated woman and man:

> You shall not bring a prostitute's fee (אֶתְנַן זוֹנָה) or a dog's hire into the house of the LORD your God to [fulfill] any vow, for both of them are an abomination to the LORD your God.

The placement of this law concerning the fee of a "prostitute" (זוֹנָה) immediately after the law concerning the "consecrated woman" (קְדֵשָׁה) in Deut 23:18 suggests that the two terms might be parallel.[105] These two words also seem to function as synonyms in the prophetic castigation in Hos 4:14 of the men of Israel "because they have gone aside with the prostitutes (הַזֹּנוֹת) and sacrificed with the consecrated women (הַקְּדֵשׁוֹת)."

Upon closer inspection, however, the term "consecrated woman" (קְדֵשָׁה) implies some sort of connection with religious aspects of life that the term "prostitute" (זוֹנָה) lacks. The root of the word itself, "to be set apart, consecrated, holy" (קָדֵשׁ), indicates this difference. In

---

[105] Some early translators of Deut 23:18–19 clearly understood the word קְדֵשָׁה as a synonym for זוֹנָה. For example, the LXX, in a remarkable double translation, renders the term קְדֵשָׁה in Deut 23:18 as πόρνη ("prostitute") as well as τελεσφόρος ("initiate in the mysteries"), the latter implying idolatry. The first of these renditions corresponds to its translation of the word זוֹנָה in Deut 23:19, indicating an understanding that the two words are synonyms. The second translation, however, reveals the translator's recognition that the two words have different semantic ranges. The strong condemnation of prostitution evident in the LXX translation of Deut 23:18 is also found in other Jewish writings of the Hellenistic period. For example, Philo *On Joseph* 43 and *On the Special Laws* 3.51 specify the death penalty for prostitution. See also Josephus *Ant.* 4.8.23§245, which maintains that prostitutes are categorically unfit for Jewish marriage, whereas biblical law only prohibits priests from marrying them (Lev 21:7).

Note that the verb in Tamar's question, "What will you give (תִּתֵּן) me so that you may go into me" (Gen 38:17), in Judah's question, "What is the pledge that I should give (אֶתֵּן) you?" (Gen 38:18), and in the narrator's report, "he gave (וַיִּתֶּן) to her" (Gen 38:18), recalls the term from the same verbal root used to designate the prostitute's fee (אֶתְנַן), rejected for payment of a vow at the temple in Deut 23:19. The verbal correspondence links Tamar's story with yet another law concerning prostitution. This observation comes from Michael Fishbane in a personal communication.

the phrase from Hos 4:14 quoted in the preceding paragraph, the consecrated women are associated with a ritual activity, namely sacrifice, that may distinguish them from the prostitutes mentioned immediately before. References to groups of consecrated men (קְדֵשִׁים) in passages from 1 and 2 Kings indicate that at least the prohibited "consecrated man" (קָדֵשׁ) of Deut 23:18 performed in a religious context. 1 and 2 Kings associate these male cult functionaries with the worship of other gods besides YHWH, especially Asherah.[106] Ugaritic texts, which repeatedly list a group of male professionals known as *qdšm* or "consecrated men," directly after another group of professionals known as *khnm*, or "priests," reinforce the idea that the "consecrated men" in 1 and 2 Kings and Deut 23:18 are temple personnel.[107] One can tentatively conclude from this evidence that the "consecrated woman" of Deut 23:18 is the female counterpart of the male cult functionary mentioned in 1 and 2 Kings.[108] The appearance of a type of "consecrated woman" (*qadištu*) with ritual duties in Akkadian texts lends credence to this view.[109]

But this discussion does not answer the question of why Hirah uses the term "consecrated woman" (קְדֵשָׁה) in his search for the woman Judah considers a prostitute. Modern answers to this question frequently assume that a distinctive conceptual connection between sexuality and religion characterized Canaanite and Mesopotamian cultures. Until recently, biblical scholarship presupposed the existence of a

---

[106] For example, 1 Kgs 15:11–12 connects Asa's dismissal of the male cult functionaries (קְדֵשִׁים) with his destruction of idols and his mother's Asherah, and 2 Kgs 23:7 mentions that the male cult functionaries (קְדֵשִׁים) had houses within the temple near to the site where women wove tapestries for Asherah. The editors of 1 and 2 Kings viewed the persistence of other cults and their functionaries in the land, and even in the temple in Jerusalem, as a great sin. 1 Kgs 14:24 castigates Rehoboam for allowing male cult functionaries (קְדֵשִׁים) to remain in the land. These editors portray the expulsion of those consecrated to idolatrous worship as a fundamental aspect of the religious reforms under Asa (1 Kgs 15:11–12), Jehoshaphat (1 Kgs 22:47), and Josiah (2 Kgs 23:7). In Job 36:14 as well, a passing negative reference to male cult functionaries (קְדֵשִׁים) suggests that association with them was disgraceful.

[107] See the discussion of the Ugaritic *qdšm* in Edwin M. Yamauchi, "Cultic Prostitution: A Case Study in Cultural Diffusion," in *Orient and Occident: Essays Presented to Cyrus H. Gordon on the Occasion of His Sixty-Fifth Birthday*, ed. Harry A. Hoffner, Alter Orient und Altes Testament 22 (Kevelaer: Butzon & Bercker; Neukirchen-Vluyn: Neukirchener Verlag, 1973) 219.

[108] If this is the case, then the female and male cult functionaries of Deut 23:18 may be of an entirely different class from the "prostitute" and the "dog" of Deut 23:19.

[109] For a discussion of the Akkadian *qadištu*, see Joan Goodnick Westenholz, "Tamar, Qědēšā, Qadištu, and Sacred Prostitution in Mesopotamia," *HTR* 82 (1989) 245–65, and Yamauchi, "Cultic Prostitution," 214–16.

widespread fertility cult involving ritualized prostitution and other forms of sacred sexual activity in various parts of the ancient Near East.[110] Within this theoretical context, an Adullamite's use of the term "consecrated woman" (קְדֵשָׁה) in his discussion of a prostitute with other area residents might simply express the deep, native association between sexuality and religion. Alternately, Hirah's usage of this term might be euphemistic, intended to intimate that Judah's relations with the unknown woman had a lofty religious purpose.[111] Or perhaps in an earlier version of the story, Tamar, possibly a Canaanite herself, actually served as a "sacred prostitute" (as the word קְדֵשָׁה has often been translated) in the fertility religion typical of Canaan and the greater ancient Near East.[112]

Some scholars, however, have recently challenged the prevailing assumption that sacred prostitution and other sexual rites were commonplace among Israel's neighbors, pointing to the paucity of documentary evidence outside of the Bible itself for this type of religious expression.[113] The biblical charges of sexual excess and religious

---

[110] For discussions of the fertility cults of the ancient Near East and the role of sacred prostitution in them, see Beatrice A. Brooks, "Fertility Cult Functionaries in the Old Testament," *JBL* 60 (1940) 227–53; Epstein, *Sex Laws and Customs*, 152–76; Raphael Patai, *Sex and Family in the Bible and the Middle East* (Garden City, NY: Doubleday, 1959) 148–52; and Karel van der Toorn, "Prostitution (Cultic)," in vol. 5 of *The Anchor Bible Dictionary*, ed. David Noel Freedman (New York: Doubleday, 1992), 510–13.

Some of the biblical passages most frequently cited as evidence for the indigenous fertility cults of Canaan include 1 Sam 2:22–24; Num 25:1–3; Isa 57:3, 5–8; Jer 2:20; 3:6; Ezekiel 16; 23:36–45.

[111] If this were the case, then the usage of this term might serve an apologetic purpose, in that it improves Judah's character. For an expression of this view, see Speiser, *Genesis*, 300. The implication that Judah engaged in sexual relations with a foreign cult functionary is not necessarily complimentary, however, given the biblical prohibitions against worship of other gods, as Bruce Vawter notes (*On Genesis: A New Reading* [Garden City, NY: Doubleday, 1977] 398).

[112] The most extensive elaboration of this view may be found in Michael C. Astour, "Tamar the Hierodule: An Essay in the Method of Vestigial Motifs," *JBL* 85 (1966) 185–96. See also C. F. Keil and F. Delitzsch, *The Pentateuch*, vol. 1 of *Commentary on the Old Testament*, trans. James Martin (Leipzig: Dörffling und Franke, 1862–72; reprint, Grand Rapids, MI: William B. Eerdmans, no date) 341, and G. R. H. Wright, "The Positioning of Genesis 38," *ZAW* 94 (1982) 523–29. According to this view, only in the final Hebraic version of the story did Tamar's status sink to that of a common prostitute, in keeping with the biblical polemic against the worship of foreign gods.

[113] For examples of this critique, see Daniel Arnand, "La Prostitution sacrée en Mésopotamie, un mythe historique?" *Revue l'histoire des religions* 183 (1976) 111–15; Robert A. Oden, "Religious Identity and the Sacred Prostitution Accusation," in *The Bible without Theology: The Theological Tradition and Alternatives to It* (San Francisco:

whoring may therefore reflect not the actual practices of surrounding cultures, but the tactics of religious polemic.[114] If this critique of one of biblical scholarship's central presuppositions is valid, then assessing Hirah's substitution of the word "consecrated woman" (קדשה) for the word "prostitute" (זונה) becomes even more difficult. Reconsideration of a type of Akkadian priestess known as the *qadištu* is especially pertinent in this discussion, since previous understanding of this figure as a "sacred prostitute" in the religious cult of Mesopotamia influenced the translation of the cognate Hebrew term (קדשה) as "sacred prostitute." A more cautious survey of Babylonian and Assyrian sources, however, reveals merely that the *qadištu* filled important religious functions involving childbirth and perhaps nursing, and that she herself could marry, bear or adopt children, and inherit property. There is no evidence that this cult functionary participated in any form of ritual sexual activity, such as sacred prostitution or reenactment of a *hieros gamos*. The new understanding of the Akkadian *qadištu* therefore reopens the question of the Hebrew term's meaning.

Whatever the nature of the "consecrated woman" (קדשה) mentioned in biblical literature, the prohibition against her office among Israelites in Deut 23:18 and the prophetic indictment against those who associate with her in Hos 4:14 might reflect negatively on Tamar in Genesis 38, since her behavior and appearance lead to Hirah's conclusion that she is one.[115] But the fact that the local men deny the existence of any consecrated woman at Enaim checks this condemnation. Actually, if one reviews Genesis 38 carefully, one notes that the biblical narrator is extremely circumspect in his portrayal of Tamar. He never directly states that Tamar was a prostitute or a consecrated woman; moreover, he never even asserts that she pretended to be either of these. In fact, Tamar's covering with a veil, although necessary for the plot, seems incongruous for someone

---

Harper & Row, 1987) 131–53; Westenholz, "Tamar, Qĕdēšā, Qadištu," 245–65; and Tikva Frymer-Kensky, *In the Wake of the Goddesses: Women, Culture, and the Biblical Transformation of Pagan Myth* (New York: The Free Press, 1992) 199–202.

The vast majority of sources referring to ritual prostitution associated with a religious cult in Mesopotamia are in fact dependent on a single report in Herodotus *Histories* 1.199.

[114] See especially Oden, "Religious Identity and the Sacred Prostitution Accusation," 131–53.

[115] Once again, however, the curious omission of any information concerning Tamar's ethnic background in Genesis 38 complicates biblical interpretation. Since Tamar is not explicitly portrayed as one of "the daughters of Israel," the biblical law in Deut 23:18 might not apply to her.

impersonating a prostitute.[116] Rather than charging that Tamar "played the harlot,"[117] the narrator merely reveals Judah and Hirah's perception of her as prostitute and consecrated woman. Later in the chapter as well, the narrator does not directly express the opinion that Tamar engaged in illicit sexual activity; rather, he presents this as the perception of those who report anonymously to Judah. Even Judah's positive evaluation of Tamar when he compares her behavior with his own (Gen 38:26) entirely sidesteps the issue of whether she acted as a prostitute, a cult functionary, or a licentious woman. Instead, it leads to a focus on his own personal failure of responsibility. Ultimately, the narrator leaves the reader to judge Tamar's actions at Enaim. Understandably, then, the interpretations examined in subsequent chapters reveal a wide variety of responses to the intertextual connections and tensions between Genesis 38 and biblical laws concerning illicit sexuality, as well as the concept of "holiness" raised by the puzzling and suggestive word "consecrated woman" (קְדֵשָׁה).

Intruder in Joseph's Story or Proleptic Key to Israel's History?

Problematic Placement of Genesis 38
The curious placement of Judah and Tamar's story within the book of Genesis has stimulated much scholarly reflection and debate. Many modern commentators consider Genesis 38 to be an intrusive addition to the larger Joseph story (Genesis 37–50).[118] Gerhard von Rad, for example, expresses this view in his commentary on Genesis 38:

---

[116] There is no other biblical evidence that prostitutes wore veils. Elsewhere in the Bible, Rebekah covers herself with a veil before meeting her future husband (Gen 24:65). Laban's deception of Jacob suggests that Leah was similarly veiled at their wedding (Gen 29:21–25). These instances suggest that the veil was a component of bridal attire.

On the subject of veiling, it is interesting to note that Middle Assyrian law no. 40, *ANET*, 183, prohibits prostitutes from wearing veils, and the violation of this rule was a capital offense. This same law also forbids the unmarried *qadištu* to wear a veil, whereas it requires the married *qadištu* to wear one. For a discussion of veiling in Middle Assyrian law 40, see Gerda Lerner, "The Origin of Prostitution in Ancient Mesopotamia," *Signs: Journal of Women in Culture and Society* 11 (1986) 248–54.

[117] This is the interpretive translation of the Hebrew verb (זָנְתָה) in Gen 38:24 in the King James Version.

[118] The canonical placement of Genesis 38 was considered problematic in earlier times as well. For example, one of the earliest post-biblical readings of Genesis, *Jubilees* (second century BCE), does not recount its version of Genesis 38 immediately after the sale of Joseph, but much later, after Joseph has risen to power in Egypt. It places its version between notices concerning the completion of the seven years of abundance (*Jub.* 40:12–13) and the beginning of the seven years of famine (*Jub.* 42:1–3).

Every attentive reader can see that the story of Judah and Tamar has
no connection at all with the strictly organized Joseph story at whose
beginning it is now inserted. This compact narrative [Genesis 38] requires for its interpretation none of the other Patriarchal narratives,
and therefore the Yahwist, who found the story in tradition, faced the
question where to insert this piece into the succession of traditions.[119]

Similarly, E. A. Speiser maintains in his commentary that

The narrative [Genesis 38] is a completely independent unit. It has no
connection with the drama of Joseph, which it interrupts at the conclusion of Act 1.[120]

It is quite remarkable that none of the characters in Genesis 38 besides
Judah plays a role in the preceding and following chapters of Genesis.[121] Chronologically as well, Genesis 38 is jarring in its present
context, immediately following the sale of Joseph in Genesis 37. The
events that transpire in Genesis 38 (including Judah's marriage, the
birth and maturation of three sons, and the birth of twins from yet
another generation) must have taken at least two decades. But with
the first verse of Genesis 39, the narrative immediately reverts to the
much earlier time of Joseph's arrival in Egypt.[122] Some historical-

---

The book of *Biblical Antiquities* withholds reference to the events of Genesis 38 even
longer, until the period of oppression in Egypt when, in response to Pharaoh's decree
that all newborn males should be drowned, Moses' father Amram extols Tamar as
a model of courage in overcoming reproductive obstacles (*Bib.Ant.* 9:5). The *Testament
of Judah*, discussed in the following chapter, substitutes a radically different narrative
context for the events in Genesis 38, specifically Judah's autobiographical account of
his own life. Although Philo suggests many allegorical interpretations of the events
in Genesis 38, he never discusses this narrative in its biblical context within the
Joseph story. Perhaps most telling, his work *On Joseph* contains no allusion to the
story of Judah and Tamar. By contrast, the rabbinic works examined below keep
Genesis 38 in its biblical narrative context, demonstrating their allegiance to the
order of the canonical text. The practice of removing Genesis 38 from its biblical
context in the Joseph story does not necessarily signal that the order of the stories
in Genesis was unknown, however. Some modern treatments of Genesis present
Genesis 38 out of order, or eliminate it completely, as does Nahum M. Sarna,
Understanding Genesis: The Heritage of Biblical Israel (New York: Schocken Books, 1970).

[119] von Rad, *Genesis*, 357.

[120] Speiser, *Genesis*, 299. For other expressions of the view that Genesis 38 is
unconnected, independent, or disruptive in its present narrative context, see the
bibliography provided by Wright, "The Positioning of Genesis 38," 523, n. 2.

[121] It must be noted, however, that Judah's sons are mentioned by name in the
list of those descending to Egypt in Gen 46:12, so they do not completely disappear
from the narrative. This same verse also notes two sons born to Perez, thereby
implying additional narratives of procreation unrecorded in the biblical text.

[122] There remains also the larger question of whether the events in Genesis 38 could
have possibly transpired before Jacob and his sons descend to Egypt in Genesis 46.

critical scholars have even suggested that Genesis 38 portrays a different period of Israelite history than the one generally presented in Genesis 37–50, or that it presupposes a different view of that history.[123] For these reasons, some modern commentators assert that Genesis 38 must stem from a different ancient source than the one behind the rest of the Joseph story.[124]

Verbal and Thematic Links between Genesis 38 and Its Immediate Narrative Context

Regardless of this narrative's prehistory, the final redaction of Genesis 38 in its present context is intentional and artful. The numerous verbal and thematic links between Genesis 38 and the larger Joseph story in which it is embedded, especially the chapters that immediately precede and follow it, point to this conclusion.[125] These links integrate Genesis 38 into its current context and emphasize certain motifs through repetition. They also stimulate intertextual comparisons and contrasts that can serve as the starting points for creative

---

Moses David Cassuto addresses this question at length in his article, מעשה תמר ויהודה [The story of Tamar and Judah], in ציונים: קובץ לזכרונו של י. נ. שמחוני ז"ל [Tsiyyunim: Memorial volume for J. N. Simchoni], ed. J. Klatzkin (Berlin: Eshkol, 1928–29) 93–100.

[123] The rest of the Joseph story depicts Jacob's sons dwelling together with their father and eventually descending to Egypt as a group, but Genesis 38 portrays the separation of Judah from the others to settle in the southwest region of Canaan, without indicating that he ever rejoined his family. Genesis 38 may therefore preserve tribal memories of Judah's settlement of this region during the period of conquest. Alternatively, it may indicate that the tribe of Judah was a late addition to the people known as Israel and therefore participated neither in the descent to Egypt nor in the Exodus. For a discussion of these positions, see Emerton, "Some Problems in Genesis 38," 345–46.

[124] Although a majority of scholars associate both Genesis 38 and the rest of the Joseph story with the J source, there are a variety of theories explaining the differences between the two. For a discussion of various scholarly opinions concerning the source of Genesis 38 and its relation to the rest of the Joseph story, see Emerton, "Some Problems in Genesis 38," 346–54. The dissonance between Genesis 38 and the larger Joseph story leads some scholars to posit a non-Israelite source for this narrative. See for example, Robert H. Pfeiffer, "A Non-Israelite Source of the Book of Genesis," *ZAW* 48 (1930) 66–73, and Emerton, "Judah and Tamar," 411–14.

[125] Recent commentators, such as Alter (*Art of Biblical Narrative*, 3–22) have criticized historical-critical scholarship for ignoring these links in their concern with the prehistory of Genesis 38, its original source, and the discontinuities with the rest of the Joseph story. The examples of verbal and thematic links discussed below are also noted by Alter and other contemporary commentators, such as Donald B. Redford (*A Study of the Biblical Story of Joseph* [*Genesis 37–50*], VTSup 20 [Leiden: E. J. Brill, 1970] 18). The same links were also noted much earlier by the authorities quoted in *Genesis Rabba*, the *Tanḥuma*, and other rabbinic works.

biblical exegesis. One example of a verbal and thematic connection
between the story of Judah and Tamar and the larger Joseph story,
specifically the repetition of the verbal root "to go down" (ירד) in
Genesis 37, 38, and 39, has already been discussed in connection
with the narrator's ironic treatment of Judah.[126] Two other examples
involving the themes of deception and seduction help to illustrate
further the craft of the biblical redactors and to point out the
hermeneutic potential inherent in these intertextual points of contact.

Genesis 37 introduces the theme of deception into the Joseph story
when it depicts the brothers misleading Jacob concerning his favorite
son's fate (Gen 37:31–33).[127] After they sold Joseph, they "sent" (וישלחו,
Gen 37:32) his distinctive garment, dipped in the blood of a he-goat
(שעיר עזים, Gen 37:31), to their father. Their command that Jacob
"Recognize!" (הכר נא, Gen 37:32)[128] the garment's owner evoked an
immediate response. Jacob rightly "recognized it" (ויכירה, Gen 37:33)
as belonging to Joseph, but erroneously concluded that a wild animal
had killed him. The brothers misled their father through an article
of clothing and thus concealed their responsibility for Joseph's disap-
pearance. In Genesis 38, a second article of clothing—this time a
veil—plays an important part in Tamar's deception of Judah (Gen
38:12–19). Because she covered herself with a veil, he failed to perceive
that she was his daughter-in-law (Gen 38:16) and mistook her for a
prostitute (Gen 38:15). Once again in Genesis 38 the motif of the
goat—here specifically a kid (גדי עזים, Gen 38:17)—marks the theme
of deception. This time, however, it stresses Judah's obliviousness to
Tamar's ruse, since he sincerely offered it as a prostitute's fee.[129] Other

---

[126] The repetition of information in Gen 37:36 and Gen 39:1 may be considered
a *Wiederaufnahme*, or "resumptive repetition," indicating that the material appearing
between these two verses (Genesis 38) is a later insertion. But this repetition also
functions as a literary device to remind the reader of an important event after a
long digression. See S. Talmon and Michael Fishbane, סוניות בסידורם של פרקי ספר
יחזקאל [Aspects of the arrangement of passages in the book of Ezekiel], *Tarbiz* 42
(1972–73) 35–38, and Jeffrey H. Tigay, "An Empirical Basis for the Documentary
Hypothesis," *JBL* 94 (1975) 338, n. 28.

[127] Deception is a general, recurrent theme in biblical literature, often leading to
the success of the less powerful over the more powerful. For a discussion of this
theme, see Susan Niditch, *Underdogs and Tricksters: A Prelude to Biblical Folklore* (San
Francisco: Harper & Row, 1987).

[128] The imperative "Recognize!" (הכר נא) may be a legal expression, employed in
conjunction with the submission of evidence. See David Daube, *Studies in Biblical
Law* (Cambridge: Cambridge University Press, 1947) 5–6.

[129] Note also that earlier in Genesis Jacob deceives his father and thereby gains
the blessing by using two kids (גדיי עזים, Gen 27:9; גדיי העזים, Gen 27:16).

words connect the brothers' deception of Jacob in Genesis 37 with Tamar's disclosure of her deception of Judah in Genesis 38. After being sentenced to death, Tamar "sent" (שלחה, Gen 38:25) Judah's distinctive personal belongings (seal, cord, and staff) to him for identification, just as the brothers "sent" (וישלחו) Joseph's coat to Jacob in Genesis 37. She commanded Judah to "Recognize!" (הכר נא, Gen 38:25), just as they asked Jacob to "Recognize!" (הכר נא, Gen 37:32), and Judah "recognized" (ויכר, Gen 38:26) the pledge immediately, just as his father "recognized" (ויכירה, Gen 37:33) Joseph's coat earlier. In Genesis 38, however, Judah's recognition of his personal belongings brings about his acceptance of responsibility for a bad situation, whereas Jacob's recognition of his son's clothing in Genesis 37 facilitates the brothers' evasion of their responsibility. The verbal and thematic parallels between these episodes are nevertheless unmistakable, and they unify the two chapters. In addition, these parallels may suggest a certain moral appropriateness to the progression of events described in the two chapters. One might conclude, for example, that Tamar's deception of her father-in-law in Genesis 38 deals Judah his just deserts for deceiving his own father in the preceding chapter. The theme of deception also reappears following the story of Judah and Tamar, in the story of Joseph and Potiphar's wife in Genesis 39. When Potiphar's wife falsely accuses Joseph of rape, she produces his clothing as incriminating evidence (Gen 39:12–18). For the third time in three chapters a garment is used to lead others to draw false conclusions, and the repetition of this motif helps cement Genesis 38 into its present position.[130] The general theme of deception reappears later in the narrative when Joseph withholds his true identity from his brothers until they prove themselves trustworthy (Genesis 42–45).

The deceptions in both Genesis 38 and 39 are practiced by sexually forward women, and the theme of seduction therefore unifies these two chapters as well. The juxtaposition of Tamar's successful seduction of Judah and Potiphar's wife's unsuccessful seduction of Joseph opens a wide range of interpretive possibilities. For example, if one understands Tamar as a parallel figure to Potiphar's wife, her

---

[130] For a discussion of the significance of various garments in Genesis 37–50, see Nelly Furman, "His Story Versus Her Story: Male Genealogy and Female Strategy in the Jacob Cycle," in *Narrative Research on the Hebrew Bible*, ed. Miri Amihai, George W. Coats, and Anne M. Solomon, *Semeia* 46 (Atlanta: Scholars Press, 1989) 141–49.

character might be developed as a lascivious temptress. Alternately, the two women might be contrasted, since Tamar's motive was apparently to conceive children, whereas Potiphar's wife was attracted by Joseph's beauty. A contrast may be drawn between Judah and Joseph as well, since the first succumbed to a woman's charms, while the second resisted.[131]

View of Israelite History Implied by the Presence of Genesis 38 in the Joseph Story
Besides these verbal and thematic connections, the prominence of Judah as a major character unifies Genesis 38 and the larger Joseph story. In fact, the sustained focus on Judah in Genesis 38 has implications that extend beyond the story of Jacob's twelve sons in Genesis 37–50. Already in Genesis 37, Judah's suggestion to sell Joseph results in events critical for Israel's history, which neither he nor his brothers could have imagined. Joseph's forced separation from his brothers and his descent into Egypt to live among foreigners ultimately lead to his ascent to political power. As an Egyptian administrator, Joseph assures his family's survival through the famine and orchestrates their relocation in Egypt. Ultimately their geographical relocation sets the scene for the defining event of the exodus under Moses.[132]

When the focus suddenly shifts from Joseph's momentous descent to Egypt brought about by Judah in Genesis 37 to Judah's own descent in Genesis 38, this diversion highlights Jacob's fourth son's continuing influence on Israelite history. Judah's descent and separation from his brothers to live among foreigners in Genesis 38 ultimately leads

---

[131] But see James Kugel's discussion of interpretations of Joseph's relations with Potiphar's wife as less than innocent in "Joseph's Change of Heart," in *In Potiphar's House: The Interpretive Life of Biblical Texts* (San Francisco: HarperSanFrancisco, 1990) 94–124. In addition, some rabbinic works, including *Genesis Rabba*, contain traditions that ameliorate Judah's behavior.

For an alternative interpretation of the juxtaposition of these two tales of seduction in Genesis 38 and 39, see Mieke Bal, "One Woman, Many Men, and the Dialectic of Chronology," in *Lethal Love: Feminist Literary Readings of Biblical Love Stories* (Bloomington: Indiana University Press, 1987) 89–103. She argues that since the proleptic depiction of Judah's seduction by a woman in Genesis 38 ultimately turns out for the best, the reader may be assured that the results of Joseph's encounter with another woman in Genesis 39 will similarly prove beneficial in the long run.

[132] It may even be that Joseph and Judah's "descents" prefigure the larger descent of Jacob's entire family to Egypt. In this regard, it is significant that Judah also goes down to Egypt before his family in Gen 46:28. The opposite of the verb "to go down" appears at the midway point in Genesis 38, when Judah "goes up" to Timnah (Gen 38:12–13), resulting ultimately in the conception of the twins. This verb signals a reversal of Judah's fortune, and may structurally correspond to the exodus from Egypt and the change of fortune that it accomplished for the Israelites.

to the birth of Perez, an ancestor of the Davidic dynasty so central in biblical literature and the Jewish imagination. Twice then, Judah's treatment of his relatives significantly shapes Israel's future, although neither when he advocates selling Joseph nor when he buys his daughter-in-law's sexual services is he conscious of the larger historical consequences. Both instances therefore suggest the mysterious unfolding of divine purpose through the imperfect matrix of human lives, and both anticipate important events in Israelite history, namely the exodus and the establishment of the Davidic dynasty.[133]

Judah's pivotal role in Genesis 37–50 brings into question the appropriateness of the common designation of these chapters as the "Joseph story." Although Joseph receives primary attention, Genesis 37–50 actually features two of Jacob's sons, Judah and Joseph, by describing the events of their lives after they part company with their brothers and by portraying their rise to positions of leadership, within the family and over Egypt, respectively.[134] Significantly, neither of these two characters is Jacob's eldest son. Judah is the youngest among Leah's first four sons, born in succession before she temporarily ceases to bear (Gen 29:31–35).[135] Joseph is the youngest of all until the birth of Benjamin, and despite the fact that eventually there is a younger son, it is Joseph who is regarded as the son of Jacob's old age (Gen 37:3). The ascendancy of Judah and Joseph illustrates the common biblical motif of the subversion of the law of primogeniture, thereby underscoring the significance of these brothers and the tribes they represent for Israelite history.[136] In keeping with the prominence

---

[133] George W. Coats similarly suggests that Genesis 38 and other secondary "parasites" within the final portion of Genesis function to incorporate the Joseph story into the larger narrative of biblical history, although he doesn't specify exactly how they accomplish this purpose ("Redactional Unity in Genesis 37–50," *JBL* 93 [1974] 15–21).

[134] Perhaps Genesis 38, with its focus on Judah, appears intrusive at least in part because Genesis 37–50 is generally viewed as Joseph's story. If one broadens one's understanding of the subject of these chapters to include events important for Israel's history, then Genesis 38 doesn't appear intrusive, but rather of paramount importance.

[135] Judah's three elder brothers Reuben, Simeon, and Levi are disqualified from leadership by their misdeeds and excesses according to Jacob's testament in Gen 49:3–7, which refers back to earlier events in Genesis 34 and 35:22. Interestingly, although David is the youngest of eight sons in 1 Sam 17:12–14, only three of his elder brothers are listed by name in 1 Sam 17:13. The fact that David is the youngest of four sons mentioned by name establishes a loose parallel with his ancestor Judah, the youngest of Leah's four sons from an early period of fertility.

[136] For further discussion of this subject, see Judah Goldin, "The Youngest Son, or Where Does Genesis 38 Belong?" in *Studies in Midrash and Related Literature*, ed.

of these two young sons, only the offspring of Judah (Gen 38:3–5, 27–30) and Joseph (Gen 42:50–52) are featured in the book of Genesis.[137] In addition, the same motif of the ascendancy of the youngest son observed in connection with Judah and Joseph repeats itself among their descendants. In the case of Judah's sons, this motif occurs in the birth account of the twins, when Perez usurps Zerah as the first son to emerge from the womb (Gen 38:27–30).[138] In the case of Joseph's sons, this motif occurs later in their lives, when Jacob reverses the expected order of the firstborn's blessing and gives it to Ephraim rather than to his older brother Manasseh (Gen 48:8–20). The portrayal of Judah and Joseph's ascendancy and of their youngest sons' ascendancy in the next generation therefore corresponds to the importance of these two tribes in later Israelite history when they become the central core of the Southern and Northern Kingdoms respectively. Indeed, while the Northern Kingdom represented by Joseph remains relatively prosperous and mighty in comparison with its weaker neighbor to the south for at least two centuries,[139] it is the

---

Barry L. Eichler and Jeffrey H. Tigay (Philadelphia: Jewish Publication Society, 1988) 121–39. The special legal status of the firstborn son is evident in the biblical law guaranteeing him a double portion of inheritance in Deut 21:15–17, but in biblical narratives younger sons, including Abel, Shem (in midrashic tradition considered the youngest of Noah's sons), Isaac, Jacob, Judah, Joseph, Ephraim, Moses, Gideon, David, and Solomon, are favored.

[137] Interestingly, both Judah and Joseph have sons by foreign women—Judah by the Canaanite daughter of Shua and by the possibly Canaanite Tamar, and Joseph by the Egyptian Asenath. For a study of post-biblical traditions concerning Asenath, see V. Aptowitzer, "Asenath, the Wife of Joseph: A Haggadic Literary-Historical Study," *HUCA* 1 (1924) 239–306.

Children born to Jacob's other sons are also noted in the list of family members who go down to Egypt (Gen 46:8–27), but the Bible provides no other information about these descendants besides their names. The exception to this generalization is the note that Simeon had a Canaanite wife (Gen 46:10).

[138] The importance of Perez is also emphasized by the inclusion of his two sons, Hezron and Hamul, in the list of these who go down to Egypt with Jacob (Gen 46:12). With the exception of Asher's two grandsons in Gen 46:17, none of Jacob's other great-grandchildren are listed among those who descend into Egypt.

There may also be an allusion to the motif of the ascendancy of the youngest son implicit in the deaths of Judah's two eldest sons by the Canaanite woman and the survival of his third son, Shelah. Apparently, Judah's youngest son by his first marriage continues to live and prosper despite his eclipse from the narrative in Genesis 38, since in 1 Chr 4:21–23 Shelah's descendants are listed and described as craftsmen. Incidentally, this genealogy indicates that Shelah's eldest son was named Er.

[139] The concentration on Joseph in Genesis 37–50 reflects the early prominence of the Northern Kingdom. Note that the Chronicler has a similar understanding of the importance of Jacob's two sons, Joseph and Judah, in 1 Chronicles 1–2. In this passage, despite Judah's strength among his brothers and despite the fact that royalty stems from him, Joseph receives the birthright after Reuben is disqualified.

Southern Kingdom represented by Judah that endures. Eventually in the post-exilic period, the name Judah becomes synonymous with the Jewish people as a whole, and the Davidic dynasty associated with Judah acquires a national and theological significance unparalleled by any royal lineage in the north.

The importance of Judah, of the tribe associated with his name, and of the dynasty stemming from it emerges from an examination of Jacob's testament in Genesis 49.[140] Jacob's address to Judah (Gen 49:8–12) is the longest of any in this chapter, with the exception of his address to Joseph (Gen 49:22–26). The fact that Judah and Joseph receive the most attention in Genesis 49 confirms their preeminent position within the rest of the narrative in Genesis 37–50 and hints at the importance of the tribes bearing their names in later periods of Israelite history.[141] An interpretation of the notoriously difficult allusions contained in Jacob's blessing of Judah is beyond the scope of this study,[142] but several features deserve mention here. In the opening verse (Gen 49:8), Jacob indicates that the brothers will praise Judah[143] and bow down to him. Jacob's assertion that the leadership position among his sons belongs to Judah counters Joseph's earlier dreams (Gen 37:5–11) that his family would bow down to him.[144] This first verse also indicates that Judah will prevail over his enemies ("Your hand shall be on the neck of your enemies"), although the identity of these enemies is left unspecified. These themes of strength and victory are developed as well in the next verse (Gen 49:9), which employs the imagery of lions at hunt and at rest. Elsewhere in biblical literature and in the iconography of the ancient Near East the lion

---

[140] Most contemporary scholars view Genesis 49 as an originally independent unit interpolated into the narrative of Jacob's sons. See for example Speiser, *Genesis*, 370–71.

[141] By contrast, Moses' blessing of the tribe of Judah in Deut 33:7 is short compared to his blessing of Joseph in Deut 33:13–17. Even in Moses' blessing of the tribes, however, Judah receives special emphasis when he is addressed second, directly after Reuben.

[142] For a bibliography on Genesis 49, see Claus Westermann, *Genesis 37–50*, vol. 3 of *Genesis*, Biblisher Commentar Altes Testament (Neukirchen-Vluyn: Neukirchener Verlag, 1982). See also Calum Carmichael's interpretation of this "blessing" as an ironic criticism of Judah's actions in Genesis 37 and 38 in "Some Sayings in Genesis 49," *JBL* 88 (1969) 435–44. Carmichael's argument is based in part on that of E. Good, "The Blessing on Judah," *JBL* 82 (1963) 427–32.

[143] This line is a play on the name "Judah" (יְהוּדָה) from the verbal root "to praise" (ידה).

[144] In this connection, it is interesting to note that Jacob's address to Joseph (Gen 49:22–26) concentrates on the themes of fruitfulness and divine blessing, rather than on the theme of royal leadership.

is a symbol of royal power,[145] so the employment of this imagery designates Judah as a mighty leader and ancestor of royalty. The following verse as well (Gen 49:10) employs terminology with royal connotations, including "staff" (שֵׁבֶט) and "scepter" (וּמְחֹקֵק).[146] This terminology points beyond the Pentateuch to the biblical genealogies leading to the Davidic dynasty, which state explicitly what the presence of Genesis 38 in the Joseph story and the allusions in Genesis 49 only imply.

Royal Offspring in a Patriarchal Narrative

The significance of Genesis 38 as a story of royal origins is never made explicit within the biblical narrative itself. Without doubt, the narrative moves towards the climactic birth of twins (Gen 38:27–30) and, judging from the unexpected reversal in birth order, Perez emerges as the more important of the two sons.[147] But although this much is internally evident, the historical significance of Perez as an ancestor of later kings must be deduced from genealogies located elsewhere in the Bible.[148]

The genealogy concluding the book of Ruth (Ruth 4:18–22) most directly traces David's ancestry back to Perez and thereby defines Genesis 38 as a story of royal origins:

> These are the generations of Perez: Perez begat Hezron, and Hezron begat Ram, and Ram begat Amminadab, and Amminadab begat Nahshon, and Nahshon begat Salmah, and Salmon begat Boaz, and Boaz begat Obed, and Obed begat Jesse, and Jesse begat David.[149]

---

[145] Within the Bible, see for example Prov 19:12; 30:30; and Ezek 19:2. The lion appears as a symbol of royal power especially in late Assyrian art.

[146] For the "staff" (שֵׁבֶט) as part of the king's royal regalia, see Ps 45:7 and Ezek 19:11, 14. For the "scepter" (מְחֹקֵק) as a royal prop, see Num 21:18. See also Ps 60:9 (108:9) where Judah is YHWH's scepter. The two terms "staff" and "scepter" also appear together in the same verse in Judg 5:14 and imply military leadership in the context of Deborah's song. For a further discussion of the royal connotations of the terms "staff" and "scepter," see Skinner, *Commentary on Genesis*, 520. These two items loosely recall the "staff" (מַטֶּה) that Judah gives to Tamar as part of the pledge.

The theme of royalty is further emphasized by the allusions in Gen 49:11 to a donkey (בְּנִי אֲתֹנוֹ, עִירֹה), an animal that Zech 9:9 portrays as the mount of a future king from the Davidic line. In Zech 9:9 two parallel terms are provided for the royal mount (חֲמוֹר and עִיר בֶּן אֲתֹנוֹת). Note also Judg 10:4 and 2 Sam 13:29.

[147] Note that an alternate genealogy in 1 Chr 4:1 places Perez first in a list of Judah's sons, thereby emphasizing his preeminence through a different means than the one employed in Gen 38:27–30.

[148] For an overview of scholarship concerning biblical genealogies, see Robert R. Wilson, "The Old Testament Genealogies in Present Research," *JBL* 94 (1975) 169–89.

[149] For discussions of the form and function of linear genealogies listing single

In addition, the allusion to Genesis 38 earlier in the final chapter of Ruth is significant. When the elders at the gate address Boaz before he marries Ruth, they include the blessing, "May your house be like the house of Perez, whom Tamar bore to Judah" (Ruth 4:12), and, thus, present Tamar, the mother of the man who heads the Davidic genealogy concluding the book, as a model for Ruth. Shortly thereafter, Ruth also emerges as a royal ancestress when she gives birth to Obed (Ruth 4:13–17). By sanctioning Boaz and Ruth's union with a reference to Genesis 38, the elders attest to a positive interpretation of the pentateuchal narrative as a story concerning royal origins.[150]

Similarly, 1 Chronicles begins its version of Judah's genealogy (1 Chr 2:3–4:23) with a reference to Genesis 38 (1 Chr 2:3–4):

> 3. The sons of Judah were Er, Onan, and Shelah—three sons were born to him by the daughter of Shua, the Canaanite woman. But Er, Judah's first-born, was evil in the eyes of the LORD, so He killed him. 4. And Tamar, his daughter-in-law, gave birth by him to Perez and Zerah. All the sons of Judah were five.

The inclusion of not only Judah's sons but also their mothers suggests the author's reliance on a narrative source in addition to traditional genealogies, such as those found in Gen 46:12 and Num 26:19–22.[151] More conclusively, the specification of the ethnic identity of Shua's daughter as Canaanite (הכנענית, 1 Chr 2:3), the verbatim

---

male progenitors from successive generations (such as the one found in Ruth 4:18–22), see Marshall D. Johnson, *The Purpose of the Biblical Genealogies with Special Reference to the Setting of the Genealogies of Jesus*, 2d ed., Society for New Testament Studies Monograph Series 8 (Cambridge: Cambridge University Press, 1988) 71–82; Abraham Malamat, "King Lists of the Old Babylonian Period and Biblical Genealogies," *JAOS* 88 (1968) 163–73; and Robert R. Wilson, *Genealogy and History in the Biblical World*, Yale Near Eastern Researches 7 (New Haven: Yale University Press, 1977) 9, 195.

[150] The blessing in Ruth 4:12 immediately follows another significant blessing in Ruth 4:11: "May the LORD make this woman coming into your house like Rachel and Leah, who together built the house of Israel. Prosper in Ephrathah, and become renowned in Bethlehem!" The juxtaposition of Rachel and Leah with Tamar in this blessing stresses that she, like them, is an ancestress of an important "house" or family, specifically in her case the "house of David."

[151] Johnson (*Purpose of the Biblical Genealogies*, 50) maintains that the Chronicler included the genealogies found in Gen 46:8–27 and Num 26:4–51, 57–62 among the sources he used in composing the extensive genealogy of all Israel in 1 Chronicles 2–8. See also Martin Noth, *Das System der zwölf Stämme Israels*, Beiträge zur Wissenschaft vom Alten und Neuen Testament 4, 1 (Stuttgart: W. Kohlhammer, 1930) 14, 21, 122–32. Noth especially emphasizes the antiquity and influence of the genealogical material presented in the form of a military census in Numbers 26. Note that in Num 26:20–22, the three major divisions of Judah are depicted as descendants of his three surviving sons in Genesis 38: Shelah, Perez, and Zerah.

quotation of Gen 38:7 concerning the fate of Er,[152] and the notation
that Tamar was Judah's "daughter-in-law" (כלתו, 1 Chr 2:4) as in
Genesis 38 all point to the Chronicler's use of the pentateuchal
narrative as a source. The brief summary of Genesis 38 presented in
1 Chr 2:3–4 introduces a much more expansive genealogy than the
one concluding the book of Ruth. It includes all the sons (and even
some daughters) of successive generations in Judah's line, as well as
other miscellaneous information (1 Chr 2:3–4:23), and forms only
part of an even larger genealogy of all of Jacob's sons. This genealogy therefore differs in form and function from the linear genealogy
culminating in David at the end of Ruth.[153] But, like the genealogy
in Ruth 4:18–22, the genealogy of Judah's family in 1 Chronicles
features David and his descendants (1 Chr 2:15; 3),[154] so important
for the Chronicler's view of Israelite history.[155] By beginning the
genealogy that includes the royal family with an allusion to Genesis
38, the Chronicler reveals that he also associates this narrative with
the origins of the Davidic kingship.[156]

---

[152] Only the last word of Gen 38:7, "the LORD" (יהוה), which is the subject of the
verb "he killed him" (וימתהו), is omitted in 1 Chr 2:3.

[153] The genealogy of Jacob's family in 1 Chronicles (1 Chronicles 2–8) functions
as a shorthand version of Israel's history and defines the constituents of the ideal
Davidic theocracy, which is a central focus of 1 and 2 Chronicles. See Johnson,
Purpose of the Biblical Genealogies, 44, 56, 74–76, 80. For a discussion of this type of
segmented genealogy, describing multiple branches of a single family tree, and its
social, political and religious functions in tribal societies, the literature of the ancient
Near East, and biblical literature, see Wilson, *Genealogy and History*.

[154] Significantly, parts of the genealogy specifying David's descendants through
Solomon's line (1 Chr 2:10–12; 3:10–14) are linear, not horizontal as are other
parts of Judah and David's genealogy. While this difference may simply indicate the
Chronicler's reliance on an earlier linear genealogy of David's dynasty, it may also
highlight the special importance of this particular succession of Davidic descendants
within Judah's family. See Johnson, *Purpose of the Biblical Genealogies*, 71.

[155] In keeping with the importance of the tribe of Judah and of David and his
descendants in 1 and 2 Chronicles, Judah's genealogy is placed before those of all
the other sons of Jacob in 1 Chronicles 2–8. Judah's genealogy is also longer than
the genealogy of any of his brothers. The divine election of Judah as his brothers'
leader implied by the prominent placement of his genealogy and by its extent is
explicitly stated in 1 Chr 28:4 (cf., 1 Chr 5:2). The importance of Judah's descendants for post-exilic resettlement of Jerusalem and its environs is similarly stressed in
1 Chr 9:3–6 (cf., Neh 11:3–6). The leadership of Judah's descendants from the line
of Perez in military affairs is depicted in 1 Chr 27:2–3.

[156] The continued association of the events in Genesis 38 with the Davidic lineage may also be discerned in Jesus' genealogy in Matt 1:1–17. The mention of
Tamar and Zerah (Matt 1:3) in a predominantly linear genealogy, generally including only one male member from each generation, reminds the reader of the story
in Genesis 38. The significance of the four women included in Jesus' genealogy in

Besides these genealogies, there are other indications within the Bible that Genesis 38 was commonly considered the foundational story of the Davidic dynasty, and that its female protagonist was regarded as the royal ancestress. David named one of his own daughters Tamar (2 Sam 13; 1 Chr 3:9), thereby invoking the memory of his ancestress. David's son Absalom also called his daughter Tamar (2 Sam 14:27), apparently as a tribute to his ill-used sister, although perhaps this choice of name also indicates his own aspirations to continue the royal dynasty through his offspring.[157]

The appearance of Genesis 38, with its depiction of the origins of David's lineage, in a larger narrative concerning Jacob and his sons anticipates later periods of Israelite and Judaean history. The presence of a royal ancestor among the patriarchs claims ancient roots for the important institution of monarchy—celebrated in many Psalms,[158] central for the narrative line of the books of Kings and Chronicles, and pivotal for the ideology expressed in some of the prophetic writings including Isaiah and Zechariah. According to the final redactors of Genesis, these roots may be traced back to a time even before the defining event of the exodus from Egypt and the settlement in Canaan, to the earliest period of Israel's formation.[159] But interestingly, Genesis 38 does not glorify the origins of the important institution of kingship.

Matt 1:1–17 has been the subject of much Christian exegesis, well beyond the scope of this study. For summaries of various exegetical trajectories, see Janice Capel Anderson, "Mary's Difference: Gender and Patriarchy in the Birth Narratives," *JR* 67 (1987) 183–202; Raymond E. Brown, *The Birth of the Messiah: A Commentary on the Infancy Narratives in the Gospels of Matthew and Luke*, The Anchor Bible Reference Library, new updated ed. (New York: Doubleday, 1993) 71–74; Johnson, *Purpose of the Biblical Genealogies*, 152–79; and Karin Friis Plum, "Genealogy as Theology," *SJOT* 11 (1989) 66–92. I think that the function of these women, including Tamar, is connected with Matthew's preoccupation with the issue of the legitimacy of Jesus, which is the central focus of the narrative immediately following the genealogy (Matt 1:18–25). Anticipating objections to his claim that Jesus was a legitimate descendant of David based on the unusual circumstances of Mary's conception, Matthew reminds his audience of other unusual biblical stories of reproduction by mentioning the names of strong, though unconventional, ancestresses of the royal family.

[157] For the latter idea, see Joel Rosenberg, *King and Kin: Political Allegory in the Hebrew Bible* (Bloomington: Bloomington University Press, 1986) 159.

A pun on the name Perez in Mic 2:13, a prophetic verse that depicts the postexilic return of Israel's remnant under the leadership of their king and the LORD, also attests to the view that this son of Judah was the progenitor of the Davidic line.

[158] See for example, Psalms 2 and 89.

[159] Similarly, Exodus, Leviticus, and Numbers trace the institution of the sacrificial cult and the observance of the religious calendar to the desert period, before there was an Israelite temple in Jerusalem.

Although the narrator of Genesis 38 encourages the reader's alignment of sympathies with Tamar, and although there are indications
that he approves of her initiative because it results in the emergence
of the royal lineage described elsewhere in the biblical corpus, the
events in Genesis 38 are morally ambivalent. The less-than-complete
affirmation of the circumstances surrounding the origins of the Davidic
genealogy corresponds to the cautionary words about the nature of
kingship elsewhere in the Bible,[160] and echoes the qualified or even
negative evaluations of some of Israel and Judah's monarchs in 1 and
2 Kings.[161] While kingship was a historical reality and a political
necessity, it is not uncritically embraced in the Hebrew scriptures.
Genesis 38 therefore narratively anticipates both the emergence of
the Davidic monarchy and the reservations about the institution of
kingship expressed more explicitly elsewhere in the Bible.

Other Mothers, Other Births

The movement through reproductive difficulties to the emergence of
the next generation occurs quite frequently in biblical literature, making
comparisons between Genesis 38 and other birth narratives almost
inevitable. Comparisons between Tamar's role in the story leading
to Perez and Zerah's births and other biblical mothers' roles in important births are potential catalysts for a range of interpretive trajectories. The following discussion reviews a number of important biblical
birth narratives that would have influenced early Jewish readers'
perceptions of Genesis 38 and explores one particular interpretive
trajectory.

A number of the most important birth narratives in the Bible focus
on the problem of female infertility. The character type known as
the "barren wife" has consequently received a great deal of attention
in biblical scholarship.[162] While Tamar herself does not exemplify

---

[160] See Deut 17:14–20 and 1 Samuel 8.

[161] See, for example, the negative evaluations of members of the Davidic dynasty
in 1 Kgs 11:1–13 and 2 Kgs 21:1–18.

[162] Examples of recent secondary literature dealing with the biblical motif of the
"barren wife" include Athalya Brenner, "Mother of Great Men," in *The Israelite
Woman: Social Role and Literary Type in Biblical Narrative* (Sheffield: *JSOT* Press, 1985)
99–105, and "Female Social Behavior: Two Descriptive Patterns within the 'Birth
of the Hero' Paradigm," *VT* 36 (1986) 257–73; Mary Callaway, *Sing O Barren One:
A Study in Comparative Midrash*, SBL Dissertation Series 91 (Atlanta: Scholars Press,
1986); Esther Fuchs, "The Literary Characterization of Mothers and Sexual Politics
in the Hebrew Bible," in *Narrative Research on the Hebrew Bible*, ed. Miri Amihai, George

this type, analysis of narratives featuring barren wives discloses a basic pattern with which Genesis 38 and more closely related birth stories may be compared and contrasted. In Genesis, all four of the matriarchs (Sarah, Rebekah, Rachel, and even Leah after the birth of her first four sons) are unable to conceive.[163] Ultimately, only divine intervention resolves these crises in the patriarchal period and permits the birth of male descendants, including Isaac, Jacob and Esau, Joseph, and Issachar.[164] The motif of the barren wife reappears in biblical literature depicting later periods of Israelite history as well. Manoah's wife, from the period of the Judges, and Hannah, from the transitional period leading to the united monarchy, are both childless until God intervenes to bring about the births of Samson and Samuel, respectively.[165]

Although the biblical narratives involving barren wives are quite varied as far as narrative content is concerned, a number of them share more than the universally present motifs of the barren wife and divine intervention resulting in birth. In some stories, for example, the women themselves try to rectify procreative stalemates by offering their handmaids to their husbands, although these human efforts are not always satisfactory.[166] Other narratives feature prayers for divine assistance, which are answered when God acts.[167] Several

---

W. Coats, and Anne M. Solomon, *Semeia* 46 (Atlanta: Scholars Press, 1989) 151–66; and James G. Williams, "The Beautiful and the Barren: Conventions in Biblical Type Scenes," *JSOT* 17 (1980) 107–19. For a discussion of the post-biblical development of this theme, see Judith R. Baskin, "Rabbinic Reflections on the Barren Wife," *HTR* 82 (1989) 101–14.

[163] Birth narratives involving the barren wife motif are often incorporated into larger biblical narratives, so it is difficult to specify exactly where each begins and ends. The motif of the barren wife is most extensively developed in connection with Sarah, whose failure to conceive is a central issue in Genesis 15–18. All other biblical narratives containing this theme therefore implicitly refer the reader back to the first and greatest of the matriarchs. Rebekah is described as barren in Gen 25:21, and Rachel in Gen 29:31. Leah's secondary inability to conceive is noted in Gen 29:35 and 30:9. The barren wife motif is the weakest in Leah's case, but passing references to her infertility present her as a parallel to the other matriarchs.

[164] Following divine intervention, Sarah gives birth to Isaac (Gen 21:2–7), Rebekah gives birth to Jacob and Esau (Gen 25:21–26), Rachel gives birth to Joseph (Gen 30:23–24), and Leah gives birth to Issachar (Gen 30:17–18). The relative unimportance of Issachar confirms that Leah's case merely echoes the barren wife motif.

[165] The story of Manoah's wife may be found in Judges 13, and the story of Hannah may be found in 1 Samuel 1.

[166] Sarah (Genesis 16), Rachel (Gen 30:3–8), and Leah (Gen 30:9–13) all employ handmaids.

[167] The stories involving Rebekah (Gen 25:21) and Hannah (1 Sam 1:10–17) include prayers.

include an announcement by God or an intermediary figure concerning the impending birth and the significance of the offspring.[168]

Birth narratives containing the barren wife motif stress God's control over the reproductive powers of the womb and over life itself. Significantly, in most of the patriarchal narratives containing the motif of the barren wife, there is no explicit mention of the husband's role in engendering the child born through divine intervention.[169] But these birth narratives also have a more specific message, related to the fact that the six women who give birth with divine assistance are all either from Abraham's family or (apparently) from the larger family of Israel; furthermore, they are all married either to members of Abraham's family or more generally to Israelites.[170] At least part of the impact

---

[168] In the story concerning Sarah, there are several such announcements (Gen 15:4–6; 17:15–22; 18:9–15). Rebekah also receives an oracle concerning the significance of the struggle within her womb, although this oracle occurs after she has conceived (Gen 25:23). An angel informs Manoah's wife that she will conceive and gives her instructions concerning her son's future (Judg 13:3–5). Hannah is blessed by Eli, the priest, after she explains that she has been praying for a son (1 Sam 1:17).

[169] Where one would expect masculine verbs with the husband as subject, such as "he went into" (ויבא אל, as in Gen 38:2, 18) or "he knew" (ידע, as in Gen 4:1), to directly precede female conception, masculine verbs with God as the subject appear. These masculine verbs include "he visited" (פקד) and "he did" (ויעש) preceding Sarah's conception (Gen 21:1); "he heeded him" (ויעתר לו) preceding Rebekah's conception (Gen 25:21); and "he remembered" (ויזכר), "he heard" (וישמע), and "he opened" (ויפתח) preceding Rachel's conception (Gen 30:22). Only in Leah's case, which, as I have pointed out above, consists of a weak application of the barren wife motif, both a masculine verb with Jacob as the subject, "he lay" (וישכב) and a masculine verb with God as the subject, "he heard" (וישמע), precede Leah's conceiving (Gen 30:16–17). The substitution in three out of four cases of masculine verbs with a divine subject for masculine verbs with a human subject emphasizes God's decisive role in the births of the patriarchs and significant ancestral figures and, therefore, in the implementation of the promises given to Abraham. The supranatural element interjected into these stories by this substitution of verbal subject is further developed in post-biblical literature.

Outside of the Pentateuch, the stories containing the barren wife motif do not emphasize God's intervention in the same way. For example, no masculine verb with God as the subject appears before Manoah's wife gives birth to Samson (Judg 13:24), although the theme of divine involvement is otherwise emphasized through the depiction of a double appearance of the LORD's messenger, who announces Samson's birth and finally ascends in the flames of a sacrifice. In the narrative leading to Samuel's birth, two masculine verbs, one with Elkhanah as the subject ("he knew," וידע) and one with the LORD as the subject ("he remembered her," ויזכרה), directly precede Hannah's conception and delivery (1 Sam 1:19).

[170] Sarah is both Abraham's half sister and his wife (Gen 20:12). Rebekah is the daughter of Abraham's nephew, Bethuel (Gen 22:23), as well as the wife of his son Isaac. Rachel and Leah are the granddaughters of this same nephew (Gen 28:2) and the wives of his grandson Jacob. The lineage of Manoah's wife is never explicitly

of these stories therefore stems from their portrayal of how the divine solicitation shown to Abraham continues into future generations of the same family. In particular, the stories of the matriarchs' difficulties in Genesis emphasize that the fulfillment of God's promise to Abraham that his numerous descendants would inherit the land and be blessed (Genesis 15, 17) depends primarily on divine benevolence and loyalty. The reappearance of the motifs of the barren wife and of divine intervention leading to childbirth in the periods of the judges and the transitional period leading to the monarchy stresses the continuity between the patriarchal period and later periods of Israelite history and underscores God's active involvement with a chosen lineage of Abraham's descendants.[171] In keeping with this important theme of continuity into future generations, each of these six birth narratives, whatever else they may convey in and of themselves, also serves as a preface to further narratives involving the son (or sons) born at its conclusion.[172] Birth narratives containing the barren wife motif therefore generally flag the birth of a male character (or characters) who will figure prominently in ensuing narratives, introduce important themes, and prefigure events in the life of these biblical heroes.[173]

Although Tamar is a fundamentally different type of mother, an

---

stated, although her husband is from the tribe of Dan (Judg 13:2); later both join together in questioning the wisdom of their son's choice of a wife from outside their own people (Judg 14:3), implying that Manoah's wife is also an Israelite. No ethnic identity is given for Hannah either, although her husband is from the tribe of Ephraim (1 Samuel 1). Perhaps the stories involving Manoah's wife and Hannah presuppose that a woman assumes her husband's ethnic identity.

[171] Similarly, Isaiah 54 metaphorically depicts restored Jerusalem as a barren wife giving birth, in order to convey this same message concerning God's continuing involvement with Israel.

[172] Admittedly, Leah's son Issachar plays no special role in the narratives which follow his birth, although he participates along with his brothers in Jacob's return from Haran and in the events centered around Joseph's descent into Egypt.

[173] It is worth noting as well, that every barren wife who becomes a mother also has a role in the subsequent narratives concerning her son's life. Sarah directs her husband to expel Ishmael and Hagar, thus ensuring Isaac a prominent position in the family (Gen 21:9–13). Rebekah schemes with her son to procure Isaac's blessing (Gen 27:1–40) and sends him off to her brother's family in Haran (Gen 27:41–28:5) where he starts his family and gains his fortune. Leah and Rachel agree with Jacob to leave their father and take their children back to their husband's homeland (Genesis 31), and they participate in Jacob's reunion with Esau (Gen 32:23–24; 33:1–7). Manoah's wife reluctantly participates with her husband in arranging the marriage which leads to Samson's destruction of the Philistines (Judg 14:1–7). Hannah brings Samuel to the temple in Shiloh after he is weaned and continues to visit him yearly (1 Sam 1:21–28; 2:11, 19–21).

important point of contact between a passage from Genesis 38 and a passage from one of the birth narratives containing the barren wife motif deserves note. Tamar's delivery (Gen 38:27–30) bears both thematic and verbal similarities to Rebekah's delivery (Gen 25:24–26). The birth scene in Gen 38:27–30 reads as follows:

> 27. At the time of her delivery (לדתה), there were (והנה) twins (תאומים) in her belly (בבטנה)! 28. As she gave birth, one put out his hand (יד), and the midwife took [it] and tied a red thread (שני) on his hand (יד), saying "This one came out (יצא) first (ראשנה)." 29. When he drew back his hand (ידו), his brother (אחיו) came out (יצא)! She said, "What a breach (פרץ) you have made (פרצת) for yourself!" And his name (שמו) was called (ויקרא) Perez (פרץ). 30. Afterwards (ואחר), his brother (אחיו), upon whose hand (ידו) was the red thread (השני), came out (יצא). His name (שמו) was called (ויקרא) Zerah.

The birth scene in Gen 25:24–26 where Rebekah is the mother reads as follows:

> 24. [When] her days to give birth (ללדת) were completed, there were (והנה) twins (תומם) in her belly (בבטנה)! 25. The first (הראשון) came out (ויצא) reddish (אדמוני), like a hairy mantle all over him (כלו כאדרת שער), and they called (ויקראו) his name (שמו) Esau. 26. After that (ואחרי כן), his brother (אחיו) came out (יצא), with his hand (וידו) grasping Esau's heel (בעקב), and they called (ויקרא) his name (שמו) Jacob (יעקב).

Both of these passages depict the births of twins, a fact that in and of itself motivates comparison, since there are no other depictions of twin births in the Bible. The similarity of the initial announcements of the presence of twins emphasizes the correspondence between the two passages. Each refers to the time of delivery for the mother (לדתה, Gen 38:27; ללדת, Gen 25:24), contains an exclamation of visual surprise (והנה, Gen 38:27; 25:24), and notes that there were twins in the woman's belly (תאומים בבטנה, Gen 38:27; בבטנה תומם, Gen 25:24). Following these opening announcements, the focus in each case turns directly to the twins, who become the main subjects of the action, and away from the mother, who is usually the subject of the verbs in birth scenes. A number of common words and themes also unify the two passages. Admittedly, some of the verbal parallels, including verbs from the roots "to come out" (יצא, Gen 38:28, 29, 30; 25:26; ויצא, Gen 25:25) and references to a twin's "brother" (אחיו, Gen 38:29, 30; 25:26), might simply be due to the common subject matter. But more striking is the special attention paid to birth order in both passages, reflected verbally in the usage of similar expressions, such

as "first" (רִאשׁנָה, Gen 38:28) and "the first" (הָרִאשׁוֹן, Gen 25:25), and
"afterwards" (וְאַחַר, Gen 38:30) and "after that" (כֵן וְאַחֲרֵי, Gen 25:26).
In both cases, determination of birth order involves attention to the
actions of the "hand" (יָד, Gen 38:28, twice; יָדוֹ, Gen 38:29, 30; וְיָדוֹ,
Gen 25:26) of the infant who ultimately emerges last from the womb.[174]
Also prominent in each birth narrative is the color red, which shows
up in the thread that the midwife ties around Zerah's hand (שָׁנִי, Gen
38:28; הַשָּׁנִי, Gen 38:30) and which characterizes Esau's entire body
(אַדְמוֹנִי Gen 25:25). In each case this color marks the twin who ultimately proves to be less central to Israel's history. Common terms
associated with naming, including verbs from the root "to name"
(וַיִּקְרָא, Gen 38:29, 30; 25:26; וַיִּקְרְאוּ, Gen 25:25) and the expression
"his name" (שְׁמוֹ, Gen 38:29, 30; 25:25, 26) itself, might be expected
given the subject matter of the two passages. More intriguing, however, is the similar disruption and prominence suggested by the names
of the more important sons from the two sets, including Perez (פֶּרֶץ,
Gen 38:29), who "breaks forth" (Hebrew root פרץ; פָּרָצְתָּ, פֶּרֶץ, Gen
38:29) unexpectedly from the womb, and Jacob (יַעֲקֹב, Gen 25:26),
who grasps his brother's heel (בַּעֲקֵב, Gen. 25:26) at birth and eventually "supplants" (Hebrew root עקב) him later in life.[175]

Although these two birth scenes are clearly not identical,[176] there
is enough similarity between them to raise the question of dependence. Is one of these birth scenes dependent on the other, or are
both simply following a conventional pattern associated with the birth
of twins, which happens to appear only twice in the Bible? To answer
this question, it might be helpful to view the two birth scenes within
their larger narrative contexts. If one of the birth scenes appears to
be more integrally related to its present context than the other, perhaps that one served as a model for the less integrally related scene.

In the shorter version, depicting the birth of Jacob and Esau (Gen
25:24–26),[177] the theme of twins clearly resonates with material in
the larger narrative context. When Rebekah goes to inquire about

---

[174] In the case of Zerah, the initial extension and subsequent retraction of his hand
signal his loss of status as the firstborn, whereas in the case of Jacob, his grasping
of his elder brother's ankle foreshadows his efforts later in life to usurp him.

[175] Gen 27:36.

[176] Notable differences between the two accounts include the role of the midwife
and the actual reversal of birth order in Gen 38:27–30, as well as the details associated with the etymologies of the twins' names in both cases.

[177] While the rule of thumb is that the shorter version is the older, more original
version, this general rule needs to be confirmed by critical analysis.

the significance of her tumultuous pregnancy, she receives an explanation from the LORD (Gen 25:23):

> Two nations are in your belly (שני גיים בבטנך), and two peoples shall
> issue forth from your loins. But one people shall be stronger than the
> other, and the elder shall serve the younger.

In Rebekah's delivery in the next verses, the twins revealed in her
belly (והנה תומם בבטנה, Gen 25:24), correspond to the two nations in
her belly (שני גיים בבטנך, Gen 25:23) foretold in the oracle. The reference in the birth scene to Esau's red coloration (אדמוני, Gen 25:25),
which is a pun on the nation Edom (אדום), and the reference to his
hairiness (כלו כאדרת שער, Gen 25:25), which is a pun on the territory of that nation, Seir (שעיר), build on the theme of the origins of
distinctive peoples introduced in the oracle. Elsewhere in the biblical
corpus, Jacob's name itself designates a distinctive people.[178] The close
attention in the birth scene to who is "the first" (הראשון, Gen 25:25)
to emerge and who appears "after that" (ואחרי כן, Gen 25:26) brings
to mind the prediction that "the elder shall serve the younger." Jacob's
grasp of his elder brother's heel (בעקב, Gen 25:26) with his hand
(וידו, Gen 25:26) involves a pun on his name, which can mean "he
shall supplant" (יעקב, Gen 25:26). This pun proleptically confirms
the oracle's vision of the outcome of the ethnic struggle nascent in
Rebekah's womb, even as it anticipates Esau's later lament that Jacob
had twice supplanted him (ויעקבני, Gen 27:36) by gaining both the
birthright and the blessing due the firstborn son. Similarly, the reference to Esau's red color (אדמוני, Gen 25:25) foreshadows the red
porridge (האדם האדם, Gen 25:30) for which he surrenders his birthright to Jacob. The birth scene in Gen 25:24–26 therefore hearkens
back to Rebekah's pregnancy and the divine oracle she receives, even
as it anticipates the continuing rivalry between Jacob and Esau
throughout their lives. In the ensuing narratives, Jacob outmaneu-
vers his elder brother through cunning, subterfuge, and diplomacy,
until finally he possesses the family birthright and blessing, great wealth,
and a large family, and returns safely to the land of his origins.[179]

---

[178] See, for example, Num 24:5, 19 and Deut 32:9.

[179] From the very beginning the two sons compete for their parent's favor, with
Isaac preferring Esau and Rebekah preferring Jacob (Gen 25:28). Jacob gains Esau's
birthright in exchange for some porridge (Gen 25:29–34). Jacob gains the firstborn's
blessing from Isaac by deceiving his father with Rebekah's help (Genesis 27). The
sons also compete for their parents' approval concerning their choice of wives (Gen
27:46–28:9). The strife between Jacob and Esau continues even into a much later

The birth scene therefore introduces the theme of sibling rivalry that dominates the Jacob cycle, ultimately resulting in the ascendancy of the younger son over his elder brother.

By contrast, specific connections between the details of the birth scene in Gen 38:27–30 and the larger birth narrative it concludes are less obvious. Tamar's delivery of two sons seems appropriate, in that it restores the number of Judah's sons to three at the end of the chapter. But the contextual significance of the twins' reversed order of emergence, described with such care at the end of the narrative, is less clear. Does this reversal reiterate in a general way what Judah learned from his experience with Tamar, that things are not always as they seem, but that the unexpected and extraordinary may sometimes work for good? Or is this reversal simply a reference to the common biblical motif of the ascendancy of the youngest son and therefore a marker for Perez's importance? Even more puzzling is the prominent presence in Gen 38:27–30 of motifs also present in the earlier birth scene in Gen 25:24–26, including the color red (שָׁנִי, Gen 38:28; הַשָּׁנִי, Gen 38:30) and an infant's hand (יָד, Gen 38:28, twice; יָדוֹ, Gen 38:29, 30). Whereas the motifs of Esau's red coloration and Jacob's grasping hand in Gen 25:24–26 fit in with larger themes in the Jacob cycle, the color red and the infant's hand have no particular resonance within the narrative context of Genesis 38 or the following chapters.[180] Just as striking is the lack of connection between the birth scene in Gen 38:27–30 and the narrative that immediately continues in Genesis 39, which focuses on Joseph in Egypt. Whereas the birth scene in Gen 25:24–26 introduces the subsequent stories of the twins' lives, the birth scene in Gen 38:27–30 serves a terminal function.[181]

---

period. When Jacob returns to Canaan with his large family and flocks, Esau meets him with a large force. Even in this final instance, Jacob overcomes Esau, this time through generous gifts and diplomacy (Gen 32:4–33:17).

[180] Some, including Franz Delitzsch, *A New Commentary on Genesis*, vol. 2, trans. Sophia Taylor (Edinburgh: T. & T. Clark, 1894) 275, argue that the reference to the bright red thread corresponds to the name "Zerah," which contains a root (זרח) that can mean "to be bright." For this meaning of זרח, see Isa 60:3. Alternatively, Frank Zimmerman, "The Births of Perez and Zerah," *JBL* 64 (1945) 377–78, suggests that there may have also been wordplay involving Zerah's name and an Aramaic word for scarlet (זחוריתא) in an oral version of Genesis 38, although this wordplay is obscured in the written text. Interesting in this connection is the fact that Zerah is depicted as an Edomite clan in Gen 36:13, 17, and 33.

[181] Whereas Jacob emerges as the younger twin in Gen 25:24–26 and gains pre-eminence over his brother through many adventures recounted in the following

Since the details of the birth scene in Gen 25:24–26 fit well within its larger narrative context and the details of the birth scene in Gen 38:27–30 do not, it seems likely that the account of Tamar's delivery of Perez and Zerah alludes to the more original account of Rebekah's delivery of Jacob and Esau. If indeed this is the case, then this intentional allusion to the earlier birth narrative has important consequences. For one thing, it establishes a correspondence between an important Israelite matriarch and the female protagonist of Genesis 38. This correspondence legitimates Tamar, whose impersonation of a prostitute and unconventional conception through intercourse with her father-in-law may otherwise devalue her in the reader's mind. The allusion also draws attention to Tamar's position as the ancestress of an important lineage, in that it presents her as a parallel figure to the mother of Israel himself. The allusion to Gen 25:24–26 at the end of Genesis 38 also highlights the importance of one of the sons born in Gen 38:27–30, in that it presents Perez, the usurping brother, as Jacob's parallel. The people of Israel and the king of Israel therefore trace their origins to similar births, and this situation implies something about the importance of both for Israelite history.[182]

But despite the significant similarities between the concluding birth scene from Genesis 38 and the birth scene from an important narrative containing the barren wife motif, Tamar's story differs fundamentally in that she is not a barren wife. Indeed, after a certain point, Tamar is not a wife at all. Tamar herself makes her lack of a partner clear when she notes that "she had not been given to him [Shelah] as a wife" (Gen 38:14). The reproductive impasse in Genesis 38 stems not from female infertility as in the case of the narratives containing the barren wife motif, but from the absence of effective procreative behavior by the male characters. Tamar's first husband, Er, is removed early in the story by divine intervention, Onan intentionally prevents conception and is consequently removed by divine intervention, and Shelah is withheld from Tamar although he has come of age. The basic problem in this narrative is therefore the lack of an appropriate sexual partner for a fertile woman brought about by a combination of divinely caused death and male recalcitrance.

---

narratives, Perez usurps his brother's place as first-born during the birth scene itself. The concluding episode in Genesis 38 thus condenses into a few phrases the ascendancy of the younger son illustrated at length in the Jacob cycle.

[182] The importance of two "houses," the "house of Israel" (בית ישראל, Ruth 4:11) and the "house of Perez" (כבית פרץ, Ruth 4:12), known later as the "house of David," is indicated in the elders' two blessings of Boaz (Ruth 4:11–12).

As in several of the birth narratives containing the motif of the barren wife, Tamar attempts to resolve the problem of childlessness through human means. Her efforts do not involve the use of another woman as a surrogate mother, however, since the problem is not female infertility but male neglect. Rather, Tamar solicits the necessary sexual services of one of the recalcitrant males by posing as another woman herself. Tamar's method of overcoming the lack of offspring is therefore based on secrecy and deception, in contrast to Sarah, Rachel, and Leah's more overt and socially acceptable method involving their handmaids.[183] In addition, Tamar ignores Shelah, the young man designated for her, and selects an older man from the previous generation. Since this man is her father-in-law, their union technically constitutes incest. But surprisingly in light of these irregularities, Tamar's unorthodox initiatives result in the birth of very important sons for Israelite history, including the ancestor of the Davidic lineage. The success of her human initiative therefore contrasts with the more qualified results of the matriarchs' human initiatives.

Because Tamar's efforts are successful, there is no narrative necessity for a prayer for divine assistance or for an announcement of impending divine intervention, as we find in some of the birth narratives with the barren wife motif. An even more striking difference is that God does not intervene in the events leading directly to the conception and birth of the twins at the end of Genesis 38; there is no masculine verb with God as the subject immediately prefacing Tamar's conception (Gen 38:18). Instead, there is a masculine verb with Judah as the human subject, "he went into" (אל ויבא, Gen 38:18). This verb is commonly used in connection with male procreative behavior in biblical literature, but in Genesis 38, Judah's action is clearly in response to Tamar's initiative. Structurally, Tamar effectively replaces God in his role of facilitator of birth in the narratives containing the barren wife motif, since she, not God, acts to continue

---

[183] Tamar's deception involves more than preventing Judah's recognition of her identity. Judah assumes that she offers sexual relations with no reproductive consequences, and therefore Tamar also deceives her father-in-law concerning the import of their encounter. By contrast, the procreative purposes that motivate the matriarchs' initiatives involving their handmaids are obvious to their husbands from the outset. Tamar's reliance on deception may be related to her lack of social and legal options for solving the basic problem underlying the narrative. For a study of the status of women and feminine deception in the Bible, see Esther Fuchs, "Who Is Hiding the Truth? Deceptive Women and Biblical Androcentrism," in *Feminist Perspectives on Biblical Scholarship*, ed. Adela Yarbo Collins (Chico, CA: Scholars Press, 1985) 137–44.

an important lineage.[184] The conception which occurs therefore appears to be the result of events that remain entirely on the human
level, in contrast to the interaction between human and divine levels
that characterizes the birth narratives containing the barren wife motif.

Three other features distinguish Genesis 38 from narratives containing the barren wife motif. One concerns Tamar's ancestry. Judging from the setting of the narrative in a land where Adullamites
and Canaanites lived (Gen 38:1–2), she was most likely a foreign
woman from outside of Abraham's family, as noted previously. The
text is mute concerning this issue and thus prevents firm conclusions,
but if this is the case, then Tamar's ethnicity contrasts with that of
the endogamous barren wives. The second distinguishing feature is
that Genesis 38 is clearly connected with the lineage of the Davidic
kings, whereas the birth narratives containing the barren wife motif
are either directly connected with the patriarchs, or else they create
a bridge between the patriarchal period and later periods in Israelite
history. The final feature that distinguishes Genesis 38 is that it is a
self-contained unit, despite its thematic and verbal connections with
the larger Joseph story. The birth of Perez and Zerah is a terminal
scene in Genesis 38 and does not serve as an introduction to further
narratives concerning their lives. This situation contrasts with the birth
scenes in the narratives containing the barren wife motif, which serve
as introductions to narratives concerning the sons' lives.

Two other biblical birth narratives—those involving Lot's daughters (Gen 19:30–38) and Ruth—have stronger affinities with Tamar's
story.[185] In both of these, the basic problem is not the infertility of a
married woman, as in the narratives containing the barren wife motif,

---

[184] In the past, some commentators have sought a divine parallel for the figure of
Tamar. For example, Skinner (*Commentary on Genesis*, 452) compares Tamar with
Ishtar, and Astour ("Tamar the Hierodule," 195–96) compares Tamar with Adonis'
mother, Smyrna. Similarly, William F. Albright ("Historical and Mythical Elements
in the Story of Joseph," *JBL* 37 [1918] 126) views Tamar as a "depotentized goddess."
These comparisons are generally based on similarities between Genesis 38 and other
texts from the ancient Near East. But there is also some internal biblical basis for
the attribution of an uncanny, almost superhuman power to Tamar, in that she
performs the role reserved for God in the stories containing the barren wife motif.

[185] For discussions of the similarities between these narratives, see Athalya Brenner,
"Naomi and Ruth," *VT* 33 (1983) 393–94; Gillian Feeley-Harnik, "Naomi and Ruth:
Building Up the House of David," in *Text and Tradition: The Hebrew Bible and Folklore*,
ed. Susan Niditch, SBL Semeia Studies (Atlanta: Scholars Press, 1990) 163–84; Fisch,
"Ruth and the Structure of Covenant History," 425–37; and André LaCocque, *The
Feminine Unconventional: Four Subversive Figures in Israel's Tradition* (Minneapolis: Fortress
Press, 1990) 104.

but the lack of an appropriate male partner for a lone, fertile woman, as in Genesis 38. In the case of Lot's virgin daughters (Gen 19:8), this lack is caused by the divine destruction of the cities of Sodom and Gomorrah and their inhabitants (Gen 19:1–29).[186] Lot's elder daughter clearly expresses her perception of this problem, when she says to her sister, "Our father is old, and there is no man on earth to come into us in the way of all the world" (Gen 19:31). In the case of Ruth, the deaths of both her husband and her husband's brother in the land of Moab leave her widowed and without a potential levir (Ruth 1:5). Death of suitable sexual partners thus unifies Genesis 38, Gen 19:30–38, and Ruth. Ruth's choice to return to Bethlehem with Naomi rather than to remain in Moab and remarry in her native land further limits her opportunities for finding a suitable mate, as her mother-in-law herself cautions (Ruth 1:11–18).

In both of these stories, as in Genesis 38, the women protagonists take direct action to overcome reproductive impasses caused by the absence of appropriate male partners. The female initiatives of Lot's daughters and Ruth are similar in nature to Tamar's, in that they involve secrecy and deception,[187] and in that they target an older relative from the previous generation, thus invoking the common theme of incest. Most straightforwardly, Lot's daughters get their own father drunk so that they can have sexual intercourse with him without his knowledge on two consecutive nights (Gen 19:31–35). The story of Ruth contains less morally offensive echoes of the themes of female sexual initiative, secrecy and deception, and incest also present in Gen 19:30–38 and Genesis 38. Lot's daughters' exploitation of their unconscious father and Tamar's deception of her father-in-law find a modified parallel in Ruth's surprise of her elder kinsman at night, when he awakens to discover her lying near him.[188] The language

[186] The theme of divine, punitive elimination of potential sexual partners thus also unites Genesis 38 and Gen 19:30–38.

[187] For the more general issue of sexual deception in the Hebrew Bible, see Wendy Doniger, "Sexual Masquerades in the Hebrew Bible: Rachel and Tamar," Loy H. Witherspoon Lectures in Religious Studies (University of North Carolina at Charlotte, March 21, 1990), and Zvi Jagendorf, "'In the Morning, Behold It Was Leah:' Genesis and the Reversal of Sexual Knowledge," in *Biblical Patterns in Modern Literature*, ed. David H. Hirsch and Nehama Aschkenazy, Brown Judaic Studies 77 (Chico, CA: Scholars Press, 1984) 51–60.

[188] Boaz reveals his lack of awareness concerning Ruth's identity and motives when he startles from sleep and asks, "Who are you?" (Ruth 3:9). The theme of secrecy is also expressed in Naomi's instructions that Ruth not let her presence at the threshing floor be known (Ruth 3:3–4), in Ruth's stealth as she approaches Boaz

describing the encounter that Ruth orchestrates with Boaz is sexually
suggestive (Ruth 3:6–15),[189] although their union appears to be delayed
until its legal aspects are resolved (Ruth 3:12–13; 4). Similarly, the
theme of incest, although suggested by references to Boaz as an elder
kinsman[190] and by allusions to levirate practice with its component of
socially sanctioned incest, is decidedly muted in Ruth's story.[191]

The stories of Lot's daughters and Ruth, like Genesis 38, emphasize female initiative leading to male sexual activity, not God's miraculous intervention. In the case of Lot's daughters, there is no mention
whatsoever of divine participation in the events of the story. In fact,
the daughters' control over the course of the narrative and over their
father's behavior is so complete that where one might expect masculine procreative verbs leading to conception, feminine forms appear.
The daughters "go into" (ותבא, Gen 19:33; ובאי, Gen 19:34) their
father and "lie" (ונשכבה, Gen 19:32; ותשכב, Gen 19:33; שכבתי, Gen
19:34; שכבי, Gen 19:34; ותשכב, Gen 19:35) with him. Elsewhere in
the Bible, these verbs denoting sexual activity appear with masculine
subjects.[192] Emphasis is also placed on a woman's initiative in the
story of Ruth. There is no indication that Boaz would have taken

---

(Ruth 3:7), and in Boaz's precaution that she return home in the dark to prevent
recognition (Ruth 3:14).

[189] Ruth accepts Naomi's instructions to beautify herself, to wait secretly at the
threshing floor until Boaz has finished eating and drinking and has gone to bed, to
uncover his feet and to lie down, and to do whatever he tells her (Ruth 3:1–5),
apparently indicating that she is sexually offering herself. The references to uncovering and lying at Boaz's feet, or more literally, "the place of his feet" (מרגלתיו) Ruth
3:4; 7, 8, 14), are particularly suggestive because the word "feet" (רגלים) is used
euphemistically for the genitals (Ezek 16:25; Deut 28:57; MT reading [qere] in
2 Kgs 18:27 [= Isa 36:12]; Isa 7:20). Also suggestive is the fact that Ruth spends
the entire night with Boaz (Ruth 3:13–14).

[190] See Ruth 2:1; 3:2, 9, 12–13; 4:3–6 for indications of Boaz's relationship to
Elimelech's widow. His seniority is indicated by the gratitude he expresses to Ruth
for choosing him instead of one of the "young men" (Ruth 3:10).

[191] See Ruth 4:5 and 7–8. For a discussion of the increase in moral sensitivity
expressed in the story of Ruth in comparison with the stories of Lot's daughters and
Tamar, see Fisch, "Ruth and the Structure of Covenant History," 425–37.

[192] Lot's eldest daughter herself expresses this general rule when she tells her younger
sister that there is no man left "to go into us" (לבוא עלינו, Gen 19:31), as is usual
in the world. Note also that Jacob actively "lay" (וישכב) with Leah (Gen 30:16) even
though she arranged their night together, and that Joseph refused to obey Potiphar's
wife's command that he actively "lie" (שכבה) with her (Gen 39:7). Lot's passivity is
emphasized even further by the double notice that he "did not know" (ולא ידע, Gen
19:33, 35) when his daughters lay down or got up. These notices are ironic in that
generally when the verb "to know" (ידע) is used in a sexual context, the man actively
"knows" the woman.

Ruth as his wife had she not ventured to the threshing floor. But in this narrative, Ruth's initiative eventually results in the appearance of familiar masculine procreative verbs with Boaz as the subject before her conception. Boaz "takes" (ויקח, Ruth 4:13) Ruth and she becomes his wife, then he "goes into her" (ויבא אליה, Ruth 4:13). It must be pointed out, however, that there is also a notice in the same verse that the LORD "gave" (ויתן, Ruth 4:13) Ruth conception, which is in keeping with the general tendency of the book to note God's presence.[193] The divine role in Ruth's pregnancy does not stand out as much as it does in the stories containing the barren wife motif, however, since the central problem has not been her inability to conceive, but her lack of a spouse.[194]

In addition, the issue of foreign ethnic identity is raised in each of these narratives, as in Genesis 38. It is true that the female protagonists in Gen 19:30–38 are the daughters of Abraham's nephew and also bear sons by the same man. But, by this point in the narrative, Lot has departed from Abraham's company, and he remains tangential to the main line of the patriarch's descendants through which the divine promises continue. The theme of foreign ethnic identity is also evoked by the names of the sons delivered by Lot's daughters. The elder daughter gives birth to Moab and the younger gives birth to Ammon, the eponymous ancestors of two of Israel's foreign neighbors (Gen 19:37–38). In the book of Ruth, the female protagonist is clearly a Moabite woman, and her foreign identity remains a prominent part of the narrative (Ruth 1:4, 15, 22; 2:2, 6, 21; 4:5, 10).[195]

Both of these stories, like Genesis 38, end with the birth of sons, and even more significantly, the offspring delivered by Lot's daughters and Ruth, like the offspring delivered by Tamar, are related in some

---

[193] For other references to the divine presence in Ruth, see Ruth 1:6, 8–9, 13, 16–17, 20–21; 2:4, 12, 20; 3:10; 4:11–12, 14.

[194] In this connection, it is especially interesting to note that in the third chapter of Ruth, where Ruth takes the initiative by going to the threshing floor, God's presence is indicated only in Boaz's blessing of her for choosing him over a younger man (Ruth 3:10). In the following scene at the gate in Ruth 4:1–12, which has been precipitated by Ruth's request that Boaz take her under his protection as a redeeming kinsman (Ruth 3:9), God's presence is indicated only in the elders' blessings of the couple's union after it has been arranged through ordinary human negotiations (Ruth 4:11–12). God's participation in Ruth's conceiving therefore appears to be a divine confirmation of the course of events initiated by Ruth.

[195] It is true, however, that she aligns herself with her Israelite husband's people (Ruth 1:16–17; 2:11–12), and her second husband is also from the tribe of Judah, as was the first (Ruth 1:1–2, 4; 2:1; 3:2; 4:3, 10, 12, 17, 18–19).

way to the Davidic lineage. In the case of Lot's daughters, the eldest
daughter gives birth to Moab, the eponymous ancestor of David's
maternal grandmother, Ruth.[196] In the case of Ruth, the connection
between her son Obed and the Davidic line is even more clearly
spelled out in the final genealogy of the book (Ruth 4:18–22).

But perhaps as striking as these two stories' connection to a future
king is the absence of contiguous narratives in which the sons born
at their conclusions function as protagonists—a feature also shared
with Genesis 38. Because of these abrupt endings, the mothers who
make the births possible remain more memorable than their sons.[197]
These abrupt endings also direct attention forward in time to David,
the distant relative of these sons, who is the hero of many biblical
narratives. In this way, as in all the other ways listed above, these
three narratives form a set that fundamentally differs from the stories
containing the barren wife motif. Because of the shared connection
between these birth narratives and the Davidic lineage, each of the
mothers—Lot's daughters, Tamar, and Ruth—may be designated as
a "royal ancestress."

In light of this discussion, it is important to note that David himself has no birth narrative whatsoever in the Bible. In fact, the only
information the Bible provides about David's mother is that David
sent her and her husband to Moab for safety during a period of war
(1 Sam 22:3–4).[198] This silence is curious, given that David is one of

---

[196] There is also a second connection between Gen 19:30–38 and the Davidic
dynasty. Lot's younger daughter gives birth to Ben-ammi, the eponymous ancestor
of the Ammonites. Naamah, Solomon's wife and the mother of Rehoboam, was an
Ammonite woman (1 Kgs 14:31; 2 Chr 12:13).

[197] Also interesting is the fact that these mothers disappear from narrative view
after the birth of their sons, recalling Tamar's eclipse from the narrative even while
giving birth. Only Ruth is mentioned again, albeit not by name, in a scene following her delivery of Obed (Ruth 4:15), when Naomi's friends praise her "daughter-
in-law," who loves her and is better to her than seven sons. But even in this scene
(Ruth 4:14–17), Naomi usurps Ruth as the focal character.

[198] There is not even a passing reference to David's mother in the descriptions of
Jesse's family in 1 Sam 16:6–11; 17:12–15; and 1 Chr 2:13–16.

By contrast, Israel's first king, Saul, apparently once had a birth narrative, as two
distinctive etymological explanations in the story subsequently associated with Samuel's
birth (1 Sam 1:20, 28) indicate. If 1 Samuel 1 originally recounted the circumstances
of Saul's birth, the presence of the barren wife motif stressed God's involvement in
the emergence of Israel's first king from the tribe of Benjamin. With David's usurpation of the kingship, however, the strong connection between Saul and the patriarchs provided by the repetition of this motif was deemed inappropriate, and the
birth narrative was applied to the prophetic figure who transferred the kingship
from Saul to David.

the most important heroes of the Hebrew Bible. Narratively, the lack
of a birth story corresponds to David's sudden entrance on the scene
as a young man in the middle of Saul's reign.[199] His appearance out
of nowhere emphasizes his intrusion into Israelite history and his upset-
ting its apparent course. Or alternatively, perhaps the lack of a Davidic
birth narrative reflects a conscious, ideological attempt to avoid idealizing Israel's kings by introducing them with birth narratives.[200]

Whatever the case, in the absence of a mother for Israel's most
celebrated king, the biblical reader may look to David's more distant
female relatives to fill the void, and in the absence of a birth narrative, the biblical reader may look to the three birth narratives with
the royal ancestress motif.[201] In fact, given the repetition of the basic
narrative pattern containing the royal ancestress motif, one might
speculate that at one time this pattern was associated with the great
king's birth as well. If so, one might further speculate that the absence
of a birth narrative directly associated with David and the presence
of birth narratives for his ancestors result from an intentional attempt
to distance the king from his own story of origins. This distancing
might be desirable because aspects of the birth narrative containing

---

[199] When he is anointed by Samuel, he is already old enough to tend sheep by
himself (1 Sam 16:11), and by the time he comes to Saul's attention he is already
an accomplished musician and warrior (1 Sam 16:18). He next appears to challenge
Goliath (1 Samuel 17).

[200] By contrast, Solomon does have a birth narrative of sorts (2 Sam 11:1–12:25),
although it is not an especially flattering one.

[201] See *Ruth Rab.* 8.1, where Tamar and Ruth are discussed as David's ancestresses,
and *Gen.Rab.* 51.8, where Lot's daughters are viewed as the messiah's ancestresses.
In post-biblical literature, the similarities between the three stories containing the
royal ancestress motif are enhanced, and additional similarities are created. For
example, in some sources Tamar remains a virgin throughout her first two marriages,
and therefore becomes aligned with Lot's daughters, who are also virgins. (A question then arises about how Lot's daughters and Tamar were able to conceive, since
it was common wisdom that a woman could not conceive as a result of her first
sexual experience, as stated in *b. Yebam.* 34a. The answer in *b. Yebam.* 34b is that all
three manually destroyed their virginity in order to be able to conceive.) Ruth becomes
assimilated to Tamar in some sources, in that she enters a levirate marriage with
her brother-in-law after her husband's death. He too, like her husband, and like Er
and Onan in Genesis 38, is killed by God because of his wickedness. Ruth is also
brought in line with Lot's daughters and Tamar in sources that portray her conception as the result of a single act of intercourse, since Boaz dies on their wedding
night. Also, in some sources Ruth and Tamar are developed as model proselytes,
thereby positively elaborating the common motif of the foreign woman. Similarly,
Tamar is implicitly compared with Abraham in some post-biblical works, just as
Ruth is implicitly compared with Abraham in Ruth 2:11. The interpretive harmonization of the three stories in these and other ways indicates that they were viewed
as a set, all dealing with the emergence of the Davidic lineage.

the royal ancestress motif are extremely unflattering. For example, the themes of foreign blood and incest would not contribute to a wholehearted endorsement of God's anointed king.[202]

Perhaps the displacement of the birth narratives containing the royal ancestress motif serves a double purpose. On the one hand, this displacement removes these stories of origin to a distant and less politically explosive past.[203] On the other hand, it foreshadows the emergence of David and his dynasty, by alluding to their origins in earlier periods of Israelite history.[204] In fact, these birth narratives with the royal ancestress motif may do more than generally project the origins of the Davidic lineage into the distant past. They may also presage certain aspects of David's character and career. No doubt the theme of foreign blood common to all of these birth narratives is an appropriate symbol for David's expansion of Israel to include a number of foreign territories and peoples. In this way, the royal ancestresses correspond to David and his son Solomon's foreign wives, as concrete expressions of this expansionist drive.[205] But the shrewdness and resourcefulness of David's ancestresses, their opportunism and daring, their effective control of history through unorthodox

---

[202] It must be admitted, however, that the biblical author does not shirk from similar themes in his depiction of David's relations with Bathsheba, the wife of Uriah the Hittite, whom he takes in adultery (1 Sam 11:1–12:25). In fact, this narrative serves as a birth narrative for Solomon, who succeeds David.

[203] In fact, each narrative containing the royal ancestress motif becomes successively less offensive, in relation to its nearness to the time of David's life. Fisch explores how Ruth contains a positive modification of some of the same basic themes contained in Gen 19:30–38 and Genesis 38 ("Ruth and the Structure of Covenant History").

[204] Redford suggests that the stories of Tamar and Ruth may be remnants of a cycle of legends dealing with David's descent, the main purpose of which was to illustrate the survival of an important line placed in jeopardy (*Study of the Biblical Story of Joseph*, 16–17).

[205] Leach deals with the basic tension between the religious idealization of ethnic purity based on endogamy (the closest type of which is incest) and the political necessity for incorporation of larger land mass and expansion of hegemony through intermarriage and integration of foreign peoples into greater Israel ("The Legitimacy of Solomon," 25–83). For another structural discussion of this same biblical tension, see Michael P. Carroll, "Genesis Restructured," in *Anthropological Approaches to the Old Testament*, ed. Bernard Lang, Issues in Religion and Theology 8 (Philadelphia: Fortress Press; London: SPCK, 1985) 130–31. For a criticism of the structural analysis provided by Leach, see J. A. Emerton, "An Examination of a Recent Structuralist Interpretation of Genesis 38," *VT* 26 (1976) 79–98. Significantly, the birth narratives containing the royal ancestress motif juxtapose the themes of incest and foreign nationality. These narratives therefore internally express the tension between the ideals of ethnic purity and political expansion in Israelite society.

means, also correspond more generally to the character of David's reign. A usurper and empire builder, David, like his royal ancestresses placed at a safe narrative distance, succeeds magnificently through the unconventional.[206]

Although the Bible itself lacks a birth narrative for David, one emerges by the medieval period. Significantly, this narrative contains important elements and themes from the earlier biblical stories with the royal ancestress motif, although there are also a number of important modifications. The transfer of material directly to David's birth suggests that by the middle ages the stories of Lot's daughters, Tamar, and Ruth were indeed associated with the emergence of the Davidic lineage and served as models for the king's own birth narrative.

According to a number of sources,[207] Jesse, David's father, was an extremely righteous man—so righteous, in fact, that he never committed a sin in his life. Having already fathered six sons, Jesse abstained from sexual relations with his wife for a period of three years. After this time, however, he became infatuated with his wife's handmaid. She informed Jesse's wife, Nazbat,[208] and the two women conspired to deceive the love-struck man. The handmaid set up a tryst, and Jesse's wife, disguised as the handmaid, met him at the appointed hour. Nazbat conceived, and the son she delivered was David. Since Nazbat did not disclose the circumstances of her conception, Jesse and his other sons erroneously thought that she had been unfaithful to her husband and that David was the offspring of an adulterous union.[209] His brothers lightly esteemed David because of the apparent circumstances of his birth and sent him off to care for the flocks. It was not until Samuel came to anoint Saul's replacement that David's

---

[206] There may also be a hint at the morally problematic quality of kingship itself in these birth narratives. In the three narratives, human women take the initiative reserved for God in the birth narratives involving the barren wife motif, and this may thematically correspond to the king's usurpation of divine leadership, expressed in some strands of the tradition (1 Samuel 8). The entirely human nature of events leading to the emergence of the royal lineage may therefore implicitly comment on the human aspect of Israelite kingship.

[207] For a list of sources containing versions of David's birth, see Louis Ginzberg, *The Legends of the Jews*, vol. 6 (Philadelphia: Jewish Publication Society of America, 1928; reprint, 1968) 246, n. 11, and Leopold Zunz, *Die synagogale Poesie des Mittelalters* (Berlin: Julius Springer, 1855) 129, n. a. The version recounted here is a harmonization of several sources.

[208] This name for David's mother appears only in *b. B.Bat.* 91a.

[209] There are other versions of this portion of the narrative. In one such alternative version, the handmaid raises David to prevent Jesse's discovery of his wife's trick.

mother revealed his true paternity. The son whose conception appeared irregular and sinful therefore proved to be legitimate in every way, and Samuel anointed David Israel's new king amidst the joyous acclamations of his father and brothers.

There are a number of obvious similarities between David's medieval birth narrative and the biblical birth narratives containing the royal ancestress motif, especially Genesis 38. The basic problem of the absence of an appropriate sexual partner, found in all three of the biblical birth narratives, reappears twice in David's birth narrative, first in Jesse's abstention from relations with his wife for three years and next in his infatuation with the wrong woman.[210] The female initiative in response to this problem that is a hallmark of the biblical birth narratives reappears in Nazbat's collaboration with her handmaid to arrange a sexual engagement for herself with Jesse. The secrecy and deception that characterize the initiatives of the other royal ancestresses also characterizes the initiative of David's mother. Specifically, David's birth narrative contains the motif of mistaken identity that plays such an important role in Genesis 38. The motif of a failure to recognize the paternity of important offspring found in Genesis 38 is also present in David's medieval birth narrative. Both Genesis 38 and David's birth narrative also contain a disclosure of the father's identity by the mother at a pivotal moment. Finally, in David's birth narrative, as in all the others containing the royal ancestress motif, there is no emphasis on divine intervention leading to the solution of the main problem of the narrative, since the female protagonist accomplishes its resolution through her own cunning and daring.[211]

But in this medieval tale, unlike in the biblical narratives, the birth of a son is accomplished without an infraction of the incest taboo. Similarly, there is no reference to the motif of foreign ethnic identity. David's own birth, although it echoes Genesis 38 and the other biblical

---

[210] Certainly there is a softening of the motifs of divine destruction and death leading to the absence of appropriate male partners emphasized in the other three birth narratives of this type. In addition, David's mother has previously given birth to six sons, and this detail shifts the narrative focus away from the issue of progeny to the issue of Jesse's virtue.

[211] The enduring popularity of this basic plot, which appears for example in Menander's *Men at Arbitration* and Shakespeare's *All's Well that Ends Well* and *Measure for Measure*, may have played a part in the application of this narrative to David's birth as well. But certainly at least one reason that this story came to be associated with David was its affinity with the biblical narratives containing the royal ancestress motif.

narratives containing the royal ancestress motif in important ways, is therefore purified and reformed. Indeed, what appears to be an illicit sexual act is in fact a legal embrace within the context of a marriage, and the son who appears to be illegitimate is ultimately revealed to be the legitimate offspring of his rightful father and mother. This medieval tale therefore represents a mutation of the pattern present in the biblical birth narratives in that the female's deception of the male is accomplished without sin—and in fact prevents sin. Whereas Genesis 38 and the two other biblical birth narratives may indicate some reservations about the origins of the Davidic dynasty, this medieval tale asserts that despite unseemly appearances, there is neither scandal nor even room for reproach. It thus serves as a corrective for the earlier biblical expressions of a similar birth pattern, and narratively argues for the legitimacy and respectability of Israel's greatest king.

Conclusions

The issues discussed in this introductory chapter resurface repeatedly in the following studies of the story of Judah and Tamar in the *Testament of Judah, Targum Neofiti,* and *Genesis Rabba.* Ancient interpreters, much like modern interpreters, often select one possible direction indicated by the biblical text itself or by its canonical contexts and develop it to the exclusion of other possible directions. The following studies therefore explore some of the decisive points at which the three interpretive writings restrict the biblical narrative in the very process of expanding upon it.

But although the preceding discussion of Genesis 38 provides a foundation for the next three chapters, it does not anticipate every feature of the biblical narrative that evokes a reaction from its early Jewish readers. These readers approach the text from particular historical perspectives, with distinctive interpretive strategies and hermeneutic agendas. Even their perceptions of the text's problematic aspects and of its central message are shaped by their traditions of interpretation and their larger cultural contexts. Precisely what these readers consider worthy of emphasis or needful of clarification in the biblical story will therefore be explored in the following chapters.

In fact, the ancient interpreters sometimes read against what appears to be the plain sense of the story of Judah and Tamar in order to

realign the narrative with their contemporary concerns. They interject material, alter details and even major aspects of the narrative,
consider episodes in isolation or out of order, shorten or lengthen
the story at certain points, and otherwise behave in ways that today
would be considered grievous breaches of an interpreter's etiquette
towards the text's integrity. Their free and paraphrastic interpretations
are nevertheless serious readings. The next chapters work on a number of levels, attending to the details of alteration and emphasis, as
well as searching for the overarching inner logic that influences choices
made by invested interpreters. In addition, these chapters reflect on
how each interpretive writing argues that its distinctive representation
of Genesis 38 expresses the narrative's authentic meaning, not a
secondary meaning concocted late in time for a particular community.

CHAPTER TWO

BIBLICAL INTERPRETATION
THROUGH LITERARY RECONTEXTUALIZATION:
DOWNFALL OF THE WARRIOR KING
IN THE *TESTAMENT OF JUDAH*

> Judah saw there the daughter of a Canaanite man, whose name was Shua, and he took her and went into her. (Gen 38:2)
>
> Judah saw her and thought she was a prostitute because she covered her face. He turned aside to her on the road and said, "Come, let me go into you," for he did not know that she was his daughter-in-law. (Gen 38:15–16a)

The *Testament of Judah*, part of the larger Hellenistic work known as the *Testaments of the Twelve Patriarchs*,[1] expresses anguished discomfort with some of the legal and moral issues raised by Genesis 38. In particular, the *Testament of Judah* reacts strongly and negatively to Judah's relations with women, specifically his marriage with a Canaanite woman and his incestuous intercourse with his daughter-in-law. This reaction is not particularly surprising, given the prohibitions against intermarriage with Canaanites and incest elsewhere in the Bible. Indeed, most early interpretations of Genesis 38 also express

---

[1] The critical edition used in this study is Marinus de Jonge, ed., *The Testaments of the Twelve Patriarchs: A Critical Edition of the Greek Text*, Pseudepigrapha Veteris Testamenti Graece, vol. 1, 2 (Leiden: E. J. Brill, 1978), based on fifteen Greek manuscripts, of which de Jonge considers MS b the best. An earlier critical edition following MS a, Robert Henry Charles, ed., *The Greek Versions of the Testaments of the Twelve Patriarchs Edited from Nine Manuscripts Together with the Variants of the Armenian and Slavonic Versions and Some Hebrew Fragments* (Oxford: Oxford University Press, 1908; reprint, Hildesheim: Georg Olms Verlagsbuchhandlung, 1960), was also consulted. English translations of this work include Harm W. Hollander and Marinus de Jonge, *The Testaments of the Twelve Patriarchs: A Commentary*, Studia in Veteris Testamenti Pseudepigrapha, vol. 8 (Leiden: E. J. Brill, 1985), and Howard Clark Kee, trans., "Testaments of the Twelve Patriarchs," in vol. 1 of *The Old Testament Pseudepigrapha*, ed. James H. Charlesworth (Garden City, NY: Doubleday, 1983) 775–828. Introductions to scholarship on the *Testaments* include Marinus de Jonge, "The Main Issues in the Study of the *Testaments of the Twelve Patriarchs*," *NTS* 26 (1980) 508–24, and *The Testaments of the Twelve Patriarchs: A Study of Their Text, Composition, and Origins*, 2d ed. (Assen: Van Gorcum, 1975).

consternation at Judah's irregular relations with the opposite sex.[2] But unlike most other early interpretations, the *Testament of Judah* makes no attempt to minimize the sexual aspects of the narrative,[3] nor does it attempt to justify Judah's behavior.[4] Instead, this work develops Judah's marriage with a Canaanite and his incestuous relations with Tamar, while eclipsing or even entirely eliminating other aspects of the story—including the final birth scene in the biblical narrative. Some of the narrative embellishments in the *Testament of Judah* appear elsewhere, most notably in the book of *Jubilees*, while others are unique to this work. But whether particular embellishments stem from earlier sources or are original to the *Testament of Judah*, the augmented episodes depicting Judah's relations with the women of Genesis 38 dominate the version of the biblical narrative embedded in this testament. The emphasis on the sexual irregularities of Genesis 38 contributes to this testament's development of Judah as an exemplar of immoral behavior, and subsequently as a model of contrition and penitence.

In addition to altering the biblical narrative itself, the *Testament of Judah* employs another exegetical technique to articulate its distinctive, moral interpretation of Genesis 38. It recontextualizes its revised version of Genesis 38 within Judah's autobiography, which he recounts to his sons on his deathbed. In the *Testaments*, each of Jacob's twelve sons addresses his descendants (and sometimes other male relatives) for a final time, imparting to them wisdom gained from personal

---

[2] An exception to this rule is *Bib.Ant.* 9:5, which emphasizes Tamar's heroic efforts to continue a threatened lineage. In this work, her bold action is held up by Moses' father Amram as a positive example to the Israelites in Egypt, in order to encourage them to procreate despite Pharaoh's order to kill the male babies.

[3] Philo *Preliminary Studies* 23, for example, shifts attention from the actual sexual encounter between Judah and Tamar by interpreting it allegorically as the encounter between the true lover of learning (Judah) and Wisdom (Tamar). In a different way, *Genesis Rabba* 85 also shifts attention from Judah and Tamar's liaison by emphasizing its divinely ordained outcome in the royal and messianic lineage. Similarly, *Tg.Neof.* Gen 38:25–26 downplays the main characters' involvement with prostitution and their act of incest by focusing on Tamar and Judah's admirable behavior when threatened with death. *Seper Hayyašar* offers a shortened version of the narrative, which eliminates the details of Judah's encounter with Tamar on the road to Timnah. Most effectively of all, Josephus deflects attention from the story of Judah and Tamar by never mentioning it.

[4] For example, *Tg.Ps.-J.* Gen 38:2 claims that Judah married the daughter of a merchant (נבר תנר) rather than a Canaanite (איש כנעני) as in the MT. *Gen.Rab.* 85.8, discussed at length in a subsequent chapter, presents an interpretation of the events at Enaim in which Judah wishes to avoid Tamar since he considers her a respectable woman, not a prostitute; however, he returns reluctantly to her as instructed by the angel in charge of desire, since kings and redeemers will be engendered through their union.

experience. This work's presentation of the ancestors' testaments parallels biblical instances of the same phenomenon, including most strikingly Jacob's testament to his twelve sons in Genesis 49;[5] final addresses to descendants also appear in other post-biblical writings from the Hellenistic period.[6] The exact definition and structure of the testament genre remains open to debate,[7] but in the *Testaments* there are generally three major parts to each final address, including an autobiographical account, moral exhortations, and prophetic predictions.[8] In general, narrative incidents presented in the autobiographical section dramatize particular virtues or vices exemplified by the patriarch.[9] These virtues or vices often reappear in the exhortations as behavior to be emulated or avoided, and they are sometimes associated with a particular tribe's future in the prophetic passages as well. The *Testaments* is therefore fundamentally an ethical treatise,

---

[5] See also Deuteronomy 33 (Moses), Joshua 23–24 (Joshua), 1 Samuel 12 (Samuel), and 1 Kgs 2:1–9 and 1 Chronicles 28–29 (David).

[6] These include the *Testament of Job* and the *Testament of Moses*. There are also a number of other works that are called "testaments," although they do not contain the final words of the speaker. These include the *Testament of Abraham*, the *Testament of Solomon*, and the *Testament of Adam*.

[7] Even the basic question of whether there are sufficient similarities between biblical and post-biblical testaments to permit an encompassing definition of the genre is debatable. For an overview of the testament genre and representatives of it, see John J. Collins, "Testaments," in *Jewish Writings of the Second Temple Period: Apocrypha, Pseudepigrapha, Qumran Sectarian Writings, Philo, Josephus*, ed. Michael E. Stone (Assen: Van Gorcum; Philadelphia: Fortress, 1984) 325–55. Testaments bear some affinities to Egyptian instruction literature, apocalyptic literature, and Graeco-Roman paraenesis, although there are differences as well, including the testament's temporal context immediately before the speaker's death. See Leo G. Perdue, "The Death of the Sage and Moral Exhortation from Ancient Near Eastern Instructions to Graeco-Roman Paraenesis," in *Paraenesis: Act and Form*, ed. Perdue and John G. Gammie, Semeia 50 (Atlanta: Scholars Press, 1990) 81–109.

[8] These three parts are framed by reports of the circumstances of the testament's delivery and of the patriarch's death. In the *Testament of Judah*, the autobiographical account appears for the most part in *T.Jud.* 1:3–12:12, the moral exhortations in *T.Jud.* 13–20, and the predictions in *T.Jud.* 21–25; these main sections are framed by a note concerning the circumstances of delivery in *T.Jud.* 1:1–2 and an account of the patriarch's death in *T.Jud.* 26. The most concentrated allusions to Genesis 38 appear within the autobiographical account, in *T.Jud.* 8 and 10–12, although additional narrative material also appears among the moral exhortations and predictions. It should be noted that the three divisions are not entirely distinct, and not all of the twelve testaments contain each of these divisions.

[9] Similar employment of biblical figures as exemplars of vices and virtues appears in the Hellenistic works of Philo, who, for example, describes Tamar as "Virtue" in *On Flight and Finding* 27. This practice is related to a larger trend in Greek and Hellenistic literature to personify vices and virtues. An example of this trend, Prodicus' representation of "Vice" and "Virtue" as two women in "Heracles' Choice," recorded in Xenophon *Memorabilia* 2.1.21–34, receives further attention later in this chapter.

presented as the final words of Jacob's sons to their descendants.

Judah's case is unusual in the *Testaments*, for unlike his brothers he exemplifies both virtues (obedience and manly courage) and vices (fornication, drunkenness, and greed).[10] As described in more detail below, the first part of Judah's autobiography in the *Testament of Judah*, based on a combination of biblical and post-biblical traditions, illustrates his virtues as a royal leader of his brothers. The second part, based primarily on Genesis 38 and elaborations on that biblical narrative, illustrates his weaknesses, especially those involving women. The final episode of Judah's life consists of his repentance and restoration. Even from this brief summary, it is obvious that the *Testament of Judah* recontextualizes Genesis 38 within the larger story of Judah's life. Instead of a perplexing digression in the Joseph story as in the Bible, Genesis 38 becomes the account of a great warrior king's downfall. The discussion below analyzes precisely how the testament's literary recontextualization of a revised version of Genesis 38 within Judah's autobiography assigns a distinctive post-biblical valence to the biblical narrative. It also shows how the *Testament of Judah* uses exegesis of Genesis 38 as a vehicle through which to make statements on a number of subjects, including the value of filial obedience and fraternal love, the nature and future of Israel's kingship, the dangers of particular vices (especially fornication, drunkenness, and greed) for both kings and common men, the efficacy of penitence and prayer, and the anthropological and cosmological forces that affect human existence in this world. By understanding the function of Genesis 38 in the *Testament of Judah*, one comes to understand something about the community behind the *Testaments*, which articulates its distinctive view of reality, at least in part, through creative interpretation of scripture.

The precise identity of this community continues to elude scholars who study this work. The exploration of the interpretive recontextualization of a version of Genesis 38 within the *Testament of Judah* here

---

[10] In general, the other brothers exemplify either vices or virtues, not a combination of the two. An exception to this rule is Gad, who exemplifies both strength and anger, although his moral vice is developed more extensively than his physical virtue. A similar imbalance occurs in Judah's case, in that his vices receive extended attention in the exhortation and prophetic sections, unlike his virtues. Perhaps the complexity within Judah's autobiography is related to the ambivalent attitude towards kingship (stemming from Judah's lineage) in the biblical tradition itself. Contrast, for example, the negative evaluation of kingship in 1 Sam 8:11–18 with the more positive portrayal in 2 Sam 7:8–16.

will not resolve, nor even address in any detail, many of the enduring enigmas concerning this work's origins and history of redaction.
For example, scholars continue to debate whether this work was
originally composed by a Jewish writer from the Hasmonean period
and repeatedly revised, finally by a Christian,[11] or whether this work
was originally composed by a Christian from the second century CE
who incorporated earlier Jewish material.[12] At least in its final form,
the work is Christian, and it was preserved and transmitted in Christian circles.[13] But the explicitly Christian material is limited, whereas
the traditional Jewish exegetical material is copious. Fragments of
semitic testaments of Levi and Naphtali from Qumran and the Cairo
Geniza suggest that the original version of the *Testaments* may have
arisen within Jewish circles.[14] The existence of parallel Hebrew accounts of the wars waged by Jacob's sons against Canaanite kings
and against Esau and his sons in the *Testament of Judah* suggests the
same thing.[15] For the purposes of this discussion, therefore, I regard
the *Testaments* as a composition originally emerging from otherwise
unknown Hellenistic Jewish circles sometime during the second or
first centuries BCE, which achieved its final form through Christian
editing during the second century CE.[16]

---

[11] As, for example, Charles argues in his introduction to *Greek Versions of the Testaments*, ix.

[12] As, for example, de Jonge argues in *The Testaments: A Study*, 116–28.
For surveys of the history of scholarship on the issues of authorship and date of
the *Testaments*, see E. Bickerman, "The Date of the *Testaments of the Twelve Patriarchs*,"
JBL 69 (1950) 245–60; Jürgen Becker, *Untersuchungen zur Entstehungsgeschichte der Testamente
der Zwölf Patriarchen*, Arbeiten zur Geschichte des Antiken Judentums und des
Urchristentums 8 (Leiden: E. J. Brill, 1970) 129–58; Henk Jan de Jonge, "Die
Patriarchentestamente von Roger Bacon bis Richard Simon," in *Studies on the Testa-
ments of the Twelve Patriarchs: Text and Interpretation*, ed. Marinus de Jonge, Studia in
Veteris Testamenti Pseudepigrapha, vol. 3 (Leiden: E. J. Brill, 1975) 3–42; H. Dixon
Slingerland, *The Testaments of the Twelve Patriarchs: A Critical History of Research*, SBL
Monograph Series 21 (Missoula, MT: Scholars Press, 1977); Collins, "Testaments,"
332–33; and Marinus de Jonge, "The *Testaments of the Twelve Patriarchs*: Christian
and Jewish: A Hundred Years after Fredrich Schnapp," *NedTTs* 39 (1985) 265–75.

[13] Whatever the truth about the origins of the work, Marinus de Jonge is correct
in his assertion that the significance of this work within the Christian communities
that preserved and transmitted it has been ignored for too long.

[14] For a discussion of a semitic version of the *Testament of Levi*, see Marinus de
Jonge, "The *Testament of Levi* and 'Aramaic Levi,'" *RevQ* 13 (1988) 369–85.

[15] These Hebrew sources include *Yalquṭ Šimʿoni* Wayyissaʿu, the *Chronicles of Yeraḥmeʾel*,
and *Seper Hayyašar. Jubilees* also contains a version of these wars.

[16] For an example of a systematic attempt to identify the different layers of tradition in the *Testaments* through literary analysis, see Becker, *Untersuchungen*, especially
306–26 concerning the *Testament of Judah*.

Although important issues of authorship and date of composition remain unresolved, the *Testaments* clearly exemplifies a creative synthesis of Hebraic and Hellenistic influences. This work's dependence on traditions from the Hebrew Bible is unmistakable, as is its reliance on early Jewish biblical exegesis and midrashic traditions in Hebrew and Aramaic.[17] Yet the current consensus maintains that this work was originally written in Greek.[18] It contains traditions found in the Septuagint translation of the Bible, moral and anthropological concepts deriving from Stoicism, and possibly even literary motifs and mythic patterns from the larger Hellenistic cultural context. The resulting product is complex and even self-contradictory at times; nevertheless, the *Testaments* expresses the ideals and presuppositions of a distinctive form of Hellenistic Judaism, and for this reason it is an especially interesting case study in the history of biblical exegesis.

---

[17] Examples of such traditions appearing in this testament that are also found in other early midrashic sources include the following: Judah the fourth son in *T.Jud.* 1:3 (see also *Genesis Rabba* 97, NV); Judah the king in *T.Jud.* 1:6 (see also *Gen.Rab.* 84.17); Judah the mighty warrior in *T.Jud.* 2–7, 9 (see also *Gen.Rab.* 93.7); war with the Amorites in *T.Jud.* 3–7 and with Esau in *T.Jud.* 9 (see also *Jubilees* 34, 36–37; *Yalquṭ Šim'oni* Wayyissa'u; the *Chronicles of Yeraḥme'el*; and *Seper Hayyašar*); Hirah as Judah's shepherd in *T.Jud.* 8:1 (see also the LXX Gen 38:12, 20); the high status of Judah's father-in-law in *T.Jud.* 8:2 (see also *Gen.Rab.* 85.4); Tamar from Aram's lineage in *T.Jud.* 10:1 (see also *Jub.* 41:1; from Seth's lineage in *Gen.Rab.* 85.10); Er, like Onan, prevents conception in *T.Jud.* 10:3 (see also *Gen.Rab.* 85.4); the Canaanite wife's responsibility for her sons' sexual behavior in *T.Jud.* 10:3, 5, 6 (see also *Jub.* 41:2, 7); Tamar a virgin at Enaim in *T.Jud.* 10:3, 4, 5 (see also *Jub.* 41:27 and *b. Yebam.* 34b); Tamar's beauty in *T.Jud.* 12:3 (see also the LXX Gen 38:14; *Tg.Onq.* Gen 38:14; and *Midr. Haggadol* Gen 38:6); royal significance of the pledge items in *T.Jud.* 12:4 and 15:3 (see also *Gen.Rab.* 85.9); Tamar's privately sending the pledges and Judah's humiliation in *T.Jud.* 12:5 (see also *Tg.Neof.* Gen 38:25; *Midr. Haggadol* Gen 38:25; *b. Soṭa* 10b); events "from the Lord" in *T.Jud.* 12:6 (see also *Tgs.Neof.* and *Ps.-J.* Gen 38:26; *Gen.Rab.* 85.12); possibility of Tamar's deceit in *T.Jud.* 12:7 (see also *Exod.Rab.* 30.19); and Judah's turning aside to Tamar before the eyes of all in *T.Jud.* 14:5 (see also *Tg.Ps.-J.* Gen 38:14). The person or persons responsible for this testament were familiar with a large number of Jewish traditions and incorporated them freely, at times with little concern for the discrepancies that these incorporations created.

For another study of Jewish exegetical traditions incorporated into the *Testaments*, see James Kugel, "The Story of Dinah in the 'Testament of Levi,'" *HTR* 85 (1992) 1–34. Kugel isolates a number of non-biblical motifs that appear in an expanded version of Genesis 34 in the *Testament of Levi* and identifies the origins of each in the exegesis of a difficult or unusual feature of the biblical text itself. Since his atomistic approach emphasizes the prehistory of individual midrashic traditions, he avoids entanglement in the larger narrative and ideological structures of the *Testaments*, which are notorious for their complexity and inconsistency.

[18] See Collins, "Testaments," 344. Scholars earlier argued that the original language was Hebrew or Aramaic. The majority of manuscripts are written in Greek, although there are also translations from the Greek into Armenian and Slavonic.

A close examination of the treatment of Genesis 38 within the *Testament of Judah* discloses some of the dynamics of scriptural interpretation within a particular religious community and reveals how this biblical narrative made sense within a Hellenistic Jewish cultural context.

GENESIS 38 IN JUDAH'S AUTOBIOGRAPHY

Genesis 38 Removed from Its Biblical Narrative Context

In the *Testament of Judah* Genesis 38 has been unmoored from its precarious biblical placement following the sale of Joseph in Genesis 37 and before his arrival in Egypt in Genesis 39. Perhaps this un-mooring is not especially surprising, given the enduring puzzlement over the placement of Genesis 38 from earliest times to the present. More surprising, however, is the fact that the *Testament of Judah* itself makes no explicit allusion whatsoever to the sale of Joseph, although Joseph's presence in Egypt is acknowledged, both by his absence in the battle scenes and by Judah's note that he and his family "came to Egypt, to Joseph, because of the famine" (*T.Jud.* 12:11). This silence is initially puzzling since in the biblical narrative Judah himself urges the brothers to sell Joseph and therefore bears responsibility for his brother's residence in Egypt (Gen 37:26–27);[19] furthermore, Judah's explicit interest in "profit" (בצע) in Gen 37:26 and the receipt of twenty silver pieces from the Ishmaelites in Gen 37:28 could easily have been interpreted as expressions of greed—one of the three vices attributed to the patriarch in the *Testament of Judah*.[20]

But in the larger context of the *Testaments of the Twelve Patriarchs*, which stresses love of one's neighbor as a cardinal virtue,[21] this silence

---

[19] The *Testament of Judah* also fails to develop the important role that Judah plays in facilitating his family's travels to Egypt by negotiating with Jacob and Joseph (Gen 43:1–15; 44:14–45:3; 46:28). This omission is also quite remarkable, because this material could have been used to illustrate Judah's leadership among his brothers. Perhaps Judah's offer to serve as Joseph's slave in Benjamin's place (Gen 44:33) was considered servile and therefore unfitting for a king.

[20] The closest the *Testaments* comes to developing the sale of Joseph as an example of Judah's greed is *T.G.* 2:3–4. In this passage, Gad conspires with Judah to sell Joseph for thirty gold pieces, and the two brothers keep ten for themselves before sharing the remaining twenty with their other brothers. But even in this expansion of the story, Gad takes complete responsibility for the covetousness leading to the sale of his brother. Similarly, in *T.Z.* 3:1 Gad, Simeon, and six other unnamed brothers (not Judah) are specified as the parties who profit from the sale.

[21] For representative expressions of the ideal of love for one's neighbor, see *T.R.* 6:9; *T.I.* 5:2; *T.G.* 4:2; and *T.B.* 3:3–4. More specifically, the importance of love

concerning Judah's heinous treatment of his own brother becomes understandable. Although Judah is a seriously flawed character, he is still second in importance only to Levi for Israel's history, as most of the testaments reiterate; moreover, in some of the testaments, especially in the clearly Christian passages, the ultimate savior figure for Israel and the gentile nations comes from Judah's line. One could imagine that Judah's association with this fundamental betrayal of his brother would disqualify him as the royal leader of his brothers and as the ancestor of the redeemer. Elsewhere, the *Testaments* interprets Judah's suggestion to sell Joseph as a desperate ploy to spare his brother from the murderous hatred of Simeon.[22] In another version of the story in this document, Judah does not advocate the sale of Joseph alone; instead he is joined by Gad, whose deep hatred and greed motivate him to hurt his brother.[23] The *Testaments* therefore exculpates Judah of this especially grievous breach of brotherly love in more than one way, while the *Testament of Judah* itself passes over the entire incident in silence.[24] These tactics preserve Judah's worthiness to become the first of Israel's kings.

---

and cooperation among brothers is indicated in *T.S.* 4:4–7; *T.G.* 6:1; and *T.Jos.* 17:1–8. The theme of cooperation among brothers is developed metaphorically in terms of waters flowing together and the members of the body under one head in *T.Z.* 9:1–4. By contrast, jealousy of one's brother is from Beliar in *T.S.* 2:7.

[22] *T.S.* 2:7–9. In *T.S.* 4:2 Simeon assumes complete responsibility for what happened to Joseph. Numerous other passages in the *Testaments* also develop the theme of Simeon and the other brothers' hatred and ill-will towards Joseph. *T.Z.* 4:11 further illustrates Simeon's hatred and desire to kill Joseph. In *T.Z.* 2:1 Gad joins Simeon in the attempt to kill their brother; in *T.D.* 1:4–9 Dan reveals that he too conspired to murder him out of jealousy; and in *T.G.* 2:1–2 Gad confesses that he hated Joseph and wanted to kill him as well. *T.Z.* 3:5 suggests that most of the brothers desired Joseph's death. By contrast, in *T.Z.* 4:2 Judah fasts for two days with Zebulun in order to watch the pit where Joseph lies and protect him from his other brothers.

[23] In *T.G.* 2:1–5 Gad initially wants to kill Joseph, but then joins Judah in selling him in order to make an unlawful profit. The deflection of Judah's guilt to his brothers in the *Testament* appears also in *Jub.* 34:11, where all the brothers first conspire to kill Joseph, then repent and sell him to the Ishmaelites.

[24] *T.Z.* 5:2–4 indicates the grievous nature of the sale of Joseph when it states that the offspring of Joseph's brothers became ill and even died because of their fathers' role in the sale. This motif is a generalization of the tradition found in rabbinic literature (for example, *Gen.Rab.* 85.3) that Judah's sons (and wife) died due to his advocacy of the sale of Joseph. Other early Jewish literature emphasizes the enormity of this sin as well. For example, *Jub.* 34:18–19 decrees an annual day of mourning for the sin of Joseph's sale.

King Judah, Manly Victor over Animal and Human Enemies

Judah Gains Kingship through Obedience

Silence about the sale of Joseph permits an alternate interpretation of Judah's character. In the *Testament of Judah* the preface to Genesis 38 consists primarily of a depiction of Judah as an exemplar of masculine courage and virtue through a series of contests with animal and human enemies (*Testament of Judah* 2–7, 9). The testament accomplishes this depiction through a mosaic of motifs based on biblical, midrashic, and Hellenistic traditions, as well as some unique motifs found nowhere else.

But even before describing Judah's courageous exploits, the very first section of the *Testament of Judah* portrays Jacob's appointment of Judah as king over his brothers. Following a brief introduction alluding to the biblical verse in which Leah names her fourth son,[25] the following notice appears:

> 1:4. I was sharp and zealous in my youth, and I obeyed my father's every word, 5. and I blessed my mother and my mother's sister. 6. And it came to pass when I became a man, that my father Jacob promised me, saying: "You will be king, succeeding in all things." (*T.Jud.* 1:4–6)

The theme of Judah's leadership, implicit in the biblical narrative through his important role in the rest of the Joseph story, through the naming of David's ancestor Perez at the conclusion of Genesis 38, and through Jacob's blessing of his fourth son with its reference to a scepter and ruler's staff (Gen 49:8–12), becomes explicit from the onset of the testament. In effect, the *Testament of Judah* transfers Jacob's recognition of his son's royal status from his final blessing in Gen 49:8–12 to his commissioning of Judah as a youth in *T.Jud.* 1:6. The emphasis on Judah's kingship in the opening section of this

---

[25] *T.Jud.* 1:3. The force of the biblical pun relating Leah's remark, "This time I will thank (אוֹדֶה, from the root ידה) the LORD" (Gen 29:35) and Judah's name (יְהוּדָה) is of course lost in its translation into Greek in the *Testament of Judah*. (A similar pun on Judah's name occurs in Jacob's final words to Judah in Gen 49:8.) Judah is specified two times as Leah's fourth son in *T.Jud.* 1:3, a detail absent in the biblical text itself. While the indication of the son's numerical position with respect to his brothers is not anomalous in the *Testaments* (see also *T.S.* 2:2; *T.I.* 1:15; *T.Z.* 1:3; *T.N.* 1:6; *T.B.* 1:6), in this instance its reiteration suggests a familiarity with the elaborate explanations of the significance of Judah's name in rabbinic literature. See for example, *Genesis Rabba* 97, NV, which notes that Judah's name (יְהוּדָה) consists of the tetragrammaton (יהוה) with the addition of the fourth letter of the alphabet (ד), indicating among other things that Judah was Jacob's fourth son. Worth noting is the fact that Judah's most important son, Perez, was also fourth in order of birth.

testament (and throughout its remaining sections) corresponds to this patriarch's royal status elsewhere in the *Testaments*, where he often appears in tandem with the priestly figure of Levi. The early and repeated emphasis on kingship in the *Testament of Judah* sets this testament apart from the others, because it thereby becomes much more than a discussion about certain virtues and vices. It also becomes a discussion about the nature of Israel's kingship, including the requisite qualities of the king and the behavior expected of him, the temptations to which he is especially prone, and the future of the institution. The *Testament of Judah* therefore retains and even emphasizes the theme of kingship that emerges from reading Genesis 38 within the canon, although it develops it quite differently.

Full exploration of the statement that the *Testament of Judah* makes concerning Israel's kingship must wait until later in this chapter. For present purposes, it is important to emphasize the basis for the patriarch's royal status, since this issue proves central for the testament's interpretation of Genesis 38. In keeping with the fundamental value of filial piety implicit in the testament genre itself, which seeks to extend the control of fathers over sons even from beyond the grave,[26] Judah's obedience to Jacob apparently earns him his royal status. In the passage cited above, Judah claims that as a youth he was obedient to his father in everything, so that upon maturity Jacob declared him king. Judah reiterates this claim later in the testament, explaining that it was actually the Lord who granted him his kingdom "because of obedience to [my] father. For I never distressed a word of Jacob my father, because I did everything whatsoever he said" (*T.Jud.* 17:3–4).

Judah's obedience has yet an additional resonance within the context of the *Testaments*. In this document, set before the revelation at Sinai, the righteous fathers orally pass on the commandments of God to their sons, generation after generation.[27] In particular, this document depicts Abraham, Isaac, and Jacob as sources of special revelation, although it also cites other pre-Mosaic figures, including Enoch, Noah,

---

[26] A clear expression of the importance of filial obedience appears in *T.S.* 7:3, where Simeon says, "Therefore, I give you all these commands, that you also may command your children that they may observe them through their generations." Other explicit expressions of the importance of filial obedience include *T.R.* 1:5; *T.L.* 10:1; and *T.Jud.* 13:1.

[27] This view of pre-Sinaitic transmission of the commandments is also more generally held in early Judaism. For pre-rabbinic expressions of this view, see, for example, *Jub.* 7:38; 21:10; 45:16; 1 *Enoch* 82:2; and 2 *Apoc.Bar.* 84:9.

and Shem. The *Testament of Benjamin* most explicitly expresses this view of pre-Sinaitic transmission of divine commandments from patriarch to patriarch:

> 10:3. Therefore, perform truth and righteousness, each one with his neighbor, and [perform] justice to establish good faith, and keep the Lord's law and his commandments. 4. For I teach you these things instead of any inheritance. And you also, therefore, give them to your children for an everlasting possession; for so did Abraham and Isaac and Jacob. 5. They gave us all these things for an inheritance, saying: "Keep the commandments of God, until the Lord will reveal his salvation to all the nations." 6. Then you will see Enoch, Noah, and Shem and Abraham and Isaac and Jacob rising on the right hand in joy. (*T.B.* 10:3–6)

Within the *Testament of Judah* itself (*T.Jud.* 13:7), Judah refers to the prohibition against marrying a Canaanite as both "the Lord's commandment" and "my fathers' commandment," with no apparent distinction in meaning. Earlier in the same section, Judah once more equates the Lord's commandment with a patriarch's commandment, when he urges his sons, "And now, whatever I command you, listen, children, to your father, and keep all my words, to perform the Lord's ordinances and to obey the Lord God's commandment" (*T.Jud.* 13:1).

Whether or not the *Testaments* equates the commandments of the fathers and God with the Tora revealed at Sinai is not entirely clear. Certainly this document emphasizes cultivating moral predispositions and general virtues, as well as avoiding pernicious vices, rather than observing the stipulations of the Tora, including its ritual observances.[28] In the passage cited above from the *Testament of Benjamin*, for example, the commandments of God are mentioned in connection with

---

[28] For example, there is no reference to the Sabbath, and circumcision is mentioned only in passing in connection with the ruse against the Shechemites following the rape of Dinah (*T.L.* 6:3). When specific reference is made to laws from the Pentateuch, they are generally interpreted allegorically or historically. For example, the levirate law from Deut 25:5–10 in *T.Z.* 3:1–8 is interpreted in terms of the sale of Joseph. In addition, descriptions of the virtues and vices exemplified by particular patriarchs are often followed by general references to God's law and commandments. See, for example, *T.R.* 6:9; *T.Jud.* 26:1; *T.I.* 5:1–3; *T.Z.* 10:5; *T.D.* 5:1–3; 6:10; *T.N.* 8:10; *T.G.* 3:1; 7:7; *T.Jos.* 19:6; and *T.B.* 3:1. The *Testaments* thus participates within the common ethic of the larger Hellenistic world. For discussions of the precise nature of this ethic, see Robert Eppel, *Le Piétisme juif dans les Testaments de Douze Patriarches* (Paris: Féliz Alcan, 1930); Herford R. Travers, *Talmud and Apocrypha: A Comparative Study of the Jewish Ethical Teaching in the Rabbinical and Non-Rabbinical Sources in the Early Centuries* (London: Soncino Press, 1933); Howard Clark Kee, "The Ethical Dimensions of the *Testaments of the Twelve Patriarchs* as a Clue to Provenance,"

general moral precepts, including acting truthfully and righteously towards one's neighbor. But regardless of the exact correspondence between the commandments of the fathers, the commandments of God, and biblical law in this work, Judah's obedience to his father is not simply submission to his elder's whims. It also indicates his compliance with the divine will and thereby suggests that he is sinless. When Judah later reveals that it was actually the Lord who established him as king over his brothers because of his filial obedience, he also notes that Abraham and Isaac blessed him in his royal office (*T.Jud.* 17:3–5). The elder patriarchs' involvement at this point confirms that the basis of Judah's royalty was indeed his compliance with the divine commandments transmitted through the righteous forefathers. The assertion that obedience, and therefore righteousness, forms the basis of Judah's divinely bestowed kingship expresses a cultural ideal. Not only does it stress the value of righteous behavior and its generous rewards, it also denies that acclamation by one's peers, military prowess, or dynastic lineage suffice for political rule. In fact, the opposite is true. Military victory and continuation of one's lineage are viewed as gifts from God as a reward for obedient behavior in the *Testament of Judah*.

The view of kingship expressed to this point generally corresponds with the biblical ideal depicted in Deut 17:14–20. According to this deuteronomic passage, the divinely chosen king rules among his brothers by scrupulously observing the laws and commandments; moreover, his righteousness guarantees the continuation of his dynasty.[29] Similarly, the *Testament of Judah* echoes themes in David's final words to his son Solomon in 1 Kgs 2:1–12, where the great king urges his son to be strong and keep the commandments, since the continuation of the dynasty depends on obedience to the LORD's charges. Because kingship in the *Testaments* depends on obedience to the fathers and,

---

NTS 24 (1978) 259–70; Harm W. Hollander, *Joseph as an Ethical Model in the Testaments of the Twelve Patriarchs*, Studia in Veteris Testamenti Pseudepigrapha, vol. 6 (Leiden: E. J. Brill, 1981); and H. Dixon Slingerland, "The Nature of *Nomos* (Law) within the *Testaments of the Twelve Patriarchs*," *JBL* 105 (1986) 3–48.

[29] The behavior of the ideal king in Deut 17:18–20 differs from that of Judah, in that the deuteronomic king studies a written copy of the law in order to learn and obey its precepts. By contrast, Judah lives prior to the revelation of the written law at Sinai, although there are some indications in the *Testaments* that a written law exists.

The warnings in Deut 17:14–20 concerning the king's wives (Deut 17:17a), greed (Deut 17:17b), and arrogance (Deut 17:20) anticipate Judah's downfall later in his life in the *Testament of Judah*. Clearly, this testament interprets Deut 17:14–20 by portraying Judah as an example of the king that the biblical passage describes.

through them, to God, a king risked losing his status and his dynastic lineage if he became disobedient. This possibility is later realized in Judah's own life when he encounters the women of Genesis 38, and he predicts that his descendants will experience similar degradation until the sinless, final king will arise.[30]

Strikingly, the sections of Judah's autobiography immediately following his rise to kingship do not emphasize the theme of obedience. One finds only hints of the young Judah's supposedly central attribute in his encounters with animal and human challengers. For example, the hunting he does for his father suggests solicitude for his elder's desires and needs (*T.Jud.* 2:2).[31] Explicit illustrations of the obedience distinguishing Judah from his brothers and qualifying him to rule are entirely lacking, however. This absence suggests that the theme of filial obedience as a prerequisite for Judah's kingship is an innovation by the compiler of the *Testaments*. This innovation would be in keeping with the ethos of the testament genre and with the compiler's view that the divine commandments were revealed and passed down through the fathers.

The omission of any specific illustrations of Judah's obedience furthermore may tacitly acknowledge that worldly leadership requires more than compliance to one's elders. The sections which follow dramatize Judah's prowess in contests between animal and human enemies, and on the surface they seem to suggest that physical and military strength are prerequisites for royal power. Certainly these sections concretely illustrate the adjectives describing Judah's essential character in the first section. In his violent exploits Judah is indeed "sharp" (ὀξύς)[32] and "zealous" (σπουδαῖος), although in the introduction these adjectives appear in connection with his obedience and respect for his parents.[33] The suspicion that Judah's physical strength constitutes the actual basis for his kingship is explicitly negated, however, by earlier assertions that his success in all his undertakings is a gift from God, subsequent

---

[30] The idea that Israel's first king is sinless corresponds to Judah's prophetic vision that the final king will be sinless as well (*T.Jud.* 24.1).

[31] Also, following the wars, Judah and his brothers as a group respect the peace that Jacob contracts with the Canaanite kings (*T.Jud.* 7:7–8), and they consult with their father before receiving Esau's sons as tributaries (*T.Jud.* 9:7–8).

[32] This word is typically used in Greek to describe the sharpness of a knife and the fleetness of a runner, both of which are good images for Judah in the testament.

[33] In *T.Jud.* 1:4 Judah's statement, "I was sharp and zealous in my youth," is qualified immediately with his assertion, "and I obeyed my father's every word, and I blessed my mother and my mother's sister."

to his filial obedience.[34] The understanding of success as a gift from
God echoes the biblical depiction of God's granting of success to
Judah's most famous royal descendant, David.[35] Judah's dominance
over animal and human opponents also illustrates the theme of divinely granted victory over enemies expressed in the blessings of both
Jacob and Moses. In Gen 49:8, Jacob tells Judah, "your hand shall
be on the neck of your enemies." In Deut 33:7, Moses states concerning Judah, "with his hands he contends for himself," and then
asks for divine assistance for this tribe when he requests that God
"be a help against his adversaries." The theme of divine protection
for Judah the king in the *Testament of Judah* therefore elaborates upon
Jacob and Moses' prophetic statements concerning this figure in their
biblical testaments.

Judah's Physical Superiority over Animals
In the second section of the *Testament of Judah*, the patriarch recalls
his encounters with a number of animals:

> 2:1. And the Lord showed me favor in all my works, both in the field
> and in the home, 2. as I saw when I raced a hind, and having caught
> it I prepared food for my father. 3. I mastered the roes in the chase
> and overtook everything that was in the plains: I overtook a wild mare,
> and, having caught it, I tamed it. 4. And I slew a lion and removed
> a kid out of its mouth. Taking a bear by its paw, I rolled it over a
> cliff, and every beast, when it turned upon me, I tore it apart like a
> dog. 5. I raced the wild boar and gaining advantage over it when I
> ran, I pulled it to pieces. 6. A leopard in Hebron leapt upon [my]
> dog, and having caught it by the tail I hurled it, and it was shattered
> in the districts of Gaza. 7. I seized a wild ox feeding in the field by the
> horns and, whirling it in circles and stunning it, I cast it from me and
> killed it. (*T.Jud.* 2:1–7)

The depiction of Judah as a successful challenger of animals is unique
to this testament. But although found neither in the Bible nor in any

---

[34] In *T.Jud.* 1:6, when Jacob promises Judah that he will be king because of his
obedience, he also assures him that he will be prosperous in all things. In *T.Jud.* 2:1,
immediately before his encounters with the animals, Judah states that "the Lord
showed me favor in all my works." Similarly, in *T.Jud.* 3:10 Jacob has no fear for
Judah in battle, because he sees a vision of the mighty angel who accompanies him
to keep him safe.

[35] See 1 Sam 18:14, which states, "And David was successful in all his undertakings, for the LORD was with him." Also in David's testament (1 Kgs 2:1–12), he
instructs Solomon to obey the divine commandments so that he will be successful in
all that he does (1 Kgs 2:3).

other post-biblical source of which I am aware, it may have originated from some suggestive passages in scripture. Returning to the biblical testaments cited above, in Gen 49:9 Jacob says, "Judah is a lion's whelp; from the prey, my son, you have gone up. He stooped down, he crouched as a lion, and as a lioness; who dares rouse him up?" The image of Judah as a fierce lion may have contributed to the development of the patriarch as superior to every kind of animal.[36] Behind the striking absence of weapons in Judah's exploits in this section may lie an interpretation of a curious phrase in Moses' blessing of the tribe of Judah. Perhaps the phrase in Deut 33:7, "with his hands he contends for himself" (ידיו רב לו), influenced the depiction of Judah as a bare-handed fighter. It must also be noted that Judah's initiation to violent heroism through his mastery of wild animals recalls similar youthful exploits by several biblical characters. His success in both field and home, epitomized by his capture of a hind and his preparation of it as a meal for his father (T.Jud. 2:1–2), brings to mind both Esau, who excelled in the field, and Jacob, who excelled at home, and their efforts to gain their father's blessing through food preparation.[37] Turning to his encounters with dangerous predators, Judah's destruction of a lion with a kid in its mouth as easily as if it were a dog (T.Jud. 2:4) recalls Samson, who under the influence of the LORD's spirit tore apart a lion with his hands as if it were a kid.[38] But Judah's dispatch of the lion and then the bear (T.Jud. 2:4) establishes an even stronger link with his royal descendant David, who recounts his own pastoral experience with lions and bears to Saul before fighting Goliath:

---

[36] Gad also prevails against animals in T.G. 1:3, and he too is compared to a lion in Moses' blessing in Deut 33:20.

Perhaps the image of Judah tying his foal and colt to the vine later in Jacob's testament (Gen 49:11) may have suggested his taming of the horse in T.Jud. 2:3.

[37] See Gen 25:27 and Genesis 27. In the Testament of Judah, Judah combines the positive qualities of Isaac's twins; furthermore, he feeds his father wild game without deceit.

[38] See Judg 14:5–6. At the end of T.Jud. 2:4, Judah remarks that he rent every beast as if it were a dog, just as Samson tore the lion as a man would tear a kid. Samson's use of his bare hands to destroy the lion may have influenced the depiction of Judah as a bare-handed fighter in the Testament of Judah. Like Judah, Samson is connected with a place named Timnah in the biblical text (Judg 14:1, 2, 5; Gen 38:12, 13, 14). There is an additional link between locations associated with Samson in the Bible and with Judah in the Testament of Judah: Samson carries the city doors of Gaza all the way to Hebron (Judg 16:1–3), and Judah swings the leopard by the tail all the way from Hebron to Gaza (T.Jud. 2:6).

17:34. Your servant used to tend sheep for his father; and when a lion came, or a bear, and took a lamb from the flock, 35. I went after him and smote him and rescued it from his mouth; and if he arose against me, I caught him by his beard, and smote him and killed him. 36. Your servant has killed both lions and bears; and this uncircumcised Philistine is like one of them, because he has defied the armies of the living God. 37. . . . The LORD who delivered me from the paw of the lion and from the paw of the bear, will deliver me from the hand of this Philistine. (1 Sam 17:34–37)[39]

The details in the *Testament of Judah*, where Judah removes the kid from the lion's mouth and seizes the bear by one of its body parts,[40] align the patriarch's actions with those of David. In addition, David defeats threatening animals as a preface to his first combat with a human enemy in war, just as Judah does in the *Testament of Judah*. Through allusions to David's bravery and strength, the testament emphasizes the genealogical connection between the two biblical characters and buttresses its development of Judah as a royal figure by presenting him as a parallel to Israel's archetypal king. Viewing Judah's similarities to Samson and David from a slightly different angle, one might conclude that they also foreshadow the patriarch's defeat at the hands of women (at least one of them a foreigner), just as the other two biblical characters have their own fateful encounters with foreign women.[41] Clearly the *Testament of Judah* draws on the exploits of heroic biblical characters to portray the patriarch himself as an unsurpassed hero. The sequential listing of Judah's victories over animal foes, however, may ultimately derive from larger cultural influences, such as the well-known Greek traditions concerning

---

[39] This biblical passage depicting David's slaying of the lion and the bear was influential in the development of more than one character in the *Testaments*. In *T.G.* 1:3 the lion and bear are among the many predators of the flock that Gad kills by grabbing their feet and swinging them to their deaths.

[40] Note that whereas Judah grabs the bear by its paw in *T.Jud.* 2:4, David grabs the lion or the bear by its beard in 1 Sam 17:35; however, David explicitly mentions the paw of the lion and the paw of the bear from which the LORD spared him later in his speech in 1 Sam 17:37.

[41] Samson experienced his downfall at the hands of the Philistine woman Delilah (Judg 16:4–21) and David sinned with Bathsheba, the wife of Uriah the Hittite (2 Samuel 11). It should be noted, however, that in both cases their encounters with these women ultimately had positive results, in that Samson was able to kill a large number of Philistines after his captivity (Judg 16:23–31) and David and Bathsheba produced Solomon, the next king of Israel (2 Sam 12:24–25). Although Genesis 38 itself also ends positively with the emergence of the royal lineage, in the *Testament of Judah* nothing positive issues from Judah's relationships with Bathshua and Tamar, except that he comes to recognize his own limitations (*T.Jud.* 19:4).

Heracles' labors. I will explore this possibility more fully later.

Within the context of the *Testaments* itself, however, Judah's defeat of animals corresponds with his high moral character, as Jacob's obedient and sinless son. Issachar, who exemplifies a simple and good lifestyle in the *Testament of Issachar*, maintains that the person who follows his example and remains sinless will experience marvelous security:

> Every spirit of Beliar will flee from you, and no action of wicked men will prevail over you, and every wild beast you will enslave, having with you the God of heaven, walking together with men in singleness of heart. (*T.I.* 7:7)[42]

According to this view, Judah's victory over so many wild beasts is overwhelming proof of his faultlessness and of God's favor in all his endeavors. In addition, Judah's superiority over animals has a messianic connotation in the *Testaments*, at least in its final form. At the prophetic conclusion of the *Testament of Joseph*, Joseph relates his vision of the savior's final appearance as a lamb resembling a lion on its left side. In this vision concerning the lamb born from a virgin of the tribe of Judah,[43] "all the beasts rushed against it, and the lamb overcame them and destroyed them to be trodden under foot" (*T.Jos.* 19:3). The lamb's victory caused angels, men, and the whole earth to rejoice. Judah's victory over animals early in the *Testament of Judah* therefore establishes a correspondence between the first and last sinless kings from Israel's royal lineage.

Judah the Royal Warrior and Military Leader
After proving himself against beasts, Judah demonstrates his competence in battle, first against a coalition of indigenous Canaanite (or Amorite) kings, and later against Esau and his sons.[44] The first fray with the Canaanites serves as a transition from Judah's encounters with animals to his encounters with human enemies:

---

[42] *T.N.* 8:4 expresses the same idea, that if one does what is good, "the wild beasts will fear you," as does *T.B.* 3:4–5 and 5:2. *T.N.* 8:6 expresses the negative corollary, that if one sins "every wild beast will master him," which loosely recalls Judah's loss of dominion to his Canaanite wife and Tamar after he boasts of his own strength and shames his brother.

[43] In a vacillation typical in the *Testaments*, this lamb of God is described both as Judah's and as Levi's descendant in *T.Jos.* 19:6.

[44] *T.Jud.* 3–7 describes the war against the Canaanites (*T.Jud.* 3:1; 7:11) or Amorites (*T.Jud.* 7:2; 12:2), as the indigenous peoples of Canaan are variously called, and *T.Jud.* 9 describes the war against Esau and his sons.

3:1. And when the two armor-sheathed kings of the Canaanites advanced against the flocks, and a multitude of people with them, I ran
out alone against [the] king [of] Hazor and seized him, and, striking
him on the greaves, I pulled him down, and so I killed him. 2. And
the other, [the] king [of] Tappuah mounted upon his horse—I killed
him, and so I scattered all the people. 3. As for Achor, the king, a
giant among men shooting arrows before and behind from his horse—
taking a stone of sixty pound weight, I hurled it at the horse and killed
it. 4. And after fighting Achor for two hours, I killed him, and having
cleft his shield into two parts, I hacked off his feet. 5. And while I was
stripping off his breastplate, behold eight men, companions of his, began to fight with me. 6. Gathering, therefore, my garment in my hand
and slinging stones at them, I killed four of them; but the others fled.
7. And Jacob our father killed Beelisah, the king of all the kings,
a giant in strength, twelve cubits tall. And trembling fell upon them
and they retreated from fighting against us. 9. Therefore, my father
was free from worry during the wars, because I was with my brothers.
10. For he saw in a vision concerning me that a mighty angel followed
me everywhere, that I should not be overcome. (*T.Jud.* 3:1–10)

In this passage, Judah defeats enemy after enemy in single combat,
just as he did when fighting the animals in the previous section. In
his initial military skirmish, even Judah's physical manner of fighting
echoes his earlier encounters with the beasts, as he races out alone,
seizes the king of Hazor (or King Hazor), strikes him on the leg armor,
and drags him down to his death (*T.Jud.* 3:1).[45] The explanation that
the Canaanites advanced against the family flocks establishes an
additional link between these human enemies and some of the wild
animals in the previous section, who also attack domesticated animals.[46]
A further transitional detail appears when Judah destroys yet another
animal, specifically giant King Achor's horse (*T.Jud.* 3:3).[47]

---

[45] Judah's first combat with a human enemy recalls how earlier he races against
the hind, the roes, the wild mare, other animals of the plain, and the wild boar,
how he seizes the bear by the paw and rolls it over a cliff (*T.Jud.* 2:4), and how he
grabs the leopard by the tail and the wild ox by the horn before throwing them to
their deaths (*T.Jud.* 2:6–7).

[46] The Canaanite enemies are like the lion that went after one of the kids of the
flock (*T.Jud.* 2:4), or, less precisely, like the leopard that leapt on Judah's dog (*T.Jud.* 2:6).

Sheep theft initiates the conflict with the indigenous kings in *Jub.* 34:1–2, 5, as
well, but in later sources, including *Yalquṭ Šimʿoni* Wayyissaʿu and the *Chronicles of
Yeraḥmeʾel*, the local kings attack Jacob and his sons after they return to Shechem
from Bethel because they don't want this family to take their land. Even these later
sources, however, present a remnant of the sheep theft motif. *Yalquṭ Šimʿoni* Wayyissaʿu
notes that at the war's end the local population returns the flocks they stole two for
one. The *Chronicles of Yeraḥmeʾel*, by contrast, emphasizes Jacob's family's largesse
when they restore double the flocks taken as booty from the local kings.

[47] Judah kills the horse only in the *Testament of Judah*. By contrast, the medieval

These transitional motifs join the description of Judah's victories over wild animals, unique to the *Testament of Judah*, to versions of widely attested traditions concerning Jacob and his sons' extrabiblical wars, first against a coalition of indigenous kings and later against Esau and his sons. The tradition concerning the war with the Canaanite (or Amorite) forces under discussion here appears in *Jubilees* 34, *Yalqut Šim'oni* Wayyissa'u, the *Chronicles of Yeraḥme'el*, and *Seper Hayyašar*.[48] The idea that Jacob's family fought a second war with the local population in addition to their violent treatment of the inhabitants of Shechem (Gen 34:13–31) apparently arose from a cryptic note in Gen 48:22. In this verse Jacob tells his son Joseph, "I have given to you instead of your brothers a certain slope (שְׁכֶם אַחַד) that I took from the hand of the Amorites with my sword and my bow." The word translated "slope" (שְׁכֶם) above could also be translated "Shechem," and the latter translation implies that Jacob fought a war in this city. But Genesis 34 clearly denies that Jacob participated in his sons' vengeful destruction of Shechem. In fact, he castigates Simeon and Levi for creating enmity between themselves and the more numerous Canaanites and Perizzites (Gen 34:30–31). In response to this apparent contradiction, the midrashic imagination conceived a second war at Shechem, setting it after Jacob sent his sons back to pasture their sheep near that city following a period of absence.[49] The earliest version of this second war, found in *Jubilees*

---

sources, although they include a horse in the opening battle scene, merely depict Judah knocking the enemy off his mount.

[48] In *Jubilees*, *Yalqut Šim'oni* Wayyissa'u, and the *Chronicles of Yeraḥme'el*, the enemies are consistently called "Amorites." In *Seper Hayyašar* they are called both "Canaanites" and "Amorites," as in the *Testament of Judah*. Even in the Bible there is some confusion about whether the indigenous population was Canaanite or Amorite. For example, Jacob himself refers to the local population of the area around Shechem as "Canaanites" (and "Perizzites") in Gen 34:30, and as "Amorites" in Gen 48:22. In Gen 10:15–16, Canaan is depicted as the father of the Amorites.

The versions in *Yalqut Šim'oni* Wayyissa'u (thirteenth century CE) and the *Chronicles of Yeraḥme'el* (fourteenth century CE) are for the most part identical. The version from *Yalqut Šim'oni* Wayyissa'u may be found in A. Jellinek, ed., בית המדרש [The house of study], 3d ed., vol. 3 (Leipzig: Vollrath, 1853–77; reprint, Jerusalem: Wahrmann Books, 1967) 1–5; an English translation may be found in Hollander and Marinus de Jonge, *The Testaments: A Commentary*, 451–56. The English translation of the *Chronicles of Yeraḥme'el* consulted is M. Gaster, trans., *The Chronicles of Jerahmeel, or the Hebrew Bible Historiale* (London: Royal Asiatic Society, 1899; reprint, New York: Ktav Publishing House, 1971).

[49] In Genesis 35 Jacob and his family travel from Shechem to Luz (Bethel), then on past Ephrath (Bethlehem) and the tower of Eder, and finally to Isaac's dwelling in Mamre (Hebron). In Gen 37:12, however, the brothers have returned to Shechem to pasture their flocks.

(second century BCE), presents Jacob as the central combatant, who personally killed with a sword the seven Amorite kings who conspired to steal the family flocks.[50] The medieval accounts *Yalquṭ Šimʿoni* Wayyissaʿu and the *Chronicles of Yeraḥmeʾel* expand the single battle at Shechem against a united coalition of kings in *Jubilees* into a six-day war against a series of kings. In these two closely related sources, as well as in the embellished account in *Seper Hayyašar*, Judah emerges as an important warrior alongside his father. The battles in these medieval sources recall the battles in the books of Joshua and Judges, and these similarities tacitly argue that as early as the patriarchal period Israel's claim to the promised land rested on military conquest, as well as on divine grant.[51]

Detailed comparisons of the versions of the war between Jacob's family and the indigenous kings may be found in a number of scholarly works,[52] and a rehearsal of these discussions would lead us beyond the scope of the present project.[53] A brief exploration of the distinctive

---

Yalquṭ Šimʿoni Wayyissaʿu and the *Chronicles of Yeraḥmeʾel* explain that a terror from God fell on all the cities around Shechem following its initial destruction by Jacob's sons and prevented the local population from immediately pursuing them (Gen 35:5), but, after Jacob's family returned to Shechem, they did attack to prevent them from possessing the land.

[50] In *Jub.* 34:2 and 4 there are seven Amorite kings, but in the list of the kings that Jacob kills in this source one is inexplicably missing.

[51] See, for example, the description of Joshua's victories over coalitions of indigenous kings in Joshua 10–11. Abraham also successfully fights a coalition of indigenous kings (Genesis 14). The war between Jacob's family and the coalition of indigenous kings therefore casts the former in the image of the earlier patriarch Abraham and the later military leader Joshua.

[52] Discussions of the relationship between different versions include Louis Ginzberg, *The Legends of the Jews* (Philadelphia: Jewish Publication Society of America, 1909–38; reprint 1967–69) vol. 1, 408–11, and vol. 5, 315, n. 292; Becker, *Untersuchungen*, 114–25; James C. VanderKam, *Textual and Historical Studies in the Book of Jubilees* (Missoula, MT: Scholars Press, 1977) 218–38; G. Schmitt, *Ein indirektes Zeugnis der Makkabäerkämpfe: Testament Juda 3–7 und Parallelen* (Wiesbaden: L. Reichert, 1983); and Hollander and Marinus de Jonge, *The Testaments: A Commentary*, 26–27, 185–86.

[53] Similarly, a comprehensive discussion of the literary influences on the battle scenes would detract us from the central purpose in this chapter. But it seems that Judah's mortal contests with the Canaanite kings are recounted with an attention to detail that is reminiscent of that classic Greek account of war, Homer's *Iliad*, although there are biblical allusions in this battle scene as well. Judah's two methods of employing stones as weapons in the third section of the testament provides a concrete illustration of the dual literary traditions operative behind his encounter with the giant King Achor and his men. To kill Achor's horse, Judah lifts an enormous stone and hurls it at the animal (*T.Jud.* 3:3), recalling Diomedes' wounding of Aeneas with a stone too big for two ordinary men to lift in Homer *Iliad* 5. (See also Athena's blow to Ares with a boundary stone in Homer *Iliad* 2.) But to kill Achor's companions,

features in the *Testament of Judah* and, at least as interesting, of the distinctive functions that traditional motifs play in the context of this work is nevertheless in order.[54] Among other things, this type of exploration demonstrates that the *Testament of Judah* does not blindly appropriate existing traditions, but rather shapes and employs them in accordance with its larger purposes. The distinctive use of traditional material in the *Testaments* has received relatively little attention in scholarly discussions to date.

For the most part, the account of the war with the Canaanites and Amorites in the *Testament of Judah* is derivative. It either paraphrases some larger work or conflates the versions in a number of works, and it shows little concern for accuracy in detail. Although the exact relationship between the extant versions of this tradition remains unclear, the similarities between the account in the *Testament of Judah* and the accounts in the medieval sources *Yalquṭ Šimʿoni* Wayyissaʿu and the *Chronicles of Yeraḥmeʾel* are stronger and more numerous than those between the testament and the earlier work *Jubilees*.[55] In general, however, the war report in the *Testament of Judah* is less precise concerning timing, geography, and other details than the medieval sources. For example, although it roughly corresponds with the carefully constructed six-day account of war in *Yalquṭ Šimʿoni* Wayyissaʿu and the *Chronicles of Yeraḥmeʾel*, the *Testament of Judah* only rarely specifies the days upon which particular battles occur.[56] Similarly, not until the initial battle is over and a new one begins "in the south" (later specified as Hebron, *T.Jud.* 4:1, 3) does the *Testament of Judah* reveal that the initial battle took place in Shechem. This failure to

---

Judah slings stones in his clothing (*T.Jud.* 3:6), recalling David's felling of Goliath with a slingshot (1 Sam 17:49). The expanded version in the *Chronicles of Yeraḥmeʾel* is perhaps even more indebted to classical influences. As in the *Iliad*, for example, the sky becomes dark with arrows, and streams of blood flow from the battlefield.

[54] The discussion above about how the *Testament of Judah* links its unique account of Judah's encounters with animals with traditional material concerning the war between Jacob's family and the indigenous kings is an example of intentional shaping and employment of received material.

[55] The similarities between the *Testament of Judah* and the more elaborate version in *Seper Hayyašar* are largely identical to the similarities between this testament and the other two medieval sources, *Yalquṭ Šimʿoni* Wayyissaʿu and the *Chronicles of Yeraḥmeʾel*.

[56] Whereas the other two sources describe what happened on each of six consecutive days, *T.Jud.* 5:1 and 7:1 refer only casually to the events of "the next day." *T.Jud.* 6:3 refers more specifically to the events of "the fifth day." (*Yalquṭ Šimʿoni* Wayyissaʿu and the *Chronicles of Yeraḥmeʾel* depict the events in the passage as occurring on "the fourth day.") These three passages contain the only references to time in the *Testament of Judah*.

specify the place of the initial battle conceals the relationship between the extra-biblical tradition and the biblical verse upon which
it is based (Gen 49:22) and indicates a lack of concern with geography. Clearly the purpose of the war account in the testament is not
to correlate an extra-biblical legend with the biblical text, nor is it to
describe accurately historical events—or even credible imaginary
events, for that matter. The primary purpose is rather to portray
Judah's accomplishments as a warrior and military leader among his
brothers by loosely employing pre-existing traditions.

In keeping with this purpose, the *Testament of Judah* features Judah's
successes in the war's opening frays, as well as throughout its dura-
tion. In this source, Judah single-handedly kills three kings, the king
of Hazor (or King Hazor), the king of Tappuah (or King Tappuah),
and King Achor, plus four other men, before his father appears to
slay the giant overlord Beelisah (*T.Jud.* 3:1–7). Immediately following
his brief participation, Jacob cedes the field completely to his son's
leadership (*T.Jud.* 3:9–10) and only reappears at the end of the war
to negotiate terms with the defeated enemy and to build a city while
Judah builds another (*T.Jud.* 7:7–9). This depiction is in marked
contrast to the shorter version of the battle in *Jubilees*, where Jacob
appears as the most important warrior. In this earlier source Jacob
kills all of the enemy kings while his sons only participate more
generally in the battle, and later after negotiating peace he single-
handedly builds two cities (*Jub.* 34:6–9). By contrast, in the more
lengthy versions in *Yalquṭ Šimʿoni* Wayyissaʿu and the *Chronicles of
Yeraḥmeʾel,* Jacob's sons assume a more significant role alongside their
father in battle. In these sources, as in the *Testament of Judah,* Judah
emerges as a leader: he slays the first enemy king in the opening
battle, he kills more enemies than any other brother, he consistently
climbs first to the tops of city walls in the battles, and he builds a
city just as his father does. But in the medieval sources, after Judah
kills the king of Tappuah in the first battle, Levi emerges to kill the
king of Gaash, and then Jacob finally kills the king of Shiloh and
routes the enemy. Just as significantly, Jacob remains an active participant in the battles that follow in these sources, performing a number
of heroic actions. In the *Testament of Judah,* neither Levi nor any of
the other brothers single-handedly kills a king. Judah alone continues
to kill king after king,[57] even four kings (*T.Jud.* 4:1) who apparently

---

[57] In the opening scene when Judah kills three kings (*T.Jud.* 3:1–6), the details

correspond to the four kings Jacob kills in the *Chronicles of Yeraḥme'el*. The repeated motif of single-handed battle between Judah and foreign kings emphasizes Judah's royal status among his brothers and demonstrates his superior strength.[58]

The *Testament of Judah* also emphasizes Judah's ferocity in battle through a telling employment of a traditional exegetical motif. Following the initial military encounters, in which Judah emerges as the main combatant, the enemies react with terror: "And trembling fell upon them and they retreated from fighting against us" (*T.Jud.* 3:8). This statement recalls Gen 35:5, which describes the local population's reaction to the departure of Jacob's family following Simeon and Levi's attack on Shechem: "And they journeyed, and the terror of God was upon the cities which were around them, and they did not chase after the sons of Israel." *Yalquṭ Šim'oni* Wayyissa'u and the *Chronicles of Yeraḥme'el* also associate this verse from Genesis with the wars against the Amorite kings. In both of these sources, however, the biblical verse appears at the very beginning of the war account, as a summary of the uneasy seven-year peace following Simeon and Levi's destruction of Shechem. The placement of a similar notice concerning the enemies' fear after Judah's heroic acts in the *Testament of Judah* thus designates Judah, and not Simeon and Levi, as the

---

actually correspond to the account of his battle with a single king, the king of Tappuah, in the medieval sources. The single combat narrative preserved in the medieval sources is divided into three distinct combat narratives in the *Testament of Judah* in order to enhance Judah's reputation as a warrior.

[58] In the *Testament of Judah* the anonymous kings of Hazor and Tappuah in the medieval sources apparently become named royal heroes, King Hazor and King Tappuah, although the text remains ambiguous on this point. Without doubt, King Achor in this source is a named warrior king (as is the giant King Beelisah that Jacob defeats). This slight change emphasizes Judah's single-handed victories over his royal equals, instead of the larger ethnic war between Jacob's sons and the indigenous peoples.

Judah's royal status is also emphasized through the similarities between his combat with the three kings in *T.Jud.* 3:1–6 and the famous battle between his distant royal descendant David and the Philistine enemy Goliath (1 Samuel 17). For example, in the *Testament of Judah*, Judah fights his opponent alone with a multitude standing by (*T.Jud.* 3:1); his opponent is covered with armor (*T.Jud.* 3:1, where the mention of greaves is especially striking, given the LXX translation of 1 Sam 17:6); he fights a giant (*T.Jud.* 3:3); he removes his opponent's armor after he kills him (*T.Jud.* 3:5); and he uses stones in a sling to kill his enemies (*T.Jud.* 3:6). The medieval accounts contain similar motifs in their description of Judah's encounter with the king of Tappuah. Although there is no slavish dependence on the biblical story of David and Goliath, there is enough overlap in combat style to establish a correspondence between Judah and Israel's greatest king.

most important warrior. There is also a second paraphrase of Gen
35:5 later in the testament, concluding the account of war with the
Canaanites: "And the Canaanites feared me and my brothers" (*T.Jud.*
7:11). Once again in this final notice, Judah singles himself out from
his brothers when he claims first that "the Canaanites feared me"
and then adds "and my brothers."

A unique religious feature appears in the account of the war with
the Canaanite and Amorite kings in the *Testament of Judah*, which
otherwise remains on the more mundane level of human history,
despite its exaggerations.[59] This feature consists of Jacob's vision following the opening battle:

> 3:9. Therefore, my father was free from anxiety in the wars, because
> I was with my brothers. 10. For he saw in a vision concerning me that
> a mighty angel followed me everywhere, so that I should not be over-
> come. (*T.Jud.* 3:9–10)

Jacob's vision appears in none of the other versions of the war, and
it therefore provides a glimpse of the anthropology and cosmology
behind the *Testaments*, in which both divine and demonic forces influence the outcome of human events.[60] Jacob's vision of special angelic
protection for Judah also corresponds with this son's special status in
this work, in which he is the representative of royal power and, with
Levi, one of the two figures associated with Israel's redemption. Significantly, in the *Testament of Levi* a guardian angel is likewise appointed
to protect Levi before he takes vengeance on the Shechemites for
their abuse of Dinah (*T.L.* 5:3–7). Elsewhere as well (for example
T.D. 5:4), there is mention of the angel who watches over Levi and
Judah to preserve them from harm, since the ultimate well-being of
Israel depends on these tribes.

Even more important for present purposes, however, the passage
describing Jacob's vision testifies to the power of cooperation in the
masculine realm of war. When Jacob delegates military leadership to
Judah, he has no fear for him or for his brothers as long as they stay
together, because he perceives the angel's presence. The image of
cooperation evoked by Jacob's vision corresponds with the ideal of

---

[59] The other versions also remain on a purely mundane level, with the exception
of the expansive version in *Seper Hayyašar*, which includes many prayers and miraculous
interventions.

[60] Whereas here an angel protects Judah in battle, later in his life a spirit of envy
and fornication conspires against him, causing him to fall into sin (*T.Jud.* 13:3).

brotherly love so central to the *Testaments*. Following Jacob's vision, the *Testament of Judah* notes that Judah joins forces with his brothers in the next battle instead of fighting the enemy single-handedly as before:

> 4:1. And in the south there came upon us a battle greater than the one in Shechem. And joining my brothers in battle array, I pursued a thousand men and I killed of them two hundred men and four kings. 2. And I went up against them upon the wall and killed two other kings. 3. And so we liberated Hebron and took all the captives of the kings. (*T.Jud.* 4:1–3)

Judah's demonstration of virtuosity in single combat in the first battle at Shechem is followed by his demonstration of leadership and bravery among the fraternal ranks in the second battle at Hebron. In fact, he kills even more enemies in the company of his brothers (two hundred men and six kings) than he did alone the previous day (three kings and four men),[61] and his increased success illustrates the power of cooperation. In the larger context of this testament, however, Judah's success in the male sphere of war also contrasts with a later time of peace, when, separated from his brothers, he experiences defeat at the hands of women.

In the midst of Judah's glory in war, another theme corresponds with his eventual downfall through feminine wiles. This theme involves military conquest through deception, which is entirely absent in *Jubilees*, *Yalquṭ Šimʿoni* Wayyissaʿu, and the *Chronicles of Yeraḥmeʾel*.[62] For example, Judah reports a stratagem employed during the battle at Areta:

> 5:2. Then Gad and I approached from the east of the city, but Reuben and Levi from the west and the south. 3. And those who were on the wall, supposing that we were alone, were drawn out against us. 4. And so the brothers stealthily climbed up the wall on both sides by means of pegs and entered the city, while they were unsuspecting. (*T.Jud.* 5:2–4)

---

[61] In this section, although Judah ostensibly joins forces with his brothers, he continues to do all the fighting! Not until *T.Jud.* 5–7 does he actually cooperate with them in specific military maneuvers.

[62] There are instances of deceptive maneuvers in the expanded account of the war with the indigenous kings in *Seper Hayyašar*, although the particular details differ considerably.

The deceptive ploys in the *Testament of Judah* recall the brothers' deception of the men of Shechem in the Bible, when they pretend to enter an alliance with the local population and then slaughter them while they are in pain from circumcision (Gen 34:13–29).

Similarly, on the fifth day, when the brothers approach the city of Makir and encounter women rolling stones from the summit, Judah recalls how "entering secretly from the rear, Simeon and I seized the heights, and we destroyed the whole city" (*T.Jud.* 6:5). Finally, Judah explains that when a mighty host from Gaash, the city of the kings, comes against the brothers:

> 7:2. Then Dan and I, pretending to be Amorites, went as allies into their city. 3. And in the depth of the night when our brothers came and we opened the gates for them, we destroyed all of them and their possessions, and, plundering all that was theirs, we demolished their three walls. (*T.Jud.* 7:2–3)

These three instances of male deception of the enemy in war anticipate the theme of female deception of the male in peace developed later in Judah's encounters with the Canaanite woman and Tamar. As noted in the previous chapter, deception is an important theme in Genesis 38 itself, in which Judah apparently deceives Tamar and then is deceived by her in turn. The *Testament of Judah* interjects the theme of deception from Genesis 38 into its version of the war with the Canaanites and Amorites, just as it later intensifies this theme in its version of the biblical narrative. Since Judah himself participates in each of the deceptive military ploys in the *Testament of Judah*, the reversal is complete when the two women of Genesis 38 ultimately deceive him during times of peace.[63]

One final distinctive feature in the *Testament of Judah* consists of the use of place names from Genesis 38 in the battle scenes. For example, Judah recounts that he was "at the waters of Chozeba" (ἐν τοῖς ὕδασι Χωζηβά) when the men of Jobal came against the brothers for war (*T.Jud.* 6:1). This location recalls Kezib (כזיב, Χασβι in the Septuagint), the place associated with Shelah's birth in the Masoretic text of Gen 38:5 and with all three of the sons' births in the Septuagint.[64] None of the other sources refers to this place. In another

---

[63] Notice also that in the *Testament of Judah* women cast stones from the hill of Makir, whereas in *Yalquṭ Šimʿoni* Wayyissaʿu and the *Chronicles of Yeraḥmeʾel* it is men who cast the stones. This change in gender may relate to the treachery of women emphasized in *T.Jud.* 8, 10–12.

[64] The use of the phrase "the waters of Chozeba" is curious, however, since waters are not mentioned in Gen 38:5. This phrase may stem from an intertextual reading of Gen 38:5 and Isa 58:11, which refers to a "spring of water whose waters do not fail" (וכמוצא מים אשר לא־יכזבו מימיו). In the verse from Isaiah, both the word "waters" (מים) and the root "to fail" (כזב), containing the same consonants as the place name

instance, the *Testament of Judah* locates the final battle at Thamna
(Ξάμνα, *T.Jud.* 7:4–6), which recalls Timnah (Ξαμνα in the Septuagint),
Judah's destination when he meets Tamar in the biblical story. There
is no corresponding battle at Timnah in *Yalquṭ Šimʿoni* Wayyissaʿu
and The *Chronicles of Yeraḥmeʾel*. In these medieval sources, the final
battle is at Gaash, which becomes the site of the second-to-last battle
in the *Testament of Judah*.[65] Significantly, in the medieval sources, all
of the brothers are insulted at Gaash, whereas in the *Testament of
Judah* this motif is transferred and Judah alone is insulted during the
final battle at Thamna.[66] Similarly, in the medieval sources, Judah is
almost killed at Gaash, whereas in the *Testament of Judah* the site of
his close brush with death is changed to Thamna. The patriarch's
humiliation and jeopardy at Thamna during war in the *Testament of
Judah* thus foreshadow his humiliation and jeopardy on his way to
this location later in peace.[67] Finally, in the *Testament of Judah* the city
that Judah builds is designated as Thamna, whereas his father builds
Rambael (*T.Jud.* 7:9). By contrast, in *Jubilees* Jacob builds both cities,
designated as Robel and Tamnatares (*Jub.* 34:8); in the *Chronicles
of Yeraḥmeʾel*, Jacob builds Timnah and Judah builds Arabeel; and
in *Yalquṭ Šimʿoni* Wayyissaʿu Jacob inclines to Timnah and Judah

---

in Gen 38:5 (כזיב), appear. (See also Mic 1:14, in which the root "to fail" appears
twice, in a passage concerning Israel's royalty.)

   The phrase "the waters of Chozeba" apparently has more than a simple geographical significance for the compiler of the *Testament of Judah*, however, since it
appears again in an explanation of why Judah sinned with Tamar. In *T.Jud.* 12:3
Judah confesses that he had become drunk "at the waters of Chozeba" (ἐν ὕδασι
Χωζηβὰ) and therefore did not recognize his daughter-in-law. In light of the connection between the waters of Chozeba and drunkenness in this second passage, one
wonders if Judah was also drunk earlier during the war when Jobal attacked in
T.Jud. 6:1. Note that in his exhortations Judah cautions that wine is the cause of
war and confusion (*T.Jud.* 16:5).

   [65] The second-to-last battle takes place at Gaas (Γαὰς), according to *T.Jud.* 7:1–3.
The *Testament of Judah* divides what in the medieval midrashic sources is a single battle
at Gaash into two battles, the first at Gaas and the last at Thamna. Significantly,
while there is a king of Gaas in *Jubilees* 34, there is no king of Thamna, and this
detail further confirms that the *Testament of Judah* introduces the latter place name to
link the traditions concerning the wars with the material from Genesis 38 that follows.

   [66] No reason is given for the enemies' taunting of Judah at Thamna (*T.Jud.* 7:4).
Thus, the general theme of humiliation becomes associated with this city, towards
which Judah is traveling when he meets Tamar in the biblical narrative. By contrast, the medieval versions specify a limited military context for the humiliation at
Gaash when they explain that the enemies taunted the brothers because they were
unable to breach the three walls surrounding that city.

   [67] It must be noted, however, that the *Testament of Judah* itself never specifies
Thamna as the place towards which Judah ascends to shear sheep (*T.Jud.* 12:1).

inclines to Arabeel. So whereas Timnah, or another similar city name, appears at the end of each of these accounts, only the *Testament of Judah* specifically associates Judah with this place as its builder. On a positive note, this association transforms the biblical city of Timnah into the site of Judah's cultural achievement, from merely his destination when he turned aside to hire a prostitute. This association also explains why Judah travels to this particular city to shear sheep in the biblical narrative. But perhaps most important, the appearance of the name of this city from Genesis 38 once more anticipates the version of the biblical narrative in the sections which follow. The combination of the tradition concerning the war between Jacob's sons and the Canaanite coalition with Genesis 38 is unique to the *Testament of Judah*, and the incorporation of place names mentioned in Genesis 38 into the battle scenes helps to fuse these disparate units into a single composition.

In summary, the *Testament of Judah* prefaces its version of Genesis 38 with a unique constellation of motifs: Judah portrays himself as an exemplar of filial obedience and righteousness, through which he gains his status as king among his brothers. He next recounts his success in various exploits, achieved with divine assistance. Judah's courage and physical dominance over animals and human enemies, his military leadership of his brothers, and his participation alongside his father in city-building mark him as a successful king and a model of masculine virtue, encapsulated by a phrase in the subtitle of this testament in many manuscripts, "Concerning Manliness" (περὶ ἀνδρείας).[68] But interwoven into the account of his early life are foreshadowings

---

[68] These words appear in the subtitle in a majority of the manuscripts (MSS b, l, d, m, k, g, e, f). The emphasis on Judah's manhood begins even in the opening section of the testament, when his father promises him the kingship once he "becomes a man" (ὡς ἠνδρώθην, *T.Jud.* 1:6). The origin of the portrait of Judah as strong man and king may ultimately stem from the last words of David to his son Solomon, where he commands him to "be strong and become a man" (וחזקת והיית לאיש, 1 Kgs 2:2). Up until this point, Judah may be viewed as an example of a "national hero" of the type described by Martin Braun, *History and Romance in Graeco-Oriental Literature* (Oxford: Basil Blackwell. 1938) 1–43, although subsequent events establish his identity as a fallen figure, in clear contrast to the examples discussed by Braun. In addition, the focus on Judah as an exemplar of manliness introduces the theme of gender that is so critical for the further development of the plot in the *Testament of Judah*.

The virtue of "manliness" (ἀνδρεία) is also very important in Graeco-Roman philosophy. For example, Aristotle *Rhetoric* 136a states that prudence and manliness (ἀνδρεία) are appropriate virtues for a man. For further discussion of this virtue, see Hollander, *Joseph as an Ethical Model*, 72; 130, n. 54. Note that Simeon also exemplifies physical strength and manliness (ἀνδρεία) in *T.S.* 2:3, 5.

of a precipitous change. The next sections of the *Testament of Judah* critique what initially appears to be a positive portrayal of masculinity and kingship. A distinctive version of Genesis 38 serves as the vehicle through which the testament makes its critique.

Gen 38:1–5 as the Royal Warrior's First Defeat

The first explicit allusion to Genesis 38 in the *Testament of Judah* immediately follows the cessation of fighting between the Canaanites and Jacob's family. This editorial juxtaposition of the Canaanite war with a version of Gen 38:1–5 occurs in no other extant source. In the *Testament of Judah*, the events in Gen 38:1–5 are incorporated into the description of Judah's life during peacetime:

> 8:1. And I also possessed many flocks, and I had as chief herdsman Hirah the Adullamite. 2. When I went to him I saw Barsan, the king of Adullam. And he made a drinking party for us, and, after persuading me, he gave me his daughter Bathshua as a wife. 3. She bore me Er and Onan and Shelah; two of these the Lord killed childless, but Shelah remained alive, and you are his children. (*T.Jud.* 8:1–3)

As noted in the previous chapter, the first five verses of the biblical narrative focus on Judah's marriage with a Canaanite woman and the birth of their sons, thereby establishing the expectation that the remainder of Genesis 38 will also deal with the theme of procreation. In the version in the *Testament of Judah* there are alterations of the biblical account concerning what happened after "Judah went down from his brothers" (Gen 38:1), including both contractions and additions that drastically change its import.

The most significant contraction of the biblical narrative is that this passage pays little attention to the Canaanite woman's conception, delivery, and naming of Judah's three sons. Their births are summarized in a single line ("She bore me Er and Onan and Shelah," *T.Jud.* 8:3), with no repetition of the female verbs of procreation as in the biblical text. The patriarch immediately proceeds from his sons' births to his two eldest sons' deaths, recounted in more detail in a later section of the testament (*T.Jud.* 10:2–5). Then he connects the story with the present by identifying his deathbed audience as Shelah's offspring, not Perez's offspring as one might expect in light of the biblical genealogies.[69] The cursory treatment of Er, Onan, and

---

[69] The identification of his audience as Shelah's descendants appears in all the manuscripts except MSS c, h, i, and j.

Shelah's births deflects the reader's attention from the theme of procreation. To jump ahead for a moment, the theme of procreation is
hardly raised at all in the version of Gen 38:6–30 presented later in
the *Testament of Judah*. Although Judah notes that Tamar became pregnant after intercourse with him (*T.Jud.* 12:4), he fails to mention
either the anonymous report of her pregnancy (Gen 38:24) or Tamar's
charge that she was with child by the man who owned the pledge
(Gen 38:25).[70] Most significantly of all, the births of Perez and Zerah
are deleted entirely from the narrative in the *Testament of Judah*. Structurally, the version of Genesis 38 in the *Testament of Judah* is not a
double tale of procreation as it is in the Bible. It is reworked for
other purposes, and these purposes may be discerned at least in part
from the additions to Gen 38:1–2 in the passage quoted above.

Judah appears in this passage as an owner of many flocks, and the
extra-biblical reference to his wealth in sheep emphasizes the theme
of success due to obedience noted above, this time in the family's traditional line of work. But in addition, it may foreshadow the revelation
of one of Judah's dominant vices, namely "greed," a vice to which
kings are particularly susceptible according to the *Testament of Judah*.
The immediate attention to the patriarch's occupation also anticipates his fateful journey to shear sheep later in the story (*T.Jud.* 12:1).

Judah's employment of Hirah the Adullamite as chief herdsman
(implying that he had other shepherds as well), similarly stresses his
wealth and high standing. The understanding of Hirah's relationship
to Judah in the *Testament of Judah* is based on the reading of the
word רעהו in the Hebrew consonantal text of Gen 38:12 and 20 as
"his shepherd" (רֹעֵהוּ) rather than as "his friend" (רֵעֵהוּ), as this word
is pointed in the Masoretic Text. Because Hirah accompanies Judah
to Timnah for the sheep shearing and because Judah charges him
with delivering the kid to the woman at Enaim, "his shepherd" (רֹעֵהוּ)
is a logical interpretation of the Hebrew consonantal text. The Septuagint attests to the reading of the Hebrew consonantal text as "his
shepherd" (ὁ ποιμὴν αὐτοῦ) in a Hellenistic cultural context. This reading grants Judah an elevated standing among his foreign neighbors,
as their leader and employer rather than as simply their equal and
companion.[71]

---

[70] Rather, she merely sends the pledges to him privately, apparently at a time of
her own choosing, and thus humiliates him (*T.Jud.* 12:5).

[71] Similarly, *Jub.* 41:14 portrays Hirah as Judah's shepherd. The rabbinic exegetical

The development of Judah's father-in-law, Barsan,[72] as the king of the Adullamites (which the *Testament of Judah* later identifies as a Canaanite people)[73] similarly stresses Judah's elevated status through his association with indigenous royalty.[74] Tellingly, Judah sees the Adullamite king when he visits his Adullamite shepherd Hirah, instead of seeing the daughter of a Canaanite man as in the biblical text. This initial meeting between two kings serves as a transitional motif from Judah's violent encounters with other kings during war to his domestic life during peace.

In addition, the *Testament of Judah* gives Judah's Canaanite wife a name. In calling her Bathshua, the author of the *Testaments* relies on a tradition that may stem from the description of her as "Shua's daughter, the Canaanitess" (בת שוע הכנענית) in 1 Chr 2:3. The initial construct chain in this phrase, "Shua's daughter" (בת שוע), was apparently understood as a personal name, "Bathshua" (בתשוע; or in the Greek of the *Testament of Judah*, Βησσουὲ). The Septuagint as well gives the Canaanite woman in Gen 38:2 a name, when it specifies that "her name was Shua" (ᾗ ὄνομα Σαυα; cf., LXX Gen 38:12) rather than "his name was Shua" (ושמו שוע), referring to her father, as in the Hebrew text. The designation of Judah's wife by name reflects her important, although negative, role in the testament's revised version of Genesis 38.

An additional motif in this passage consists of the enemy king's grant of his daughter to the hero at a drinking party (*T.Jud.* 8:2). This curious motif has no basis whatsoever in the biblical version of Genesis 38,[75] nor does it appear outside of the *Testament of Judah*. In legends, including those from Hebrew and Greek cultures, leaders

---

tradition that Hirah in Genesis 38 is none other than King Hiram of Tyre, David's long-lived friend (*Gen.Rab.* 85:4), may have influenced the Masoretic pointing "his friend" (רֵעֵהוּ) in Gen 38:12 and 20.

[72] The name Barsan (Βάρσαν) is unique to the *Testament of Judah*, although the LXX calls the king of Gomorrah in Gen 14:2 Barsa (Βαρσα). Perhaps his name derives from an Aramaic version of the expression "Shua's daughter" in Gen 38:12 and 1 Chr 2:3 (בת שוע).

[73] *T.Jud.* 10:2, 6; 11:1, 3; 14:6. Joshua and the Israelites also overthrow an Adullamite king in Judg 12:15, as part of their conquest of Canaan.

[74] The view that Judah's Canaanite father-in-law was an important leader of his people is found in rabbinic literature as well. *Gen.Rab.* 85.4, for example, calls the Canaanite woman's father a leading "light" in his region.

[75] Notice, however, how this extra-biblical motif is inserted between material that makes specific allusion to the biblical narrative. Through this technique of embedding, the author incorporates this motif as part of the biblical narrative.

commonly give their daughters to successful heroes after battles. Two biblical examples are King Saul's offer of his daughter Michal to David in exchange for one hundred Philistine foreskins (1 Sam 18:17–29) and Caleb's offer of his daughter Achsah to the man who could conquer Kiriath-sepher (Judg 1:11–15).[76] But in the *Testament of Judah* the king who offers his daughter is a Canaanite, a former enemy and a member of a wicked race (*T.Jud.* 11:1); moreover, he pressures Judah to marry his daughter (*T.Jud.* 8:2). These details lend a sinister valence to this motif.[77] Following Judah's successful military leadership of his brothers against a coalition of Canaanite kings, he encounters one final Canaanite king alone. But whereas in the masculine realm of war Judah always prevails against the enemy through violence, in peace he ultimately suffers defeat at the hands of a Canaanite enemy through the medium of a woman. The portrayal of Judah's marriage with the Canaanite woman in the *Testament of Judah* 8, therefore, introduces the themes of the dangerous power of women and the destructive passions to which kings are particularly vulnerable. Similarly, the theme of drunkenness, another of Judah's vices to which his royal descendants are also prone, is suggested in this version of the first verses of Genesis 38 through the introduction of the detail of the drinking party. To summarize, the *Testament of Judah* develops Gen 38:1–2 to emphasize Judah's royal status and to suggest the three vices (drunkenness, lust, and greed) that lead to the downfall of this great warrior king.

Additional details later in Judah's exhortations to his sons articulate the negative valence of the events in Gen 38:1–2 implied in the *Testament of Judah* 8. The deceptive wiles of the evil Adullamite king to destroy Judah through the snare of his daughter are most fully elaborated in a narrative passage embedded within Judah's opening exhortations to his sons:

> 13:4. And I said to my father-in-law, "I will consult with my father and then I will take your daughter." But he showed me a measureless amount of gold in his daughter's name, for he was a king. 5. And

---

[76] For some examples of this motif in Greek legend, see the comparison between Judah and Heracles below. In Greek legend, the motif of the banquet at which the king offers his daughter sometimes appears, whereas this is not a Hebrew motif. Perhaps the closest parallel in biblical literature to the motif of the drinking party appears when Laban deceptively gives Leah to Jacob after holding a wedding feast for him in Gen 29:22.

[77] Note also that in 1 Sam 18:21 King Saul plots to ensnare David when he offers his daughter Michal.

having adorned her with gold and pearls, he made her pour wine for us at the meal, with the beauty of women. 6. And the wine distorted my eyesight, and pleasure blinded my heart. 7. And desiring her, I met her, and I transgressed the Lord's commandment and my fathers' commandment, and I took her as a wife. 8. And the Lord repaid me according to the disposition of my heart, because as I took no delight in her children. (*T.Jud.* 13:4–8)

Barsan plots to destroy the very basis of Judah's kingship in this passage, which is his obedience to his father. Once again the central issue of obedience, introduced in the very first lines of this testament, reappears, although here Judah's conduct is far from exemplary. Like a good son, Judah initially desires to consult with his father, but the Adullamite king distracts him. Appealing to Judah's greed, Barsan shows him his daughter's dowry;[78] relying on the power of wine to pervert judgment, he has his daughter pour at the banquet;[79] and trusting in the seductive charms of feminine beauty, he presents his daughter in an expensive costume of gold and pearls.[80] Just as the

---

[78] Judah's fatal attraction to wealth, which contributed to his sinful marriage with Bathshua, is reiterated in *T.Jud.* 17:1. According to *T.Jud.* 19:2 Judah almost lost his children because of his love of money.

[79] Judah's drunkenness as a factor contributing to his sinful relationship with Bathshua is developed in *T.Jud.* 11:2; 14:6; and 16:4. The image of the princess pouring wine at the banquet in the passage cited above (*T.Jud.* 13:5) and earlier (*T.Jud.* 11:2) transforms a gesture of hospitality into a stratagem of the enemy. Other literary works from the Graeco-Roman period, including the New Testament book of Revelation and the *Tabula* of Cebes of Thebes, similarly employ the image of a woman offering wine as a negative symbol. Rev 17:1–6 depicts Babylon as a harlot dressed in rich, jeweled clothes (including gold and pearls), with a golden cup in her hand full of abominations and the impurities of her fornication. Concerning her, an angel explains that she is the harlot "with whom the kings of the earth have committed fornication, and with the wine of whose fornication the dwellers on earth have become drunk" (Rev 17:2). In a later passage, another angel explains that Babylon has fallen "for all nations have drunk the wine of her impure passion, and the kings of the earth have committed fornication with her, and the merchants of the earth have grown rich with the wealth of her wantonness" (Rev 18:3). This verse strikingly depicts the same three vices associated with Judah: drunkenness, uncontrollable lust, and greed. An earlier association between Babylon and an intoxicating golden cup appears in Jer 51:7. In the *Tabula* of Cebes of Thebes, the similarities are more general. According to this source, all who enter life drink from a cup filled with ignorance offered by a woman called "Deceit."

[80] The patriarch's vulnerability to the beauty of women, which led to his association with Bathshua, is reiterated in *T.Jud.* 17:1.

The Canaanite king's dressing of his daughter in alluring clothing aligns her more closely with Tamar, who dresses deceptively in Genesis 38. Later, the *Testament of Judah* develops Tamar as a sinister parallel to the seductively and expensively dressed Canaanite woman. Feminine dress and adornment are particularly sensitive issues for the author of the *Testaments*.

king planned, Judah's three vices of greed, drunkenness, and lust conspire against him, and he violates the commandments of the Lord and his fathers by taking a Canaanite as his wife. The undefeated warrior king thus suffers moral defeat at the hands of the enemy's daughter, who ensnares him with the three vices associated with royalty.[81] The augmented version of Gen 38:1–2 in the *Testament of Judah* fills in the mysterious silence in the biblical version concerning the reason that Judah married a forbidden Canaanite woman. If this version of the narrative does little to relieve Judah's responsibility for his actions, at least it explains them.

A few observations concerning the specific vices attributed to Judah are in order. Wine and libido are commonly associated in Hebraic thought, as the stories of Lot and his daughters (Gen 19:30–38) and of Noah and Ham (Gen 9:20–27) illustrate.[82] More closely related to Judah's experience in the *Testament of Judah*, in Prov 31:3–5 a king's mother warns him against strong drink and women because they will destroy his power and pervert his rule. The portrait of Judah as a drunkard may also have been motivated by some rather puzzling phrases in Jacob's blessing of his son. In Gen 49:11–12a, Jacob states concerning Judah, "Tying his foal to the vine, and to the choice vine his donkey's colt, he washed his clothing in the wine, and in the blood of grapes his vesture; [his] eyes were red from wine." The many references to vines and wine in these verses, especially to his bloodshot eyes, suggests that Judah consumed alcohol liberally.

Judah's association with greed, on the other hand, may stem from more mundane observations about the graft which often plagues political leadership, and this may be true of his lascivious behavior as well. Biblical kings, such as Solomon, were famous for both their wealth and numerous wives. The negative depiction of kingship in 1 Sam 8:11–18 stresses the king's acquisitive nature, in its description of his seizure of sons and daughters, land, produce, servants, and

---

[81] Judah confirms that kings are particularly prone to greed, drunkenness, and lust when he warns his royal descendants against these vices (*T.Jud.* 13:1; 14:1–8; 16:1–5; 17:1; 18:2–6; 19:1), even while recognizing the futility of his warnings (*T.Jud.* 17:2; 18:1; 21:7–8; 23:2).

[82] See also Rev 17:2 and *m. Soṭa* 1.4 for additional examples of the association between drunkenness and fornication. For further examples of the connection between wine and sexual potency in the Bible and in the larger Mediterranean world, see H. Hirsch Cohen, *The Drunkenness of Noah*, Judaic Series 4 (University: University of Alabama Press, 1974) 1–11.

livestock for his own possession.[83] Even closer in detail is the description of prohibitions for Israel's kings in Deut 17:14–17. According to this passage, the king should "not multiply wives for himself so that his heart be turned aside, nor greatly multiply silver and gold for himself" (Deut 17:17).[84] No doubt political figures contemporary with the author of the *Testaments* were similarly subject to the corruptions which power affords and would have provided more immediate models for the author's portrayal of Judah as king.[85] The first part of Genesis 38 in the *Testament of Judah* therefore provides the focal image for the introduction of Judah's three vices; furthermore, the biblical material is developed to show how Judah is ultimately defeated, albeit on a moral rather than a physical battlefield, through his marital alliance with a Canaanite woman.[86]

---

[83] The prophetic description of Judah's descendants in *T.Jud.* 21:7 ("they will enslave free daughters and sons, they will plunder houses, lands, flocks, money") is a certain allusion to 1 Sam 8:11–18.

[84] There is also a prohibition against the multiplying of horses or returning his people to Egypt to acquire horses. The reference to horses recalls Judah's taming of a mare in *T.Jud.* 2:3.

[85] The gravity of the three vices associated with Judah in the *Testament of Judah* is indicated by the counter example of Issachar. As an exemplar of the simple and good life in the *Testament of Issachar*, this patriarch swears that he has never committed a serious sin. Issachar specifies the very three vices (fornication, drunkenness, and greed) associated with Judah at the beginning of his declaration of innocence (*T.I.* 7:1–3), and defines simplicity as disinterest in gold and women, among other things (*T.I.* 4:2–5).

[86] The idea that a defeated enemy might ultimately triumph over one of Jacob's descendants through the seductions of his daughter also appears in a rabbinic interpretation of the law concerning the woman captured in war in Deut 21:10–14. An interpretive tradition from *Sipre Debarim* 211–12 (Louis Finkelstein, ed. [Berlin: Jüdischer Kulturbund in Deutschland, 1939; reprint, New York: Jewish Theological Seminary Press, 1969] 245–47) focuses on the stipulation that the captive woman "shall put off her captive's garb" (Deut 21:13) when she enters her captor's house: "This explains that the captor must divest her of her attractive garments and clothe her in widow's weeds, for these accursed nations make their daughters adorn themselves in time of war in order to make the others [i.e., their foes] go awhoring after them." (This translation was supplied by David Stern, during an oral presentation at the University of Chicago Divinity School, February 1994, entitled "The Captive Woman: Hellenization, Rabbinic Judaism, and the Graeco-Roman Novel.") The concern in the larger context of *Sipre Debarim* is that intermarriage leads to idolatry. By contrast, although Judah worries about his sons falling into idolatry through their love of money and their mingling in the abominations of the gentiles (*T.Jud.* 19:1; 23:1–2), he himself does not succumb to this particular danger. Rather, because of his disobedience and participation in vice, he almost loses the kingship and almost dies childless (*T.Jud.* 17:1–3; 19:2).

Return to the Masculine Realm of War

Immediately following the allusion to events in Gen 38:1–5 in section 8, Judah relates another of his successes in the masculine realm of war, this time against Esau and his sons. A number of other sources, including *Jubilees* 36–37, *Yalquṭ Šimʿoni* Wayyissaʿu, and the *Chronicles of Yeraḥmeʾel* also describe this conflict. Once again, it is difficult to determine the relationship between these sources.[87] In any event, the version in the *Testament of Judah* 9 is by far the shortest, and its main purpose is to reiterate Judah's bravery and military prowess. According to this testament, soon after Esau and his sons attack, Jacob shoots his own brother with a bow and routs the enemy forces. Jacob's family then pursues the sons of Esau and unsuccessfully besieges their iron-walled city for twenty days. Finally, Judah ascends on a ladder holding a shield to deflect the heavy stones thrown down on his head. Once upon the wall, he kills four mighty men. The next day, after some additional heroism on the part of Reuben and Gad,[88] Esau's sons ask for terms of peace and become tributaries until Jacob's family goes down to Egypt.

Yalquṭ Šimʿoni Wayyissaʿu and the *Chronicles of Yeraḥmeʾel* place the war with Esau and his sons immediately after the war with the Canaanite kings. Apparently these two descriptions of Jacob and his sons' military ventures were brought together because of their similar subject matter. In *Jubilees*, the two wars appear in the same order, but they are separated by other material, including narratives recounting the sale of Joseph, the deaths of Bilhah, Dinah, and Leah, and the efforts of Rebekah to reconcile Jacob and Esau, as well as a list of the wives of Jacob's twelve sons (including Judah, who married "Betasuel, a Canaanite"). Only in the *Testament of Judah* do these two wars appear separated by events from Genesis 38 and nothing else. This configuration may reflect an attempt by the author to present the most important events of Judah's life in chronological order.[89]

---

[87] There is even less specific correspondence between the *Testament of Judah* and the other sources concerning this war than there is concerning the war with the Canaanite (or Amorite) kings.

[88] Inexplicably, these brothers kill either six (mss g, d, m, e, a, f, c, h, i, j) or sixty (mss b, l) men, dwarfing Judah's exploits of the previous day.

[89] The author's interest in the order of events in Judah's life is indicated by his specification that the patriarch was twenty years old at the end of the war with the Canaanite and Amorite enemies (*T.Jud.* 7:10) and forty years old at the beginning of the war with Esau and his sons (*T.Jud.* 9:2). The chronological presentation in

But in addition, this arrangement confirms that the contrast in the *Testament of Judah* between Judah's success in the masculine realm of war and his failure in a more personal fight against vices—especially those involving women—is intentional. Just as the successful war with the Canaanite kings prefaces Judah's moral defeat by a Canaanite woman, the successful war with Esau and his sons, who are relatives, precedes the introduction of a female relative who will similarly cause his downfall. This female relative is Tamar, who according to this testament is the daughter of Aram and comes from Mesopotamia (*T.Jud.* 10:1). In this latter detail, she is similar to one of the biblical matriarchs, Rebekah, who also comes from Mesopotamia according to the *Testament of Judah*.[90] Judah and his brothers' military victory over male relatives therefore foreshadows the patriarch's corresponding defeat at the hands of a female relative, whom he encounters in a time of peace without his brothers.[91]

Gen 38:6–12 as Judah's Continuing Subservience

But even before the encounter between Tamar and Judah, the *Testament of Judah* 10–11 illustrates Judah's loss of masculine authority within his own family to his domineering Canaanite wife and disobedient sons:

> 10:1. After these things my son Er took as a wife Tamar from Mesopotamia, a daughter of Aram. 2. But Er was wicked, and he had a difficulty concerning Tamar because she was not from the land of Canaan. And an angel of the Lord killed him on the third day, at night. 3. And he had not known her on account of the villainy of his

---

the *Testament of Judah* may be based on a prior tradition, judging from the appearance of events in the same order in *Jubilees*. While the events are not contiguous in this earlier source, the war with the Canaanite kings (*Jub.* 34:1–9) precedes the brief allusion to Judah's marriage with a Canaanite woman named Betasuel (*Jub.* 34:20), and the lengthy version of the war with Esau and his sons (*Jub.* 37:1–38:14) precedes the story of Judah and Tamar (*Jubilees* 41). But even if the author of the *Testament of Judah* drew on *Jubilees* or a similar source for his chronological schema, he certainly develops the significance of the order of events in a distinctive way.

[90] *T.Jud.* 9:1 presents Mesopotamia as Laban's home, and therefore it is Rebekah's home as well.

[91] The author of the *Testament of Judah* clearly considers Judah's relations with Tamar as incest. In *T.Jud.* 13:3, Judah describes Tamar as the woman "espoused to my sons," and in *T.Jud.* 14:5, he notes that he committed a terrible sin by uncovering "the cover of my son's shame." Similarly, *Jubilees* focuses on Judah's relations with Tamar as incest and describes his recognition that by laying with his daughter-in-law "he uncovered the robe of his son" (*Jub.* 41:23).

mother, for he did not want to have children by her. 4. In the days designated for the bridal chamber, I gave Onan to her in levirate marriage; and he also, in wickedness, did not know her, though he was with her a year. 5. And when I threatened him, he came together with her, but spilled the seed on the ground, according to his mother's command; and he also died in wickedness. 6. And I wanted to give Shelah to her also, but my wife Bathshua did not permit it, for she maltreated Tamar because she was not of the daughters of Canaan, as she was.

11.1. And I knew that the race of Canaan is wicked, but the disposition of youth blinded my heart. 2. And when I saw her pouring out wine, I was deceived through the intoxication of wine, and I met with her. 3. In my absence, she went and took for Shelah a wife from the land of Canaan. 4. Realizing what she had done, I cursed her in the anguish of my soul. 5. And she also died because of the wickedness of her sons. (*T.Jud.* 10:1–11:5)

Many of the events in this passage stem from Gen 38:6–11, or actually Gen 38:6–12, since the passage ends with the death of Judah's wife. But whereas in the biblical narrative Gen 38:6–11 depicts the frustrated attempts at procreation leading up to Tamar's actions, here the augmented version illustrates the disastrous consequences of Judah's marriage to a Canaanite woman. A number of the details in this elaborated version of Gen 38:6–12 may also be found in *Jubilees* 41, but many that are unique to this document emphasize Judah's humiliation by his Canaanite wife.

This passage from the *Testament of Judah* consistently alters the biblical story to present the patriarch as a passive and anguished observer of his family's behavior. This alteration exaggerates the theme of Judah's ineffectiveness implied by Genesis 38 itself. First of all, Er takes his own wife instead of waiting for his father to act as in the biblical story. Then Judah helplessly notes Er's difficulty with Tamar because she is not a Canaanite like his mother,[92] and he explains that his eldest son's wickedness consists of abstention from intercourse with her to avoid having children. This explanation of Er's unspecified wickedness deserving of divine punishment involves a transfer of

---

[92] Er's disdain for Tamar because she is not a Canaanite in this testament is incredible, given the fact that he himself chooses her. The version in *Jubilees* is much more consistent, in that it depicts Er rebelling against his father's selection of a wife for him because he wants to marry a Canaanite like his mother (*Jub.* 41:1–2). Apparently, the author of the *Testament of Judah* wants to emphasize Judah's passivity, as well as to stress the patriarch's lack of responsibility for Tamar's situation.

Onan's desire to prevent conception onto his elder brother.[93] In the process of this transfer, the issue in both cases becomes Tamar's ethnicity, not distaste for levirate responsibilities as in Onan's case in the Bible. The unique detail that an angel kills Er in the night several days after the wedding corresponds with the testament's view that Er dies because he abstains from sexual relations.[94]

Following Er's death, Judah briefly asserts his paternal authority when he gives Onan to Tamar in levirate marriage during the remaining days of the wedding celebration. But Judah's specific instructions to his second son to raise up seed for his brother (Gen 38:8) are missing in the *Testament of Judah*, and an entire year passes during which Onan neglects to have intercourse with Tamar. Only after this long period of inaction does Judah finally threaten his son. Even then his threats prove ineffective, as Onan goes into her, spills his semen on the ground, and dies because of his wickedness as in the biblical narrative. In the *Testament of Judah*, both Judah and his son must be urged before having sexual relations with a woman. But whereas Judah was urged by a former enemy king and should have resisted, Onan is urged by his father to have intercourse with an appropriately endogamous woman and should comply.[95]

After Onan's death, Judah sincerely plans to give Shelah to Tamar, but once again his intentions are thwarted. Shelah eventually marries a Canaanite woman that his mother chooses for him during her husband's absence, and quite against his wishes. Throughout this expanded form of the biblical narrative, Judah's Canaanite wife, not the patriarch himself, controls the behavior of their sons. The sons' disobedience is particularly striking in the context of this testament,

---

[93] The idea that Er and Onan share the same aversion to having children with Tamar is a common Jewish exegetical tradition. For example, *Jub.* 41:2 also depicts Er as refusing to have intercourse with Tamar because she is not a Canaanite. In rabbinic literature as well, for example in *Gen.Rab.* 85.4, Er's wickedness is explained by portraying him as a parallel figure to Onan, although the emphasis of the comparison differs. According to this rabbinic source, Er like Onan prevents conception through his prophylactic style of intercourse, expressed euphemistically as "plowing on roofs." The gap in the biblical narrative concerning the nature of Er's wickedness is thus filled by repeating a motif already present in Genesis 38.

[94] The addition of an angel is in keeping with the multi-layered spirit world of the *Testaments*, and it also softens God's punitive character in the biblical narrative by attributing Er's death to an intermediary.

[95] Another way of expressing this contrast is to note that whereas Judah took a foreign wife without his father's consent, his sons refuse to consummate their marriage with a woman of proper descent even, in Onan's case, after the threats of their father.

where Judah distinguishes himself as an obedient son to his own
father.[96] Er refrains from intercourse with Tamar on account of the
craftiness of his mother,[97] Onan spills his seed on the ground in accordance with her command and in disregard of his father's threats,[98]
and Shelah marries the woman of his mother's choice rather than of
his father's.[99] In each of these instances, Judah's wife's special area of
control is sexuality. Just as she elicited from Judah inappropriate sexual
desire when they first met, she later demands inappropriate sexual
restraint from her sons. Whether the problem is promiscuity or irre-
sponsible avoidance, women are blamed for the sexual misconduct
of men in the *Testament of Judah*. This blame corresponds with a general
tendency in the *Testaments* to vilify women as the embodiment of
sexuality and its moral ambiguities.

The testament's portrayal of Judah's dysfunctional family reopens
the issue of intermarriage raised earlier by his own marriage to a
Canaanite. Judah himself later admits to his sons that marrying a
Canaanite woman was against the commandments of the Lord and
his fathers (*T.Jud.* 13:7); however, in the *Testament of Judah* 10–11 the
ideal of marriage within one's own race is held most strongly not by
any member of Abraham's family, but rather by a member of the
very Canaanite race that Israel is advised to avoid in biblical law.
Judah's wife rejects Tamar as an inappropriate spouse for her sons
and aligns her sons with her on this issue (*T.Jud.* 10:2–3, 5, 6; 11:3).
The *Testament of Judah* presents Tamar as a descendant of Aram
from Mesopotamia (*T.Jud.* 10:1),[100] and there are a number of hints
that suggest she would have been an appropriate endogamous spouse
for one of Judah's sons. For one thing, Aram was a descendant of
Shem, and therefore distantly related to Abraham and his descendants. In addition, as noted above, in the *Testament of Judah* some of

[96] The Canaanite woman's control over the sons explains why they are "wicked"
even though they have a father noted for his filial obedience.
[97] *T.Jud.* 10:3. This same motif may be found in *Jub.* 41:2.
[98] *T.Jud.* 10:5. In both the biblical account and in the *Testament of Judah*, Onan's
actions are identical, but the motivations differ. Whereas in Genesis 38 Onan acts
so as to prevent heirs for his brother, in the *Testament of Judah* he acts in accordance
with his mother's instructions, apparently motivated by ethnic prejudice.
[99] *T.Jud.* 10:6 and 11:3. The Canaanite wife in *Jub.* 41:7 also prevents Shelah
from marrying Tamar, although she doesn't find him a Canaanite wife.
[100] Similarly, *Jub.* 41:1 depicts Tamar as a daughter of Aram. For a slightly different
view, that she was the descendant of Shem, the father of Aram, see *Gen.Rab.* 85.10
and parallel passages in rabbinic literature.

the matriarchs, including Rebekah, come from Mesopotamia. Finally, Judah clearly considers Tamar a fitting partner for his sons, and one assumes that he would have learned from his own negative experience with a Canaanite wife about the value of endogamy. The xenophobia implicit in the biblical prohibitions against marriage with Canaanites is therefore imputed to the Canaanite wife in this testament. This transference of concern for ethnic purity to the foreign enemy corresponds with the numerous positive expressions of universalism in the *Testaments*, which depicts ultimate salvation for both Israel and the gentiles.[101] In this connection, it is notable that one of Judah's reflections on his mistake of marrying a Canaanite woman emphasizes that the Canaanites are an evil people, not that exogamy in itself is wrong (*T.Jud.* 11:1).[102]

The treatment of levirate marriage in the *Testament of Judah* 10–11 also reveals some of the larger perspectives and concerns of the *Testaments*. Through its specification that Er never consummated his marriage with Tamar and its implication that Onan simply took his brother's place as groom during the wedding festivities (*T.Jud.* 10: 3–4),[103] and through its deletion of language specifically recalling the levirate law in Deut 25:5–10,[104] the *Testament of Judah* alters the biblical narrative to accord with its marital ideal of lifelong monogamy

---

[101] See for example, the numerous passages which mention the salvation of "humankind" or the "nations" without specific reference to Israel (*T.R.* 6:11; *T.S.* 6:5–7; *T.L.* 2:11; and many others listed in Hollander and Marinus de Jonge, *The Testaments: A Commentary*, 64).

[102] The evil of the Canaanites is defined as their rapacious sexuality in *T.L.* 6:8–10, where Levi charges that they tried to mistreat Sarah just as they did Dinah and claims that they make a regular practice of taking other men's wives by force. The depiction of the Canaanites as sexual perverts is generalized to apply to all the gentiles in *T.D.* 5:5, where Dan associates them with abominations and lawless fornications. (*Jub.* 25:1 also claims that the Canaanites are filled with fornication and lust.) In light of these passage, it is no wonder that Eppel holds a different view and argues that marriage with gentiles is an abomination in the *Testaments* (*Le Piétisme juif*, 161). It is true that Isaac specifically tells Levi not to take a gentile wife (*T.L.* 9:10), in accordance with the biblical stipulations concerning the priest's wife (Lev 21:7, 13–15). But there is no negative evaluation of Joseph's marriage to his Egyptian master's daughter (*T.Jos.* 18:3). In fact, Joseph presents his marriage to a wealthy Egyptian woman as a reward for his moral rectitude.

[103] In *Jub.* 41:27 as well, Er never actually consummates the marriage.

[104] *T.Jud.* 10:4 does employ a technical term when it specifies that Judah arranged a levirate marriage (ἐπεγάμβρευσα) between Onan and Tamar, but there is no explicit statement concerning the purpose of this arrangement, nor is there any significant overlap of terminology between Deut 25:5–10 and the narrative in the *Testament of Judah*.

for both sexes.[105] The ideal that men as well as women should have only one sexual partner is also evident from Judah's assumption that once Shelah married his Canaanite wife, he was permanently disqualified from levirate marriage with Tamar.[106] Apparently, a literal understanding of levirate marriage in the Bible was morally abhorrent to those responsible for the *Testaments*, since this practice suspends normal rules governing sexual conduct and contradicts the later ideal of lifelong monogamy. In the context of the *Testaments*, the levirate law in Deut 25:5–10 therefore loses its prescriptive force and instead becomes commentary on a particular biblical event—the brothers' treacherous sale of Joseph. The *Testament of Zebulun* refers to a law of Enoch that resembles the deuteronomic law when it stipulates "whoever does not want to raise up seed for his brother, his sandal should be pulled off, and he should be spat upon in the face" (*T.Z.* 3:4). Zebulun applies this law to the brothers, who did not want Joseph to live and so sold him and bought sandals with the money from the sale. In time, however, they had their sandals pulled off their feet in Egypt by Joseph's servants and were spat upon while bowing down to their brother.[107] The application of this law with its strong component of shame to the brothers' mistreatment of Joseph once again stresses the importance of brotherly love as an ideal in the *Testaments*— an ideal that the brothers violated. This application also indicates a rejection of the idea implicit in the custom of levirate marriage that a genealogical lineage must be continued even if that means setting aside ordinary regulations of sexual behavior.

A final important aspect of the version of Gen 38:6–12 in the *Testament of Judah* is its creation of a disjunction between the events in the first half of Genesis 38 involving the Canaanite wife and her

---

[105] In this connection, it is interesting to note how the *Testaments* treats Jacob's polygamous marriage with Leah and Rachel. In the *Testament of Issachar* (*T.I.* 1:6–13), the sisters argue not about which of them is more loved by their husband, but about which of them is his legitimate wife.

[106] After Shelah's marriage, Judah curses his wife so that she dies, but he still does not arrange a levirate marriage between his youngest son and Tamar, even though he had wanted to do so earlier and his wife can no longer prevent him from doing so.

[107] The interpretation of the levirate law in *T.Z.* 3:4–7 is more complex than this summary indicates. For example, according to this passage God also pulls off the brothers' "sandal," allegorically interpreted as Joseph. A detailed discussion of this passage, however, is beyond the scope of this study. For the motif of the brothers' purchase of sandals with money from the sale of Joseph (associated with imagery from Amos 2:6), see also *Tg.Ps.-J.* Gen 37:28 and the sources cited in Ginzberg, *Legends*, vol. 5, 330, nn. 51–2.

sons (Gen 38:1–12) and the events in the second half involving Tamar (Gen 38:13–26). In the testament's embellished and restructured account of the biblical narrative, the Canaanite wife's complete control over her sons absolves Judah of all responsibility for his daughter-in-law's unfortunate plight. Unlike the biblical narrative, which suggests a certain duplicity in Judah's dismissal of Tamar to her father's house, this testament stresses his sincere intentions towards her. The patriarch himself claims that he would have indeed given his third son to Tamar, and he doesn't express any reservations even about Shelah's youth. But his wife prevents him from following through with his plan and ultimately makes other arrangements in his absence. The *Testament of Judah* thus resolves the ambiguity of the biblical narrative in Judah's favor.[108] Judah's lack of culpability for Tamar's liminal situation is further emphasized in this testament by the fact that he never verbally promises her his third son. In fact, Judah's distance from Tamar is first indicated when Er, not his father, selects her as his wife. The improvement of Judah's character that these alterations effect simultaneously destroys the internal dynamics of the biblical narrative. Since Judah has left no explicit promise to his daughter-in-law for an appropriate sexual partner unfilled, Tamar has no motive for extracting justice through deception. Instead, the *Testament of Judah* bifurcates the biblical story into two separate illustrations of Judah's basic character flaws and their consequences. Whereas the Bible presents Genesis 38 as a double tale of procreation (Gen 38:1–5 and Gen 38:6–30), the *Testament of Judah* transforms it into a double tale of Judah's fall to temptation, each revolving around his sinful relations with one of the women from Genesis 38 (corresponding roughly to Gen 38:1–12 and Gen 38:13–26).

Two features of the *Testament of Judah* 11 emphasize this secondary closure of the biblical narrative at midpoint. One of these features consists of Judah's reflection on his error in marrying the Canaanite woman. Judah admits that he knew the Canaanites were an evil people, but laments that youth, feminine beauty, and wine nevertheless caused him to sin (*T.Jud.* 11:1–2). This type of reflection appears frequently in the patriarch's exhortations to his sons following his autobiographical account (beginning in the *Testament of Judah* 13), and it therefore signals the termination of an important episode. The other feature consists of the unique explanation in the *Testament of Judah*

---

[108] Similarly, in *Jub.* 41:7 Judah sincerely desires to match Tamar with Shelah.

that Judah's curse upon learning about Shelah's marriage caused his wife's death (*T.Jud.* 11:4–5). This explanation of her death as the moral consequence of wickedness fills a gap in the biblical narrative in a manner consistent with the testament genre's ethical focus. In addition, however, this explanation serves to bring the narrative to full closure as Judah terminates his subjugation to his most pernicious enemy to this point by ending her life, just as earlier he vanquished his animal and human foes by killing them.

Gen 38:13–26 as Judah's Second Defeat

Finally freed from his first oppressor, Judah suffers a second, climactic onslaught of feminine intrigue in the concluding section of his autobiography:

> 12:1. And after these things, while Tamar was a widow, having heard after two years that I was going up to shear the sheep and having adorned herself in bridal array, she sat in the city of Enaim by the gate. 2. (For it was a law of the Amorites that she who was about to marry should sit publicly by the gate for seven days for fornication.) 3. Now, having become drunk at the waters of Chozeba, I did not recognize her because of the wine, and her beauty deceived me through the fashion of adornment. 4. And turning aside to her I said, "Let me go into you!" And she said to me, "What will you give me?" And I gave her my staff and my armor and the diadem of kingship, and after I went in with her, she conceived. 5. And not knowing what she had done I wanted to kill her; but, secretly sending the pledges, she humiliated me. 6. And when I called her I heard also the words of mystery that I spoke while lying with her in my drunkenness. And I could not kill her, because it was from the Lord. 7. But I said. "Perhaps she acted deceitfully, having received the pledge from another woman." 8. But I did not again approach her until my death, because I had done this abomination in all Israel. 9. And those who were in the city said that there was no initiate in the gate, for having come from another region she sat for a short while in the gate. 10. And I supposed that nobody knew that I had gone in unto her. 11. And after this we came into Egypt, towards Joseph, because of the famine. 12. I was forty-six years old, and seventy-three years I lived there. (*T.Jud.* 12:1–12)

After a respectable period of two years (during which Judah presumably mourned his Canaanite wife),[109] Tamar learns about her father-

---

[109] This unique detail in the *Testament of Judah* amends the patriarch's unfeeling character in the biblical narrative by suggesting a period of mourning and abstinence between Judah's involvement with the two women of Genesis 38.

in-law's travels from an anonymous source, as in Gen 38:13. In the context of this testament, however, Tamar's specific targeting of Judah is doubly without motive. First of all, as noted above, her father-in-law owes her nothing in this version of the story. Additionally, her public solicitation of his sexual services merely follows an Amorite law specifying that all women who were soon to marry should prostitute themselves at the city gate for seven days (*T.Jud.* 12:2). Through this detail, the author of the *Testament of Judah* interprets Tamar's status as a "consecrated woman" (קְדֵשָׁה) in Gen 38:21 and 22 in light of the Mesopotamian custom described by Herodotus *Histories* 1.199.[110] Later, when the local men deny that there was an "initiate" (τελισκομένην) at the gate (*T.Jud.* 12:9), the wording recalls the Septuagint's second translation of the prohibition against the "consecrated woman" (קְדֵשָׁה, τελεσφόρος) and the "consecrated man" (קָדֵשׁ, τελισκόμενος) in Deut 23:18.[111] According to the *Testament of Judah*, Tamar blatantly violates a pentateuchal law, which might be considered one of the commandments of the fathers and God centrally featured in this work's definition of morality, and obeys instead the perverse law of the Amorites.[112]

The novel detail of Tamar's dress in this work perhaps stems from the veil that she puts on in the biblical narrative, which suggests a bride's costume. It may also have been suggested by the Septuagint's translation of the word "daughter-in law" (כַּלָּה, Gen 38:11, 16, 24), describing Tamar's relation to Judah. In keeping with the range of the Hebrew word itself, which designates both "daughter-in-law" and "bride," the Septuagint offers the Greek word νύμφη, which most commonly designates "bride," although it may refer to any married woman or marriageable maiden. The depiction of Tamar as a bride may improve the main characters slightly, in that it suggests that perhaps Tamar intended to marry Judah. In any event, this motif eliminates the idea that she intentionally dressed as a prostitute, and it also removes the charge that Judah responded to a prostitute. But

---

[110] The *Testament of Judah* is therefore an early forerunner of the widespread view in biblical scholarship (until recently) that ritual prostitution was common in the ancient Near East, discussed in the previous chapter.

[111] As noted in the previous chapter, the LXX provides a double translation of these terms, the first referring to simple prostitution and the second referring to a religious function.

[112] Tamar is thus guilty of the serious sin described in *T.A.* 7:5 of "not giving heed to the law of God, but to commandments of humans."

despite this slight amelioration, in this section of the *Testament of Judah*
Tamar's role has been reduced to that of an immoral temptress who
causes her father-in-law to succumb to vice yet a second time.

Tamar's conformity to the customs of Judah's former enemies recalls
the patriarch's own impersonation of an Amorite in the war with the
indigenous kings. As noted earlier, Judah and Dan pretend to be
Amorites and enter Gaash undetected in *T.Jud.* 7:2–3. The repeated
motif of Amorite impersonation suggests a connection between war
and moral temptation.[113] But whereas Judah's impersonation facilitates the invasion and conquest of a hostile city, here Tamar's adop-
tion of immoral Amorite ways accomplishes the enticement and defeat
of the patriarch himself.

Again in this section, the *Testament of Judah* employs Judah's encounter with a woman from Genesis 38 to illustrate his characteristic vices,
here specifically drunkenness and lust. The motif of Judah's drunkenness during the sheep shearing season has at least some basis in
scripture, since sheep shearing in the Bible is elsewhere associated
with festivities which include wine drinking. The explanation that
Judah did not recognize Tamar because he had become drunk "at
the waters of Chozeba" (ἐν ὕδασι Χωζηβὰ, *T.Jud.* 12:3) in this passage recalls the note that he had been "at the waters of Chozeba"
(ἐν τοῖς ὕδασι Χωζηβά, *T.Jud.* 6:1) when attacked by the enemy in the
Canaanite war. The reappearance of the same phrase emphasizes
that Judah faces an enemy assault here of at least as great a challenge
as that of his military foes earlier. Significantly, one of the meanings
of the three letter Hebrew verbal root (כזב) that appears in the place
name Kezib (כזיב, Gen 38:5; Χασβι, LXX) is "to deceive," and the
Testament of Judah suggests that meaning of the Hebrew word when

---

[113] When Tamar acts in accordance with an Amorite custom, she aligns herself
with Judah's foreign enemies in war and with his Canaanite wife. More positive
traditional interpretations of her character nevertheless show through this overarching
trajectory of interpretation. We have already seen in the previous sections (*T.Jud.*
10–11) that she and Judah were allied as part of the same extended family (since
she is Aram's daughter from Mesopotamia) against the Canaanite wife for control
of Judah's sons. She remains a virgin through her marriage with Er, and at least for
a whole year after her marriage with Onan. (In *Jub.* 41:27, she is still a virgin when
she meets Judah outside of Enaim.) As just noted, she dresses, not as a prostitute,
but as a bride (*T.Jud.* 12:1), and she is called an "initiate" instead of a "prostitute"
by the local men when they deny knowing her whereabouts (*T.Jud.* 12:9). Later, she
sends Judah the pledge items privately, instead of publicly, although even so the
result is his humiliation (*T.Jud.* 12:5). Tamar's character in the *Testament of Judah* is
therefore ambivalent, and in this regard the testament retains some of the complexity
of Genesis 38 itself and its history of interpretation.

it associates Judah's drunkenness at Chozeba with Tamar's deception of him.[114]

Judah's charge that Tamar intentionally enhanced her feminine beauty to arouse his lust has no basis in the Hebrew text, which simply indicates that she concealed her identity when she "wrapped herself" (וַתִּתְעַלָּף, Gen 38:14) in a veil; however, the Septuagint translates this Hebrew word as "she beautified her face" (ἐκαλλωπίσατο).[115] The *Testament of Judah*, with its reference to Tamar's seductive beauty (τὸ κάλλος αὐτῆς) brought out through her manner of adornment (διὰ τοῦ σχήματος τῆς κοσμήσεως), accentuates the Septuagint's implication that she manipulated her looks in order to heighten Judah's desire.[116] The interpretation of Judah's encounter with Tamar in Genesis 38 as a second example of the patriarch's fornication was no doubt facilitated by the presence of the word "prostitute" in the biblical narrative (זוֹנָה, Gen 38:15; πόρνην, LXX; cf., Gen 38:24; קְדֵשָׁה, Gen 38:21, 22; πόρνη, LXX). The Septuagint's translation of the word "prostitute" (πόρνη) is related to the word "fornication" contained in a subtitle of the *Testament of Judah* that appears in some manuscripts: "Concerning Manliness, Greed, and Fornication (πορνείας)."[117]

Apparently the author of this testament found it too difficult to illustrate explicitly Judah's third vice of greed through the pre-existing narrative in Genesis 38, although the reference to Tamar's bridal array suggests an opulence that would be attractive to this patriarch, judging from his reaction to Bathshua's adornment with gold and pearls (*T.Jud.* 13:5). While the details of Judah's second solitary encounter with a woman during peacetime differ from his first (due at least in part to the influence of the biblical narrative), essentially the *Testament of Judah* presents it as a repetition of his earlier moral defeat.

---

[114] In 1 Samuel 25 and 2 Sam 14:23–29 (as well as in Gen 31:19–21 which lacks the specific reference to wine) the sheep shearing season occasions some form of deception, as it does in Genesis 38 and in the *Testament of Judah*.

[115] Similarly, *Tg.Onq.* Gen 38:14 translates the Hebrew verb וַתִּתְעַלָּף into Aramaic as וְאִיתְקַנַת ("she adorned herself"). In *Jub.* 41:9 as well, Tamar "beautified herself." These translations of the verb are supported by the usage of the root עלף in Cant 5:14, which reads, "his loins are ivory work, adorned (מְעֻלֶּפֶת) with sapphires."

[116] These phrases are from *T.Jud.* 12.3, but earlier in this section as well (*T.Jud.* 12:1), Judah claims that Tamar "adorned herself in bridal array" (κοσμηθεῖσα κόσμῳ νυμφικῷ).

[117] Variations of this subtitle are found in mss b, l, d, and m; the subtitle in ms e also contains the word "fornication." But note that all explicit references to Tamar as a prostitute are eliminated from the version of the story in the *Testament of Judah*, where she becomes a bride.

Judah's encounter with Tamar in the *Testament of Judah* follows the
biblical narrative closely at certain points, but the surface similarities
mask deeper transformations. For example, in a rare instance of
reported dialogue in the testament, Judah relates part of his conversation with Tamar after he turns aside to her (*T.Jud.* 12:4): "I said,
'Let me go into you!' And she said to me, 'What will you give me?'"
The wording of this conversation resembles the opening lines of the
longer biblical dialogue beginning in Gen 38:16. Since Tamar lacks
the constructive purpose that motivates her seduction of Judah in
the biblical narrative, however, she also lacks her biblical cunning
in exacting the pledge that will prove her father-in-law's paternity.
Instead, after Tamar asks what he intends to give her, Judah answers
non-verbally by immediately surrendering to her significant possessions related to his status as king.[118] There is no indication here that
Judah intends these items as a surety for later payment, nor is there
any mention in the short allusion to Hirah's search for the mysterious woman (*T.Jud.* 12:9) of an attempt to retrieve them through the
payment of a kid. Instead, Judah voluntarily surrenders the symbols
of his royal authority to a woman engaged in impure behavior. Even
in this passage, the significance of this transfer of articles is suggested
by a designation of them that differs radically from the one found in
the biblical narrative. According to the Hebrew text of Gen 38:18,
the three items of the pledge include Judah's seal (חתמך), his cord
(ופתילך), and his staff (ומטך). The Septuagint follows the Hebrew fairly
closely in identifying them as his ring (τὸν δακτύλιόν σου), his cord
(τὸν ὁρμίσκον), and his staff (τὴν ῥάβδον). Of the three items in the
Septuagint, the *Testament of Judah* retains only Judah's staff or scepter
(τὴν ῥάβδον μου), replacing the other two with more powerful symbols of royal authority, including his armor (τὴν ζώνην), and, even
more explicitly, his royal diadem (τὸ διάδημα τῆς βασιλείας). The significance of this transfer as a stripping of Judah's royal status is
explicitly confirmed later in his exhortations, when he identifies his
staff as the support of his tribe, his armor as his power, and his
diadem as the glory of his kingship (*T.Jud.* 15:1–3). The *Testament of
Judah* recasts Judah's encounter with Tamar as his abdication of royal

---

[118] In *Jub.* 41:11 as well, Judah, rather than Tamar, suggests the three items,
although in that source they correspond more closely to those listed in the biblical
narrative, and they are clearly designated as a temporary pledge as in Genesis 38.

status among his brothers, even as earlier it portrays his marriage
with a Canaanite in disregard of God and his fathers' commandments as a threat to his claim to kingship as an obedient son.

Not knowing what Tamar has done,[119] Judah's first impulse (apparently upon learning of her pregnancy) is to kill her, as he has killed
those who have previously challenged his dominance, including his
Canaanite wife. The legal context suggested by Judah's biblical command for Tamar's death in Gen 38:24 ("Take her out and let her
be burned") is therefore eliminated in the *Testament of Judah*. It is
replaced by the patriarch's personal desire to assert mastery through
violence so typical of his character in this testament. Following the
order of the biblical narrative, Judah next reports Tamar's return of
the pledge—or rather multiple pledges in this version of the story.[120]
This motif's appearance here is somewhat mechanical, however, since
Judah has unconditionally forfeited the three items earlier in this same
passage. Also, Tamar does not present the items publicly so that
Judah's responsibility becomes obvious to all, including her father-in-
law himself who acknowledges the justice of her claims (Gen 38:25–
26). Rather, Tamar privately sends the pledges to Judah, and the
result is solely his personal humiliation.[121] Once again, the *Testament
of Judah* discards the public, legal tenor of this scene in the biblical
narrative, emphasizing instead the patriarch's emotional reaction.
Instead of proof of Judah's paternity, the pledges are visible signs of
the patriarch's degradation and relinquishment of sovereignty.

In the *Testament of Judah*, unlike in the biblical narrative, the pledge
alone remains insufficient to convince Judah that Tamar's charges

---

[119] In this version of the story, exactly what Tamar had done remains unclear.
The previous line explicitly notes that she conceived, but there is no subsequent
mention of her delivery of twins, so apparently she is not spared because of her role
in carrying on an important lineage. Perhaps what Tamar did was carry out the
Lord's punishment for Judah's boasting and humiliation of his brother.

Note that the wording in this passage contains a variant on an earlier scene
involving Judah's discovery of a woman's secret deeds. In *T.Jud.* 11:3 Judah reveals
that, "knowing what she had done" (that Bathshua had found a Canaanite wife for
Shelah), he cursed her so that she died. Here in *T.Jud.* 12:5 Judah reveals that, "not
knowing what she had done," he wished to kill Tamar.

[120] The Hebrew considers all three items as a single pledge (עֵרָבוֹן), as do the
LXX (τὸν ἀρραβῶνα) and a later line in this passage (*T.Jud.* 12:7), where Judah
considers the possibility that the pledge (τὸν ἀρραβῶνα) may have changed hands.

[121] The themes of privacy and humiliation also appear in connection with Tamar's
presentation of the pledge in *Tg.Neof.* Gen 38:25–26, although this source develops
Tamar in a positive light through the introduction of these themes.

are valid.[122] After privately receiving the pledge items, Judah calls Tamar to question her further. When he hears the secret words that he spoke while sleeping with her in a drunken state, he seems convinced of his culpability—at least momentarily. The secret words may consist of the divine commandments passed orally from patriarch to patriarch in accordance with the understanding in the *Testaments* of pre-Sinaitic revelation, or they may include visions of the future similar to those disclosed at the end of the testaments in this work. These explanations of Judah's secret words to Tamar are supported by his later confession that he also revealed "the commandments of God and the mysteries of Jacob" to his Canaanite wife when drunk (*T.Jud.* 16:4). The repetition of Judah's disclosure of esoteric lore received from worthy male ancestors and God to licentious women emphasizes the grievous nature of his sin.

Within the passage under discussion itself, however, Tamar's revelation of mysteries spoken in bed intrudes upon Judah's more general reflections about the value of the pledge items themselves for conclusive identification. Judah speculates that the pledge might have changed hands from woman to woman, although his speculation incongruously follows Tamar's definitive revelation of the secret words![123] In this part of the *Testament of Judah* the main issue becomes the identity of the woman who seduced the patriarch, not the identity of the man responsible for Tamar's difficult situation. This development corresponds to the general mistrust of women expressed in the *Testaments*.

Judah ultimately refrains from acting on his desire to kill his daughter-in-law when he realizes that "it was from the Lord" (παρὰ κυρίου ἦν, *T.Jud.* 12:6). This assessment paraphrases the traditional reassignment of the prepositional phrase "from me" (ממני) in Judah's biblical evaluation of Tamar in Gen 38:26, "She is more righteous than I" (צדקה ממני), to a divine voice. As indicated in the introduction to this book, this exegetical tradition depicts God's acceptance of responsibility for the events of Genesis 38 when he declares, "From

---

[122] In rabbinic tradition as well, the theme of doubt concerning Tamar's truthfulness appears. In *Exod.Rab.* 30.19, for example, Judah's ancestors and brothers do not believe her charges until Judah confirms them with his confession. In the *Testament of Judah*, by contrast, it is Judah himself who doubts Tamar's charges; therefore, the motif of the patriarch's exemplary public confession is lacking.

[123] If Judah were correct and Tamar had received the items from another woman, the patriarch would still be guilty of promiscuity, but he would be cleared of incest with his daughter-in-law.

Me!"[124] In the context of this testament, however, there is little joy in Judah's acknowledgment of divine intention behind the narrative. His words, "it was from the Lord," suggest that the events of Genesis 38 are his punishment from God. Behind this view may lie an interpretation of Judah's entire declaration, "She is more righteous than I" (צדקה ממני), as God's statement, "[This is] a righteous decree from me." The understanding of events in Genesis 38 as God's punitive intervention in Judah's life echoes the two divine intrusions in the biblical narrative to punish Er and Onan. The biblical motif of divine punishment is transferred to Judah in the *Testament of Judah*, although unlike his sons he escapes death. The theme of punishment is more explicitly developed at the very beginning of Judah's exhortations to his living descendants, immediately following the account of his relations with Tamar:

> 13:1. And now, whatever I command you, listen, children, to your father, and keep all my words, to perform the righteous decrees of the Lord and to obey the commandment of the Lord God. 2. And do not walk after your lusts, nor in the stratagems of your dispositions, in the arrogance of your heart; and do not boast of the works of your youthful strength, for this also is evil in the eyes of the Lord. 3. For when I, too, boasted that in wars no beautiful woman's face had deceived me, and reproved Reuben my brother concerning Bilhah my father's wife, the spirit of envy and fornication arrayed itself in me, until I met with Bathshua the Canaanite and Tamar who was married to my sons. (*T.Jud.* 13:1–3)

In this passage, Judah reveals two previously unreported instances in which he expressed overconfidence in his own strength. During the height of his masculine power in war, Judah brags of his invulnerability against female attractions;[125] he also humiliates his brother Reuben by scolding him for his incestuous relations with Bilhah. Using language that recalls the LORD's negative evaluation of Er and Onan in the biblical narrative, Judah urges his sons to avoid similar arrogant behavior, since it "is evil in the eyes of the Lord" (*T.Jud.* 13:2; cf., Gen 38:7, 10).[126] Because he overestimated his own powers, the

---

[124] This motif is discussed in the following two chapters as well, since it appears (with distinctive functions) in both *Targum Neofiti* and *Genesis Rabba*.

[125] It is unclear whether Judah bragged that he never raped a foreign woman, or whether he declined to take a wife from among the defeated people as described in the law of the captive bride in Deut 21:10–14.

[126] Note that Levi's sons will similarly be prone to arrogance (*T.L.* 14:7–8). By contrast, Joseph refrains from shaming his brothers after he is sold into slavery, even

spirit of envy and fornication plots against him, causing him to commit the very sins to which he considered himself immune, namely
to have sexual relations with a Canaanite woman and with a relative.[127] The depiction of Judah's punishment for arrogance concerning his sexual restraint through his own licentious behavior accords
with the anthropology of the *Testaments*, in which human immorality
separates one from God and cedes control over the soul to the forces
of Beliar.[128] By attributing Judah's immoral behavior in Genesis 38
to demonic forces at work in God's absence, the *Testament of Judah*
explains the strange lack of divine presence throughout most of the
biblical narrative.

Before the conclusion of Judah's autobiography with a note about
his descent to Egypt (*T.Jud.* 12:11–12), the theme of humiliation,
raised first in the testament when Tamar privately presents the pledge
items to Judah, reappears. This theme is developed through a brief
allusion to Judah and Hirah's search for the mysterious woman at
Enaim in Gen 38:20–23 (*T.Jud.* 12:9–10). As noted in the previous
chapter, the biblical episode itself raises the theme of public embarrassment, by indicating that Judah had Hirah abandon the search so
that they wouldn't become ridiculous. The *Testament of Judah* highlights Judah's humiliation by concluding his autobiography with this
biblical episode, which epitomizes his degrading experience in Genesis 38. A consternated Judah reveals that he thought his sexual sin
remained secret, since the inhabitants of the city denied the presence
of a woman at the gate.[129] Judah's preoccupation with reputation
reappears later in his exhortations to his sons as well, and this repetition suggests that for the author of the *Testament of Judah* public opinion

---

when his silence concerning his identity leads to a beating and imprisonment (*T.Jos.*
10:4–11:1; 11:2–16:6; 17:1–18:2), and he thus becomes an exemplar of brotherly love.

In light of the many allusions earlier in the *Testament of Judah* to the statutes
concerning Israel's king in Deut 17:14–20, Judah's sin of arrogance may be an
additional interpretation of a phrase from that deuteronomic passage. In Deut 17:20,
the king is instructed to guard against "acting arrogantly towards his brothers" so
that his kingdom and that of his descendants may endure. In the *Testament of Judah*,
Judah's arrogance leads ultimately to his loss of royal status.

[127] Judah's punishment is in accordance with the precept of measure for measure
(common also in rabbinic literature), expressed in the *Testaments* by Gad's observation,
"For by what things a man transgresses, by the same he is also punished" (*T.G.* 5:10).

[128] Dan expresses a similar idea: "When the soul is disturbed continually, the
Lord departs from it and Beliar rules over it" (*T.D.* 4:7). See also *T.S.* 5:2–3.

[129] The gravity of secret sexual relations, including incest, is developed at length
in Sir 23:16–27.

holds an almost equal importance to one's actual deeds.[130] There is therefore no development in the *Testament of Judah* of the motif of Judah's exemplary public confession, which figures prominently in rabbinic exegesis of Genesis 38. In this document, public knowledge of Judah's sin is utterly humiliating.

To conclude the autobiographical section of the *Testament of Judah* with the image of the patriarch's disgrace suggested by the unsuccessful search scene in Gen 38:20–23, the author of the *Testament of Judah* drastically alters the structure of the biblical narrative. First of all, he awkwardly places the allusion to the search after Tamar's production of the pledge items and Judah's reaction, so that its only narrative function is to express the patriarch's deep shame. In addition, he radically truncates the narrative in Genesis 38 in order to conclude the autobiographical section with an allusion to this scene. He eliminates Judah's positive comparison of Tamar's behavior with his own in Gen 38:26, so that the concept of "righteousness" is never associated with this temptress.[131] An even more fundamental change is his deletion of any reference to the climactic birth of twins in Gen 38:27–30. The curious eclipse of Tamar's active presence in the birth scene in the biblical narrative becomes the elimination of any mention whatsoever of her delivery of twins in the *Testament of Judah*. Just as the author greatly expands the first part of Genesis 38 to portray Judah's defeat at the hands of a woman, so he abbreviates the second part to accomplish the same end.

---

[130] In *T.Jud.* 14:5 there is a second allusion to the public humiliation associated with the search for the woman in Gen 38:20–23. In this passage, Judah points out that he was not ashamed of the multitude in the city when he turned aside to Tamar "before the eyes of all." The phrase "before the eyes of all" (ἐν ὀφθαλμοῖς πάντων) appears to be an interpretation of the Hebrew phrase "the entrance of Enaim" (פתח עינים), which may be translated literally as "opening of eyes," describing where Tamar waited for Judah (Gen. 38:14). Additional references to Judah's humiliation appear elsewhere in the exhortations (*T.Jud.* 14:4, 8; 15:1).

The emphasis on public opinion in this testament accords with the heroic ethos of honor and shame typical of Graeco-Roman culture. For a discussion of this Graeco-Roman code of honor and shame emphasizing heroic military virtues of active domination in men, see John Milbank, *Theology and Social Theory Beyond Secular Reason* (Cambridge, MA: B. Blackwell, 1990).

[131] Immediately after Judah recounts his recognition that he had sexual relations with his daughter-in-law, he exhorts his sons to perform the "righteous decrees" (δικαιώματα) of the Lord (*T.Jud.* 13:1). It may be that the root meaning of the verb "she was righteous" (צדקה, Gen 38:26; δεδικαίωται, LXX) that Judah uses to describe Tamar in the biblical narrative has been displaced in the *Testament of Judah* to Judah's exhortation of his sons to righteous behavior.

In its treatment of the second part of Genesis 38, the *Testament of
Judah* focuses on both the scandal of the biblical narrative and the
theme of kingship implicit in it, but it radically alters the tension-
filled relation between these two elements. Rather than the means
through which royalty emerges, Judah's sexual union with Tamar pre-
cipitates this warrior king's fall from the throne and nearly terminates
his dynastic lineage.[132] The most explicit expression of this reversal
appears in Judah's exhortations to his sons, where the patriarch elaborates on the significance of the items he willingly gives to Tamar:

> 15:2. For even if a man is king when he acts lasciviously, he goes away
> stripped of his kingship, having become the slave of fornication, as I
> myself was stripped. 3. For I gave my staff, that is the support of my
> tribe, and my armor, that is the power, and the diadem, that is the
> glory of my kingship. (*T.Jud.* 15:2–3)

Judah's shameful abdication of kingship also finds an echo in the
testament's final lines, where he instructs his sons concerning his burial:

> 26:2. I die today before your eyes, a hundred and nineteen years old.
> 3. Let no one bury me in expensive raiment, nor embalm my body,
> for this is what those who reign as kings are accustomed to do. (*T.Jud.*
> 26:2–3)

In his final words, the royal son of Jacob humbly declines interment
befitting a king, in keeping with the hard lesson he has learned concerning his own fallibility. The theme of knowledge from Genesis 38
is therefore developed in the *Testament of Judah*, although in the latter
work Judah comes to recognize not Tamar's righteousness but the
limits of human nature, even for the strongest of men—the king.
Whereas in the biblical narrative Judah's increased knowledge contributes to the emergence of the next generation, in the testament it
leads to acts of remorse and contrition and to the patriarch's assumption of the role of teacher for the next generation.[133]

---

[132] In both Genesis 38 and in the *Testament of Judah*, there is a threat to Judah's
lineage, but whereas in the biblical narrative the threat is biological, due to the
failure of Judah's sons to procreate with Tamar, in the testament the threat is moral,
since the king has disobeyed his fathers' and God's commandments and therefore
has lost his claim to royalty. In the biblical narrative Tamar rights the problem of
childlessness through her ruse, whereas in the testament her ruse is one of two
sexual ordeals that the patriarch fails. In the *Testament of Judah*, the crisis of childlessness
is resolved through Judah's repentance and acts of penance and his father's prayers.

[133] See also *T.Jud.* 19:4 for an expression of the self-knowledge that Judah gains
through his experience.

Alternate Ending to Genesis 38

The autobiographical portion of the *Testament of Judah* proper ends with Judah's second disgrace through his association with a woman, but in the exhortations and predictions which follow an alternate ending to the narrative replaces the one found in Genesis 38. In these concluding portions, the story continues with Judah's recognition of his error and his repentance for his sins. As an expression of his penitence, he abstains from meat and wine until his old age and experiences no merriment (*T.Jud.* 15:4; 19:2). In addition, his father Jacob intercedes on his behalf through prayer (*T.Jud.* 19:2).[134] Eventually, through these means Judah receives divine pardon for the sins that he committed in ignorance while under the control of the Prince of Error (*T.Jud.* 19:3–4). Judah is furthermore assured descendants who will inherit the royal leadership over Israel that Jacob and the Lord granted him early in his life because of his obedience (*T.Jud.* 17:6; 19:2–3).[135]

The identity of Judah's royal descendants in the *Testament of Judah* reveals the horror with which the author viewed the story of incest between Judah and Tamar in the second part of Genesis 38. In clear contradiction to the biblical genealogies,[136] these descendants are the offspring of Shelah, Judah's only remaining son in this document.[137] In the *Testament of Judah*, as in the biblical narrative, there is a threat to the continuity of Judah's lineage. But in the testament, this threat stems ultimately from Judah's sins associated with his marriage to the Canaanite woman. When Judah explains that "for the sake of

---

[134] Judah mourns, makes supplication, and ultimately gains divine forgiveness also in *Jub.* 41:23 .

[135] Judah's life, with its elements of sin, repentance, and forgiveness provides a variation on a personal level of the Deuteronomic pattern of corporate sin, exile, and return that is very common in the prophetic predictions in the *Testaments*. Hollander and Marinus de Jonge discuss this recurring pattern in the predictions (*The Testaments: A Commentary*, 51–56).

[136] The discrepancy between *Testament of Judah* and the genealogies in 1 Chr 2:3–3:24 and in Ruth 4:12 and 18–22 concerning the royal lineage raises the question of whether the author of the *Testaments* was familiar with the biblical material and consciously contradicted it, or whether he had no knowledge of it. If the latter were the case, perhaps it would indicate something about the relative unimportance of the Writings at the time of this work's composition.

[137] Shelah also appears as a notable ancestor from Judah's line in 1 Chr 4:21–23, although clearly he is of lesser importance than Perez. This genealogy states that according to ancient records Shelah's offspring settled in the towns of the Shephelah, to the southwest of Adullam, and included craftsmen for the royal house.

money I lost my children" (*T.Jud.* 19:2), he connects the deaths of Er and Onan with the greed that compelled him to marry their mother.[138] When Judah maintains that but for his sincere repentance and the prayers of Jacob "I would have died childless" (*T.Jud.* 19:2), he implies that these religious practices stayed the compassionate and merciful God of his fathers from slaying Shelah as well. The view that Shelah, and not Perez, is Judah's royal descendant may be connected with a reading of the puzzling Hebrew consonantal text of Gen 49:10 as "The scepter shall not depart from Judah, nor the ruler's staff from between his feet, until Shelah comes (עד כי יבא שילה), and to him shall be the obedience of the peoples."[139] For a royal ancestor, the author of the *Testament of Judah* found a son from Judah's intermarriage with an evil Canaanite, who himself marries a Canaanite, preferable to an illegitimate son born of an incestuous relationship with a woman acting in obedience to an immoral Amorite law. The choice between the two potential ancestresses for the royal lineage must have been a difficult one. Clearly, even if Tamar had been chosen, the author of the *Testament of Judah* would never have developed her character as the heroic ancestress of kings.

The story of Judah's moral failure and restoration involving the events in Genesis 38 has implications beyond his death as well, and therefore to disclose the story's ultimate ending, the patriarch describes the future of Israel until the eschatological age. Judah relates that although his offspring are destined to be Israel's kings and therefore hold a status second in importance only to the priestly offspring of Levi (*T.Jud.* 17:6; 21:1–6), they will repeat their ancestor's sins and experience a similar loss of sovereignty (*T.Jud.* 17:2–3; 18:1–6; 21:6–22:2; 23:1–4; cf., *T.D.* 5:7). Like their royal ancestor, they too will repent and experience God's pardon.[140] This pattern of history

---

[138] Similarly, *T.Jud.* 13:4–8, where Barsan shows Judah his daughter's gold and dresses her in gold and pearls, ends with the patriarch's observation, "And the Lord rewarded me according to the disposition of my heart, inasmuch as I had no joy in her children," alluding to Er and Onan's deaths because of their father's greed.

By contrast, the theme of greed is not explicitly developed in the passages depicting Tamar's seduction of Judah, so the connection in *T.Jud.* 19:2 between Judah's love of money and his loss of offspring does not apply to Perez and Zerah. Rather, the twins are entirely excised from the story in this testament.

[139] Shelah's name appears in Genesis 38 without the letter י (שלה), but the puzzling word in Gen 49:10 could be interpreted as a full spelling of his name. The reading (qere) of the consonants שילה in the MT as שִׁילוֹ argues against interpreting this word as Shelah's name.

[140] *T.Jud.* 23:5. Like their father, Judah's sons participate in the common Deuter-

will continue until the appearance of Judah's sinless descendant, who
will judge Israel and the gentiles eternally in righteousness and save
all who call on the Lord.[141] Following his appearance, the patriarchs
will arise to life, Beliar's spirit of deceit will be cast into eternal fire,
and a world characterized by unity, justice, joy, and praise will emerge
(*T.Jud.* 25:1–5). The *Testament of Judah* therefore presents the events
in Genesis 38 as part of a template for the behavior of Israel's fallible kings, until Judah's final descendant breaks the pattern and
inaugurates a new age.

Summary of Genesis 38 in the Testament of Judah

In the literary context of the *Testament of Judah*, the story told in
Genesis 38 is divided and reshaped into two parallel narratives illustrating the seduction and defeat of a successful warrior king. Once
removed from his brothers' company in the heroic wars against the
Canaanites and against Esau and his sons, he becomes vulnerable to
solitary defeat on the moral battlefield of the soul. The two women
of Genesis 38, one a Canaanite and the other a relative, accomplish
this defeat, succeeding where their male counterparts failed. Ultimately,
Judah's defeat stems from his overconfidence in his own strength
and his arrogant treatment of his brother. Judah's temporary loss of
royal status through his association with the women of Genesis 38
teaches him to assess his strengths and weaknesses more realistically.
With new wisdom and humility, Judah is able to counsel his own
descendants about the dangers inherent in the worldly leadership which
they inherit, although he recognizes that his warnings will prove
ineffectual. Instead of a story of royal origins as in the biblical narrative, in the *Testament of Judah* Genesis 38 becomes the story of a
warrior king's moral failures, which will be repeated in history by
Israel's kings until the coming of the sinless royal descendant. It becomes, at the same time, a cautionary tale for the common man
regarding the wiles of women and their power to accomplish the
destruction of even a mighty king.

---

onomic sin, exile, return pattern discussed in Hollander and Marinus de Jonge, *The
Testaments: A Commentary*, 51–56.

   [141] *T.Jud.* 22:2–3; 24:1–6.

SOURCE OF THE STORY OF JUDAH AND TAMAR
IN THE *TESTAMENT OF JUDAH*

As obvious from the discussion above, the *Testament of Judah* often
disregards the details and even the basic structure of Genesis 38 in
its reworking of the biblical narrative. The glaring deviations make
one wonder if the biblical text of Genesis 38 lies behind the work at
all, or if perhaps some "rewritten bible" similar to *Jubilees* serves as
the source from which the narrative allusions are drawn.[142] There
are in fact many extra-biblical motifs shared by the *Testament of Judah*
and *Jubilees*, some of which appear in no other extant sources. These
similarities include 1) the identification of Hirah as Judah's shepherd
(*T.Jud.* 8:1; *Jub.* 41:14); 2) the naming of Judah's Canaanite wife,
even though the name is different in each source (Bathshua in *T.Jud.*
8:2; 10:6; 13:3; 17:1; Betasuel in *Jub.* 34:20; and Bedsuel in *Jub.*
41:7); 3) the specification of Tamar as the daughter of Aram (*T.Jud.*
10:1; *Jub.* 41:1); 4) the revelation that Er never slept with Tamar
because she was not a Canaanite like his mother (*T.Jud.* 10:2–3; *Jub.*
41:2); 5) the portrayal of Judah's sincere desire to give Tamar to
Shelah in marriage (*T.Jud.* 10:6; *Jub.* 41:7); 6) the Canaanite woman's
role in preventing Shelah from marrying Tamar (*T.Jud.* 10:9; 11:3;
Jub. 41:7); 7) Tamar's beautification of herself before meeting Judah
(*T.Jud.* 12:1, 3; *Jub.* 41:9); 8) the transfer of the choice of pledge
items from Tamar to Judah (*T.Jud.* 12:4; *Jub.* 41:11); 9) the clear
identification of Judah's sin with Tamar as incest (*T.Jud.* 13:1; 14:5;
Jub. 41:23); 10) the depiction of Judah's penitence and the motif of
supplication for forgiveness (*T.Jud.* 15:4; 19:2–3; *Jub.* 41:23); 11) the
notice that Judah received divine forgiveness (*T.Jud.* 19:3; *Jub.* 41:25);
and 12) the elimination or radical shortening of the biblical scene
depicting Tamar's delivery of twins (*Jub.* 41:21, which simply notes,
"And after this she bore two children, Perez and Zerah").

A number of the similarities between the *Testament of Judah* and
Jubilees listed above correspond to features of the Septuagint's translation of Genesis 38 into Greek, possibly indicating a common dependence on this translation. As pointed out in the context of previous
discussions, the Septuagint depicts Hirah as Judah's shepherd (ὁ ποιμὴν
αὐτοῦ, Gen 38:12, 20); it gives Judah's Canaanite wife a name, Shua

---

[142] For the concept of the "rewritten bible," see Géza Vermès, *Scripture and Tradition in Judaism: Haggadic Studies*, 2d rev. ed. (Leiden: E. J. Brill, 1973) 10, 95, 229.

(Σαυα, Gen 38:2, 12), although this name differs from the one found in either the *Testament of Judah* or *Jubilees*; and it also explains that Tamar beautified herself to attract Judah (καὶ ἐκαλλωπίσατο, Gen 38:14). In addition, the *Testament of Judah* contains words and phrases that either directly correspond to those found in the Septuagint or paraphrase them. For example, the depiction of Tamar as a bride in *T.Jud.* 12:1–2 may have originated from the Septuagint's translation of the Hebrew description of Tamar as Judah's "daughter-in law" (כלה, Gen 38:11, 16, 24) with the Greek word νύμφη, which may also mean "bride." Similarly, the local men's denial of the presence of an "initiate" (τελισκομένην) at the gates (*T.Jud.* 12:9) draws upon one of the Septuagint's translations of the terms "consecrated woman" (קדשה, τελεσφόρος) and "consecrated man" (קדש, τελισκόμενος) in Deut 23:18. A final example of a more extended type of correspondence is the dialogue between Judah and Tamar in *T.Jud.* 12:4, which resembles the Septuagint's translation of Gen 38:16 to a certain degree.[143]

The *Testament of Judah* may therefore directly employ the Septuagint or some other Greek translation of the biblical narrative, freely paraphrasing it and incorporating additional exegetical traditions current in the larger sphere of Hellenistic Judaism.[144] Some deviations may simply illustrate the common practice in biblical interpretation of slighting the text's plain sense in order to express through it more immediate concerns. In the *Testament of Judah*, motifs and episodes from ancient scripture are recontextualized in Judah's autobiography to portray a religious and ethical anthropology and a concept of kingship unimaginable to the biblical author. Precisely because this testament makes its statement at least in part through the vehicle of scriptural allusion, it buttresses its own understanding of reality with the authority of the canonical writings.

---

[143] *T.Jud.* 12:4 reads καὶ ἐκκλίνας πρὸς αὐτὴν εἶπον· Εἰσέλθω πρός σε. καὶ εἶπέ μοι· Τί μοι δώσεις; This dialogue contains several phrases from the LXX version of Gen 38:16 (corresponding phrases underlined): ἐξέκλινεν δὲ πρὸς αὐτὴν τὴν ὁδὸν καὶ εἶπεν αὐτῇ Ἐασόν με εἰσελθεῖν πρὸς σέ· οὐ γὰρ ἔγνω ὅτι ἡ νύμφη αὐτοῦ ἐστιν. ἡ δὲ εἶπεν Τί μοι δώσεις, ἐὰν εἰσέλθῃς πρός με;

Note also that one manuscript family (mss c, h, i, j) entirely replaces *T.Jud.* 12: 6–10 with a long biblical quotation (LXX Gen 38:20, 24–30).

[144] Marinus de Jonge explores the correspondence between the *Testament of Issachar* and the LXX in *The Testaments: A Study*, 78, 118.

Of course, similarities between the *Testament of Judah* and the LXX do not rule out the possibility that the former relied on an intermediary source that employed the LXX as its base.

CENTRAL THEMES IN
THE *TESTAMENTS OF THE TWELVE PATRIARCHS*
AND THE INTERPRETATION OF GENESIS 38

So far, I have limited the discussion primarily to the internal dynamics of the *Testament of Judah*, especially to how its version of Genesis 38 functions within this context. But because the *Testament of Judah* appears as part of a much larger work, it is important to consider how its employment of Genesis 38 corresponds with the thematic perspectives of the *Testaments of the Twelve Patriarchs* as a whole. Themes emphasized throughout the *Testaments* reveal the perspectives and central concerns of the community behind this work, and thereby indicate why Genesis 38 received its distinctive form and function within the *Testament of Judah*. In particular, the religious and ethical anthropology and the concept of kingship expressed by the *Testaments* bear upon the interpretation of Genesis 38 in the *Testament of Judah*.

Religious and Ethical Anthropology

According to the *Testaments*, each individual is the locus of a struggle between forces of good and evil. This struggle is complex, having cosmic, psychological, and ethical dimensions. Since God and his angels contend with Beliar and his spirits for control of the soul, the good person's goal is to align himself with the former and reject the latter through conscious choice.[145] The goal of becoming single-mindedly aligned with God is complicated, however, by the construction of human nature itself, which includes a number of spirits given by Beliar at creation.[146] The surest recourse one has, therefore, is

---

[145] In *T.D.* 4:7–5:3 either the Lord or Beliar rules over the soul, depending on the attitudes and actions of the individual. See also *T.Jud.* 20:1–5, which explains that the spirit of the mind's understanding may turn to either the spirit of truth or the spirit of deceit; *T.N.* 3:1, which advises that one hold fast to the will of God and cast away the will of the devil; and *T.A.* 1:2–9, which describes the two paths of good and evil.

[146] In *T.R.* 2:1–3:8 the spirits given by Beliar include very basic components of human existence, including life, sight, hearing, smell, speech, taste, procreation and intercourse, and sleep. All of these spirits are mingled with spirits of deceit, including impurity, desire, fighting, flattery, arrogance, lying, and unrighteousness. According to this passage, there are obstructions within each person's constitution for choosing what is good.

The goal of becoming single-mindedly aligned with God is further complicated by the fact that in the *Testaments* one's vision of good and evil is often distorted by spirits and passions. See, for example, *T.Jud.* 19:4, where Judah is blinded by the

obedience to the commandments of God and the fathers, although other practices, including the cultivation of moral attitudes and virtues, hard work and self-denial, and prayer and fasting are also valuable.[147]

This brief summary of the religious and ethical anthropology of the *Testaments* indicates the centrality of conflicting opposites—opposites including God and Beliar, spirits of truth and deceit, light and darkness, and good and evil. In light of the importance of moral dichotomies in this work, yet another basic dichotomy of human existence takes on a distinctive valence. This basic dichotomy consists of the natural occurrence of two genders, male and female. According to the anthropology underlying this work, women are naturally weaker than men,[148] and they are therefore far more susceptible to invasion by the demonic forces of Beliar (*T.R.* 4:6–7). In the *Testaments* fornication (πορνεία) is the most typical manifestation of domination by evil spirits.[149] As Reuben explains, "if fornication does not overpower the mind, also Beliar will not overpower you" (*T.R.* 4:11). Because of their weakness, women are by their very nature more prone to fornication than men. Their proclivity towards amoral sexual behavior threatens men as well, since they try to engage the opposite sex in their sinful activities. Reuben summarizes a lesson about the danger of women that he learned from an angel: "women are overcome by the spirit of fornication more than man, and in their heart they scheme

---

prince of deceit himself. Interestingly then, the theme of sight which figures so prominently in Genesis 38 in its biblical version reappears in this work, although it is given a moral valence, whereby sight becomes a metaphor for the ability to discern correct moral decisions and blindness becomes a metaphor for the lack of this ability. So, whereas Judah "sees" the Canaanite woman and Tamar and consequently has sexual relations with them in Genesis 38, in the *Testament of Judah* the patriarch is "blind" to the truth in his encounters with them and therefore has sexual relations with them.

In its interest in the psychological mechanisms that contribute to ethical choice, the *Testaments* is reminiscent of Stoic philosophy. See Kee, "Ethical Dimensions of the *Testaments*," 259–70.

[147] The anthropology of the *Testaments* is neither systematic nor consistent. For further discussion, see Hollander and Marinus de Jonge, *The Testaments: A Commentary*, 41–50. For a comparison between the anthropology and ethics of the *Testaments* and the literature from Qumran, see Collins, "Testaments," 340–41. For the ascetic ideal underlying this work, see S. D. Fraade, "Ascetical Aspects of Ancient Judaism," in *Jewish Spirituality from the Bible to the Middle Ages*, ed. A. Green, vol. 13 of *World Spirituality* (New York: Crossroads, 1986) 253–88. See also Eppel, *Le Piétisme juif.*

[148] This view is a common one in Greek thought, articulated systematically, for example, by Aristotle *Politics.*

[149] The emphasis on chastity and prevention of fornication is discussed in Eppel, *Le Piétisme juif,* 154–57.

168   CHAPTER TWO

against men" (*T.R.* 5:3). Contact between men and women, especially of an illicit sexual nature, thus offers a vulnerable point of entry for defiling passions into the male soul. It might be said that in the battle between good and evil depicted in the *Testaments*, men and women frequently fight on opposite sides.[150] While the central ethos of this work is summarized in the recurrent injunctions to love God and one's neighbor,[151] this "neighbor" is always another man, usually a brother, in positive examples of cooperation and consideration.[152] There appears to be a negative corollary to the positive emphasis on brotherly love, consisting of a basic distrust and even abhorrence of women and the contagion of passions they arouse.[153]

The *Testaments* emphasizes the dangers of fornication through a variety of means. The dominant theme of the opening testament, the *Testament of Reuben*, is fornication, and this introduction establishes the tone for the remainder of the work. In addition, repeated warnings against promiscuity and fornication throughout the various testaments attest to this work's preoccupation with the dangers of illicit sexuality. While one might expect warnings concerning fornication in the *Testament of Reuben*, the *Testament of Judah*, and the *Testament*

---

[150] The application of war terminology to the relations between the sexes is sometimes quite explicit. For example, when Judah claims that the spirit of envy and fornication "arrayed" (παρετάξατο) itself in him, until he "encountered" (συνέπεσα) the Canaanite woman and his daughter-in-law Tamar (*T.Jud.* 13:3), he employs verbs commonly used to describe military maneuvers.

[151] Commandments to love both God and one's neighbor are found in *T.I.* 5:2; 7:6; *T.D.* 5:3; *T.B.* 3:3–5.

[152] We have seen Judah's cooperation with his brothers in war in *T.Jud.* 4–7, 9. Zebulun shows compassion for his brother Joseph when his other brothers first threaten to kill him and then sell him into slavery (*T.I.* 1:4–5:5). Joseph also serves as a positive exemplar of consideration for one's neighbor, when he refuses to shame his brothers by revealing that they sold him into slavery (*T.Jos.* 11:2–15:7). He even refuses to shame a dishonest Egyptian eunuch (*T.Jos.* 16:1–6).

[153] Commentators have lauded the positive emphasis on brotherly love, but do not seem to notice its negative corollary. For example, Charles praises this work, "so noble in its ethical side" (*Greek Versions of the Testaments*, ix). Travers is even more generous with his accolades. He notes that the greater part of the *Testaments* is "purely ethical, and that of a very high order, so much so that it stands out from and above all the other non-canonical books" (*Talmud and Apocrypha*, 233). Travers also states that this "noble book" (234) reaches "new ethical heights" (243), and that the author remains "unequaled in purity and depth of his ethical teaching. We reverently salute him and pass on" (243).

It should be noted that the misogyny expressed in the *Testaments* is not unique for its time, and that similar deprecations and expressions of mistrust of women appear in other Hellenistic Jewish works, including Ecclesiastes, Sirach, and the Wisdom of Solomon.

of Joseph, since they deal with biblical narratives containing seductions, the appearance of similar warnings in other testaments without such narratives illustrates the perceived gravity of the threat. For example, when in the *Testament of Levi* Isaac teaches Levi about "the law of priesthood," the opening words of his instruction are "Beware, child, of the spirit of fornication, for this will persist and will certainly defile the holy things by your seed" (*T.L.* 9:9). In the *Testament of Simeon*, where the dominant themes are envy and jealousy, Simeon nevertheless warns his sons, "beware of committing fornication, for fornication is the mother of all evils, separating from God and bringing near to Beliar" (*T.S.* 5:3).[154] In the final testament, the *Testament of Benjamin*, this patriarch concludes his exhortations with a discussion of the proper attitude of men towards women:

> 8:2. He who has a pure mind in love does not look at a woman for the purpose of fornication, for he has no defilement in his heart, because the spirit of God rests in him. 3. For as the sun is not defiled though in contact with manure and mud, but rather dries up both and drives away the stench, so also the pure mind, though constrained by the defilements of the earth, is not itself defiled, but rather edifies. (*T.B.* 8:2-3)

This passage brings the exhortations within the *Testaments* to closure by reiterating the opening theme of fornication in the *Testament of Reuben*. It accomplishes this closure through a telling metaphor that likens the man with pure love in his heart to the sun and the woman he sees to manure and mud that he is able to denature.

Yet another means through which the *Testaments* emphasizes the dangers of fornication is its portrayal of the downfall of Israel's tribes and institutions through this vice in prophetic passages containing a Deuteronomic pattern involving sin, exile, and return. Fornication even leads to the downfall of several tribes whose eponymous ancestors are not directly implicated in this vice in the narrative sections of the *Testaments*. These tribes include Simeon (*T.S.* 5:4), Issachar (*T.I.* 6:1), Dan (*T.D.* 5:5–6), and Benjamin (*T.B.* 9:1). Fornication is also the cause of the predicted degradation of the priesthood, because Levi's descendants will "pollute married women, defile virgins of Jerusalem, be joined with prostitutes and adulteresses, take as wives

---

[154] The *Testament of Judah* illustrates this precept by associating Judah's sexual immorality with other vices, including greed, drunkenness, and disobedience to his fathers' and God's commandments.

daughters of the Gentiles, purifying them with an unlawful purification" so that their union "will be like Sodom and Gomorrah in ungodliness" (*T.L.* 14:6; cf., *T.D.* 5:6). At least in part because of the lascivious behavior of Levi's sons, "the temple which the Lord will choose will be desolate in uncleanness" (*T.L.* 15:1).[155] As previously noted, fornication is also a major cause of the downfall of the institution of Israel's kingship, because Judah's descendants will be prone to this vice, as was their ancestor.[156]

Ironically, in this work that ostensibly endeavors to suppress immoral sexuality, there is a florid development of biblical stories containing irregular sexual encounters, obsessive in its detail. We have already observed this type of development of Genesis 38 in the *Testament of Judah*. The brief biblical report of Reuben's incest with Bilhah is similarly expanded in the *Testament of Reuben*. Gen 35:22 itself simply notes that "while Israel dwelt in that land Reuben went and lay with Bilhah his father's concubine; and Israel heard of it." By contrast, in the *Testament of Reuben* when the patriarch warns his sons about the danger of a woman's beauty, he discloses his voyeurism and consuming lust, culminating in his rape of his drunken step-mother:

> 3:11. For if I had not seen Bilhah bathing in a sheltered place, I would not have fallen into the great lawlessness. 12. For my mind, conceiving the female nakedness, did not let me to sleep until I had done the abomination. 13. For while Jacob our father was absent [visiting] Isaac his father and we were in Gader, near to Ephratah, house of Bethlehem, Bilhah was drunk and sleeping, lying uncovered in her bedroom. 14 And I, having entered and seen her nakedness, I did the impiety, and leaving her sleeping I went out. 15. And immediately an angel of God revealed my impiety to my father Jacob, and when he came he mourned over me, never touching her again. (*T.R.* 3:11–15)[157]

In this version of the story, Bilhah's passivity and complete lack of consciousness contrasts markedly with Reuben's compulsive wakefulness until he commits the shameful sexual act.[158] Yet, Reuben blames his

---

[155] In *T.Jud.* 23:1–5, the burning of the temple is connected with Judah's sins, including immoral sexual practices.

[156] *T.Jud.* 17:1–3; 18:1–2; 23:1–4.

[157] The motif of the bathing woman in *T.R.* 3:11, associated with Bathsheba (2 Sam 11:2) in the biblical corpus and Susanna (Susanna 15–21) in the Hellenistic period, is also incorporated into the story of Reuben and Bilhah in *Jub.* 33:2.

[158] In this passage, Jacob learns of his son's action only through an angel's revelation, since Bilhah sleeps through the whole episode. By contrast, in *Jub.* 33:3–7, although Bilhah is sleeping when Reuben approaches her, she suddenly wakes to find him in her bed and later tells Jacob what happened.

step-mother, and women in general, for inciting male sexual excesses. He describes their wiles in graphic detail:

> 5:1. Evil are women, my children, because, having no authority nor strength over man, they use wiles, alluring him to them by appearances. 2. And the one whom she cannot defeat by strength, him she overcomes by guile. 3. For also concerning them the angel of God informed me, and he taught me that women are overcome by the spirit of fornication more than man, and in their heart they scheme against men, and by their adornment they deceive first their minds, and by their glance they spread the venom, and then they capture them by the act, 4. for a woman cannot force a man. 5. Flee, therefore, fornication my children, and order your wives and daughters, so that they do not adorn their heads and faces, because every woman who uses these wiles has been reserved for eternal punishment. 6. For thus they bewitched the Watchers before the flood: As [the Watchers] looked at them continually, they were filled with lust for one another, and they conceived the act in their mind, and they changed into human form, and when [the women] were together with their husbands, they appeared to them. 7. And [the women], lusting in their mind after their phantasms, bore giants, for the Watchers appeared to them as reaching unto heaven. 6:1. Beware, therefore, of fornication, and if you wish to be pure in mind, guard your senses from every female. 2. And command the woman likewise not to associate with men, so that they, too, may be pure in mind, 3. for continuous meetings, even though the impiety is not committed, are to them an incurable disease and to us an eternal reproach of Beliar. (*T.R.* 5:1–6:3)[159]

As this passage makes clear, the *Testament of Reuben* employs the story of Reuben and Bilhah as a prelude to warnings concerning the dangers of feminine beauty and adornment, the weakness of women to the deceptions of Beliar, and the advisability of maintaining a safe distance from them.[160] It also emphasizes the enormity of feminine evil by claiming that the flood was caused by their fornication. This passage, appearing in the very first testament of the *Testaments* in association with a woman who plays no active role in seducing Reuben, assures that the active seductions of Judah by the Canaanite princess and Tamar will be read in an extremely negative light. For example, just the mention of Bathshua's adornment with gold and pearls or of Tamar's beautification of herself in the *Testament of Judah*

---

[159] Other warnings against women's machinations in this testament may be found in *T.R.* 3:10; 4:1, 6–11.

[160] Examples in rabbinic literature of exhortations to avoid women include *b. Ber.* 61a and *b. ʿAbod.Zar.* 20a.

is enough to associate them with all the charges contained in the
opening testament. The *Testament of Reuben* also introduces the theme
of loss of status through association with a woman, in this case
Reuben's loss of status as first-born through incest with Bilhah, at
the beginning of the work. It thus anticipates Judah's loss of royal
status through the two women of Genesis 38.

If even the passive Bilhah becomes a temptress in the *Testaments*,
an actual biblical temptress has a predictable fate in this work. In
the *Testament of Joseph*, the wiles and seductions of the Egyptian woman
are multiplied and intensified,[161] and her association with Beliar is
explicitly noted (*T.Jos.* 7:4, 8). These developments accentuate Joseph's
patient resistance to her seductions[162] and present him as a positive
counter-example to Reuben and Judah who fall to similar temptations. For his righteousness, Joseph is "enthroned with kings" (*T.L.*
13:9),[163] in contrast to Judah, who loses the kingship through his
associations with women.[164]

Issachar, the exemplar of the simple and innocent life, similarly
illustrates proper male resistance to women. This patriarch "did not
think of pleasure with a woman" and only took a wife relatively late
in life, when he was thirty years old (*T.I.* 3:5; cf., 4:4). Levi also
waited to select a chaste wife until he was twenty-eight years old
(*T.L.* 11:1). These two figures appear to express a cultural ideal concerning relations between the sexes, but in Issachar's case, his wife is
never mentioned again, and in Levi's case, the only other mention

---

[161] *T.Jos.* 2:2; 3:1–9.5; cf., *T.R.* 4:8–10. Many of the embellishments of Joseph's
encounter with Potiphar's wife bear the influence of the Greek Phaedra legend, as
discussed by Braun, *History and Romance*, 44–104.

[162] He even treats her kindly and prays for her to be freed from the power of
Beliar (*T.Jos.* 3:10; 7:4–8; 9:4).

[163] For a more general assertion that the good person wears a crown, see *T.B.* 4:1
(cf., *T.D.* 5:13).

[164] Joseph expresses most fully the ethical ideal of the *Testaments*. See George
Nickelsburg, Jr., ed., *Studies on the Testament of Joseph*, SBL Septuagint and Cognate
Studies 5 (Missoula, MT: Scholars Press, 1975); H. Dixon Slingerland, "The *Testament of Joseph*: a Redactional Study," *JBL* 96 (1977) 507–16; Hollander, *Joseph as an
Ethical Model*; and Jean Daniel Dubois, "Joseph et la vertu dans le judaïsme hellénistique et le christianisme ancien," *Foi Vie* (1987) 25–33. Joseph's two virtues, patient
endurance illustrated by his resistance to the Egyptian woman and silent humility
illustrated by his refusal to disclose his identity to the Egyptians and thereby shame
his brothers, contrast with Judah's vices when he yields to the Canaanite woman
and Tamar and when he shames his brothers through boasting and through scolding Reuben. Ironically, as a reward for his righteousness, Joseph is wedded to the
daughter of a prominent foreigner who brings into the marriage plenteous gold
(*T.Jos.* 18:3)—thus resembling Judah's wicked wife Bathshua!

of his wife Melcha entails her delivery of children. This silence implies that while marriage is an antidote for fornication (*T.L.* 9:9–10), and while children are a greatly desired blessing,[165] even within the context of marriage sexual relations remain problematic, or at least distracting. In the *Testament of Naphtali*, for example, this patriarch advocates periods of abstinence within marriage for prayer (*T.N.* 8:8). Another illustration of this ambivalence towards sexual activity even within marriage occurs in connection with the biblical story about Rachel's bargaining with Leah for the mandrakes that Reuben picked (Gen 30:14–24). In the version of this story in the *Testament of Issachar* (*T.I.* 1:2–2:5), God rewards Rachel with two sons because she surrenders her marital rights to Leah for two nights in exchange for two mandrakes that she offers God (*T.I.* 2:5). Rachel's chastity demonstrates that she was not interested in intercourse with Jacob for pleasure, but only for procreation (*T.I.* 2:3). An angel announces the consequences of her abstinence to Jacob: "Two children will Rachel bear, because she has despised intercourse with a man and has chosen continence" (*T.I.* 2:1). By contrast, Leah is deprived of the two sons that she would have otherwise borne because she paid two apples (as the mandrakes are interpreted in this testament) in order to have intercourse with her husband (*T.I.* 2:2). Later, Rachel conceives Benjamin after a period of praying and fasting (*T.B.* 1:4).[166] This testament thus proposes that children arise from piety and ascetic abstinence rather than sexual intercourse. A similar dynamic may be operative in the *Testament of Judah*, where the sexually active Tamar never gives birth to sons, and where Judah resolves his crisis of childlessness through repentance, humiliation, and prayer.

Given the misogynistic anthropology of the *Testaments*, any reading of Judah's two encounters with women in Genesis 38 other than as his moral downfall would have been impossible. In the *Testament of Judah*, women conquer the strong king, who previously prevailed against all enemies. The broader implication of this testament is that if even a warrior king can be conquered by women, the general

---

[165] Judah's consternation that two of his sons died childless (*T.Jud.* 8:3) and that he himself almost died childless as well (*T.Jud.* 19:2) illustrates the value placed on children.

[166] But notice that even though Rachel is developed as a model of feminine chastity in association with her delivery of Joseph and Benjamin, she is later implicated in the sexual deception generally associated with women, when she tricks her husband into sleeping with her maid (*T.N.* 1:6).

male readers of the *Testaments* must doubly protect themselves from
the female sex—although perhaps the hope that precautions might
be effective is a delusion. Judah expresses this pessimistic view in his
exhortations to his sons, claiming that his knowledge of women's
pernicious power stems from divine revelation:

> 15:5. And the angel of God showed me that women have eternal
> dominion over both king and beggar; 6. and from the king they take
> away his glory, and from the valiant man his power, and from the
> beggar even that little which supports [him] in poverty. (*T.Jud.* 15:5–6)

Israel's Kingship

Earlier in this chapter, I showed how the *Testament of Judah* accords
Judah a unique status among his brothers, since through his obedience to his father and to the divine commandments he becomes Israel's
first king. The recognition of Judah's special status is not limited to
this testament, but occurs in several of the other testaments as well,
generally in the context of predictions concerning Israel's future. There
the patriarchs encourage their offspring to give their allegiance to
this patriarch and his descendants as Israel's kings, as well as to Levi
and his descendants as Israel's priests.[167] The precise relationship
between Judah and Levi is not entirely consistent within the *Testaments*, although generally Levi is superior to Judah. Some testaments
depict the final savior figure as coming from both tribes, although
others depict him as coming from either Levi or Judah.[168] In any
event these two patriarchs have a unique status in Israel's history
and redemption as the ancestors of royal and priestly tribes.[169]

In light of the special attention given to Judah as a royal figure in
the *Testaments*, the limited positive development of the theme of kingship in the *Testament of Judah* itself is remarkable. While Judah's courage, physical strength, and military competence are stressed in the

---

[167] Examples of statements stressing the importance of Judah and Levi for Israel's
future include *T.R.* 6:5–8, 10–12; *T.S.* 7:1–2; *T.I.* 5:7–8; *T.D.* 5:4–10; *T.N.* 8:2–3;
T.G. 8:1; and *T.Jos.* 19:6.

[168] *T.S.* 7:1–2; *T.L.* 2:11; *T.D.* 5:10; *T.N.* 8:2; *T.G.* 8:1; and *T.Jos.* 19:6 all depict
the final savior from both Levi and Judah. For an example of the final savior from
Levi, see *T.L.* 18:10–12, and from Judah, see *T.L.* 8:14 and *T.Jud.* 24:1–6.

[169] The stress placed on Levi and Judah is similar to the importance placed on
the anointed king and priest in Zech 4:14 and on the messiahs of Aaron and Israel
in the Qumran literature. Similarly, *Jub.* 31:5 singles Levi and Judah out for a
special blessing from Jacob.

opening sections of this testament, other responsibilities associated with kingship that one might expect, for example the dispensation of justice and the administration of a kingdom, are curiously absent. Instead of focusing on positive functions such as these, the *Testament of Judah* critiques the corruptions to which worldly leaders are vulnerable. Lust, drunkenness, and greed are the specific vices that it associates with the archetypal royal figure and his descendants. Hubris is an even more fundamental problem for the worldly ruler, since a false sense of invincibility and superiority may lead to further sins, including boasting and shaming one's brother. Even Judah's military success, which initially appears to be a positive aspect of kingship in the *Testament of Judah*, becomes qualified later in an exhortation concerning drunkenness. At the very conclusion of a list of problems that drinking causes, Judah notes that "wine is a cause also of war and confusion" (*T.Jud.* 16:5).[170] This statement implies that even Judah's valorous actions in battle may have been somehow connected with one of his greatest faults. In any event, the *Testament of Judah* critiques the idea that military leadership qualifies one for kingship by depicting the moral downfall of the mighty warrior king. Judah's graphic predictions of his descendants' similar moral failings (*T.Jud.* 17:2–3; 18:1; 21:6–22:2; 23:1–4) confirm that the *Testament of Judah* holds a very low opinion of earthly kingship in general. There is no praise for any of Israel's historical kings in the *Testament of Judah*, nor elsewhere in the *Testaments*. Not even David, Hezekiah, or Josiah receive mention in this work.[171] The one absolutely positive result of Judah's royal status is that, at least according to some passages, the sinless king will ultimately arise from his lineage and rule in justice.[172]

Several passages in the *Testaments* qualify the importance of kingship represented by Judah and his lineage in yet another way, by ranking this tribe second after Levi and his lineage, who represent priesthood.[173] The prominence of Levi over Judah appears in a number

---

[170] In the prophetic portion of the testament, the sinful reigns of Judah's descendants are also marked by continuous wars, leading to the end of the dynasty among foreign nations (*T.Jud.* 21:1).

[171] In its negative attitude towards historical kingship, this work echoes the biblical critique of kingship in 1 Sam 8:11–18.

[172] See for example *T.Jud.* 24. It is only in association with this figure, who at least in the latest recension of the work is equated with Christ, that any positive function of kingship besides military prowess is mentioned. For example, *T.Jud.* 24:6 portrays Judah's sinless descendant dispensing righteous judgment.

[173] Note that in *T.R.* 6:10–12 Levi is associated with kingship as well.

of testaments, but perhaps it is the most striking when it appears in
the *Testament of Judah* itself:

> 21:1. And now, children, love Levi, so that you may endure, and do not
> exalt yourselves against him, so that you may not be utterly destroyed.
> 2. For to me the Lord gave the kingship and to him the priesthood,
> and he set the kingship beneath the priesthood. 3. To me he gave the
> things upon the earth, to him the things in the heavens. 4. As heaven
> is higher than the earth, so is the priesthood of God higher than the
> kingship on earth, unless it falls away from the Lord through sin and
> is dominated by the earthly kingship. 5. For also the Lord chose him
> rather than you to draw near to him and to eat of his table, even the
> first fruits, the choice things of the sons of Israel. (*T.Jud.* 21:1–5)

Besides exhortations like the one above, the relative ranking of Levi
over Judah is graphically depicted in contrasting events that occur in
the *Testament of Levi* and the *Testament of Judah*.[174] An obvious example
consists of the fact that Levi marries an appropriate wife, and they
have children who live and thrive (*T.L.* 9:10; 11:1). In this important
area Levi is superior to Judah, who first marries an evil Canaanite
woman and begets disobedient sons that perish, and then enters an
incestuous and unproductive sexual relationship with Tamar, who
conceives but apparently never gives birth. The same dynamic of
rank is operative in the comparison implicit between Levi's two visions of the heavenly realms and of the future (*T.L.* 2:3–6:2; 8:1–19)
and Judah's blindness through lust, greed, and wine which leads to
his defeat by seductive women (*T.Jud.* 11:1; 13:6). Another contrast
arises when Levi practices appropriate restraint and does not reveal
his visions to his family (*T.L.* 6:2; 8:18–19), while Judah drunkenly
discloses mysteries and divine commandments to impure women
(*T.Jud.* 12:6; 16:4). Perhaps most striking is a contrast involving the
treatment of the clothing that identifies the function of each of these
patriarchs in Israel's future. In Levi's second vision, seven angels invest
him with priestly apparel:

> 8:2. And I saw seven men in white raiment, saying to me, "Arise, put
> on the robe of priesthood and the crown of righteousness and the

---

[174] See also *T.N.* 5:3–4, which depicts Levi capturing the sun and Judah capturing the moon, implying a hierarchy between the two patriarchs. Another expression
of Levi's superiority over Judah may be found in *T.Jud.* 25:1–2.

In Levi's predictions of the future, he notes that his descendants will pervert their
essential nature through their sins, suffer degradation, and ultimately be replaced by
a new priesthood established by the Lord (*T.L.* 14:1–18:14).

breastplate of understanding and the garment of truth and the plate of faith and the turban of sign[s] and the ephod of prophecy." 3. And each of them carried one of these things and put them on me, and said, "From now on become a priest of the Lord, you and your seed forever." (*T.L.* 8:2–3)[175]

In marked contrast, Judah divests himself of his royal apparel upon seeing a beautiful woman in order to engage her sexually. Although I have already cited short sections of the following passage in earlier discussions, Judah's full assessment of his encounter with Tamar merits repeating in this context:

> 15:1. He who fornicates does not perceive when he suffers loss, and he is not ashamed when dishonored. 2. For even if a man is king when he acts lasciviously, he goes away stripped of his kingship, having become the slave of fornication, as I myself was stripped. 3. For I gave my staff, that is the support of my tribe, and my armor, that is the power, and the diadem, that is the glory of my kingship. 4. And repenting these things I did not take wine or meat until my old age, nor did I see any merriment. 5. And the angel of God showed me that women have eternal dominion over both king and beggar; 6. and from the king they take away his glory, and from the valiant man his power, and from the beggar even that little which supports [him] in poverty. (*T.Jud.* 15:1–6)[176]

Through his surrender of the symbols of kingship in fornication, Judah loses his royalty and becomes enslaved to a woman. Through these contrasts, which in the case of the *Testament of Judah* involve allusions to Genesis 38, the *Testaments* portrays and justifies the inferior rank of Judah to Levi in Israel's future.

JUDAH AND HERACLES COMPARED: TWO HELLENISTIC "STRONG HEROES"

The discussion above described how the author of the *Testament of Judah* employs the figure of Judah and narrative elements from Genesis 38 to articulate the anthropological, religious, and historical

---

[175] This passage continues with a further description of the angels' investiture and commissioning of Levi as Israel's priest (*T.L.* 8:4–17). Compare this passage from the *Testament of Levi* with Exod 28:3–43, which describes the holy garments designed for Aaron and his sons, and with Eph 6:13, which contains an allegorical explanation of armor in spiritual terms.

[176] See also *T.Jud.* 12:4.

perspectives of a particular variety of Hellenistic Judaism. Additional resonances of Judah's character and his role in Genesis 38 in this testament may be amplified by broadening the focus of discussion from the immediate documentary context of the *Testaments of the Twelve Patriarchs* to the larger context of the Hellenistic cultural sphere within which this work emerged. The means employed to do so entail a close comparison between Judah and a legendary figure of the same basic type from Greek literature, designated here as the "strong hero" and defined as a male character known both for his exceptional physical strength and for his correspondingly large physical appetites.

Heracles, one of the most popular and enduring characters from Greek legend and literature, fits this definition of the strong hero and thereby emerges as a promising candidate for comparison with Judah in the *Testament of Judah*.[177] Indeed, the general typological correspondence between the Greek hero and the Jewish hero is strengthened by the fact that their legendary biographies hold a number of specific narrative motifs in common and raise several identical themes. Perhaps as striking, Heracles frequently functions as an exemplary figure in Greek philosophical and moral writings on subjects similar to those addressed in the *Testament of Judah*, including the nature of kingship, the potentialities and limitations of human existence, and the definition of the virtuous life. The narrative, thematic, and functional correspondences between these two strong heroes therefore suggest that a careful comparison might highlight points of both interface and disjunction between the community reflected in the *Testaments* and the surrounding Hellenistic culture. The similarities and differences between Judah and Heracles and the values these two heroes exemplify may offer insight into some of the complex negotiations involved in maintaining Jewish cultural identity within a dominant Greek cultural sphere. More specifically for present purposes, this comparison may further intimate why the *Testaments* interprets

---

[177] The popularity and endurance of Heracles in literature from the time of Homer through the Hellenistic period implies that his life and character were in some way paradigmatic for the Greeks and those who followed in their cultural and literary wake. Because of this paradigmatic quality, Heracles may be employed as a representative of some of the literary patterns and cultural values typical of the Hellenistic world within which the *Testament of Judah* emerged. For a discussion of the multifaceted depictions of the character of Heracles in Greek and Roman literature, as well as in literature from later periods of western civilization, see G. Karl Galinsky, *The Herakles Theme: The Adaptations of the Hero in Literature from Homer to the Twentieth Century* (Oxford: Basil Blackwell, 1972).

Genesis 38 as it does and may reveal nuances of the revised story of Judah and Tamar within Hellenistic Judaism that would otherwise be lost on modern readers.[178]

In surveying some of the common narrative motifs, themes, and functions associated with the two strong heroes in the following discussion, it will be difficult to avoid speculating about the possible influence of traditions concerning Heracles on the development of Judah's character and life in the *Testament of Judah*.[179] But since the points of correspondence between the two heroes are sometimes inexact, it would be unwise to argue for direct dependence of the portrayal of Judah in the *Testament of Judah* on any single literary depiction of Heracles.[180] Putting the difficult question of literary dependence aside, one may still imagine that in the Hellenistic world readers would have inevitably understood the figure of Judah in the *Testament of Judah* as a parallel to Heracles because of the many similarities between their stories, the common themes that these stories raise, and the similar employment of these figures in larger cultural discussions. The natural association between these two heroes within a Hellenistic cultural context would highlight certain aspects of the figure of Judah, his role in the events of Genesis 38, and the statement made through the example of his life in the *Testament of Judah*. My primary goal in the following comparison of strong heroes is therefore not to identify areas of dependence of the figure of Judah on a Greek prototype such as Heracles, although I do not entirely rule out the possibility of this type of cultural borrowing. It is rather

---

[178] For these reasons, a comparison between Judah and Heracles is worthwhile, despite the fact that this comparison will be complicated by the wealth of often contradictory depictions of Heracles in Greek literature. The difficulty of doing justice to the unwieldy mass of Heracles legends was noted already in an earlier age by Diodorus of Sicily 4.8: "For as regards the magnitude of the deeds which he accomplished it is generally agreed that Heracles has been handed down as one who surpassed all men of whom memory from the beginning of time has brought down an account." Galinsky describes the major interpretive trajectories concerning the character of Heracles in Graeco-Roman literature from Homer to Seneca (*Herakles Theme*, 1–184).

[179] Braun (*History and Romance*, 44–104) similarly argues that the elaboration of Joseph's encounter with Potiphar's wife (Genesis 39) in the *Testaments* is dependent on the Greek Phaedra myth.

[180] In fact, there may have been ancient Near Eastern influences on the development of the Greek hero Heracles. See Joseph Eddy Fontenrose, *Python: A Study of Delphic Myth and Its Origins* (Berkeley: University of California Press, 1959), 321–58. If Fontenrose is correct, then some of the correspondences between Heracles and Judah may ultimately reflect Oriental, rather than Greek, mythology and narrative patterns.

to point to some of the dynamics that must have been operative, at either a conscious or unconscious level, in the minds of the author and early readers of the *Testament of Judah*.

Narrative motifs and themes associated with both Judah in the *Testament of Judah* and Heracles in Greek legend forge a link between these two characters. One prominent theme associated with both the Jewish strong hero and the Greek strong hero is the theme of kingship. In the *Testaments*, Judah is king over his brothers, and his descendants are destined to rule Israel in future generations. Similarly, in Greek literature from the Hellenistic and early Roman periods, Heracles is cast as king over all Greece—or even over the entire world.[181] As an archetypal king, Heracles becomes the mythological counterpart and ancestor of important rulers, including Alexander himself, the Ptolemies, and many Roman emperors, perhaps most notably Augustus.[182] The means through which these two heroes ascend to royal power in the *Testament of Judah* and in some Greek

---

[181] See for example, Dio Chrysostom *Discourses* 1.59–61, where Heracles is the king not only of Argos, but of all Greece and even the entire world, since his shrines may be found from the farthest point east to the farthest point west. See also Pseudo-Lucian *The Cynic* 13, where Heracles is the master of both land and sea.

[182] The view that Alexander and the Macedonian kings were from the lineage of Heracles is summarized and documented by A. S. F. Gow (*Theocritus: Edited with a Translation and Commentary*, vol. 2 [Cambridge: Cambridge University Press, 1950] 331). A relatively late, but explicit, expression of the view that Heracles was Alexander's ancestor may be found in Dio Chrysostom *Discourses* 4.62, 70–73. In *Discourses* 32.95, Dio Chrysostom portrays Alexander as Heracles' brother. Alexander's father, Philip of Macedon, and all the Greek kings of his generation are similarly described as Heracles' descendants in Isocrates *Orations* 5.109–15, 132. In a bid for legitimacy as Alexander's successors, the Ptolemies also claimed to be from Heracles' stock, as expressed by Theocritus in an encomium on Ptolemy II Philadelphus 17.20–33. Also among Heracles' descendants were the kings of Scythia, according to Herodotus *Histories* 4.8–10; the Spartan kings, according to Herodotus *Histories* 6.52, 7.204, and 8.131, Diodorus of Sicily 4.58.1–4, and Apollodorus *Library* 2.8.2–3; the king of Rhodes, according to Diodorus of Sicily 4.58.7–8; Croesus, the king of Sardis, according to Apollodorus *Library* 2.7.8; and Latinus, the king of the Aborigines of the Italian peninsula, according to Dionysius of Halicarnasus *Roman Antiquities* 1.43–44. For the association between Heracles and Augustus, see Horace *Roman Odes* 3.3.9–12 and *Letter to Augustus* 2.1.5–14, as well as other sources cited in Galinsky, *Herakles Theme*, 132–41 (where there is also a discussion about the associations between the legendary Greek hero and other Roman emperors). Even through the medieval period, the association between Heracles and historical kings continued, as the courts of Burgundy, Castile, and Navarre traced their lineage to the Greek hero, as did the Hapsburgs and some courts in England, according to Galinsky, *Herakles Theme*, 191. Tracing one's genealogy to Heracles was not the exclusive prerogative of royalty in ancient Greece, but was a common practice among important families, judging from Plato *Lysis* 205C–D and *Theaetetus* 24B.

sources roughly correspond as well. In each instance, the hero's filial obedience and piety motivates his father to confer royal status upon him. In the case of Judah, his human father Jacob promises him that he will be king because of his filial obedience.[183] As noted above, obedience to one's father is generally an important virtue within the testament genre, but this is particularly true within the *Testaments*, in which the commandments of the fathers are often identified with the commandments of God.[184] In the case of Heracles, in some sources his divine father Zeus appoints him king over Greece, or indeed the entire world, because of his zeal to implement the supreme god's law, identified as justice.[185]

It must be noted at this point, however, that the Hellenistic and Roman presentation of Heracles as an archetypal king conflicts with earlier mythology, in which the theme of lost kingship predominates. According to a legend recounted already in Homer's *Iliad*,[186] Zeus

---

[183] See *T.Jud.* 1:4–7. But in *T.Jud.* 17:3, it is the Lord, and not Jacob, who entrusts Judah with royal status because of his obedience to his father. Similarly, in *T.Jud.* 21:2 the Lord gives Judah the kingship.

[184] For examples of this identification, see *T.Jud.* 13:1, 7; and 16:4. See also the discussion in Hollander and Marinus de Jonge, *The Testaments: A Commentary*, 41–42, which demonstrates that in the *Testaments* God's commandments are handed down from patriarch to patriarch, beginning as early as the time of Enoch, Noah, and Shem. The loose identification of paternal and divine commandments in the *Testaments* corresponds with the confusion in the *Testament of Judah* over whether it was Jacob or God who conferred kingship upon Judah because of his obedience.

[185] Already in Euripides *Madness of Heracles* 798–814, Heracles is viewed as worthy of ruling because of his opposition to tyranny and his struggle to implement the justice that Zeus approves. In a later period, Dio Chrysostom maintains that Zeus entrusted Heracles with kingship after he proved himself to be an opponent of wicked tyrants and an advocate of just government (*Discourses* 1.83–84). A variation on this theme entails Zeus' conference of immortality upon Heracles because of his efforts to establish the divine law of justice on earth. For expressions of this variation, see Isocrates *Orations* 5.132; Diodorus of Sicily 4.15.1; and Dionysius of Halicarnassus *Roman Antiquities* 1.40.2. The mythological and often amoral Heracles found in the writings of Homer is already recast as a moral force of justice and order in the writings of Hesiod, where he kills lawless and destructive creatures (*Theogony* 295–332) and uses violence to make the pilgrimage routes to Delphi safe (*Shield of Heracles*— if this work may be attributed to Hesiod). Heracles is also associated with Zeus' law of justice in Bacchylides *Odes* 12(13); Pindar *Law, the Lord of All* frg. 169(151); *Nemean Odes* 1.62–66; and *Olympian Odes* 10.13–59.

[186] Homer *Iliad* 19.95–133. This story is summarized by subsequent writers, including Apollodorus (*Library* 2.4.5) and Diodorus of Sicily (4.9.4–5). Pausanias *Description of Greece* 9.11.3 also alludes to Hera's hindrance of Heracles' birth. *Homeric Hymn* 15, "To Heracles the Lion-Hearted," describes Heracles' service to Eurystheus, which the previously listed sources associate with Heracles' birth narrative. It is interesting to note that Dio Chrysostom, who depicts Heracles as an ideal ruler in his discussions of kingship, finds it necessary to refute the legend of Heracles' loss of

indeed intended to grant his son by the mortal Alcemene royal status. When Heracles was due to be delivered, the chief god swore that the human child from his stock born that day would have dominion over all his peers. The jealous Hera subverted his plan, however, by forbidding the goddesses of childbirth to attend to Alcemene and by hastening the premature birth of Eurystheus, from the lineage of Zeus' mortal son Perseus. Heracles thus lost the kingship intended for him; moreover, the theme of lost kingship is further dramatized through Heracles' performance of the many tasks assigned to him by the usurper Eurystheus.[187] Significantly, the theme of lost kingship present in the Greek myth is also present in the *Testament of Judah*, which emphasizes Judah's fall from royal status. In addition, a similar structural pattern undergirds both narratives. In each case, the hero's father confers kingship on his son early in life, but the hero subsequently loses his royal status due to feminine intrigue and becomes enslaved to an inferior. The manifestation of this structure in the *Testament of Judah* involves Judah's loss of the kingship granted in his youth by his father Jacob through the deceptive seductions of the Canaanite woman and Tamar (*T.Jud.* 11:1–2; 12:3), and his subsequent servility towards these women (*T.Jud.* 10:3, 5, 6; 11:3; 15:1–6).

Yet despite this structural similarity, differences in detail and emphasis between the two narratives are obvious as well, and these differences indicate fundamentally different perspectives. For example, in the Greek myth, Heracles' near achievement of royal status depends entirely on the identity and power of his divine father, and his loss of that status reflects an internal conflict among members of the pantheon. By contrast, Judah gains his royal status through obedience to his father and God, and subsequently loses it through his acts of hubris and disobedience, specifically illustrated by his relations with the women of Genesis 38. In the *Testament of Judah*, therefore, we see

---

the throne to Eurystheus as an idle tale. In *Discourses* 1.58–60, Dio Chrysostom maintains that Eurystheus falsely appeared to be king of Argos because Heracles was constantly absent from his kingdom on military expeditions. Similarly, Pindar describes Heracles' birth without explicit reference to the theme of lost kingship (*Pythian Odes* 9.78–91 and *Nemean Odes* 1.33–72), in keeping with his idealized depiction of the hero.

[187] An echo of this theme of lost kingship from the mythology persists through the Hellenistic and Roman periods, specifically in the Cynic and Stoic portrayals of Heracles as the ideal sage and suffering king, who endures the insult of service to an inferior and the hardship of toil voluntarily and without complaint. See for example, Epictetus *Discourses* 3.22 and 26.

a clear moralization of the theme of kingship, gained and lost, which is absent in the Greek myth concerning Heracles' birth.[188]

A second area of correspondence between the two strong heroes consists of their demonstrations of physical excellence by overcoming fleet and powerful animals. As noted above, a number of Judah's encounters with animals in the *Testament of Judah* recall the encounters of other biblical characters with animals. But it should also be noted that in this testament the patriarch surpasses all other biblical characters in his victories over representatives from the animal world. The sequential listing of Judah's many exploits, as well as some of the specific animals mentioned and the details of the encounters, most vividly brings to mind not another biblical character, but Heracles and his legendary feats of strength performed at Eurystheus' behest.[189] In fact, in some sources, Heracles' mighty acts are called his "works" (ἔργα),[190] which is the same word Judah uses to preface the account of his exploits in the second section: "And the Lord showed me favor in all my works (τοῖς ἔργοις μου), both in the field and in the home."[191]

Heracles' victories over mythological monsters and wild animals form an essential part of his vita even in the earliest strands of the tradition;[192] however, it is the later, semi-canonical lists of Heracles' twelve labors under Eurystheus from the Hellenistic and early Roman periods that bear most resemblance to Judah's engagements with animals in the *Testament of Judah*.[193] For example, the hind (τῇ ἐλάφῳ)

---

[188] By the Hellenistic and Roman periods, however, Heracles' royal status takes on a moral dimension as well, as discussed below.

[189] Marc Philonenko similarly notes parallels between Judah and Heracles' engagements with animals ("Juda et Héraklès," *Revue d'histoire et de philosophie religieuses* 50 [1970] 61–62). The depiction of Judah as victor over the animal world is unique in this testament, which contains a number of other parallels to the figure of Heracles.

[190] See, for examples, Pindar *Law, the Lord of All* frg. 169(151) (ἔργοισιν); Diodorus of Sicily 4.8 (ἔργοις); and Pausanias *Description of Greece* 5.26.7 (ἔργων).

[191] *T.Jud.* 2:1. It must also be noted, however, that this line also echoes Deut 14:29, which speaks of divine blessing on all the "works" of one's hands. The pertinent part of this verse is translated in the LXX as ἵνα εὐλογήσῃ σε κύριος ὁ θεός σου ἐν πᾶσιν τοῖς ἔργοις, οἷς ἐὰν ποιῇς.

[192] Early descriptions of Heracles' encounters with monsters and animals appear in Homer *Odyssey* 9.617–26; Hesiod *Theogony* 285–332, 978–83; Pindar *Nemean Odes* 1.33–72; *Olympian Odes* 3.25–34; Bacchylides *Odes* 8(9).1–9; *Odes* 12(13).46–57; Euripides *Alcestis* 479–504; and Sophocles *Women of Trachis* 1089–102.

[193] Later descriptive lists of Heracles' twelve labors that vary slightly only in order of performance may be found in Apollodorus *Library* 2.5.1–12 (who technically recognizes only ten labors, since two labors performed by Heracles are subsequently discounted by Eurystheus) and Diodorus of Sicily 4.11.3–4.26.4. Euripides *Madness of Heracles* 348–441 contains an earlier list of Heracles' mighty acts that differs in

184   CHAPTER TWO

that Judah outruns and captures (*T.Jud.* 2:2) corresponds to the Ceryneian hind (ἡ ἔλαφος), which in some sources Heracles captures only
after extended pursuit.[194] Judah's race with the female gazelles (τὰς
δορκάδας, *T.Jud.* 2:3) constitutes an amplified echo of this same Her-
culean labor; significantly, one classical source refers to the Ceryneian
hind as a gazelle (τάν . . . δόρκαν).[195] The wild mare that Judah captures
and tames (*T.Jud.* 2:3) recalls the savage Thracian mares of Diomedes
that Heracles subdues and brings to Eurystheus.[196] The lion (λέοντα)
that Judah slays (*T.Jud.* 2:4) brings to mind the famous Nemean lion
(λέων) that Heracles kills as one of his first demonstrations of strength.[197]

---

only four instances from those in Apollodorus and Diodorus. Frank Brommer argues from the combined evidence of artistic renditions and literary descriptions that
the familiar twelve labors (depicted for example on Zeus' temple at Olympia) appear together as a series only from the third century BCE on (*Heracles: The Twelve
Labors of the Hero in Ancient Art and Literature*, trans. Shirley J. Schwarz [New Rochelle,
NY: Aristide D. Caratzas, 1968]).

[194] Descriptions of Heracles' capture of the golden-horned Ceryneian hind dedicated to Artemis appear in Apollodorus *Library* 5.3 and Diodorus of Sicily 4.13.1.
Pindar *Olympian Odes* 3.29–32 provides an earlier description of this same feat.
Apollodorus states that Heracles hunted the hind for an entire year and captured it
only after it tired of the chase. Diodorus emphasizes the swiftness of this hind and
records the opinion of those who maintained that Heracles exhausted it by running
it down. Pindar also stresses Heracles' endurance in the chase by noting the great
distance he traversed to reach the hind's northern habitat.

[195] Euripides *Madness of Heracles* 375–79.

[196] Heracles' encounter with Diomedes' man-eating mares is described in Apollodorus *Library* 2.5.8; Diodorus of Sicily 4.15.3; and Philostratus *Imagines* 2.25.1; however, in these sources the word designating the mares (τὰς . . . ἵππους) differs from
the word used to designate the mare in *T.Jud.* 2:3 (φοράδα ἀγρίαν). Other sources
refer to this incident as well, although in Euripides *Alcestis* 479–504 and *Madness of
Heracles* 380–86 Diomedes' horses are stallions, not mares. Heracles' breaking in of
Diomedes' horses is also the subject of a recently discovered fragment of a work by
Pindar, the continuation of frg. 169, discussed by Carlo Pavese ("The New Heracles
Poem of Pindar," *HSCP* 72 [1967] 47–88).

[197] Heracles' victory over the Nemean lion is among the best attested episodes in
his mythology. According to Brommer, it is the "most frequently represented theme
in all of Greek art" (*Heracles: The Twelve Labors*, 7). This episode is described in
Apollodorus *Library* 2.5.1 and Diodorus of Sicily 4.11.3, as well as in earlier works
including Hesiod *Theogony* 326–32; Bacchylides *Odes* 8(9).6–1; *Odes* 12(13).46–57; Pindar
Isthmian Odes 6.47–49; Sophocles *Women of Trachis* 1091–93; Euripides *Madness of
Heracles* 153–54, 359–63; and Theocritus 25.153–281. Most of these sources specify
that Heracles kills the lion with his bare hands, which also seems to be the case in
Judah's encounter with the lion. The motif of the struggle between human and lion
may have its origins in the ancient Near East. See Brommer, *Heracles: The Twelve
Labors*, 8. For a discussion of the motif of the lion hunt in the ancient Near East,
see Leo Bersani and Ulysse Dutoit, *The Forms of Violence: Narrative in Assyrian Art and
Modern Culture* (New York: Schocken Books, 1985).

Clearly, however, the primary allusion at this point is to David, who protects his
flock from the lion and the bear in 1 Sam 17:34–37, as previously noted.

The wild boar that Judah races and rends (*T.Jud.* 2:5) corresponds to the wild Erymanthian boar that Heracles subdues through brute strength.[198] Finally, the wild ox (βοῦν) that Judah hurls to death (*T.Jud.* 2:7) suggests either the unruly Cretan bull[199] or the cattle (βοῦς) of Geryon[200] that Heracles drives to Eurystheus.

Admittedly, Judah's hunting exploits do not correspond exactly with the canonical twelve labors of Heracles. For example, Judah's destruction of the leopard who attacks his dog (*T.Jud.* 2:6) is anomalous; it has no parallel among Heracles' labors—nor among the deeds of other biblical characters for that matter.[201] On the other side of the equation, Heracles' labors involving fabulous beasts such as the Lernaean hydra and the Stymphalian birds find no parallel in the *Testament of Judah.*[202] But although Judah's hunting exploits do not

---

[198] Apollodorus *Library* 2.5.4 and Diodorus of Sicily 4.12.1 describe Heracles' capture of the Erymanthian boar, although the word that they use to designate this animal (τὸν ... κάπρον) differs from the word used in *T.Jud.* 2:5 (τῷ χοίρῳ τῷ ἀγρίῳ). Sophocles *Women of Trachis* 1097 and Pausanias *Description of Greece* 8.24.5 also allude to Heracles' contest with the wild boar of Erymanthus, although they too employ different terms (θήρα and ὗν, respectively) to describe this animal.

[199] Heracles' adventure with the Cretan bull (τὸν ... ταῦρον) is depicted in Apollodorus *Library* 2.5.7 and Diodorus of Sicily 4.13.4, as well as in Pausanias *Description of Greece* 1.27.9 and 5.10.9.

[200] Heracles' encounter with Geryon and subsequent procurement of his cattle are frequently depicted in Greek literature. It is mentioned in Apollodorus *Library* 2.5.10 and Diodorus of Sicily 4.17.1, as well as in numerous earlier sources, including Hesiod *Theogony* 287–94, 979–83; Hecataeus frg. FGH 1 F 26 (= Arrian 2.16.50); Pindar *Law, the Lord of All* frg. 169(151); Herodotus *Histories* 4.8; Plato *Gorgias* 484B–C; Euripides *Madness of Heracles* 422–24; and Aeschylus frg. 37(74N) of *Children of Heracles*. The Roman appropriation of Heracles' mythology focuses on this particular labor as well, for according to tradition it was while the hero was returning through Italy with Geryon's cattle that he first was worshipped as a divine hero in that land—long before the time of Romulus. Significantly, in both the Greek and Roman versions of this labor, Heracles' journey home with the cattle is the occasion for battles with outlaws and unjust rulers, and for his subsequent establishment of cities and culture. In this respect, there is a structural affinity with the material in the *Testament of Judah*, in which Judah's encounter with the wild ox also prefaces his encounter with human enemies (*T.Jud.* 3–7, 9) and his establishment of a city (*T.Jud.* 7:9).

[201] It should be noted, however, that the leopard does appear as a swift and powerful animal in the Hebrew Bible. For example, in Dan 7:6, a winged, four-headed leopard represents Achaemenid Persia. Other biblical references to leopards alluding to their characteristic strength and rapacity include Isa 11:6; Jer 5:6; Hos 13:7; and Hab 1:8.

Apparently the predatory animals killed by Judah comprised a stock list for the author of the *Testaments*. The animals that Gad kills while watching the family flocks in *T.G.* 1:3 (lion, leopard, bear, and other wild beasts) are identical to the beasts of prey that Judah kills, with the exception of the additional wolf.

[202] The world of the *Testaments* is generally as ordinary as the animals Judah defeats, although angelic interventions, heavenly visions, and prayerful intercessions occasionally

correspond exactly with the canonical twelve labors of Heracles, the similarities between the actions of the Israelite patriarch and the popular Greek hero would have made a comparison between the two almost inevitable in a Graeco-Roman cultural context. Judah, like Heracles, exemplifies the physical excellence and courage often associated with ideal manhood in the Graeco-Roman world.[203] In fact, in the gratuitous violence he displays, Judah sometimes surpasses Heracles, who frequently brings animals back alive to Eurystheus.[204]

Reflecting on Judah's physical excellence from a slightly different angle, we find that in his encounters with animals (as well as with human enemies in subsequent sections) the patriarch distinguishes himself as an athlete. Judah displays his swiftness of foot when he

---

link the mundane and divine realms. The lack of fabulous creatures in the *Testament of Judah* brings to the fore important differences in perspective concerning the nature of the world and the approximation of the lives of legendary characters to those of ordinary people.

Philonenko nevertheless suggests that the dog mentioned in this testament (*T.Jud.* 2:4, 6) may be an allusion to Cerberus, the mythical dog of the underworld that Heracles brings up to Eurystheus ("Juda et Héraklès," 62). Similarly, although there is also no parallel to Heracles' defeat of the Amazons in the *Testament of Judah*, the theme of hostile women is by no means absent. It is also interesting to note that while a parallel to Heracles' procurement of golden apples (μῆλα) from the distant, enchanted garden of the Hesperides (attested to in Hesiod *Theogony* 215, 275, 517; Apollodorus *Library* 2.5.11; Hyginus *Fabulae* 30; *Poetica Astronomica* 2.3) is lacking in this testament, the procurement of apples from a special place appears later in the *Testament of Issachar* (*T.I.* 1:5). In a gloss describing the mandrakes Reuben obtained for his mother, this testament explains, "Now these [mandrakes] were the sweet-smelling apples (μῆλα) which the land of Aram produced on a high place below a ravine of water." Significantly, in this testament Rachel refrains from eating the apples and instead dedicates them to the Lord's house, by giving them to the priest of the Most High (*T.I.* 2:5). This curious detail finds a rough parallel in the Greek myth. After Heracles obtains the golden apples for Eurystheus, the king gives them back to the hero, who in turn brings them to the goddess Athena, who ultimately returns them to the garden of the gods.

[203] The majority of manuscripts (mss b, l, d, m, k, g, e, f) specify in a subtitle that the *Testament of Judah* illustrates the attribute of "manliness" (περὶ ἀνδρείας), as well as other less positive attributes. Similarly, Heracles is called "the best of men" (ἄνδρ᾽ ἄριστον) in Aristophanes *Clouds* 1048–50. Other sources containing versions of this appellation include Sophocles *Women of Trachis* 811 and Euripides *Madness of Heracles* 183. See also the *Homeric Hymn to Heracles* 1–2. (Note that even Heracles' original name, Alcides, evokes the idea of physical power, due to its correspondence with the Greek word "strength" (ἀλκή). Similarly, a common title applied to the Greek hero, "the force of Heracles" (Βίη Ἡρακληείη), emphasizes his might (Homer *Odyssey* 11.601; Hesiod *Theogony* 289, 315, 332, 943, 982; *Shield of Heracles*, 52, 69.)

[204] For example, in most sources Heracles subdues the Ceryneian hind, the Erymanthian boar, and the Cretan bull without killing them, whereas in the *Testament of Judah* the patriarch kills the hind and the roes, the boar, and the bull.

outruns the hind,²⁰⁵ the gazelles and other animals of the plains,²⁰⁶ the wild mare,²⁰⁷ and the boar;²⁰⁸ he continues to demonstrate his racing ability in the following section, when he rushes out alone against the king of Hazor.²⁰⁹ Judah's bare-handed victories over the bear, the wild boar, the leopard, the wild ox, and other beasts (and possibly over the lion and human enemies as well) confirm his athletic prowess in other areas as well, including wrestling and throwing.²¹⁰ In these respects, Judah once again corresponds to Heracles, the Graeco-

---

²⁰⁵ In *T.Jud.* 2:2, Judah races (συνέδραμον) a hind and catches (πιάσας) it before preparing it as a meal for his father.

²⁰⁶ In *T.Jud.* 2:3 Judah masters the gazelles in the chase (ἐκράτουν διὰ τοῦ δρόμου) and overtakes (κατελάμβανον) all that is in the plains.

²⁰⁷ In *T.Jud.* 2:3 Judah overtakes (κατέλαβον) a wild mare before taming it.

²⁰⁸ In *T.Jud.* 2:5 Judah races (συνέδραμον) the wild boar and gains advantage over it through his running (προλαβὼν ἐν τῷ τρέχειν με) before he tears it to pieces.

²⁰⁹ In *T.Jud.* 3:1 Judah races out alone (κἀγὼ μόνος δραμὼν) to confront the enemy king. This detail is entirely absent in *Jubilees'* version of the war with the indigenous kings (*Jubilees* 34). In the other versions of this war in *Yalquṭ Šimʿoni* Wayyissaʿu, the *Chronicles of Yeraḥmeʾel*, and *Seper Hayyašar*, Judah is indeed first to spring onto the battlefield, but the image of this patriarch as a foot racer is lacking.

Judah's fleetness of foot is already suggested in the introductory section (*T.Jud.* 1:4) by the adjective ὀξὺς (which can mean "swift" or "quick") that he uses to describe himself as a youth. Although Judah's racing ability immediately brings to mind the Greek hero Achilles (commonly described as "swift of foot"), the patriarch's versatile prowess in all types of athletic endeavors aligns him more closely with Heracles.

²¹⁰ In *T.Jud.* 2:4 Judah takes the bear by the paw and rolls it into pit. In *T.Jud.* 2:5 he tears the wild boar into pieces, just as he does to the other unspecified beasts at the end of *T.Jud.* 2:4. In *T.Jud.* 2:6 he swings the leopard by the tail to its death. (The description of the leopard's demise may obliquely allude to boxing, in that it states that the leopard "was knocked out" [ἐρράγη] in Gaza, which is a form of a verb [ῥήγνυμι] used to describe defeat in boxing matches.) Finally, in *T.Jud.* 2:7 Judah grapples with the wild ox by the horns before he throws it to its demise. In *T.Jud.* 2:4, the means through which Judah kills the lion are left unspecified; however, since in his encounters with other animals he uses the brute strength of a wrestler and not the weapon of a hunter or warrior, we might assume that the same is true in this case. At least in the case of Judah's first encounter with a human enemy (*T.Jud.* 3:1), the language also suggests unarmed, single combat, in that he seizes the king of Hazor, strikes him on his lower leg armor, drags him to the ground, and thus kills him. (But later in this section, Judah uses weapons, including a large stone in *T.Jud.* 3:3 and a sword or knife in *T.Jud.* 3:4.) The depiction of Judah as an unarmed fighter forges yet a further connection with Heracles, who conquered a number of beasts (including the Nemean lion and the Erymanthian boar) with his bare hands and was commonly known as a master wrestler. As pointed out above, however, the depiction of Judah fighting with his hands may present an interpretation of the biblical phrase from Moses' blessing of Judah in Deut 33:7, ידיו רב לו, as "his hands were sufficient for him" against his adversaries.

Judah's ability to throw heavy objects long distances is indicated by his treatment of the leopard (*T.Jud.* 2:6) and the wild ox (*T.Jud.* 2:7) and by his employment of a massive stone as a weapon later in his fight with the foreign kings (*T.Jud.* 3:3).

Roman athlete *par excellence* [211] and the legendary founder and patron of the Olympic games and other important athletic contests.[212] According to one version of the legend, Heracles himself won all the events of the original Olympic games, including the foot races,[213] although his special expertise was the pancration (a rugged combination of boxing and wrestling).[214] Heracles' close association with athletic

---

Judah's superhuman physical prowess is expressed in other ways as well throughout the war scenes in *T.Jud.* 3–7 and 9. For example, in *T.Jud.* 4:1–2 he pursues a thousand men, kills two hundred of them along with four kings, climbs up on the wall of Hebron to kill two more kings, and thus conquers the city. See also *T.Jud.* 7:5 and 9:5.

[211] Philistratus *Imagines* 24.3 compares Heracles' mighty arms and thighs to those of the best athletes of Sparta. Even writers attempting to redefine Heracles in terms of his moral and spiritual qualities attest to the common perception of him as an athlete in their refutation of it. See for example, Epictetus *Discourses* 3.22 and Dio Chrysostom *Discourses* 8.26–35.

[212] Heracles is depicted as the founder of the Olympic games in Pindar *Olympian Odes* 2.3–4; 3.11–45; 6.67–69; 10.13–59; Philostratus *Life of Apollonius of Tyana* 6.10; and Diodorus of Sicily 4.14.1–2. Compare with Pausanias *Description of Greece* 5.7.6–5.8.4.

[213] Diodorus of Sicily 4.14.1–2 depicts Heracles as winning every event of the original Olympic games and emphasizes the magnitude of this accomplishment by noting that generally athletes who excel at running do not also win events requiring heavier musculature, such as boxing and wrestling. Significantly, in the works of Euripides, Heracles employs the metaphor of running when he describes his labors as "races" (δρόμων in *Madness of Heracles* 425; cf., *Alcestis* 489).

[214] Heracles is depicted as the archetypal wrestler in Bacchylides *Odes* 12(13).46–57 (where his wrestling with the Nemean lion is a model for later participants in the pancration); Plutarch *Moralia* 56.12; Apollodorus *Library* 2.5.10–11; Diodorus of Sicily 4.14.1; and Pausanias *Description of Greece* 5.8.4. Epictetus *Discourses* 3.26 states that Heracles won all his victories "unarmed and single-handed." Euripides *Madness of Heracles* 954–62 maintains that even in a fit of madness Heracles continued to wrestle with an imaginary opponent. There are also numerous accounts of Heracles' legendary wrestling matches in mythology, including with King Eryx of northwestern Sicily in Diodorus of Sicily 4.23.2–3; Apollodorus *Library* 2.5.10; Pausanias *Description of Greece* 3.16.4–5 and 4.36.4; Virgil *Aeneid* 5.400–19, 772–73; and with the Libyan giant Antaeus in Pindar *Isthmian Odes* 4.52–55; Apollodorus *Library* 2.5.11; and Philostratus *Imagines* 2.21.3. Some sources depict Heracles raising his victims above his head and dashing them to the ground, just as Judah does to the leopard and the wild ox. For example, in Sophocles *Women of Trachis* 779–82 Heracles seizes a young man by the foot and hurls him onto a rock in the sea, crushing his skull and spilling his blood and brains. For a later repetition of this same motif, see Seneca *Madness of Heracles* 1005–7. Note that the same technique is also used by Gad in *T.G.* 1:3. Attempting to lift an opponent prior to throwing him to the ground is a standard device of ancient wrestling, judging from artistic representations, according to Timothy Gantz, *Early Greek Myth: A Guide to Literary and Artistic Sources* (Baltimore: Johns Hopkins University Press, 1993) 417. A more detailed discussion of the literary and artistic representations of the pancration and the Greek wrestling match (including depictions of Heracles' participation in these sports) may be found in E. Norman Gardiner, *Greek Athletic Sports and Festivals* (London: MacMillan, 1910) 435–50, 372–401.

games in the Graeco-Roman world was expressed by the practice of calling victorious contestants the "sons of Heracles."[215] The portrayal of Judah as an athlete in the *Testament of Judah* therefore indicates a superimposition of Hellenistic physical ideals associated most commonly with Heracles onto this biblical character.[216]

Judah and Heracles are also similar in that they are both undefeated warriors, who prove victorious in single combat against powerful enemies (including other kings) and in organized military action against entire cities.[217] For example, the *Testament of Judah* depicts Judah's personal defeat of the kings of Hazor (*T.Jud.* 3:1) and Tappuah (*T.Jud.* 3:2), the giant King Achor (*T.Jud.* 3:3–4), and six unnamed kings at Hebron (*T.Jud.* 4:1–2).[218] It also portrays him leading his brothers in successful military attacks against the cities of Hebron (*T.Jud.* 4:1–3),[219]

---

[215] See for example, Pausanias *Description of Greece* 5.21.10; Galen *Exhortation for Medicine* 9–14; and Lucian *How to Write History* 10. There are also descriptions of athletes who modeled themselves after Heracles, including Pulydamas the pancration winner (Pausanias *Description of Greece* 6.5.1–9) and Dioxippus the Athenian fighter (Diodorus of Sicily 17.100–1). At one point in history, the practice of considering winners of both the boxing and wrestling contests "successors of Heracles" was abolished because of the arrogance that it caused. See Gardiner, *Greek Athletic Sports*, 174.

[216] This athletic ideal influences the development of other patriarchs in the *Testaments* besides Judah. Gad is also depicted as a strong man in *T.G.* 1:2–3, where (much like Judah with the leopard and the wild ox in *T.Jud.* 2:6–7) he pursues predators, swings them around by their feet, and throws them incredible distances to their deaths. Naphtali is also portrayed as an athlete—specifically a runner—in *T.N.* 2:1, where his fleetness in bearing his father's messages is compared to that of a deer. This passage is an interpretation of Jacob's blessing of Naphtali in Gen 49:21: "Naphtali is a hind sent forth—the one giving excellent words" (נפתלי אילה שלחה הנתן אמרי־שפר). It is important to note, however, that a number of positively depicted patriarchs, including Levi, Joseph, Issachar, and Benjamin, are not developed as athletes. Indeed, as we shall conclude below, the *Testament of Judah* contains an implicit critique of the athletic ideal, in that Judah's moral character is essentially flawed despite his phenomenal physique.

[217] With the depiction of Judah as hunter, athlete, and warrior, the *Testament of Judah* presents him as the equal of any highly bred Greek, who as a class "endeavor to excel in hunting lions, bearing arms, Olympic running," according to Menander *Men at Arbitration* 11.320.

[218] With the exception of his father Jacob (who kills Beelisah, the king of all kings, in *T.Jud.* 3:7), Judah is the only character in *T.Jud.* who kills foreign kings. His victories over kings further emphasizes his royal status in this testament. In addition, Judah also personally kills four of Achor's men in *T.Jud.* 3:6, two hundred men at Hebron in *T.Jud.* 4:2, and four mighty men of Esau's city in *T.Jud.* 9:5. (The only time any of Judah's brothers are explicitly credited with personal military victories is in *T.Jud.* 9:6, where Reuben and Gad kill six or [sixty men] of Esau's city.)

[219] In this instance, as in most of the others, Judah's military leadership is evident, in that after joining his brothers in common pursuit of a thousand men, he alone kills soldiers and kings, and he alone climbs on the wall to liberate Hebron. But even when this patriarch's leadership role is not explicitly portrayed, as in the

'Areta (*T.Jud.* 5:1–5), Tappuah (*T.Jud.* 5:6–7), Makir (*T.Jud.* 6:4–5), Gaash (*T.Jud.* 7:1–3), Thamna (*T.Jud.* 7:4–8),[220] and the city of Esau's sons (*T.Jud.* 9:4–8).[221] Turning to the figure of Heracles, we find the instances of his single combat with enemies too numerous to list. For present purposes, his legendary victories over King Geryon of Erytheia,[222] King Busiris of Egypt,[223] King Emathion of Aithiopes,[224] the usurper King Lycus of Thebes,[225] the giant Alcyoneus,[226] Ares' son Kyknos,[227] and (in his Roman reception) Vulcan's son Cacus[228]

---

case of the battle with Tappuah (*T.Jud.* 5:6–7), his father's earlier vision of the angel protecting Judah from defeat (*T.Jud.* 4:10) singles him out as the central figure in the ensuing military maneuvers.

[220] The brothers' siege of Thamna ends before they destroy it, since its inhabitants flee and negotiate peace terms with Jacob.

[221] Similarly, the brothers do not destroy this city, since Esau's sons negotiate peace.

[222] Hesiod *Theogony* 287–94, 981–83; Pindar *Law, the Lord of All* frg. 169(151); Diodorus of Sicily 4.18.2; and Apollodorus *Library* 2.5.10.

[223] Diodorus of Sicily 4.18.1; 4.27.3; Apollodorus *Library* 2.5.11; and Hyginus *Fabulae* 31, 51. Compare with Herodotus *Histories* 2.45.

[224] Emathion is called king of Aithiopes in Diodorus of Sicily 4.25.3. For depictions of Heracles' defeat of Emathion, see Diodorus of Sicily 4.27.3 (set on the Nile) and Apollodorus *Library* 2.5.11 (set in Arabia). Compare with Hesiod *Theogony* 984–85.

[225] Euripides *Madness of Heracles* 726–814; Hyginus *Fabulae* 32.

[226] Pindar *Nemean Odes* 4.25–30; *Isthmian Odes* 6.31–35; Apollodorus *Library* 1.6.1. Heracles was generally known as a killer of giants. He was noted especially for his assistance of the gods in the battle against the giants. See Pindar *Nemean Odes* 7.90; Sophocles *Women of Trachis* 1058–59; Euripides *Madness of Heracles* 177. In light of Heracles' status as a giant slayer, the references to the giants that Judah and his father slay in the *Testament of Judah* ("Achor, the king, a giant," *T.Jud.* 3:3; "Beelisah, the king of all kings, a giant in strength," *T.Jud.* 3:7) take on an additional resonance.

[227] Hesiod *Shield of Heracles* 57–58; Apollodorus *Library* 2.5.11; 2.7.7.

[228] Dionysius of Halicarnassus *Roman Antiquities* 1.39–40, 41, 80; Virgil *Aeneid* 8.184–272; Propertius 4.9.1–20; Livy 1.7, 3–15; Strabo 5.3.3; Origo 6.8. Compare with Diodorus of Sicily 4.21. A detail from this Roman appropriation of the Greek hero further connects the stories of Heracles and Judah. According to the sources listed above, Heracles was returning through Italy with his newly acquired cattle after victory over Geryon, when Cacus stole some of his livestock and hid them in a cave. Upon discovery of this theft, Heracles fought and defeated the guilty Cacus. Similarly, the *Testament of Judah* depicts the theft of family flocks as the reason why Judah initially attacked the foreign kings (*T.Jud.* 3:1). It must be conceded that this detail naturally corresponds to Jacob and his sons' occupation as shepherds elsewhere in Genesis and that it is not unique to the version of the war account found in the *Testament of Judah*. (The motif of cattle theft also opens the version of the war with the local kings in *Jubilees* 34, and the theme of restoration of flocks concludes the versions in *Yalqut Šim'oni* Wayyissa'u and the *Chronicles of Yeraḥme'el*.) It nevertheless has an additional resonance within the context of this testament's development of Judah as a parallel to Heracles. Note that in the *Testament of Judah*, when the focus returns from the war between the sons of Jacob and the Canaanites back to Judah, attention is once again given to the possession of large flocks (*T.Jud.* 8:1). Needless to say, unlike Heracles in the Roman legend, Judah is not deified in the *Testament*

suffice to illustrate his unrivaled skill as a fighter.[229] Similarly, legend portrays Heracles as the "sacker of cities,"[230] including Orchomenus,[231] Troy,[232] Elis,[233] Pylos,[234] Sparta,[235] and Oechalia,[236] although, unlike Judah, Heracles does not typically employ deceit to conquer the enemy. Emphasis on the Greek hero as a military leader and civilizing force continued well into the Hellenistic and early Roman periods; of special interest are the euhemerist interpretations of Heracles as the greatest general of his age, who led a large army across the known world to defeat tyrants, build cities, and establish just governments.[237] In light of this portrayal of Heracles, it is interesting to note that following Judah's successful leadership against the Canaanite coalition, the patriarch also builds a city, specifically the city of Thamna.[238] This action suggests that Judah too acted as a civilizing force and cultural hero, parallel to Heracles.

Parallels between the two strong heroes appear during times of peace as well. Following their violent victories over animal and human

---

of Judah after his violent defeat of the cattle thieves. This difference reflects a basic divergence in religious outlooks.

[229] Heracles' other opponents include King Eryx of Elymoi, the giant Antaeos, and Theiodamas, king of the Dryopes.

[230] The appellation "sacker of cities" is taken from Hesiod *Ehoia* frg. 25MW, cited in Gantz, *Early Greek Myth*, 432. Bacchylides *Odes* 5.56–59 refers generally to Heracles' destruction of city gates without specifying the names of these cities. Even in the grip of madness, Heracles continues his attack of cities in Euripides *Madness of Heracles* 935–1015.

[231] Allusions to Heracles' conquest of Orchomenus, which resulted in the imposition of a heavy tribute, appear in Euripides *Madness of Heracles* 48–50, 220–21 and Diodorus of Sicily 4.10.3–5.

[232] See Homer *Iliad* 5.628–51; 14.250–51, 265–66; 20.144–48; Pindar *Nemean Odes* 4.22–27; *Isthmian Odes* 6.27–35; Isocrates *Orations* 5.111–12; Diodorus of Sicily 4.32.1–5; 4.49.3–6; and Apollodorus *Library* 2.5.9; 2.6.4.

[233] See Pindar *Olympian Odes* 10.34–38; Diodorus of Sicily 4.33.1–4; and Apollodorus *Library* 2.7.2. Compare also Pausanias *Description of Greece* 5.2.1–2.

[234] See Hesiod *Shield of Heracles* 359–61 and Apollodorus *Library* 2.6.2.

[235] See Diodorus of Sicily 4.33.5–6; Apollodorus *Library* 2.7.3; and Pausanias *Description of Greece* 3.15.4–5.

[236] Allusions to Heracles' conquest of Oechalia, leading ultimately to his own demise, appear in Homer *Odyssey* 21; Bacchylides *Dithyrambs* 15(16).13–35; Sophocles *Women of Trachis* 248–80; Diodorus of Sicily 4.31.1–2; 4.38; Apollodorus *Library* 2.6.1; 2.7.7; and Ovid *Metamorphosis* 9.101–272.

[237] For an example of this type of euhemerist interpretation, see Dionysius of Halicarnassus *Roman Antiquities* 1.41–44.

The interpretation of Heracles' violence as a salvific and civilizing force is by no means unique to these late sources, however, but may be found in the works of Hesiod and other early writers. See Hesiod *Theogony* 270–335; *Shield of Heracles* 22–29; Pindar *Olympian Odes* 10; *Nemean Odes* 7.

[238] *T.Jud.* 7:9.

opponents, Judah in the *Testament of Judah* and Heracles in Greek legend marry princesses and engender sons by them.[239] Soon after Judah's victories over the Canaanite kings, another of the indigenous kings, namely Barsan the king of Adullam, gives Judah his daughter Bathshua in marriage; this couple has three sons.[240] In the case of Heracles, variations upon the motif of marriage (or simply sexual union) with royal women after combat recur throughout his legendary life. A single example will suffice to illustrate it here. After the hero's defeat of King Erginus and the Minyans of Orchomenus, King Creon of Thebes rewards Heracles by giving him his daughter Megara in marriage, and this couple has sons.[241]

---

[239] The motif of the hero's marriage with the princess bears upon the depiction of Judah and Heracles as kings discussed above, in that it portrays them as worthy of union with royalty.

[240] *T.Jud.* 8:2–3. In this passage from the *Testament of Judah*, Hirah's Adullamite ethnic identity in the biblical narrative (Gen 38:1) is transferred to Shua, the Canaanite man with a daughter (Gen 38:2), who is elevated to royal status. According to *T.Jud.* 11:1, Bathshua (and by implication her father) are Canaanites (*T.Jud.* 7:11). The fact that it is the defeated enemy king who gives his daughter to the successful victor in order to defeat him lends a sinister aspect to the story that is developed more fully in *T.Jud.* 13:4–7. The motif of Judah's marriage with a foreign princess after the war with the Canaanites is found only in this source.

[241] Depending on the source, the number of sons ranges from two to eight. Diodorus of Sicily 4.10.6 and Apollodorus *Library* 2.4.11 provide two Hellenistic versions of the narrative. Similarities in detail between these two sources and the *Testament of Judah* are striking, especially if one looks at the larger contexts within which the accounts of Heracles' marriage to Megara are set. Leading up to his marriage with Megara, Heracles single-handedly kills King Erginus (Diodorus of Sicily 4.10.5; Apollodorus *Library* 2.4.11; cf., *T.Jud.* 3:1, 2, 3–4; 4:1, 2) and most of the men who accompany him (Diodorus of Sicily 4.10.5; Apollodorus *Library* 2.4.11; cf., *T.Jud.* 3:5–6; 4:1; 9:5), slips secretly into the city of Orchomenus (Diodorus of Sicily 4.10.5; cf., *T.Jud.* 7:2–3) and burns it (Diodorus of Sicily 4.10.5; cf., *T.Jud.* 4:5, 7), and exacts a high tribute from the Minyans (Apollodorus *Library* 2.4.11) or at least ends the yearly tribute formerly demanded by the Minyans (Diodorus of Sicily 4.10.2–4; cf., *T.Jud.* 9:7–8). Following his marriage, Heracles has three sons with Megara (Apollodorus *Library* 2.4.11; cf., *T.Jud.* 8:3), but upon being reminded that he must serve his inferior, King Eurystheus, he falls into a frenzied madness and kills them (Diodorus of Sicily 4.11.1–2; cf., *T.Jud.* 11:4–5).

Other examples of Heracles' union with princesses include the following: During Heracles' ultimately successful hunt of the lion of Cithaeron, King Thespius arranges for the hero to sleep with his fifty daughters, each of whom bears a son (Herodorus frg. 31F20, summarized in Gantz, *Early Greek Myth*, 379; Apollodorus *Library* 2.4.9–10; Diodorus of Sicily 4.29.2–3; Pausanias *Description of Greece* 9.27.6–7). After Heracles' successful wars in the Peloponnesus and his defeat of the river monster Achelous, the hero marries King Oeneus' daughter Deianeira who bears him Hyllus (Bacchylides *Odes* 5.165–75; Sophocles *Women of Trachis* 555–77; Diodorus of Sicily 4.34.1; 4.35.3–5; Apollodorus *Library* 2.7.5–6). Note also that following his defeat of Sparta, Heracles engenders a child with Auge, daughter of King Aleos (fragments of plays by Sophocles and Euripides, summarized by Gantz, *Early Greek Myth*, 428–29;

One might argue that the motif of the hero's marriage to the princess in the *Testament of Judah* should more appropriately be compared with a biblical parallel. After all, Judah's descendant David marries Michal, the daughter of King Saul, after he collects one hundred Philistine foreskins in battle.[242] Significantly, this biblical parallel portrays the king's sinister attempt to cause the hero's downfall through his offer of a daughter—a motif that also appears in the *Testament of Judah*. Saul hopes that David will be killed during his combat with the Philistines, just as Barsan apparently plots Judah's destruction when he tempts him with his daughter's wine, wealth, and beauty.[243] But there is one significant detail in the *Testament of Judah* that strengthens the connection with the Heracles legends. This detail consists of the drinking party following Judah's victories that serves as the setting for Barsan's duplicitous grant of his daughter's hand.[244] Depictions of

---

Diodorus of Sicily 4.33.7–8; Apollodorus *Library* 2.7.4; Pausanias *Description of Greece* 8.4.9). Significant variations of this pattern also occur. For example, Heracles takes the daughter of the enemy King Phyleus by force after defeating the Thesprotians and begets Tlepolemus (Diodorus of Sicily 4.36.1; Apollodorus *Library* 2.7.6). Another variation consists of Heracles' marriage to Omphale, the Lydian queen. After he defeats a number of monsters and outlaws during his period of servitude to her, they have a son Lamos (Sophocles *Women of Trachis* 248–53, 274–78; Diodorus of Sicily 4.31.5–8; Apollodorus *Library* 2.6.2–3). Since Omphale is a widowed queen and not a young princess, she functions in the dual role of the authority figure facilitating the hero's marriage into the royal family and of the bride herself. A third variation appears when King Eurytos refuses to give Heracles his daughter Iole after the hero has completed his labors and won an archery contest (Apollodorus *Library* 2.6.1–3; 2.7.7; cf., Sophocles *Women of Trachis* 248–80; Diodorus of Sicily 4.31.1–2; 4.38; and other fragmentary sources cited by Gantz, *Early Greek Myth*, 434–37). This deviation from the expected pattern leads ultimately to Heracles' demise. A final variation of this narrative pattern appears at the end of the hero's life, when all of his struggles with animals, monsters, and kings are completed. At this time, Zeus, the king of the gods, grants Heracles his daughter Hebe, with whom he lives immortally (Apollodorus *Library* 2.7.7).

[242] 1 Sam 18:17–29. But note that they have no sons (2 Sam 6:23).

[243] *T.Jud.* 8:2; 11:2; 13:4–7; 14:4–6; 17:1.

It is interesting to reflect upon the significance of the fact that the king's daughter pours the hero's wine at the drinking party in the *Testament of Judah*. At least in Greek culture, respectable women of the family (virgin daughters and wives) would not be present at men's parties, although courtesans would. The depiction of the princess at Barsan's drinking party therefore assimilates her character to the "singing girls" (μουσικὰς) and "harlots" (δημοσίας) associated with the abominable sexual behavior of the gentiles in *T.Jud.* 23:2.

[244] This drinking party (πότον) is specifically mentioned in *T.Jud.* 8:2, and additional details, many focusing on wine consumption, are given in *T.Jud.* 11:2; 13:4–7; 14:4–6; 17:1. Reference to a party or banquet is entirely absent in the story of David and Michal in 1 Sam 18:20–30 and also in the story of Othniel and Achsah in Judg 1:11–15.

banquets including copious drinking after successful military ventures and other violent exploits are common in Greek literature and may stem from a formulaic type scene characteristic of oral poetry.[245] Whatever the case, for our purposes it is important to note that at least twice some type of party including wine consumption serves as the setting for Heracles' amorous involvements with princesses; moreover, in both of these cases, the royal father deceives the hero in one way or another. In the first instance, King Thespius entertains Heracles during his hunt of the lion of Cithaeron, and, possibly with the help of the copious wine served, he induces his unwitting guest to sleep with each of his fifty daughters to beget fifty grandsons.[246] The second instance of the banquet scene in connection with Heracles' affairs occurs at King Eurytos' palace in Oechalia, following the hero's completion of all his labors.[247] This instance contains a deception with more grievous consequences. The outlines of the original story must be pieced together from literary and artistic evidence, but it seems probable that King Eurytos proposed an archery contest at a banquet, with his daughter Iole as the prize. Heracles won the contest, but Eurytos then reneged on his offer and expelled the hero after a drunken brawl.[248] This insult led Heracles to destroy Oechalia

---

[245] An example of this banquet scene appears in Pindar *Isthmian Odes* 6.35–56, where Heracles participates in a banquet following his victory over Troy. Another consists of Heracles' participation in a sacrifice and feast following his defeat of the cattle thief Cacus, in Dionysius of Halicarnassus *Roman Antiquities* 1.20.

[246] This version of the story, found in Apollodorus *Library* 2.4.9–10, implies that Heracles was so drunk that he never noticed that there was a different virgin in his bed each night. Similarly, Diodorus of Sicily 4.29.2–4 hints at Heracles' drunken state by maintaining that King Thespius invited the hero to a sacrifice and lavishly entertained him before sending his daughters in to him one by one, apparently in a single night. Another allusion to this story with different details may be found in Pausanias *Description of Greece* 9.27.6–7.

[247] This placement of Heracles' affair with Iole after the completion of his labors occurs in Diodorus of Sicily 4.31.1 and Apollodorus *Library* 2.6.1–3.

[248] Sophocles *Women of Trachis* 260–68 describes King Eurytos' boast of his sons' superiority in archery and his expulsion of a drunken Heracles from a banquet. This same source later describes Heracles' thwarted love for Iole, suggesting that Eurytos denied the hero his daughter as a trophy (351–70, 476–78). Early Corinthian and red-figure art on pottery vessels (described by Gantz, *Early Greek Myth*, 435–36) depicts a banquet at Eurytos' palace, during which Heracles participates in an archery contest, with Iole looking on. This archery contest is also described in Herodorus frg. 31F37 (summarized by Gantz, *Early Greek Myth*, 436) and in Apollodorus *Library* 2.6.1–3, with no reference to the banquet motif in either source. Diodorus of Sicily 4.31.1–2 omits even the archery contest in his description of Heracles' unsuccessful bid for Iole. Both he and Apollodorus explain that Eurytos refused to give Iole to Heracles because he feared for the safety of their offspring, given the hero's history of madness.

and to capture Iole. Ultimately these events precipitate the hero's own death at the hands of his jealous wife Deianeira, if we follow the story to its conclusion.[249]

The common motif of the drinking party in the *Testament of Judah* and in the legends of Heracles also alerts one to broader character propensities shared by the two strong heroes. Both characters exhibit strong physical appetites to match their great physical strength. More specifically, both are known for their copious alcohol consumption and ardent sexual passion.

The *Testament of Judah* depicts the patriarch drunk from too much wine more than once[250] and develops the dangers of wine as one of its central moral themes.[251] Similarly, the figure of Heracles was commonly associated with copious consumption of wine. Artistic representations on pottery vessels (including cups) portray the Greek hero reclining and drinking at a banquet, sometimes in the company of Dionysius, the god of wine.[252] In narrative art as well, Heracles'

According to tradition, Eurytos was the master bowman of his day. See Homer *Odyssey* 8.223–28, where Odysseus admits that even he could never rival the archers of the previous generation, namely Heracles and Eurytos. Note that Apollodorus *Library* 2.4.9, 11 portrays Eurytos as Heracles' archery teacher.

[249] References to the destruction of Oechalia as revenge for Eurytos' insult, the capture of Iole, and Heracles' death appear in Bacchylides *Dithyrambs* 15(16).13–35; Sophocles *Women of Trachis* 240–85, 531–1278; Diodorus of Sicily 4.37.5–4.38.5; and Apollodorus *Library* 2.7.7.

Note that there is yet another instance in which Heracles participates in a banquet in the company of a king's daughter. This instance occurs after his death and apotheosis, when the hero reclines at a banquet among the gods, with Hebe the daughter of Zeus at his side (Homer *Odyssey* 11.602–4).

[250] Judah's wine consumption and drunkenness are depicted in *T.Jud.* 11:2; 12:3; 12:6; 13:5–6; 14:5–6; 16:4. None of the other patriarchs is developed as a drunk in this manner.

[251] The dangers of wine are explicitly enumerated in *T.Jud.* 14:1–8 and 16:1–5. One manuscript (MS g) specifies in the subtitle to this testament that it deals with the subject of drunkenness (μεθύσκεσθαι).

[252] Examples of artistic depictions of Heracles reclining and drinking at a banquet may be found in *LIMC*, vol. 4.2, 543–46. Verbal descriptions of the pottery depicted on these pages, plus many other examples of "Herakles *symposiastes*," may be found in *LIMC*, vol. 4.1, 817–21. According to this source, Heracles was the first Greek hero to be artistically represented reclining at a feast; later representations of this theme clearly portray the hero in a drunken state. Heracles appears reclining with Dionysius on the pottery described in *LIMC*, vol. 4.1, 818–19. Other artistic representations of Heracles in the company of Dionysus or Bacchus (and sometimes the satyrs) are described in *LIMC*, vol. 5.1, 154–60, examples of which may be found on the plates in *LIMC*, vol. 5.2, 144–49. Also of special interest are the pottery decorations portraying Athena, King Zeus' daughter, attending Heracles as he reclines at a banquet, described in *LIMC*, vol. 4.1, 817–18. This image corresponds

enjoyment of wine and his inebriation at banquets are much repeated themes.[253] In particular, comic treatments of this character emphasize his reputation as a drunk.[254] Significantly, in more than one instance, Heracles' consumption provides the occasion for reflection on the effects of wine, in much the same way that Judah's does in the *Testament of Judah*.[255]

Turning to the heroes' common propensity towards promiscuous sexual behavior, we find that in the *Testament of Judah* the patriarch has more than one sexual relationship due to his susceptibility to the passions.[256] None of the other sons of Jacob in the *Testaments* has more than one sexual partner.[257] Of course, Judah's double involvement with the Canaanite woman and Tamar is based on the biblical narrative in Genesis 38. But the explicit development of his relations with these two women as a sequential repetition of his fundamental weakness to feminine beauty and guile is unique. Intriguingly, in one

---

with a similar motif in the *Testament of Judah*, in which the king's daughter serves Judah wine at a party (*T.Jud.* 11:2; 13:5–6).

The association between Heracles and Dionysius is also comically dramatized in Aristophanes *Frogs*, in which Dionysius impersonates Heracles and descends to Hades to enjoy the wine and women (and food) found there. Significantly, in the writings of Diodorus of Sicily, his discussion of Dionysius (4.2–6) immediately precedes his discussion of Heracles (4.8–39, 57–58).

[253] Hesiod *Marriage of Ceyx* frg. 2.263–65, attests to Heracles' love of banquets, to which he goes even if uninvited. Panyassis of Halikarnassos *Herakleia* frgs. 12–14K, describes a host urging Heracles to drink at a banquet. Sophocles *Women of Trachis* 268–69 alludes to Heracles' humiliating expulsion from King Eurytos' banquet, at which he had been drinking. Euripides *Alcestis* 747–802 deals at length with Heracles' consumption of wine. Note also that Heracles' battle with the centaurs begins with a dispute about some wine reserved for the hero by Dionysius. See Diodorus of Sicily 4.12.3–12.

[254] Aristophanes *Frogs* 107–14, 503–18, 549–67 dramatizes Heracles' reputation in Hades as a drunk (as well as a glutton and womanizer). The extant fragments of Menander *Counterfeit Heracles* similarly refer to drink, women, and food—themes commonly associated with the comic Heracles. Dio Chrysostom *Discourses* 32.94–95 reports that the drunken figure of Heracles on the stage consistently evoked laughter.

[255] Depending on the source, these effects are either positive or negative. For example, in Euripides *Alcestis* 773–802 Heracles himself extols the pleasures of wine, without which life is not worth living. By contrast, in Panyassis of Halikarnassos *Herakleia* frgs. 13–14K, Heracles' host describes the dangers of wine after expelling his drunken guest.

[256] His relations with the Canaanite princess are described in *T.Jud.* 8:2; 11:1–2; 13:3–7; 14:6; 17:1; and with Tamar in *T.Jud.* 12:1–4 and 14:5.

[257] Even the *Testament of Reuben*, which most fully develops the dangers of female sexuality and fornication, portrays only one sexual relationship (that of Reuben and Bilhah). Jacob's polygamous marriage with Leah and Rachel is retained, since it is part of the biblical story, but even in this case the *Testaments* pointedly discusses its irregularity. See *T.I.* 1:6–13.

textual family there is an allusion to yet a third woman, named Aknan (or Anan), with whom the patriarch also has sexual relations.[258] In keeping with his negative experience as the promiscuous lover of the *Testaments*, Judah warns his sons repeatedly concerning the dangers of illicit sexual behavior.[259] Similarly, in Greek thought Heracles is the great lover, who experienced more of desire and its fulfillment than any other man.[260] The list of Heracles' amours is extensive, but perhaps the most graphic expression of this hero's phenomenal libido is the story mentioned above concerning his impregnation of the fifty daughters of Thespius. At least one source maintains that the hero accomplished this feat in a single night.[261] While the Greek hero is portrayed as a lover of women in a wide variety of literary genres, it is once again the comic Heracles whose promiscuity is most exaggerated.[262] Note, however, that whereas Heracles' prodigious love life is either positively associated with his great physical strength in legend and tragedy or parodied in the comedies, the serious moral tone of the *Testaments* assures that Judah's status as the greatest lover among his brothers is neither celebrated nor treated humorously.[263]

---

[258] In *T.Jud.* 13:13, three manuscripts (MSS h, i, and j) refer to Judah's sexual relations with an otherwise unknown woman named Aknan (ακναν); a variant (MS c) refers to a woman named Anan (αναν).

[259] *T.Jud.* 13:3, 5–7; 14:3–8; 17:1; 18:2; 23:2. The subtitle of this testament in many manuscripts (MSS b, l, d, m, e, f) indicates that it deals with the subject of "fornication" (πορνείας). It is interesting to note, however, that the *Testament of Reuben* contains lengthier passages concerning the dangers associated with women, since that is the primary focus of that testament.

[260] Heracles' own wife Deianeira offers this assessment of the hero in Sophocles *Women of Trachis* 459–60. Elsewhere in the same work, she describes Heracles' passionate nature as a disease (445, 491, 544).
Pottery decorations depicting Heracles' relationships with women are described in *LIMC*, vol. 4.1, 821–24, examples of which are shown on the plates in *LIMC*, vol. 4.2, 547–49.

[261] Pausanias *Description of Greece* 9.27.6–7 explicitly states that Heracles had intercourse with Thespius' daughters (except one who refused) on a single night, and Diodorus of Sicily 4.29.2–4 implies the same.

[262] In the comic portrayals of Heracles, the hero's amorous affairs are associated with his consumption of wine, as is the case with Judah in the *Testament of Judah*. A good example of this may be found in Aristophanes *Frogs* 107–14, 503–18, 549–67, where Heracles' reputation in Hades is based on his past conduct as a glutton, drunk, and womanizer. For a discussion of the comic Heracles, including additional sources depicting the hero as a sot and womanizer, see Galinsky, *Herakles Theme*, 81–100. More generally, Eva C. Keuls (*The Reign of the Phallus: Sexual Politics in Ancient Athens* [New York: Harper & Row, 1985] 191) points out the emphasis on "greed, bibulousness, and unsatiable lust"—the very vices associated with Judah in the *Testaments*—in Greek comedy.

[263] Note that Judah's third weakness, his love of money (φιλαργυρίας) indicated in

Despite this difference, there is a further important similarity between Heracles' relationships with women and Judah's. This similarity consists of the theme of a woman's humiliating enslavement—or even destruction—of the unconquered hero. In the *Testament of Judah* the undefeated hunter and warrior ultimately succumbs to enemy forces during peacetime through his attraction and marriage to a Canaanite woman. Judah describes his subsequent shameful subordination to Bathshua in the domestic sphere when he recounts how his wife manipulated their sons without his consent or knowledge (*T.Jud.* 10:2–6). Similarly, he describes how he lost his claim to the kingship through his relations with Tamar, to whom he freely surrendered the symbols of his royal power for illicit and incestuous love. From personal experience and from wisdom gained through angelic revelation, Judah warns every man of woman's power to enslave (*T.Jud.* 15:5–6). The theme of thwarting, feminine control over the male hero is also present in the Heracles legends.[264] We have already noted Hera's deflection of the royal status intended for this hero even before his birth. Shifting our attention from the beginning of Heracles' life to its end, we find yet another illustration of the theme of destructive female power. Heracles' jealous wife Deianeira sends him a tunic smeared with deadly Centaur's blood (mixed with semen in later sources) that she mistakenly thinks is a love potion, just as he returns from a successful military campaign.[265] One of the most developed portrayals of this episode, Sophocles' *Women of Trachis*, explicitly notes the irony of the hero's destruction—not by a fierce

---

the subtitle of many of the manuscripts (mss b, l, d, m, k, f), is not generally associated with Heracles. But while the Greek hero is not depicted as particularly avaricious, he does at least demonstrate a greed for food in the comedies. See for example, Aristophanes *Wasps* 60 and *Frogs* 549–67. In Aristophanes *Peace* 745 the comic figure of Heracles is characterized as "needy and seedy and greedy:" The theme of avarice is explicitly raised—if only to be refuted—in some of the moralizations of Heracles' character in Greek ethical writings. For example, Prodicus depicts Heracles' rejection of luxury and wealth in his "Heracles' Choice," according to Xenophon *Memorabilia* 2.1.21–34.

[264] The social and psychological dynamics behind the fear of female domination expressed in the Heracles legends are discussed in Philip E. Slater, *The Glory of Hera: Greek Mythology and the Greek Family* (Princeton: Princeton University Press, 1968).

[265] Heracles' death at the hands of Deianeira is described in Bacchylides *Dithyrambs* 15(16).23–35; Sophocles *Women of Trachis* 531–1278; Apollodorus *Library* 2.7.7; and Diodorus of Sicily 4.38.1–5. In the latter two sources, the supposed love charm is composed of the centaur Nessus' blood and semen (Apollodorus *Library* 2.7.6 and Diodorus of Sicily 4.36.3–5), whereas in Sophocles *Women of Trachis* 555–77 it is composed simply of his clotted blood.

enemy in combat as might be expected, but by a weak, unarmed woman.[266] A final narrative episode depicting Heracles' humiliation by a woman consists of his enslavement under the Lydian queen Omphale, which at least in later sources includes romantic involvement between the hero and his mistress.[267] A number of sources emphasize Heracles' subjection to Omphale by portraying his transfer of characteristic attributes, including his lion-skin, bow, and arrows (or club), to the foreign queen.[268] Heracles' surrender of his identifying articles in these sources recalls Judah's surrender of his staff, armor, and diadem to Tamar in the *Testament of Judah*.[269] In general, however,

---

[266] Sophocles *Women of Trachis* 1058–63, 1089–117. The name "Deianeira" (Δηιάνειρα) itself suggests that she is a "man-slayer." The theme of the mighty hero felled by a woman is raised earlier in *Women of Trachis* 351–74 as well, since Heracles' attack of Oechalia because of his passionate love for Iole leads ultimately to his demise.

The theme of Heracles' death at the hands of a woman is also present in Bacchylides *Odes* 5.68–175. Bacchylides presents Heracles as an unwitting parallel to Deianeira's brother Meleager, whom he encounters in Hades. After Heracles expresses wonder about the man who could have killed such an outstanding warrior, Meleager explains that it was no man at all, but a woman (specifically his mother) who caused his death. Heracles' expression of interest in marrying Meleager's sister (Deianeira) portends that he will meet the same fate.

[267] Allusions to this degrading episode appear in literary sources from the classical period to the Hellenistic and Roman periods, including Homer *Odyssey* 11.601–26; Sophocles *Women of Trachis* 69–71, 248–57, 274–78; Aeschylus *Agamemnon* 1035–46; Herodorus frg. 31F33, summarized by Gantz, *Early Greek Myth*, 439; Diodorus of Sicily 4.31.5–8; Apollodorus *Library* 2.6.2–3; and Dio Chrysostom *Discourses* 4.72–73. The latter three sources attempt in various ways to ameliorate the humiliation of Heracles' legendary service under Omphale. By contrast, a number of other later sources, including Ovid *Heroides* 9.53–118; Lucian *How to Write History* 10; *Dialogue of the Gods* 15(13).237; and Plutarch *Moralia*, "Old Men in Public Affairs," 785, emphasize the degradation of the hero. Ovid *Heroides* 9.103–18 makes explicit the theme of the manly victor defeated by a weak woman in his depiction of Heracles' enslavement by Omphale. This enslavement is of course simply a further permutation of the more general theme of the hero's humiliating bondage to an inferior, expressed in the legends about Heracles' labors for Eurystheus.

[268] Artwork from as early as the sixth century BCE depicts Omphale's appropriation of Heracles' lion-skin, bow, and arrows, according to Gantz, *Early Greek Myth*, 439. Later artwork and literary sources go even farther in depicting the hero's humiliation. Not only does Heracles give Omphale his own clothing and arms, but he also dons the queen's luxurious dress and takes up the feminine tools of the carding comb and spindle. For literary examples of this depiction of Heracles' cross-dressing, see Ovid *Heroides* 9.53–118; Lucian *How to Write History* 10; *Dialogues of the Gods* 15(13).237; Plutarch *Moralia*, "Old Men in Public Affairs," 785; and Dio Chrysostom *Discourses* 32.94.

The theme of sex-role inversion also appears in Sophocles *Women of Trachis*, where Deianeira stabs herself like a man (instead of hanging herself like a woman) upon learning that she has caused her husband's suffering (930), while Heracles weeps like a girl because of his pain (1071–75).

[269] *T. Jud.* 12:4 and 15:2–3. The *Testament of Judah* initially depicts these items as

because of the strong association between women, fornication, and Beliar in the *Testaments*,[270] there are moral and cosmological dimensions to Judah's involvement with Bathshua and Tamar that are absent in Heracles' involvement with Deianeira and Omphale in Greek myth, which emphasizes the irony of fate.[271]

These are not the only correspondences in theme and narrative detail between Judah in the *Testament of Judah* and Heracles in Graeco-Roman legend. For example, because these two characters represent the extremes of human strength, they are also prone to commit acts of hubris;[272] consequently, both must undergo penitential regimens to

---

an outright gift to Tamar, symbolizing his abdication of royal power, not as a pledge for later payment (*T.Jud.* 12:4; 15:3), although subsequently Judah refers to a pledge (*T.Jud.* 12:5, 7), as in the biblical narrative. Even the allusion in *T.Jud.* 12:9–10 to Hirah's attempt to reclaim the pledge (Gen 38:20–23) contains no reference whatsoever to a pledge. Rather, the emphasis is on Judah's false perception that no one knew of his sin, which in turn emphasizes the humiliation of its public disclosure.

[270] See for example, *T.R.* 3:9–4:11 (especially 4:7 and 4:11) and *T.R.* 5:1–6:4 (especially 5:3 and 6:1).

[271] Of special interest, however, is an even later phase of this trajectory, expressed by the sixth-century Christian writer Fulgentius, who allegorizes and moralizes the episode as a depiction of unconquered Virtue's defeat by Eros (*Fables* 2, "The Fable of Hercules and Omphale"). This permutation of the common motif of the strong hero's weakness to the female sex is similar to that found in the *Testament of Judah*. For further examples of Heracles overcome by Eros, see Galinsky, *Herakles Theme*, 124, n. 29.

[272] In *T.Jud.* 13:2–3 Judah discloses that, overconfident in his own strength, he boasted of his abstinence during war and chided his brother Reuben for the incident with Bilhah. His hubris activated the spirit of envy and fornication against him, until he succumbed to the very temptations to which he considered himself immune. Judah more realistically assesses the limits of his strength after his experience with Bathshua and Tamar in *T.Jud.* 19:4. (Interestingly, in *Homeric Hymns* 5, "To Aphrodite," 45–255 Zeus causes Aphrodite to experience irresistible desire for a mortal man and to bear a child by him so that she will no longer be able to mock the gods for their inappropriate matings with mortal women. In this episode, the Greek goddess is similar to Judah in that she must abandon her posture of prideful superiority after she succumbs to the same temptation.) Heracles, especially in the works of Homer, also transgresses the limits set for human behavior. For example, he violates the boundaries between the human and divine realms when he dares to attack and wound members of the pantheon, namely Hera and Hades (*Iliad* 5.381–404). Similarly, he violates accepted codes of hospitality when he kills his guest, Iphytos (*Odyssey* 21.22–30). But even the mighty and irrepressible Heracles cannot escape death, humanity's common fate (*Iliad* 18.117–19; *Odyssey* 11.601–26). Much later comparisons between famous athletes and Heracles (in Pausanias *Description of Greece* 6.5.1–9 and Diodorus of Sicily 17.100–1) also emphasize the theme of the legendary hero's overweening pride and ultimate death. More positively, Pindar *Nemean Odes* 3.20–27 portrays the hero stretching the outward limits of human potential and accomplishment, symbolized by the famous pillars that the hero sets in the sea. For the motif of the pillars of Heracles, see also Isocrates *Orations* 5, "To Philip," 112.

atone for grievous transgressions.[273] It is also interesting to note that the theme of unrecognized sexual intercourse between Judah and Tamar present in Genesis 38 and in the version of this biblical story in the *Testament of Judah* is also present in the legend about Heracles' rape of Auge.[274]

---

[273] In *T.Jud.* 15:4 Judah discloses that he repented of his transgression with Tamar, refrained from wine and meat, and experienced no joy in his life. (Compare with Reuben's similar forms of repentance in *T.R.* 1:10.) In *T.Jud.* 19:2 Judah once again recalls the repentance of his flesh, his humiliation, and the prayers of Jacob which served as the means of his restoration.

Heracles must perform penance more than once in his life. Because he killed his guest, Iphytos, he consults an oracle and learns that he must serve as Omphale's slave for a fixed period of time as an expiation. See Sophocles *Women of Trachis* 248–80; Apollodorus *Library* 2.6.2; and Diodorus of Sicily 4.31.2–17. Similarly, after killing his sons and his wife in a fit of madness, Heracles must atone for his terrible crime. See for example, Hyginus *Fabulae* 32; Pausanias *Description of Greece* 10.29.7; and Tzetzes on Lycophron 38, in which Heracles goes to Delphi to atone for the murder of his family. Alternately, see the ending of Euripides *Madness of Heracles* 1088–429 in which he follows Theseus to Athens to perform penance, mourning and lamenting as he goes.

Incidentally, Heracles' murder of his wife and sons when out of his senses bears at least a slight resemblance to Judah's anguished cursing of his wife, which leads to her death soon after two of their sons have already died due to their wickedness (*T.Jud.* 11:4–5). This additional detail in the *Testament of Judah* also lends a different sense to Judah's later desire to kill Tamar (*T.Jud.* 12:5–6). In the biblical narrative, Judah calls for Tamar's death as a punishment for her sexual misconduct; however, in the *Testament of Judah*, this patriarch's earlier dispatch of his first wife marks him as a killer of the women with whom he becomes involved. In the testament, Judah does not give orders to others that Tamar be burned, but rather he himself person-ally wishes "to kill" (ἀνελεῖν) her (*T.Jud.* 12:5–6). The verb employed here removes Judah's desire that Tamar die from the semantic sphere of legal proceedings im-plied in the biblical version and places it within the semantic sphere of his own violent exploits against animal and human enemies, to which category Tamar, as a representative of deceptive and treacherous womankind, belongs.

[274] In *T.Jud.* 12:3 and 5, Judah's failure to recognize his daughter-in-law is stressed, as in the biblical narrative, although in the *Testament of Judah* the reason he does not recognize her is different. Whereas in the biblical narrative, the veil Tamar wears conceals her identity, in the later source Judah's drunkenness and Tamar's beautiful adornment prevent his recognition.

The theme of unrecognized paternity also appears in connection with Heracles, in the story of his relations with Auge. There are many different versions of the story, but its basic outline is as follows: King Aleos learned that if his daughter Auge were ever to bear a child, that grandson would endanger the lives of Aleos' own sons. He therefore dedicated Auge as a priestess of Athena. Once while drunk after being entertained by King Aleos, Heracles raped this priestess, not knowing that she was his host's daughter, and she thereby became pregnant. When Aleos learned that his daughter was with child, he wanted to kill her. In one source (Diodorus of Sicily 4.33.7–12), he did not believe her when she claimed that Heracles was the father of her child. The story has several different endings which need not concern us here (summarized by Gantz, *Early Greek Myth*, 428–29), except to note the ultimate recognition of the child's (Telephus') ancestry, which recalls the recognition of the unborn sons' paternity in Genesis 38. Versions of the story may be found in Sophocles

The similarities discussed above suggest that Judah's character in the *Testament of Judah* may have been developed as a rough parallel to the popular Greek hero. The fact that the figures of Judah and Heracles appear in larger cultural discussions about the same issues further collaborates this hypothesis. Two examples of how these heroes function within discussions of broader issues, specifically those concerning the moral life and kingship, point out that although both Heracles and Judah were used to define moral values and royal ideals in Greek philosophical writings and in the *Testaments*, respectively, the resulting definitions contrast sharply. These final examples therefore illuminate some of the complex dynamics of Jewish thought within a dominant Hellenistic cultural context—dynamics that include borrowing and adaptation, as well as rejection and substitution.

As the best and strongest of men, Heracles was widely used as an exemplar in ethical discussions within the Greek speaking world.[275] This practice was perhaps most consistent among the Cynics, who appropriated him as one of their primary behavioral models,[276] although it was certainly not limited to these philosophers, nor did it begin with them. Already in earlier times, Hesiod, Bacchylides, and Pindar credited Heracles with the establishment of justice and law on earth. These writers thus imbued his legendary acts of violence

---

Telepheia (now lost, but summarized by the fourth-century Athenian Alkidamas); Euripides *Telephos*; Diodorus of Sicily 4.33.7–12; Apollodorus *Library* 2.7.4; and Pausanias *Description of Greece* 8.2.9.

The motif of disputed paternity, often resolved by the evidence of identifying marks or trinkets, is a common one in Greek literature, especially in the new comedy of the fourth century BCE. For example, Menander *Men at Arbitration* portrays a courtesan obtaining a ring belonging to a well-bred man, who seduced a well-bred girl and afterwards gave her his ring. With this prop, the courtesan pretends to be the mother of the child born of the illicit union between the lovers, in order to gain her freedom. Note that the version of Genesis 38 in the *Testament of Judah* is similar to this story, in that even when Tamar produces the pledge items, Judah still speculates that she may have procured them from another woman, as is the case in the Greek comedy.

There may even be some sort of implicit association between the two strong heroes on the basis of the similarities between Heracles' birth narrative and Judah's twin sons' birth narrative at the end of Genesis 38. This comparison remains implicit, however, because the birth of the twins at the end of Genesis 38 has been entirely eliminated in the version in the *Testament of Judah*. But, it should be mentioned that Heracles' birth involves a sexual deception and the birth of twins with one destined for greatness, as does the birth of Perez and Zerah at the end of Genesis 38.

[275] Gilbert Murray, "Heracles the Best of Men," in *Greek Studies* (Oxford: Clarendon Press, 1946) 106–26.

[276] Galinsky, *Herakles Theme*, 101–25, and Ragnar Höistad, *Cynic Hero and Cynic King: Studies in the Cynic Conception of Man* (Uppsala: Karl Bloms Boktryckeri, 1948).

with a positive moral valence.[277] More important for our discussion here, however, is a work by Prodicus (a contemporary of Socrates) depicting "Heracles' Choice." In this work, unfortunately lost but summarized at length by Xenophon,[278] Prodicus depicts Heracles as a youth at a crossroads, making a choice between Vice and Virtue, represented as two women.[279] Each of these women describes the benefits and style of life that she offers the hero.[280] Vice, depicted as a short woman seductively dressed to display her charms, tempts Heracles with a life of ease, sensual pleasures, and luxuries. Significantly in light of our present comparison with Judah in the *Testament of Judah*, the attractions she mentions include plenteous drink, the delights of love, and the wealth of others gained without toil.[281] By contrast, Virtue, depicted as a tall woman with a straightforward and noble bearing, offers Heracles a life of exertion and austerity in the service of others and the pursuit of worthwhile activities. Heracles' choice of Virtue in this work radically transforms the Greek hero almost beyond recognition with its suppression of his impulsive, violent aspects and his excessive indulgences from the mythology. In this moralizing interpretation, Heracles' legendary physical struggles and

---

[277] In Hesiod *Theogony* 289–94, 313–18, 326–32, 526–32, Heracles destroys terrible monsters that plague the land; in Bacchylides *Odes* 12(13), he quells violent arrogance and establishes law for mortals; and in Pindar *Law, the Lord of All* frg. 169(151), Heracles' violence against Geryon is justified as in keeping with the law of the cosmos.

[278] In Xenophon *Memorabilia* 2.21–34, Socrates recounts Prodicus' work in a discussion concerning the proper education for rulers and all those who desire to lead a worthwhile life. It is also presented with significant variations in Philostratus *Life of Apollonius of Tyana* 6.10. In addition, it is mentioned briefly in a number of other sources, including Plato *Symposium* 177; Philostratus *Lives of the Sophists* 482–83; pseudepigraphal letter of Aristippus 13, "To Simon," in Abraham J. Malherbe, ed., *The Cynic Epistles: A Study Edition*, SBL Sources for Biblical Studies 12 (Missoula, MT: Scholars Press, 1977) 250–53; and Cicero *De Officiis* 1.118.

[279] Although it may not be surprising that Prodicus represents Vice and Virtue as women due to the feminine gender of these Greek words (Κακία and Ἀρετή), in this particular case the employment of women may bear an additional resonance because of Heracles' legendary reputation as a lover. Here, the hero's characteristic attraction to women is transformed into a moral choice between two distinctive ways of life.

[280] "Heracles' Choice" is dependent on the story of Paris' choice between Aphrodite, Hera, and Athena. It should be remembered that in the earlier story as well each of the goddesses offers their judge a reward, should he choose her, and that Paris' choice of Aphrodite and her subsequent gift of Helen precipitate the Trojan war. In Prodicus' allegory, by contrast, Virtue recalls Athena, Heracles' patron goddess.

[281] The very temptations to which Judah succumbs in the *Testament of Judah* are included in Vice's description of the life that she offers, although there are other attractions as well, including dainty foods, physical comforts, and leisure.

204 CHAPTER TWO

appetites are replaced with equally strong desires and exertions of an ethical and spiritual nature, and the hero thus becomes a moral paragon. Prodicus' image of Heracles' deliberate choice of Virtue over Vice was well-known in the Graeco-Roman world, and it came to influence a long philosophical and literary tradition extending through the Renaissance and beyond.[282] In addition to Prodicus' work, however, there were many other moral interpretations of Heracles' life, consisting primarily of allegorical explanations of his labors and other physical feats as spiritual struggles and victories against vices. To mention just one example as an illustration, Herodorus of Heraklea explained that the three golden apples Heracles obtained after killing a dragon with his club represent the three virtues he gained through philosophy, specifically the virtues of not getting angry, not loving money, and not being fond of pleasure.[283] This type of interpretation of the Heracles legends is in keeping with a wider trend in the Graeco-Roman world to offer allegorical explanations of physical struggles in mythology. These allegorical explanations include an implicit critique of the sufficiency of physical excellence for the ideal of manhood. In addition, they forward a redefinition of virtue in moral terms.[284] Because it would be impossible to discuss all the variations of the moral interpretation of Heracles' life and exploits here, it must suffice to reiterate that this hero was commonly employed as an exemplar of the ethical way of life in philosophical writings and to note, moreover, that he provided a flexible vehicle for the expression of quite a range of positive cultural ideals by authors of different philosophical persuasions.[285]

---

[282] See Johann Alpers, *Hercules in bivio* (Göttingen: Dieterichium, 1912), and Galinsky, *Herakles Theme*, 185–230.

[283] Herodorus of Heraklea frg. 31F14, quoted by Galinsky, *Herakles Theme*, 56. Herodorus' list of the three vices conquered by Heracles recalls the three vices to which Judah succumbs in the *Testament of Judah*, not only because of their number, but also because of the specific references to love of money and pleasure. Additional examples of allegorical interpretations of Heracles' labors may be found in Heraclitus *Homeric Allegories* 33, in Félix Buffière, ed., *Héraclite, Allégories d'Homère* (Paris: Belles Lettres, 1962) 39–40; Dio Chrysostom *Discourses* 5.16–23; and Lucretius *De Rerum Natura* 5.22–54. Similarly, in Philostratus *Life of Apollonius of Tyana* 6.10, the representation of Prodicus' allegory of Heracles' choice between Vice and Virtue stresses the interpretation of the hero's labors as moral struggles. The discussion concludes with the promise that if one chooses Virtue as Heracles did, one accomplishes the equivalent of all the hero's legendary labors.

[284] See Victor C. Pfitzner, "The Agon Motif in Greek and Hellenistic Philosophy," in *Paul and the Agon Motif: Traditional Athletic Imagery in the Pauline Literature*, NovTSup 16 (Leiden: E. J. Brill, 1967) 23–37.

[285] For example, in retelling Prodicus' allegory, Philostratus *Life of Apollonius of Tyana* 6.10 radically redefines the Virtue that Heracles chooses. Instead of the social

Turning to the *Testament of Judah*, we first note that the theme of the choice between vice and virtue present in the moral interpretation of Heracles' life is also emphasized in this Hellenistic Jewish source. This theme appears both in Judah's accounts of the mistaken choices that he made at important points in his own life and in his instructions to his sons to avoid similar poor choices.[286] Significantly, in this testament a youthful Judah[287] encounters two women, as the youthful Heracles encounters two women in Prodicus' allegory. Admittedly, the presence of two women in the *Testament of Judah* stems ultimately from Genesis 38 itself, and they remain actual characters with names (Bathshua and Tamar) rather than pure personifications of abstract ideas, and neither is a good choice, like Virtue. But despite these qualifications, and especially given the other similarities between Judah and Heracles noted above, it is difficult to ignore the affinities between this testament and Prodicus' depiction of "Heracles' Choice." In the *Testament of Judah*, then, the very same moral issue of choice of lifestyle presented in Prodicus' work is raised by the two women that the young hero meets. In this way the testament participates in a greater trend in the Graeco-Roman world to moralize the message of important narratives and to express through legendary figures lessons of an ethical nature.

---

value of working for the common good stressed in Xenophon's version, Philostratus emphasizes asceticism and the cultivation of personal character traits associated with the Pythagoreans. Another example of a distinctive understanding of Heracles' virtue is the one held by the Cynics. According to a variety of sources, Diogenes and the Cynics portrayed Heracles' labors and exploits as the vicissitudes and hardships of fate that the truly wise person endures willingly and without complaint. For references to Heracles as the exemplar of the Cynic way of life, see the pseudepigraphal letters of Diogenes 26, "To Metrocles;" 39, "To Crates;" 4, "To Monimus" (where incidentally, the worthless activities of "possessing more, eating, drinking, and indulging in one's lusts" recall Judah's vices); the pseudepigraphal letter of Heraclitus 4, "To Hermodorus;" Diogenes Laertius *Antisthenes* 6.2; *Diogenes* 6.71; Epictetus *Discourses* 3.22, 24, 26; 4.8, 10; Dio Chrysostom *Discourses* 8.21–36; and Pseudo Lucian *The Cynic* 13. See also Höistad, *Cynic Hero and Cynic King*.

[286] For example, Judah reflects on his mistaken choice of a wicked Canaanite wife in *T.Jud.* 11:1–2; 13:4–8; 14:6; 16:4; 17:1; 19:2–4; and on his poor judgment in having sexual relations with his daughter-in-law in *T.Jud.* 12:3–10; 14:5; 15:1–6. He warns his sons to avoid the vices of drunkenness, greed, and fornication that led to his downfall in *T.Jud.* 13:2; 14:1–4, 7–8; 16:1–3; 17:1; 18:1–6; 19:1; 20:1–5. A more abstract expression of the necessity to make choices between truth and deceit may be found in *T.Jud.* 20:1–5.

[287] References to Judah's youth in this testament include *T.Jud.* 7:10, where he is depicted as a young man of twenty years at the conclusion of the Canaanite wars, and *T.Jud.* 11:1, where he laments that his youth blinded his eyes when he saw the Canaanite woman. The patriarch's youth is also indicated in *T.Jud.* 13:2–3.

In keeping with the misogynistic outlook of the *Testaments*, however, both of the women Judah encounters are viewed negatively as
temptresses to vice. They are dressed seductively,[288] as is Vice in
"Heracles' Choice," and they elicit behavior from Judah very much
in keeping with the vision that Vice offers Heracles, including drunkenness, acquisition of the wealth of others, and promiscuous sexuality.[289]
And instead of making a single positive choice as Heracles does, Judah
makes two negative choices. Whereas Heracles chooses Virtue and
therefore comes to represent moral excellence instead of merely physical excellence, Judah succumbs to his characteristic three vices through
his association with Bathshua and Tamar. He therefore becomes a
negative exemplar and illustrates the uselessness of physical strength
in matters of morality. To a certain extent, Judah's fall in these two
instances echoes the critique of the ideal of manhood as hunter, athlete,
and fighter accomplished in a very different way through the positive allegorical interpretations of the Heracles legends. But the critique
of this masculine ideal is even stronger in the *Testament of Judah*, because
this work assigns no positive moral or spiritual qualities to Judah to
replace the physical strength that proves useless in the more important ethical struggles of life.[290] The testament may therefore provide
an oblique critique of the Greek hero's character and role in contemporary moral discussions.

But whether or not this is the case, it is still possible to gain an
understanding about this testament's guarded view concerning the
human potential to be a positive moral agent from these differences
with the Heracles material, although some caution is needed in this
endeavor. After all, Judah is the royal figure in the *Testaments*, and
the negative depiction of him may tell more about this document's

---

[288] Bathshua is irresistibly beautiful because of her adornment in *T.Jud.* 13:5 (cf.,
T.Jud. 17:1), and Tamar is the same in *T.Jud.* 12:3.

[289] It must be acknowledged, however, that Bathshua and Tamar are not entirely
responsible for Judah's errant behavior in the *Testament of Judah*. Even before he
meets these women, the spirit of envy and fornication plots against him to insure
that he is punished through his irregular sexual relations for his boasting and his
humiliation of a brother (*T.Jud.* 13:2–3). Note also that Judah is already drunk when
he meets Tamar (*T.Jud.* 12:3), so that she is not the actual cause of his drunkenness;
nevertheless, it is only in the stories of his involvement with the two women that his
excessive drinking becomes evident, so the two women at least act to bring his vices
into focus.

[290] Judah's only redeeming spiritual qualities are his recognition of error and his
sincere repentance. See for example *T.Jud.* 19:2–4.

view of kingship than anything else.[291] Indeed there are other patriarchs, including Joseph and Issachar, who are presented in a more
positive light, and these figures suggest a more optimistic perspective
on the human potential for choosing and achieving a life of piety.
But even in the testaments associated with these more positive exemplars, just as in the *Testament of Judah*, there is an emphasis on the
internal conflict between psychological and spiritual forces for good
and evil, corresponding to the larger cosmic conflict between God
and Beliar, which is absent from the allegorical interpretations of
Heracles' life.[292] To some extent, these larger dynamics curtail the
freedom of an individual's choice to lead a virtuous life, although
certainly the ethical tenor of the *Testaments* ultimately demands that
each person become a responsible moral agent. The complicating
psychological, spiritual, and cosmological dynamics underlying the
anthropology expressed in this document are especially evident in
the *Testament of Judah*. Early in this testament, in response to Judah's
filial obedience, the Lord watches over him and grants him success
in all he does (*T.Jud.* 2:1), and an angel protects him in battle (*T.Jud.*
3:10). But after Judah boasts of his own moral superiority and humiliates his brother because of his failure, the spirit of envy and fornication plot against him (*T.Jud.* 13:3). He becomes blinded by a number
of forces, including youth, wine, pleasure, feminine beauty, and the
prince of deceit himself, so that he can no longer discern righteousness from sin.[293] Finally, after falling into error, Judah's penitential
behavior and his father's prayers, not a choice to do better in the
future, activate divine forgiveness and restoration (*T.Jud.* 19:2–3). In
addition to these narrative illustrations of the constant interaction
between an individual's choice and the larger forces of the spiritual

---

[291] But the *Testament of Judah* also makes Judah a model for the rest of humanity
in many passages, such as in his extrapolation from his experience about the dangers
of wine (*T.Jud.* 14:1–8) and women (*T.Jud.* 15:1–6).

[292] A similar interest in the psychological and spiritual forces influencing moral
choice may be detected in some of the writings of the Stoic philosophers, although
in these sources the interest in religious themes evident in the *Testaments* is absent.

[293] In *T.Jud.* 11:1, the disposition of youth blinds Judah; in *T.Jud.* 11:2 and 13:6,
wine blurs his vision; in *T.Jud.* 13:6, pleasure blinds him; in *T.Jud.* 12:3, feminine
beauty deceives him; and in *T.Jud.* 19:4, the prince of deceit himself blinds the
patriarch. In the moral exhortations as well, a number of forces are noted as the
general causes of moral blindness, including wine (*T.Jud.* 14:1), impurity, and love of
money (*T.Jud.* 17:6). In the prophetic predictions concerning the future, Judah notes
that the eyes of his descendants will be blighted because of their sins (*T.Jud.* 23:3),
until finally at the end of time the deceit of Beliar is destroyed by fire (*T.Jud.* 25:3).

world, a number of passages in the *Testament of Judah* explicitly describe some of the psychological and cosmological struggles centered in the soul.[294] We may therefore conclude that the *Testament of Judah* pays more attention to the psychological and cosmological influences contributing to one's choices than does Prodicus' allegory and some of the other allegorical interpretations of the Heracles material. In fact, by emphasizing the possibility that one may be blinded by external forces, the *Testament of Judah* asserts that sometimes one cannot even discern the true nature of one's choices. With its recognition of severe limits even to the perception of moral options, the testament offers a more qualified perspective on the human potential to become an effective moral agent than the more optimistic Heracles material. This perspective accords with the religious world view of the *Testaments*, in which obedience to God's commandments and the commandments of the fathers is emphasized as an ideal, rather than the exercise of rational will to choose and implement the moral life.[295] The emphasis in this document is therefore on the importance of tradition, of what has been revealed in the past as divine intention for human life, and this viewpoint is entirely different from anything in the Greek material. The heroic choice of one's own moral destiny that is intrinsic to the portrayals of Heracles in ethical writings such as Prodicus' "Heracles' Choice" is therefore muted in the *Testament of Judah* by a number of factors.[296]

Another area of larger cultural concern in which the heroes appear involves discussions of the nature of kingship. As briefly noted above, Heracles becomes the model of ideal kingship, in an interpretive move that contradicts the mythological portrait of the rightful king denied his throne. For example, in addressing Philip of Macedon

---

[294] See, for example, *T.Jud.* 16:1–3, 18:2–6, and especially 20:1–5, which concludes Judah's exhortations to his sons with a description of how the mind's understanding must discriminate between the spirits of truth and deceit.

[295] As noted previously, these laws do not appear to be biblical laws, but rather are often equated with broad ethical principles.

[296] Heracles is subject to the same faults as Judah in the writings of the church fathers, who had to contend with the Greek hero's challenge to Jesus as a legendary figure worthy of worship. Later, once religious loyalty to Heracles had safely declined and Christianity had secured its place in the Roman empire, Heracles emerged as a positive figure in Christian thought, representing virtue and strength. An interesting Christian usage of this figure appears in Fulgentius *Fables* 2, "The Fable of Hercules and Omphale," which notes that despite Heracles' great strength and virtue, he was overcome by lust. Fulgentius' moral employment of the figure of Heracles is remarkably similar to the employment of Judah in the *Testament of Judah*.

(the father of Alexander), Isocrates invokes the example of Heracles to spur this ruler to military action in Asia on behalf of all Greeks.[297] Isocrates emphasizes Heracles' intelligence, love of justice, and willingness to fight for the well-being of all Greeks as royal qualities worth emulating, and he thereby articulates his ideal of kingship through the legendary hero. Similarly, in an allegory based on Prodicus' work "Heracles' Choice," Dio Chrysostom depicts Heracles choosing between Royalty and Tyranny, represented as two women.[298] Royalty is more beautiful and stronger by far, and she is surrounded by good counselors. By contrast, Tyranny is dressed in gaudy dress, and she is avaricious and flirtatious. As in Prodicus' piece, Dio Chrysostom's Heracles chooses the right woman, and in this instance, his father Zeus makes him king of all Argos because of his clear judgment. This allegory was written for the eyes of Trajan,[299] and it articulates the ideals of political leadership for the emperor through the vehicle of the Greek hero.

Both Isocrates and Dio Chrysostom demonstrate an interest in defining the qualities and behavior of the ideal political leader in their employment of Heracles as a royal exemplar. By contrast, Cynic and Stoic philosophers redefine kingship as the ethical person's control of his passions and indifference to the hardships and vicissitudes of life. For example, in a spurious letter attributed to the Cynic Diogenes, slavery and kingship are given a moral valence:

> Opinion has it that the souls that indulge the body are worthless and servile, while the souls that are not like these are good and carry their heads high (for they live as leaders of all, giving commands with sovereign authority), undertaking as a consequence of this only what is just and very easy to accomplish. . . . For when it is a question of possessing more, eating, drinking, and indulging in one's lusts, they are all worthless and no different from animals.[300]

---

[297] Isocrates *Orations* 5.109–15.

[298] Dio Chrysostom *Discourses* 1.58–84.

[299] The prophetess who describes Heracles' choice between Royalty and Tyranny specifies that the person who would benefit most from hearing it is "a mighty man, the ruler of very many lands and peoples," apparently Trajan.

[300] Pseudepigraphal letter of Diogenes 39, "To Monimus, do well," in Malherbe, ed., *Cynic Epistles*, 167. This letter was written in the second to first centuries BCE and describes similar vices to those discussed in the *Testament of Judah*.

For another example of this type of moralization of the concept of kingship, see Epictetus *Discourses* 4.8, which declares that "Zeus has deemed [the Cynic as a person free from passion, tumult, and vainglory] worthy of crown and scepter."

In this moralization of kingship, Heracles is frequently depicted as the archetypal "king," free from all passion and attachment, whom every person can and should emulate. For example, in a discussion of the futility of striving for wealth, the Stoic philosopher Epictetus writes:

> If he [God] does not provide me with much or with abundance, his will is for me to live simply; for he did not give abundance to Heracles, his own son; another than he was king of Argos and Mycenae, and he was subject to him and suffered toils and discipline. Yet Eurystheus was the man he was, no true king of Argos and Mycenae, for he was not king over himself, while Heracles was ruler and commander of all land and sea, cleansing them from lawlessness and wrong, and bringing in justice and righteousness, and this he did unarmed and single-handed.[301]

Similarly, a spurious letter attributed to the Cynic Heraclitus depicts the philosopher crowning himself after emulating Heracles' struggles:

> Was not Heracles born a man? According to Homer's lies he even murdered his guests. What then, made him a god? His own goodness and the most noble of his works when he had concluded such great labors. Therefore, sirs, am I myself not also good? I made a mistake in even asking you, for even if you answer to the contrary, nevertheless, I am good. Indeed, I have perfectly performed even of the most troublesome labors. I have overcome pleasures, I have overcome money, I have overcome ambition, I overthrew cowardice, I overthrew flattery, fear does not contradict me, drunkenness does not contradict me, grief fears me, anger fears me. It is against these that I struggle. And I crowned myself, at my own behest, and not at that of Eurystheus.[302]

The employment of Heracles as a royal figure in these philosophical writings has very little to do with statecraft and everything to do with the definition of the moral life. In Cynic and Stoic thought, therefore, the functions of Heracles as royal figure and moral exemplar coalesce.

As noted in previous discussions, the *Testaments* similarly presents Judah as the archetypal king, and the *Testament of Judah* discusses the origins of kingship, its strengths and limitations, and its future. Judah's departure from obedience and his near loss of kingship, however,

---

[301] Epictetus *Discourses* 3.26, trans. P. E. Matheson, in *The Stoic and Epicurean Philosophers: The Complete Extant Writings of Epicurus, Epictetus, Lucretius, [and] Marcus Aurelius*, ed. Whitney J. Oates (New York: Random House, 1940) 404.

[302] Pseudepigraphal letter of Heraclitus 4, "To Hermodorus," in Malherbe, ed., *Cynic Epistles*, 191–93.

sharply critique Israel's royalty. The first king's particular weaknesses—love of wine, women, and wealth—are vices that plague all of Israel's royalty, until the coming of the final sinless king. This work accordingly expresses no interest in Israel's historical kings, failing to mention even the greatest of them all: David, Hezekiah, Josiah, and the post-biblical Maccabees. Only the ultimate sinless savior from Judah's lineage receives affirmation. This perspective on kingship fundamentally differs from the more positive perspective expressed in the literature depicting Heracles as the ideal monarch.

The *Testament of Judah* also redefines kingship in moral terms, much as Greek philosophy does. While the patriarch ostensibly addresses the royal descendants who will govern after him, he also addresses the common man, who similarly experiences threats to his sovereignty over life and the passions.[303] But whereas Heracles presents a positive model for how a person may be "king" in everyday life through control of his passions, Judah presents a negative model of how even the king may fall due to the wiles of women and warns that all classes of men are similarly endangered (*T.Jud.* 15:5–6). Once again, this difference emphasizes the pessimistic attitude concerning human capabilities in the *Testament of Judah*.

Conclusions

In the previous pages, I have shown how the *Testament of Judah* reshapes Genesis 38 and recontextualizes it within Judah's autobiography in order to portray the fall of the mighty warrior king through his encounters with women. I have also examined how the treatment of Genesis 38 within this testament corresponds with the larger perspectives on women, the ethical life, and the nature of Israel's kingship

---

[303] Other passages in the *Testaments* also redefine kingship in moral terms. For example, in *T.B.* 4:1, following a discussion of Joseph as a model of the good man, Benjamin concludes, "See children, the end of the good man. Be followers, therefore, of his compassion with a good mind, that you also may wear crowns of glory." Similarly, in *T.L.* 13:9 Levi urges his sons to be righteous and seek wisdom and concludes that if a person teaches and practices these things, "he will be enthroned with kings, as was also Joseph our brother." Note also *T.D.* 5:13, which states that at the eschatological age when the Holy One reigns over Israel and Jerusalem in humility and poverty, "he who believes in him will be king in truth in the heavens." In its employment of the image of the king as the moral person, the *Testaments* participates in a larger trend in Graeco-Roman philosophy illustrated by the Cynic and Stoic usage of the figure of Heracles.

expressed in the *Testaments of the Twelve Patriarchs*. Finally, I have explored some possible connections with the larger Hellenistic world through a comparison between Judah and Heracles, with respect to common themes and motifs appearing in their narratives and to their employment within larger cultural discussions concerning morality and kingship.

At the conclusion of this discussion of the *Testament of Judah*, it is appropriate to return to the genre of "testament" and to reflect on the impact that this genre itself exerts on the interpretation of Genesis 38. Perhaps one of the most obvious impacts of the testament genre is that it introduces a consistent narrative point of view. As noted earlier, the perspective in the biblical text switches between the narrator and various characters, and this technique sets up a complicated dynamic. It aligns the reader's sympathy with Tamar even though she remains marginal to the narrative focus, and it implies an ironic attitude towards Judah even though he is more prominently featured. The *Testament of Judah* resolves this tension between sympathy and perspective. The single voice of Judah, sincerely recounting his flawed life to his offspring, eliminates both the biblical author's implied support of Tamar and his ironic attitude towards Judah. Instead, in this testament Judah himself bids for his descendants' sympathy and respect—and by extension for the general reader's sympathy and respect—by fully disclosing his sincere motives, his honest failures, and his deep remorse, and by portraying the actions and motivations of the women in Genesis 38 in extremely unflattering detail.

Besides introducing a unifying perspective, the *Testament of Judah* simplifies the biblical narrative in other ways. Although the version of Genesis 38 in the testament is an embellished narrative, containing additional narrative motifs and explanations, it is at the same time less complex. In keeping with the ethical purposes of the testament genre, this work interprets Genesis 38 as a moralistic tale of the patriarch's two failed sexual temptations. In the process, many of the intriguing gaps and ambiguities in the biblical narrative are filled in or ignored. For example, the suggestion in the biblical narrative that Judah may have held Tamar responsible for his sons' deaths and that he therefore never intended to give her to Shelah is entirely eliminated by the introduction of Bathshua's xenophobic schemes. More fundamentally, the *Testament of Judah* eliminates the implication that Tamar's bold sexual initiative outside of a socially sanctioned context was justified because it overcame a reproductive stalemate.

The context of the patriarch's testament to his sons also provides a moral justification for the retelling of a scandalous biblical story. The didactic purpose of its retelling insures that Genesis 38 will not be taken as a titillating tale of voyeuristic interest, but as a useful pedagogical tool for instructing the next generation. The testament genre therefore helps transform what appears to be a morally ambiguous biblical narrative into a bearer of moral truth. This transformation occurs even though Genesis 38 is used in a discussion of negative behavior to be avoided, rather than positive behavior to be emulated. The testament genre also justifies the retelling of Genesis 38 despite its scandal because of its implication that what has happened in the past will continue to affect the future. Judah portrays the story of his weakness as paradigmatic for the future of his tribe and of the institution of Israel's kingship until the eschatological age. It is therefore worth repeating so that members of future generations will at least be forewarned.

Finally, the testament genre suggests that, despite its deviations from the biblical narrative, the version of Genesis 38 in the *Testament of Judah* is authoritative. Since Judah was present when the events of Genesis 38 took place, his account may be trusted. The pseudepigraphic aspect of the testament genre, then, attempts to lend credibility to the revisions of the biblical narrative. The testament genre therefore facilitates the expression of much later issues and ideals through the medium of reworked scripture, since Judah himself urges his descendants and the readers who form a more extended audience to "Listen, children, to your father" (*T.Jud.* 13:1).

CHAPTER THREE

READING GUIDED BY NARRATIVE EXPANSION:
"SANCTIFICATION OF THE [DIVINE] NAME"
IN *TARGUM NEOFITI*

> As she was being brought out, she sent to her father-in-law, "By the
> man to whom these belong I have conceived." She said, "Recognize!
> To whom do this seal, cord, and staff belong?" Judah recognized
> and said, "She is more righteous than I, because I did not give her
> to Shelah my son." He never knew her again. (Gen 38:25–26)

Targum Neofiti, an expansive Aramaic translation[1] of the Pentateuch,
contains additions of plot and dialogue at the climax of the story of
Judah and Tamar (Gen 38:25–26) that completely recast the narrative
as an illustration of the concept "sanctification of the [divine] Name."
Genesis 38 becomes a story of divine providence, and its characters
are reformed into exemplars of ethical behavior under duress. The
goal of this chapter is to delineate the unique interpretation of Genesis 38 that is accomplished in *Targum Neofiti* through its non-biblical
expansion of the narrative at the pivotal point of the story.

A few background words about the history and nature of the
document under investigation are in order. *Targum Neofiti*, a manuscript copy of a complete Aramaic version of the Pentateuch made
in 1504, had been wrongly catalogued in the Vatican library as a
copy of *Targum Onqelos*, a fairly literal Aramaic translation which
received its final recension in Babylon and eventually ascended to
prominence as the official targum in both eastern and western Judaism. Alejandro Díez Macho brought *Targum Neofiti* to public attention in 1959, when he correctly identified it as a representative of a

---

[1] The simple sense of the Aramaic word *targum* (תרגם) is "translation." This word
may stem from the Hittite verb *tarkummāi*, meaning "to announce, explain, or translate," or from the Akkadian noun *targumānu*, meaning "interpreter," from the root
rgm, meaning "to speak or to call out." See Chaim Rabin, "Hittite Words in Hebrew," *Or* 32 (1963) 134–36. The verbal root תרגם appears in the Bible only in
Ezra 4:7, which precedes an Aramaic section of the book. Generally in rabbinic
literature, the word *targum* designates biblical translation into Aramaic, although in
a few passages it includes translation into other languages (for example, into Greek
in *Gen.Rab.* 36.8).

set of texts known as the Palestinian targums.[2] These texts are interpretive Aramaic translations of the first five books of the Bible, which may have originated and circulated orally in Palestine before they received their written form.[3]

During the post-exilic period in Palestine, there was a significant linguistic shift from Hebrew to Aramaic, which gave rise to the general phenomenon of biblical translation.[4] Evidence from the Mishna

---

[2] Alejandro Díez Macho, "The Recently Discovered Palestinian Targum: Its Antiquity and Relationship with the Other Targums," VTSup 7 (1959) 222–245.

[3] Each text records a different version of a fluid, yet relatively fixed, tradition. The abbreviations for the targums in the footnotes in this chapter are as follows:

Tg.Neof.: *Targum Neofiti*, Alejandro Díez Macho, ed., *Neophyti 1: Targum Palestinense MS de la Biblioteca Vaticana*, vol. 1 (Madrid: Consejo Superior de Investigaciones Científicas, 1968).

Frg.Tg.: *Fragmentary Targum*, Michael L. Klein, ed., *Texts, Indices, and Introduction*, vol. 1 of *The Fragment Targums of the Pentateuch According to Their Extant Sources* (Rome: Biblical Institute Press, 1980), including:

Frg.Tg. P: *Fragmentary Targum*, MS Paris Hebr. 110.

Frg.Tg. V: *Fragmentary Targum*, MS Vatican Ebr. 440.

Gnz.Tgs.: Geniza Targums, Michael L. Klein, ed., *Genizah Manuscripts of Palestinian Targums to the Pentateuch*, vol. 1 (Cincinnati: Hebrew Union College Press, 1986), including:

D: Cambridge MS T-S B 8.3 f. 2.

X: Oxford Bodleian MS Heb. c 75r (tosepta).

FF: Cambridge MS T-S NS 184.81r, 182.2r (tosepta).

E: Oxford Bodleian MS Heb. 343, ff. 66–67r.

Tg.Ps.-J.: *Targum Pseudo-Jonathan*, E. G. Clark, ed., *Targum Pseudo-Jonathan of the Pentateuch: Text and Concordance* (Hoboken, NJ: Ktav Publishing House, 1984). Although this targum has linguistic affinities with *Targum Onqelos*, it will be used in this discussion because it contains a version of the narrative expansion found in the other Palestinian targums.

Tg.Onq.: *Targum Onqelos*, Alexander Sperber, ed., *The Pentateuch According to Targum Onkelos*, vol. 1 of *The Bible in Aramaic* (Leiden: E. J. Brill, 1959), which will be used for comparative purposes.

t. Tg.Onq.: *Targum Onqelos Tosepta*, Sperber, *Pentateuch According to Targum Onkelos*, which also contains a version of the narrative expansion.

For an introduction to targumic literature see Roger le Déaut, *Introduction à la littérature targumique*, vol. 1 (Rome: Instituto Biblico de Roma, 1966), and "The Current State of Targumic Studies," *BTB* 4 (1974) 3–32; Martin McNamara, "Targums," in *IDBSup*, 856–61; and Alejandro Díez Macho, *El Targum: Introducción a las traducciones Arámicas de la Biblia*, Textos y estudios "Cardenal Cisneros," vol. 21 (Madrid: Consejo Superior de Investigaciones Científicas, 1979).

[4] Jewish tradition, recorded in *y. Meg.* 4.1; *Gen.Rab.* 36.8; *b. Meg.* 3a; and *b. Ned.* 37b, projects the practice of translating the first five books of the Bible to the time of Ezra. The word "interpreting" (actually a passive participle describing the book as "interpreted," מפרש) in Neh 8:8, which states that Ezra's assistants "read from the book, from the Tora of God, *interpreting* and giving sense, so that [the people assembled] understood the reading," is equated with the targum in all four of these sources. The likelihood that the interpretive activity mentioned in Neh 8:8 has any correlation with the written targums is slight, however. See Michael Fishbane, *Biblical*

attests that already in the tannaitic period (first and second centuries
CE) oral recitation of an Aramaic translation had been integrated
into the liturgical reading of scripture in the synagogue.[5] While one
cannot be certain of the degree of correspondence between the targum
mentioned in the Mishna and the written Palestinian targums, it is
likely that these written versions are based on an early Palestinian
oral tradition which emerged in the context of the synagogue and
the academy.[6] If this hypothesis is correct, the Palestinian targums
provide an invaluable glimpse at popular interpretation of biblical
literature in Palestine.

Each of the extant Palestinian targums contains a version of the
narrative expansion found in *Tg.Neof.* Gen 38:25–26. For the sake of
simplicity, however, I have elected to concentrate on this single text
rather than to work with a number of related, but slightly different,
texts. *Targum Neofiti* is the most suitable text for this study for two

---

Interpretation in Ancient Israel (Oxford: Clarendon Press, 1988) 108–9, for a discussion
of the original semantic content of the term "interpreting" (מפרש). In any event,
Neh 8:8 does suggest that at an early period biblical Hebrew was incomprehensible
to some segments of society. This loss of linguistic competency is also noted in Neh
13:24. The presence of Aramaic material in two of the latest biblical books (Ezra
and Daniel, written in the fourth to second centuries BCE) also points to a linguistic
shift. Aramaic translations of Job and of Leviticus 16 found at Qumran provide
additional evidence for an early date of biblical translation. See Michael Sokoloff,
ed., *The Targum to Job from Qumran Cave XI* (Ramat Gan: Bar Ilan University, 1974).

[5] See, for example, *m. Meg.* 4.4 which gives instructions about the delivery of the
targum following the reading of scripture. See also *y. Meg.* 4.1; *b. Meg.* 23b, 24a;
b. Soṭa 39b; *b. Ber.* 45a; and *b. Meg.* 32a. Special instructions concerning the reading
and translation of certain sensitive biblical passages are listed in *m. Meg.* 4.10 (and
more fully discussed in *y. Meg.* 4.11 and *b. Meg.* 25a, b). Evidence of written targums
appears in *m. Meg.* 2.1 (for Esther); *m. Yad.* 4.5 (for Ezra and Daniel); and *m. Šabb.*
16.1 (for Job). For additional evidence of written targums, see *y. Meg.* 4.1; *t. Šabb.*
13.2; *b. Šabb.* 115a; and *Pesiq.R.* 4.5. Targum study also constituted part of the
educational curriculum, judging from the indications that minors were allowed to
translate in the synagogue in *m. Meg.* 4.6 and *b. Meg.* 24a. The use of targum in
private study is mentioned in *b. Ber.* 8a, b.

[6] See P. S. Alexander, "The Targumim and the Rabbinic Rules for the Delivery
of the Targum," VTSup 36 (1985) 14–28, and Anthony D. York, "The Targum in
the Synagogue and in the School," *JSJ* 10 (1979) 74–86. Martin McNamara (*Targum
and Testament: Aramaic Paraphrases of the Hebrew Bible: A Light on the New Testament* [Shan-
non, Ireland: Irish University Press, 1972] 187–88) notes that a targum similar to
Tg.Neof. is cited by Palestinian rabbis from the second to fourth centuries CE, as well
as by Nathan b. Yehiel in his twelfth-century lexicon, *Aruk*, and argues that *Tg.Neof.*
consists of a faithfully transmitted copy of a "semi-official" Palestinian targum. The
theory that these targums originated in Palestine is supported by the fact that most
of the rabbinic traditions incorporated into the narrative expansion in *Tg.Neof.* Gen
38:25–26 are attributed to second-, third-, and fourth-century Palestinian authorities
in other midrashic sources.

reasons. First, *Targum Neofiti* offers an Aramaic rendition of the entire Tora, unlike many of the other extant targums.[7] I can therefore draw upon the traditions of translation and interpretation found elsewhere in this targum, both in the other verses of Genesis 38 and in other parts of the Pentateuch, to shed light on the material found in this narrative expansion.[8] The second reason involves the position of the version of Gen 38:25–26 in *Targum Neofiti* in the evolutionary development of the narrative expansion, which can be roughly reconstructed through a comparison of the material in the different Palestinian targums. Despite the opinion of Díez Macho and other scholars that *Targum Neofiti* records an early form of the Palestinian targum tradition,[9] the narrative expansion found in Gen 38:25–26 is relatively late in comparison to the versions recorded in other extant targumic manuscripts. In addition to containing the full range of motifs found in the other Palestinian targums, *Targum Neofiti* occasionally alters traditional material and adds its own expressions to articulate a distinctive interpretation of the chapter.[10] The other Palestinian targums

---

[7] For example, *Frg.Tg.*, Gnz.Tgs. X and FF, and *t. Tg.Onq.* consist of selected interpretive passages, including the narrative expansion which is the focus of this chapter. Only fragments of other targums, such as Gnz.Tgs. D and E, have been preserved.

[8] While *Tg.Ps.-J.* is also a complete targum to the Tora, using this targum would raise a number of questions about its linguistic affinities to *Tg.Onq.* which are outside the scope of this discussion.

[9] Díez Macho argues that *Tg.Neof.* is basically pre-Christian ("Recently Discovered Palestinian Targum," 222–45). In general, those scholars who wish to use *Tg.Neof.* to illuminate traditions recorded in the New Testament, including Díez Macho, McNamara, and Paul Kahle, assign to it an early date, based on criteria including the presence of legal traditions contrary (and therefore supposedly prior) to mishnaic halakha and the presence of other early aggadic material. There is no proof, however, for Kahle's presupposition that what is anti-mishnaic is pre-mishnaic, and the assumption that the presence of early traditions marks an entire document as early is untenable, as Anthony D. York points out ("The Dating of Targumic Literature," *JSJ* 5 [1974] 49–62). The fact that the Aramaic of *Tg.Neof.* is later, from the third to fourth centuries according to Martin McNamara, trans., *Targum Neofiti 1: Genesis*, vol. 1A of *The Aramaic Bible* (Collegeville, MN: Liturgical Press, 1992) 3, points to a later date of composition.

[10] While a comparison of the texts suggests that many of the differences between them are simply due to distinctive oral presentations of the same material, it appears that Gnz.Tg. E is the earliest version of this expansion and *Tgs.Neof.* and *Ps.-J.* are the latest, or at least the most developed. The relationship between the different Palestinian targums has received much discussion. See, for example, Renée Bloch, "Note sur l'utilisation des fragments de la Geniza du Caire pour l'étude du Targum Palestinien," *Revue des études juives* 111–116 (1954–57) 5–35, which presents a textual comparison of *Tg.Onq.*, *Tg.Ps.-J.*, *Frg.Tg.* P, Gnz.Tgs. D and E, as well as the Peshitta, for Gen 38:17–30. Through this study, she establishes that *Frg.Tg.* P and Gnz.Tgs.

will be mentioned, either in the text or in the notes, when they clarify
ambiguous aspects of *Targum Neofiti*, when they offer significantly different readings, or when they are otherwise relevant to the discussion
of the interpretation presented in the Palestinian targum tradition.

NARRATIVE EXPANSION IN *TARGUM NEOFITI*
GEN 38:25-26

The climax of Genesis 38 is narrated with few words, illustrating the
understated style typical of biblical literature. Judah's command in Gen
38:24 that his daughter-in-law be executed by burning immediately
follows the report that she is pregnant due to illegitimate sexual activity
and leads up to the swift reversal in Gen 38:25–26:

> As she was being brought out, she sent to her father-in-law, "By the
> man to whom these belong I have conceived." She said, "Recognize!
> To whom do this seal, cord, and staff belong?" Judah recognized and
> said, "She is more righteous than I, because I did not give her to
> Shelah my son." He never knew her again.

By contrast, the presentation of the events of Gen 38:25–26 in *Targum
Neofiti* is dramatically augmented with additional elements of plot and
dialogue lacking in the Hebrew text:

> Tamar went out to be burned in the fire, and she sought the three
> witnesses but did not find them. She raised her eyes to the heights and
> said, "I beseech mercy from before you, LORD. You are he who answers
> the oppressed in the hour of their oppression. Answer me in this hour
> which is the hour of my distress, O God who answers the distressed.
> Illumine my eyes and give me the three witnesses. And I will raise up
> for you three righteous ones in the valley of Dura: Hananiah, Mishael,
> and Azariah. When they go down into the burning fire, they will sanc-
> tify your holy Name."

D and E contain many similarities in language and content. *Tgs.Onq.* and *Ps.-J.*
have linguistic affinities, although *Tg.Ps.-J.* contains a version of the narrative expansion which is absent in *Tg.Onq.* The relationship of *Tg.Neof.* (published by Díez Macho
in 1968 after Bloch's study) to these other texts is complicated. While in language
Tg.Neof. most resembles *Frg.Tg.* P and Gnz.Tgs. D and E in Gen 38:17–24 and
27–30, at a few points it differs and corresponds to *Tg.Onq. Tg.Neof.* also contains
several midrashic elements not present in *Frg.Tg.* P and Gnz.Tgs. D and E, but
found in *Tg.Ps.-J.* The composite nature of *Tg.Neof.* suggests a relatively late date of
composition.

Immediately the LORD heard the voice of her prayer and said to Michael, "Go down and give them, his three witnesses, to her." Her eyes were illumined and she saw them.

She gave them to the judge[11] and said to him, "The man to whom these belong—by him I am pregnant. As for me, even if I am burned I will not identify him. But my Witness,[12] who is between him and me, he will place in his heart [the willingness] to see them in this hour, and he will redeem me from this great judgment."

Immediately Judah rose to his feet and said, "I beseech you, brothers and men of my father's house, listen to me. It is better for me to burn in this world with extinguishable fire, so that I do not burn in the world to come which is the fire that consumes fire. It is better for me to be ashamed in this world which is a passing world,[13] so that I am not ashamed before my righteous fathers in the world to come. Listen to me, my brothers and my father's house, with the measure with which a man measures it will be measured to him, whether a good measure or a bad measure. And happy is every man whose deeds are revealed. Because I took the garment of Joseph, my brother, and dyed it with the blood of a goat and said to Jacob, 'Recognize! Recognize! Is this your son's garment or not?' now it is said to me, 'The man to whom these, the signet ring, the cord, and the staff, belong—by him I am pregnant.' Tamar my daughter-in-law is innocent. By me she is pregnant. Far be it from Tamar, my daughter-in-law—she is not pregnant with sons through illicit intercourse!"

A voice[14] went out from heaven and said, "Both of you are innocent. From before the LORD is the decree."

And Judah recognized and said, "Tamar my daughter-in-law is innocent because[15] I did not marry her to Shelah, my son." And he did not know her again.

---

[11] The text has a single "judge" (דיינא), which a later scribe changed to the plural "judges" (דייניא) by adding the letter ' above the line. See Díez Macho, *Neophyti 1*, vol. 1, 255.

[12] The word "Witness" (שהדי) could also be read "the witnesses," or even "his witnesses," but God is clearly the subject of the verbs in this sentence.

[13] The text reads "a created world" (עלם עבוד), but Díez Macho corrects it to "a passing world" (עלם עביר), which corresponds to *Tg.Ps.-J.* (*Neophyti 1*, vol. 1, 255).

[14] *Tg.Neof.* has the spelling ברם קלא, which Díez Macho corrects to ברת קלא, literally, "a daughter of a voice," as it appears in all the other Palestinian targums (*Neophyti 1*, vol. 1, 255).

[15] The phrase בנין כך is found only in *Tg.Neof.* Díez Macho emends it to בנין כן (*Neophyti 1*, vol. 1, 255). For a discussion of this phrase see McNamara, *Targum Neofiti 1*, 178, n. 16.

Biblical Translation in New Narrative Context

One would never mistake the passage above for a literal translation of the Hebrew text of Gen 38:25–26. Here and there, one can nevertheless identify fragments of the biblical verses translated amidst a new narrative context. Often these biblical citations are altered in surprising ways, however. For example, the first verb in the Aramaic passage appears in an active form, "went out" (נפקת), which replaces the passive masoretic Hebrew, "was brought out" (מוּצֵאת). Another change is that the transfer of the three pledge items occurs not once but two times in the Aramaic text, and the verb employed is "give" (root יהב) rather than "send" (root שלח) as in the Hebrew text. In addition, the items are given once to Tamar and once to a judge, and never to Tamar's father-in-law.

Tamar's first biblical statement concerning the significance of the pledge is translated quite literally. Her second statement containing a direct imperative to her father-in-law undergoes drastic revision, however. It is reassigned to Judah and atomized in typical midrashic style into two separate utterances. Tamar's biblical command that her father-in-law "Recognize!" (הכר נא) the three items becomes in *Targum Neofiti* Judah's recollection of another command, that his father Jacob "Recognize!" (אכר אכר כען) Joseph's coat in Gen 37:32. The last half of Tamar's second biblical statement becomes part of Judah's paraphrastic repetition of her first biblical statement.

Judah's comparative evaluation of Tamar as "more righteous than I" (צדקה ממני) from the Hebrew text is also severed into two parts which become the core of two separate statements. These consist of a declaration of innocence, "Tamar my daughter-in-law is innocent" (וזכאה היא תמר כלתי), and a direct confession of his paternity, "From me she is pregnant" (מיני היא מעברה), missing in the Hebrew text. The abrupt and jarring return to the biblical text in Gen 38:26 with Judah's tardy and anti-climactic recognition of the three items and his redundant declaration of Tamar's innocence signals the end of the expansive portion of the text.

Obviously, the words of Gen 38:25–26 do not account for all the material which appears at this point. An additional movement in the plot, the loss of the three items, elicits an extended prayer from Tamar. Divine response through an angelic intermediary is immediate. Tamar once more places her life in danger with her refusal to shame her father-in-law. Judah responds immediately with a public address in which he employs aphorisms to reveal his willingness to accept punishment for his misdeeds, confesses to not one but two sins, and clears Tamar of the charges against her. Both apparently would have been burned for their sexual relations, but a voice from heaven intervenes.[16]

Yet, as will become clear in the following discussion, the task of translation is far from abdicated in this narrative expansion. In addition to the words of Gen 38:25–26, *Targum Neofiti* translates into Aramaic particular rabbinic traditions of exegesis of these verses, which also appear in other midrashic sources including *Genesis Rabba*, the *Tanhuma*, and the Babylonian Talmud. This translation of exegetical commentary is accomplished with some significant alterations, however. In the targum, the individual lemmatic bits of commentary are stripped of their attributions to particular authorities and of their particular connections to features of the Hebrew text, narrativized, and used as the raw material for the construction of an original composition that presents its own unique understanding of the story of Judah and Tamar.

In the pages that follow, I will discuss the component parts of the narrative expansion in *Targum Neofiti*, exploring the rabbinic exegetical traditions that lie behind the text of the targum, considering their origins and history of development, and describing how this traditional material functions within its new framework. I will also highlight aspects of the narrative expansion which appear nowhere but in the Palestinian targums or in *Targum Neofiti* itself. But no matter how interesting discussions of particular features of the narrative expansion may prove to be, the final step must consist of a discussion of the comprehensive statement made by *Targum Neofiti* about the significance of the biblical narrative. Many details of the narrative expansion work together to provide a thematic translation of the characters and events of Genesis 38 into the terms of a larger post-biblical discussion summarized by the phrase "sanctification of the [divine] Name." This unique targumic depiction will be the focus of an extended study with which I will conclude the chapter.

---

[16] This same basic structure is found in all the Palestinian targums, although Gnz.Tg. D is broken at the end, Gnz.Tg. E lacks many elements from Judah's speech and the intervention of the heavenly voice, Gnz.Tgs. X and FF and *t. Tg.Onq.* lack Tamar's statement of willingness to burn rather than identify Judah, and the order of the elements in Judah's speech varies from targum to targum. This situation suggests stages in the development of the narrative expansion, although many of the differences may be due simply to idiosyncratic oral presentations of the same basic material.

Components of the Narrative Expansion

Witnesses: Lost and Found

The first addition to the plot is Tamar's inability to find the three items which she had cleverly procured from her father-in-law to safeguard her life. As noted in the first chapter, in the biblical story the pledge is central to the resolution of the plot, and its importance is emphasized by Tamar's biblical silence except to acquire the three items and to identify Judah with them. The halt of the flow of the biblical narrative provided by the targumic notice that "she sought the three witnesses but did not find them" creates an opening for post-biblical changes in the story.

The new direction of the story is highlighted by the use of a different legal term to designate the personal items that Judah gives to Tamar. The biblical text uses the term "pledge" (ערבון), designating a legal security for a debt. In Genesis 38, Judah thinks that he surrenders the items only until he pays for the prostitute's sexual services. The targum introduces the term "witnesses" (שהדי/סהדי), guiding readers from the business of prostitution to the semantic world of legal courts and justice which permeates the drama of the narrative expansion.[17] The introduction of witnesses also points forward to the unexpected appearance in Tamar's vow of the three saints at Dura, who by their willingness to die rather than worship an idol attest to the importance of their God and become witnesses to his power to save. Finally, the term anticipates the intervention of the divine Witness of all things, in whom Tamar places her trust in her statement before the court.

Despite the clear deviation from the biblical narrative initiated by the introduction of the lost items, a number of midrashic sources besides the Palestinian targums specifically connect this motif to a feature of the Hebrew consonantal text. These sources articulate a secondary interpretation of the letters of the first verb of Gen 38:25

---

[17] This shift relieves Judah of the appearance of an arbitrary and hasty family head who sentences Tamar to death without even questioning her, since the term "witnesses" suggests due process. Three witnesses are one more than the two generally required to establish a point of fact in court, although here the witnesses are inanimate items. All of the Palestinian targums call the three items "witnesses," with the exception of *Tg.Ps.-J.*, which employs the Aramaic word "pledges" (משכוניא), the singular of which it uses in Gen 38:17, 18, and 20, in agreement with *Tg.Onq.* Most of the commentaries that contain the motif of the lost items do not use the term "witnesses." For instance, *Tanḥ.* Wayyešeb 9.17 retains the Hebrew word "pledge" (ערבון) in one of its versions of the motif. An exception to this rule is *Midr. Haggadol* Gen 38:25, which employs the Hebrew word "witnesses" (עדים).

(מוצאת). In addition to reading the verb as derived from the Hebrew root "to go out" (יצא), which is the root indicated in the masoretic pointing,[18] each of these sources also contains a secondary reading of the same verb from the Hebrew root "to find" (מצא).[19] The proximity of Judah's command to "bring her out" (הוציאוה) in the biblical text of Gen 38:24 (a causative imperative from the root "to go out," יצא) suggests that the root "to go out" (יצא) may be appropriate and sufficient for understanding the first verb of Gen 38:25. Early translations, including the Septuagint, *Targum Onqelos*, the Samaritan Targum, and the Peshitta uniformly represent this verb with a passive form from the same root contained in Judah's command in Gen 38:24.[20] It is true, however, that only a few verses earlier Judah and Hirah fail to find the woman they seek. The verbal root "to find" (מצא) is repeated in Gen 38:20, 22, and 23, each time preceded by the negative particle "not" (לא).[21] This secondary interpretation therefore echoes a narrative element which is already present in the biblical narrative.[22]

The *Tanḥuma* presents a simple version of the conclusions arising from understanding the verb to mean "she found" in the name of R. Judah bar Shallum the Levite (fourth-century Palestinian):

> As she was going out, the Holy One Blessed be He illuminated her eyes and she found (ומצאה) them [the three items] after she had lost them, because [the word] "finding" (מציאה) always implies something that had

---

[18] The MT pointing מוצאת defines this verb as a passive participle from the causative stem of the root "to go out" (יצא), meaning "she was brought out."

[19] See *Tanḥ.* Wayyešeb 9.17; *Gen.Rab.* 85.11; *b. Soṭa* 10b; and later sources, including *Yal. Šimʿoni* Gen 38:25 and *Midr. Haggadol* Gen 38:25.

[20] Since early translators had no difficulty with this form, it is unlikely that the double reading of the Hebrew word מוצאת originated in an attempt to explain a difficult verbal form, notwithstanding James Kugel's understanding of the generative potentiality in the difficult features of the biblical text itself (*In Potiphar's House: The Interpretive Life of Biblical Texts* [San Francisco: Harper, 1990] 3–4, 247–51). Rather, hermeneutic pressures to rewrite Genesis 38 as a story of divine providence motivated exegetes to interact creatively with a pliable point in the Hebrew text. The possibility of multiple readings made the first verb in Gen 38:25 a productive focus for the shaping of the distinctive contours of aggadic tradition.

[21] It is interesting to note that *Tg.Neof.* Gen 38:22 alters the subject of the verb in Judah's description of the failure to find the woman, when it depicts him as saying "I did not find her" (לא אשכחית יתה). In *Tg.Neof.* it is Judah, not Hirah, who fails to find Tamar. The targum aligns the two main characters through their common failure to find something important.

[22] Similarly, the traditional intertextual reading of Gen 37:32 with Gen 38:25 due to the presence of the imperative "Recognize!" in each may have introduced the concept of finding the object sent for identification from Genesis 37 into Genesis 38, since Gen 37:32 states, "This we have found (מצאנו). Recognize!"

been lost (אבדה). As it is written, "Or found (מצא) something that had been lost (אבדה)" (Lev 5:22).[23]

According to this source, R. Judah bar Shallum maintains that the secondary reading of the verb as "she found" implies that previously she had lost the three items. He supports his explanation that this verb includes its opposite by citing a biblical law concerning lost items that are later found, which employs these two words.

The exegetical conclusion that Tamar loses the items and then finds them is incorporated into the narrative in *Targum Neofiti*, as well as into all the other Palestinian targums. The verbal connection between this motif and the biblical text is lost in the translation, however, since the Aramaic root meaning "to find" (שכח) bears no resemblance to the Hebrew root meaning "to find" (מצא), nor to the Aramaic root "to go out (נפק)".[24] Only the narrative content of the tradition is preserved.

One of the most significant things about this passage in the *Tanhuma* is the notice that "the Holy One illumined her eyes." This narrative addition is inserted without comment and without biblical justification. Divine aid in finding the items is not required by the reading of the verb as "she lost and then found." In the proof text itself (Lev 5:22), the lost pledge is found by ordinary human means, without divine assistance. There is, in fact, a line in *Midraš Haggadol*, a thirteenth-century Yemenite work which preserves a wealth of early material, that simply states "When she went out she found the original [items]." *Midraš Haggadol* incorporates the tradition that Tamar finds the items with no divine assistance into a more complex type of the motif of the lost and found pledge, but it seems likely that the original form of this motif may have lacked divine assistance. Apparently, hermeneutic pressures to read Genesis 38 as an episode of religious history force the interjection of divine intervention into the crack created in the biblical text by the secondary reading of the first verb as "she found."[25]

---

[23] *Tanh.* Wayyešeb 9.17. Although this tradition is associated with R. Judah bar Shallum, one cannot precisely date midrashic material from the traditional attributions. The material may be earlier and simply repeated by a scholar from a later generation, or conversely, it may be later and attributed to a famous scholar from an earlier generation.

[24] Multiple translations of the same word in the Palestinian targums, such as the dual translation of the Hebrew word מוצאת as both נפקת and אשכחת in *Tg.Neof.*, are not uncommon and reflect contemporary exegetical traditions.

[25] The masculine pronoun "he" (הוא) at the beginning of Gen 38:25 in the conso-

Lighting Tamar's eyes is not the only type of divine action introduced at this point in the story in midrashic literature, as I demonstrate below in the typology of different kinds of divine intervention. Before leaving the passage from the *Tanḥuma*, however, we need to examine further the curious phrase "to illumine the eyes," since a similar expression occurs in *Targum Neofiti*.[26] It is not clear whether the use of this expression emerges out of some sort of word play with the consonants of Gen 38:25,[27] whether it stems from an intertextual reading of some other portion of scripture in conjunction with Genesis 38,[28] or whether it is simply an idiomatic expression reflecting a common theory of sight in the Hellenistic world.[29] Whatever the origins of this expression, the emphasis on Tamar's vision reflects an appreciation for the importance of eyes and sight in the biblical story of Genesis 38. As noted in the first chapter, major events in the biblical story are initiated by visual perception, and this tradition adds a further important instance of sight at the narrative's climax. It may be that the expression describing where Tamar waited for Judah, "the entrance of Enaim" (פתח עינים)—literally, "opening of eyes"—suggested that God "opened [Tamar's] eyes," and therefore contributed to the version of the motif of the lost and found pledge in the *Tanḥuma*.

Turning to other versions of the motif of the lost pledge, we find that rabbinic exegetes exercised considerable creativity in resolving the problem they introduced in parsing the Hebrew verb (מוצאת) as "she found" and understanding that verb as "she did not find." In a

---

nantal Hebrew text may have also suggested the action of someone besides Tamar, although the reading (qere) of this pronoun as "she" (הוא) is quite common in the MT.

[26] The Hebrew expression in *Tanh.* Wayyešeb 9.17 is האיר עיניה, and the Aramaic expressions in *Tg.Neof.* are ואנהר עייני and ואנהדון עיניה.

[27] Perhaps the first verb in Gen 38:25 (מוצאת) suggested the root "to kindle or ignite" (יצת), which triggered the image of flashing eyes. *Midr. Haggadol* Gen 38:25 presents a reading of the verb based on this root, although not in connection with eyes. Alternatively, perhaps the emphasis on sight arose through a bilingual pun on the word "her father-in-law" (חמיה) in Gen 38:25, which related this word to the Aramaic root "to see" (חמי).

[28] For example, Psalm 56 refers to Tamar's plight when the pledge was lost, according to *b. Soṭa* 10b. This psalm ends with the phrase "the light of the living" (באור החיים), which includes the same root as in the expression "he illuminated her eyes" (האיר עיניה) in the *Tanḥuma*.

[29] This theory regards vision as the result of light emanating from the eye onto external objects and blindness as the absence of such light. There is a clear loss of the understanding of this theory in a number of the targums including *Frg.Tg.* and Gnz.Tgs. D and E which depict Tamar's eyes lighting up, with joy perhaps, after she sees the objects. For example, Gnz.Tg. E states, "As soon as she saw them, her eyes lit up" (כוון דחמת יתהון אנהרין עיניה).

second type of divine intervention, God's action is even more dramatic than in the first type. Instead of lighting Tamar's eyes so that she finds the three items that Judah gave her, he providentially replaces the original items. This second type also appears in a simple form in the *Tanḥuma*, this time anonymously:

> As she was going out, she sought the pledge and did not find them [the three items]. In that hour, she raised her eyes to the heavens. Immediately, the Holy One Blessed be He sent (שלח) her others.[30]

This version of the tradition maintains a tenuous link with the biblical text by employing the verbal root "to send" (שלח) from Gen 38:25 in its description of God's delivery of mysterious "others" in response to Tamar's appeal for divine assistance.[31]

Reference to the divinely sent alternate items also appears in a passage from *Genesis Rabba*. This document interjects the second type of divine intervention into the statement attributed to R. Judah bar Shallum, which we have seen in a more cogent and original form in the *Tanḥuma*. *Genesis Rabba* portrays this authority as explaining what happened at this point in the story in the following manner:

> They [the three items] were lost, and the Holy One Blessed be He provided (המציא) others to replace them. As scripture says, "Or found (מצא) something that had been lost" (Lev 5:22).[32]

In this passage, the replacement items are linked to the biblical text of Gen 38:25 through an employment of the root "to find" (מצא) that differs from R. Judah bar Shallum's employment of the same root to demonstrate that Tamar initially lost the pledge.[33] In this passage from *Genesis Rabba*, the verb appears in the causative form, which can mean "to furnish or provide with,"[34] and takes God as the subject.

---

[30] *Tanḥ*. Wayyešeb 9.17. This tradition is presented immediately before the explanation attributed to R. Judah bar Shallum, quoted above.

[31] Apparently the verb and preposition in the biblical phrase "she sent to" (שלחה אל) in Gen 38:25 are being read as "God sent to her." Elsewhere in rabbinic literature as well, for example in *Gen.Rab*. 98.2 and 3, the preposition "to" (אל) is read as the noun "God" (אל).

[32] *Gen.Rab*. 85.11. See also *Yal. Šimʿoni* Gen 38:25 for a similar description of this type of divine intervention.

[33] *Genesis Rabba* intentionally places two cases of word play on the root "to find" (מצא) together in this passage. The second type of divine intervention to replace the lost items is connected to the biblical word "she was brought out" (מוצאת) here in *Gen.Rab*. 85.11, whereas it is connected to the biblical word "she sent" (שלחה) in *Tanḥ*. Wayyešeb 9.17.

[34] Marcus Jastrow, *A Dictionary of the Targumim, the Talmud Babli and Yerushalmi, and the Midrashic Literature* (New York: Judaica Press, 1971) 825.

This multiple interpretive employment of a single biblical word constitutes a complex pun, ensuring a concrete connection between non-biblical expansions of the narrative and the biblical text itself.

The intrusion of the replacement pledge provided by God in this passage in *Genesis Rabba* confuses the simple explanation attributed to R. Judah bar Shallum in the *Tanḥuma* that Tamar found what she had lost. In fact, in *Genesis Rabba*, there is no explicit indication that she finds the items she had lost. Since God replaces the originals with others, the verse from Lev 5:22 about lost items that have been found dangles uselessly at the end of this passage. *Genesis Rabba* offers an artless merging of two types of the motif of the lost pledge.[35]

A conflation of two originally independent traditions describing how Tamar regained possession of the items is more logically accomplished in an extended passage from *Midraš Haggadol*, to which I have briefly alluded above. This passage is worth quoting at length, both because of its elaborate version of the events in Gen 38:25–26 and because of its distinctive literary style consisting of midrashic narrative interjected with the guiding voice of a commentator:

> She went and sought the witnesses which he gave to her, but she did not find them. What did the Holy One Blessed be He do for her? He created (ברא) others for her. But when she went out she found the original ones. How do we know this? R. Judah bar Shallum said, "'She went out' (יוצאת) is not written, but 'she found' (מוצאת). Concerning this matter, it is written, 'Or found something that had been lost' (Lev 5:22)." Our teachers say that she sent and said to him, "Here are the witnesses which you gave me. If you try to deny [it], here are the witnesses which the Holy One Blessed be He gave me." It is written, "Recognize, please, to whom (למי) . . ." (Gen 38:25). [The phrase] "to whom" (למי) is written here, and elsewhere it is written "Abner sent to David a messenger to say, 'To whom (למי) belongs the earth?'" (2 Sam 3:12). Just as [the answer to the one question] is God's presence [the Shekhina], so [the answer to the other question] is God's presence [the Shekhina]. [The words] "the seal" (החותם) and "the cord" (הפתיל) are not written here, but, "To whom do 'the seals' (החותמת) and 'the cords' (הפתילים) belong? See, these are yours and those are the ones that the Holy One Blessed be He gave me." At that time, he was not able to deny, but he confessed, as it says, "Judah recognized" (Gen 38:26).

---

[35] A later line in *Gen.Rab.* 85.11 suggests that Tamar found both the original set and the divinely created set, because she orders her reluctant father-in-law to "recognize your creator in these, for they are yours and your creator's." A double finding is not clearly articulated in the passage attributed to R. Judah bar Shallum in *Genesis Rabba*, however.

228   CHAPTER THREE

In this passage, God first replaces the original pledge with a specially created pledge. The verb describing God's action is identical to the one found in the creation story in Genesis 1 ("he created," ברא), and this detail defines the "other" items that God provides for Tamar in the *Tanḥuma* and *Genesis Rabba* as special creations. After receiving the newly created items, Tamar finds the originals as well. Two versions of how Tamar recovers the lost items are depicted as two chronological events, resulting in Tamar's possession of two sets of items. With the two pledges, she is able to overcome Judah's attempt to conceal his responsibility for her pregnancy.

In *Midraš Haggadol*, each of Tamar's statements concerning the significance of the pledge in Gen 38:25 introduces her presentation of a different set of items. Since Judah is unwilling to confess his ownership after Tamar's first statement, she presents a second set and commands Judah to recognize the items created by God.[36] This passage explains that Tamar's second statement points to God's ownership of one of the pledges through its inclusion of the phrase, "to whom" (למי). This phrase is found elsewhere in the Bible in Abner's question to David about the ownership of the earth (2 Sam 3:12). Certainly Abner himself would have been surprised to hear his question answered in theological rather than military or political terms. The editor of *Midraš Haggadol*, however, assumes what is explicitly stated elsewhere in the biblical corpus, that "the earth is the LORD's (ליהוה הארץ)" (Ps 24:1). According to the logic of the passage, the pledge must also be the LORD's, since both questions contain the same interrogative and therefore must have the same answer. Additional biblical support for the midrashic presence of two pledges is provided by the curious different forms of the first two items in the lists in Gen 38:18 and 25. This passage interprets the forms in the latter list as plurals which signal the presence of more than one set of pledge items.[37]

---

[36] See also *Leqaḥ Ṭob* Gen 38:25; *Yal. Šimʿoni* Gen 38:25; *Tanḥ.* Wayyešeb 9.17; and *b. Soṭa* 10b. All of these sources depict Tamar demanding that Judah recognize the work of the divine creator when he tries to conceal his guilt. Judah's attempt to keep his sexual relations a secret is an ancient motif, as its inclusion in the *Testament of Judah* indicates. Judah's initial refusal to reveal what he knows makes him doubly culpable in light of Lev 5:1, which states, "Any person who sins in that he hears the voice of adjuration and he is a witness or he has seen or he knows, and yet he does not tell, he will bear his iniquity."

[37] In Gen 38:18, Tamar requests "your seal, your cord, and your staff" (חתמך ופתילך ומטך). When she demands that Judah recognize the implication of the pledge

In the different types of the motif of the lost and found pledge, there is an escalation of the importance of God in the story. In the simplest original type, suggested by the line from *Midraš Haggadol*, Tamar finds the pledge herself without divine intervention. In the first type that refers to divine intervention, recorded in the *Tanḥuma*, God enables Tamar to regain the original three items by improving her sight. In the second type of divine intervention, recorded in both the *Tanḥuma* and *Genesis Rabba*, God performs a miracle to provide replacement items so that she will not go out empty-handed. In the version in *Midraš Haggadol*, he creates a special set of items which are presented to Judah along with the original ones, forcing the reluctant patriarch to confess. The dual ownership of the pledges may also implicate God as one of the parties responsible for Tamar's pregnancy.

There is also a final type of intervention involving conflict between good and bad angels, recorded in a number of the tosepta targums and in *b. Soṭa* 10b. In the tosepta targums the wicked angel Samael conceals the pledge items from Tamar, making it impossible for her to find them.[38] In the version in the Babylonian Talmud, an even more aggressive Samael removes them to a distant place after Tamar finds them.[39] In both instances, the angel Gabriel restores them to her, at the command of God in the targums and apparently by his own initiative in the Talmud. Midrashic literature frequently depicts Samael and Gabriel competing, especially in the last days before the messianic age. One of the Geniza fragments that depicts this angelic conflict contains a messianic conclusion: the voice from heaven exhorts everyone to rejoice because the LORD's messiah will come forth from Perez to rule the nations and lead the people from exile to the temple.[40]

---

in Gen 38:25, however, the first and second words of this list appear in slightly different forms. The second word "and the cord" (והפתילים) bears a plural ending, and the first word "the seal" (החתמת) bears either a marker for feminine gender (as pointed in the MT) or a defective plural ending.

[38] The root of the word "to conceal" (טמר) may be a pun on Tamar's name. Samael and Gabriel appear in Gnz.Tgs. X and FF (which are tosepta targums) and *t. Tg.Onq*, and in the tosepta to the *editio princeps* of *Tg.Ps.-J.*, according to Michael Maher, trans., *Targum Pseudo-Jonathan: Genesis*, vol. 1B of *The Aramaic Bible* (Collegeville, MN: Liturgical Press, 1992) 19–20.

[39] This version is presented in the name of R. Eleazar (fourth-century Palestinian), as an introduction to an interpretation of the superscription of Psalm 56 in light of Tamar's loss of the pledge. This superscription contains the plural adjective "distant" (רחקים), which *b. Soṭa* 10b interprets as a description of the pledge items after Samael took them.

[40] This fragment is Gnz.Tg. FF.

Given these various types of divine intervention that arose to resolve the post-biblical problem posed by the loss of the pledge, which
tradition or traditions lie behind *Targum Neofiti*'s depiction of events?
The double appearance of the expression "to illumine the eyes" in
Targum Neofiti emphasizes its relation to the first type of divine intervention, which is presented in the name of R. Judah bar Shallum in
the *Tanḥuma*.[41] There is also, however, a reference in *Targum Neofiti*
to Tamar's raising of her eyes in prayer which prefaces the sending
of replacement items in the second type as it is expressed in the
Tanḥuma. In addition, Tamar's request that God "give" her the witnesses and God's command that Michael "give" her the items suggest that the items are in heaven, as they might be if stolen by an
angel or newly created for angelic delivery.[42] In any event, although
there is a conflation of the language from different types of this motif
in *Targum Neofiti*, there is no indication that there are two sets of
pledges as in the version in *Midraš Haggadol*.

In its inclusion of an angel, *Targum Neofiti* also resembles the final
type of solution to the problem of the lost pledge found in *b. Soṭa*
10b and the tosepta.[43] Unlike these sources, *Targum Neofiti* depicts
only one angel instead of two, and the angel who appears is Michael

---

[41] It appears in Tamar's prayerful request and in the narrative report of the results
of divine intervention. In Tamar's public statement before the court she expresses
her trust in God's ability to improve Judah's sight as well, although a different verb
is used. The expression "to illumine the eyes" also appears in *Tg.Ps.-J.*, *Frg.Tg.*, and
Gnz.Tgs. D and E.

[42] Tamar's request and the divine instruction containing the word "give" are
superfluous. Tamar also asks for her eyes to be illumined and the result of Michael's
visit is that her eyes are illumined. She is given nothing, but instead she herself
gives the items to the judge. Note the gloss in God's command to Michael in *Tg.Neof.*
which I have set off with commas in the translation: "Go down and give them, his
three witnesses, to her." The words "his three witnesses" do not appear in any of
the other Palestinian targums. While this phrase may simply refer to Judah's three
possessions, it may indicate that whoever added this phrase was aware of the tradition that God created a divine set, designated here as "his [God's] three witnesses."
(On the other hand, the interjection of the verb "to give" may simply be an attempt
to integrate the narrative expansion into the biblical story. The use of this verb
echoes Tamar's request that she be given the items in Gen 38:17 and the report
that she was given the items in Gen 38:18. The difference is that here she requests
and receives the items from God.)

[43] God's sending of an angel to help Tamar see in *Tg.Neof.* and some of the other
targums may involve a reading of the Hebrew line "she sent to her father-in-law"
(שלחה אל חמיה) as "he sent her an angel [to enable] her seeing." The translation of
the consonants אל as "angel" is not uncommon in post-biblical texts. See for example *Gen.Rab.* 87.3.

and not Gabriel;[44] nevertheless, God acts through an intermediary instead of directly as in the *Tanhuma, Genesis Rabba,* and *Midraš Haggadol.* The appearance of a named intermediary in a place where the biblical text lacks an angelic presence is actually quite rare in the Palestinian targums, with the exception of *Targum Pseudo-Jonathan.*[45] The angel Michael, for example, is mentioned by name in *Targum Neofiti* only in this passage. *Targum Pseudo-Jonathan,* however, depicts the angel Michael performing a number of important tasks in keeping with his role as guardian angel of Israel.[46] Perhaps most important in connection with Genesis 38 is that he appears in this targum to redeem Israel.[47] In the *Tanhuma,* the angel Michael also intervenes to ensure that a reluctant Judah sexually engage a woman he has shunned as a prostitute in order to engender kings.[48] The appearance of Michael in *Targum Neofiti* therefore signals that Genesis 38 is a story about Israel's well-being and future redemption, even though the narrative expansion does not emphasize royal and messianic themes.

Having discussed the exegetical traditions that lie behind the motif of the lost and found pledge in *Targum Neofiti,* it is necessary to ask how this motif functions in this narrative expansion itself. For one thing, it heightens the dramatic tension of the narrative by placing Tamar's life in even greater danger than in the biblical story. This heightening of the climax of a story is a common technique within aggada, pointing to its creative, folkloric nature and its delight in the dynamics of narrative. A similar attenuation of the climax appears when Tamar places herself in danger a second time by refusing to identify her father-in-law.[49]

---

[44] Other targums that depict Michael as the angel responsible for returning the items are *Tg.Ps.-J., Frg.Tg.,* and Gnz.Tgs. D and E.

[45] See Avigdor Shinan, "The Angelology of the 'Palestinian' Targums on the Pentateuch," *Sefarad* 43 (1983) 188–91.

[46] For example, he announces the creation of the Levite community (*Tg.Ps.-J.* Gen 32:25), calls Moses to ascend Sinai (*Tg.Ps.-J.* Exod 24:1), praises God and Israel (*Tg.Ps.-J.* Deut 32:9), and offers Moses a place to sit prior to his death (*Tg.Ps.-J.* Deut 34:6).

[47] *Tg.Ps.-J.* Deut 34:3.

[48] *Tanh.* Wayyešeb 9.17; cf., *Gen.Rab.* 85.8, in which an anonymous "angel in charge of desire" performs the same function.

[49] Another example of this literary technique may be observed in the midrashic traditions concerning the delay of the exodus while Moses searched for Joseph's bones, discussed in Joseph Heinemann, ויקח משה את עצמות יוסף עמו [And Moses took Joseph's bones with him] in אנדות ותולדותיהן: עיונים בהשתלשלותן של מסורות [Aggadic traditions and their development: Studies on the evolution of traditions] (Jerusalem: Keter Publishing House, 1974) 49–63.

But even more significantly, this motif accomplishes a basic transfer of power over the plot's forward movement from its human protagonist in the biblical version to its divine overseer in the post-biblical version. This same transfer of narrative control manifests itself once again when the voice from heaven intervenes and asserts that the matter was "from before the LORD." The voice's claim of divine providence at the conclusion of the story is credible at least in part because of God's earlier intervention to restore the pledge.

Through the introduction of the motif of the lost and found pledge items, Genesis 38 becomes a story of divine guidance in history. The divine presence, which is strangely absent after the initial swift executions of Judah's two wicked sons, reasserts itself, this time ultimately to save two righteous people from execution. Judging from the major change that is affected, the hermeneutic pressure that channeled the development of this motif was the desire to read Genesis 38 as the story of divine intervention in human history, not simply the story of a clever woman who outwits her recalcitrant father-in-law.

The loss of the three items in *Targum Neofiti* also initiates a pious transformation of the character of Tamar, whose cunning and strength in the biblical narrative are replaced by gentler, more comfortable characteristics. In the targum, Tamar's careful procurement of Judah's personal items proves insufficient, and she loses her control over the events of the narrative. This plot development provides an opportunity to portray her under duress. In this revision of the biblical narrative, Tamar responds to crisis with prayer. It is to this prayer that we now turn to explore more fully who she has become in this targumic version of the story.

Tamar's Prayer

Under the threat of death in *Targum Neofiti*, Tamar assumes a common prayerful posture when she raises her eyes to the heights.[50] The addition of a prayer at this point is not especially surprising, given

---

[50] All the Palestinian targums assert that Tamar raised her eyes to heaven in prayer and present a version of her petition. For another example of the prayerful gesture of raising the eyes, see the explanation in *Tg.Neof.* Gen 29:17 that Leah's eyes were "weak" (רכות, Gen 29:17) because she constantly raised them in prayer to request that she be married to Jacob. Similarly, *Tg.Neof.* Gen 24:63 maintains that Isaac's purpose was to pray when he went out to the field and lifted his eyes before meeting Rebekah. Tamar's raising her eyes once again highlights the importance of sight and eyes in Genesis 38, as pointed out above.

the abundance of prayers composed for biblical characters in post-biblical literature, from the second-temple period forward.[51] But when we look at the wider corpus of rabbinic literature, we find that the words of Tamar's prayer at this point of the narrative are not depicted in any source outside of the Palestinian targums. Even the *Tanḥuma*, which is the only other source that portrays Tamar raising her eyes in prayer when she cannot find the pledge, does not present the contents of her prayer.[52] This is not to say that Tamar is not depicted as a person of prayer in other rabbinic sources. Her intercession with heaven outside of the Palestinian targums, however, appears as she sits waiting for Judah at the gate of Enaim. The introduction of a prayer at this point in the narrative is justified in *Genesis Rabba* by an explanation in the name of Rabbi (Judah the Patriarch, second-century Palestinian) of the phrase "the entrance of Enaim," or "the gate of Enaim" (פתח עינים). Since this place is not otherwise mentioned in biblical literature, the phrase is taken as an indication that she lifted her "eyes" (עינים) to the "gate" (פתח) to which all eyes appeal for help.[53] In *Genesis Rabba*, Tamar prays for success in her venture, "May it be your will that I do not go out empty from this house."[54] This brief prayer is especially appropriate in this source, which emphasizes the importance of the birth of the ancestor of the messiah through the events in Genesis 38.[55]

Perhaps the motif of lifting the eyes to heaven, which introduces Tamar's prayer in *Targum Neofiti*, derives from this traditional understanding of the words "the gate of Enaim," and is then transferred

---

[51] See for example the prayers of Esther and Mordecai in the Greek version of the book of Esther. For a discussion of early Jewish prayer, see Roger le Déaut, "Aspects de l'intercession dans le Judaïsme ancien," *JSJ* 1 (1970) 35–57, and Joseph Heinemann, *Prayer in the Talmud: Forms and Patterns*, Studia Judaica 9 (Berlin and New York: Walter de Gruyter, 1977).

[52] See *Tanḥ*. Wayyešeb 9.17, cited above in the discussion of the lost and found pledge. It is striking that *b. Soṭa* 10b portrays Tamar as completely mute when the three items are removed by Samael, although perhaps this silence is intended to reflect her refusal to shame Judah by identifying him.

[53] A similar explanation of the phrase "the gate of Enaim" is found in *Tanḥ*. Wayyešeb 9.17, attributed to R. Joshua b. Levi, a third-century Palestinian. See also *b. Soṭa* 10a and *y. Ketub*. 13.1. The association between an upward gaze toward the gate of heaven and prayer appears also in Jacob's description of Bethel as the "gate of prayer set aside unto the height of the heavens" in *Tg.Neof.* Gen 28:17.

[54] *Gen.Rab.* 85.7. See also *Tanḥ*. Wayyešeb 9.17 and *y. Ket*. 13.1 for versions of this prayer.

[55] The *Tanḥuma*, which also contains this prayer, similarly emphasizes the messianic significance of this biblical chapter.

in the Palestinian targums to this later point when she is in danger of being burnt.[56] The appearance of this fairly substantial additional prayer in the targums reflects their tendency to emphasize prayer to an even greater extent than many of the other documents in the larger midrashic corpus. Certainly the liturgical context in which the targums were used contributed to the proliferation of references to prayer and examples of prayer in them.[57] Tamar's request that the God who answers the oppressed answer her follows a typical pattern in the penitential Seliḥot prayers used for times of distress, public fast days, and the Day of Atonement,[58] and this fact confirms the liturgical awareness of this prayer's author.

But the recognition that the presence and form of Tamar's prayer correspond to a general trend in targumic literature does not address the importance of its specific content for reconstructing the distinctive perspective of the Palestinian targums, and of *Targum Neofiti* in particular, in which her prayer is longer than in any of the others. My discussion here will therefore anticipate the discussion in the final section concerning the unique contribution of the targum tradition to the history of interpretation of Genesis 38. One important aspect of Tamar's prayer, the significance of her vow of the three righteous men, will be introduced here and discussed more fully in that final section.

Tamar's prayer consists of three parts: an address, which includes a description of the nature of the God to whom she prays; a petition for help in her present crisis; and a vow, which she will fulfill if her prayer is answered. This basic form, which recalls the individual laments in the book of Psalms, is found in all of the Palestinian targums. The address and petition in *Targum Neofiti* serve to identify

---

[56] *Tg.Neof.* does not mention prayer as Tamar sits waiting for her father-in-law, and the interpretation of פתח עינים in *Tg.Neof.* Gen 38:14 (and 21) is "crossroads," as in *Tg.Onq.*, the Peshitta, the Vg, Jerome *Hebrew Questions* 46, and *Tg.Ps.-J.* According to *Tg.Ps.-J.* Gen 38:14 the "crossroads" are the place "where all eyes look" on the road.

[57] See Avigdor Shinan, צלותהון ובעותהון: תפילותיהם של ראשונים בראי התרגומים לתורה [Their prayers and intercessions: Prayers of the ancestors in light of the targums to the Tora], *Sinai* 78 (1975) 89–92. For further examples of prayer in the targums, see McNamara, *Targum Neofiti 1*, 40–41.

[58] See B. Barry Levy, *Targum Neophyti 1: A Textual Study*, vol. 1, Studies in Judaism (London and Lanham, NY: University Press of America, 1986) 229, and Heinemann, *Prayer in the Talmud*, 150–54. Heinemann, 150, translates an Aramaic form of the Seliḥot prayer with wording that is very similar to Tamar's prayer: "May he who answers the afflicted answer us!"

God as merciful, especially to those who are oppressed.[59] They also identify Tamar as one of the oppressed to whom the God of mercy responds in time of crisis.[60] Through the wording of this prayer, *Targum Neofiti* argues that Tamar is not guilty of the sexual impropriety for which she is being unjustly executed. She is one of the many innocent sufferers in the world for whom God shows special concern.

An appeal to divine mercy in order to avert an unjust death sentence is found elsewhere in *Targum Neofiti*. In its version of Gen 20:4, after Abimelek has been told in a dream that he is about to die because he has taken Sarah into his house, he prays, "I beseech mercy from before you, LORD! Shall also innocent people be killed in justice?"[61] Another prayer in the targum which appeals to God's mercy is the prayer of Abraham inserted in *Tg.Neof.* Gen 22:14, directly following the story of the binding of Isaac.[62] This prayer opens with a line identical to that found in *Tg.Neof.* Gen 20:4 and *Tg.Neof.* Gen 38:25 in which Abraham says, "I beseech mercy from before you, LORD!" Although Abraham does not request that his own life or the life of his son be spared in this prayer, he does request that God spare Isaac's innocent descendants from suffering in future generations:

> At the time when his sons find themselves in the hour of affliction, remember the binding of Isaac, their father, and listen to the voice of their prayer and answer them and deliver them from all tribulation,

---

[59] God's mercy is invoked by Tamar in *Tg.Ps.-J.*, *Frg.Tg.* P, and Gnz.Tg. E. The phrase "from before you, LORD" (מן קדמיך ייי) is a typical expression of respect in *Tg.Neof.*, as well as in other targums. See McNamara, *Targum Neofiti 1*, 33–34. Other titles, including "the living God" (Gnz.Tg. X and *t. Tg.Onq.*), "the living and enduring God," and "God of Abraham, Isaac, and Jacob, my fathers" (Gnz.Tg. FF), are also used in the Palestinian targums.

[60] Two other targums, *Frg.Tg.* V and Gnz.Tg. D, also identify Tamar as one of the oppressed. Others refer to the hour of her distress, obliquely assigning her to the category of the distressed (*Tg.Ps.-J.*, *Frg.Tg.* P, perhaps Gnz.Tg. FF which is somewhat broken, and Gnz.Tg. E). Two targums (Gnz.Tg. X and *t. Tg.Onq.*) have changed the reference to the hour of her distress to a plea of innocence: "the hour in which I am innocent." Only *Tg.Neof.* stresses the identity of God as the one who answers the oppressed by repeating the title two times. Although this repetition could be an unintentional dittography, as Levy maintains (*Targum Neophyti 1*, vol. 1, 229), it does emphasize Tamar's status as one of the oppressed, in keeping with the larger thematic emphases of *Tg.Neof.*

[61] The opening lines of the prayers in *Tg.Neof.* Gen 38:25 and in *Tg.Neof.* Gen 20:4 are identical (בבעו ברחמין מן קדמיך ייי).

[62] A version of Abraham's prayer after the binding of Isaac is found in all the extant targums, according to le Déaut, "Aspects de l'intercession," 41. It also appears in other midrashic sources as well, including *Gen.Rab.* 56.10.

because the generations to arise after him shall say, "On the mountain
of the sanctuary of the LORD, where Abraham offered Isaac his son,
on this mountain the glory of the presence [the Shekhina] of the LORD
was revealed."

In language recalling Tamar's prayer, Abraham asks that God "answer" his descendants in generations to come in their "hour of oppression" because of the merit of the perfect sacrifice which he had been
willing to perform in Genesis 22.[63]

As noted in passing above, Tamar's address and petition resemble
the Seliḥot prayers used on the Day of Atonement and other public
fast days. Significantly, the first petition in the Seliḥot prayer listed
in the Mishna (*m. Taʿan.* 2.4) refers to a prayer offered by Abraham.
This petition begins: "He who answered Abraham on Mt. Moriah
will answer you and hear the voice of your cry this day." Abraham's
prayer in *Tg.Neof.* Gen 22:14 attests to an awareness of this Seliḥot
prayer through the wording of his request that God listen to the
voice of the prayers of his descendants in the time of their distress
and answer them. With its allusions to the Seliḥot prayers, *Targum
Neofiti* portrays Abraham setting up a bank of merits upon which
later generations may draw when they suffer[64] and casts Tamar as
one of the many suffering souls in the world who can expect a hearing from God because of the merits of righteous figures such as
Abraham and Isaac.

Although the similarity of terminology between their prayers tacitly evokes the presence of Abraham in Tamar's prayer, Tamar does
not explicitly draw attention to the actions of Abraham and Isaac in
the past. Instead, she points to the future through her vow to raise
up three righteous men who will sanctify God's name in return for

---

[63] Abraham's prayer contains the words "answer them" (ועני יתהון) which are echoed
in Tamar's address to the God "who answers the oppressed" (דעני לעיקי) and in her
request that he "answer me" (עני יתי). Reference to a time of oppression is found in
both Abraham's prayer (בשעת עקתא) and Tamar's prayer (בשעת עקתהון). For a discussion of the significance of the binding of Isaac in Jewish tradition, see Shalom
Spiegel, *The Last Trial, On the Legends and Lore of the Command to Abraham to Offer Isaac
as a Sacrifice: The Akedah*, trans. Judah Goldin (New York: Pantheon Books, 1967)
and Jon D. Levenson, *The Death and Resurrection of the Beloved Son: The Transformation
of Child Sacrifice in Judaism and Christianity* (New Haven: Yale University Press, 1993).
[64] For the concept of the merits of the fathers, see Ephraim E. Urbach, *The Sages:
Their Concepts and Beliefs*, trans. Israel Abrahams (Cambridge, MA: Harvard University
Press, 1975; reprint, Jerusalem: Magnes Press, 1979) 496–508, especially 502–7 on
the binding of Isaac.

her life.[65] What will become more evident in the final section, however, is that the introduction of these three saints into Tamar's prayer does not merely project the drama of the story into the future. It also forces us to read Tamar's willingness to be burnt in *Targum Neofiti* in light of the three men's willingness to be burned at Dura. If Hananiah, Mishael, and Azariah's willingness to enter the furnace rather than worship the idol is meritorious, then Tamar's willingness to be burned rather than embarrass her father-in-law is similarly commendable. The comparison of Tamar with the three men at Dura, triggered by their introduction in her vow, also subtly transforms the relationship of her story to the events in Genesis 22. Drawn into the semantic sphere of self-sacrifice through her similarity to Hananiah, Mishael, and Azariah, she becomes not only a petitioning member of a later generation but also a figure parallel to Isaac, who in Jewish tradition distinguished himself with his willingness to die for God's glory.[66]

For now, it is important to mention two of the other enhancements of Tamar's character that are accomplished through her vow of the three righteous men at Dura.[67] One is that with this vow Tamar is depicted as possessing a prophetic grasp of biblical history and of the interrelationship of events from patriarchal to exilic periods. In connecting the events in Genesis 38 and Daniel 3, she acts as a precursor to the rabbinic exegetes who endeavor through their intertextual readings of scripture to create of it a seamless whole.

The other is that Tamar is shown in a positive light through an allusion to the language of the levirate law in her vow. Tamar's promise that she will "raise up" (מקיימה)[68] three righteous ones and her specification that they will sanctify God's "Name" (שמך) echo the

---

[65] All of the Palestinian targums depict Tamar as vowing the three men at Dura, although only *Tg.Neof.* and *Tg.Ps.-J.* specify that they will sanctify the divine Name.

[66] In some rabbinic sources Isaac and the three men at Dura are explicitly brought together as exemplars of laudable surrender to death. See for example *Gen.Rab.* 56.11, where all four devote their lives to study after divine deliverance from death.

[67] The simple fact that Tamar vows in time of distress is itself praiseworthy, according to *Gen.Rab.* 70.1–3, which states "It is meritorious to vow [in a time of trouble]."

[68] This verb is from the root "to rise" (קום), which is the same root used in the levirate law in Deut 25:5–10. This root can also mean "to vow" something, as it does in this context. This root is found in all the Palestinian targums, except for *t. Tg.Onq.*, which uses the root "to give" (יהב). The verbal root קום appears twice in Genesis 38 itself. The report that Tamar "rose up" (ותקם, Gen 38:19) to return to her father's house after conceiving, especially after Onan's failure to "raise up" (ותקם, Gen 38:8) seed for Er according to his father's instructions, marks her as the party who actually accomplishes the central purpose of the levirate custom in Genesis 38.

terminology of the levirate law in Deut 25:5–10, which concerns "raising up" (יָקִים, Deut 25:6; לְהָקִים, Deut 25:7) a "name" (שֵׁם, Deut 25:6, 7) for the dead.[69] This allusion shows Tamar as willing to fulfill for God the responsibility of a levir, which Onan had failed to do for a human brother.

To summarize, Tamar's prayer depicts her as a model of piety and trust in time of danger, as well as a prophetess, a biblical savant, and the true, spiritual levir in contrast to Onan. It also introduces through her vow of the three men the central theme of "sanctification of the Name," discussed at length in the final section of this chapter, and suggests that she, like Hananiah, Mishael, and Azariah, is an innocent and principled sufferer, who willingly faces death. Certainly Tamar's prayer and her subsequent statement to the court fill in the spare lines of her biblical character and resolve the tension between her important role in the story line and her marginal position in the narrative surface.

Tamar's Statement before the Court

Tamar's statement before the court follows her transfer of the three items, not to her father-in-law as in the biblical text, but to a judge. This change in the person who receives the pledge from Judah to a judge provides an appropriate context for the discussion of her new evidence by setting it in a legal court.[70] Tamar's statement in *Targum*

---

[69] Concern for the "name" of the dead, absent in the biblical text of Gen 38:8–9 but repeated three times in the law of the levir in Deut 25:5–10 (twice in Deut 25:6 and once in Deut 25:7), is also interjected into *Tg.Neof.* Gen 38:8–9. It is introduced into Judah's instructions to his second son, into Onan's perception of his situation, and into the narrator's description of the effect of Onan's sexual practices. For example, in *Tg.Neof.* Judah instructs Onan to "Raise up seed of sons for the name of your brother," whereas the biblical text simply reads "Raise up seed for your brother." Onan's concern in the Hebrew text that "the seed would not be his" is transformed in *Tg.Neof.* to a concern that "the sons would not be called by his name." Similarly, Onan adopts his style of intercourse in *Tg.Neof.* not simply "to not give seed to his brother" as in the Hebrew text, but "to not raise up sons for the name of his brother." This type of paraphrastic translation in order to bring two biblical texts into alignment is common in the Palestinian targums, according to Michael L. Klein, "Associative and Complementary Translation in the Targumim," *Eretz Israel* 16 (H. M. Orlinsky vol., 1982) 134–40.

[70] *Tg.Neof.* alone among the targum manuscripts has a single judge. The other Palestinian targums all contain the plural "judges," which more closely corresponds with a midrashic tradition identifying Isaac, Jacob, and Judah as the three judges who hear this case. See for example *Tanḥ.* Wayyešeb 9.17 and *Yal. Šim'oni* Gen 38:25. A later hand inserted the letter ' above the line in *Tg.Neof.* in order to make

Neofiti begins with a biblical quotation, "The man to whom these belong—from him I am pregnant," before continuing with a traditional rabbinic explanation concerning the peculiar wording of her accusations in Gen 38:25.[71]

Although in the biblical text Tamar speaks twice concerning the significance of the pledge, she never explicitly names Judah as the owner of the three items and the father of her unborn children. A passage in *b. Soṭa* 10b registers surprise at this omission with the exclamation "She should have told [the messenger his name]!" This source also focuses on Tamar's silence in its interpretation of the superscription of Psalm 56, in which she is called a "silent dove" or "silent sufferer" (יונת אלם) when the pledge items are lost.[72]

In the biblical text, Tamar's reliance on the pledge's visual impact implies that its owner's identity is obvious. Since its mere presence implicates Judah, she has no need to identify him by name. In particular, Tamar's second statement in the biblical text, which contains a direct imperative to her father-in-law to recognize his personal effects, is not meant to be vague or non-incriminating. It is intended to force Judah to admit to himself and to the others present his responsibility for the situation, and his public admission is far stronger that any accusation Tamar herself could have made.[73]

---

the word plural and bring it in line with the rest of the targums, but the singular possessive suffix on the word "in his hands" (בידוי) and the singular object in the prepositional phrase "to him" (ליה) confirm that originally a single judge was intended. Perhaps the tradition that Tamar gave the items to a judge arose out of yet another reading of the phrase "she sent to her father-in-law" (שלחה אל חמיה) as "she sent [to the] judge [after] she saw [them]," since the word אל is sometimes interpreted as "judge" in *Tg.Neof.* See for example *Tg.Neof.* Gen 6:2, in which the "sons of God" are called "sons of judges." In any event, since *m. Sanh.* 1.4 indicates that twenty-three judges are required for a capital case, neither the tradition included in *Tg.Neof.* nor the tradition in the other targums accords with the halakha of the Mishna.

[71] The technique of inserting extra-biblical material into the targum text in the middle of a verse is a common one, through which the extraneous material is incorporated neatly into the body of the translation. See Levy, *Targum Neophyti 1*, vol. 1, 55.

[72] *b. Soṭa* 10b may be associating the word "dove" (יונה) with the Hebrew root "to oppress" (ינה). If this is the case, then the theme of innocent suffering expressed in Tamar's prayer in *Tg.Neof.* is present also in the Talmud. Note that in *Cant.Rab.* 2.14 an interpretation of the line "My dove in the clefts of the rock" picks up on the verbal similarity between the Hebrew words "dove" and "to oppress" when it describes the dove as Israel entrapped by the Egyptians at the sea.

[73] Self-incrimination is seen in other parts of the Bible as well, for example in the stories involving Judah's descendant David in 2 Samuel 12 and 14. As we will see in the discussion of Judah's confession, this theme of self-condemnation is picked up and celebrated in the midrash as a laudatory, voluntary disclosure.

Targum Neofiti modifies the calculating and assertive character implied by the biblical narrative, however, when it presents Tamar's
statement that she will under no circumstances publicly reveal the
identity of the man who impregnated her.[74] Not only does Tamar's
refusal to speak accentuate and prolong her concealment of knowledge in the biblical narrative, it also ascribes to this concealment a
positive value. Tamar's statement portrays her as an advocate of an
ethos in which publicly shaming another is one of the worst crimes
possible. Other sources, such as *b. Soṭa* 10b, also point to her as a
model of considerate discretion. In this source, a number of authorities are listed as the author of the following observation: "It is better
that a person throw himself into the midst of the furnace of fire than
embarrass his neighbor in public. How [do we know this]? From
[the example of] Tamar."[75]

Because *Targum Neofiti* desires to paint a portrait of thoughtful, self-
sacrificing reserve, Tamar's second statement in Gen 38:25, with its
confrontational imperative ("Recognize!" הכר נא), is taken away from
her and reassigned to Judah. Other Palestinian targums preserve the
statement beginning with this imperative as the words of Tamar but
transform it from a command to her father-in-law into a pious statement of trust that God "will place in his heart [the willingness] to
recognize them, to whom this ring, cord, and staff belong."[76]

Targum Neofiti preserves the content of Tamar's statement of trust
found in other manuscripts when it quotes her declaring that God
"will place in his heart [the willingness] to see them,"[77] but it severs

---

[74] This statement is found in most, but not all, of the other Palestinian targums,
including *Tg.Ps.-J.*, *Frg.Tg.*, and Gnz.Tgs. D and E. It is lacking in Gnz.Tgs. X and
FF and *t. Tg.Onq.*

[75] This is a well attested rabbinic tradition. See *b. Ketub.* 67b; *b. B.Meṣ.* 59a; *b. Ber.*
43b; *Midr. Haggadol* Gen 38:25; and *Yal. Šimʿoni* Gen 38:25 for similar statements
attributed to various second- and third-century authorities. See also the discussion
in Urbach, *Sages*, 253.

[76] This is a translation of Gnz.Tg. E. There is a similar statement in *Frg.Tg.*

[77] Whereas Gnz.Tg. E and *Frg.Tg.* preserve the biblical verb "to recognize" in
Tamar's statement of trust that God "will place in his heart [the willingness] to
recognize them," *Tg.Neof.* substitutes the verb "to see" in her statement that God
"will place in his heart [the willingness] to see them." This substitution suggests an
allusion to Lev 5:1, which discusses the obligation each person has to testify if that
person is a witness, or has seen something, or knows something. The Aramaic word
used in *Tg.Neof.* Lev 5:1 to express the concept of visual perception (חמי) is from the
same verbal root that appears in Tamar's statement that God will make Judah
willing "to see" (למיחמי) in *Tg.Neof.*

the verbal connection with the biblical verse and adds additional material. For example, it adds a description of God as the Witness between Tamar and Judah of things which no one else could have seen.[78] It also adds an additional line of confidence in God's ability to free her from her sentence of death, which anticipates the intervention of the voice from heaven that concludes the passage.[79] In these ways, *Targum Neofiti* interjects a positive divine presence into the narrative.

Tamar's reformation into a model of modest propriety occurs earlier in *Targum Neofiti* as well. When the biblical narrative states in Gen 38:15 that Judah thought she was a prostitute because she covered her face, this targum adds a gloss summarizing a traditional explanation of this verse. This gloss explains that she covered her face "in Judah's house, so that Judah did not recognize her."[80] This portrayal of Tamar as an extremely modest daughter-in-law arose out of a perceived discrepancy between what is stated in the biblical text and a common sense observation that prostitutes do not cover their faces.[81] One lesson drawn from this incident is the importance of men becoming familiar with their female relatives to prevent such incidents of incest from occurring.[82] Another is that Tamar's exceptional modesty merited that she should be the mother of kings and prophets.[83] The

---

[78] See the description of God as a witness between Laban and Jacob in Gen 31:50. See also the description of God as a witness between Judah (used as a personification of the tribe in the biblical text) and the wife of his youth in Mal 2:14, cited in *Tanḥ*. Wayyešeb 9.9 in connection with Genesis 38. God is called as a witness also in *Frg.Tg.* and Gnz.Tg. E. All the others lack this feature, which may have been added under the influence of God's presence as a witness in Samuel's court in the midrashic reading of 1 Sam 12:5. In the LXX, Samuel describes God as a witness in 1 Sam 12:6. See the discussion below about the heavenly voice in the court.

[79] Only *Tgs.Neof.* and *Ps.-J.* have this statement of reliance on God's deliverance. The others presuppose that Judah's recognition of the items will be sufficient to spare her, as in the biblical story. Tamar's reliance on God in *Tg.Neof.* contrasts positively with Joseph's trust in a human butler to free him from jail, which is evaluated negatively in *Tg.Neof.* Gen 40:43.

[80] For this same tradition, see *Gen.Rab.* 85.8; *Tanḥ*. Wayyešeb 9.17; *b. Soṭa* 10b; and *b. Meg.* 10b.

[81] See *Gen.Rab.* 85.8 and *b. Soṭa* 10b, which express the objection that prostitutes do not cover their faces. *Tg.Onq.* also presents Tamar without a veil at Enaim with its alteration of Gen 38:14 to read "she despised the veil and beautified herself."

[82] See *Gen.Rab.* 85.8 and *Tanḥ*. Wayyešeb 9.17.

[83] See *b. Soṭa* 10b and *b. Meg.* 10b. See also the favorable comparison of Tamar with Rebekah because both wear veils in *Gen.Rab.* 60.16 and 85.7. Each modest woman is rewarded with twins.

explanation that her zealous conformity to conventional decorum is the basis for her position as the ancestress of important genealogical lines remakes her as a model of behavior for ordinary women.[84] In the process of this transformation, the focus is shifted away from the extraordinary and unconventional actions which actually earn her that status in the biblical story. The biblical Tamar's actions were apparently regarded as contrary to ordinary ideals of morality and to a woman's role in society. Before she could be offered as an exemplar of behavior for later generations, she was denatured and assimilated to traditional mores.

To summarize, Tamar's address to the court in this narrative expansion remakes her into an exemplar of considerate discretion and strong faith, even in the face of death. Her statement of confidence in God as the Witness of the events at the entrance of Enaim and as the prompter of Judah's confession emphasizes the divine role in shaping the course of events in this post-biblical version of the story.

Confessions of Judah

The next section, consisting of Judah's public statement before the court, is the longest section in the narrative expansion in *Targum Neofiti*,[85] and also one of the fullest representations of Judah's confession contained in any targumic or rabbinic document.[86] Judah appears frequently as an exemplar of voluntary confession of sin in rabbinic

---

[84] This same decorum is emphasized in another detail in *Tg.Neof.*, found in none of the other Palestinian targums. In *Tg.Neof.* Tamar places the pledge items in the hands of the judge rather than throwing them at the feet of the judges as in the other targums. This latter gesture is more dramatic, but not in keeping with the self-restrained and unassuming woman depicted in *Tg.Neof.*

[85] The desire to supplement the limited biblical material concerning Judah because of the importance of the tribe associated with his name in later history is seen also in two other narrative expansions in *Tg.Neof.* The first, which appears in *Tg.Neof.* Gen 44:18–19, stresses his great physical strength and his royal status in Canaan. The second appears in *Tg.Neof.* Gen 50:1, in which he leads his brothers in planting a cedar tree on their father's grave.

[86] *Frg.Tg.*; Gnz.Tgs. D, X, and FF; and *t. Tg.Onq.* contain confessions which are comparable in length. *Tg.Ps.-J.* contains similar material, but some of it is depicted as the private thoughts of Judah as he decides whether or not to confess. Gnz.Tg. E, which has a very brief confession, also includes a shorter version of Judah's private deliberations leading to his confession. The words of Judah's confession before the court are never presented in such length in rabbinic literature outside of the targums, although, as described in the previous chapter, the *Testament of Judah* contains a lengthier, more explicit confession on his deathbed. For an example of the importance of repentance in *Tg.Neof.*, see *Tg.Neof.* Gen 6:3, in which the possibility of repentance to avert the flood is raised.

literature.[87] In fact, the motif of Judah's confession acquired such prominence in the rabbinic exegesis of Genesis 38 that *b. Meg.* 25b singles it out as the main point of the biblical narrative. The relevant passage occurs in a discussion of rules concerning the reading and translation of a number of sensitive biblical texts within the context of the synagogue service:

> The story of Tamar and Judah is both read and translated. Certainly! We might think that [we should forbear] out of respect for Judah. Therefore we are told [that this is no objection]; [the passage] really redounds to his credit, because [it records that] he confessed.[88]

Rather than an unseemly story about a tribal ancestor's deception of his daughter-in-law, his association with a woman he considers a prostitute, and his unwitting incestuous relations, the story becomes a record of Judah's commendable behavior when confronted with his guilt.

Judah's confession is associated with a number of rewards in different rabbinic sources. It is singled out as the reason why Judah's brothers praised him in Gen 49:8;[89] described as the means through which Judah gained life in the world to come;[90] regarded as the decisive factor through which Judah's offspring merited the kingship of the people;[91] specified as the reason why the tribe of Judah remained so long in the land where they settled,[92] and why they were victorious in war over their enemies;[93] portrayed as the reason his descendants

---

[87] For an overview of the origins and development of this motif, see C. E. Hayes, "The Midrashic Career of the Confession of Judah (Genesis 38:26)," parts 1 and 2, *VT* 45 (1995) 62–81, 174–87.

[88] This translation is from Isidore Epstein, ed., *The Babylonian Talmud* (London: Soncino Press, 1935–48). The reason why Genesis 38 is both read and translated is not explicitly stated in the short version of this tradition in *m. Meg.* 4.10, but the quotation of Job 15:18–19 in the discussion of forbidden texts in *y. Meg.* 4.11 implies that the reason is that Judah confessed.

[89] See *Tanḥ.* Wayehi 12.12 and *Genesis Rabba* 97, NV; 98.6.

[90] *Num.Rab.* 9.17 and *Genesis Rabba* 97, NV.

[91] *Exod.Rab.* 30.19 states that although Isaac and Jacob did not believe Tamar's claim that Judah was responsible for her pregnancy, he himself cleared her and thereby gained the kingship. *Tanḥ.* Wayehi 12.12 also implies that Judah merited that the messiah be among his descendants because of his confession. Not all sources are so enthusiastic about the value of Judah's confession, however. In a discussion between R. Tarfon and his students, the suggestion that Judah merited the kingship through his confession is rejected with the objection that confession only suffices to remove the guilt of the crime. See *Mek.* Bešallaḥ 6; *t. Ber.* 4.18; and *Midr. Tehillim* Ps 76:2

[92] See *y. Meg.* 4.11, based on a reading of Job 15:18–19.

[93] *Genesis Rabba* 97, NV.

were spared from death in the exile;[94] associated with the fact that
the Jewish people are called by his name;[95] and, finally, seen as the
reason that Judah merited that all the letters of the tetragrammaton
be included in his name.[96]

The understanding that Judah's confession constitutes the main point
of the biblical story and results in these positive consequences is curious
in light of the biblical narrative itself. In Genesis 38, Judah does not
appear especially eager to avail himself of the opportunity for extended,
public confession. Presented with irrefutable evidence, Judah does
immediately compare his daughter-in-law favorably with himself and
admit that he should have arranged a marriage for her with his son
Shelah; however, he does not explicitly confess his incestuous sexual
relations with her nor his paternity of the children soon to be born.
Genesis Rabba's treatment of Genesis 38, discussed in the next chapter,
also fails to develop the motif of Judah's confession.[97] Rather, several
traditions in this commentary maintain Judah's innocence in ingenious
and sometimes incredible ways. How then did the motif of Judah's
confession arise and become featured so prominently in the targums?

Certainly the basic generating force behind the ascendancy of the
motif of Judah's confession is the desire to view Israel's ancestors in
a positive light, as models of behavior and piety. Since the events in
the early part of the biblical narrative make such a reading of this
patriarch extremely difficult, the focus shifts to Judah's behavior after
Tamar presents the pledge items in the new setting of a legal court.
In the midrashic version of the story, Judah is faced with the difficult
choice of either confessing or denying his responsibility for Tamar's
pregnancy.[98]

---

[94] Hananiah, Mishael, and Azariah are spared because Judah spared Tamar and
her unborn children from the fire with his confession in *Genesis Rabba* 97, NV; *b. Soṭa*
10b; and *Tanḥ.* Wayyešeb 9.17 (where Daniel is also spared). See also *Num.Rab.* 13.4
and *Exod.Rab.* 16.4.

[95] *Tanḥ.* Wayehi 12.12; *Gen.Rab.* 98.6; and *Midr. Haggadol* Gen 49:8. *Genesis Rabba*
97, NV, attributes this honor to Judah's efforts to save Joseph from his brothers'
plot to kill him.

[96] *b. Soṭa* 10b. Judah's name (יהודה) with the fourth letter (ד) removed spells the
name of God (יהוה). The significance of the fourth letter, which also has the numerical value of four, is discussed at length in *Genesis Rabba* 97, NV.

[97] The motif does appear, however, in the material commenting on Judah's blessing in Gen 49:8–12 in *Genesis Rabba* 97, NV.

[98] Judah's initial reluctance to confess is depicted in a number of sources, including the *Testament of Judah* 12; *Gen.Rab.* 85.11; *Tanḥ.* Wayyešeb 9.17; *Midr. Haggadol*
Gen 38:25; *Yal. Šimʿoni* Gen 38:25; and *Leqaḥ Ṭob* Gen 38:25. In *Genesis Rabba* 97,

Besides this basic motivation to present him as an exemplar of behavior, other factors contributed to the development of the portrait of Judah as the confessing sinner. Judah's name itself, which contains the same root as the verb "to confess" (ידה), undoubtedly played a big part in the development of this motif.[99] Word play on aspects of his name is evident in most of the passages summarized above concerning the rewards that Judah gained due to his confession.

The project of recreating Judah into a repentant sinner finds a pliant point of entry in the biblical text in his first words after recognizing the three items: "She is more righteous than I" (צדקה ממני).[100] As pointed out earlier, later interpreters employ an atomizing technique common in rabbinic exegesis, splitting the phrase into its two components. Each word then serves as a core for two separate sentences: "She is righteous" (צדקה). "From me" (ממני) is the pregnancy. This division eliminates the comparison with Tamar, unflattering to the patriarch, and inserts an explicit verbal confession into Judah's utterance.[101] The pervasive nature of this interpretation in rabbinic Judaism is indicated by its inclusion in the generally literal translation of *Targum Onqelos*.[102] *Targum Neofiti* and the other Palestinian

---

NV, he is praised because he conquered the evil inclination to deny responsibility for Tamar's pregnancy. Judah's reluctance to confess becomes plausible only if one assumes that his identity is not immediately apparent after Tamar's presentation of the pledge.

[99] *Gen.Rab.* 71.5 acknowledges Judah and a number of his family members (including Leah, David, and Daniel) for their confessions and praises, in an extended play on the Hebrew root of Judah's name (ידה).

[100] The comparative phrase is also preserved in the Samaritan targum, the LXX, and the Peshitta, indicating that the grammar of the biblical phrase was not especially difficult to understand. Judging from this evidence, it was not a problem in the biblical text which motivated the splitting of this phrase in rabbinic exegesis, but rather other hermeneutic pressures which found in these two words an opening for the presentation of Judah as a repentant sinner.

[101] In *Gen.Rab.* 71.5, Judah's statement "She is more righteous than I" (צדקה ממני) is quoted as the basis for his fame as a confessing sinner.

The explicit verbal confession "from me" is so significant that *Tg.Neof.* carefully prepares for its appearance by repeating the preposition "from" (מין) earlier in the narrative expansion. Tamar states concerning the man who owns the items that "from him" (מיניה) she is pregnant, even though in the original Hebrew text the prepositions used in her accusation in Gen 38:25 (לו) and in the comparative phrase in Gen 38:26 (ממני) are different. The same preposition appears in Judah's paraphrase of Tamar's statement when he addresses the court (מיניה). By the time Judah confesses that Tamar is pregnant "from me" (מיני), one is primed to accept his confession as part of the biblical narrative. Note that Judah's double address to his family also includes this preposition each time (קבילו מיני).

[102] *Tg.Onq.* contains the reading "She is innocent. From me she is pregnant" (זכאה מני מעדיא).

targums emphasize the motif of Judah's confession by augmenting the two statements "She is righteous" and "From me" with additional material. The component parts of Judah's public statement before the court will be discussed below with special attention to the traditional material which they contain and the history of development of the confession which appears in *Targum Neofiti*.

In *Targum Neofiti*, Judah's response to Tamar's statement is immediate, as was God's response earlier to Tamar's prayer. The word "immediately" (מיד) serves as a structural marker for the sections in which God and Judah react to Tamar's words. The speed of Judah's response to Tamar's statement of trust in divine providence echoes the rapid pace of the biblical narrative at this point and, in fact, surpasses it. *Targum Neofiti*, in contrast to the biblical text and all of the other Palestinian targums, portrays Judah as speaking even before he recognizes his personal property in Gen 38:26. Perhaps his swift reaction in *Targum Neofiti* implies that it is not the undeniable evidence of the three items that forces him to confess, as in the biblical story. It is rather the stirrings of divine intervention within his heart, to which Tamar alludes in her address to the court, that prompt him to offer his courtroom confession.[103] On a more prosaic level, Judah's immediate confession and the awkward and anti-climactic placement of his recognition of the pledge after his statement may be due to the reassignment of Tamar's statement beginning with the imperative, "Recognize!" (הכר נא), as part of Judah's speech in *Targum Neofiti*. In following the order of the biblical text in which this imperative precedes Judah's recognition, *Targum Neofiti* creates a jarring seam between the narrative expansion and the resumption of the translation of the biblical text when Judah belatedly recognizes the items in Gen 38:26.[104]

In *Targum Neofiti*, Judah rises to his feet and publicly addresses his relatives present at the court. The initial word Judah uses to request

---

[103] There is a tradition recorded in *Tanh.* Wayyešeb 9.17, partially reconstructed at this point in Solomon Buber, ed., *Midraš Tanhuma* (Vilna: Romm, 1885), which lends support to this interpretation of Judah's immediate confession in *Tg.Neof.* In this tradition, a heavenly voice commands Judah to acknowledge that Tamar is pregnant by him. Although initially reluctant, he confesses because of the divine command. While *Tg.Neof.* portrays Judah as eager to confess, it may be drawing on traditions such as this one, which depict God as intervening to insure his proper response.
[104] Other Palestinian targums, including *Frg.Tg.*; Gnz.Tgs. D, X, FF, and E; and *t. Tg.Onq.*, which allow Tamar to keep a revised version of her second biblical statement, do not have this problem of Judah's anticlimactic recognition of the three items.

their attention is the same one which Tamar uses to request God's attention in her prayer (בבעו). This word therefore serves as a verbal marker introducing the words of both Tamar and Judah.[105] A similar address to his family members is repeated later in his statement, structurally dividing his confession into two parts. One might be surprised at the presence of Judah's brothers and his father's relatives at Tamar's trial in *Targum Neofiti*.[106] Although the biblical text implies that there is a crowd of people present throughout the events recorded in Gen 38:25–26,[107] it does not specify that it consists of members of Judah's family. In fact, Gen 38:1 clearly notes that Judah separated himself from his family following the sale of Joseph. Judah's unexpected appeal to his family members may be based in part on a conventional address formula used by leaders before an assembly. In 1 Chr 28:2, for example, David prefaces his disclosure that he will not build the temple because of his involvement with war by rising to his feet and saying, "Hear me, my brothers and my people."

But there are other reasons for the presence of Judah's family members at the court based on intertextual readings of certain biblical verses in conjunction with the motif of Judah's confession. For example, Jacob's blessing in Gen 49:8–12 begins with a pun, "Judah, your brothers shall praise you," in which both Judah's name and the verb "praise" come from the same verbal root (ידה). Some sources

---

[105] Although I have translated this word as a verb in this passage, it is in fact a prepositional phrase containing an abstract noun, meaning literally "in seeking" or "in request." The repetition of this word here and elsewhere in *Tg.Neof.* indicates that it functions as a formulaic marker for monologues, whether they take the form of prayers or public speeches. The same root (בעי) is used to express Tamar's search for the three items, as well as Judah and Hirah's search for the woman on the road. It is one of the many roots which are repeated throughout *Tg.Neof.*'s treatment of Genesis 38. See for example the repetitions of the roots נפק, עבר, שכח, חמי, יהב, יקד, and קום. This technique of repeating verbal roots creates connections between the more literal translation of Gen 38:1–24, 27–30 and the narrative expansion, thereby tacitly arguing for the unity of the presentation of Genesis 38 in *Tg.Neof.*

[106] An address to Judah's brothers and his father's house is found in *Frg.Tg.*; Gnz.Tgs. D, X, and FF (two times); and *t. Tg.Onq.* It is lacking in *Tg.Ps.-J.* and Gnz.Tg. E, which present some of the material found in Judah's public address in *Tg.Neof.* as his internal deliberations over whether or not to confess.

[107] The notice that Judah "was told" about his daughter-in-law's condition in Gen 38:24 implies the presence of others, as does his plural imperative to "bring her out" in the same verse. The indication that Tamar "sent" the three items and her two messages to her father-in-law in Gen 38:25 implies the presence of at least one intermediary, and Judah's declaration of Tamar's greater righteousness because of his failure to marry her to Shelah also suggests the presence of an audience.

extend the pun and associate this brotherly praise with Judah's willingness to "confess," which is also from the same root (ידה). The
association between the brother's praise and Judah's confession implies
that the brothers were present when Judah confessed.[108]

Another biblical verse associated with Judah's confession is Job 15:18,
"What wise men have told and have not hidden from their fathers."[109]
According to one tradition based on this intertextual reading, both
Judah's father, Jacob, and Tamar's father, Shem, were present at
the court when he bravely confessed.[110] In harmony with the interpretation of Job 15:18 as an indication that Judah admitted his sin before
his fathers, another tradition depicts Judah's father, Jacob, and his
grandfather, Isaac, as judges along with Judah at Tamar's trial.[111] All
of the sources which read Job 15:18 as a description of Judah's confession regard his willingness to confess before his elders and other family
members in a positive light. Judah's public disclosure of secret information becomes the complement of Tamar's earlier guarding of secret
information in the courtroom. The biblical theme of concealed and
revealed knowledge is therefore developed in *Targum Neofiti* in a unique
way that furthers a positive interpretation of both main characters.

The body of Judah's confessional statement in *Targum Neofiti* consists of two parallel aphorisms which apply especially well to Judah's
particular case. These aphorisms stress that, in light of post-biblical
eschatology, acceptance of punishment and public humiliation in this
world are preferable to the consequences which denial would bring
in the world to come.[112] The first maxim indicating Judah's choice
to burn in this world rather than in the world to come indicates that

---

[108] See *Tanḥ.* Wayehi 12.12; *Genesis Rabba* 97, NV; 98.6. A number of sources,
including *Genesis Rabba* 97, NV, and *Tanḥ.* Wayyešeb 9.17, contain a tradition associated with Deut 33:6–7 that Reuben heard Judah's confession and consequently
confessed his own incestuous relations with Bilhah. As noted in the previous chapter, the *Testament of Judah* depicts Judah confessing on his deathbed in the presence
of family members, specifically his sons, in accordance with the testament genre.

[109] *Genesis Rabba* 97, NV, and *Tanḥ.* Wayyešeb 9.17 refer to this verse in connection with the motif of Judah and Reuben's confessions. See also *Num.Rab.* 9.17.

[110] See *Num.Rab.* 13.4. For the tradition that identifies Shem as Tamar's father,
see the discussion in the final section of this chapter concerning "sanctification of
the Name."

[111] See *Tanḥ.* Wayyešeb 9.17 and *Yal. Šimʿoni* Gen 38:25. See also *Exod.Rab.* 30.19,
in which Isaac, Jacob, and all of Judah's brothers try to defend Judah against Tamar's
charge, before Judah himself comes forward with the truth.

[112] The relationship between events in this world and in the world to come is seen
also in Joseph's reasoning that he should not lie with Potiphar's wife in this world
to avoid being joined with her forever in the world to come (*Tg.Neof.* Gen 39:10).

he expects to share Tamar's punishment after confessing his guilt.[113] Since Judah condemned Tamar to death by burning, he himself expects to burn. This assumption is entirely absent in the biblical narrative, in which Judah's life is never endangered and in which he is apparently free to reverse his earlier decree concerning Tamar's fate. A number of biblical laws, however, stipulate that both the man and the woman are to be executed for sexual misconduct. Especially pertinent in this connection is the law in Lev 20:12: "Any man who lies with his daughter-in-law, both of them shall certainly be put to death. They have done an abominable thing. Their blood is upon them."

The rabbinic assumption that both Judah and Tamar are liable for the same punishment finds expression in an exclamation attributed to R. Huna (fourth-century Palestinian): "She went out! Both she and he must go out!"[114] This insistence that both parties deserve punishment is supported by appeal to a feature of the biblical text. The first pronoun in Gen 38:25 is actually written with the consonants indicating a masculine subject, "he" (הוא), although traditionally it is read as a feminine subject, "she" (היא). According to the tradition attributed to R. Huna, the discrepancy between the consonantal writing of the pronoun and the traditional reading indicates that both Tamar and Judah should have gone out together to be burned.[115] This understanding that both parties are liable to punishment according to biblical law affects the narrative in more than one way. It removes the control that Judah exercises over Tamar's life and, therefore, over the narrative plot, and it emphasizes both the binding force of legal statutes and the power of God to deliver from death portrayed at the end of Judah's confession.

---

[113] All of the Palestinian targums contain this aphorism and its implication that Judah accepts punishment by burning.

[114] *Gen.Rab.* 85.11. See also *Midr. Haggadol* Gen 38:25.

[115] The assumption that Judah's confession includes his acceptance of punishment by burning is highlighted in a number of the Palestinian targums through their placement of this maxim at the very end of his statement (Gnz.Tgs. X and FF, and *t. Tg.Onq.*). The voice from heaven intervenes immediately afterwards, saving both parties from death. Of all the Palestinian targums, *Tg.Ps.-J.* most explicitly depicts the voice as saving them both from punishment when it says, "This decree is from me: The two of them are saved from judgment." A number of targums (Gnz.Tgs. X and FF, and *t. Tg.Onq.*) contain a different second aphorism, which replaces the theme of embarrassment with the theme of judgment. The two aphorisms in *t. Tg.Onq.*, for example, clearly confirm that Judah expects to be punished: "It is better for me to be judged in this world, than be judged in the world to come. It is better to be judged in the extinguishable fire than to be judged in the consuming fire."

In addition to the assumption that both parties are liable to punishment, the first maxim contains a second rabbinic assumption, that acceptance of punishment is expiatory. If Judah accepts his deserved punishment in this world, he will spare himself from the fire of Gehenna, which was created after the expulsion from the Garden of Eden, according to *Tg.Neof.* Gen 3:24.[116] The idea that repentance and acceptance of a deserved death earn one a place in the world to come is expressed in a number of places in rabbinic literature.[117]

Judah's second aphorism compares the embarrassment that confession brings here in this world and in the next,[118] and picks up on the biblical theme of embarrassment raised in Gen 38:23 by Judah's unwillingness to be a laughingstock. The willingness to be embarrassed before those assembled indicated by this aphorism remakes the character of Judah. He is no longer primarily concerned with his worldly reputation, but instead considers the long-term gain to be had by humiliating himself through confession before the court.

A statement attributed to Ben Zoma (second-century Palestinian), associated with Judah's confession in a passage in *Exodus Rabba*, contains vocabulary similar to that in the two aphorisms in *Targum Neofiti*:

> If you have been put to shame in this world, you will not be put to shame before God in the world to come, for he is a consuming fire. Why is this? Because the shame of this world is nothing compared to the shame of standing before him in the world to come.[119]

---

[116] This placement of the creation of Gehenna after the expulsion from Eden in *Tg.Neof.* contrasts with another rabbinic view expressed in *Pirqe R.El.* that both Eden (paradise) and Gehenna were created at the same time in fulfillment of God's original plan for the cosmos.

[117] As pointed out above, Judah's confession earns him eternal life in *Num.Rab.* 9.17 and *Genesis Rabba* 97, NV. For a discussion of the concept of repentance in rabbinic literature, see Urbach, *Sages*, 462–71. *Lev.Rab.* 10.5 provides a representative expression of the rabbinic idea that repentance is expiatory. See also the examples of repentant acceptance of death in Arthur J. Droge and James D. Tabor, *A Noble Death: Suicide and Martyrdom among Christians and Jews in Antiquity* (San Francisco: HarperSanFrancisco, 1992) 97 ff. The two examples found in *Gen.Rab.* 65.22 are particularly fitting, in that they describe the acceptance and even self-infliction of the death penalty by guilty parties who subsequently gain eternal life. By contrast, *Gen.Rab.* 26.6 states that where there is no punishment below, punishment above awaits.

[118] A number of other Palestinian targums (*Tg.Ps.-J.*, *Frg.Tg.*, and Gnz.Tgs. D and E) also include this aphorism about embarrassment, although in each of these targums the order of the two aphorisms is reversed from that in *Tg.Neof.*

[119] *Exod.Rab.* 30.19.

References to types of shame, the consuming fire,[120] and the two worlds suggest that the aphorisms in *Targum Neofiti* may derive from this statement attributed to Ben Zoma. In *Targum Neofiti*, however, the theme of burning, central to the biblical story and to the narrative expansion, is emphasized through the creation of a second aphorism concerning burning that formally imitates the aphorism concerning shame. In addition, in keeping with the theme of confession before family members introduced in Judah's initial words, the shame of confession in the world to come is heightened by the presence of righteous ancestors.

Two targums containing both aphorisms present in *Targum Neofiti* portray them as Judah's private calculations, as he decides whether or not to admit his responsibility for Tamar's pregnancy.[121] This internal weighing of options is fitting for a man who advocates selling his brother rather than killing him because it is more profitable, who promises his daughter-in-law his third son while apparently intending to withhold him from her, and who abandons his efforts to pay the mysterious woman when things threaten to become embarrassing. It is also in harmony with the tradition depicting Judah as a reluctant confessor, noted above in the discussion of lost and found witnesses. In addition, there is a smooth fit between biblical text and extra-biblical expansion in these two texts. After Judah recognizes the pledge, as in the opening of Gen 38:26, he privately weighs the advantages of confession with the words of the extra-biblical aphorisms, and then he speaks his biblical lines before the court.[122] This depiction of the two aphorisms as the private thoughts of Judah may therefore be the earliest form of their presentation in the Palestinian targum tradition.[123]

In *Targum Neofiti*, these two aphorisms have been transformed from Judah's private assessment of his situation into part of his public confession. This reassignment from thought to word recreates Judah

---

[120] The phrase "consuming fire" in the statement attributed to Ben Zoma comes from Deut 4:24 and 9:3, where it describes God.

[121] *Tg.Ps.-J.* and Gnz.Tg. E.

[122] This internal deliberation prolongs the suspense of the narrative climax, since it halts the rapid progress from recognition to reversal of Judah's verdict in the biblical story.

[123] Gnz.Tg. E, one of the targums which presents these aphorisms as Judah's private deliberations, is possibly the earliest of the Geniza targums. Interestingly, the second section of Judah's confession in *Tg.Neof.* beginning with the words "With the measure with which a man measures" is lacking in Gnz.Tg. E, which contains only the biblical core of Judah's confession.

as a moral exemplar, free from the self-interest which marks him in the biblical story and in some rabbinic portraits of his character. It also presents him as a teacher of ethical wisdom, and this characterization of Judah as sage continues in the next section of his confession, where he turns biblical exegete, commenting on the significance of biblical narratives in which he himself plays a role.[124]

The second section of Judah's public confession in *Targum Neofiti* opens with a familiar rabbinic dictum, "With the measure with which a man measures it will be measured to him."[125] The aphorisms about fire and shame in the first section raise the expectation that the sin which Judah is about to confess involves Tamar, since he alludes to the method decreed for her execution in Gen 38:24 and the possibility of embarrassment in Gen 38:23. This general dictum about appropriate punishments, however, prepares the way for a second confession about a different, but linguistically related, crime committed earlier in the Joseph story in Genesis 37.

But before turning to Judah's double confession, one needs to note that the dictum about just measures and the interpretation which follows it also stir recollections of yet other bad deeds mentioned in *Targum Neofiti* Genesis 38. The contrast between good and bad (בישא) measures and the declaration that every person whose deeds (עובדוי) are revealed is fortunate evoke the memory of Judah's sons. In *Tg.Neof.* Gen 38:7, Er is portrayed doing "bad deeds" (עובדין בישין), explaining why he was considered "evil" (רע) in God's sight in the biblical narrative. In *Tg.Neof.* Gen 38:9–10, what his brother Onan "did" (דעבד) is described as "bad" (ובאש) before the LORD because he destroyed his "deeds" (עובדוי) on the ground. *Targum Neofiti* affirms in a number of places, independently of the biblical text, the fundamental moral principle that good deeds are rewarded and bad deeds

---

[124] Judah is depicted as a teacher of Tora elsewhere in midrash. For example, in *Tanḥ.* Wayyigaš 11.12 and *Gen.Rab.* 95.3, he goes before his family into Egypt (Gen 46:28) to set up a Tora school. *Tg.Neof.* Gen 49:10 states that Judah's descendants will not only be kings, but also scribes who teach Tora generation after generation.

[125] This expression is found in all the Palestinian targums except Gnz.Tg. E. Similar expressions appear in *m. Soṭa* 1.7; *Mek.* Bešallaḥ 6, Širata 6, and 'Amaleq 2; and *Tg.Neof.*, *Frg.Tg.* P, and *Tg.Ps.-J.* For a discussion and more examples, see H. P. Ruger, "Mit welchem Mass ihrmesst, wird euch gemessen werden," *ZNW* 60 (1969) 174–82, especially 177–79 which discuss the various forms this expression takes in the Palestinian targums to Gen 38:25–26. In *Gen.Rab.* 9.11 "measure for measure" is described as the consistent rule for punishments, established with the creation of the world.

punished.[126] In this targum, both of Judah's sons die because of their bad deeds, which are never brought to light through public confession. In contrast, Judah, whose bad deeds are revealed through confession, is ultimately delivered from death. The contrast in *Targum Neofiti* between the fates of Judah and his sons, who are all guilty of wrongful actions, tacitly argues for the efficacy of confession to deliver one from deserved death.

The first bad deed which Judah confesses to the assembled court in *Targum Neofiti* is the deception of his father with Joseph's bloodied coat in Gen 37:32. The difficulty of confession before a father, which *Targum Neofiti* implies and other sources more clearly articulate, makes Judah's confession that he deceived his own father particularly poignant. In the biblical story, and also in *Tg.Neof.* Gen 37:32, the brothers act in concert to deceive their father.[127] In the narrative expansion, however, Judah admits sole culpability, in keeping with the interpretation of his predicament in Genesis 38 as a consequence of this deception.

In his confession, Judah discerns the causal relation between two contiguous biblical stories, Genesis 37 and 38, which superficially have little connection. He links these two stories through the repetition of the imperative "Recognize!" (הכר נא) in both chapters. Because he deceived his father with this command, he was destined to hear this command again after his daughter-in-law deceived him. The story in Genesis 38, therefore, does not consist of random events which merely happen to follow those depicted in Genesis 37. Instead it portrays the moral consequences which follow the sale of Joseph and the deception of Jacob.

A number of midrashic sources link Genesis 37 and 38 as cause and effect by means of the identical imperatives these chapters contain.[128]

---

[126] For example, Cain and Abel's debate in the field in *Tg.Neof.* Gen 4:8 concerns this principle, with Cain denying and Abel affirming the connection between deeds and rewards and punishments. *Tg.Neof.* Gen 6:9 describes Noah as perfect in doing good works, and *Tg.Neof.* Gen 33:18 describes Jacob as perfect in good deeds, which win for him the garment of the first man in *Tg.Neof.* Gen 48:22. By contrast, in *Tg.Neof.* Gen 21:9 Ishmael is expelled into the desert because of his bad deeds, specifically those involving idolatry.

[127] The plural verbs in this verse in both the biblical text and in *Tg.Neof.* indicate that all of the brothers participate in the deception.

[128] In a number of these sources, the connection is strengthened by drawing attention to the double appearance of a goat in Gen 37:31 (שעיר עזים) and Gen 38:17 and 20 (גדי עזים).

In some, the verbal and causal connections are pointed out anonymously.[129] In others, this traditional association is attributed to a
scholar.[130] A number of these sources portray this rabbinic tradition
as emanating from the mouth of God himself or from a laughing
Tora.[131] In no other place besides the Palestinian targums, however,
does Judah himself recognize the relation between his deeds and words
in Genesis 37 and the events and words in Genesis 38.

Admittedly, the association of the two chapters in this manner is
a bit strained in *Targum Neofiti*, since Tamar never directly commands
her father-in-law to "Recognize!" in this version of the story. Instead,
the imperative is reassigned to Judah, who presents it as a repetition
of his own words to his father in Gen 37:32. In reassigning this
command to Judah, the targum effaces the very basis for the rabbinic joining of the two chapters. This insensitive presentation of the
content, but not the textual basis, of a rabbinic tradition is typical of
Targum Neofiti. Apparently, the parties responsible for the targum so
thoroughly assumed that scripture and traditional commentary form
one seamless whole that they felt free to obliterate the very details of
the biblical text that motivated and supported particular exegetical
conclusions. It may be, however, that the dittography of the imperative ("Recognize! Recognize!") in *Targum Neofiti* is not entirely accidental, but rather calls attention to the double appearance in Genesis 37
and 38 of the same command, obscured by the targum's treatment
of the biblical material.[132]

Judah's confession of the additional crime, the deception of his
father, and his linkage of that episode with Genesis 38 have a number
of results. Paradoxically, his confession of multiple sins reflects positively on his character; it makes him more sympathetic by portraying him as a reflective and sincere person with a sensitive conscience.

---

[129] *Num.Rab.* 13.14 and *Leqaḥ Ṭob* Gen 38:25.

[130] In *b. Soṭa* 10b, this association is attributed to R. Hama b. R. Hanina; in *Gen.Rab.*
85.9, to R. Judah b. Nahman in the name of R. Simeon b. Laqish; and in *Gen.Rab.*
84.19 and *Gen.Rab.* 85.11, to R. Johanan.

[131] *Gen.Rab.* 84.19; 85.9, 11; *Leqaḥ Ṭob* Gen 38:25.

[132] In the expansion in *Tg.Neof.*, the double imperative uttered by Judah (אכר אכר
כען) preserves the root of the Hebrew imperative in Gen 38:25 (הכר נא), whereas
the imperative in *Tg.Neof.* Gen 37:32 is translated into Aramaic (חכם כען). Levy
concludes from this fact that the narrative expansion is not originally part of *Tg.Neof.*
(*Targum Neophyti 1*, vol. 1, 57). This may indeed be the case, but in any event the
retention and repetition of the Hebrew root in *Tg.Neof.* Gen. 38:25–26 flags the
duplication of this root in Genesis 37 and 38, otherwise obscured by the targum's
reassignment of dialogue in the narrative expansion.

This treatment softens the ironic stance of the biblical narrator towards Judah.

His double confession also presents him as a biblical scholar, able to draw verbal and causal links between the events in Genesis 37 and 38 even as they occur. Not only is the story about him, but he joins the interpretive endeavor of rabbinic Judaism, drawing the moral lessons which come to dominate the aggadic traditions about him and introducing a whole set of dimensions absent from the biblical story, including the two worlds, punishments and rewards after death, and the value of confession.

The introduction of a second confession also diverts some of the focus from Judah's incestuous relations with Tamar. His description of what he did to Jacob is certainly longer and more graphic than his description of what he did to Tamar. At the same time, this augmented confession increases his guilt significantly. The deception of Jacob brings to mind the sale of Joseph, which was Judah's idea in the biblical narrative. A tradition revealing how seriously rabbinic circles took Joseph's sale states that the ten companions of R. Akiva, who were martyred during the Hadrianic persecution, lost their lives because of this sin.[133] Having much to confess, Judah becomes an even better exemplar of public repentance.

Judah's statement concludes with his declaration of Tamar's innocence, his admission of paternity, and his explicit refutation of the charge that Tamar is pregnant through illicit sexual relations. The latter charge is left standing in the biblical text, although the fact that Tamar's life is spared implies that she is acquitted of it. Apparently the implication that the royal and messianic genealogy began through illicit sexual relations was considered too explosive to leave unanswered, and *Targum Neofiti* emphasizes that Tamar's sons are not illegitimate by concluding Judah's address with this assertion.[134] The voice from heaven confirms Judah's human assertion of Tamar's innocence.

---

[133] This tradition appears to be quite early, although it was rejected by the tannaim and amoraim. For an expression of this tradition, see the words attributed to R. Joshua b. Levi in *Midr. Mišle* 1.13, in Solomon Buber, ed., *Midraš Mišle* (Vilna: Romm, 1893) 45. See also the discussion in Urbach, *Sages*, 521–22 and 921, n. 46.

[134] Other sources refute the charge in other ways, such as explaining that Tamar's lewdness consisted of beating on her belly in the bathhouse and bragging about how she was pregnant with kings and prophets. See *Gen.Rab.* 85.10; *Tanḥ.* Wayyešeb 9.17; and *Midr. Haggadol* Gen 38:17–18.

Following the intervention of the heavenly voice, *Targum Neofiti* returns to a fairly literal translation of the biblical text, although the transition is not accomplished gracefully. The placement of the notice "Judah recognized" from Gen 38:26 after his lengthy confession renders this biblical event narratively useless in the targum. Similarly, Judah's repetitive assertion "Tamar my daughter-in-law is innocent" falls flat since her innocence has already been established by the higher authority of heavenly decree. Interestingly, in the version of Gen 38:26 in *Targum Neofiti*, Judah's explicit confession of paternity based on the second word of the biblical comparative phrase, "from me" (ממני), is omitted. Perhaps the final editor of *Targum Neofiti* considered the lengthy confession in the narrative expansion sufficient. With Judah's reference to Shelah and the notice that Judah did not know her again, *Targum Neofiti* completes its transition from biblical expansion to biblical translation.

In summary, Judah's lengthy confession functions in a number of ways in *Targum Neofiti*. It prolongs and even amplifies the crisis of the biblical narrative, since Judah joins Tamar on the verge of execution. The character of Judah becomes a model of public confession and repentance, as well as a teacher and biblical exegete, and Tamar is cleared of the biblical charges against her. In addition, Judah's confession interjects a rabbinic world view into the biblical story, by introducing the concepts of rewards and punishments in the world to come, asserting that Judah himself is liable to judgment under biblical law, and emphasizing the value of repentance. The material in Judah's confession also argues that the Tora is an interconnected, seamless whole, with moral and causal relations between its parts. Finally, this passage sets the scene for the dramatic intervention of the divine voice which closes the narrative expansion.

Verdict from Heaven

The final addition to the plot in *Targum Neofiti* consists of a second instance of divine intervention, this time through the means of a voice from heaven that is heard in the courtroom.[135] The heavenly voice, literally a "daughter of a voice,"[136] delivers a verdict of innocence for both characters, thereby granting them a reprieve from

---

[135] This motif is found in all of the Palestinian targums except Gnz.Tg. E.
[136] In Hebrew, בת קול. In *Tg.Neof.*, according to Díez Macho's reconstruction, בר[ת] קלא (*Neophyti 1*, vol. 1, 6, n. 14).

death by burning.[137] The words attributed to the voice are clearly an expansive interpretation of the same biblical phrase in Gen 38:26 that lies behind the motif of Judah's confession, "She is more righteous than I" (צדקה ממני).[138] In *Targum Neofiti*, the first word of the Hebrew phrase is transformed from Judah's recognition of Tamar's integrity ("She is righteous," צדקה) to a divine judgment upon both Tamar and Judah ("Both of you are innocent," תריכון זכיין). This transformation is in keeping with the legal setting of the narrative expansion, where the apparently unlawful behavior of both characters becomes the central issue. The second word of the biblical phrase, "from me" (ממני), is paraphrased as the voice's assertion that this verdict of innocence is authoritative, since "From before the LORD is the decree" (מן קדם ייי הוה פתגמא).[139] As previously noted, other sources also explicitly link the interjection of a divine point of view into Gen 38:26 to the prepositional phrase "from me" (ממני) in Judah's comparative statement. This prepositional phrase becomes a divine utterance in midrashic tradition, claiming responsibility for the events in Genesis 38. In *Genesis Rabba*, for example, R. Jeremiah explains, in the name of R. Samuel b. R. Isaac (fourth-century Palestinian), that in court, "The holy spirit said, 'From Me (ממני) were these events.'"[140] The exact interrelation between the wording of biblical text and midrashic tradition preserved in *Genesis Rabba* and other rabbinic sources, including all but one of the other Palestinian targums, is lost in *Targum Neofiti*.[141] Once again, *Targum Neofiti* displays a willingness

---

[137] The heavenly voice also appears in *Tg.Neof.* Gen 22:10, in the context of the story of the binding of Isaac, which contains a prayer (*Tg.Neof.* 22:14) with thematic elements similar to those found in Tamar's prayer; in *Tg.Neof.* Gen 27:33; and in *Tg.Neof.* Num 21:6. The voice also appears in *Tg.Ps.-J.* Deut 28:15. See McNamara's discussion of the heavenly voice in *Targum Neofiti 1*, 39.

[138] Just as the word מוצאת provides the textual basis for a cluster of interpretive activity, the phrase צדקה ממני also serves as the basis for more than one exegetical expansion of the story.

[139] In *Tg.Neof.* and the other Palestinian targums, the expression "before the LORD" is a common one, which, like the phrase "the memra of the LORD" in *Tg.Onq.*, functions as an expression of respect. See McNamara, *Targum Neofiti 1*, 22–24.

[140] *Gen.Rab.* 85.11; cf., *Deut.Rab.* 'Ekeb, in Saul Liebermann, ed., *Midraš Debarim Rabba*, 2d ed. (Jerusalem: Wahrmann Books, 1964) 72; *Eccl.Rab.* 10.18; *b. Mak.* 23b; and *Midr. Tehillim* Ps 72:2. A voice also speaks following Judah's words in Gen 38:26 according to *b. Soṭa* 10b, but the words attributed to it are different.

[141] *Frg.Tg.* V has the same paraphrase ("From before the LORD is the decree"). All the others containing the motif of the verdict from heaven maintain a connection to the biblical prepositional phrase: *Tg.Ps.-J.* and *Frg.Tg.* P have מן קדמי; Gnz.Tgs. X and FF and *t. Tg.Onq.* have מני. Gnz.Tg. D is broken at this point.

to paraphrase the sense of an exegetical tradition in a manner that obscures the original basis for that tradition.[142]

According to rabbinic tradition, there were three instances of divine intervention in court cases in the Bible. These cases were heard in the courts of Shem, Samuel, and Solomon.[143] The events in Genesis 38 were considered to have been discussed in the court of Shem, a famous judge and, in some sources, the father of Tamar. The case involving Judah and Tamar was therefore the first instance in which heaven intervened to clarify something that could not be known by the humans judging the case and to vindicate individuals whose innocence was not obvious.[144]

In the cases involving Samuel and Solomon, tradition also ascribes features in the biblical text to a voice from heaven. In Samuel's farewell address in 1 Samuel 12, he calls on God and his anointed as witnesses that he has never defrauded anyone. Immediately after Samuel asserts that God is his witness in 1 Sam 12:5, the Hebrew text reports that someone said "witness" (עד ויאמר). The subject of this singular verb is understood in the Lucianic recension of the Septuagint as a collective, "the people," who agree with Samuel that God is the witness between them.[145] In rabbinic tradition, however, the subject of the singular verb is regarded as God or a heavenly voice which proclaims "I am a witness."[146] As *Midraš Šemu'el* explains:

> "They said, 'We are witnesses'" (עדים ויאמרו) is not written, but rather "He said, 'I am a witness'" (עד ויאמר). The Holy One, Blessed be He said to them, "You testify about him concerning what is revealed, and I will testify about him concerning what is secret."[147]

---

[142] Whether this willingness attests to a later date than that of some of the other targumic manuscripts, to a lack of sensitivity to the origins of the traditions it preserves, or simply to a desire to present a coherent narrative is debatable.

[143] See *Gen.Rab.* 85.12; *Eccl.Rab.* 10.16; *Midr. Tehillim* Ps 72:2; and *b. Mak.* 23b.

[144] The versions in *Midr. Tehillim* Ps 72:2 and *b. Mak.* 23b both specify that it was not humanly possible to know if Tamar had consorted with other men in the same way that she did with Judah. The heavenly voice therefore settled a question that was otherwise unanswerable.

[145] The Lucianic recension reads, καὶ εἶπεν ὁ λαος. The Peshitta, several targum manuscripts, and the Vg have similar readings. Some Hebrew manuscripts indicate in the margin that the verb should be a plural. See the note in K. Elliger and W. Rudolph, eds., *Biblia Hebraica Stuttgartensia*, 2d ed. (Stuttgart: Deutsche Bibel Gesellschaft, 1984).

[146] Perhaps this tradition depicting God as Samuel's heavenly witness influenced the presentation of God as Tamar's witness in *Tg.Neof*.

[147] *Midr. Šemu'el* 14.9, מ. The expression that "X is not written, but rather X" (X אלא כתוב אין X) often introduces an anthropomorphic interpretation and is intended

The case in Solomon's court during which a divine voice intervenes concerns the two prostitutes who both claim to be the mother of the same child in 1 Kgs 3:16–28. The conclusion "She is his mother" (היא אמו) in 1 Kgs 3:27, which follows Solomon's order to give the child to the woman who surrenders him to preserve his life, was considered beyond the knowledge of any human judge. It therefore came to be regarded as a divine decree, confirming the wisdom of the king and preventing the execution of Solomon's order to cut the child in two. As *b. Mak.* 23b explains:

> "She is his mother" (היא אמו). How did he [Solomon] know this? Perhaps she had acted cunningly! A voice came forth and said, "She is his mother."[148]

In the narrative expansion in *Targum Neofiti*, the intervention of the voice also eliminates any lingering doubts about Tamar and Judah's guilt, by extending to both the same verdict of innocence that Judah grants Tamar immediately above.[149] It also precludes the view that Judah and Tamar escape punishment through a fluke of history by stating that the decree of innocence stems "from before the LORD." The positive closure that this motif provides the narrative expansion is irrefutable, since it comes from heaven. The divine verdict of innocence remains a bit jarring, however, since immediately before it Judah confesses and accepts punishment alongside Tamar, presumably for incest.

Targum Neofiti *Gen 38:25–26 and Rabbinic Exegesis*

As the previous discussion shows, much of the material in the narrative expansion stems from larger exegetical discussions of Gen 38:25–26

---

to demonstrate that this interpretation arises from a feature of the biblical text itself. See also *Gen.Rab.* 85.12 and *Eccl.Rab.* 10.17, in which the holy spirit says "I am a witness," and *b. Mak.* 23b and *Midr. Tehillim* Ps 72:2, in which a heavenly voice says, "I am a witness."

[148] See also *Midr. Tehillim* Ps 72:2, in which a voice also says these words, and *Gen.Rab.* 85.11 and *Eccl.Rab.* 10.17, in which the holy spirit says these words. In *Eccl.Rab.*, the first part of 1 Kgs 3:27, "Give her the living child and do not kill it!" is also reassigned to God, who intervenes to spare the child from Solomon's reckless judgment.

[149] *Frg.Tg.*, Gnz.Tg. X, and *t. Tg.Onq.* all declare that both Judah and Tamar are innocent. Gnz.Tgs. D and FF are broken at this point. By contrast, *Tg.Ps.-J.* contains no declaration of innocence by the voice which nevertheless intervenes to save them both from judgment. Judah's innocence is confirmed in *Tg.Neof.* Gen 49:9, where he is declared innocent in the incident with Tamar.

in rabbinic Judaism. This correspondence is not especially surprising, given the fact that both the Palestinian targums and the exegetical commentaries and other midrashic literature arose out of the same rabbinic milieu. What is also clear, however, is that *Targum Neofiti*'s versions of exegetical traditions are relatively late and dependent on earlier forms. This conclusion does not necessarily indicate that *Targum Neofiti* is directly dependent on midrashic works such as *Genesis Rabba* and the *Tanḥuma*. Rather, both the targum and these other documents may rely on earlier oral exegetical traditions, although the prehistory of these texts is difficult to determine. A fundamental difference, however, is that in the other rabbinic documents the original exegetical links between biblical text and midrashic tradition are preserved, whereas often in *Targum Neofiti* they are obscured. Indeed, at times only the narrative content of a tradition is presented.

Certainly part of this loss of connection with the features of the biblical text is due to the fact that the language of targum is Aramaic and not Hebrew. Returning to an earlier example, we have seen how the first Hebrew verb of Gen 38:25 (מוצאת) provides the starting point for the creative verbal play lying behind the traditions about the lost and found pledge, since this word may be read either as "she was brought out" or "she finds." This link between the word in the biblical text and the post-biblical motif is lost in *Targum Neofiti*, as well as in all of the other targums, because the Aramaic word "to go out" (נפק) bears similarity to neither the Aramaic word "to find" (שכח) nor the Hebrew verb "to find" (מצא).

But even when there are sufficient similarities between Aramaic and Hebrew to indicate the exegetical links between biblical text and midrashic tradition, *Targum Neofiti* does not always take advantage of the possibility of doing so. We have seen, for example, how *Targum Neofiti* obscures an important basis for midrashic comparison of Genesis 37 and 38 when it reassigns Tamar's imperative "Recognize!" to her father-in-law, as he remembers the identical imperative in Gen 37:32. We have also seen how *Targum Neofiti* paraphrases the tradition that the heavenly voice uttered the biblical phrase, "from me," with the phrase, "from before the LORD."[150] In *Targum Neofiti*, traditional

---

[150] James Barr maintains that "because of the considerable overlap between Hebrew and Aramaic, and because the targum was not read alone but with the accompaniment of the Hebrew text itself, this rendering was able to provide hints and plays upon phenomena of the Hebrew, along with explanations of names and clarifications

exegetical elaborations based on lemmatic features of the biblical text sometimes become autonomous narrative elements. The genre of pure narrative reasserts itself over against a type of rabbinic commentary which interweaves details of the biblical text and post-biblical narrative elements.

These considerations contradict Renée Bloch's assertion that the targums are a source from which midrashic documents borrowed their themes.[151] On the contrary, the versions of exegetical traditions recorded in *Targum Neofiti* are derived from earlier forms of exegetical commentary, written in Hebrew, on the biblical text. The same may generally be said of the other Palestinian targums, although there are instances in which some of them adhere more closely to the particulars of the lemmatic exegetical traditions.

In comparison with some of the other Palestinian targums, *Targum Neofiti* assumes a great deal of freedom in its presentation of traditional material and in its development and articulation of a particular direction of interpretation. This fact challenges the position of Díez Macho and others that *Targum Neofiti* is perhaps a copy of the earliest targum which has been preserved. Whatever the case with the rest of *Targum Neofiti*, its particular version of Genesis 38 is not early in comparison with the versions in the other Palestinian targums.[152]

Although the narrative expansion in *Targum Neofiti* is not the oldest, it is perhaps the most interesting in the way it articulates a trajectory of interpretation which remains implicit in some of the other Palestinian targums. Now that we have explored the component sections of the narrative expansion in *Targum Neofiti* and noted when and how

---

of obscurities" ("Which Language Did Jesus Speak? Some Remarks of a Semitist," *BJRL* 53 [1971] 9–29). While this is often the case, in many instances *Tg.Neof.* fails to preserve the original point in the Hebrew text which triggered particular exegetical traditions, despite the possibility of doing so in the new language of translation.

[151] Bloch, "Note sur l'utilisation des fragments de la Geniza," 30.

[152] The general principle that a shorter version of a tradition is earlier than a longer version, since the longer version contains within it later developments grafted onto the earlier version, may hold true in the case of *Tg.Neof.* But each instance must be decided separately, since a shorter version could indicate rejection of material considered offensive or unimportant for the purposes at hand. An example of a version of Genesis 38 which is much later than the biblical version and also much shorter may be found in *Seper Hayyašar*. This source attempts to reform the narrative morally by eliminating any mention of Judah's perception of Tamar as a prostitute, of their bargaining about the fee and the pledge, of Judah and Hirah's search for a consecrated woman, of the uncomplimentary report of Tamar's behavior, and of Judah's order that she be burned.

this targum employs traditional material, it is time to delineate its distinctive and unexpected reading of Genesis 38 in terms of the larger concept of "sanctification of the Name."

Targum Neofiti's Overarching
"Translation" of Gen 38:25–26:
"Sanctification of the [Divine] Name"

In addition to translating the words of Gen 38:25–26 and a number of rabbinic exegetical traditions into Aramaic and presenting them as part of a sustained narrative, *Targum Neofiti* also accomplishes a broader type of "translation" in this passage. By introducing thematically charged material throughout the narrative expansion, the targum systematically carries the story of Judah and Tamar into a new semantic field designated by the phrase "sanctification of the [divine] Name" (קידוש השם). Tamar uses a form of this significant phrase to describe the three men from Daniel 3 in her prayer, when she promises God that they will "sanctify your holy Name" (ומקדשין שמך קדישא) by descending into the fire.[153]

"Sanctification of the Name" is a term with a rich history of meaning.[154] In Tamar's vow in *Targum Neofiti*, the adjectival form of this expression describing Hananiah, Mishael, and Azariah presupposes that specific, exemplary actions by humans, such as the descent of the three men into the fire, positively affect God's status and perhaps even his potency in the world. The Hebrew Bible itself, however, does not employ the phrase "sanctification of the Name" to describe this type of positive connection between human actions and the holiness of God. A form of this expression in which the subjects of the verb are humans appears only in Isa 29:23, where God says that the offspring of Jacob "will sanctify my Name" (יקדישו שמי). In this verse, however, the expression denotes a recognition of God's power to redeem rather than specific human deeds.[155] The

---

[153] While all the Palestinian targums depict Tamar as vowing to raise up the three men at Dura, only *Tg.Neof.* and *Tg.Ps.-J.* specify that they will sanctify the divine Name.

[154] For an overview of the history of this concept see Ithamar Gruenwald, קידוש השם: בירורו של מושג ["Sanctification of the Name:" Explanation of a concept], *Molad* 24 (1967–68) 476–84, and Samuel Safrai, קידוש השם בתורתם של התנאים ["Sanctification of the Name" in the teachings of the tannaim], *Zion* 44 (1979) 28–42.

[155] Similarly, the phrase "the Lord of hosts you will sanctify" (את יהוה צבאות אתו תקדישו) in Isa 8:13 designates recognition of God's status rather than specific human

single human action in the Pentateuch evaluated in terms of God's
sanctification consists of Moses and Aaron's behavior at the waters
of Meribah at Kadesh. This example is a negative one, however, for
God chides Moses when he says, "you did not sanctify me (לא קדשתם
אותי) in the midst of the sons of Israel" (Deut 32:51).[156] The lack of
positive examples is significant, given the importance of the holiness
of God and his Name in the Bible.[157] In biblical literature, especially
in the book of Ezekiel, God sanctifies his own Name and manifests
his own holiness before Israel and the other nations of the world
through displays of power.[158] Interestingly, while God alone enhances
the sanctity of his Name, people desecrate his Name in numerous
scriptural passages.[159] In these passages, "desecration of the [divine]
Name" (חילול השם) occurs through specific human infractions of justice and violations of God's commandments which lessen his status,
especially in the eyes of foreign nations.

In discussions traditionally associated with the tannaitic period (the
first two centuries of the common era), however, the expression
"sanctification of the Name" appears not only in connection with
the miracles and displays of power through which God enhances his
own status, but also in connection with a variety of human actions
which reflect positively on the divinity. During this period, the meaning of "sanctification of the Name" is enlarged to include the opposite
of the biblical expression "desecration of the Name." For example,
human praise of the divine Name in a liturgical context constitutes
"sanctification of the Name" in traditions attributed to this period.
In a discussion of the "Additional Prayer" for the New Year, both
the anonymous voice of the Mishna and R. Akiva call the third

acts. *Targum Jonathan*'s rendition of Isa 29:23 and Isa 8:13, however, interprets Israel's
sanctification as verbal acknowledgment of God's holiness, which does constitute the
specific act of speech.

[156] Deut 32:51; cf., Num 20:12 and 27:14 (in both verses להקדישני).

[157] "Holy" (קדוש) is a commonly used adjective describing God in many biblical
passages, including Isa 6:3; Lev 19:2; and Ps 22:4. God's Name is described as holy
in Lev 20:3; 22:2, 32; Amos 2:7; nine times in Ezekiel; 1 Chr 16:10; Ps 33:21;
103:1. God's Name itself is "Holy One of Israel" (קדוש ישראל) in Isa 1:4; 5:19; etc.
(a total of 25 times in Isaiah); Jer 50:29; 51:5; Ps 71:22; 78:41; 89:19; or "Holy One
of Jacob" (קדוש יעקב) in Isa 29:23.

[158] God sanctifies his own Name and acts for the sake of his holy Name in Ezek
36:22–23. See also Ezek 20:44 and 39:25. God manifests his own holiness in Ezek
20:41; 28:22, 25; 38:16; 39:27; Isa 5:16; and Lev 10:3.

[159] See Lev 18:21; 19:12; 20:3; 21:6; 22:2, 31–32; Ezek 20:39; 36:16–20; Amos
2:7; Jer 34:16; Mal 1:12. Lev 22:32 implies, however, that when people refrain from
desecrating God's Name, his holiness is enhanced.

blessing recited by the congregation the "sanctification of the Name" (קדושת השם).[160] "Sanctification of the Name" by humans is also the goal in legal proceedings, according to a tradition attributed to R. Akiva. In an argument with R. Ishmael, he maintains that Jewish law should not be bent in cases involving gentiles in order to acquit the Jewish party because the primary goal in these legal proceedings should be "sanctification of the Name" (קידוש השם).[161] The phrase "sanctification of the Name" was also applied to the exemplary actions of biblical characters. For example, a tradition ascribed to R. Tarfon, a contemporary of R. Akiva, explains that the tribe of Judah merited the kingship because at the time of the exodus Nahshon led this tribe in jumping first into the waves of the sea before it had parted. God responded to Nahshon's eagerness to obey his command to enter the sea by saying, "The one who sanctified my Name (מי שקדש את שמי) at the sea will come and rule over Israel."[162]

The expression "sanctification of the Name" eventually assumed yet another connotation in rabbinic literature. It came to designate the ultimate human testimony of faith: the willingness to die rather than repudiate religious beliefs and practices.[163] This meaning of the term gradually assumed dominance, until in the middle ages "sanctification of the Name" became synonymous with martyrdom for the Jewish faith. The initial application of this expression to martyrdom may have been a response to the Hadrianic persecution following the failure of the Bar Kokhba revolt, which resulted in the deaths of R. Akiva and his ten companions, but the phenomenon of martyrdom itself was not new to Jewish history. Jews gave their lives for their religious commitment during the reign of Antiochus IV (Epiphanes) in the second century BCE and during the period of Roman rule

---

[160] m. Roš Haš. 4.5.

[161] b. B.Qam. 113a.

[162] Mek. Bešallaḥ 6, in Jacob Z. Lauterbach, ed., Mekilta de Rabbi Ishmael, vol. 1 (Philadelphia: Jewish Publication Society, 1933) 237. The same tradition appears in t. Ber. 4.18 and Midr. Tehillim Ps 76:2. At root, this tradition is an interpretation of Ps 114:1, which reads, "When Israel went out from Egypt, the house of Jacob from a people of strange speech, Judah became his sanctuary, Israel his dominion" (בצאת ישראל ממצרים בית יעקב מעם לעז היתה יהודה לקדשו ישראל ממשלותיו).

[163] Willingness to die to fulfill God's command is implicit in Nahshon's action in the previous example, although the discussion in the Mekilta stresses his obedience and the reward that he receives. Similarly, in Gen.Rab. 43.2 R. Nehemiah (middle of the second century) states that Abraham was willing to fall in war against the foreign kings in Genesis 14 to sanctify the Name of the Holy One. Although Abraham does not ultimately die, he was willing to do so in order to sanctify God's Name.

leading up to and following the destruction of the temple in Jerusalem.[164] But the term "sanctification of the Name" is never used to describe this type of principled death in literature before the Hadrianic persecution. Instead, one reads in the early references to martyrdom that pious Jews died so as "not to desecrate the holy covenant" (μὴ βεβηλώσωσιν διαθήκην ἁγίαν)[165] or that "they gave their souls for the commandments" (נותנין נפשם על המצוות).[166] Even in descriptions of the deaths of R. Akiva and his ten companions during the reign of Hadrian, one does not always find the expression "sanctification of the Name." At times other, more traditional, expressions appear, such as "they devoted themselves to slaughter for the words of Tora" (מסרו עצמן לשחיטה על דברי תורה).[167]

One of the earliest uses of the expression "sanctification of the Name" in connection with martyrdom is found in a passage associated with the name of R. Ishmael, R. Akiva's contemporary, in *Sipra*, an early commentary on *Leviticus*.[168] In this passage, R. Ishmael begins

---

[164] See the accounts in 1 Macc 1:60–63; 2 Maccabees 6–7; 4 Maccabees; and Josephus *Ant.* 12.255–56, 281–82 for examples of martyrdom during the reign of Antiochus IV (Epiphanes). Especially significant is the recurrent story of the pious mother who encourages her sons to die rather than transgress the commandments. This motif is echoed in Tamar's vow, where she approvingly alludes to her descendants' willingness to enter the furnace rather than worship an idol. For willingness to die rather than transgress Jewish law during the Roman occupation see Josephus *Ag.Ap.* 1.43; 2.218–19, 233–35; and Philo *Embassy to Gaius* 117, 192, 215, 233 ff. In addition, see the rabbinic sources discussed by Gruenwald, "Sanctification of the Name," 477–79.

[165] 1 Macc 1:63.

[166] These words are attributed to R. Nathan, a fourth-generation tannaitic scholar, in *Mek.* Baḥodeš 6, in Lauterbach, *Mekilta*, vol. 2, 247. For other examples of expressions used to describe martyrdom in earlier periods, see Gruenwald, "Sanctification of the Name," 477–79.

[167] *b. Sanh.* 110b.

[168] Two other passages employing the expression "sanctification of the Name" to denote martyrdom appear in *Sipra*. In a passage commenting on Lev 22:32 (Isaac Hirsch Weiss, ed., *Sipra* [Vienna: Jacob Schlossberg, 1862] 99) the divine statement, "I will be sanctified" (ונקדשתי), introduces a gloss: "Devote yourself and sanctify my Name" (מסור את עצמך וקדש שמי). The expression "to devote oneself" is a traditional designation for martyrdom, as noted above. Another anonymous tradition (Weiss, *Sipra*, 99) continues, "On this condition did I bring you out of the land of Egypt: on the condition that you devote yourselves to sanctify my Name" (שתמסרו עצמכם לקדש את שמי). Safrai, "Sanctification of the Name," 31, n. 17, notes, however, that these expressions are lacking in Vatican MS 66 and cannot be considered original. For a similar expression, see *Cant.Rab.* 2.7, in which the words "Give your soul for the sanctification of the Name" (תן נפשך על קידוש השם) appear in a discussion attributed to R. Hiyya (early third century) concerning the persecution under Hadrian. A version of R. Hiyya's discussion also appears in *Pesiq.Rab.Kah.* 11.14. Martyrdom during the

with an interpretation of the injunction in Lev 18:5 to live through the commandments and moves to an interpretation of the connection between the holiness of God, the holiness of the people, and the observation of the commandments in Lev 22:31–33. The discussion continues with material of special significance for discovering the larger interpretive background of the narrative expansion in *Targum Neofiti*:

> "Live through them" (Lev 18:5), not die through them. R. Ishmael said, "Where do you find in scripture that if they say to someone privately, 'Worship idols or you will be killed!' he should worship and not be killed? Scripture says, 'Live through them,' not die through them. Does this imply that even if they speak to him publicly he should obey them? Scripture says, 'You shall not profane my holy Name (ולא תחללו את שם קדשי), so that I may be sanctified (ונקדשתי)' (Lev 22:32). If you sanctify my Name (מקדישים אתם את שמי), I myself will sanctify my Name through you." Just as Hananiah, Mishael, and Azariah did. When all the nations of the world were stretched out before the image, they were standing, resembling palm trees (דומים לתמרים). Concerning them it is explained in the Writings, "This is your stature: you are like the palm tree" (דמתה לתמר), etc. "I will go up (אעלה) in the palm tree (בתמר) and seize its branches" (Cant 7:8–9). I was exalted (אני מתעלה) through them in the eyes of the nations of the world, those denying the Tora. Today I am punishing those who hate them for them. Today I am reviving the dead for them. "I am the Lord" (Lev 18:5; 22:31, 32, 33). I am a judge who punishes and who is faithful in giving rewards.[169]

The basic intent of the first part of this passage ascribed to R. Ishmael is to limit Jewish suffering and death at the hands of foreign enemies while still preserving God's sanctity. To this end, R. Ishmael introduces a distinction between private and public compliance with pressure to pay homage to other gods. Most likely in reaction to the recent blood bath of the great Hadrianic persecution, he argues that under duress one is allowed to break commandments pertaining to idolatry privately, since the commandments were given to foster life and not to bring death. On the other hand, one must refrain from publicly worshipping idols even if this means that one will be martyred, because to comply would desecrate God's Name and detract from

---

Hadrianic persecution is also called "sanctification of the Name" in *b. Ber.* 20a and *Midr. Tehillim* Ps 16:4.

[169] *Sipra* 'Aḥare Mot 14 (Weiss, *Sipra*, 76). The reference to God as judge in the final line of this passage recalls the court setting of the narrative expansion in *Tg.Neof.* God's deliverance of the faithful and his desire to reward positive behavior in *Sipra* also have loose parallels in the targum.

his status in the eyes of all those present. The contrast between private and public actions introduced here in the name of R. Ishmael appears elsewhere in reference to "sanctification of the Name" in rabbinic literature. It may even be the case that *Targum Neofiti* alludes to this aspect of the rabbinic discussion through Tamar's refusal to identify Judah publicly and through Judah's willingness to confess his sins publicly.[170]

Of special importance is *Sipra*'s association of the phrase "sanctification of the Name" with the willingness to die rather than publicly defile the Name of God by practicing idolatry. Significantly, this association occurs in a paraphrase of Lev 22:32, not in the actual biblical text. While the biblical verse forbids human desecration of God's Name so that God may be sanctified, the paraphrase of this verse which immediately follows positively enjoins human sanctification of God's Name, and it promises a corresponding reaction from God to sanctify his own Name through those who do so. With this paraphrase, there is a subtle transition from R. Ishmael's discussion of the proper response to actual threats to life triggered by recent historical tragedy to a discussion of a biblical example in which ultimately no one loses his life. In this example, Hananiah, Mishael, and Azariah's willingness to sanctify God's Name by accepting death rather than publicly worshipping Nebuchadnezzar's idol evokes a corresponding willingness on God's part to sanctify his own Name by miraculously delivering them in the presence of many people. The focus shifts from a real historical dilemma to a literary pattern of human devotion and divine intervention. This passage portrays both human and divine efforts to sanctify the Name in some detail, with the quotation of phrases from Song of Songs serving as the point of transition between the descriptions of the actions of the three men and those of God.[171]

---

[170] The public nature of Judah's confession is positively contrasted with the private nature of Joseph's refusal of Potiphar's wife's sexual advances in *b. Soṭa* 10b, where both are explicitly described as sanctifying God's Name.

[171] Safrai concludes that in this passage from *Sipra* "the emphasis of 'sanctification of the Name' lies on the acts of salvation that the Holy One Blessed be He does, just as he did in the story of Hananiah, Mishael, and Azariah" ("Sanctification of the Name," 32). This conclusion does not take seriously the dialectical relationship between human and divine actions to sanctify God's Name in this source. There are other rabbinic texts, including Louis Finkelstein, ed., *Sipre Debarim* (Berlin: Jüdischer Kulturbund in Deutschland, 1939; reprint, New York: Jewish Theological Seminary Press, 1969) 342–43, and *y. Ber.* 9.1, that focus exclusively on God's miracle in

It is not clear whether the paraphrase of Lev 22:32 beginning
with the expression "If you sanctify my Name" and the presentation
of the example based on Daniel 3 were originally associated with
R. Ishmael, or whether they were later accretions to the discussion.
In *b. Sanh.* 74a and in *b. 'Abod.Zar.* 27b, the distinction between private and public acquiescence to threats involving idol worship attributed to R. Ishmael concludes with the biblical quotation from Lev
22:32, but it is possible that the discussion has been shortened to suit
the halakhic purposes of these talmudic passages. The evidence of
variant manuscripts is similarly not decisive in answering the question of whether or not the second half of this passage was originally
associated with the figure of R. Ishmael.[172] Whatever the case, the
important thing for this discussion is that at some point in the history of Jewish thought, whether during R. Ishmael's life or later,
Hananiah, Mishael, and Azariah become archetypal exemplars of
the human side of the concept "sanctification of the Name."[173]

It is no accident that the type of death which these three archetypes of "sanctification of the Name" accept consists of burning. Fire
has a special connection to God's holiness in the literature of the
Hebrew Bible.[174] Theophanies, such as those at the burning bush
and at Sinai, are frequently accompanied by fiery manifestations. The
entire sacrificial system which evokes the presence of God has fire at
its center. It is the Seraphs, or "fiery ones," who proclaim God's

---

saving the three men. This passage in *Sipra*, however, begins with a discussion of
when it is appropriate for Jews to die for religious convictions and celebrates both
human and divine sanctification of the Name.

[172] See the discussion of the manuscript evidence in Safrai, "Sanctification of the
Name," 32.

[173] The archetypal status of these three men is apparent elsewhere in rabbinic
literature as well. They are described as sanctifying God's Name in *b. Pesaḥ.* 53b
and in *Cant.Rab.* 7.8 (in which they are also listed as the three pillars on which the
world is established, like Abraham, Isaac, and Jacob). When the question is raised
in *y. Ber.* 9.1 of whether or not a blessing should be said at places where miracles
have occurred to persons through whom the heavenly Name has been sanctified,
Hananiah, Mishael, and Azariah appear as the examples of such persons. In pre-
rabbinic literature as well, these three men figure prominently in speeches of encouragement given in times of persecution, although the term "sanctification of the
Name" does not appear. See for example, 4 Macc 13:9; 16:21; and 3 Macc 6:6.
The persistence of the status of these three men as archetypes of the concept of
"sanctification of the Name" in the sense of martyrdom may be seen in Maimonides'
employment of them in his discussion of this concept in *Seper Hammiṣwot* 9 and
Fundamental Principles of the Tora 5.

[174] See the discussion of the connection between God's holiness and fire in James
Muilenberg, "Holiness," in vol. 2 of *IDB*, 617–18.

holiness in Isa 6:2–3. The judgment of God is often depicted as accomplished through fire, and, in fact, God is called a "consuming fire" in Deut 4:24 and 9:3. An instance in which God sanctifies himself in Lev 10:1–7 involves the deaths of Nadab and Abihu through a blast of divine fire at the dedication of the tent of meeting. Interestingly, some sources honor these two sons of Aaron because they contributed their lives for God's holiness.[175]

The archetypal nature of the narrative pattern found in Daniel 3, including its fire motif, may also be seen in its extension in the aggada to other biblical characters, including the patriarch Abraham himself. In a number of sources, Abraham is depicted as willing to enter the burning "furnace of the Chaldeans," which is a midrashic interpretation of the biblical phrase "Ur of the Chaldeans" (אוּר כַּשְׂדִּים), rather than commit idolatry.[176] In at least one source, Abraham, like the three righteous men, is delivered by the angel Michael,[177] and this angelic intervention dramatizes the power of God before many people. Significantly, a number of sources describe Abraham's acceptance of a fiery death with the term "sanctification of the Name,"[178] and he is frequently coupled with the three men at Dura in discussions within the midrashic corpus.[179] *Targum Neofiti* reveals its awareness of

---

[175] In *Lev.Rab.* 12.2 Moses and Aaron marvel at the honor that God bestows on Nadab and Abihu by choosing them to sanctify his house at its dedication. See also *b. Zebaḥ.* 115b.

[176] See Louis Ginzberg, *The Legends of the Jews,* vol. 5 (Philadelphia: Jewish Publication Society of America, 1925; reprint 1968) 212–15, nn. 33, 34, and 40, for sources describing Abraham's descent into the furnace.

[177] The angel Michael assists both the three men and Abraham in *Gen.Rab.* 34.13. In other sources, however, the angel who aids the three men at Dura is Gabriel, the angel responsible for fire, not Michael nor God himself, as in the traditions concerning Abraham.

[178] See, for example, *Gen.Rab.* 42.3, 7; 44.13.

[179] See, for example, *b. Pesaḥ.* 118a, in which a discussion of the words of Hananiah, Mishael, and Azariah as they went in and came out of the furnace digresses into a discussion of why God himself saved Abraham from the fire and then returns to a discussion of how Gabriel came to save the three men from the fire. See also the discussion in *Gen.Rab.* 34.9, in which God accepts the sacrifice of Noah because of the good smell of Abraham and Hananiah, Mishael, and Azariah as they came out of the fire. References to Abraham and the three men also appear side by side in *b. Sanh.* 93a. In this latter source, yet other biblical characters, the lying prophets Ahab and Zedekiah of Jer 29:21–22 and Joshua the High Priest of Zech 3:1–2, are also cast into the furnace by Nebuchadnezzar, with less favorable outcomes. Besides biblical characters, R. Akiva and his companions are also compared to Hananiah, Mishael, and Azariah in *b. Sanh.* 110b, as righteous men who are burned for the sake of the Tora. Similarly, in *Gen.Rab.* 34.9 the martyrs of the Hadrianic persecution give off a pleasing savor, as do Abraham and the three men at Dura. The

this aggadic assimilation of Abraham to Hananiah, Mishael, and Azariah when it presents the words of God to Abraham in Gen 15:7 as "I am the Lord who brought you out of the furnace of fire of the Chaldeans (אנה ייי דאפקת יתך מן אתון נורהון דכשׂדאי) to give you this land that you might inherit it."[180]

Similarly, the narrative expansion in *Tg.Neof.* Gen 38:25–26 assimilates Tamar and, to a lesser extent, Judah to the basic pattern of "sanctification of the Name" exemplified by the three saints in Daniel 3. One of the most striking means through which the narrative expansions accomplishes this assimilation is its emphasis on burning and fire. The motif of burning is already present in Gen 38:24 in Judah's command to bring Tamar out "and let her be burned" (ותשׂרף), and this specification of execution by burning may have been at least partially responsible for the original association of Genesis 38 with Daniel 3. But *Targum Neofiti* significantly amplifies the motif of burning. For example, at the very beginning of the narrative expansion, the targum adds the phrase, "to be burned with fire" (למתוקדה בנורא), explaining why Tamar went out.[181] While this phrase may initially appear to be a redundant expansion of the second part of Judah's command in Gen 38:24 to bring her out "and let her be burned" (ותתוקד in *Tg.Neof.* Gen 38:24), on further examination it proves to be much more than a superfluous embellishment.

For one thing, its inclusion of this expanded phrase signals that *Targum Neofiti* stands within an interpretive trajectory that understands Tamar's sentence in light of the biblical law in Lev 21:9.[182] This biblical verse states, "The daughter of a priest who defiles herself by having illicit intercourse defiles her father. She shall be burnt with fire" (באשׁ תשׂרף). The fact that *Targum Neofiti*'s translation of the punishment specified in Lev 21:9 (בנורא תתוקד) contains the same verb and noun that appear in the phrase at the beginning of the narrative

reference to a pleasing savor introduces imagery of the sacrificial cult into the discussion of those who sanctify God's Name by demonstrating a willingness to give their lives.

[180] Other allusions to the tradition of Abraham and the Chaldean furnace appear in *Tg.Neof.* Gen 11:28, 31; 16:5.

[181] The complete phrase "to be burned with fire" is found also in *Frg.Tg.*, Gnz.Tgs. D (although somewhat broken) and FF, and *t. Tg.Onq.* A shorter notice that she went out "to be burned" is found in all the remaining manuscripts (*Tg.Ps.-J.* and Gnz.Tgs. X and E).

[182] *Gen.Rab.* 85.10 and *Tanh.* Wayyešeb 9.17 explicitly associate Lev 21:9 with Genesis 38.

expansion in Gen 38:25–26 confirms the intentional link between the two biblical passages.[183] The original basis for this intertextual reading of narrative and law clearly lies in the common themes of "illicit intercourse" (Hebrew root זנה) and execution by "burning" (Hebrew niphal נשׂרף).[184] Once these biblical passages are brought together, however, their juxtaposition opens potential interpretive directions for the biblical narrative and its characters. For example, a number of sources present Judah as an exemplar of Tora obedience before Sinai when he orders that Tamar be burned in compliance with biblical law.[185] Other sources focus on the specification that the woman under discussion in the law is "the daughter of a priest" and enhance Tamar's character by providing her with a famous priestly father, namely Shem, who was also known by the name Melchizedek.[186]

While the mere presence of the phrase from Lev 21:9 may trigger memory of these interpretive traditions, the primary significance of the phrase "to be burned by fire" lies elsewhere in *Targum Neofiti*. In this targum the phrase introduces a central theme of the passage which unites its component sections. A quick review of the narrative expansion locates the next appearance of the words "burning" and

---

[183] This example once again illustrates the phenomenon described in Klein, "Associative and Complementary Translation in the Targumim," 134–40.

[184] The fact that the verbal root in the expression "desecration of the Name" (חילול השם) appears twice in Lev 21:9 ("defiles herself," תחל; "defiles her father," את אביה היא מחללת) is also suggestive, in light of *Tg.Neof.*'s interpretation of Genesis 38 as an example of its opposite, "sanctification of the Name."

[185] See for example *Tg.Ps.-J.* Gen 38:24; *Gen.Rab.* 85.10; and *Tanḥ.* Wayyešeb 9.17. Judah's order that Tamar be burned in the biblical narrative may appear unusual in light of the fact that stoning is the form of execution specified in the law for sexual sins in Deut 22:21, which contains the same word for sexual misconduct which appears in Genesis 38 (Hebrew, root, זנה), and in Deut 22:24. Burning is prescribed in Lev 20:14, however. Judah is also depicted as an early keeper of Tora when he implements the levirate law in *Gen.Rab.* 85.5; *Lev.Rab.* 2.10; *Cant.Rab.* 1.2.5; and *Pesiq.Rab.Kah.* 12.1.

[186] Examples of texts which name Shem as Tamar's father include *Tg.Ps.-J.* Gen 38:6; *Tanḥ.* Wayyešeb 9.17; *Gen.Rab.* 85.10; and *Ruth Rab.* 8.1 (which does not consider this genealogy in a positive light). The equation of Shem with Melchizedek, the priest of the Most High God and king of Salem, is a common one in rabbinic literature and is recorded also in *Tg.Neof.* Gen 14:18. The traditions which portray Shem, whose midrashic development is too extensive to discuss here (see Ginzberg, *Legends*, vol. 5, 187, n. 51; 209–10, n. 13; 225–26, n. 102), as Tamar's father provide her and the Davidic line with a royal and priestly maternal pedigree. In addition, the tradition of Tamar's priestly parentage justifies Judah's command that she return to her father's house when widowed (see Lev 22:13). It also assimilates Judah's character to that of Joseph in the biblical narrative by depicting him as producing two sons with a priest's daughter, just as his younger brother does.

"fire" at the conclusion of Tamar's prayer. Here she vows that she will produce three saints who will go down "into the burning fire" (בנורא יקידתא) if her prayer for divine assistance is answered.[187] This phrase, which once again contains the same words that appear in Lev 21:9, is also almost identical to the last part of an Aramaic phrase that recurs throughout Daniel 3. This phrase is "the furnace of burning fire" (אתון נורא יקדתא, Dan 3:6, 11, 15, 17, 20, 21, 23, 26), which describes Nebuchadnezzar's instrument of death into which Shadrach, Meshach, and Abednego willingly enter rather than worship the idol. It is remarkable how the final editor of the narrative expansion in *Targum Neofiti* has clipped this phrase from Daniel 3 of its first word, "furnace" (אתון), to exaggerate the verbal similarities between the fates of Tamar and the three men at Dura.[188]

Reference to burning next appears in Tamar's address to the judge, where she states, "As for me, even if I am burned (יקדה) I will not identify him." The explicit use of the word "fire" (נורא) found in the two earlier occurrences of the motif of burning is missing in this statement. But the correspondence between Tamar and the three men at Dura already carefully established twice through exact verbal correspondence is reinforced in yet another way here. Tamar's readiness to burn echoes Shadrach, Meshach, and Abednego's readiness to burn in Dan 3:16–18. In the biblical passage these men express their willingness to enter the furnace rather than worship the golden image, whether or not their God chooses to deliver them. They emphasize their active choice and personal risk in entering the furnace. In *Targum Neofiti*, Tamar also expresses her willingness to burn rather than violate an ethical principle. Looking back at the opening of the narrative expansion, one finds that Tamar's active choice to burn rather than humiliate her father-in-law is expressed in its very opening words, through the transformation of the passive masoretic reading, "She was brought out" (הוא מוצאת), to the active targumic

---

[187] The exact phrase describing the three men's descent "into the burning fire" occurs only in *Tg.Neof.* Different expressions alluding to their entrance into the furnace are found in *Tg.Ps.-J.*, Gnz.Tgs. X and FF, and *t. Tg.Onq.* In *Frg.Tg.* and Gnz.Tgs. D and E, Tamar names the three men without specifying what they would do.

[188] In *Tg.Ps.-J.*, Tamar refers to "the furnace of fire" (לאתון נורא) from Daniel 3, and in Gnz.Tg. FF, she employs the whole phrase "the furnace of burning fire" (אתון נורא יק[דהא]) from that biblical chapter. These targums make the allusion to Daniel 3 more explicit, whereas *Tg.Neof.* emphasizes the shared fate of Tamar and the three men at Dura.

reading, "Tamar went out" (תמר נפקת).[189] Through Tamar's principled acceptance of death, the punitive burning, prescribed as a means of execution for sexual immorality by Judah in Gen 38:24 and by the law of the priest's daughter in Lev 21:9, takes on a different valence in *Targum Neofiti*. It becomes the means through which Tamar, like her pious descendants in Babylon after her, proves that she is a person of integrity, who would rather accept an unjust sentence than violate a central ethical principle.

The final appearance of the motif of burning occurs in Judah's confession before the court, when he explains to his family members, "It is better for me to burn (יקד) in this world with extinguishable fire (באשא טפיא), so that I do not burn (ניקוד) in the world to come which is the fire that consumes fire (אשא אכל[א] אשא)."[190] This aphorism provides a fitting final appearance of the motif, despite the fact that the word for "fire" (אשא) differs from the word for "fire" (נורא) used earlier in connection with Tamar.[191] Underlying Judah's confession in court and his acceptance of death by burning lie two post-biblical interpretive assumptions. One is that, even after Tamar produces the pledge items, Judah's identity remains unknown, and so he is free either to remain quiet or to confess. A second interpretive assumption is that, as the party responsible for Tamar's pregnancy, Judah will share her fate if he confesses. His immediate confession with its expression of willingness to die a fiery death in *Targum Neofiti* is therefore a pious action.

Admittedly, the correspondence between Judah and the three exemplars of the concept "sanctification of the Name" is complicated by the fact that in *Targum Neofiti* he merely accepts just punishment for his sins. The strong traditional interpretation of Judah as an exemplar of penitent confession conflicts with *Targum Neofiti*'s project of portraying the characters of Genesis 38 in light of the events of Daniel 3. Despite

---

[189] A number of targums besides *Tg.Neof.* have this active reading, including *Frg.Tg.* and Gnz.Tgs. D, FF (partially broken at this point), and E. A more literal translation retaining a passive verb is found in *Tg.Ps.-J.*, Gnz.Tg. X, and *t. Tg.Onq.*

[190] All the targums contain this aphorism, but only *Tg.Neof.* presents it as Judah's first words to the court.

[191] The word for "fire" (אשא) in this aphorism is drawn from the phrase "consuming fire" (אש אכלה) which describes God in Deut 4:24 and 9:3 and in Ben Zoma's statement in *Exod.Rab.* 30.15. In *Tg.Neof.* an expanded Aramaic form of the biblical phrase, "the fire that consumes fire" (אשא אכל[א] אשא), describes punishment in the world to come.

this fundamental conflict, Judah's opening aphorism emphasizes that he, like Tamar and the three men, is willing to die in flames.

But although both Tamar and Judah express their willingness to burn, ultimately they are spared through a salvific type of divine intervention entirely lacking in the biblical narrative. The heavenly voice acquitting Tamar and Judah and sparing them from a fiery death ("Both of you are innocent. From before the LORD is the decree.") is a traditional motif incorporated, rather than invented, by *Targum Neofiti*. Its presence nevertheless recreates Genesis 38 as a story of divine providence illustrating God's power to deliver those who piously surrender their lives, similar to Daniel 3.

Even before the voice actually sounds from heaven, Tamar introduces the motif of divine intervention when she expresses confidence that God will deliver her: "But my Witness, who is between him and me, He will place in his heart (the willingness) to see them in this hour, and He will redeem me from this great judgment." This verbal expression of faith in the power of God to save once again recalls the story of Hananiah, Mishael, and Azariah. In Dan 3:17 these three men also express the possibility that their God might save them, although they are not as certain as Tamar that he will choose to intervene. It is worth noting that the expression "my Witness" (שׂהדי), which Tamar uses to describe God in her statement of confidence, and the term "witnesses" (שׂהדי), which earlier specifies the three items of the pledge, themselves evoke the concept of willingness to die for one's beliefs central to "sanctification of the Name." In Greek a "martyr" (μάρτυς) is a "witness" of faith through voluntary death; in rabbinic thought, Hananiah, Mishael, and Azariah "witness" (מעידין) not only to their own faith but also to God's power through their descent into the furnace.[192]

Through its alignment of the characters of Genesis 38 with the three archetypes of "sanctification of the Name," *Targum Neofiti* translates the biblical narrative in terms of larger cultural and religious discussions. In particular, these discussions concern the absolute claims of certain moral principles, the relative value of human life on this earth, and the power of God to deliver those who trust in him. It is

---

[192] *Deut.Rab.* 'Eqeb 74 contains God's description of Hananiah, Mishael, and Azariah as "those who witness (מעידין) for me, that I saved them from the fire."

The three witnesses that make up the pledge in *Tg.Neof.* Gen 38:25 therefore link Genesis 38 with Daniel 3, which also features three "witnesses."

true, however, that the correspondence between Tamar and Judah and the three men at Dura created in this narrative expansion is not as complete as that between Abraham and these men in aggadic literature. For example, hostile foreigners and the theme of idolatry are absent from *Targum Neofiti*'s depiction of Genesis 38. These differences may be explained at least in part by the fact that the targum is working within and around pre-existing biblical material and traditional exegetical motifs, rather than creating an independent legend such as the legend of Abraham's descent into the Chaldean furnace.

Evidence from the larger exegetical sphere of rabbinic Judaism confirms that the characters and events of Genesis 38 were indeed once interpreted in light of the concept "sanctification of the Name" exemplified by Daniel 3. In fact, the passage from *Sipra* cited above contains one such piece of evidence, at the point where phrases from Song of Songs appear in the discussion about the three men at Dura. The biblical material from Song of Songs quoted in this passage contains two references to a "palm tree" (תמר), which is also Tamar's name in Hebrew. The passage interprets this Hebrew word in Cant 7:8–9 literally as "palm tree," judging from its use of the plural form "palm trees" (תמרים) in its figurative description of the three men's erect posture before the idol immediately preceding the scriptural quotations. But the curious interjection of these phrases containing the word "palm tree" or "Tamar" from Song of Songs into the context of the discussion of "sanctification of the Name" is highly suggestive. It motivates a search for further evidence within the midrashic corpus for an interpretation of them which directly compares Hananiah, Mishael, and Azariah with the biblical character Tamar.

An explicit comparison of these characters appears in *Song of Songs Rabba*. Following an extended elaboration of the story of the three men in Daniel 3, a brief alternate interpretation of the first part of Cant 7:8 appears:

> "This is your stature: You are like Tamar" (דמתה לתמר, Cant 7:8). Just as Tamar (תמר) was condemned to be burned (ננזרה עליה שריפה) but wasn't burned (ולא נשרפה), these [Hananiah, Mishael, and Azariah] were condemned to be burned (ננזר עליהם שריפה) but weren't burned (ולא נשרפו).[193]

---

[193] *Cant.Rab.* 7.8, in *Midraš Rabba*, vol. 2 (Vilna: Romm, 1884–87) 75. The connection between Tamar and the three men at Dura in this tradition is confirmed by

This passage compares Tamar and the three men on the basis of the similarities between their stories. It must be admitted, however, that this tradition points only to their shared condemnation to be burned and its reversal, and not explicitly to any common willingness to be burned to sanctify God's Name.

The paragraph directly preceding this passage in *Song of Songs Rabba*, however, emphasizes even more than Daniel 3 itself that Hananiah, Mishael, and Azariah actively decide to sacrifice their lives. In the midrashic portrayal of the events on the plain of Dura in this source, the prophet Ezekiel informs God that the three men "desire to give their lives for the sanctification of your Name" (מבקשים ליתן נפשם על קדושת שמך). Ezekiel then inquires if the deity plans to save their lives. To test the three men, God replies that he will not intervene. But Hananiah, Mishael, and Azariah nevertheless proclaim their determination to follow through with their plan: "Whether he stands by us or does not stand by us, we are giving our lives for the sanctification of his Name" (אנו נותנין נפשותינו על קדושת שמו).[194]

This strong presentation of the three men's willingness to burn for the purpose of exalting God colors the comparison between them and Tamar that directly follows. Reading the passage in this context, one cannot help but conclude that Tamar's condemnation to be burned must also have involved some sort of laudable behavior that sanctified the divine Name. It is tempting to reconstruct a hypothetical reading of the phrases from Cant 7:8–9 associated with Daniel 3 in *Sipra* that also alludes to Tamar's enhancement of God's status. These biblical phrases may have once been understood in the following manner: "This is your [Hananiah, Mishael, and Azariah's] stature: You are like Tamar (דמתה לתמר) . . . I was exalted (אעלה) by Tamar (בתמר) and grasp her branches." In this hypothetical reading, the word "I will go up" (אעלה) in Cant 7:9 is interpreted "I was exalted" (אני מתעלה) as in the explanation in *Sipra*. The means through which God is exalted, however, is not the three men symbolized by the palm tree as in *Sipra*, but Tamar herself. In this reading, Tamar's "branches" signify her three descendants in Babylon, whom God

---

an interpretation in *Cant.Rab.* 7.9, which reads, "'Let your breasts be as clusters of the vine' (Cant 7:9). This refers to Perez and Zerah. Just as Perez and Zerah were condemned to be burned but weren't burned, so these [three men] were condemned to be burned but weren't burned." *Cant.Rab.* 7.8–9 is the only source besides the Palestinian targums that explicitly associates Hananiah, Mishael, and Azariah with Tamar and not with Judah.

[194] *Cant.Rab.* 7.8, in *Midraš Rabba*, vol. 2, 37b.

"grasps" to save from the fire. There is, in fact, another source which interprets the word "branches" as Hananiah, Mishael, and Azariah.[195] This reading of phrases from Song of Songs, although unsubstantiated by any extant interpretive record, might have contributed to the developing link between Tamar and the three men. Once this link between characters became established, the strong association of Hananiah, Mishael, and Azariah with the concept "sanctification of the Name" would in turn begin to shape Tamar's exaltation of God into a corresponding example of "sanctification of the Name."

Some late sources, including *Midraš Haggadol*, heighten the similarities between the stories of Tamar and the three men at Dura noted in *Song of Songs Rabba* in a dramatic way. Focusing once more on the versatile first verb of Gen 38:25, *Midraš Haggadol* presents the following tradition:

> Another interpretation of "She was brought out" (הִיא מוּצֵאת): Don't read "she was brought out" (מוּצֵאת), but "she was set on fire" (מוּצָת), as the wording in "He kindled (וַיַּצֶּת) a fire in Zion" (Lam 4:11). According to this interpretation, she was being burned (בִּשְׂרֵיפָה).[196]

This interpretation identifies the root of the first word of Gen 38:25 as "to kindle" (יצת), rather than "to go out" (יצא) as in the Masoretic text. The effect of this interpretation is to align the character of Tamar more closely with the three archetypes of "sanctification of the Name" by describing her physical contact with fire. She, like Hananiah, Mishael, and Azariah, actually enters the fire.[197]

This midrashic intensification of the biblical narrative finds confirmation in a list of teachings attributed to R. Zutra that immediately follows in *Midraš Haggadol*. This list concludes with the didactic statement:

> It is better that a person fall into the midst of the furnace of fire (שִׁיפּוֹל לְתוֹךְ כִּבְשַׁן הָאֵשׁ) than embarrass his neighbor in public (יַלְבִּין פְּנֵי חֲבֵירוֹ בָּרַבִּים). How [do we know this]? From [the example of] Tamar. As it is written, "She was brought out" (or "she was set on fire").[198]

---

[195] See *b. Sanh.* 93a, in which this interpretation is attributed to R. Samuel b. Nahmani in the name of R. Jonathan; however, this passage interprets the palm tree as all of Israel, not as Tamar.

[196] *Midr. Haggadol* Gen 38:25. The same tradition is also presented in *Leqaḥ Ṭob* Gen 38:25.

[197] The heightened danger to Tamar's life in this late source parallels what happens to Isaac in late sources, where he is actually slain by Abraham. See Spiegel, *Last Trial*.

[198] A version of the teachings attributed to R. Zutra appears also in *b. Ber.* 43b. The particular didactic statement quoted here may be found also in *b. Sota* 10b;

The citation of this statement in close proximity with the earlier interpretation of the Hebrew word "she was brought out" (מוצאת) as "she was set on fire" (מוצת) reinforces the idea that Tamar actually entered the fire rather than humiliate her father-in-law.[199] In addition, the description of the pious person exemplified by Tamar, "who falls into the midst of the furnace of fire" (שיפול לתוך כבשן האש), reinforces the association between Tamar and the three men at Dura, who similarly "fell into the midst of the furnace of burning fire" (נפלו לגוא אתון נורא יקדתא) in Dan 3:23.[200]

However, the particular expression "sanctification of the Name" commonly associated with Hananiah, Mishael, and Azariah is not directly associated with Tamar in the sources examined thus far. But there is another source which does employ this expression in its portrayal of Tamar's actions in Genesis 38. This source is a seventh-century poem written by the liturgical poet Yannai, who typically takes biblical events as his subject matter. Yannai's depiction of Tamar as a proselyte who risks her life to align herself with the people of Israel through bearing Judah's offspring differs significantly from the depiction in *Targum Neofiti*; nevertheless, his poem confirms that the expression "sanctification of the Name" was associated with this biblical character in the Palestinian milieu. In his poem, Yannai praises Tamar through an extended play on the Hebrew verbal root meaning "to be holy" (קדש):

> Holy (הַקְּדוֹשָׁה) Tamar sanctified the Name (קִידְּשָׁה שֵׁם) when she longed for consecrated (קְדוֹשָׁה) seed. She dissembled and became a consecrated woman (קְידֵשָׁה) and her Holy One (קְדוֹשָׁה) made her way successful.[201]

Clearly in his eulogy Yannai develops a complicated pun on the biblical term "consecrated woman" (קְדֵשָׁה) which appears in Hirah's

---

b. Ketub. 67b; *b. B.Meṣ.* 59a; *b. Ber.* 43b; and *Yal. Šimʿoni* Gen 38:25. See also Urbach, *Sages*, 253.

[199] This statement also reveals another resonance in rabbinic exegesis between Genesis 38 and the biblical law in Lev 21:9 concerning the priest's wayward daughter. Before specifying the sentence of death by burning, the levitical law states that "the daughter of a priest who defiles herself by having illicit intercourse defiles her father" (את אביה היא מחללת). The interpretive tradition extends the concern for the status of the father in the levitical law to Tamar's concern for the reputation of her father-in-law.

[200] The biblical allusion is obvious, despite the fact that the statement in *Midr. Haggadol* is in Hebrew instead of in Aramaic as is the text of Daniel 3.

[201] Menahem Zulay, ed., פיוטי יניי [Liturgical poems of Yannai] (Berlin: Shoken, 1938) 54.

question about Tamar's whereabouts to the local men in Gen 38:21 and in his report to Judah in Gen 38:22. But the root "to be holy" (קדשׁ) at the base of the noun describing Tamar in Gen 38:21 and 22 is rich with semantic associations in Hebrew, as Yannai's liturgical poem illustrates. In one of his variations on the root, Yannai claims that Tamar herself "sanctified the Name" (קִידְּשָׁה שֵׁם). She may therefore be considered an exemplar of this concept, although the precise range of its meaning in Yannai's thought remains unclear.

It may be that the semantic associations of the verbal root "to be holy" (קדשׁ) applied to Tamar in Genesis 38 contributed to the development of the biblical narrative in terms of the concept "sanctification of the Name." Another factor may have been the application of the root "to be righteous" (צדק) to Tamar by Judah in Gen 38:26, when he declares "She is more righteous than I" (צדקה ממני). Those who sanctify God's Name are commonly called "righteous ones" (צדקים) in rabbinic literature.[202] Significantly, the roots "to be holy" (קדשׁ) and "to be righteous" (צדק) applied to the figure of Tamar in Genesis 38 are never applied to this figure in *Targum Neofiti*. In this targum, the same word for "prostitute" (נפקת בר) used earlier in its translation of Gen 38:15 is used in Gen 38:21 and 22,[203] and Judah declares Tamar "innocent" (וזכאה) rather than "righteous" as in the Hebrew version. The two roots "to be holy" (קדשׁ) and "to be righteous" (צדק) reappear in Tamar's vow as descriptions of Hananiah, Mishael, and Azariah, who are the "righteous ones" (צדיקין) destined to sanctify the holy Name (ומקדשׁין שׁמך קדישׁא).[204]

One final problematic aspect of the understanding of Tamar as an exemplar of the concept "sanctification of the Name" emerges in light of the evolving discussion within Judaism of when one should surrender one's life rather than transgress certain commandments. According to the passage from *Sipra* quoted above, R. Ishmael proposed that one need lay down one's life only when coerced into

---

[202] For example, Hananiah, Mishael, Azariah, and R. Akiva and his companions are called "righteous ones" in *b. Sanh.* 110b; Hananiah, Mishael, Azariah, and Abraham are called "righteous ones" in *b. Pesaḥ.* 118a; and Joshua the High Priest, who enters a furnace and emerges alive in a midrashic story in *b. Sanh.* 93a, is also called a "righteous one."

[203] By contrast, as noted in the first chapter, the biblical narrative uses the common word "prostitute" (זונה) in Gen 38:15 and the word "consecrated woman" (קדשׁה) in Gen 38:21 and 22.

[204] All the other Palestinian targums call the three men "righteous ones," except for *Tg.Ps.-J.*, which calls them "holy ones" (קדישׁיא).

publicly worshipping idols. The example of the three men at Dura
who "sanctified the Name" by refusing to bow down to the golden
statue before the assembled people fits well into his discussion. An
alternate ruling was more stringent, however, in that it eliminated
the distinction between private and public actions and specified two
additional commandments that one should not transgress, even at
the cost of one's life. According to the tradition found in *b. Sanh.*
74a, by a majority vote in Lod it was resolved:

> Concerning transgression of any law of the Tora, if they say to a man,
> "Transgress, so that you will not be killed," he should transgress and
> not be killed, except for idolatry, incest, and shedding blood (ושפיכות
> דמים).

Targum Neofiti demonstrates its awareness of this ruling when it charges
the people of Sodom with three sins in its version of Gen 13:13:

> And the people of Sodom were evil, each man towards his neighbor,
> and they were very guilty of incest, of shedding blood (ובשפיכות אדמייה),
> and of idolatry before the Lord.[205]

In view of the placement of incest among the three weightiest transgressions, it becomes difficult to understand Tamar's character positively, since in the biblical story she deliberately seeks sexual union
with her father-in-law. *Targum Neofiti* and other rabbinic sources therefore take a drastic measure to preserve Tamar's reputation. Rather
than evade the issue, they meet it head on and present Tamar not
as a shirker of the minimum standards set at Lod, but as a keeper
of a high moral standard who would willingly die even to prevent
her father-in-law's humiliation. The focus on her zeal for this ethical
principle functions as a kind of sleight of hand, preventing too much
reflection on her voluntary transgression of one of the three commandments that one should never transgress.

Later sources, such as *Midraš Haggadol* recognize this problematic
aspect of the biblical text and of the midrashic interpretation of Tamar
in light of discussions about when one should die rather than transgress
a commandment. In a discussion appearing in conjunction with the

---

[205] Similarly, a marginal note in *Tg.Neof.* describes how Laban cleansed his house
of these three great sins in preparation for receiving Jacob as his guest in Gen
24:31: "I have cleansed the house. I have cleansed [it] for worship. I have set it in
order from three harsh works that stood within it: from idolatry, from incest, and
from shedding innocent blood (שפיכות דם זכאי). And I have set a place in order for
the camels."

traditions quoted earlier concerning Tamar's entrance into the fire, this source moralizes the list of three commandments and argues that embarrassing one's neighbor is actually among the three greatest sins—perhaps the only sin through which one forfeits all hope for a part in the world to come.[206] *Midraš Haggadol* introduces a teaching attributed to R. Nahman b. Isaac at this point in the discussion: "Everyone who embarrasses his neighbor with words (כל המלבין פני חבירו בדברים) is the same as one who sheds blood (שופך דמים)."[207] Through R. Nahman's equation of embarrassment of one's neighbor and murder, Tamar is once more drawn into the sphere of discussion concerning "sanctification of the Name." Tamar's refusal to identify the father of her unborn children becomes equivalent to a refusal to commit murder. She is therefore equal to one who refuses to transgress one of the three great commandments designated through the vote at Lod (shedding blood), just as the three men at Dura refuse to transgress another of these three (idolatry).[208] The discussion in *Midraš Haggadol* therefore confirms the hypothesis that *Targum Neofiti* follows a larger exegetical trend when it recreates Tamar's character in keeping with the larger cultural values expressed by the phrase "sanctification of the Name."

As far as the figure of Judah is concerned, his assimilation to the narrative pattern of his three descendants at Dura is less developed than Tamar's in *Targum Neofiti*, but other sources draw the connection much more forcefully.[209] At least one source explicitly states that Judah sanctified the divine Name when he confessed his involvement with Tamar. After discussing the addition of a letter to Joseph's name as a reward for his sanctification of the Name in private when he

---

[206] Adultery and calling people names are the other two listed in *Midr. Haggadol* Gen 38:25. This same list of three sins is also found in the Talmud, for example in *b. B.Meṣ.* 59a.

[207] This tradition is also recorded in *b. B.Meṣ.* 58b and *Yal. Šim'oni* Gen 38:25.
Note that the expression "everyone who embarrasses his neighbor with words" (כל המלבין פני חבירו בדברים) basically corresponds to the expression in the statement attributed to R. Zutra that it is better to fall into a furnace (as Tamar did) than "embarrass one's neighbor in public" (ילבין פני חבירו ברבים) in *Midr. Haggadol* Gen 38:25.

[208] Significantly, in the concluding section of Philo *On the Virtues*, Tamar (220–22) follows Abraham (211–19) as an example of true nobility because of her rejection of idolatry. Willingness to burn is not part of Philo's presentation of either of these characters, however.

[209] For example, see *b. Soṭa* 10b; *Exod.Rab.* 16.4; *Num.Rab.* 13.4; *Deut.Rab.* 'Eqeb (Liebermann, *Midraš Debarim Rabba*, 74); and *Genesis Rabba* 97, NV.

refused the sexual advances of Potiphar's wife, *b. Soṭa* 10b continues
with a discussion of Gen 38:26:

> "Judah, who sanctified the heavenly Name (ש"ש שׁקְדֵשׁ) in public mer-
> ited that the whole of his name should be called after the Name of the
> Holy One Blessed be He. When he confessed and said, "She is more
> righteous than I," a voice issued forth and said, "You rescued Tamar
> and her two sons from the fire. By your life, I will rescue through your
> merit three of your descendants from the fire." Who are they? Hananiah,
> Mishael and Azariah.[210]

In this passage, Judah's sanctification of the Name through confession results in the honor of bearing the letters of the Tetragrammaton
in his own name. The emphasis here is on Judah's willingness to
save Tamar and her sons through acceptance of responsibility for
her pregnancy, in contrast to the emphasis in *Targum Neofiti* on Judah's
willingness to burn alongside her for his wrongdoing. But despite
this difference, this passage demonstrates that a linkage between
Judah's confession, the three men at Dura, and the concept "sanctification of the Name" existed in the larger exegetical sphere of
Palestinian Judaism.

As demonstrated above, *Targum Neofiti* and other rabbinic sources
bring Genesis 38 into the semantic circle of "sanctification of the
Name" by portraying especially Tamar, but to a lesser extent also
Judah, as parallel figures to the three archetypes of this concept,
Hananiah, Mishael, and Azariah. The development of this theme in
Targum Neofiti transforms Tamar and Judah from the morally ambiguous characters of the biblical narrative to conscientious individuals
who exemplify the most principled adherence to ethical standards
through their willingness to give their lives. This development shifts
attention from the royal ancestors' involvement with deception, prostitution, incest, and perversion of justice, and resignifies Judah and
Tamar as exemplars of post-biblical piety and morality, worthy of
emulation by those standing in the shadow of biblical tradition. The
divine intervention concluding the narrative expansion also corresponds
to the pattern set by Daniel 3 and transforms Genesis 38 into a
story illustrating God's power to deliver the faithful. The story thus
becomes a dignified and inspiring chapter in Israelite history and a
meaningful paradigm for human piety and behavior under duress.

---

[210] This teaching is attributed to R. Hanin b. Bizna, who cites R. Simeon the Pious.

CONCLUSIONS

The narrative expansion incorporated into the translation of Genesis 38 in *Targum Neofiti* fights its battles with the biblical text selectively. By concentrating its wealth of material at the climax of the story and having very little expansive material elsewhere in the chapter, *Targum Neofiti* deflects the focus of attention from other potentially problematic issues in the biblical story, such as Judah's marriage to a Canaanite, his evil sons, his incestuous sexual encounter with Tamar, as well as Tamar's deception of her father-in-law in order to engage him sexually. Because it does not expand on the importance of the birth of the twins, *Targum Neofiti* also de-emphasizes the royal and messianic implications of the story,[211] although there is evidence that it is aware of these implications.[212] The important heroes of the future whom this story explicitly anticipates are not the Davidic kings or an eschatological messiah, but three righteous men under duress in exile who, like Tamar and Judah, would have willingly burned if not for the intervention of the God in whom they place their trust.

The real tasks assumed by this narrative expansion are to transform the characters of the story into exemplars of seemly comportment under threat of death and to interject a decisive divine presence into what appears on the surface to be a story of human initiative. In this

---

[211] Although Renée Bloch ("'Juda engendra Pharès et Zara de Thamar,' Matth. 1,3," in *Mélanges bibliques rédigés en l'honneur de André Robert*, Travaux de l'Institute Catholique de Paris 4 [Paris: Bloud & Gay, 1957] 381–89) cites the Palestinian targums extensively when she creates a composite rabbinic portrait of Tamar to explain this woman's inclusion in Jesus' genealogy in Matt 1:3, she is insensitive to the absence of any indication in the targumic material that Tamar "ardently desired to participate in the messianic blessing" by being the messiah's ancestress.

[212] *Tg.Neof.* presupposes that Genesis 38 describes the origin of the kingly and messianic lines without emphasizing or even explicitly stating that this is the case. Evidence for this tacit understanding of the story includes the interpretation of Judah's "seal" in Gen 38:18 and 25 as his "signet ring" (עזקה), which is the same word used to specify the ring that Pharaoh gives to Joseph in *Tg.Neof.* Gen 41:42. Other targums, including *Frg.Tg.*; Gnz.Tgs. D, X, FF (slightly broken), and E; and *Tg.Onq.*, also have the translation "signet ring" with its royal connotations, although *Tg.Ps.-J.* retains the meaning of "seal" in its translation. A number of sources comment on the royal significance of this item, including *Gen.Rab.* 85.9; *Leqah Tob* Gen 38:18; and *T.Jud.* 12:4 and 15:3. Further evidence appears in the interpretation of the midwife's exclamation concerning the reversal of the birth order in *Tg.Neof.* Gen 38:29 as "How strong you are and how strong you will become." This same translation is found in *Tg.Ps.-J.*, Gnz.Tg. E, and *Tg.Onq.* In *Tg.Ps.-J.* the royal dimensions of this interpretation are explicitly articulated through an additional phrase concluding the midwife's exclamation: "For you are destined to possess the kingship." In Gnz.Tg. FF the messianic connotations of the story are made explicit by the voice from heaven.

transformation, Tamar becomes a pious and prayerful woman, an exemplar of modest consideration for another's reputation, and an illustration of the multifaceted concept of "sanctification of the [divine] Name." Judah becomes a teacher of ethics and a biblical exegete, as well as an exemplar of willing confession of sin. With the introduction of divine activity bringing the plot to its happy conclusion, the story becomes religious history, appropriate to its status as scripture. Guided by the expansion, the reader lifts his or her eyes up to heaven like Tamar, to the source of events which take place on earth.

As we have seen in our analysis of the additional elements of plot and dialogue in the narrative expansion, some of its features are based on traditional rabbinic exegesis of these verses which are also recorded in other midrashic sources. Others are unique to the Palestinian targum tradition or to *Targum Neofiti* itself, and many of these unique features work together to present the story as an illustration of the concept of "sanctification of the Name" in keeping with the influences of larger cultural and religious discussions.

But whether transmitting traditional lore or presenting its own interpretation of the biblical narrative, *Targum Neofiti* argues for a particular understanding of the biblical story through the means of narrative. With the reassertion of the narrative genre, the gap between the written biblical text and traditional, originally oral, exegesis on aspects of that text is closed. Biblical narrative and biblical commentary appear translated into Aramaic as one continuous whole. Characters both inhabit the story and assign moral meaning to it through additional words and actions. At the end a divine voice ratifies as revelation what has already been determined by rabbinic commentary: both Tamar and Judah are innocent and the events are divinely ordained.

At the end of this discussion about the narrative expansion in *Tg.Neof.* Gen 38:25–26, the liturgical setting of targum recitation deserves attention. A good starting point for reflection is the curious instructions found in *m. Meg.* 4.10, concerning translation of Genesis 38 into Aramaic during public worship. This passage in the Mishna, which contains a list of sensitive biblical passages and special stipulations concerning their liturgical reading and translation, presents the "story of Tamar" after another tale of incest, namely the "story of Reuben." But unlike the tale of Reuben and Bilhah, which is to be read in Hebrew but left untranslated, the Mishna specifies that "the story of Tamar is to be read and translated."

Since according to other passages, including *m. Meg.* 4.4, verse by verse alternation of reading from the Tora and oral translation into Aramaic is portrayed as the norm in the synagogue liturgy, these explicit instructions to proceed as usual in the case of Genesis 38 are puzzling. Perhaps they indicate that at an earlier time Genesis 38, like the report of Reuben's sexual relations with Bilhah in Gen 35:22, was only read but not translated because of the unseemly nature of its contents.[213] The inclusion of positive interpretative material into the translation of this chapter, such as that found in the expansion in *Targum Neofiti*, may have secured the meaning of the text and thereby altered the attitude towards public presentation of a targum to Genesis 38.

While it cannot be demonstrated conclusively that the Aramaic version contained in *Targum Neofiti* was ever actually used in synagogue services,[214] one can easily understand why such an expanded translation would have been desirable in this context. With the presentation of the narrative expansion in the silence after the reading of the Hebrew text of Gen 38:25 and 26, those listening would be guided in understanding the chapter in a manner concordant with contemporary moral and religious sensibilities and ideals. The requirement that the biblical text be accompanied by its targum would therefore serve as a guarantee that the story would not be misunderstood. Or perhaps more precisely, it would guarantee that it would be properly misunderstood as conveying edifying truths worthy of scripture.

---

[213] P. S. Alexander notes that the category of passages which are to be read and interpreted is a redundant category and indicates an earlier, more restrictive phase ("The Rabbinic Lists of Forbidden Targumim," *JJS* 27 [1976] 181–82). But he suggests that by the tannaitic period the necessity for this sort of restriction passed away, perhaps because of developments in the history of interpretation of this material. It is interesting to note that, in the discussion of the woman accused of adultery in *Num.Rab.* 9.17, the affairs of Reuben with Bilhah and of Judah with Tamar are both described as "things which neither she nor all the families of her father's house deserve to hear," possibly alluding to this earlier phase in which Genesis 38 was considered in the same category with Gen 35:22.

[214] Michael L. Klein discusses evidence from the margins and bodies of targumic manuscripts, including *Tg.Neof.*, that suggests the presentation of targum within the synagogue liturgy ("Not to Be Translated in Public," *JJS* 39 [1988] 80–91). Díez Macho points out that a number of liturgical addresses to an audience, such as "O, my people," and "O, sons of Israel," may be found in *Tg.Neof.*, suggesting a liturgical context (*Neophyti 1*, vol. 1, 59).

CHAPTER FOUR

POETICS OF EXEGETICAL ANTHOLOGY:
ROYAL AND MESSIANIC ORIGINS IN *GENESIS RABBA* 85

> At the time of her delivery, there were twins in her belly! As she
> gave birth, one put out his hand, and the midwife took [it] and tied
> a red thread on his hand, saying "This one came out first." When
> he drew back his hand, his brother came out! She said, "What a
> breach you have made for yourself!" And his name was called Perez.
> Afterwards, his brother, upon whose hand was the red thread, came
> out. His name was called Zerah. (Gen 38:27–30)

In the previous chapter I drew upon a variety of sources, including
Genesis Rabba, the *Tanḥuma*, *Midraš Haggadol*, and the Babylonian
Talmud, in order to analyze the traditional exegetical material incorporated into *Targum Neofiti* Gen 38:25–26. Comparing parallel passages from different documents facilitated comprehension of important
aspects of individual interpretive motifs, including their origins in and
points of connection with the biblical text itself, their development
and distinctive forms within different written works, and ultimately
their function within the narrative expansion itself, which illustrated
the concept "sanctification of the Name." Although comparing short
passages from different literary contexts aided understanding of *Targum
Neofiti*'s distinctive hermeneutic dynamics, it simultaneously prevented
identification of other overarching interpretive trajectories within rabbinic Judaism. Closer examination of the sources cited above reveals
that *Targum Neofiti*'s presentation of Tamar and Judah as moral exemplars under duress and its dramatization of God's power to deliver
pious and penitent individuals are by no means omnipresent rabbinic strategies for positively reading Genesis 38. These documents,
although they contain many of the same exegetical traditions found
in *Targum Neofiti*, assign strikingly different meanings to the biblical
chapter as a whole and rework its narrative details accordingly.

  This situation, in which a common exegetical heritage concerning
certain lemmatic features of the biblical narrative does not effectively
determine the general direction of interpretation, presents itself as a
productive area for exploration of the relation between written text,
historical readers standing within an interpretive tradition, and the

meaning of a biblical narrative. The multiplicity of overarching interpretive trajectories, even within the single exegetical sphere of rabbinic Judaism, emphasizes the abundant potentialities for the creation
of scriptural meaning—potentialities that stem both from the surplus
of the biblical narrative itself, including its various points of interface
with other canonical texts, and from the diverse perspectives of historically situated readers that frame the interpretive process. It is
therefore worthwhile to investigate more fully the larger structural
dimensions of at least one other interpretation of Genesis 38 from
the exegetical sphere of rabbinic Judaism.

The interpretation of Genesis 38 found in the rabbinic commentary on the book of Genesis generally known as *Genesis Rabba* presents
itself as an ideal candidate for this study.[1] As the most ancient extant
verse-by-verse commentary on this biblical book, *Genesis Rabba* provides an invaluable witness to early Jewish biblical interpretation of

---

[1] *Genesis Rabba* is an Anglicization of the Hebrew title *Berešit Rabba* (בראשית רבה).
This commentary is also designated by several other names, including *Berešit de Rabbi
Hošaʿya*, which refer to the third-century Palestinian authority credited with the opening
proem of this work. The inclusion of this first generation amoraic scholar in the title
subsequently led to the traditional, though erroneous, view that he edited the entire
commentary. For a discussion of the significance and history of this work's title, as
well as an introduction to other issues, see C. Albeck's מבוא לבראשית רבא [Introduc-
tion to *Genesis Rabba*], in vol. 3 of *Midraš Berešit Rabba*, ed. J. Theodor and Albeck
(Berlin: Defus Tsevi Hirsch Ittskavski, 1903–36; reprint, Jerusalem: Wahrmann Books,
1965) 1–138. This critical edition in three volumes serves as the primary text for the
present study, unless otherwise indicated. It is based upon a twelfth-century manuscript, MS British Museum Codex Add. 27169, but in addition, it notes variants
from eight other manuscripts in the critical apparatus. Among these manuscripts is
an eleventh-century manuscript from the Vatican library (MS Vat. Ebr. 30), recognized ultimately by Theodor and Albeck themselves as a superior witness to the
original. For a discussion of the history of scholarship concerning MS Vat. Ebr. 30
and of the claims for its superiority, see Lewis M. Barth, *An Analysis of Vatican 30*,
Monographs of the Hebrew Union College 1 (Cincinnati: Hebrew Union College
Press, 1973) 1–13. More recently, an ancient fragment of *Genesis Rabba* from the
Cairo Geniza (MS 2) has been identified as a possible *Vorlage* for ms Vat. Ebr. 30.
See Michael Sokoloff, ed., *The Geniza Fragments of Bereshit Rabba* (Jerusalem: Ben Zvi
Printing Enterprises, 1982). General introductions to *Genesis Rabba* in English in-
clude J. Theodor, "Bereshit Rabbah," in vol. 3 of *The Jewish Encyclopedia* (New York
and London: Funk and Wagnalls, 1901–1906) 62–65, and Moshe David Herr,
"Genesis Rabbah," in vol. 7 of *Encyclopaedia Judaica* (Jerusalem: Keter Publishing
House, 1971) 399–401. Translations into English which occasionally inform the translations of passages in this chapter include H. Freedman, trans., *Genesis*, vols. 1 and 2
of *Midrash Rabbah*, ed. Freedman and Maurice Simon (London: Soncino Press, 1939),
and Jacob Neusner, trans., *Genesis Rabbah: The Judaic Commentary to the Book of Genesis:
A New American Translation*, 3 vols., Brown Judaic Studies 106 (Atlanta: Scholars Press,
1985).

Genesis.[2] Recent scholarly consensus views this work as a collection
of exegetical traditions—most of which emerged out of Palestinian
academic institutions and synagogues of the tannaitic (first to second
centuries CE) and amoraic (third to fourth centuries CE) periods—
that assumed its basic documentary shape in the late fourth and early
fifth centuries CE.[3]

In addition to its early date and its commentary genre, which
contrasts to the genres of testament and paraphrastic translation
explored earlier, *Genesis Rabba* makes a promising subject for analysis
in the context of this study for two other reasons. This commentary
contains a constellation of interpretive traditions at the narrative climax

---

[2] It predates by centuries the verse-by-verse explications on Genesis found in later
exegetical anthologies such as *Midraš Haggadol* and *Yalquṭ Šimʿoni*. It also predates the
commentaries on the other books of the Pentateuch and the Scrolls included in the
larger corpus known as *Midraš Rabba*. The antiquity of *Genesis Rabba* has long been
acknowledged. The medieval work *Halakot Gedolot*, for example, classifies this commentary along with midrashic literature from the tannaitic period (*Sipra, Sipre,* and
the *Mekilta de Rabbi Ishmael*) rather than with the other Rabba literature. In fact, it
may be the earliest extant rabbinic commentary of its type, in which direct quotation
of almost every verse of an entire biblical book is followed by pertinent exegesis.
The introductory proems, which head all but a few of the approximately one hundred
chapters of *Genesis Rabba* and which bear some resemblance to the homiletic expositions found in the *Tanḥuma* and the *Yelammedenu* literature, are discussed below.

[3] Some of the traditions included in this work predate the common era. For
example, the citation of Joshua ben Sira (second century BCE) and the incorporation
of material found also in other documents from the period of the second temple
attest to the antiquity of certain traditions in *Genesis Rabba*. See the list of quotations
of ben Sira, as well as traditions with parallels in the works of Philo and Josephus,
in Albeck, "Introduction to *Genesis Rabba*," 84–89. But despite the presence of traditions from literally centuries of biblical exegesis, there is no question that the basic
editorial shaping of this work took place at the end of the fourth century CE, at the
earliest. Some of the most convincing arguments for this date include the frequent
citation of members of the final generations of amoraic scholars (late fourth century), the references to historical events including the reign of the Roman emperor
Diocletian (late fourth century), and the correspondence in content and language
(Hebrew and Palestinian Aramaic) to other late fourth-century sources, especially
the Jerusalem Talmud. For a critique of the sixth-century date of compilation assigned
by Leopold Zunz and an advancement of a late fourth- or early fifth-century date,
see Albeck, "Introduction to *Genesis Rabba*," 93–96. Later accretions to the basic
document, however, are evident in the final chapters of this work. For example, the
passages corresponding to the entire annual lectionary pericope Wayyiggaš and the
beginning of the pericope Wayehi in the great majority of the manuscripts do not
conform to the genre of verse-by-verse commentary typical of this work as a whole,
but rather exemplify the homiletic genre typical of the later *Tanḥuma* or *Yelammedenu*
commentaries. These anomalous passages are a later intrusion into an earlier document, as the presence of a more original verse-by-verse commentary on these pericopes
in MS Vat. Ebr. 30 confirms. For a discussion of the early version of the final chapters in MS Vat. Ebr. 30, see J. Theodor, "Drei unbekannte Paraschas," in *Festschrift
zum siebzigsten Geburtstage Jacob Guttmans* (Leipzig: G. Fock, 1915).

of Genesis 38 similar to those found in the narrative expansion in
Targum Neofiti Gen 38:25–26.[4] This is perhaps not unexpected, since
both *Genesis Rabba* and *Targum Neofiti* arose from a common matrix of
rabbinic exegetical activity in the land of Palestine.[5] But beyond
confirming the shared hermeneutic heritage of these two documents,
the constellation of common interpretive traditions can provide a
heuristic point of entry into the running commentary on Genesis 38
in *Genesis Rabba* which, in comparison to the simple expansion of a
single section of the biblical narrative in *Targum Neofiti*, is unwieldy
and therefore difficult to synthesize. The unwieldy quality of *Genesis
Rabba* derives from more than mere abundance of material, but also
from the various levels of commentary possible for any given biblical
verse and from the frequent juxtaposition of multiple, and sometimes
contradictory, exegetical traditions. With respect to the possible levels
of commentary, for example, one may find after the citation of a
biblical verse an explanation of one or more of the following: a single
word; a problem of grammar or a peculiarity of spelling; the significance of a name, a place, or an action; an intertextual connection
with another passage of scripture; a broader, relevant theme; a connection between the biblical text and contemporary customs or historical events; or the moral and legal implications of biblical precedent.
In addition, within any one of these levels of commentary, there is
the possibility of interpretive multiplication, in which a list of divergent traditions on a single feature of the text is presented without
further evaluation as to their relative validity.

The resulting complexity renders the procedure that I followed in
the previous chapter of discussing each exegetical motif in its order of

---

[4] The repeated references to *Genesis Rabba* in the previous discussion of *Tg.Neof.*
Gen 38:25–26 may have already suggested this correspondence. The constellation
of common interpretive traditions begins with *Gen.Rab.* 85.11 and continues through
the first part of *Gen.Rab.* 85.12, that is, the sections which offer commentary on Gen
38:25–26.

[5] The conclusion that this work is of Palestinian origin is based on considerations
including the predominance of Palestinian authorities cited in the work, its similarity
in language and content to other Palestinian documents including the Jerusalem
Talmud, and the correspondence of many of its divisions of Genesis with the readings of the three-year Palestinian lectionary cycle. For a study of the latter, see
Jacob Mann, *The Palestinian Triennial Cycle: Genesis and Exodus*, vol. 1 of *The Bible as
Read and Preached in the Old Synagogue* (Cincinnati: Mann Sonne Publication Committee, 1940; reprint, New York: Ktav Publishing House, 1971); the earlier discussion
by J. Theodor, "Die Midraschen zum Pentateuch u. der dreijährige pal. Cyclus,"
MGWJ 34–36 (1885–87); and Joseph Heinemann, מבנהו וחלוקתו של מדרש בראשית
רבה [The Structure and divisions of *Genesis Rabba*], *Bar Ilan* 9 (1971) 279–89.

appearance in *Targum Neofiti* impractical and even counter-productive in the case of *Genesis Rabba*. Instead, to achieve a synthetic understanding of the overarching statement this commentary makes about Genesis 38, I identify the thematic emphases which recur and significantly shape its dominant structural presentation of the story of Judah and Tamar. A preliminary exploration of the distinctive forms and editorial arrangement of the constellation of traditions which *Genesis Rabba* holds in common with *Targum Neofiti* can initiate discovery of their relation to the broader thematic emphases of this early commentary. Seen as part of the structural whole presented by *Genesis Rabba*, some of the exegetical traditions previously explored in the context of the discussion of *Targum Neofiti* acquire new significance. Others are left undeveloped, unincorporated, and therefore structurally insignificant in *Genesis Rabba*, whatever their inherent value as witnesses to the ongoing enterprise of biblical interpretation within the field of rabbinic Judaism. Therefore, while this investigation begins with a discussion of material that *Genesis Rabba* holds in common with *Targum Neofiti*, it will ultimately achieve a clear view of the distinctive concretization and reformulation of Genesis 38 within the early commentary.

These observations concerning the relation between the overall orientation of *Genesis Rabba* and the individual traditions that appear in this work lead to the second reason that this document makes a promising subject for study. In addition to recording numerous and even contradictory traditional explanations of particular features of the biblical text, *Genesis Rabba* does in fact forward its own distinctive statement about the general significance of Genesis 38. This thesis, that *Genesis Rabba* makes a cogent statement of its own through an intentional process of selecting and editing traditional material, is by no means universally accepted in academic circles.[6] In fact, some of

---

[6] An exception is Jacob Neusner, who in a recent work argues that *Genesis Rabba* is a unified work on the basis of formal/rhetorical analysis, as well as on the basis of the overall thematic statement that this work makes about "Israel's salvific history" through the vehicle of commentary on Genesis (*Comparative Midrash: The Plan and Program of "Genesis Rabbah" and "Leviticus Rabbah,"* Brown Judaic Series 111 [Atlanta: Scholars Press, 1986]). Neusner's focus on the formal features of *Genesis Rabba* and on its most general purposes and thematic messages, however, prevent him from seriously grappling with the question of how this work makes unified statements on particular passages of Genesis while simultaneously acknowledging contradictory traditional material. The study here of *Genesis Rabba*'s treatment of Genesis 38 will therefore supplement Neusner's discussion of the unity and intentionality of *Genesis Rabba* through a close examination of the specific contents of a single chapter of this work.

the scholars most familiar with the text of *Genesis Rabba* itself and its history of transmission view this work as a collection of random, unconnected traditions on specific features of the first book of the Bible.[7] Turning from the field of Jewish studies to contemporary literary criticism, *Genesis Rabba* and other rabbinic documents are sometimes celebrated for their presentation of multiple, equally valid interpretations of scriptural passages, which is regarded as a refusal to constrict the inherent multivalency of the biblical text or even as an attempt to shatter the illusion of univocal reading.[8]

But while the layers of interpretation visible in *Genesis Rabba* should be neither denied nor minimized, this commentary stands in sharp relief to later commentaries, such as the *Tanḥuma, Midraš Haggadol,* and *Yalquṭ Šimʿoni.* In these later works, the proclivity to pay homage to the authority of traditional biblical interpretation by indiscriminately listing exegetical explanations in encyclopedic fashion makes discernment of distinctive documentary perspectives difficult, if not impossible. *Genesis Rabba,* by contrast, through its method of controlled anthological presentation, argues for a particular reading of the biblical narrative and presents a corresponding adaptation of its events and characters. It is to the task of discovering the unique reformulation of Genesis 38 accomplished by *Genesis Rabba* through its poetics of anthology which I now turn.

---

[7] For example, Theodor presupposes an unmotivated accumulation of exegetical traditions in his description of the compilation of *Genesis Rabba* ("Bereshit Rabbah," 62a). He writes: "with the notoriously loose construction of the haggadic exegesis, it became easy to string together on every verse, or part of a verse, a number of rambling comments, or to add longer or shorter haggadic passages, stories, etc., connected in some way with the exposition of the text. This process of accretion took place quite spontaneously in the *Bereshit Rabbah.*"

[8] See for example, Susan Handelman, *The Slayers of Moses: The Emergence of Rabbinic Interpretation in Modern Literary Theory* (Albany: State University of New York Press, 1982); Geoffrey H. Hartman and Sanford Budick, eds., *Midrash and Literature* (New Haven: Yale University Press, 1986); and José Faur, *Golden Doves with Silver Dots* (Bloomington: Indiana University Press, 1986). For a critique of this understanding of midrash, see Howard Eilberg-Schwartz, "Who's Kidding Whom?: A Serious Reading of Rabbinic Word Plays," *JAAR* 55 (1987) 765–88.

UNIFIED COMPOSITION OR
RANDOM COLLECTION OF RABBINIC
EXEGETICAL TRADITIONS?

Case Study 1: Genesis Rabba's *Commentary on Gen 38:25–26*

In the eighty-fifth chapter of *Genesis Rabba*, devoted entirely to the
explication of Genesis 38, a constellation of exegetical traditions
appears as commentary on the climax of the biblical chapter (Gen
38:25–26):

> "She was brought out (היא מוצאת)" (Gen 38:25). R. Judan said, "They
> [the three items] were lost (אבדו), and the Holy One Blessed be He
> provided (והמציא) others to replace them. As it says, 'Or found (מצא)
> something that had been lost (אבדה)' (Lev 5:22)."
>
> R. Huna said, "'She (היא) was brought out!' Both she (היא) and he
> (הוא) should have gone out."
>
> "She sent to her father-in-law," etc. (Gen 38:25). He sought to deny
> [it]. She said to him, "Recognize your creator concerning these [pledge
> items], for they are yours and your creator's."
>
> "Recognize! (הכר נא) To whom (למי) do the seal (החתמת)," etc. (Gen
> 38:25). R. Johanan said, "The Holy One Blessed be He said to Judah,
> 'You said to your father "Recognize! (הכר נא)" (Gen 37:32). By your
> life, Tamar will say to you, "Recognize! (הכר נא)" (Gen 38:25).'"
>
> "Judah recognized," etc. (Gen 38:26). R. Jeremiah said in the name of
> R. Samuel b. R. Isaac, "In three places the Holy One Blessed be He
> revealed himself: in the court of Shem, in the court of Samuel, and in
> the court of Solomon." In the court of Shem: "And Judah recognized
> and he said, 'She is more righteous than I (צדקה ממני)'" (Gen 38:26).
> R. Jeremiah said in the name of R. Samuel b. R. Isaac, "The holy
> spirit said 'From me' were these things (ממני היו הדברים).'" In the court
> of Samuel: "The LORD is a witness against you and his anointed one
> is a witness," etc. . . . "And he said 'I am a witness.'" (1 Sam 12:5).
> Who said "I am a witness?" R. Jeremiah said in the name of R. Samuel
> b. R. Isaac, "The holy spirit said, 'I am a witness.'" In the court of
> Solomon: "Give her the living child and certainly do not kill it. She is
> his mother" (1 Kgs 3:27). Who said, "She is his mother?" R. Jeremiah
> said in the name of R. Samuel b. R. Isaac, "The holy spirit said, 'She
> is his mother.'"[9]

---

[9] *Gen.Rab.* 85.11–12.

Most of the traditions that appear in the passage above are already familiar from the earlier discussion of the narrative expansion in *Targum Neofiti*. *Genesis Rabba* also groups together the motif of the lost and restored pledge, the assumption that both Tamar and Judah deserve punishment for their shared guilt, the claim that Tamar's deception of Judah corresponds to his earlier deception of his father in Genesis 37, and the motif of divine intervention in court.

But despite the similarities in content, there are obvious differences as well between this passage and the narrative expansion in *Targum Neofiti*. One of the most striking differences is a formal one, related to the genre of commentary which characterizes *Genesis Rabba*. In contrast to the consistent narrative presentation of biblical text and exegetical traditions in the targum, *Genesis Rabba* oscillates in this passage between introductory citation of the biblical text and clearly demarcated, external discourse about it.[10] The attribution of exegetical traditions to five different authorities commonly associated with the academy at Tiberias,[11] separated temporally from each other by generations and from the original biblical narrative by centuries, initially seems to emphasize the distinction between biblical text and ongoing rabbinic commentary.

But *Genesis Rabba* mediates this apparent gap between text and commentary, albeit through a different mechanism than that employed by *Targum Neofiti*. In each unit of commentary in this passage, whether cited in the name of a rabbinic authority or anonymously, there is a clear link with some particular feature of the biblical text. I have already discussed a number of these connections forged between later commentary and the biblical text in the discussion concerning the traditional exegetical motifs in *Targum Neofiti* above, but a quick summary is nevertheless in order to facilitate comprehension of the consistent poetics through which *Genesis Rabba* argues that post-biblical

---

[10] In this particular passage, the only exception to this oscillation between biblical quotation and extra-biblical commentary consists of the lack of a biblical quotation before the explication attributed to R. Huna, but this omission is understandable in light of the fact that his comment deals with another aspect of the opening words of Gen 38:25, cited at the head of this section and again internally within his own comments.

[11] These include R. Judan or Judah b. Shallum, late fourth century CE; R. Huna, Babylonian emigrant to Palestine, late fourth century; R. Johanan, founder of the school in Tiberias, middle of the third century; and R. Jeremiah, Babylonian emigrant, early fourth century, who speaks in the name of R. Samuel bar R. Isaac, another Babylonian emigrant, late third to early fourth century.

exegesis arises immediately from scripture itself. To legitimate the
addition of the narrative motif of the lost and restored pledge as
emerging from the biblical text itself, the first verb in Gen 38:25,
"she was brought out" (מוּצֵאת), is parsed twice as being from the
root "to find" (מצא), once implicitly in the note that the pledge items
were lost as "she did not find" (לֹא מֹצֵאת) and once explicitly as "he
produced" (הִמְצִיא). To substantiate the assumption that both Judah
and Tamar were liable for punishment, which has no basis in the
biblical narrative itself although it is indicated in some biblical laws
concerning sexual misconduct,[12] the pronoun subject at the head of
Gen 38:25, written consonantally as the masculine "he" (הוּא) but
pointed as the feminine "she" (הִוא), is read as a prescriptive double
subject for the verb "was brought out" (מוּצֵאת). The anonymous tradition concerning Judah's reluctance to confess and Tamar's command
that he recognize divine providence behind the events of the story is
presented as an explanation for Tamar's curious double statement
concerning the importance of the pledge in Gen 38:25, although it
is probably tacitly linked to other features of the biblical text as well.[13]
The moralizing commentary from heaven correlating Judah's deception of his father with Tamar's subsequent deception and public exposure of him is connected with the double occurrence of the imperative
"Recognize!" (הכר נא) in Genesis 37 and 38. Finally, the narrative
motif of divine acceptance of responsibility in court is argued from a
reassignment of the prepositional phrase "from me" (ממני) in Judah's
biblical declaration of Tamar's relative righteousness to the holy spirit.

   Through the technique of explicitly incorporating details of the
biblical text within later commentary employed in each of the five
cases described above, the gap between scripture and exegesis is mediated. In the context of *Genesis Rabba*, therefore, the format in which
authorities from different generations appear in tandem, each commenting on a different aspect of the biblical verses under consideration,

---

[12] For example, see Lev 20:12, as well as the laws which precede and follow this verse.

[13] This anonymous tradition in *Genesis Rabba* may allude to the whole complex of
traditions recorded fully in *Midraš Haggadol* concerning Tamar's presentation of
duplicate pledges. The latter source, discussed at length above in the third chapter,
explicitly connects exegetical motifs with specific features of the biblical text, including the different forms of the first two items of the pledge in Tamar's second statement (חתמך and פתילך in v. 18; החתמת and הפיתלים in v. 25, interpreted as plurals).
Interestingly, just as *Genesis Rabba* presents this tradition anonymously, so *Midraš
Haggadol* presents its whole complex of traditions anonymously, as the teaching of
"our rabbis."

does not signal an approval of exegetical relativism. Rather, this format imputes to rabbinic exegesis a timeless validity, tacitly arguing that it emerges directly from the biblical text itself, through the ongoing process of academic discussion of its distinctive features.

The commentary on Gen 38:25–26 appearing in this passage goes far beyond mere clarification of difficulties in the biblical text. At least as important as explaining problematic features of scripture, *Genesis Rabba* also interjects later rabbinic values into the biblical text. This commentary achieves this purpose by discussing selected lemmata that provide productive points of entry for post-biblical concerns into earlier biblical writings.[14] In the passage under consideration, for example, *Genesis Rabba* recreates the Bible as a rabbinic document by adding extra-biblical narrative elements[15] and moral evaluations,[16] presented on the authority of various sages as interpretation of details of the biblical narrative itself.

Interestingly, in this passage no single lexical item from Gen 38:25–26 receives more than one explanation. This economy does not universally characterize the treatment of biblical verses and words in *Genesis Rabba*, in which multiple, alternative interpretations are often listed one after another.[17] The simplicity of this passage raises the question of how one should best read this chain of traditions. Is this sequence of comments attributed to different sages from different times to be read as a unified composition with a consistent point of view, or as an eclectic selection of unrelated or even discordant explanations of discrete aspects of the biblical text? Judging from the evidence of

---

[14] The fact that the commentary in *Genesis Rabba* revolves around certain selected details of the biblical narrative confirms that its primary intention is not to explicate evenly all the words of the text, but to accomplish a broader cultural explication of scripture for contemporary generations.

[15] These include the loss and divine replacement of the pledge, Judah's reluctance to confess, Tamar's call for discernment of the hand of providence in the narrative events, and the divine intervention and assumption of responsibility in court.

[16] These include the negative evaluations of Judah through the assertions that he too is liable for punishment, that he tries to conceal his guilt, and that his predicament in Genesis 38 is linked to his involvement in the deception of his father in Genesis 37, as well as the more positive evaluation implicit in the divine acceptance of responsibility for the outcome of the larger narrative.

[17] Multiple interpretations of single verses and words are especially prominent in the beginning chapters of *Genesis Rabba* (specifically in the first twenty-nine chapters which cover only the first pericope of the annual lectionary cycle, known as Berešit), although they are not uncommon elsewhere. Within *Genesis Rabba* 85 itself, there are instances of multiple interpretations, concerning, for example, the significance of Judah's descent from his brothers (*Gen.Rab.* 85.1, 2, 3).

the expansion in *Targum Neofiti*, one early answer to the question of how to read a similar list of traditions was to consider it as a skeletal frame upon which to construct a coherent, secondary narrative. But in the context of the present discussion, the answer to this question can only emerge through an examination of the relation of the individual traditions in this passage to each other.

A productive method through which to determine if the five exegetical comments on Gen 38:25–26 contribute to a harmonious statement would be to examine their portrayal of the characters in Genesis 38. Remarkably, in light of his absence at this point in the biblical story, the dominant character in this passage is God, who figures prominently in all but one of the five comments.[18] For example, in the version of the motif of the lost pledge in *Genesis Rabba*, God is the only active character, and the additional narrative element of his special creation of a replacement pledge emphasizes that the outcome of the story is divinely determined. In the third, anonymous tradition, God's effective presence is once again stressed when Tamar exhorts Judah to recognize both his own role and the role of his creator in shaping the events of the narrative. In the following tradition concerning the double appearance of the imperative "Recognize!" in Genesis 37 and 38, it is God himself who acts as biblical exegete and chidingly interprets for Judah the significance of this verbal repetition, unlike in *Targum Neofiti*, where Judah himself makes the connection. In the final comment, the human drama of Judah's biblical reversal of judgment is eclipsed by God's immediate and complete assumption of responsibility for the events of the preceding narrative.

The majority of traditions contained in this passage therefore argue that the biblical events of Gen 38:25–26, and perhaps other earlier events of Genesis 38 as well, fulfill a divine intent. While this consistent emphasis on the pervasive role of God in the narrative corresponds to a general tendency in *Genesis Rabba* and other rabbinic literature to interject an explicit divine presence even where there is none in the biblical text, it also directly corresponds to more localized purposes of this commentary in its particular concretization of Genesis 38. Further elaboration of the exact nature of this correspondence will have to wait for the articulation of *Genesis Rabba*'s distinctive perspective on Genesis 38 in the pages which follow, but

---

[18] Only the remark attributed to R. Huna lacks any explicit interjection of a divine presence into the narrative at this point.

for now it is crucial to note that at least with respect to their emphasis on divine control over the narrative, the traditions grouped together
at this point in *Genesis Rabba* form an integrated set.

The emphasis on the active role of God is further underscored by
the absence of substantial positive development of the two characters
who actually do appear at this point in the biblical narrative. For
example, in marked contrast with *Targum Neofiti*'s expansive development of Tamar as a model of piety and self-sacrifice, *Genesis Rabba*
virtually neglects her character in this passage. Most significantly,
she is entirely absent in the version of the motif of the lost pledge
presented in this commentary, whereas the version of the same motif
in *Targum Neofiti* serves as the starting point for its distinctive elaboration of her character. In fact, the only addition to her biblical role
in this passage in *Genesis Rabba* occurs in the anonymous tradition, in
which she points beyond herself to the divine hand which guides the
narrative events. The taciturn treatment of Tamar in this passage
suggests that one must search other parts of *Genesis Rabba*'s commentary on Genesis 38 to discern the nature of its development of this
character in consonance with its larger perspectives on the biblical
narrative.

The puzzling and possibly inconsistent depiction of Judah raises
most forcefully the question of whether *Genesis Rabba* is merely a
random collection of unconnected traditions or whether it makes its
own distinctive statement even while incorporating some traditional
material at odds with it. The three traditions commenting on Gen
38:25 that refer to Judah portray him in a negative light, although
the misdeed of which he is accused varies in each. According to the
comment attributed to R. Huna, Judah is as guilty as Tamar of a
sin—presumably incest—deserving punishment by death. His guilt is
compounded in the anonymous tradition that immediately follows,
when he attempts to deny responsibility for Tamar's pregnancy.
Finally, the comment attributed to R. Johanan further discredits Judah
through the divine correlation of his earlier deception of Jacob in
Genesis 37 with its fitting consequence of Tamar's deception and
public humiliation of him in Genesis 38.[19]

---

[19] This tradition is also incorporated into this commentary's discussion of Gen
37:32 (*Gen.Rab.* 84.19). Elsewhere in *Genesis Rabba* as well, Judah is singled out as the
brother who brought the bloodied coat to Jacob for identification (*Gen.Rab.* 84.8;
95.2), even though the biblical text depicts all of the brothers acting in concert to
deceive their father.

Strikingly, *Genesis Rabba* presents these three traditions emphasizing Judah's guilt in close proximity and fails to include at this point
a single tradition ameliorating his behavior. Nor does *Genesis Rabba*
depict Judah as a contrite confessor of sins, as do *Targum Neofiti* and
many other rabbinic sources. In fact, in the second of these three
traditions involving Judah, he explicitly declines an opportunity to
repent publicly, and in the third his guilt and its consequence must
be pointed out to him by another character, namely God.

This failure to develop a natural opening for Judah's reformation
as a penitent sinner is especially remarkable in view of the importance of the theme of repentance in *Genesis Rabba* as a whole. In this
work, God contemplates the creation of repentance even before he
actually begins the creation of the world.[20] He mercifully offers an
opportunity for repentance to Adam in the garden of Eden,[21] to the
generation of the flood,[22] to the builders of the tower of Babel,[23] and
to the people of Sodom.[24] Repentance is of such value that God
destines Abraham himself to promote its increase throughout the
world.[25] Its significance extends to post-biblical generations as well,
since it is a human act with the power to end droughts,[26] to nullify
malevolent astrological influences of stars and planets,[27] and to drive
away attacking enemies.[28] Repentance is also the prerequisite for the
coming of the messianic age[29] and a means for gaining access to the
garden of Eden after death.[30] Outside of the context of its commentary on Genesis 38, *Genesis Rabba* does hold up particular individuals

---

[20] *Gen.Rab.* 1.4. In addition to contemplating the creation of repentance, God
creates the Tora and the throne of glory, and contemplates the creation of the
patriarchs, Israel, the temple, and the name of the messiah before creating the world.
[21] *Gen.Rab.* 21.6. Cain is also preserved through the power of repentance in *Gen.Rab.*
22.12, 13.
[22] *Gen.Rab.* 32.7.
[23] *Gen.Rab.* 38.9.
[24] *Gen.Rab.* 49.6. In addition, individual characters such as Ishmael and Esau,
whom *Genesis Rabba* consistently develops as villains despite scripture's relatively be-
nign portrayals of them, are similarly presented with the opportunity to repent. See
Gen.Rab. 38.12 and 75.11.
[25] *Gen.Rab.* 30.8.
[26] *Gen.Rab.* 13.14.
[27] *Gen.Rab.* 44.12. Prayer and righteousness (or charity) are similarly effective in
this tradition, as well as changing one's name and location, good deeds, and fasting.
[28] *Gen.Rab.* 44.16, if Freedman's interpretation is correct (*Genesis*, vol. 1, 372, n. 1).
[29] *Gen.Rab.* 2.4.
[30] *Gen.Rab.* 65.22. See also *Gen.Rab.* 65.9 and the version of *Genesis Rabba* 97 that
appears in MS Vat. Ebr. 30, which explain that God began to cause repeated illness
before death in order to promote repentance.

as examples of the virtue of repentance, but Judah is mentioned in this connection only once.[31] The lack of significant development of Judah as a model of repentance despite the general importance of this theme suggests that *Genesis Rabba* has another agenda in its treatment of this character and of the biblical narrative as a whole.

One can begin to appreciate this distinctive agenda through a closer analysis of *Genesis Rabba*'s commentary on Gen 38:26. As noted earlier in the discussion of the narrative expansion in *Targum Neofiti*, this biblical verse is the classical locus for the extra-biblical development of the motif of Judah's confession. The atomistic reading of the prepositional phrase "from me" (ממני) in Judah's biblical comparative statement "She is more righteous than I" (צדקה ממני) as an acknowledgment of his guilt is so wide-spread that even the relatively literal *Targum Onqelos* presents it as his confession, "She is pregnant by me" (מני מעדיא).[32] But in its treatment of Gen 38:26, *Genesis Rabba* does not forward any version of Judah's acceptance of responsibility for Tamar's situation—neither an acknowledgment of his negligence to give her to Shelah as in the biblical text, nor a confession of his incestuous sexual relations with his daughter-in-law as in other midrashic sources.

In fact, *Genesis Rabba* passes over most of Gen 38:26 without comment. In a clear testimony to the selectivity of this apparently comprehensive verse-by-verse commentary, only a single lexical item, the prepositional phrase "from me" (ממני), receives explication in a tradition

---

[31] In *Gen.Rab.* 71.5 Judah is celebrated, in the context of an extended wordplay on the Hebrew root "to acknowledge" (ידה), as a member of a genealogical lineage, including Leah and David, distinguished for its practice of praise and confession. Other figures, however, such as Cain (*Gen.Rab.* 22.12, 13) and Reuben (*Gen.Rab.* 82.11; 84.19) are presented more frequently as exemplary penitents. The atypical emphasis on the motif of Judah's confession in the New Version of the commentary on Jacob's blessing in Gen 49:8–12 (*Genesis Rabba* 97, NV) may be disregarded in this discussion, for while this homiletic expansion is found in a majority of the manuscripts, it is universally acknowledged to be a later interpolation. The same holds true for the brief allusion to Judah's confession in an alternate commentary on Jacob's blessing that exhibits affinities with the New Version (*Gen.Rab.* 99.8 in a Yemenite MS, Theodor/Albeck, vol. 3, 1279). By contrast, the more authentic version of the commentary on Jacob's blessing of Judah found in MS Vat. Ebr. 30 lacks explicit development of Judah's confession of his sexual relations with Tamar. See Theodor/Albeck, vol. 3, 1199, 1245, for discussion about the variant endings of *Genesis Rabba*. For a more general discussion of the additions and deletions in the manuscripts and printed editions of *Genesis Rabba*, see Albeck, "Introduction to *Genesis Rabba*," 103–4.

[32] This disparity in the interpretation of Gen 38:26 is but one example of a general lack of correspondence between *Genesis Rabba* and *Targum Onqelos*, pointing to the different communities of interpretation responsible for these two works.

about three divine interventions in human courts of law.[33] Certainly
the exclusive presentation of a tradition which isolates this phrase
and designates it as the speech of the holy spirit corresponds to the
emphasis on divine responsibility for the events of the biblical narrative in *Genesis Rabba*. But in addition to this emphasis, the exclusive
presentation of the motif of divine acceptance of responsibility also
contributes to a particular understanding of the character of Judah
in *Genesis Rabba*.

Targum Neofiti incorporates the motif of divine intervention into its
larger literary pattern of human willingness to die and divine salvation
based on Daniel 3; however, this motif plays a different function in
the context of this passage in *Genesis Rabba*. The immediate clarification of the providential nature of the preceding events in *Genesis Rabba*'s
commentary on Gen 38:26 overrides the biblical drama of Judah's
acceptance of responsibility and reversal of judgment and precludes
any development of the post-biblical motif of confession. Additionally, the focus on divine acceptance of responsibility deflects attention from any wrongdoing on Judah's part. In fact, if one reads *Genesis
Rabba*'s commentary on Gen 38:26 independently of the three preceding exegetical traditions concerning Gen 38:25, which stress Judah's
guilt, one might conclude that it intends to whitewash this character
by implying that his sexual relations with his daughter-in-law were
in innocent compliance with the larger designs of providence.[34]

---

[33] This instance is only one of many in which the appearance of a consistent
treatment of each verse in the biblical text masks the active judgments made within
Genesis Rabba about the larger significance of the scriptural material it explicates.
Genesis Rabba makes its argument concerning the significance of this narrative through
the technique of uneven commentary.

[34] Corresponding to the minimization of attention to Judah's sexual guilt here in
its commentary on Gen 38:26, *Genesis Rabba* does not elsewhere significantly develop
this figure as a negative example of immoral sexual behavior. This is not to say that
elsewhere in this commentary Judah's involvement with Tamar is completely ignored.
In *Gen.Rab.* 87.6, for example, R. Jose responds to a matron's charge that the biblical record falsifies its account of Joseph's encounter with Potiphar's wife in order
to preserve his reputation by reading "the stories of Reuben and Judah," whose
guilt is explicitly chronicled. See also the passing mention of "the story of Tamar"
in *Gen.Rab.* 92.9; 96, MSV; and 97.4. But despite the fact that Judah's actions in the
biblical narrative would amply allow for a similar critique, he is exempted from the
searing castigations which *Genesis Rabba* heaps upon Lot (*Gen.Rab.* 41.7; 51.9; 52.1,
3, 4), Ishmael (*Gen.Rab.* 53.11), and Esau (*Gen.Rab.* 63.10, 12; 65.1; 82.12, 14) for
their sexual immorality. The lack of development of the biblical motif of Judah's
incestuous relations with Tamar, especially in a commentary which so emphasizes
the serious nature of sexual deviation that it depicts it as the cause of the flood
(*Gen.Rab.* 23.2; 26.4; 26.5; 28.8; 30.2; 32.7), indicates intentional tact in the treatment of this important event in Israelite history.

An explanation in *Deuteronomy Rabba* of precisely the same heavenly words that appear in *Genesis Rabba*, "From me were these things" (ממני היו הדברים), supports this conclusion.[35] This explanation appears within a discussion of God's acclamation of Judah's special status as executor of the divine will in Ps 60:9:

> "Judah is my scepter" (Ps 60:9). Everything that Judah, who was the leader of the tribe, did, he did for my sake. As it is written, "Judah recognized and said, 'She is more righteous than I' (צדקה ממני)" (Gen 38:26). What does "from me" (ממני) mean? R. Huna said in the name of R. Idi, "Don't say that Tamar prostituted herself nor that Judah desired to commit fornication. Rather, 'From me were these things'" (ממני היו הדברים). That is what is meant by "Judah is my scepter" (Ps 60:9).[36]

The interpretation of the divine words, "From me were these things," in this passage explicitly rejects any notion of misconduct on the part of either Tamar or Judah in Genesis 38, since they were merely acting in accordance with divine intention. This same curious protestation of innocence through a shift of responsibility for immoral human behavior to God may tacitly lie behind the shorter version of the tradition of heavenly intervention in *Genesis Rabba* as well.

Genesis Rabba also implies Judah's innocence by placing an addendum immediately after the tradition concerning the holy spirit's intervention in human courts. This addendum consists of a clarification of two instances in which biblical characters are judged guilty of grievous sins:

> What does [scripture] say concerning the sons of Eli? "The sin of the youths was great," etc. (1 Sam 2:17). [And it is written, "that they lay with the women who were serving," etc. (1 Sam 2:22).] Is it really possible that the sons of the righteous Eli did this? Rather, when [the women] would bring their bird offerings for [their] purification, [his sons] would make them spend one night outside of their own homes. On account of this deed, the Holy One Blessed be He held them accountable as if they had acted immorally with [the women].

---

[35] In *Deuteronomy Rabba* this explanation is attributed to R. Huna in the name of R. Idi (fourth-century Palestinian). If the latter authority is R. Idi II, then he is yet another of the sages associated with the academy of Tiberias who figure so prominently in this section of commentary on Gen 38:25–26 in *Genesis Rabba*.

[36] *Deut.Rab.* 'Eqeb (Saul Liebermann, ed., *Midraš Debarim Rabba*, 2d ed. [Jerusalem: Wahrmann Books, 1964] 72). Other sources also record this tradition, including *Yalquṭ Siqili* and *Midraš Haggadol* on Genesis, and Nahmanides' introduction to the book of Job.

Similarly [concerning the sons of Samuel], "His sons did not walk in his ways, but they turned aside after profit," etc. (1 Sam 8:3). Is it really possible that the sons of the righteous Samuel did this? R. Berekiah said, "A caravan would pass through Beer-sheba, and [his sons] would neglect their public duties and attend to their personal business. On account of this deed, the Holy One Blessed be He held them accountable as if they had taken a bribe."[37]

In both cases, scripture portrays sons of righteous fathers receiving harsh judgment for serious infractions, despite the fact that they are only guilty of much lesser misdeeds. The question of why the discussion of Eli and Samuel's sons appears at this point in the commentary is an important one for reconstructing its portrayal of Judah. One possible answer to this question is that this addendum depicting two additional divine judgments is somewhat gratuitously grafted onto *Genesis Rabba*'s commentary on Gen 38:26 because of its association with the tradition of the three divine judgments in human courts in some earlier source.[38] If this is the case, then the discussion of the sons of righteous fathers makes no significant contribution to *Genesis Rabba*'s portrayal of Judah and may be safely ignored.

But the tradition about the sons of Eli and Samuel is not connected with the tradition of the three divine interventions in human courts in other extant sources,[39] and there are also internal reasons for carefully considering the implications that this addendum has for

---

[37] *Gen.Rab.* 85.12. Both the tradition concerning the sons of Eli and the tradition concerning the sons of Samuel are also found in *y. Ketub.* 13.1; *y. Soṭa* 1.4; *Midr. Šemu'el* 7; and *b. Šabb.* 55b–56a. The tradition concerning the sons of Eli is found independently in *b. Yoma* 9a–b and *'Ag.Ber.* 41.

[38] Neusner, for example, maintains that the traditions concerning the sons of Eli and Samuel "have nothing to do with the present matter at all" and concludes that all of *Gen.Rab.* 85.12 "obviously formed a syllogistic proposition before it was included here" (*Genesis Rabbah: New American Translation*, vol. 3, 216). There is no doubt that at various points *Genesis Rabba* does present small collections of previously edited material, in which only the initial tradition is immediately germane to the biblical verse under discussion. See for example *Gen.Rab.* 85.3, where the discussion of Judah's failure to go far enough in delivering Joseph from his brothers' murderous intent continues with an additional discussion about Moses' unrealized attempt to bury Joseph's bones in Shechem. Similar complexes of traditions connecting Judah's sale of Joseph with Moses' attention to Joseph's bones may be found in other sources, including *b. Soṭa* 13b.

[39] None of the other sources that refer to all three divine court appearances, including *b. Mak.* 23b; *Eccl.Rab.* 10.16–17; and *Midr. Tehillim*, printed ed., addendum to Ps 17:15–17, continue with a discussion of the sons of Eli and Samuel. The traditions about these sons of righteous fathers are similarly absent from sources that focus on only one of the three divine interventions in human court, including *b. Soṭa* 10b; *Deut.Rab.* 'Eqeb (Liebermann, *Midraš Debarim Rabba*, 72); and *Midr. Šemu'el*, 14. Of special interest, however, are the intriguing cases in which the two traditions

the characterization of Judah in *Genesis Rabba*. The introduction of other sons of righteous fathers in the context of a discussion of a story concerning one of the sons of Jacob, who is consistently described as "righteous" in *Genesis Rabba* despite his biblical frailties,[40] sets up an implicit comparison. This comparison between the sons of Eli and Samuel and the fourth son of Jacob is made all the more compelling by the fact that the sins imputed to the former in scripture—sexual impropriety and perverting justice for monetary gain—resemble those committed by Judah in Genesis 38 and 37, where he engages in incestuous relations with his daughter-in-law and leads his brothers in selling Joseph for profit.

With this comparison operative, the double denial that the sons of righteous fathers could possibly have perpetrated the heinous crimes attributed to them in the biblical record subtly argues for Judah's innocence as well. If Eli's sons are guiltless of serious sexual sin despite a clear scriptural statement to the contrary, Jacob's son too might be guiltless of a similar sin with Tamar imputed to him in the biblical text. If Samuel's sons are innocent of perverting justice by taking bribes, Jacob's son too might be innocent of intentionally perverting justice for profit by selling his own brother.[41]

Within the framework of the comparison established by the juxtaposition of these traditions in *Genesis Rabba*, Judah's innocence is further emphasized by the discrepancy in divine treatment of the sons of Eli and Samuel and of this son of Jacob. Whereas in the two traditions

---

concerning the sons of Eli and the sons of Samuel are joined with a third tradition concerning Tamar's public loitering at the entrance of Enaim in *y. Ketub.* 13.1; *y. Soṭa* 1.4; and *Midr. Šemuʾel* 7. The version recorded twice in the Palestinian Talmud ingeniously explains how the seemingly unfavorable biblical reports concerning the behavior of Tamar, Eli's sons, and Samuel's sons "are intended to express praise." In the passage in *Gen.Rab.* 85.12 currently under consideration, the traditions about the sons of Eli and Samuel are still connected with an event in Genesis 38, although a transfer of focus from the questionable behavior of Tamar to the questionable behavior of Judah has been effected. Perhaps the editors of *Genesis Rabba* intended this new configuration of traditions "to express praise" for the figure of Judah as well.

[40] For example, Jacob is described as "righteous" (צדיק), often in contrast to his evil brother Esau, in *Gen.Rab.* 65.15; 68.2, 5; 69.7; 72.3; 74.13; 75.8; 76.2.

[41] Significant in this regard are the attempts in *Gen.Rab.* 84.17 and 85.3 to portray Judah's suggestion to sell Joseph not as a mercenary scheme, but as a commendable effort to spare his younger brother from the murderous intent of his other siblings, although *Gen.Rab.* 85.3 does point out that he could have better served his younger brother by returning him safely to their father. Alternatively, the theme of perversion of justice might suggest Judah's failure to fulfill his promise to give Tamar to Shelah. As discussed more fully below, *Genesis Rabba* consistently minimizes Judah's guilt in withholding the son promised his daughter-in-law, most explicitly in *Gen.Rab.* 85.5, which approves of his caution.

in the addendum God charges the former with grave crimes in scripture despite the fact that they committed lesser offenses, this same harsh
judge brings no charge whatsoever against Judah in the midrashic
tradition about the divine voice. Instead God accepts full responsibility when the holy spirit declares "From me were these things."

This analysis of *Genesis Rabba*'s portrayal of the character of Judah
in its commentary on Gen 38:25–26 suggests that this work is inconsistent. On the one hand, it presents traditions depicting Judah as a
figure who is guilty of a capital sin, who furthermore attempts to
obfuscate the truth and must be divinely chastised. On the other,
this commentary's editorial selection and organization of materials
related to Gen 38:26 suggests that Judah is an innocent party who
acts in accordance with the larger plans of providence.

Genesis Rabba's inconsistent development of the character of Judah
underscores questions that are at the heart of this discussion of biblical interpretation through anthological commentary. Does this document argue through its presentation of traditions at tension with each
other for the relativity of biblical interpretation, in which equally
valid exegetical options may either be accepted or rejected by students of scripture? Or does *Genesis Rabba* make a larger, consistent
statement concerning the significance of Genesis 38, which transcends
the project of recording sometimes contradictory trajectories of traditional interpretation?

In order to begin to answer these questions, one must first turn
from *Genesis Rabba*'s commentary on the climax of the biblical narrative to its commentary on Judah's initial encounter with Tamar at
the entrance of Enaim in Gen 38:15–16. Examination of the portrayal of Judah's behavior and motives vis-à-vis Tamar in this earlier
part of the document will determine whether the binary depiction of
this character first as guilty and than as innocent in its commentary
on Gen 38:25–26 is merely a fluke, or whether it is the result of an
intentional editorial policy. Additionally, this section will suggest a
direction of inquiry leading to comprehension of the distinctive emphasis of *Genesis Rabba*'s interpretation of Genesis 38.

Case Study 2: Genesis Rabba's *Commentary on Gen 38:15–16a*

In Gen 38:15–16a, the narrator emphasizes both Judah's ignorance
of the identity of the woman he takes for a prostitute and his verbal
initiative in the encounter:

Judah saw her and thought she was a prostitute, for she covered her face. He turned aside to her on the road and said, "Come now, let me come into you," for he did not know that she was his daughter-in-law.

In *Genesis Rabba*, two comments on this biblical passage appear in tandem, defining in contrasting terms Judah's perception of the woman, his motivation for approaching her, and the nature of their union:

> "Judah saw," etc. (Gen 38:15). R. Aha said, "A man should familiarize himself with his wife's sister and his female relatives. Why is this? So that he doesn't stumble concerning one of them. And from whom do you learn this? From Judah: 'He thought she was a prostitute' (Gen 38:15). Why is this? 'Because she covered her face' (Gen 38:16) when she was in her father-in-law's house."

> Another interpretation of "Judah saw" (Gen 38:15): He did not look at her. Because she covered her face he said, "If she were a prostitute, would she cover her face?" R. Johanan said, "He wanted to pass by, but the Holy One Blessed be He assigned the angel in charge of desire to him. He said to him, 'Where are you going, Judah? From whence are kings and redeemers to arise?' 'And he turned aside to her' (Gen 38:16) under compulsion and not of his own free will."[42]

The first of these very different understandings of the biblical encounter at Enaim focuses on Judah's failure to recognize his daughter-in-law. In the biblical narrative this failure functions as an important condition

---

[42] *Gen.Rab.* 85.8. There is in fact another version of the initial encounter between Judah and Tamar at the entrance of Enaim in the concluding portion of *Gen.Rab.* 85.7, immediately preceding the two traditions quoted here. A discussion of the curious phrase "the entrance of Enaim" (פתח עינים) in Gen 38:14, which may also be translated as "gate of eyes" or "opening of eyes," provides the context for this third version, concentrating on Tamar's role in facilitating the narrative events rather than on Judah's. This tradition first presents Tamar as a prayerful intercessor for the success of her venture "to the gate to which all eyes are lifted" (לפתח שכל העינים תלויות לו). It next portrays her soliciting Judah's interest, or "opening [his] eyes" (שפתחה את העינים), by declaring her availability with the words, "I am clean, and I am unmarried." The motif of Tamar's prayer at Enaim and the significance of its contents will be discussed further below. As for the motif of Tamar's sexual initiative, although it is somewhat in keeping with her portrayal in the *Testament of Judah* as a temptress, it also functions to dramatize Judah's moral discretion in choosing a sexual partner who is neither menstruating nor married. A similar version of the tradition concerning Tamar's seduction of Judah is found in *y. Ketub.* 13.1 and *y. Soṭa* 1.4. A longer version is found in *b. Soṭa* 10b, in which Judah's fastidious effort to select an appropriate partner is explicitly expressed through his probing questions to the woman he meets on the road, which Tamar answers with claims to be a proselyte, an unmarried woman, an orphan, and not a menstruant.

for the success of Tamar's stratagem and offers an ameliorating cir-
cumstance for the act of incest which follows. The midrashic interpretation attributed to R. Aha (fourth-century Palestinian), however,
alters the reason that Judah does not recognize Tamar. Whereas in
the biblical narrative he does not recognize her because her face is
covered, in this tradition he does not recognize her because her face
is exposed for the first time in his presence, since she constantly veiled
herself when she lived with him as a daughter-in-law.[43]

This shift in location of Tamar's veiling in accordance with contemporary conventions of dress positively attributes to her character
a habit of modest decorum, but it does not go beyond the biblical
narrative in providing an excuse for Judah's behavior. In fact, this
tradition makes explicit the charge of unwitting incest implicit in the
biblical explanation in Gen 38:16 that "he did not know she was his
daughter-in-law." The lesson of how to avoid stumbling through inad-
vertent sexual relations with female relatives derived from this episode unmistakably marks Judah as guilty of this very deed. In addition,
it also imputes a further fault to this character, consisting of his earlier
failure to acquaint himself with his daughter-in-law as a precaution.[44]

By contrast, the second reformulation of the encounter—clearly
demarcated from the first by the formulaic phrase "another interpretation"—labors to acquit Judah of all charges of inappropriate
intention and behavior. In this second midrashic version of events,
Judah does see a veiled woman on the way to Timnah as in the
biblical narrative, but he declines the opportunity even to appraise
her charms, since it is obvious from her conservative dress that she
is not a prostitute.[45]

---

[43] Tamar's seemly comportment in her father-in-law's house is also discussed in
the previous chapter, in connection with a gloss in *Tg.Neof.* Gen 38:15. The tradition that Tamar covered her face in her father-in-law's house may also be found in
b. Meg. 10b and *b. Soṭa* 10b, although these sources focus on Tamar's meritorious
modesty rather than Judah's negligence. Criticism of Judah's failure to acquaint himself with his daughter-in-law is also found in *Yal. Šimʿoni* Gen 38:15 and in an abbreviated form in *Tanḥ.* Wayyēšeb 9.17.

[44] Interestingly, in this tradition there is no censure on the activity which Judah
himself intends in the biblical narrative, namely, consorting with a prostitute. Similarly in the tradition which directly follows, Judah does not attempt to avoid contact
with a prostitute, but with a respectable, modestly veiled woman.

[45] Possibly underlying this change in events is an inelegant but more flattering
reading of the biblical phrase "he thought she was a prostitute" (חשבה לזונה) as "he
thought she was not a prostitute" (חשבה לא זונה), by separating the preposition ל
from the noun "prostitute" (זונה) that it marks as a secondary object of the verb "he
thought" and revocalizing this preposition as the negative particle (לא). The convention for women's dress outside of the home presupposed by this tradition is explicitly

To this second, anonymous tradition, *Genesis Rabba* joins an additional account of extra-biblical events attributed to R. Johanan (third-century Palestinian, founder of the school of Tiberias). This account further emphasizes Judah's lack of immoral intentions towards Tamar by portraying his attempt to pass by this respectably covered woman. In addition, it illustrates his willingness to comply piously with divine directives—even those contrary to his own desires—when it depicts his return to fulfill the heavenly purpose of bringing Israel's kings and redeemers into the world articulated by the angel.[46]

Besides improving Judah's reputation, the second midrashic interpretation of the biblical narrative interjects a controlling divine presence into verses of scripture which remain consistently on a mundane level. In the *Tanḥuma*'s version of this expansion, a feature of the biblical text is specified as the clue that supernatural forces lie behind Judah's decision to approach the woman on the side of the road.[47] This feature is the usage of the verb "to turn aside" (נטה) at the beginning of Gen 38:16 (ויט), which is also used to describe the action of Balaam's she-ass after seeing the angel of the LORD in Num 22:23 (ותט). Since an angel sent by God is responsible for the donkey's swerving from the road in Numbers, an angel sent by God is introduced into the drama of Judah's swerving from the road in this midrashic reading of the Genesis narrative. Through its inclusion of this midrashic tradition, *Genesis Rabba* argues that the sexual encounter at Enaim, with its historically important outcome, is not the result of human intrigue and lust; instead, it is an expression of divine providence.[48] The emphasis on the guiding role of God in this tradition therefore echoes the

---

stated in *Gen.Rab.* 17.8, which specifies that women should cover their heads when they go out in public.

[46] This tradition is also recorded in *Yal. Šimʿoni* Gen 38:15–16. A variant of this description of events is recorded in *Tanḥ.* Wayyešeb 9.17, where Judah scorns the woman he considers a prostitute until God sends the angel Michael, the guardian angel of Israel, to summon him reluctantly to his procreative duties. The divine intention to bring forth royal and messianic antecedents from Judah and Tamar's union is also expressed in *'Ag.Ber.* 63(64), although in a different manner. Concerning *Genesis Rabba*'s depiction of Judah's intercourse with Tamar as disinterested religious duty, it is significant that *Gen.Rab.* 85.5 anticipates this concept earlier in its expansive discussion of the levirate law. This early discussion of the suspension of incest laws for a greater social good predisposes one to interpret Judah and Tamar's incestuous union more sympathetically, since it produced a lineage of vital importance for Israel's well-being.

[47] *Tanḥ.* Wayyešeb 9.17.

[48] The importance of Judah and Tamar's union in *Genesis Rabba*'s version of Israel's history is emphasized by God's sending of an angel to ensure its accomplishment.

strong divine presence already noted in the earlier discussion of *Genesis Rabba*'s commentary on Gen 38:25–26.

But to return to the portrayal of the character of Judah, *Genesis Rabba*'s commentary on the encounter at Enaim in Gen 38:15–16a presents the same basic bifurcation between Judah the guilty and Judah the innocent noted previously in its commentary on the narrative climax in Gen 38:25–26. The first midrashic reading in this section, with its emphasis on Judah's guilt, corresponds to the three traditions portraying this character in a negative light in *Genesis Rabba*'s commentary on Gen 38:25. The second midrashic reading, with its emphasis on Judah's innocent intentions and his compliance with divine designs, corresponds to the material edited in *Genesis Rabba*'s commentary on Gen 38:26. Because this juxtaposition of interpretive trajectories at tension with each other occurs twice within *Genesis Rabba*'s commentary on Genesis 38, it is most likely not accidental, but rather indicative of an intentional editorial policy.

But what is the significance of this intentional juxtaposition of disparate portraits of Judah in *Genesis Rabba*? These two interpretive directions actually articulate a tension inherent in the biblical narrative itself when read within its larger canonical context. As noted in the first chapter, reading the biblical story of Judah and Tamar's encounter in light of biblical laws against incest between father-in-law and daughter-in-law such as Lev 20:12 suggests that both characters are guilty of a capital offense. On the other hand, their illicit union leads not to punishment by death but to the origins of the royal and messianic lineage.[49] Reading backwards from this positive outcome of Judah's sexual association with Tamar, the midrashic imagination attributes to these characters the most pious motives and behavior.

In the two sections examined so far, *Genesis Rabba* does not resolve this tension by forwarding one potential interpretation of the biblical

---

The births of Perez and Zerah do not match the birth of Isaac to Abraham and Sarah in importance, however, since, according to *Gen.Rab.* 53.6, in the latter case God acts directly to ensure Sarah's pregnancy and not through the agency of an angel. But an angel has a vital role in arranging another important match in biblical history in *Gen.Rab.* 59.10, when he leads both Rebekah and Abraham's servant to the well, thus initiating the negotiations that result in the former's marriage to Isaac. God devotes much of his attention to arranging marital unions, according to *Gen.Rab.* 68.4.

[49] In *Genesis Rabba* Israel's kingship is generally viewed as a positive institution, and the messianic age is viewed as the longed-for end of hostile Roman occupation or more generally as a period of justice and peace. By contrast, the biblical evaluation of kingship is not as uniformly positive (1 Sam 8:4–22; Deut 17:14–17).

narrative and its characters and suppressing the other. Instead, both interpretations are presented side by side in the highly articulated form of midrashic traditions, with no attempt at harmonization. Through this technique, the contradictory voices within scripture itself are amplified, so that they may be easily heard by the reader of *Genesis Rabba*.[50] But does *Genesis Rabba* do more than record the range of rabbinic exegesis on an ambivalent biblical text? Does it make any pervasive argument about the significance of Genesis 38 over and beyond its secretarial duty of recording disparate traditions about various aspects of this biblical narrative?

In connection with this question, it is interesting to note that in both *Genesis Rabba*'s commentary on the events at Enaim in *Gen.Rab.* 85.8 and its commentary on the climax of the biblical narrative in *Gen.Rab.* 85.11–12, the portrait of Judah as an innocent and obedient pawn in heaven's designs follows the portrait of Judah as a sexual miscreant. This posterior placement in both cases may indicate an unwillingness to let traditions emphasizing Judah's culpability stand unchallenged.[51] Additionally, the passages which depict Judah as an innocent accomplice to divine purposes outweigh in sheer length the passages which depict him as a culpable lecher.

Regardless of whether or not position and length are generally indicators of emphasis in *Genesis Rabba*, important thematic connections between the two passages depicting Judah as innocent examined above and material found elsewhere in this commentary's treatment of Genesis 38 suggest that structurally this second portrait is more significant than the first. One theme repeated in the two depictions of Judah as innocent and in other parts of the commentary on Genesis 38 is the firm control which God exerts over the events of the biblical narrative. Another theme found in the depiction of Judah as innocent at Enaim in *Gen.Rab.* 85.8 and emphasized elsewhere in *Genesis Rabba* is the inception of the royal and messianic lineage through Judah and Tamar's union.

Indeed, these two themes are inseparable in the argument *Genesis Rabba* makes through selection and arrangement of exegetical traditions

---

[50] For a discussion of the midrashic representation of contradictory potentialities within scripture in the *Mekilta de Rabbi Ishmael*, see Daniel Boyarin, "Voices in the Text: Midrash and the Inner Tension of Biblical Narrative (Ex. 16)," *RB* 93 (1986) 581–97.

[51] Neusner, *Comparative Midrash*, 27, similarly argues in a discussion of *Gen.Rab* 1.1 that the final position in the presentation of two different interpretations enjoys prominence.

that, whatever else certain verses of Genesis 38 may teach, this biblical narrative as a whole is fundamentally the story of God's intervention at the very beginning of Israel's history to prepare for the
important institution of kingship. One expression of divine control
over the establishment of this institution for the leadership and restoration of Israel has already been noted in *Gen.Rab.* 85.8, when God
sends the angel of desire to guide Judah back to Tamar with the
questions, "Where are you going Judah? From whence are kings and
redeemers to arise?" Other passages in *Genesis Rabba* reiterate that
the central point of Genesis 38 is God's concern to provide king and
messiah for Israel. In fact, the introductory section which prefaces
the subsequent verse-by-verse commentary on the biblical narrative
portrays divine providence at work, establishing the royal and messianic genealogy for the well-being of Israel's future.

ROYAL AND MESSIANIC THEMES

Four Prophetic Introductions

Genesis Rabba's division of Genesis into approximately one hundred
sections[52] is highlighted by the presence of one or more introductions at the head of the vast majority of these divisions.[53] Formally,
these introductions exemplify the most widely attested type of literary construction in the rabbinic corpus, commonly known as the
"proem" (פתיחה).[54] The definitive characteristic of the proem consists
of its presentation of a secondary scriptural verse selected from the
Writings, or less commonly from the Prophets or the Pentateuch, as
a preface to the opening verse of the biblical passage under primary

---

[52] In general, printed editions of *Genesis Rabba* are divided into one hundred chapters, each dealing with a different passage of scripture. The manuscripts, however,
vary, containing as few as ninety-seven and as many as one hundred and one chapters. The latter number represents the number of chapters in MS Vat. Ebr. 30. Although most of the discrepancies between divisions occur in the final chapters, the
printed editions and the manuscripts disagree in the numbering of chapters 40–43
as well. As a general rule, the early chapters in *Genesis Rabba* (particularly 1–29)
treat much shorter passages of scripture than the later chapters, occasionally merely
a single verse.
[53] Albeck cites only seven exceptions to the general rule that each chapter opens
with a formally distinctive introduction ("Introduction to *Genesis Rabba*," 11).
[54] For a classic discussion of the proem, see Wilhelm Bacher, *Die Proëmien der alten
jüdischen Homilie: Beitrag zur Geschichte des jüdischen Schriftauslegung und Homiletik* (Leipzig:
J. C. Hinrichs, 1913).

consideration.[55] Typically, exposition of the forwarded secondary verse illuminates some aspect of the primary verse which concludes the proem. Even in its most rudimentary form, however, when the proem consists merely of two juxtaposed biblical verses, the former serves to guide the interpretation of the latter through its establishment of a specific textual context within which the opening verse of a biblical passage should be read.

In scholarly reconstructions of its origins and cultural setting, the classic type of proem found in *Genesis Rabba* and other early rabbinic works is generally associated with synagogue homiletics, although the exact relationship between proem and sermon remains unresolved.[56] Similarly, the complicated relation between the divisions of Genesis in *Genesis Rabba* marked by the presence of one or more proems and the divisions of the triennial Palestinian lectionary cycle continues to defy solution, although there may be a closer correspondence between the two than a superficial overview might suggest.[57] Regardless of the exact relation between the proems in *Genesis Rabba* and synagogue sermons based on the pericopes of the lectionary cycle, this commentary's consistent introduction of its own internal divisions with one or more proems reveals an editorial intentionality, at least with respect to form.[58]

---

[55] According to Albeck, 199 of the proems in *Genesis Rabba* cite a verse from the Writings, 37 from the Prophets, and 10 from the Pentateuch ("Introduction to *Genesis Rabba*," 12–13).

[56] The question of whether the proem constitutes an introduction to the sermon or the sermon itself has been answered in various ways by scholars including Joseph Heinemann, הפתיחתות במדרשי האגדה: מקורן ותפקידן [The proems in aggadic midrashim: Their origin and function], *WCJS* 4 (1965) 3–47; P. Schäfer, "Die Peticha—ein Proömium?" *Kairos* 12 (1970) 216–19; and K. E. Grözinger, "Prediger gottseliger Diesseitszuversicht," *FJB* 5 (1977) 42–64. Discussion of the subsequent development of the proem as a complex literary genre in later works such as the *Tanḥuma* may be found in M. Bregman, פתיחתאות מעגליות ופתיחתאות "זו היא שנאמרה ברוח הקודש" [Circular proems and proems beginning with the formula "this is what is said through the holy spirit"], in מחקרים באגדה תרגומים ותפלות ישראל לזכר יוסף היינמן [Studies in aggada, targum, and Jewish liturgy, in memory of Joseph Heinemann], ed. E. Fleischer and J. J. Petuchowski (Jerusalem: Magnes Press; Cincinnati: Hebrew Union College Press, 1981) 34–51.

[57] Heinemann, for example, asserts that the influence of the triennial lectionary cycle on the structure of *Genesis Rabba* may be clearly seen if one eliminates from consideration chapters headed by defective, false, or solitary proems ("Structure and Divisions of *Genesis Rabba*").

[58] Heinemann ("Structure and Divisions of *Genesis Rabba*," 288–89) and Neusner (*Comparative Midrash*, 89–90) both point to the editorial hand evident in the formal organization of this commentary.

This formal intentionality alerts one to watch for corresponding thematic intentionality in the proems that preface *Genesis Rabba*'s verse-by-verse commentary on Genesis 38. The preface to this biblical narrative, universally attested to in extant lectionary lists as an independent pericope of the triennial Palestinian lectionary cycle,[59] consists of the following list of four proems:

> "At that time," etc. (Gen 38:1). "Judah has been false," etc. (Mal 2:11). He [God] said to him [Judah], "You have denied, Judah. You have lied, Judah." "An abomination has been committed in Israel," etc. (Mal 2:11). "For Judah has profaned (כי חלל יהודה)" (Mal 2:11). You have become profane, Judah (נעשתה חולין יהודה), "the holiness of the Lord (קדש יי") whom He loves, and have married the daughter (בת) of a foreign god" (Mal 2:11). "At that time, [Judah] went down (וירד)," etc. (Gen 38:1).

> "I will yet bring the dispossessor to you, inhabitant of Moreshah. As far as Adullam will come the glory of Israel (כבוד ישראל)" (Mic 1:15): the Holy One of Israel (קדושו שלישראל). As far as Adullam will come the king of Israel (מלכן שלישראל). "As far as Adullam he will come:" "At that time," etc. (Gen 38:1).

> R. Samuel b. Nahman began [his discourse with the verse]: "For I know the thoughts (המחשבות)," etc. (Jer 29:11). The tribes were busy with the sale of Joseph, Jacob was busy with his sackcloth and fasting, Judah was busy taking a wife, while the Holy One Blessed be He (והקב"ה) was creating the light of the king messiah (מלך המשיח). "At that time (ויהי בעת ההיא)," etc. (Gen 38:1).

> "Before she labored, she gave birth" (Isa 66:7). Before the first oppressor (משעבד הראשון) was born, the final redeemer (גואל האחרון) was born. "At that time" (Gen 38:1).[60]

In each of these four proems a verse from a different prophetic book appears in the initial position, despite the fact that verses from the Writings are much more commonly cited in the proems of *Genesis Rabba*.[61] Although the exclusive reliance on the prophets to introduce this narrative may be due simply to a coincidental presence of

---

[59] The chart in Mann, *Palestinian Triennial Cycle*, Appendix 1, liv, presents a concise summary of the evidence from lectionary lists, indicating that Genesis 38 figured as the thirty-first, thirty-third, thirty-fourth, or thirty-fifth pericope in different versions of the Palestinian lectionary cycle.

[60] *Gen.Rab.* 85.1.

[61] The prominence of verses from the Writings in proems is by no means an exclusive feature of *Genesis Rabba*, but rather is a general phenomenon of the genre.

appropriate verbal and thematic material in these books, it immediately imparts at least a superficial unity to this list of four proems. The appearance of unity must be tested by further analysis, however, to determine whether these four proems may be read as a cohesive statement concerning the significance of Genesis 38, or whether they must be read independently as discrete and unrelated introductions to the chapter.[62]

The following analysis begins with an examination of each of the four proems, including comparison with related material from other sources. It then identifies specific verbal and thematic connections between the four proems attesting to the intentional editorial activity behind their collection, and it finally articulates the overarching statement made through the editorial juxtaposition of these four proems. This overarching statement is of particular importance, for the rest of *Genesis Rabba*'s commentary on Genesis 38 must be read in light of the proems' emphasis on royal and messianic origins.

In the first proem phrases from Mal 2:11, occasionally interspersed with paraphrastic explanations, serve as an introduction to Gen 38:1:

> "At that time," etc. (Gen 38:1) "Judah has been false," etc. (Mal 2:11). He [God] said to him [Judah], "You have denied, Judah. You have lied, Judah." "An abomination has been committed in Israel," etc. (Mal 2:11). "For Judah has profaned (חלל יהודה)" (Mal 2:11). You have become profane, Judah (נעשתה חולין יהודה), "the holiness of the LORD (קדש י"י) whom he loves, and have married the daughter (בת) of a foreign god" (Mal 2:11). "At that time, [Judah] went down (וירד)," etc. (Gen 38:1).[63]

In its biblical context, Mal 2:11 is part of a general prophetic indictment of the males of the early second temple period community—designated collectively as Judah—for desecrating the sanctuary through intermarriage with foreign women. This verse charges:

> Judah has been false, and an abomination has been committed in Israel and in Jerusalem, for Judah has profaned the LORD's sanctuary, which he loves, and has married the daughter of a foreign god.

---

[62] The slightly abbreviated version of the same four proems in identical order in *Yal. Šimʿoni* Gen 38:1 and the altered and augmented presentation of similar material in *Tanḥ.* Wayyešeb 9.9–11 suggest that these four proems were viewed as a single, integrated unit, although not a rigidly fixed one.

[63] Versions of this proem are found in *Yal. Šimʿoni* Gen 38:1; *Yal. Šimʿoni* Mal 2:11; and *Tanḥ.* Wayyešeb 9.9.

314	CHAPTER FOUR

In its application to the opening events in Genesis 38, however, this
verse is interpreted as a direct divine rebuke of one particular man,
namely Jacob's son Judah, for his marriage with a Canaanite woman.
This reinterpretation is made explicit in the paraphrase of the general third person charge in the Bible, "Judah has been false,"[64] as
God's rebuke of a single individual, "He said to him, 'You have
denied, Judah. You have lied, Judah.'"[65]

The most obvious connection between this verse from Malachi
and the narrative events of Genesis 38 consists of the former's concluding phrase, "he has married the daughter (בת) of a foreign god,"
which thematically and verbally recalls Judah's marriage with "the
daughter (בת) of a Canaanite man" in Gen 38:2.[66] This point of
contact between the biblical passages, as well as the general emphasis on the theme of intermarriage in the larger prophetic context of
Mal 2:10–16, tempts one to make sense of the entire proem in terms
of Judah's deviant foreign marriage. If this is the case, then God's
accusations in the gloss of the opening phrase of Mal 2:11 ("He said
to him, 'You have denied, Judah. You have lied, Judah.'") refer to
Judah's treachery against the spirit of Abraham and Isaac's prohibitions of marriage with Canaanite women for their own sons.[67]

The choice of the verbs "to deny" (כפר) and "to lie" (שקר) in this
gloss remains puzzling, however, given the fact that in the opening
verses of Genesis 38 there is no explicit fraudulence. Indeed, in the
larger context of this commentary, these verbs recall the tradition in
Gen.Rab. 85.11 discussed above, in which Judah "sought to deny"
(לכפר) his involvement with Tamar. In addition, the understanding
of this proem solely in terms of Judah's marriage with a Canaanite
does not entirely explain one of its most curious features. If the entire

[64] The Hebrew form of the verb in this phrase from Mal 2:11 (בגדה) is a bit
unusual, however, in that it appears to have a feminine ending. Perhaps this irregularity facilitated the switch from third to second person, which ends in the same
long final vowel (בגדתה).

[65] The divine speaker is identified explicitly in two manuscripts, MS Paris 149 and
MS Mincaan 97, which read, "The Holy One, Blessed be He, said to him, 'You
have denied, Judah. You have lied, Judah.'"

[66] The fact that this proem forges an important connection with the second verse
of the biblical chapter is not unusual in Genesis Rabba, in which proems conclude
with either the first or second verse of the biblical passage under discussion. See the
discussion in Albeck, "Introduction to Genesis Rabba," 12.

[67] See Gen 24:3 and 28:1. Theodor, in his commentary Minḥat Yehuda, which
appears underneath the apparatus in Theodor/Albeck, 1029, argues in this fashion.
Also worthy of note is the explicit development of the theme of Judah's falsity in
marrying a Canaanite in the expanded version of this proem in Tanḥ. Wayyešeb 9.9.

verse in Mal 2:11 is intended to refer to his marriage, why is it segmented through various means into four distinctive phrases, only some of which receive additional explanation?[68] Significantly, a similar subdivision of Mal 2:11 into four phrases occurs in the version of this proem found in *Midraš Haggadol*:

> Another interpretation of "Judah went down:" This is what scripture says: "Judah has been false, and an abomination has been committed in Israel" (Mal 2:11). "Judah has been false" in that he said to his father, "Recognize!" (Gen 37:32). "And an abomination has been committed in Israel" in that they sold Joseph. "For Judah has profaned the holiness of the LORD" (Mal 2:11) in that he departed from his brothers and from his father's house. "And he married the daughter of a foreign god" (Mal 2:11) in that he married a Canaanite woman. What was his punishment? "The LORD will cut off for the man who does this [every-one who is] vigilant (ער) and responsive (וענה)" (Mal 2:12). So Er (ער) and Onan (אונן) died. What brought all of this upon Judah? The fact that he counseled the sale of Joseph.[69]

In this passage, each of four phrases from Mal 2:11 is correlated with a different sin committed by Judah: his deception of his father, his part in the sale of Joseph, his abandonment of his family, and his marriage with a Canaanite. The following verse, Mal 2:12, is then interpreted as referring to the death of his sons as a consequence of these sins—especially his advocacy of the sale of his brother, reiterated at the conclusion of this proem.[70] This interpretation of Mal 2:12 as

---

[68] The first phrase "Judah has been false" (בגדה יהודה) is terminated by the abbreviation "etc." (וגו') and set apart from the next phrase by a gloss. The second phrase, "an abomination has been committed in Israel" (ותועבה נעשתה בישראל), lacks the final biblical word "and Jerusalem" (ובירושלם) in the best MSS (as well as in the version of this proem found in *Midr. Haggadol* Gen 38:1), perhaps since the inclusion of a reference to this city would make application of this phrase to Judah's story difficult. It concludes instead with the abbreviation "etc." (וגו'), although there is no gloss intervening between it and the next biblical phrase. The third phrase "For Judah has profaned" (כי חלל יהודה) is set apart by the interpretive gloss which follows. The final phrase "the holiness of the LORD whom he loves, and have married the daughter of a foreign god" (קדש י"י אשר אהב ובעל בת אל נכר) concludes with the quotation of the opening words of Gen 38:1.

[69] *Midr. Haggadol* Gen 38:1. A similar division of Mal 2:11 into four phrases, each alluding to a different sin, may be found in *b. Sanh.* 82a and *Yal. Šim'oni* Mal 2:11. The version in these sources, however, presents a general catalogue of vices that have serious consequences, especially for the leaders of the community, not a list of Judah's sins leading to the deaths of his sons.

[70] The special emphasis on the brothers' sale of Joseph with which this passage from *Midr. Haggadol* concludes suggests an application of Mal 2:10, the verse immediately before the one opening the proem under discussion, to the events in Genesis 37. This prophetic verse reads, "Do we not all have one father? Has not one God

316 CHAPTER FOUR

a record of just punishment is accomplished through a reading of
the difficult words translated above as participles ([every one who is]
"vigilant" [ער] and "responsive" [עונה]) as the names of Judah's sons
(Er [ער] and Onan [אונן]), who are killed by God in Gen 38:7 and 10.[71]

Exact verbal correspondence between the glosses of Mal 2:11 in
the first proem in *Genesis Rabba* and the glosses in the version of the
proem in *Midraš Haggadol* are lacking, and even the exact manner of
dividing the prophetic passage differs in the two documents. The
inexplicable division of the prophetic passage into four parts in *Genesis
Rabba*, however, may indicate a dependence on some form of the
tradition found in *Midraš Haggadol*. The correlation between the focus
on Judah's denial and lying in the gloss of the first phrase of Mal
2:11 in *Genesis Rabba* and the focus on the brother's deception of
Jacob in the gloss of the same phrase in *Midraš Haggadol* lends some
support to this theory of dependence.

But even if *Genesis Rabba*'s version of the proem is based to some
extent on an earlier tradition, in emphasis it deviates strikingly from
the version we have seen in *Midraš Haggadol*. Whether or not its broken
presentation of Mal 2:11 alludes to a well-known list of Judah's tres-
passes, *Genesis Rabba* shows no interest in fully cataloguing them in
this proem. Instead, it focuses on Judah's debasement through his
treachery in marrying a foreign woman.

Attention to Judah's decline in status begins with the gloss of the
third phrase from Mal 2:11: "'For Judah has profaned (חלל יהודה')
(Mal 2:11): You have become profane, Judah (נעשתה חולין יהודה)."[72]

---

created us? Why do we act falsely, each man against his brother, to profane the
covenant of our fathers?" This verse may have been interpreted as the self-accusation
of Jacob's sons concerning their treatment of Joseph.

[71] This intertextual reading of passages from Genesis and Malachi may have
influenced the standardization of the Hebrew consonantal text of Mal 2:12. The
LXX translates the first of the two puzzling participles identified above as the preposition "until" (ἕως), which indicates that the Hebrew text before the translator must
have read "until" (עד). These consonants may also be read as the noun "witness"
(עֵד), in which case the parallelism "witness and respondent" (ער ועונה) appears. In
some contemporary biblical translations, such as the *Revised Standard Version*, a decision that these parallel words constitute the preferred reading lies behind the translation "any to witness or answer." By contrast, the Jewish Publication Society's 1985
translation renders these two words collectively as "descendants," perhaps recalling
Judah's sons Er and Onan, although it indicates that the meaning of the Hebrew
text is uncertain.

[72] For similar expressions that someone "has become profane" (נעשה חולין) in *Genesis
Rabba*, see the description of the degradation of Enosh in *Gen.Rab.* 23.6 (24.6) and
of Noah in *Gen.Rab.* 36.3.

This gloss initiates a fundamental reinterpretation of the prophetic charge that the post-exilic community has profaned the temple through their immoral behavior. Within this proem, it is not the people who collectively desecrate a holy place, but rather a single individual, Judah, who himself becomes profane.[73] Next, the object of the desecrating actions of the people in Mal 2:11, "the LORD's sanctuary, which he loves (קדש יהוה אשר אהב)," is transformed in the grammar of the proem into a noun in apposition with Judah: "You have become profane, Judah, 'the holy one of the LORD whom he loves (קדש יהוה אשר אהב).'"[74] The quotation of the conclusion of Mal 2:11 provides the explanation that this change in status was affected when he "married the daughter of a foreign god."

Through the techniques of glossing and careful placement of words, this proem depicts Judah's decline in status from holy to profane, especially through his aberrant marriage to a Canaanite in Gen 38:2. In so doing, it semantically positions the reader to hear in the opening words of Gen 38:1 much more than a simple description of a geographical journey. Following on the heels of this introduction, the words "At that time, Judah went down" foreshadow his moral and social debasement through intermarriage. This proem, therefore, provides an extended explanation of the first verb of Gen 38:1, "he went down" (וירד), as Judah's decline in status.

The second proem begins with a full quotation of Mic 1:15 and continues with explanatory glosses and repetitions of phrases from the prophetic verse before concluding with an allusion to Gen 38:1:

---

[73] Although the targum to Mal 2:11 retains the biblical understanding that the term "Judah" refers to a community and not an individual, it also assumes that the change in status from holy to profane is a reflexive one within the people themselves, not a debasement of the temple. In the targum, this verse reads, "The people of the house of Judah have been false, and an abomination has been committed in Israel and in Jerusalem; for the people of the house of Judah have profaned their soul which was holy before the LORD [and] which he loved, and they have chosen to marry wives from the daughters of the nations."

[74] The implicit identification of Judah as "the holy one of the LORD" in this apposition is made explicit in the more expansive version of this proem in *Tanh.* Wayyešeb 9.9, which quotes Ps 114:2, "Judah, you have become his holy one" (היתה יהודה לקדשו), to support this application of the title. The Hebrew noun קדש signifies a range of concepts, including the abstract quality of holiness; sacred places such as the tabernacle, Zion, and the temple; and things and persons set aside as holy. See the biblical usages of this noun listed in BDB, 871–72. In Mal 2:11 the interpretation of this word as a reference to the temple is indicated by the larger context of the book, which repeatedly refers to the temple and the priestly perversion of the sacrificial cult there.

"I will yet bring the dispossessor to you, inhabitant of Moreshah. As far as Adullam will come the glory of Israel (כבוד ישראל)" (Mic 1:15): the Holy One of Israel (קדושו שלישראל). As far as Adullam will come the king of Israel (מלכן שלישראל). "As far as Adullam he will come:" "At that time," etc. (Gen 38:1).[75]

The common denominator between Mic 1:15 and Gen 38:1 that motivates their juxtaposition in this proem consists of the portrayal of a journey to Adullam in each. In Gen 38:1, the journey to the environs of this city is implied by Judah's descent to a place where he encounters an Adullamite. In Mic 1:15 the journey to Adullam is explicitly described, although the identity of the subject of this movement, "the glory of Israel" (כבוד ישראל), remains elusive. Not even the larger context of this verse, the prophetic lament in Mic 1:2–16 over the destruction of Samaria and the towns surrounding Jerusalem during the Assyrian campaign of the late eighth century BCE, aids in solving this puzzle to the satisfaction of the modern reader.[76]

It is exactly this ambiguity of subject in the second half of Mic 1:15 that the proem addresses in the glosses following the quotation. But rather than providing a single answer to this problem, the proem emphasizes the potential for multiple interpretations of the phrase "the glory of Israel" in its presentation of two explanations, one after the other. The first explanation appears in the form of the paraphrastic gloss identifying "the glory of Israel" as "the Holy One of Israel" (קדושו שלישראל). "The Holy One of Israel" (קדוש ישראל) appears as a title for God in the Bible, especially in the book of Isaiah, and similar divine titles containing a form of the verbal root "to be holy" (קדש) are common in rabbinic literature.[77] The choice of the title

---

[75] *Yal. Šimʿoni* Mic 1:15 also presents a version of this proem. *Yal. Šimʿoni* Gen 38:1 quotes Mic 1:15 following the first proem in its collection of proems at the head of the chapter, but, other than an introduction with the phrase "as it is said" (שנאמר), it offers no additional comment on this verse. Both *Tanḥ.* Wayyešeb 9.10 and *'Ag.Ber.* 63(64) have expositions relating Mic 1:15 to Genesis 38, but neither of these resembles the second proem in *Genesis Rabba. Yal. Makiri* Mic 1:15 both quotes material from the *Tanhuma* and cites a simplified version of the second proem in *Gen.Rab.* 85.1.
[76] Delbert R. Hillers, *Micah*, Hermeneia (Philadelphia: Fortress Press, 1984) 28, n. u, expresses absolute frustration at the indecipherable second half of the verse: "Again we miss the point, even in a general way. What is the 'glory of Israel?' Why will it come down to Adullam?" An earlier witness to the difficulty of understanding the expression "the glory of Israel" in this context is *Targum Jonathan*, which simply eliminates all reference to this phrase in its translation of Mic 1:15 as a description of foreign invasion: "Again I will bring dispossessors upon you, inhabitants of Moreshah. They will go up to Adullum and arrive at the border of the land of Israel."
[77] See, for example, Isa 12:6 and 37:23. A discussion of divine titles employing

"the Holy One of Israel" to identify God as the subject of the journey
to Adullam is significant, in that it interjects into the second proem
the concept of "holiness" already introduced in the first proem in
the description of Judah before his debasement. This repetition provides cohesion between the two proems on a verbal and thematic
level. It also forges a symmetrical link between Judah, "the holiness
of the LORD" (קדש יי׳) in the first proem, and God, "the Holy One
of Israel" (קדוש שלישראל) in the second proem, a link that will become
important for final reflection about the general implications of this
second proem.

The second explanation of the term "the glory of Israel" is presented within a paraphrastic quotation of the second half of Mic
1:15, which changes only a single word. Instead of the sentence, "As
far as Adullam will come the glory of Israel," the interpretive quotation reads, "As far as Adullam will come the king of Israel" (מלכן
שלישראל).[78] There are grounds for concluding that the expression "the
King of Israel" is yet another title for God, parallel to the earlier
title "the Holy One of Israel." For one thing, God is repeatedly portrayed as Israel's king in biblical literature[79] and also elsewhere in
Genesis Rabba.[80] In addition, one manuscript of *Genesis Rabba* replaces
the expression "the king of Israel" with "the King of the universe"
(ומלכו של עולם), who can be no other than God.[81] *Yalquṭ Šimʿoni*'s
commentary on this verse in Micah similarly alters the genitive of
the construct chain in its conflation of the two glosses found separately

---

the adjective "holy" (קדוש) and the abstract noun from the same root, "holiness"
(קדש), may be found in Ephraim E. Urbach, *The Sages: Their Concepts and Beliefs*,
trans. Israel Abrahams (Cambridge, MA: Harvard University Press, 1975; reprint,
Jerusalem: Magnes Press, 1979) 75–79.

[78] The reference to "the king of Israel" in this gloss may have been facilitated by
the discussion of Israel's kings in the second half of Mic 1:14, immediately preceding the verse quoted in this proem: "The houses of Achzib (אכזיב) have become a
stream which fails (לאכזב) for the kings of Israel (למלכי ישראל)." The pun on the
place name Achzib in this line recalls the note in Gen 38:5 that Judah was "at
Kezib" (בכזיב) when Shelah was born, forging another link between this prophetic
passage and Genesis 38.

[79] See in particular the biblical descriptions of the LORD in Isa 44:6 ("king of
Israel," מלך ישראל); Zeph 3:15 ("king of Israel," מלך ישראל); Isa 41:21 ("king of
Jacob," מלך יעקב); Ps 24:8 ("the king of glory," מלך הכבוד); and Isa 43:15 ("your
Holy One," קדושכם; "the creator of Israel," בורא ישראל; "your king," מלככם).

[80] Some examples are *Gen.Rab.* 1.11; 12.1; 14.1; 33.2; 42.5; 43.5. In addition, the
numerous parables involving a comparison between a human king and God suggest
that the latter is also a king, although of a completely different order. In the first
chapter alone, parables comparing and contrasting God with a human king include
Gen.Rab. 1.1, 4, 5, 12, 15.

[81] MS Paris 149.

in *Genesis Rabba*'s version of the proem: "As far as Adullum will come the Holy One and King of the universe" (קדושו ומלכו של עולם). In this source, there is no doubt that both "Holy One" and "King" are titles for the same divine subject.

In *Genesis Rabba*'s version of the second proem, however, a suggestive ambiguity remains concerning the referent of the title "the king of Israel." Directly following the paraphrastic rendition of the second half of Mic 1:15 containing this royal title, a repetitious quotation of the first phrase of this half-verse, highlighting the journey to Adullam ("As far as Adullam will come"), serves as a direct introduction to Gen 38:1. Since the opening verse of Genesis 38 describes Judah's journey to Adullam, it is possible to conclude that "the king of Israel" of the gloss refers to him. The identification of "the king of Israel" as Judah is made more plausible by the inclusion at an earlier point in *Genesis Rabba* of a tradition describing how the sons of Jacob appointed Judah as their king.[82]

If the expression "the king of Israel" does refer to Judah, then this proem describes a journey to Adullam by two distinct parties, both exalted as "the glory of Israel." Implicit in the second proem is the view that Judah, "the holiness of the LORD" as he is described in the first proem, is accompanied by "the Holy One of Israel" in his descent to Adullam in Gen 38:1.[83] The coordination of movement between holy divine and holy human travelers in the second proem stands in marked contrast to the oppositional relationship indicated by God's castigations of Judah in the first proem. The second proem, therefore, functions to shift focus from Judah's guilt in marrying a Canaanite at the beginning of Genesis 38 to the larger implications of the biblical narrative for the origins of the royal genealogy.[84]

---

[82] See *Gen.Rab.* 84.17 which states "On three occasions Judah spoke before his brethren, and they made him king over them." The simple version of the second proem in *Gen.Rab.* 85.1 found in *Yal. Makiri* Mic 1:15 also supports the reading of "the king of Israel" as Judah. It does this by presenting a version of the second proem with no complicating reference to the "Holy One of Israel" directly after a discussion of Judah's marriage to a Canaanite, despite the fact that he was the leader among his brothers: "'As far as Adullam will come the glory of Israel' (Mic 1:15). As far as Adullam will come the king of Israel." Judah's royal status is also indicated in *Gen.Rab.* 70.15; 71.5; 72.5; 85.2; 92.5; 93.2, 5, 6, 12; 96.5; 95, MSV; 97, NV; 98.4; 100.8.

[83] '*Ag.Ber.* 63(64) more explicitly develops the theme of God's accompaniment of Judah in his descent to Adullam in its discussion of Mic 1:15.

[84] A comparison with the proem based on Mic 1:15 in *Tanh.* Wayyešeb 9.10 highlights the distinctive statement which this second proem in *Gen.Rab.* 85.1 makes

In light of these considerations, it is tempting to speculate that this proem intends a different reading of the first verb of Gen 38:1, "he went down" (וירד), from the one we have noted in the first proem. As part of a discussion of the actions of "the king of Israel." in this proem, this verb may have been viewed as a derivative from the root "to rule" (רדה).[85] If read as "At that time, Judah ruled," the opening line of Gen 38 becomes a proleptic hint of the dominion of this patriarch's line through Perez, whose birth is recorded at the conclusion of the narrative. It may even be that in the context of this proem the first part of Mic 1:15 should be read not as a divine threat ("I will yet bring the dispossessor to you"), but a divine prom- ise for offspring who will inherit hegemony over the land ("I will yet bring the heir to you").[86] In any event, the theme of royal leadership introduced through the title "the king of Israel" (מלכן שלישראל) in this proem dominates the remaining two proems, which concentrate on God's provisions for the emergence of Israel's messiah and re- deemer through the events of Genesis 38.

The third proem, which alone of the four proems in this section is attributed to a specific rabbinic authority (R. Samuel b. Nahman),[87] opens with a quotation of the first line of Jer 29:11 and continues with an elaboration of a theme which this verse suggests:

---

as an introduction to the biblical chapter. Unlike the proem in *Genesis Rabba*, the proem in the *Tanḥuma* continues the focus on the theme of Judah's irregular mar- riage. The concluding point of this second proem in the *Tanḥuma* seems to be simi- lar to that of the first proem: through his marriage to a Canaanite at Adullam, Judah lost his honor.

[85] *Gen.Rab.* 86.2 interprets a verb from the same root, "to go down" (ירד), in the phrase from Gen 39:1, "Joseph was brought down (הורד) to Egypt," as stemming from the root "to rule" (רדה). According to this interpretation, Joseph ruled over the Egyptians. One of the biblical verses quoted in support of this interpretation, Ps 72:8, contains a verb from the root "to rule" (רדה), which has the same consonantal spelling (וירד) as the verb found in Gen 38:1. For another pun on the verbal roots "to go down" (ירד) and "to rule" (רדה), see *Gen.Rab.* 8.12.

[86] The Hebrew word הירש can mean either "the dispossessor" or "the heir." The exposition of Mic 1:15 in *'Ag.Ber.* 63(64) opens with a similar assumption that the first half of this verse alludes to the divine promise given to Abraham that his descend- ants would inherit the land. The exposition in this source takes an unexpected turn, however, when it argues that the second half of this verse refers to the humiliation Israelite prisoners experienced at Adullam when their captors required them to strip and march into exile without their clothes, or, in the words of the biblical verse, without their "glory."

[87] The great majority of the proems in *Genesis Rabba* (170 out of 246 according to Albeck, "Introduction to *Genesis Rabba*," 14) are anonymous.

R. Samuel b. Nahman began [his discourse with the verse]: "For I
know the thoughts (המחשבות)," etc. (Jer 29:11). The tribes were busy
with the sale of Joseph, Jacob was busy with his sackcloth and fasting,
Judah was busy taking a wife, while the Holy One Blessed be He
(והקב"ה) was creating the light of the king messiah (מלך המשיח). "At
that time (ויהי בעת ההיא)," etc. (Gen 38:10).[88]

In its biblical context, the opening verse of this proem occurs within
a letter sent by the prophet Jeremiah to the Judaean community in
exile. In this letter, he urges them to embrace their lot in Babylon,
since their relocation there is part of a larger divine plan that includes
return to their native land after seventy years. In the context of this
proem, however, the verse serves to introduce a contrast between
the limited preoccupations of the human characters of Genesis 37
and 38 and the more comprehensive purposes of God for ultimate
redemption.

It may be that this contrast was initially inspired by a verse in Isa
55:8, which also contains the word "thoughts" (מחשבות) in its explicit
comparison between the intentions and behavior of humanity and
God: "For my thoughts (מחשבותי) are not your thoughts (מחשבותיכם),
and my ways are not your ways. An oracle of the LORD." Expositions on this verse from the book of Isaiah appear in the *Tanhuma*
immediately following proems based on Mal 2:11 and Mic 1:15,
indicating that Isa 55:8 was the third prophetic verse brought forward to illuminate Gen 38:1 in an alternate version of the series of
proems in *Gen.Rab.* 85.1.[89]

But the portion of Jer 29:11 left unquoted in the third proem
contains thematic material especially appropriate for the subsequent
exposition, which explains why this verse rather than Isa 55:8 appears
in *Genesis Rabba*. In its entirety, Jer 29:11 reads, "For I know the
thoughts that I think about you, an oracle of the LORD: thoughts for
peace and not for evil, to give you an end (אחרית) and a hope." One
suggestive feature of the second half of this prophetic verse consists

---

[88] Versions of this proem are also found in *Yal. Šimʿoni* Gen 38:1 and *Midr. Haggadol*
Gen 38:1.

[89] See *Tanh.* Wayyešeb 9.11. None of the three expositions of Isa 55:8 in this
source contains a similar contrast between divine and human purposes, although
the final exposition mentions the brothers' sale of Joseph and the preparation for
the king messiah's appearance: "Another interpretation of 'For my thoughts,' etc.
(Isa 55:8): His brothers sold Joseph to the Midianites, and the Midianites sold him
to the Egyptians. Before Joseph went down, Judah went down to establish the final
redeemer, who is the king messiah."

of the contrast between thoughts for peace and thoughts for evil. This verbal contrast corresponds to the contrast between the grand divine activity of providing for the messiah's final reign of peace and the limited human activities, which are either reprehensible (as are the brothers' sale of Joseph and Judah's marriage to a Canaanite) or misinformed (as is Jacob's incessant mourning for a son still living).[90] The other significant feature consists of the final phrase of the verse, "to give you an end (אחרית) and a hope," which articulates the motive behind God's intervention in the events of Genesis 38, to establish the lineage of the messiah for ultimate redemption.

In this third proem, there is an intensification of emphasis on the purposefulness of divine intervention in human history, already implied in the second proem with the depiction of God's accompaniment of Judah to Adullam. The theme of royalty introduced in the second proem through the title "the king of Israel" (מלך שלישראל) is further developed in the third proem as well, with the assertion that the overarching significance of Genesis 38 lies in the providential preparation for the emergence of the "light of the king messiah" (מלך המשיח). An additional link between the second and third proems may be seen in the employment of the title "the Holy One Blessed Be He" (abbreviated הקב"ה) to identify God, which corresponds to the divine title "the Holy One of Israel" (קדוש שלישראל) in the previous proem. These links establish a continuity between these two proems, despite the fact that the third proem concentrates more specifically on God's teleological plans for Israel's final redemption implemented through his creation of the light of the royal messiah.[91]

---

[90] Various MSS of *Genesis Rabba* and other sources provide alternate lists of human behaviors. The text of MS British Museum Codex Add. 27169 itself replaces Jacob with Joseph, who busies himself with sackcloth and fasting, although the text is corrected between the lines to refer to Jacob. Joseph's mourning is included alongside Jacob's in some manuscripts of *Genesis Rabba*. Other manuscripts, as well as the printed editions, introduce Reuben in the list, who also busies himself with mourning. *Yal. Šimʿoni* Gen 38:1 replaces Jacob with Reuben, who busies himself with sackcloth and fasts. *Midr. Haggadol* Gen 38:1 supplements the list in *Genesis Rabba* with a description of Joseph, who busies himself with his work. For more information about these variations, see the apparatus of Theodor/Albeck, 1030, as well as Theodor's commentary on the same page.

[91] In *Genesis Rabba*, the light that God creates on the first day is hidden following Adam's sin (*Gen.Rab.* 11.2; 12.6) and stored up for the righteous in the messianic future (*Gen.Rab.* 3.6). Alternatively, this primal light dwells with the messiah (*Gen.Rab.* 1.6). In *Midraš Haggadol* by contrast, God busies himself not with "the light (אורו) of the king messiah" as in *Genesis Rabba* and other sources, but with "the blood relative of the king messiah" (בשאירו שלמלך המשיח), apparently Perez.

The final allusion to Gen 38:1 in the third proem seems to have
two functions. One is to highlight the simultaneity of divine and human
activities at loggerheads with each other through its reference to a
specific point in time, indicated by the temporal marker, "At that
time" (ויהי בעת ההיא). In addition, the opening words of Genesis 38
have been transformed from a specific reference to events occurring
early in the chapter, such as Judah's marriage in the first proem and
Judah's descent to Adullam in the second proem, to a shorthand
reference to the narrative as a whole, with its outcome in the birth
of Perez and his brother. This more general function of the first
verse appears again in the final proem.

The fourth and final proem in *Gen.Rab.* 85.1 begins with a quotation of the first half of Isa 66:7 and continues with an interpretation
of this prophetic verse in terms of redemptive history:

> "Before she labored, she gave birth" (Isa 66:7). Before the first oppressor
> (משעבד הראשון) was born, the final redeemer (גואל האחרון) was born.
> "At that time" (Gen 38:1).[92]

In its original context in Isaiah, the verse cited partially in this proem
alludes to the sudden restoration of Jerusalem after the Babylonian
exile, metaphorically depicted in two synonymous half-lines as a mother
painlessly delivering a baby even before her contractions begin: "Before
she labored, she gave birth; before pangs came upon her, she delivered a male child." Later apocalyptic writings, however, commonly
appropriate images of labor pains and birth similar to those found in
Isaiah to portray the tribulations preceding the end time and the
emergence of a new cosmic order. The fourth proem partially con-
forms to this apocalyptic usage with its reference to a period of oppression and to the appearance of "the final redeemer."

But the fourth proem also interprets Isa 66:7 in a distinctive fashion
befitting its application to Gen 38:1. The proem literalizes the marvelous birth which the biblical author employs as a metaphor for Jerusalem's restoration, and which later writers employ as a metaphor for
the final days; moreover, the proem understands the double description

---

[92] The reading in the body of MS British Museum Codex Add. 27169 is actually
"Before the final oppressor was born, the first redeemer was born," but this is corrected in the margin to the reading presented above. The great majority of the MSS
(all except for MS British Museum Codex Add. 27169, MS Vat. Ebr. 30, and MS
Stuttgart 32) also refer to "the first oppressor" and "the final redeemer," as do *Yal.
Šim'oni* Gen 38:1; *Yal. Šim'oni* Isa 66:7; Rashi's commentary; and other sources cited
by Theodor in his commentary (Theodor/Albeck, 1030).

of this birth in Isa 66:7 as referring to not one but two different births. According to this proem, the prophetic verse describes two human mothers giving birth to real babies. Since the references to labor and pain in the verse recall Israel's historical suffering, and since each half verse contains a phrase describing the time before the period of travail, the proem presents a providential chronology of salvation. Even before Israel's first oppressor, Pharaoh, was born, the ancestor of Israel's final redeemer, Perez, was born. Later in its commentary on Genesis 38, *Genesis Rabba* incorporates the theme of miraculous birth suggested by Isa 66:7 into its depiction of Tamar's rapid delivery of twins, born before their gestation period is complete.[93]

Besides emphasizing that the most important event in Genesis 38 is the birth of Perez, this proem offers a theory about the significance of the editorial placement of Genesis 38 within the Joseph story. The proem suggests that the position of Genesis 38 before Genesis 39 is not intrusive, but attests to the providential ordering of Israelite history. According to this proem, the birth of the final redeemer's ancestor precedes Joseph's enslavement in Egypt, which prefigures Israel's first period of oppression under Pharaoh.

A number of thematic and verbal features link the fourth proem to the preceding proem. For example, the reference to the birth of "the final redeemer" in this proem continues the focus of the third proem on the future appearance of "the king messiah," anticipated through the birth of Perez at the end of Genesis 38. An explicit verbal connection between the word "final" (הָאַחֲרוֹן) describing the redeemer in this proem and the word "end" (אַחֲרִית) occurring as part of God's promise for "an end and a hope" in the prophetic verse cited in the third proem (Jer 29:11) highlights the common teleological emphasis of these two concluding proems. Just as important, both the third and fourth proems express an interest in the timing of biblical events, motivated perhaps by the opening phrase of Gen 38:1, "At that time" (וַיְהִי בָּעֵת הַהוּא). But whereas the third proem focuses on the simultaneity of the contrasting activities of human and divine characters, the fourth proem focuses on the linear order of events implied by the placement of Genesis 38 within the Joseph

---

[93] The parallel descriptions of birth in Isa 66:7 apparently suggested the birth of twins, thereby providing another link between Genesis 38 and the prophetic verse. The motif of Tamar's miraculous delivery depicted in *Gen.Rab.* 85.13 is discussed in further detail below, in connection with *Genesis Rabba*'s development of her character as a worthy royal ancestress.

story.[94] Thus, this final proem provides closure for the opening section of *Genesis Rabba* 85, through its reiteration of the important theme of future redemption introduced in the third proem, and it functions as a transitional passage to the more extensive discussion of the placement of Genesis 38 within its biblical context in *Gen.Rab.* 85.2.

The overarching statement made by this introductory collection of four proems predisposes the reader to view the events of Genesis 38 in a certain way and to attend more carefully to the exegetical traditions in *Genesis Rabba* that accord thematically with it. Only the first proem concentrates on Judah's marriage with a Canaanite woman in Gen 38:2, although this marriage is mentioned in passing again in the third proem. Instead, the three proems that follow shift the focus away from Judah's guilt to the larger implications of the biblical narrative for Israelite history. The second proem depicts God's accompaniment of Judah to Adullam, suggesting divine involvement with the biblical events leading to the origins of Israel's royal bloodline. The third and fourth proems explicitly develop the theme of God's providential intervention in history and project the ramifications of the biblical narrative further into the future with their focus on messianic redemption. With respect to its general progression of ideas, *Gen.Rab.* 85.1 therefore loosely corresponds with the other passages from *Genesis Rabba* examined earlier, which present traditions concentrating locally on Judah's guilt first and follow them with traditions emphasizing the larger divine purposes implemented through the biblical narrative.

Relatively few proems in *Genesis Rabba*, besides the final three in this collection, accentuate royal or messianic themes. This fact emphasizes the distinctive function that Genesis 38 performs in the larger economy of this commentary. Regardless of the diverse lexical, geographical, legal, and moral lessons presented in the context of *Genesis Rabba*'s subsequent treatment of Genesis 38, the emphasis on kings, messiahs, and redeemers in the opening collection of proems highlights related thematic material in the body of its commentary.[95] Even

---

[94] The appearance of a similar expression of time in Gen 38:27, "At the time of her delivery" (ויהי בעת לדה), to that in Gen 38:1, "At that time" (ויהי בעת ההוא), facilitates the movement from the opening verse of the biblical narrative to the birth scene at its end evident in this proem.

[95] By contrast, a strong, overarching interpretation of Genesis 38 in terms of royalty and redemption is not found in *Tanh.* Wayyešeb 9.9–11. For one thing, the *Tanhuma* presents material similar to that found in *Gen.Rab.* 85.1 not at the head of its dis-

before the actual verse-by-verse commentary on Genesis 38 begins,
these proems articulate a distinctive direction of interpretation for
the biblical chapter, and the use of prophetic verses to argue for the
understanding of Genesis 38 as the story of royal and messianic origins
buttresses traditional rabbinic exegesis with the authority of scripture.

Concluding Prophetic Allusion

As might be expected given the opening proems' emphasis on the
origin of the royal and messianic lineage, *Genesis Rabba* marks the
special significance of Perez' birth in Gen 38:29 by incorporating yet
another prophetic quotation into a revised version of the midwife's
etiological utterance:

> "When he drew back his hand," etc. (Gen 38:29). "This one is greater
> than all those who will make breaches (הפרצים), [for] from you will be
> established [the one about whom it is written], 'The breaker (הפרץ)
> will go up before them' (Mic 2:13)."[96]

In commenting on Gen 38:29, *Genesis Rabba* does not explicitly quote
either the biblical depiction of Perez' unexpected emergence following
the retraction of Zerah's hand ("his brother came out!" והנה יצא אחיו)
or the midwife's biblical etiology for Perez' name based on his unusual
birth order ("What a breach you have made for yourself!" מה פרצת
עליך פרץ). This ellipsis, signaled by the word "etc." (וגו'), would not
be significant in itself; however, in this particular case *Genesis Rabba*
replaces the unquoted material with an alternate etiology for Perez'
name, presumably offered by the midwife as in the biblical narrative.

In keeping with Perez' importance for Israel's future redemption
in *Genesis Rabba*, the midwife forgoes reference to the vagaries of his
birth order and instead presents a prophetic comparison between this
newborn and others who "make breaches" (הפרצים), apparently intending by this expression other conquerors and royal leaders. She buttresses her prognostication of Perez and his descendant's greatness

---

cussion of Genesis 38, but in the middle of its discussion of Genesis 37. In addition,
the particular versions of the proems and related material in the *Tanḥuma* do not
consistently emphasize the emergence of Israel's kings and royal redeemer, but instead address a wider variety of topics suggested by the first verse of Genesis 38 and
by this chapter as a whole.

[96] *Gen.Rab.* 85.14. Mic 2:13 is presented as commentary on the significance of
Gen 38:29 in a number of other sources as well, including *Yal. Šim'oni* Gen 38:29;
Yal. Makiri Mic 2:13; and *'Ag.Ber.* 63(64).

by quoting the opening phrase from Mic 2:13, "The breaker (הפרץ) will go up before them."[97]

In its biblical context, the verse from which the midwife cites this prophetic phrase (Mic 2:13) is puzzling:

> The breaker (הפרץ) will go up before them. They will break out (פרצו), pass through the gate, and go out of it. Their king will pass through before them, and the LORD will be at their head.

The promise of restoration for a remnant in this verse and in the previous verse (Mic 2:12) contrasts strikingly with the condemnations of injustice and predictions of devastation which precede and follow them in the book of Micah. The dissimilarity of tone and subject matter has led some to view these verses as a later interpolation from the exilic or post-exilic period. But whether they express Micah's own anticipation of a restoration of the Northern Kingdom after Israel's defeat by the Assyrians in the late eighth century or whether they express a later vision of restoration, these verses describe a return from exile under the dual leadership of Israel's king and the LORD.[98]

Judging from the opening proems' development of the theme of eschatological redemption, *Genesis Rabba*'s recontextualization of the opening phrase from Mic 2:13 in a discussion of Perez' birth indicates an assumption that these two verses refer to eschatological events. This conclusion is confirmed in an earlier passage in *Genesis Rabba*, in which Mic 2:13 is quoted as an indication of what will happen "in the messianic future."[99] The application of the prophetic phrase, "The breaker will go up before them," to a descendant of Perez therefore clinches the identification of this figure as the ancestor of the final eschatological king.[100]

An important verbal link facilitates the application of the phrase "The breaker will go up before them" (עלה הפרץ לפניהם) from Mic

---

[97] Indeed, the midwife's words before the explicit quotation of the first part of Mic 2:13 may be an interpretation of that prophetic phrase, to the following effect: "Perez, the breaker (הפרץ), is eminent (עלה) over all others (לפניהם) who break out (פרצו)."

[98] Alternately, the two phrases "their King" and "the LORD" could be interpreted as parallel appellations for the deity, although this interpretation runs counter to the employment of Mic 1:15 in *Gen.Rab.* 85.1.

[99] See *Gen.Rab.* 48.10, concluding statement.

[100] Indeed, in *'Ag.Ber.* 63(64), the identification of Perez with the messiah is even stronger: "'When he drew back his hand,' etc. (Gen 38:29). Perez is the messiah, as it says [in scripture], 'The breaker will go up before them' (Mic 2:13)."

2:13 to the figure of Perez in Gen 38:29, about whom the midwife in the biblical narrative exclaims "What a breach you have made for yourself!" (מה פרצת עליך פרץ). This verbal link consists of the appearance of words from the root "to break forward" (פרץ) in both the midwife's exclamation (פרץ, פרצת) and the prophetic phrase (הפרץ).[101] It may be that the author of Mic 2:13 himself is alluding to Perez as the royal ancestor through a pun on his name. In *Genesis Rabba*, the substitution of an etiology for Perez' name that captures the dimension of royal leadership expressed in Mic 2:13 extends the import of the midwife's comment. Rather than the simple rupture of the order of birth that gains Perez his name in Gen 38:29, it is his descendant's royal leadership in bursting forth from the confines of exile that gains him his name in *Genesis Rabba*. The inclusion of Mic 2:13 in this context defines the words of the midwife concerning this son as a prophetic insight into the historical significance of the newborn from the moment it emerges from the womb.

Genesis Rabba's prophetic allusion to Mic 2:13 in its final section of commentary on Genesis 38 (*Gen.Rab.* 85.14) explicitly relates the birth of Perez to the introductory proems with their themes of king, messiah, and redemption. This closure is atypical in *Genesis Rabba*, which characteristically ends its chapters not with a thematic conclusion, but with ordinary discussions of features of the biblical text.[102] It is true that this final section continues somewhat anticlimactically with a discussion of Zerah's disreputable descendant, Achan.[103] Yet, the

[101] See also the verb "they broke through" (פרצו) immediately following the phrase quoted from Mic 2:13. Other less forceful similarities also facilitate the juxtaposition of these verses. For example, the preposition "upon yourself" (עליך) in Gen 38:29 contains the same two initial consonants as those found in the first verb in Mic 2:13, "goes up" (עלה). Also, the concept of precedence implied in the unexpected emergence first from the womb in Gen 38:29 is echoed in the preposition "before them" (מפניהם) in Mic 2:13.

[102] Unlike the beginnings of divisions in *Genesis Rabba*, which are marked by proems, the endings are not marked by any formal characteristics. See Neusner's tally of the formal/rhetorical features of *Genesis Rabba* and his conclusions (*Comparative Midrash*, 68–91).

[103] But even in the concluding discussion of Achan and the four accursed things that he took, the focus centers on the purple robe of Shinar, a symbol of royalty. This robe, in fact, may function as a transitional motif from *Genesis Rabba*'s discussion of Genesis 38, with its thematic emphasis on kingship and the origins of the royal lineage, to its discussion of the following biblical chapters portraying Joseph's rise to power. Joseph, like the vizier from Jericho who wears the purple robe of the Babylonian king in the final section of *Genesis Rabba* 85, also comes to wear the royal garments that Pharaoh gives him.

citation of Mic 2:13 at the beginning of this final section provides an uncharacteristic sense of closure, and ensures that the opening proems are recalled precisely at the moment of the birth of David's ancestor.

Kings and Redeemers Elsewhere in Genesis Rabba 85

The opening and concluding sections of *Genesis Rabba* 85 are not the only places where kings, redeemers, and messiahs are interjected through commentary into Genesis 38, which is itself remarkably taciturn about these subjects for a story of royal origins. For example, *Genesis Rabba* introduces the theme of royalty into its commentary on Gen 38:1 in a discussion of the identity of Judah's Adullamite friend, Hirah:

> "And he turned aside to an Adullamite man, whose name was Hirah (חירה)" (Gen 38:1): The rabbis say, "This Hirah (חירה) here is the same as the one in the days of David: 'For Hiram (חירם) was a lover of David all the days (כל הימים)' (1 Kgs 5:1). This teaches that this man was a lover of this tribe."[104]

The similarity of the names Hirah (חירה), Judah's Adullamite companion, and Hiram (חירם), the king of Tyre during David's reign, suggested to this anonymous group of teachers that these names designate one and the same man. Perhaps the reference to Hiram's enduring love for David "all the days" (כל הימים) in 1 Kgs 5:1 also motivated an imaginative extension into the distant past of this man's love for David's tribal ancestor.[105] Their common foreign ally emphasizes the dynastic connection between Judah and his royal descendant David, thereby highlighting the monarchic standing of Jacob's fourth son.[106] Judah's superior social connections support more explicit claims elsewhere in *Genesis Rabba* of his kingship over his brothers.

---

[104] *Gen.Rab.* 85.4. Immediately following this anonymous tradition, the voice of R. Judah b. Simon protests: "Hiram was a different person." Following this dissenting view, however, the position of the anonymous group of rabbis is reintroduced in a comparison of Hirah's age at death according to these two theories: "According to the view of the rabbis, he lived to be almost 1100 years, whereas according to the view of R. Judah, he lived to be almost 500 years."

[105] 1 Kgs 5:1 itself illustrates how Hiram's friendly relations with David extended forward to his dynasty, by describing the Tyrian king's agreement with Solomon to provide raw material for the construction of the temple. *Genesis Rabba* elsewhere depicts Hiram less positively, as a wicked claimant to divine status, similar to Nebuchadnezzar (*Gen.Rab.* 9.5).

[106] Judah's status is also enhanced through the comment concerning Shua, his father-in-law, immediately following the discussion of Hirah's identity in *Gen.Rab.*

The theme of royalty and redemption is also interjected through *Genesis Rabba*'s commentary on Judah's journey to Timnah. The reference to kings and redeemers in the angel's questions, which send Judah dutifully back to Tamar in *Gen.Rab.* 85.8, has already been noted. But even before this, when Judah's journey is first reported to Tamar in Gen 38:13, the second of *Genesis Rabba*'s three comments on the significance of Judah's ascent to Timnah explicitly focuses on the positive outcome of their union:

> "It was reported to Tamar, 'See, your father-in-law is going up to Timnah,'" etc. (Gen 38:13).

> Rab said, "There were two [places called] Timnah, one [mentioned in connection] with Judah and the other [mentioned in connection] with Samson."

> R. Simon said, "There was but one Timnah. Why then is both ascent and descent mentioned in connection with it? Merely because for Judah it was an ascent, since he produced kings, whereas for Samson it was a descent, since he married a heathen woman."

> R. Aibu b. Nagri said: "It was like Beth Maon, to which one ascends from Tiberias but descends from Kefar Shobethai."[107]

This passage contains an example of what may be called a branched commentary, in which three possible explanations are given for the contradictory description of Samson's descent (Judg 14:1) and Judah's ascent (Gen 38:13) to a place called Timnah. The first explanation given in the name of Rab is that they are two different places, one low in elevation and the other high, that just happen to have the same name. The final explanation given in the name of R. Aibu b. Nagri is that there is only one place called Timnah, but, since it is located midway on an incline, whether one goes up or down to reach it depends on one's point of departure.

Both of these explanations concern geography, whereas the middle explanation shifts to a moral and historical evaluation of the results of the two journeys. Like the final tradition, the explanation given in the name of R. Simon assumes that there is only one place called Timnah. But instead of topographical direction, the words "descend"

85.4: "He was a native and a light of that place." In *Genesis Rabba*, Judah's marriage into a distinguished local family emphasizes his high status by association, as did his friendship with Hirah.

[107] *Gen.Rab.* 85.6.

and "ascend" point to the different results of each man's journey. Since Samson's journey resulted in a reprehensible marriage with a foreign woman, he is described as descending.[108] But since Judah's journey resulted in the establishment of future kings, he is described as ascending. Through this comparison, the theme of royalty is once again reintroduced into the discussion of Genesis 38. Also, through the concentration on the positive historical outcome of Judah and Tamar's encounter, the morally problematic aspects of their sexual relations are minimized. Although *Genesis Rabba* presents all three traditions concerning Timnah without explicitly judging the validity of each, its emphasis elsewhere on the emergence of kings through Judah and Tamar's union highlights this second interpretation.

The themes of kingship, political leadership, and messianic redemption are also interjected into the glosses of the significance of the three pledge items that Tamar requests in Gen 38:18:

> "He said, 'What is the pledge,'" etc. . . . "She said, 'Your seal, your cord, and your staff,'" etc. (Gen 38:18). R. Hunia said, "The holy spirit was kindled within her: 'Your seal (חותמך)' refers to kingship, as [scripture] says, 'Though Coniah, the son of Jehoiakim the king of Judah were a seal (חותם),' etc. (Jer 22:24). 'Your cord (ופתילך)' refers to the Sanhedrin, as [scripture] says, 'That they put upon the fringe of each corner a cord (פתיל) of blue,' etc. (Num 15:38). 'And your staff (ומטך)' refers to the king messiah, as [scripture] says, 'The staff (מטה) of your strength the LORD will send from Zion' (Ps 110:2)."[109]

Whereas in the biblical story Tamar specifies the three items of the pledge because they unmistakably identify their owner, *Gen.Rab.* 85.9 presents a tradition in the name of R. Hunia which associates them prophetically with powerful institutions of national leadership: the kingship of the biblical past, the Sanhedrin of the recent present,[110] and the royal messiah of the future restoration. In this fashion, *Genesis Rabba* once again highlights the royal outcome of the events of this chapter and specifies the narrative's importance for Israelite history.

---

[108] Judah's earlier journey resulting in his marriage to a Canaanite woman is described as a descent in Gen 38:1.

[109] *Gen.Rab.* 85.9. The same tradition is also found in *Yal. Šimʿoni* Gen 38:18.

[110] *Gen.Rab.* 98.10 claims that a majority of the members of the Sanhedrin were descended from Judah. The interpretation of Judah's personal effects as symbols of political leadership in *Genesis Rabba* recalls the interpretation of them as symbols of royalty in *T.Jud.* 12:4 and 15:3, although in the latter work the focus is on kingship lost rather than kingship gained through the events in Genesis 38.

Genesis Rabba's commentary on the anonymous report concerning Tamar's behavior in Gen 38:24 reiterates the theme of royalty by depicting her cognizance that she bears "kings and redeemers:"

> "Moreover, she has also conceived through illicit sexual relations! (לזנונים)" (Gen 38:24). This merely teaches that she would beat upon her seat and exclaim, "I am big with kings and redeemers."[111]

Exactly how the anonymous report to Judah in the biblical text teaches that Tamar bragged about the important status of her unborn children is not entirely clear. Perhaps the phrase "through illicit sexual relations" (לזנונים) describing the nature of Tamar's pregnancy seemed redundant following the explicit charge of immorality in the first part of Gen 38:24, which states, "Tamar, your daughter-in-law, has had illicit intercourse" (זנתה). Or just as likely, this phrase's implication that Perez and Zerah were the offspring of immoral sexual relations was considered scandalous and untenable. In any event, a different meaning was determined for the phrase "through illicit sexual relations" (לזנונים).[112] Perhaps the object of the preposition in this phrase suggested a word for "armor" (זוני), used in rabbinic literature as a symbol of magisterial office.[113] With this replacement, the sense of the second part of the report to Judah becomes, "moreover, she has also conceived [offspring who will wear] armor" (i.e., kings and redeemers).

In the rabbinic version of the report, Tamar herself heralds her pregnancy and announces the theme of royal and messianic origins central to *Genesis Rabba*'s commentary on Genesis 38. Her prophetic role in this midrashic tradition therefore corresponds to her role as prophetess when she earlier discerns the royal significance of the pledge items. These last two passages, therefore, not only articulate the royal and messianic importance of the biblical chapter, but also illustrate

---

[111] *Gen.Rab.* 85.10.

[112] *Tanḥ.* Wayyešeb 9.17 explicitly asks "What is the meaning of 'through illicit sexual relations?'" before presenting its distinctive version of this motif. This source, unlike *Genesis Rabba*, attempts to modify the charge of sexual immorality into lesser charges of immodesty and rudeness through its depiction of Tamar's scornful treatment of other women in a bathhouse, as she boasts of the contents of her womb.

[113] The Hebrew word זוני is a cognate of the Greek word ζώνη, meaning "armor." For examples of the usage of this object as a symbol of office, see Marcus Jastrow, *A Dictionary of the Targumim, the Talmud Babli and Yerushalmi, and the Midrashic Literature* (New York: Judaica Press, 1971) 388 (cf., *T.Jud.* 12:4; 15:2–3). Alternatively, perhaps the word זנונים suggested the word "weapon" (זיין), which also implies power appropriate to a king. For these explanations, see Theodor's commentary on *Gen.Rab.* 85.10 in Theodor/Albeck, 1044.

another of *Genesis Rabba*'s projects, namely the transformation of Tamar and Judah into worthy royal ancestors.

Worthy Progenitors of the Royal Lineage in Genesis Rabba

Judah the Worthy Royal Ancestor

In conjunction with its emphasis on royal origins, *Genesis Rabba* repeatedly presents David's ancestors in a positive light, as worthy of the honor to head an important lineage. In the case of Judah, while *Genesis Rabba* does not clear him of the charges of marrying a foreigner,[114] of advocating the sale of Joseph,[115] or of deceiving Jacob,[116] it does take measures to improve his reputation as far as his relations with Tamar are concerned. We have already observed the tradition in *Gen.Rab.* 85.8 that presents Judah as merely complying with divine instructions when he approaches his daughter-in-law at Enaim, and we have also seen the tradition in *Gen.Rab.* 85.12 that confirms the role of providence behind the events of the narrative through the voice of the holy spirit. While these traditions contain narrative additions that alter the dynamics of the biblical narrative, they function to clear Judah of possible charges of immorality and stress his constructive role in the origins of the Davidic lineage.

Other traditions in *Genesis Rabba* stress Judah's moral behavior towards Tamar. According to this commentary, Judah piously administers the levirate law recorded in Deut 25:5–10[117] and appropriately sentences Tamar to burn according to the law of the priest's daughter recorded in Lev 21:9,[118] even before the legislation at Sinai. His knowledge of the law attests to his righteous standing within a tradition of pre-Sinaitic revelation entrusted first to Abraham,[119] passed

---

[114] For example, the first proem in *Gen.Rab.* 85.1, discussed previously, stresses Judah's guilt in marrying a Canaanite woman.

[115] Although Judah's idea to sell Joseph is depicted as an attempt to save his brother's life in *Gen.Rab.* 84.17 and 93.9 (as well as in *Genesis Rabba* 97, NV), his sin in this matter is emphasized in *Gen.Rab.* 99.1, as well as in 85.2 and 3.

[116] See *Gen.Rab.* 84.19 and 85.11. In *Gen.Rab.* 84.8 and 95.2, Judah is singled out as the brother who deceives Jacob.

[117] *Gen.Rab.* 85.5 claims that "Judah began levirate marriage."

[118] *Gen.Rab.* 85.10.

[119] *Gen.Rab.* 49.2 and 64.4 contend that Abraham was familiar with each new law taught daily by God in the heavenly courts, and *Gen.Rab.* 95.3 states that he kept all of the minutiae of the Tora. *Gen.Rab.* 61.1 explains that Abraham internally absorbed Tora through his kidneys, whereas *Gen.Rab.* 44.14 specifies that God himself taught this patriarch the rules of the sacrificial system. Another tradition, recorded in *Gen.Rab.* 43.6, claims that Shem (equated with Melchizedek) taught Abraham about the sacrificial system and about other matters of Tora.

from Shem and Eber to Isaac and Jacob,[120] and then from Jacob to his sons.[121] Through Judah's conscientious attention to the details of the law, this biblical character—who at least in Genesis 37 and 38 is of questionable morality—is reformed into one of the pre-Sinaitic sages of Tora. In this way, he becomes a mirror for the value of Tora learning and observance characteristic of rabbinic Judaism.[122]

In addition, *Genesis Rabba*'s commentary on Gen 38:11 depicts Judah as correctly withholding his son Shelah from Tamar:

> "Judah said to Tamar," etc. (Gen 38:10). R. Eleazar said, "Though divination is futile, yet a portent may be true. For he said, 'Lest he die also like his brothers' (Gen 38:11)."[123]

With the inclusion of this comment attributed to R. Eleazar, *Genesis Rabba* justifies Judah's withholding of Shelah in Genesis 38 as a responsible decision, given the deaths of his two eldest sons. It clarifies the biblical narrative's ambiguity concerning Judah's treatment of Tamar by declining the possible reading that his dismissal of her was deceptive or reprehensible.[124] Corresponding to its sympathetic understanding of Judah's withholding of Shelah, *Genesis Rabba* omits development of his later failure to fulfill his promise. For example, it does not comment on Tamar's recognition that Shelah had not been given to her although he had matured in Gen 38:14, although in the biblical narrative her recognition of the situation implies a negative evaluation

---

[120] See *Gen.Rab.* 56.11, where Isaac begins to study with Shem immediately after his life is spared in Genesis 22. Jacob also studies Tora with Shem and Eber in *Gen.Rab.* 63.10; 68.5, 11. He, like his father before him, never sleeps in his zeal for Tora study in *Gen.Rab.* 66.1 and 68.1. In *Gen.Rab.* 68.11 and 74.11, Jacob engages in a pre-Davidic recitation of all the psalms, and in *Gen.Rab.* 82.14 he fulfills the entire Tora.

[121] In particular, *Gen.Rab.* 84.8 depicts Jacob teaching all that he learned from Shem and Eber to Joseph. See also *Gen.Rab.* 94.3, which explains that Jacob was discussing Deuteronomy 21 concerning the heifer (עגלה) with Joseph before he was sold into captivity.

The pre-Sinaitic oral Tora in *Genesis Rabba* recalls the understanding of divine commandments passed from patriarch to patriarch in the *Testaments*.

[122] This same retrojection of halakhic observance into pre-Sinaitic times is also portrayed in *Gen.Rab.* 42.8 and 48.12, where Abraham eats unleavened bread in observance of Passover, and in *Gen.Rab.* 79.6 and 92.4, where Joseph keeps the Sabbath. In *Gen.Rab.* 95.3 (and *Genesis Rabba* 95, MSV), Judah goes down to Egypt before his brothers to establish an academy for the study of Tora.

[123] *Gen.Rab.* 85.5.

[124] It may be that *Genesis Rabba* reads the final part of Gen 38:11, "For he said, 'Lest he die also, like his brothers,'" not as a silent aside indicating Judah's duplicity, but as his straightforward explanation of his fears to Tamar.

of Judah's behavior. *Genesis Rabba* also leaves Judah's explicit admission of failure to provide Tamar with an appropriate mate in Gen 38:26 without comment, by concentrating solely on the divine acceptance of responsibility for the events of the narrative. Of the three times Genesis 38 mentions Judah's unwillingness to give Tamar to Shelah, therefore, *Genesis Rabba* explicitly recognizes only the first, and it does so only to applaud his caution.

The silence in *Genesis Rabba* concerning Judah's failure to pair Tamar with Shelah is yet another example of how this verse-by-verse commentary selectively treats the biblical text to further its own point of view. Related to this particular silence is the absence of a gloss explaining the meaning of Shelah's name in *Genesis Rabba*'s commentary on the Canaanite woman's three sons in Gen 38:3–5, despite the fact that the meanings of Er and Onan's names are explained.[125] This remarkable omission corresponds to the more general effort in *Genesis Rabba* to eclipse the presence of Judah's third son, whose role even in the biblical narrative consists of being denied a role. This eclipse is necessary, since even Shelah's minimal presence in the biblical narrative raises serious questions concerning Judah's honesty and thereby complicates *Genesis Rabba*'s efforts to present Genesis 38 as the divinely guided story of the origins of Israel's kingship through two worthy progenitors.

The positive depiction of Judah as the worthy progenitor of the royal and messianic genealogy is also articulated through *Genesis Rabba*'s inclusion of a tradition explaining the prepositional phrase "by him" (לו) in the clause "and she [Tamar] conceived by him (לו)" (Gen 38:18). In the biblical narrative, this phrase may simply be pleonastic,[126] or it may function to confirm unequivocally Judah's paternity. But in *Genesis Rabba*, this prepositional phrase is given a different significance:

> "He gave them to her," etc. "And she conceived by him (לו)" (Gen 38:18): Mighty men like himself (גיבורים שיוצא בו) and righteous men like himself (וצדיקים שיוצא בו).[127]

---

[125] See *Gen.Rab.* 85.4. Er's name (ער) signifies that "he would go childless (הוערה) from the world." Onan's name (אונן) signifies that "he would bring grief (אנינה) upon himself." By contrast, *Genesis Rabba*'s commentary on the birth of Shelah in Gen 38:5 concentrates on the cessation of the mother's childbearing after his birth.

[126] This prepositional phrase is lacking in the earlier descriptions of conception in Gen 38:3–5.

[127] *Gen.Rab.* 85.9. Note that in *Gen.Rab.* 74.13 Jacob's sons are similarly described as "mighty" and "righteous" like their father.

Since in midrashic interpretation of scripture, every feature of the biblical text is assumed to be significant, the presence of the odd prepositional phrase presented an opportunity to forward a positive, non-biblical assertion about the characters of Judah and his sons by Tamar. The description of Judah as a mighty warrior attests to familiarity with old traditions which portray him as a hero in wars with local kings and with Esau and his sons. *Genesis Rabba* itself illustrates Judah's strength by extensively developing the biblical scene when he confronts Joseph, who threatens to detain Benjamin in Egypt (Gen 44:18–34).[128] In the context of *Genesis Rabba*, which emphasizes the royal aspects of his character, the description of Judah and his sons as mighty men also highlights his correspondence to the character of David, who was the greatest warrior of his own generation.

But the additional description of Judah as the righteous father of righteous sons is unexpected, especially in the context of his behavior early in the Joseph story (Genesis 37–38) where he is portrayed as a fallible human being. This description, therefore, reveals the general tendency of *Genesis Rabba* to depict Judah as the morally worthy ancestor of the Davidic dynasty. It furthermore endows his sons with the same moral quality desirable at the beginning of this lineage.[129]

Genesis Rabba also emphasizes the positive character of Judah's twin sons in its commentary on their birth in Gen 38:27:

> "There were twins," etc. (Gen 38:27): [Here the word] "twins" (תאומים)
> is written fully, [indicating that] both [Perez and Zerah] were righteous
> (צדיקים), whereas above [in Gen 25:24 the word] "twins" (תאומם) is

---

[128] See *Gen.Rab.* 93.6, where Judah draws near to Joseph for battle according to one tradition. In this same section, the strength of Judah's anger manifests itself through his chest hairs, which pierce his clothing, and through his teeth, which grind iron bars into powder. *Gen.Rab.* 93.7 and 9 depict the strength of all of Jacob's sons, whereas *Gen.Rab.* 95.4 discusses the extraordinary might of Judah and a number of his brothers. Judah's status as the "mighty one" (נביר) among his brothers is stressed in *Genesis Rabba* 97, NV, and the strength of his sons is emphasized in *Gen.Rab.* 98.9. Judah's physical strength is a traditional motif, found in second temple literature (including the *Testament of Judah*, discussed above in the second chapter), the Palestinian targums, and the Talmud (including *b. B.Qam.* 92a).

[129] Interestingly, *Genesis Rabba* develops a parallel between Judah and his twin sons by Tamar, whom the biblical text refrains from evaluating in moral terms, whereas it ignores another possible comparison, that between Judah and his two eldest sons by the Canaanite woman, who are explicitly described as "evil." This creative forging of a genealogy of righteousness while ignoring the implied negative reflection of the eldest sons on their father is simply one more example of how *Genesis Rabba* goes far beyond simple commentary in its concretization of the significance of Genesis 38.

written defectively, [indicating that] one [Jacob] was righteous (צדיק)
and one [Esau] was wicked (רשע).[130]

In this tradition, a small discrepancy between the spelling of the word
"twins" in the very similar birth narratives in Genesis 25 and Genesis 38 offers an opportunity to reflect on the character of the two
sets of sons.[131] A full spelling indicates a fully developed moral character, whereas a defective spelling indicates an inferior moral character. The description of Judah's twin sons as "righteous" here and
in the passage above which also points to their father's righteousness
is intriguing from another angle as well. In Genesis 38 itself, the root
"to be righteous" (צדק) is used only by Judah to describe Tamar's
greater righteousness (Gen 38:26). But *Genesis Rabba* does not even
quote Judah's positive evaluation of Tamar, much less develop her
righteousness at this point in the narrative, as *Targum Neofiti* does.
Rather, in *Genesis Rabba*, there is an extension of this quality of righteousness to the male members of the family, rendering them morally
appropriate as ancestors of the royal lineage.[132]

Tamar the Worthy Royal Ancestress
Genesis Rabba's efforts to develop Tamar into an appropriate forebear
surpass those that it makes in connection with the character of Judah.
This special exertion may be due in part to the relative opacity of
the biblical text concerning her character and the corresponding
opportunity to shape it in any direction. But no doubt it also stems
from a desire to ameliorate, or at least counterbalance, her dubious
behavior in the biblical narrative. Her posing as a prostitute, deceiving her father-in-law, conceiving illegitimate sons through an act of
incest, and humiliating Judah by publicly exposing his own failure of
responsibility were considered intolerable for a royal ancestress.

---

[130] *Gen.Rab.* 85.13. *Gen.Rab.* 85.14, however, qualifies the righteousness of Zerah's
lineage with a discussion of the sin committed by one of his descendants, namely
Achan.

[131] In fact, the MT spelling of the word "twins" (תומם) in Gen 25:24 is even more
defective than the one which MS British Museum Codex Add. 27169 of *Gen.Rab.*
85.13 records (תאומם). Several other MSS spell the word תומים, which is still not as
defective as the form in the MT. See the apparatus in Theodor/Albeck, 1048. In
Genesis Rabba, Esau is portrayed as an evil character whereas Jacob is portrayed as
a righteous character, in keeping with this commentary's frequent contrast between
Rome (typified by Esau) and Israel (typified by Jacob).

[132] A tradition in *Gen.Rab.* 12.6, which concludes from the full writing of the
word "generations" (תולדות) in Gen 2.4 and Ruth 4:18 that the first man (Adam)
and the last man (the messiah, who comes from Perez) are both as perfect, echoes
the motif of Judah and Tamar's righteous twins.

Genesis Rabbah emphasizes instead Tamar's awareness of the significance of the events in Genesis 38 for Israel's history. We have already seen how *Genesis Rabba*'s commentary on Gen 38:25–26 portrays Tamar as Judah's teacher, when she instructs him to recognize the work of his creator behind the biblical events.[133] Tamar's understanding of the implications of her conception marks her as a person worthy to establish the Davidic genealogy, as does her prophetic grasp of the royal significance of the pledge:

> "He said, 'What is the pledge,'" etc. .... "She said, 'Your seal, your cord, and your staff,'" etc. (Gen 38:18). R. Hunia said, "The holy spirit was kindled within her: 'Your seal' refers to kingship, as [scripture] says, 'Though Coniah, the son of Jehoiakim the king of Judah were a seal,' etc. (Jer 22:24). 'Your cord' refers to the Sanhedrin, as [scripture] says, 'That they put upon the fringe of each corner a cord of blue,' etc. (Num 15:38). 'And your staff' refers to the king messiah, as [scripture] says, 'The staff of your strength the LORD will send from Zion' (Ps 110:2)."[134]

In this passage, Tamar selects the three items of the pledge in accordance with the holy spirit kindled within her. The inspired nature of her choices is demonstrated by the correlation between these items and significant passages of scripture, interpreted as referring to manifestations of Israel's royal leadership. This tradition grants Tamar prophetic powers to appreciate the significance of biblical events, and perhaps even to preview the pre-existent, but not yet revealed, Tora. *Genesis Rabba* also indicates Tamar's prophetic awareness of the nature of her pregnancy with its presentation of the tradition that she would "beat upon her seat and exclaim, 'I am big with kings and redeemers'" (*Gen.Rab.* 85.10).

Tamar's insight into the ramifications of her pregnancy in these three passages recalls *Genesis Rabba*'s general assertion that "the matriarchs are prophets."[135] This commentary maintains that Rebekah's knowledge of Esau's plot to kill Jacob[136] and Rachel's entreaty for only one additional son following the birth of Joseph[137] illustrate this

---

[133] *Gen.Rab.* 85.11.
[134] *Gen.Rab.* 85.9.
[135] *Gen.Rab.* 67.9 and 72.6. A tradition in *Gen.Rab.* 45.10 (cf., 48.20; 63.7) qualifies the nature of their prophecy, however, by maintaining that God never spoke directly to the matriarchs (except to Sarah in Gen 18:15), but rather spoke through an angel or through the mediation of Shem.
[136] *Gen.Rab.* 67.9.
[137] *Gen.Rab.* 72.6.

general rule. It also presents Sarah's idea to give Hagar to Abraham
as inspired by the holy spirit.[138] Although *Genesis Rabba* never explicitly calls Tamar a matriarch, her prophetic insight concerning the
nature of her pregnancy brings her into alignment with the four
women of Genesis commonly regarded as Israel's matriarchs.[139]

Similarly, *Genesis Rabba* explicitly compares Tamar and Rebekah,
implicitly arguing for the former's status as a significant and respectable Israelite mother:

> "She removed her widow's garments from upon her," etc. (Gen 38:14).
> Two covered themselves with a veil and gave birth to twins: Rebekah
> and Tamar. Rebekah: "She took her veil and covered herself" (Gen
> 24:65); Tamar: "She covered herself with a veil and wrapped herself"
> (Gen 38:14).[140]

The correspondence between the two women on the basis of their
veiling and their delivery of twins positively reflects on Tamar, just
at the point where the biblical narrative introduces her morally
ambiguous plot to conceive outside of a socially sanctioned context.
It diverts attention from her impersonation of a prostitute and highlights her similarities with an important biblical matriarch, whom
Genesis Rabba elsewhere describes as "righteous."[141] Rebekah is an especially appropriate choice for this comparison, because in addition
to the two similarities noted in the midrash above, she, like Tamar,
decisively influences Israelite history through deception of an important male character.[142] The tradition comparing the two women also
appears as *Genesis Rabba*'s commentary on Rebekah's veiling when
she first sees Isaac in Gen 25:65.[143] This comparison therefore introduces Tamar for the first time in this commentary, ensuring a positive reading of her character as equal to one of Israel's matriarchs
even before her appearance in Genesis 38.

---

[138] *Gen.Rab.* 45.2.

[139] *Gen.Rab.* 39.11 presents the traditional view that there were three patriarchs
and four matriarchs (Sarah, Rebekah, Leah, and Rachel), and *Gen.Rab.* 70.7 reiterates that there were four matriarchs.

[140] *Gen.Rab.* 85.7.

[141] Rebekah is described as "righteous" in *Gen.Rab.* 63.5, for example. In a different
and strange way, the depiction in *Gen.Rab.* 80.1 of Leah's adornment as a harlot
when she goes out to meet Jacob in Gen 30:16 obliquely argues that Tamar's behavior in Gen 38:14–19 does not disqualify her from the roster of important Israelite mothers.

[142] Genesis 27.

[143] *Gen.Rab.* 60.15.

In fact, further comparison in *Genesis Rabba* between these two women regarding the circumstances of their deliveries and the quality of their sons actually gives Tamar an advantage over Rebekah:

"At the time of her delivery (ויהי בעת לדתה)" (Gen 38:27). Here [the days of Tamar's gestation period] were reduced, whereas in [Rebekah's] case (Gen 25:24) they were complete. "There were twins," etc. (Gen 38:27): [Here the word] "twins" (תאומים) is written fully, [indicating that] both [Perez and Zerah] were righteous, whereas above [in Gen 25:24 the word] "twins" (תאומם) is written defectively, [indicating that] one [Jacob] was righteous and the other [Esau] was wicked.[144]

The two comparisons between Tamar and Rebekah in this passage are based on slight differences in wording and spelling between the remarkably similar birth accounts in Gen 25:24–26 and Gen 38:27–30. As noted previously, the different spellings of the word "twins" are used to justify different moral evaluations of the two sets of boys. The fact that both of Tamar's sons are righteous whereas only one of Rebekah's sons is righteous reflects positively upon the former.[145]

But this passage also contains a motif not yet discussed, namely Tamar's reduced period of gestation. This motif is suggested by the absence of the phrase "her days for delivery were completed" (וימלאו ימיה ללדת), which prefaces Rebekah's delivery of twins in Gen 25:24. Instead, Gen 38:27 prefaces Tamar's delivery of twins with the simple temporal marker, "At the time of her delivery" (ויהי בעת לדתה), without noting the completion of her full term. To the midrashic imagination, this omission suggested a temporal miracle related to Tamar's labor. *Genesis Rabba* frequently weaves extra-biblical miracles into biblical narratives,[146] and several times these providential measures insure a matriarch's delivery of an important son.[147] Tamar's miraculous

---

[144] *Gen.Rab.* 85.13. A doublet of this comparison of the details of Rebekah and Tamar's deliveries appears earlier in *Genesis Rabba*'s commentary on Gen 25:24 (*Gen.Rab.* 63.24). The righteousness of one of Rebekah's sons and the wickedness of the other is also associated with her mounting of a camel—an animal that has one mark of a clean animal and one mark of an unclean animal—in *Gen.Rab.* 60.14.

[145] In fact, in *Gen.Rab.* 65.4, Rebekah is viewed as less than an ideal matriarch because her parents were idolatrous priests and because she gave birth to a wicked son. By contrast, Tamar's father was the righteous priest Shem, according to rabbinic tradition.

[146] A tradition attributed to R. Muna in *Gen.Rab.* 65.17 claims that "Everything [in connection with the land of Palestine] is miraculous."

[147] See, for example, God's special creation of an ovary for Sarah in *Gen.Rab.* 47.2 and 53.5 and for Rebekah in *Gen.Rab.* 63.5. Leah as well bears her sons miraculously in *Gen.Rab.* 72.1, since she has no womb. Sarah and Rebekah experience

delivery once again aligns her character with the other matriarchs and emphasizes the importance of her offspring for Israel's history.

In addition, Tamar's premature delivery plays an important function internally within *Genesis Rabba*'s commentary on Genesis 38, in that it recalls the final proem in the introductory section. As noted above, this proem quotes the phrase, "Before she labored, she gave birth," from Isa 66:7. Tamar's delivery of twins before the period of her pregnancy is completed corresponds to the imagery of the prophetic verse in this proem.[148] It thereby graphically reminds the reader of the messianic import of Genesis 38 articulated in the fourth proem, just at the moment when the twins are born.

It may be that the arguments for Tamar's equivalence or even superiority to Rebekah in this tradition reveal a special urgency to reform a character whose sexual behavior is unconventional and suspect. In fact, behind the positive depiction of Tamar's delivery and offspring may lie traditions concerning births to women who have been cleared of suspicions of adultery. According to Num 5:28, if a suspected adulteress proves to be innocent, she will conceive children. In light of this biblical verse, the fact that Tamar has children in Genesis 38 in and of itself suggests her innocence. The Jerusalem Talmud (*y. Soṭa* 3.4) elaborates upon the positive aspects of the cleared woman's delivery and offspring:

> If she used to give birth with pain, now she will give birth in comfort. If she used to produce females, now she will produce males. If she used to produce ugly children, now she will produce pretty babies. If she used to produce dark ones, now she will produce fair ones. If she

---

other miracles associated with procreation as well. In *Gen.Rab.* 53.9 Sarah's breasts become fountains gushing milk after the birth of Isaac, and all the noble gentile babies who suckle from her gain fear of God and worldly dominion, at least until they refuse to accept the law at Sinai. In *Gen.Rab.* 59.11 and 60.1, 5, 6, 15, God performs a number of miracles to ensure Isaac and Rebekah's marital union. He marks the way to Haran for Abraham's servant Eleazar with meteors and lightning and allows him to accomplish this long trip in a single day. He ensures that Rebekah approaches the well just as the servant finishes his prayer, and he causes the water in the well to rise to meet Rebekah's pitcher as she waters the camels. In addition to Tamar's miraculous, early delivery, a number of other early births are reported in *Genesis Rabba*, including the births of two boys and three girls in a single night to Eve (*Gen.Rab.* 22.2, 3; 24.7) and the births of babies after a three-day gestation period in the era before the flood (*Gen.Rab.* 36.1).

[148] The appearance of the same phrase "at the time" (ויהי בעת) in Gen 38:1 and in Gen 38:27 may have facilitated the interweaving of these verses and Isa 66:7, with its emphasis on temporal sequence.

used to produce short ones, now she will produce tall ones. If she used to produce one by one, now she will produce two by two.[149]

A number of the descriptions of the children born to women proven innocent resonate with Tamar's sons in *Genesis Rabba*. Since Tamar is spared the discomfort of a full term pregnancy, she has less pain in childbearing than most women. She has male, not female children, and she has twins, not a single child. The biblical text reveals nothing about the physical characteristics of Perez and Zerah, so one cannot determine if they exhibit the remainder of the advantages promised in the Jerusalem Talmud. But *Genesis Rabba* states that both sons are righteous, and therefore at least morally ideal. Admittedly, the correspondence between the details in this passage from the Jerusalem Talmud and the details in *Genesis Rabba*'s description of Tamar's delivery and children is not exact. But given that the extensive similarities in language and content between these two works indicate a common cultural milieu, if not actual dependence,[150] we can assume that the reader of *Genesis Rabba* would be familiar with the traditions concerning the suspected adulteress recorded in the Jerusalem Talmud. This being the case, the positive details of Tamar's delivery and her children's characters would implicitly argue for her innocence against charges of sexual impropriety. Elsewhere, *Genesis Rabba* explicitly quotes Num 5:28 in one of its discussions of Sarah's conception after her emergence from the houses of Pharaoh and Abimelech.[151] In this passage, Sarah's conception through God's intervention at this point in the biblical narrative proves that she remained undefiled while with these foreign kings.[152]

Other measures in *Genesis Rabba* modify Tamar's audacious biblical character. Returning to the double interpretation of Judah's perceptions and actions at Enaim discussed earlier, one finds that in both cases Tamar is depicted as a proper, respectable woman. For example, the midrashic elaboration on Gen 38:15, which asserts that Judah did not recognize Tamar because she covered her face "in her father-in-law's house," imbues her character with a conscientious

---

[149] A similar tradition, lacking only the final reference to the birth of twins, is recorded in *b. Soṭa* 26a (cf., *t. Soṭa* 2.3).

[150] For a discussion of the extensive material found in both the Jerusalem Talmud and *Genesis Rabba*, see Albeck, "Introduction to *Genesis Rabba*," 66–84.

[151] *Gen.Rab.* 53.6.

[152] See also the generalization in *Gen.Rab.* 54.2 that righteous people produce children—a generalization that is discredited in *Gen.Rab.* 45.4.

modesty.[153] The second midrashic elaboration on this same biblical verse in *Genesis Rabba* also enhances her reputation, in that it depicts her as a respectably dressed woman whom Judah intends to pass by, not as a seductively dressed prostitute.[154] This transformation of Judah's biblical appraisal ensures a positive evaluation for Tamar's character even at the expense of the internal plot dynamics of the narrative, for only the subsequent introduction of an angel reestablishes the flow of events.

Tamar's motives at Enaim are also clarified in *Genesis Rabba* so as to eliminate any suggestion that she acted merely to satisfy her own desires, to gain financial advantage, or to humiliate or punish her father-in-law. *Genesis Rabba* accomplishes this task through a surprising comparison between Tamar and Potiphar's wife, appearing in the section immediately following the opening proems. This second section presents a number of reasons for the placement of Genesis 38 in its present context in the Joseph story. Following a brief identification of two verbal connections between Genesis 38 and its immediate biblical context,[155] this section continues with a more extended, final reflection upon the textual proximity of the sexually forward women in Genesis 38 and Genesis 39:

> R. Samuel b. Nahman said, "[The biblical placement of Genesis 38 is] in order to juxtapose Tamar's story and Potiphar's wife's story. Just as one [acted] for the sake of heaven, so the other [acted] for the sake of heaven." As R. Joshua b. Levi said, "She [Potiphar's wife] had seen in her horoscope that she was destined to produce a son by him [Joseph], but she did not know whether it was to be from her or from her daughter. As it is written, '[Now let] the monthly prognosticators [stand up and save you] from the things that shall come upon you (מאשר יבאו עליך)' (Isa 47:13)." R. Abin said, "[From] 'some of the things' (מאשר), but not [from] all of the things (כל אשר)."[156]

This passage concentrates on the comparison between Tamar and Potiphar's wife facilitated by the placement of Genesis 38 immediately before Genesis 39. But whereas the biblical juxtaposition might lead to a negative explanation of Tamar's obscure motives and actions, were the reader to fill in some of the gaps in Genesis 38 with details

---

[153] *Gen.Rab.* 85.8.
[154] *Gen.Rab.* 85.8.
[155] These include the references to "descent" in Gen 38:1 and Gen 39:1 and the dual appearances of the imperative "Recognize!" (הכר נא) in Gen 38:25 and Gen 37:32.
[156] *Gen.Rab.* 85.2.

from the story of the more developed seductress of the next chapter, *Genesis Rabba* takes pains to prevent such an interpretive move. In marked contradiction to its otherwise negative portrayal of Potiphar's wife as a lustful adulteress,[157] this passage portrays her as a well-intentioned character, despite her lack of precise information. She approaches Joseph only for the purpose of producing the descendants that she vaguely discerns will arise from a union with the Hebrew slave, although unbeknownst to her it is her daughter Asenath who is destined to bear these children.[158]

The sympathetic development of Potiphar's wife in this anomalous passage stresses that Tamar as well acts only for the next generation, not for personal gratification or advantage. The placement of this comparison between the two female characters who act "for the sake of heaven" even before Tamar's introduction in *Genesis Rabba*'s verse-by-verse commentary on Genesis 38 therefore constitutes a preemptive strategy of positive interpretation for her character. Interestingly, whereas the two women are portrayed as similar with respect to their worthy motives, Potiphar's wife's limited ability to see the future through astrology contrasts with Tamar's clear prophetic insight into the royal significance of her offspring with Judah.[159] This

---

[157] For example, she is equated with the seductive adulteress of Prov 7:5–27 in *Gen.Rab.* 87.1. In addition, she is frequently described as a dangerous she-bear in *Gen.Rab.* 42.3; 84.7, 19; 86.4; 87.3, 4. She is called other unflattering names in *Gen.Rab.* 86.1; 87.2, 4; 87.5, 10. Other female characters in *Genesis Rabba* motivated alternately by the worthy purpose of procreation and by immoral desires are Lot's daughters and Ruth (*Gen.Rab.* 51.9, 10, and 11). The commentary never explicitly compares Tamar with these ambiguous characters, although aspects of their stories are similar.

[158] *Gen.Rab.* 89.1 explicitly states that Joseph marries the daughter of his mistress. Behind *Genesis Rabba*'s depiction of Potiphar's wife here lies a midrashic tradition that views Joseph's wife Asenath, who bore him Ephraim and Manasseh, as the daughter of his Egyptian master Potiphar and his wife. This tradition stems from the conclusion based on a similarity of names that Potiphar (פוטיפר), Pharaoh's chief steward and Joseph's master (Gen 39:1), and Potiphera (פוטי פרע), the priest of On and Asenath's father (Gen 46:20), were one and the same man. The conflation of the two characters is explicitly made in *Gen.Rab.* 86.3. See V. Aptowitzer, "Asenath, the Wife of Joseph: A Haggadic Literary-Historical Study," *HUCA* 1 (1924) 239–306, for this and other midrashic traditions concerning Asenath. Within the world of midrashic legend, therefore, there is an inverted generational jump in the narratives in both Genesis 38 and 39. Unlike in Genesis 38, in which the younger generation (Shelah) was designated but the older generation (Judah) accomplished the task of procreation, here Potiphar's wife thought that the older generation (herself) was responsible, when in fact the younger generation (Asenath) was destined for this role.

[159] This passage comparing Tamar and Potiphar's wife (*Gen.Rab.* 85.2) captures *Genesis Rabba*'s ambivalent evaluation of heavenly portents and other divinations.

comparison highlights Tamar's superiority to her female counterpart
of Genesis 39.

Genesis Rabba also develops Tamar's status as an ancestress of kings
and redeemers by providing her with a suitable father. Tamar's pedigree is presented in this commentary's discussion of Judah's curious
order in Gen 38:25 that she be burnt for her promiscuous behavior:

> Ephraim the disputant, the student of R. Meir, [said] in the latter's
> name, "Tamar was the daughter of Shem, for it is written, 'The daughter
> of a priest who defiles herself by having illicit intercourse (לִזְנוֹת),' etc.
> (Lev 21:9). [Consequently], 'Judah said, "Take her out and let her be
> burned (תִּשָּׂרֵף)"' (Gen 38:25)."[160]

The complete biblical law found in Lev 21:9 partially quoted in this
tradition reads, "The daughter of a priest who defiles herself by having
illicit intercourse (לִזְנוֹת) defiles her father. She shall be burned (תִּשָּׂרֵף)
with fire." The presence of forms of the verb "to have illicit intercourse" (זנה) in both Gen 38:24 and Lev 21:9 and of the passive
verb "to be burned" (niphal, נִשְׂרַף) in both Gen 38:25 and Lev 21:9
establishes a connection between the biblical narrative and the priestly
law. When read intertextually, these biblical passages suggest that
Tamar is the daughter of a priest.[161] The difficulty of this conclusion,
however, lies in the setting of the biblical narrative before there was
a distinctive class of priests in Israel. But there is one figure in the
earlier chapters of Genesis who is described as "a priest of God Most
High" (Gen 14:18): Melchizedek, who brings out bread and wine
following the war against the coalition of kings, blesses Abram, and

---

This ambivalence may be seen in its tacit acceptance of the efficacy of astrological
arts in some passages (*Gen.Rab.* 1.4; 10.6, 7; 26.5; 44.10; 63.2; 68.12) and in its
explicit polemic against astrology in others (*Gen.Rab.* 44.12). *Gen.Rab.* 85.2 modifies
the ironic, absolute denial of the efficacy of astrology in Isa 47:13 to the qualified
stance that the knowledge gained through this means is partial. It does this by assigning a partitive value to the preposition מִן, which prefaces the phrase "from the
things that shall come upon you" (מֵאֲשֶׁר יָבֹאוּ עָלַיִךְ), thereby rendering it "some of
the things that shall come upon you." In the context of this passage, the phrase "for
the sake of heaven" (לְשׁוּם שָׁמַיִם), describing the motivation of the two women, suggests a double valence. In the case of Potiphar's wife, the allusion to "heaven"
brings to mind the stars and planets upon which she relies for her information
about the future. In the case of Tamar, on the other hand, the allusion to "Heaven"
recalls the frequent use of that term as an epithet for God, as described by Urbach,
Sages, 66–79. For another reference to Potiphar's wife's reliance on astrology, see
Gen.Rab. 87.4.

[160] *Gen.Rab.* 85.10.

[161] Note the discussion in the previous chapter concerning the distinctive employment of this connection between Gen 38:24–25 and Lev 21:9 in *Targum Neofiti*.

receives from him a tithe of the spoils. These priestly actions mark this mysterious figure as the Hebrew patriarch's equal, or even superior.[162] In *Genesis Rabba* and other rabbinic literature, Melchizedek is frequently identified as Shem, one of Noah's three sons,[163] and this composite character is developed in a number of ways. Not only is Shem depicted as a priest[164] and as a mediator between God and certain human characters,[165] he is also portrayed as a teacher of the esoteric details of the sacrificial system and other matters of Tora,[166] and as a judge with a famous legal court.[167] The midrashic Shem makes an especially appropriate father for the woman destined to bring forth the royal and messianic lineage, for in addition to his status as priest, teacher, legal expert, and judge, he himself is a king, specifically "the king of Salem" (as Gen 14:18 describes Melchizedek). *Genesis Rabba* therefore replaces the disturbing biblical taciturnity concerning Tamar's background with its specification of Shem as her priestly and royal father.[168]

Genesis Rabba also highlights Tamar's status as a worthy ancestress through its depiction of her prayerful piety. Although Tamar also prays in *Targum Neofiti*, she prays a different prayer at a different point in the narrative in *Genesis Rabba*, and these distinctive details contribute to the development of her character as an important Israelite mother. In this commentary, Tamar's prayer appears in a discussion of the significance of the phrase, "the gate of Enaim," where she sits waiting for Judah:

---

[162] See *Gen.Rab.* 44.7 and 46.5, which point out the similarities between these two characters, and *Gen.Rab.* 56.10, which depicts the equal consideration God gives both righteous men when he renames Jerusalem.

[163] This identification is obvious in *Gen.Rab.* 44.7, for example.

[164] *Gen.Rab.* 30.6 and 36.4 recount how Shem offered the first sacrifices after the flood because his father Noah was disqualified when a lion castrated or otherwise maimed him. *Gen.Rab.* 26.3 notes that the temple will be built in Shem's city, Jerusalem, since he is the high priest.

[165] See for example his delivery of divine messages to Hagar in *Gen.Rab.* 20.6; to Rebekah in *Gen.Rab.* 45.10 (cf., 48.20; 63.7); and to Abraham's idolatrous family in *Gen.Rab.* 52.11.

[166] For example, Shem is depicted as a teacher in *Gen.Rab.* 43.6; 63.10; and 68.5.

[167] For example, Shem is depicted as a judge, along with Eber, in *Gen.Rab.* 67.8 (cf., *Gen.Rab.* 85.12). In addition, he makes some surprising midrashic appearances in biblical narratives. For example, he helps Noah build the ark in *Gen.Rab.* 44.7, and he buries Sarah in Abraham's cave in *Gen.Rab.* 62.3.

[168] A miraculous detail concerning Shem's birth decisively links him to his distant royal descendant, David. In *Gen.Rab.* 26.3; 43.6; and 84.6, Shem is born circumcised, as are Jacob and Joseph. Significantly, in *b. Soṭa* 10b David is born circumcised as well.

"And she sat at the entrance of Enaim (פתח עינים)" (Gen 38:14): Rabbi said, "We have reviewed the whole of scripture and found no place called 'the entrance of Enaim' (פתח עינים). Then what is the significance of [the expression] 'the entrance of Enaim?' It merely teaches that she lifted up her eyes to the gate (פתח) to which all eyes (עינים) are lifted and said: 'May it be your will that I do not leave this house empty.'"[169]

This passage provides a fascinating glimpse at the rabbinic process of biblical interpretation. It alludes to an unsuccessful attempt to identify the geographical location where Tamar waited for Judah through examination of other biblical texts. Since the rest of the biblical corpus fails to illuminate the phrase under discussion, an opportunity arises to promote other non-geographical readings of "the entrance of Enaim."[170] The tradition quoted above draws on the early Jewish image of heaven's entrance as a "gate" (commonly שער, but here פתח) and on the typical gesture of raising the "eyes" (עינים) in prayer to portray a pious Tamar.[171] This midrashic explanation of the biblical phrase locates Tamar's prayer immediately before her successful encounter with Judah, thereby highlighting the significance of her conception.

The content of her prayer, which is entirely an imaginative creation with no explicit verbal links to the biblical text, emphatically reiterates the importance of Tamar's plan to conceive for Israel's redemptive history. Her supplication, "May it be your will that I do not leave this house (מבית זה) empty," hints at the theme of dynastic lineage with its reference to a "house" (בית),[172] and calls for a divine ratification of her efforts to conceive. If read in tandem with the tradition depicting the angel of desire's guidance of Judah in *Gen. Rab.* 85.8, Tamar's prayer is answered when she becomes pregnant with royal and messianic offspring.[173] In *Genesis Rabba*, therefore, Tamar

---

[169] *Gen.Rab.* 85.7.

[170] The fact that Enam (העינם) in Josh 15:34 was overlooked in this search, especially in light of the reference to the place where Tamar sat as Enaim (עינים) in Gen 38:21, may indicate a desire to open the text at this productive point to midrashic exegesis rather than simply to identify a geographical location.

[171] For the image of heaven's entrance as a gate and the gesture of raising the eyes in prayer, see the discussion in the previous chapter of Tamar's prayer for the restoration of the witnesses in *Tg.Neof.* Gen 38:25–26. In *Gen.Rab.* 75.13, Jacob lifts his eyes to heaven in prayer.

[172] "This house" apparently refers to Judah's lineage. The dynastic sense of the word "house" is evident in its biblical usage in phrases such as "the house of David" (בית דוד, 2 Sam 3:1, 6; 7:26; and other places).

[173] In *Gen.Rab.* 41.1, the prayer of one of the matriarchs is similarly answered by

is not merely a pious figure who petitions heaven in time of personal need. Instead, she is an intercessor for Israel's future generations, who will rely on the leadership of the Davidic kings and experience ultimate redemption in the messianic age.[174]

Through a variety of means, then, *Genesis Rabba* argues that Tamar is an appropriate ancestress for the royal and messianic lineage. The portrayals of Tamar's prophetic insight, her similarities with the biblical matriarchs, her marvelous delivery of righteous children, her modesty and pure motives, her distinguished genealogical background, and her prayerful intercession for Israel's future all work together to insure a positive popular perception of this lightly sketched biblical character, in keeping with this commentary's emphasis on the origins of kingship in Genesis 38.

CONCLUSIONS

Two significant transformations of Genesis 38 occur in *Genesis Rabba*. First, this commentary interjects a pervasive divine presence into a biblical narrative in which God makes only two brief punitive appearances. Rather than a puzzling tale of human intrigue and happenstance, *Genesis Rabba* portrays the events of Genesis 38 as the means through which God brings to fulfillment his intentions to provide Israel with political leaders and eschatological redeemers. Non-biblical additions to the narrative, including God's dispatch of an angel to guide Judah to Tamar, his special creation of a replacement pledge, and his acceptance of responsibility in court for the preceding events, move the plot unfalteringly to its divinely ordained goal. In addition, frequent commentaries on the events of the narrative provided by prophetic scriptural passages, by the holy spirit, by an angel, and by

---

the dispatch of an angel. This matriarch is Sarah, who prays for protection in Pharaoh's house. Subsequently, an angel appears to guard her from the Egyptian king's immoral advances. By contrast, in Tamar's case the angel appears to encourage what under ordinary circumstances might be considered an immoral sexual encounter.

[174] Judith R. Baskin examines the development of other important Israelite mothers, especially Hannah, as intercessors in "Rabbinic Reflections on the Barren Wife," *HTR* 82 (1989) 112–14. In *Genesis Rabba* itself, God causes Israel's matriarchs to be barren because he yearns to hear their prayers and supplications (*Gen.Rab.* 45.4). When the matriarchs unite to pray for Rachel to conceive, therefore, their prayer is answered (*Gen.Rab.* 72.6; 73.3). Another matriarch in *Genesis Rabba* with a special intercessory role not related to childbearing is Rachel, who prays for mercy for the Babylonian exiles who pass her grave (*Gen.Rab.* 72.10; 97, NV).

God himself emphasize the theme of divine involvement to establish Israel's historical kings and eschatological messiah.

The second significant transformation of Genesis 38 effected by *Genesis Rabba* consists of the recreation of Judah and Tamar as distinguished and moral forebears of an important royal and messianic lineage. In part, this interpretive move corresponds with the broader program evident in *Genesis Rabba* of recasting biblical characters associated with Israel's history in an unambiguously positive light.[175] But in addition, this commentary's positive understanding of Judah and Tamar as worthy ancestors functions to interject contemporary moral values and religious ideals into the story of origins of important historical and transhistorical realities. Since Israel's kingship and other forms of political leadership are idealized in *Genesis Rabba*, their origins in the relations between one man and one woman are correspondingly represented in positive and uncomplicated terms.

These two basic transformations are accomplished often at the expense of the internal dynamics of the biblical narrative. The constant intervention of God and the positive behavior of Judah and Tamar in *Genesis Rabba* flatten Genesis 38 into a tale of divine intention and human compliance for the emergence of future kings and redeemers, and often this ideological modification is less than elegant. For example, Judah's sexual restraint in passing by the respectable woman on the road in *Gen.Rab.* 85.8 ruptures the forward movement of the narrative and requires the introduction of an angel to restore it. But this measure in turn wreaks havoc on the original biblical narrative, for once Judah is informed by the angel of his duty to produce kings and redeemers, his subsequent search for the prostitute and his sentencing of Tamar for sexual immorality become unnecessary, and even incongruous. Similarly, the positive evaluation of Judah's decision to withhold Shelah in *Gen.Rab.* 85.5 robs Tamar of the moral advantage over her father-in-law upon which the biblical narrative depends. Also, if Tamar's pregnancy "through illicit

---

[175] This broader program includes a corresponding recasting of biblical characters outside of the immediate Israelite family in an unambiguously negative light. The perfect example of this dynamic consists of *Genesis Rabba*'s portrayal of Jacob as a righteous man, despite his biblical frailties, and of Esau as a wicked man, despite the biblical author's relatively sympathetic portrayal of him. Through this moral contrast between Rebekah's twin sons, *Genesis Rabba* expresses a moral contrast between the Jewish people and their Roman oppressors. *Genesis Rabba* makes similar contrasts between righteous Abraham and wicked Lot, and between righteous Isaac and wicked Ishmael.

sexual relations" merely means that she publicly announced her conception of future kings and redeemers as *Gen.Rab.* 85.10 maintains, then Judah's order that she be burned becomes incomprehensible. In these and other cases, *Genesis Rabba* sacrifices the art of the biblical narrative for the greater glory of Israelite history and for the articulation of the divine plan for ultimate redemption.

How does *Genesis Rabba*'s emphasis on kings and messiahs in this chapter relate to the commentary's broader understanding of the history and salvation of Israel? There is a repeated celebration of Israel's most famous king, David, in *Genesis Rabba*,[176] and references to an eschatological messiah or a messianic age are not absent. But concerning the latter, Jacob Neusner rightly cautions against assuming that messianic expectations dominated Jewish thought of the rabbinic period. He has argued instead for the critical appraisal of the function of traditional messianic motifs within particular documents.[177]

A survey of the content of *Genesis Rabba* suggests that eschatological redemption through the mediation of a messianic figure is far from the exclusive, or even primary, focus of this document. For example, very few of the proems that introduce the chapters in *Genesis Rabba* concern themselves with eschatological redemption. Those few which do seldom discuss the completion of history in terms of the appearance of a messiah, but employ a wide range of teleological motifs, including "the world to come,"[178] "the future to come,"[179] "the hereafter,"[180] the final "judgment,"[181] and the "resurrection."[182] Others refer generally to the "messianic future" but display no specific interest in a messianic figure.[183]

But while the almost complete absence of a royal messiah in the proems cautions against exaggerating the importance of this figure in the thought system of *Genesis Rabba*'s editors, the messianic implications of Genesis 38 are not entirely anomalous in this document. Messianic

---

[176] A few examples of the many positive references to David include *Gen.Rab.* 39.10; 44.20 (cf., 62.2); 88.7.

[177] Jacob Neusner, *Messiah in Context: Israel's History and Destiny in Formative Judaism* (Philadelphia: Fortress Press, 1984).

[178] *Gen.Rab.* 33.1.

[179] *Gen.Rab.* 95.1.

[180] *Gen.Rab.* 77.1.

[181] *Gen.Rab.* 80.1.

[182] *Gen.Rab.* 78.1 and 95.1.

[183] *Gen.Rab.* 40.2 and 48.6. See also *Gen.Rab.* 74.1, where a messiah is mentioned, but only to specify the period of time, "the days of the messiah," in which the dead will be resurrected.

motifs are employed occasionally in *Genesis Rabba* as vehicles to express religious truths. For example, God's preparation for Israel's ultimate redemption through the messiah even before the world's creation functions to illustrate the depths of divine involvement in the destiny of a particular people.[184] The promise of restoration of Israel's land[185] and wealth,[186] the rebuilding of the temple,[187] and the healing and resurrection of the righteous[188] associated with the messianic era in *Genesis Rabba* all function to illustrate God's continuing concern for this people, despite the historical experience of foreign conquest.

Perhaps it is in light of its recurrent references to oppressive foreign governments, including the contemporary Roman Empire, that the significance of *Genesis Rabba*'s development of Genesis 38 as a story of kings and messiahs may best be understood.[189] The period of this commentary's compilation in the late fourth and early fifth centuries CE witnessed repressive legislation concerning Jewish subjects by Christian emperors. In this difficult political climate, appeal to the concept of autonomous and righteous Israelite leadership no doubt played an important, though not exclusive, role in the larger project of community self-definition. The idealized recollection of strong and just kingship from the biblical past and the expectation of its restoration in the future defined the contemporary period of oppression under foreign government as a temporary aberration in Israel's history. *Genesis Rabba*'s positive development of Genesis 38 as the story of origins of Israel's kings, redeemers, and eschatological messiah corresponds to this imaginative positioning of the Jewish community upon a divinely guided time line. It thereby contributes to the construction of a religious perspective that transcends and endures the harsh realities of history.

One final issue in *Genesis Rabba*'s interpretation of Genesis 38 concerns the genre of exegetical anthology which characterizes this commentary. As pointed out earlier, in addition to defining Genesis 38

---

[184] See *Gen.Rab.* 1.4, in which the name of the messiah is contemplated before creation.

[185] *Gen.Rab.* 64.3.

[186] *Gen.Rab.* 78.12; 83.4.

[187] *Gen.Rab.* 2.5; 56.10; 65.23; 69.7.

[188] *Gen.Rab.* 20.5; 96.5.

[189] See for example the discussion of the end of foreign oppression with the appearance of a messiah in *Gen.Rab.* 2.4 and 42.4. But even more frequently *Genesis Rabba* discusses the end of Israel's oppression without explicit reference to a messianic figure, as in *Gen.Rab.* 16.4; 21.1; 56.9; 70.8.

as the story of Israel's kings and redeemers, *Genesis Rabba* presents numerous other exegetical traditions that are unrelated, or even contradictory, to this overarching interpretation of the biblical chapter. This presentation of diverse traditions from different generations of rabbinic authorities tacitly argues that the true significance of the biblical text emerges through academic study by a particular class of learned men. In turn, the fact that *Genesis Rabba*'s dominant interpretation of Genesis 38 as a royal and messianic narrative emerges through the medium of exegetical anthology suggests that this interpretation is not contrived. Rather, it results from the exegetical efforts of generations of scholars to express the revelatory sense of the biblical chapter.

It may even be that the title of the commentary itself, *Genesis Rabba*, or, literally, "The Great Genesis," reflects the desire to validate rabbinic midrash as a locus of biblical revelation. Several explanations of this curious title have been proposed.[190] But most suggestive for our purposes is one forwarded by Leopold Zunz, who maintains that this commentary is called "The Great Genesis" because it is much lengthier than the biblical book of Genesis itself. His comparison between the actual lengths of Genesis and *Genesis Rabba* offers a starting point for a slightly different reflection on the relation between scripture and commentary within the rabbinic document itself. Certainly *Genesis Rabba* accords to Genesis the priority and respect due to authoritative scripture, both by structuring the entire work according to the order of the biblical text and by consistently quoting its verses, or at least phrases from them, before offering later exegetical reflections. But while Genesis provides the focus and structure for this document, the many voices of rabbinic commentary predominate resoundingly in terms of sheer volume.[191] In its concrete illustration of the interplay between written and oral Tora characteristic of rabbinic Judaism, *Genesis Rabba* favors the latter. It may be that the title of this commentary emphasizes the rabbinic view that Tora's revelation includes much more than the written words of the biblical text. The true "greatness" of Genesis manifests itself only through the transformative study and creative appropriation of this biblical artifact

---

[190] For a summary of these explanations, see Albeck, "Introduction to *Genesis Rabba*," 93–94.

[191] The fact that *Genesis Rabba* often abbreviates its quotations of the biblical text exaggerates this disproportion, although it may have been assumed that every reader would be familiar with the endings of verses only partially quoted.

by later generations; therefore, scripture and its traditional commentary together comprise "The Great Genesis." *Genesis Rabba*'s articulation of Genesis 38 as the divinely guided origins of Israel's royalty and redemption provides an example of how written and oral Tora conjoin to offer a revelatory message for contemporary generations. Concerning this synthesis of tradition and innovation, an anonymous expression of amazement and appreciation in *Genesis Rabba* seems particularly appropriate: "See how ancient words become new in the mouth of the sage!"[192]

---

[192] *Gen.Rab.* 63.8.

AFTERWORD

"What a breach you have made for yourself!" (Gen 38:29)

The previous studies of the *Testament of Judah*, *Targum Neofiti*, and *Genesis Rabba* reveal three very different treatments of the story of Judah and Tamar. Comparisons between these interpretive works on a number of different levels naturally lead to final reflections concerning appropriate methods for comparative midrash, as well as to more general conclusions concerning the hermeneutic enterprise in ancient Judaism.

Since comparative midrash generally concentrates on the origins and development of single exegetical motifs, it makes sense to start with a comparison on this level between the *Testament of Judah*, *Targum Neofiti*, and *Genesis Rabba*. Let us return to the extra-biblical motif of the divine voice that accepts responsibility for the events in Genesis 38, since a variant of this motif appears in all three interpretive works. In *Genesis Rabba*, the holy spirit cries out in the courtroom, "These things were from me" (ממני היו הדברים).[1] In *Targum Neofiti*, a heavenly voice delivers the verdict, "Both of you are innocent. From before the LORD is the decree" (מן קדם ייי פתגמא).[2] In the *Testament of Judah*, the actual divine utterance is missing, but it is paraphrased by Judah, who refrains from killing Tamar when he realizes that what has happened "was from the Lord" (παρὰ κυρίου ἦν).[3] In each of these interpretive works, the motif of divine acceptance of responsibility appears in connection with the interpretation of Gen 38:26, which contains Judah's declaration that Tamar "is more righteous than I" (צדקה ממני). At some point in the exegetical history of this particular lemma, Judah's unfavorable comparison of himself with Tamar was broken into two parts, and the second part, "from me" (ממני), was designated as divine speech. This reassignment of a fragment of Judah's speech to the divine voice was widely known, and the parties responsible for the *Testament of Judah*, *Targum Neofiti*, and *Genesis Rabba* inherited

---

[1] *Gen.Rab.* 85.12.
[2] *Tg.Neof.* Gen 38:26.
[3] *T.Jud.* 12:6.

it as part of the body of lemmatic biblical exegesis that they used to construct their larger interpretive structures.

An exploration of the factors motivating the emergence of this exegetical motif and the distinctive employments of it within the three interpretive works addresses methodological questions within the field of comparative midrash. The first question that arises concerning this motif is whether or not the biblical phrase "She is more righteous than I" (צדקה ממני) was actually problematic for early Jewish readers of scripture and therefore required a creative solution, such as the introduction of a divine voice. Significantly, some of the earliest translators of Genesis 38 had no difficulty with the phrase. For example, the Septuagint translates the Hebrew phrase as "Tamar is more righteous than I" (Δεδικαίωται Θαμαρ ἢ ἐγώ). This translation is quite literal, with only the addition of Tamar's name to specify the subject of the verb. The Samaritan Targum and the Peshitta also preserve the comparative sense of this phrase. Perhaps, then, the difficulty lay not in the grammar of this phrase, but in its content. The comparison casts an extremely negative light on Judah, since through it he acknowledges the superiority of his daughter-in-law, who intentionally tricked him into having incestuous relations by assuming the identity of a prostitute. Perhaps as a first stage in the development of this exegetical tradition, Judah's negative comparison of himself with Tamar was severed into two parts, to become a declaration of Tamar's righteousness ("She is righteous," צדקה) and an admission that he was the father of the important twins that emerge at the end of the chapter ("It was from me," ממני). *Targum Neofiti* presents both of these statements in an expanded, interpretive form, when Judah declares "Tamar my daughter-in-law is innocent. By me she is pregnant" (וזכאה היא תמר כלתי מיני היא מעברה).

But what then motivated the reassignment of the second part of the phrase "It was from me" (ממני) to a divine voice? This question is especially perplexing in light of the clear specification in the Hebrew text that Judah spoke these words: "Judah recognized and said (ויכר יהודה ויאמר), 'She is more righteous than I.'" The interjection of divine speech at this point in the narrative contradicts the plain and simple sense of the biblical text. The reassignment therefore does not respond to a problem in the Bible. In fact the opposite appears to be the case. The interjection of divine speech appears to be a response to a problem that pious readers had as they pondered the text. As members of religious communities, these readers expected scripture to depict aspects of the relationship between humanity and divinity. But except for two punitive interventions, God is not an active presence in Genesis 38. To correct this situation, some bold interpreter found a pliant point in the Hebrew text at which to interject an active divine presence into the narrative. This pliant point occurred at the dramatic climax of the biblical narrative in the phrase "It was from me" (ממני). Perhaps the interpreter's reassignment of this phrase to a divine voice was inspired by other traditions concerning divine intervention in difficult legal situations. Whatever the case, by designating the phrase as divine speech, this unknown interpreter indicated that the events in Genesis 38 happened by the design of providence, not merely by chance. The reassignment of a single phrase from Judah to the divine voice therefore indicates a religious interpretation of Genesis 38 as an example of God's involvement with human history.

Thus, the impetus for individual exegetical motifs may be found not only in the problematics of the Hebrew text, but also in the perspectives of later readers. Certainly rabbinic exegesis does involve close attention to and manipulation of the orthography, word choice, and grammar of scripture. But to concentrate on difficulties in the Hebrew text as the primary motivating force in exegesis is to miss some of the more interesting and important dynamics of biblical interpretation. Comparative midrash at its best should include as part of its method serious attention to the transformative role of interpreters, who bring to the biblical text a wide variety of strategies of reading, verbal associations, theological presuppositions, and cultural perspectives.

The important role of interpreters is once again highlighted as we turn from the origins of the motif of the divine voice to its distinctive functions within the *Testament of Judah*, *Targum Neofiti*, and *Genesis Rabba*. The fact that each of these three interpretations employs this motif highlights the contribution that traditional lemmatic exegesis makes towards the emergence of post-biblical narrative configurations. But although the motif of the divine voice serves as an inherited building block, it does not ultimately determine the shape of the larger interpretive structures. Rather, each work employs this same motif distinctively, in keeping with its larger purposes. In *Genesis Rabba*, when the holy spirit cries in the courtroom, "These things were from me" (ממני היו הדברים), these words suggest that the events of Genesis 38 are part of a providential design leading to the origins of Israel's kings and redeemers, themes emphasized in a variety of ways in this commentary. In *Targum Neofiti*, when the voice from heaven proclaims, "Both of you are innocent. From before the LORD is the decree" (מן קדם ייי פתגמא), these words reprieve Tamar and Judah from the fiery death that they had willingly accepted as exemplars of the concept "sanctification of the [divine] Name" and demonstrate the power of God to save those who trust in him. In the *Testament of Judah*, Judah's recognition that what had happened to him "was from the Lord" (παρὰ κυρίου ἦν) implies that the events of Genesis 38 were a punishment for his sins of hubris and humiliation of his brother. Each interpretive work interjects an active divine presence into Genesis 38 through the motif of the divine voice, but each also specifies a distinctive purpose for God's involvement in the story.

Reflection on how this common motif is employed within the larger narrative and thematic structures of these three interpretations therefore ultimately leads to a deeper appreciation of their very different emphases. Comparative midrash that concentrates exclusively on the origins and diachronic development of individual exegetical motifs may overlook their recontextualization within larger synchronic structures. In so doing, it misses the broader view of how a particular biblical narrative makes sense within various religious communities. So, while it might be illuminating to trace the historical evolution of the motif of the divine voice (for example, to note that in *Genesis Rabba* it retains its connection with the biblical phrase "from me" [ממני], whereas in the paraphrases in *Targum Neofiti* and the *Testament of Judah* this connection is already lost), this attention to diachronic development does not touch upon the more interesting issue of how interpreters employ these variants in larger interpretive structures to articulate the religious significance of Genesis 38. The previous chapters provide models for a type of study of biblical interpretation that focuses on larger interpretive structures, while still acknowledging the contribution that prior exegesis makes to those larger interpretive structures.

Although comparative midrash generally operates at the level of the individual exegetical motif or tradition, there are also a number of other more encompassing levels that might permit fruitful comparison. These levels include theme, narrative structure, cultural influences, and the poetics of interpretation. Comparing the *Testament of Judah*, *Targum Neofiti*, and *Genesis Rabba* on these different levels highlights the distinctiveness of each interpretation and therefore reemphasizes the critical role of historically situated readers for determining the religious meanings of a biblical narrative.

The theme of kingship presents itself as a natural choice for a comparison on the thematic level. All three of the interpretations demonstrate an awareness of the association between Genesis 38 and the theme of kingship implicit in the biblical narrative through its conclusion with the birth of David's ancestor, Perez. Two of them, *Genesis Rabba* and the *Testament of Judah*, develop this theme extensively. Using a variety of techniques, *Genesis Rabba* repeatedly and consistently interprets Genesis 38 as the story of the origins of Israel's kings and redeemers. Its commentary on Genesis 38 opens with prophetic passages containing royal and messianic allusions and closes by linking the birth of Perez with yet another prophetic passage with messianic implications. *Genesis Rabba* also interjects narrative material that maintains the focus on this theme, including the angel of desire's guidance of Judah to beget Israel's kings and redeemers and Tamar's boasting that she is pregnant with kings and redeemers. Through these and other means, *Genesis Rabba* highlights the significance of the birth scene towards which Genesis 38 moves. The *Testament of Judah* also stresses the theme of kingship, but in contrast to *Genesis Rabba*, it reverses the relationship between the events of Genesis 38 and the origins of Israel's royalty. In the *Testament of Judah*, the events of Genesis 38 become not the means through which king and messiah are brought into being, but rather the sins through which Judah nearly loses his royal status and dynastic lineage. In contrast to the other two works, *Targum Neofiti* does not develop the theme of kingship in its narrative expansion of Gen 38:25–26, although there are hints in its more literal translation of the rest of the biblical story that it is aware of the narrative's royal implications. Instead of the theme of kingship, *Targum Neofiti* develops alternate themes of pious behavior under duress and divine salvation associated with the concept "sanctification of the Name."

The various treatments of the theme of kingship in the *Testament of Judah*, *Targum Neofiti*, and *Genesis Rabba* may be concretely illustrated through their interpretations of a motif from Genesis 38 itself, namely the pledge that Judah gives Tamar. The pledge is clearly a crucial motif in the biblical narrative, since it alone holds the potential to disclose truth and thereby to save Tamar's life. Repeated references to the pledge keep it in the narrative foreground (Gen 38:17, 18, 20, 23, 25–26), and its importance is further emphasized by the fact that Tamar only speaks in order to obtain it and to point out its implications (Gen 38:16–18, 25). Each of the three treatments of Genesis 38 demonstrates sensitivity to the importance of the pledge by developing

this motif and assigning to it an important value in keeping with the
larger thematic emphases of the particular interpretation. *Genesis Rabba*,
with its emphasis on the origins of kingship, positively equates each
of the three pledge items with an important political institution or
royal figure that emerges as a result of the events in Genesis 38.
When Tamar specifies the three items, she demonstrates her prophetic awareness of the import of her relations with Judah, since the
seal signifies kingship, the cord signifies the Sanhedrin, and the staff
signifies the king messiah.[4] Judah's transfer of the three items to her
therefore predicts the positive results of their union for Israel's history.
The *Testament of Judah* also assigns values connected with political
leadership to the three pledge items. In fact, it alters their identity in
order to stress this connection, so that Judah gives his scepter (τὴν
ῥάβδον μου), his armor (τὴν ζώνην), and his royal diadem (τὸ διάδημα
τῆς βασιλείας) to Tamar.[5] But in the *Testament of Judah*, each item
stands not for an important institution or figure charged to lead Israel
as in *Genesis Rabba*, but for an aspect of Judah's own royal status.
This difference corresponds to the emphasis on Judah's personal experience in the testament. The scepter signifies the stay of Judah's tribe,
the armor signifies his power, and the diadem signifies the glory of
his kingship.[6] The transfer of these items with their royal significance
to Tamar denotes not the origins of kingship as in *Genesis Rabba*, but
its abdication as Judah voluntarily surrenders his power to a seductive woman. Thus, even though *Genesis Rabba* and the *Testament of
Judah* both develop the theme of kingship and even similarly assign
royal value to the pledge items, the two nevertheless take radically
different interpretive directions. By contrast, *Targum Neofiti* does not
associate the three pledge items with the theme of kingship. Instead
they become three "witnesses," in keeping with the court scene depicted in the narrative expansion. By presenting the pledge items as
witnesses, the targum also stresses the behavior of the three men at
Dura mentioned in Tamar's prayer, who witness to their faith through
their willingness to die, and it points to God, who is the Witness of
the events at Enaim. The loss and recovery of the items emphasize
the danger that Tamar experiences, as well as the potential for divine
intervention and delivery that recurs later when the divine voice grants

---

[4] *Gen.Rab.* 85.9.
[5] *T.Jud.* 12:4.
[6] *T.Jud.* 15:2–3.

a reprieve. *Targum Neofiti* therefore expresses its lack of interest in the theme of kingship through its radically different employment of the three pledge items in the narrative expansion.

What conclusions may one draw from this comparison on the thematic level? Once again, this comparison stresses the distinctiveness of the three interpretations with respect to the theme of kingship, a distinctiveness that is evident even between the two works that develop this theme extensively. Because it emphasizes the connection between the events of Genesis 38 and the emergence of important offspring, *Genesis Rabba* remains true to a basic impulse of the biblical story itself, although it goes far beyond it through the addition of thematic and narrative material. By contrast, the *Testament of Judah* takes the theme of kingship traditionally associated with Genesis 38 and inverts its relationship with the events of Genesis 38. This inversion, whereby Genesis 38 becomes the story of Judah's loss of kingship, constitutes a radical transformation of the import and structure of the biblical story. It should nevertheless be taken seriously as an indication of the mortification that the community behind this work felt about the sexual irregularities of Genesis 38. *Targum Neofiti* demonstrates yet another option open to interpreters of Genesis 38, which is to sidestep a theme implicit in the biblical narrative in order to develop a completely different thematic trajectory. Thematic material in a biblical narrative may therefore be developed, altered, or ignored by interpreters. Only the larger context within which exegesis takes place and the overarching purposes of the hermeneutic endeavor determine which option an interpreter chooses. Once again this comparison emphasizes the importance of interpreters in the establishment of the meanings of a biblical narrative. Practitioners of comparative midrash should therefore be sensitive to the treatments of biblical themes in various interpretations, since these treatments indicate the concerns and perspectives of religious communities as they read and interpret scripture.

We can also make productive comparisons at the level of narrative structure. Certainly the three interpretations all refer to characters, motifs, and episodes from Genesis 38, since this biblical narrative is their common point of departure. But a comparison between these works reveals that they emphasize different parts of Genesis 38. *Genesis Rabba* emphasizes the final birth scene towards which the biblical narrative moves (Gen 38:27–30). *Targum Neofiti* emphasizes the dramatic climax of the biblical narrative depicting the crisis and resolution of the embedded plot development, in which Tamar risks her life to engender the next generation (Gen 38:25–26). The *Testament of Judah* emphasizes Judah's questionable relations with the women of Genesis 38 and the problem of his evil sons (Gen 38:2–12, 13–26).

Upon closer inspection, one notices that not only do these works selectively emphasize portions of Genesis 38, but they also alter the plot structure of the biblical narrative in order to express later values. In the first chapter, I discussed Genesis 38 in terms of a double pattern of procreation, in which Tamar emerges as the protagonist who restores the broken pattern of procreation in the second part. Of the three interpretations analyzed in this study, *Genesis Rabba* follows the plot of the biblical narrative most closely through its repeated emphasis on the final birth scene toward which the narrative moves. But it also adds a number of narrative embellishments and thematic discussions. Many of these attribute a divine intentionality to the emergence of the lineage of Israel's kings and redeemers. Others serve to ameliorate the behavior of the main characters of the story and to develop them as worthy ancestors of this important lineage.

The alterations of plot in the other two interpretations are far more radical. While it is true that *Targum Neofiti* recounts most of the biblical story through a fairly literal translation, it also interjects a lengthy narrative expansion at the climax (Gen 38:25–26). This expansion emphasizes the biblical moment that discloses the truth concerning Judah and Tamar's encounter, but it also transforms the nature of this truth. In place of truth about their morally problematic relations, *Targum Neofiti* reveals truth about Judah and Tamar's pious character under duress and about the power of God to save. Although *Targum Neofiti* leaves the rest of the biblical narrative virtually unchanged, the addition of thematically charged elements of plot and dialogue at the dramatic climax of Genesis 38 fundamentally alters the narrative structure and the import of the biblical story. The *Testament of Judah* goes even farther than the other two interpretations in its alteration of the plot structure of Genesis 38. In this work, there is not even a passing reference to the birth of twins towards which the biblical narrative moves. Rather, it divides Genesis 38 into two stories illustrating Judah's weakness for women and other vices that lead to his loss of royal status (Gen 38:1–12 and Gen 38:13–26). Narrative elements of the biblical plot are used freely and recombined into new structures according to the larger purposes of the interpretation. For example, the *Testament of Judah* transfers the biblical search for the mysterious woman (Gen 38:20–23) to the very end of its version of Genesis 38 in order to conclude with the theme of shame suggested by this episode. In addition, this work recontextualizes its version of Genesis 38 within the longer narrative of Judah's autobiography, so that accounts of Judah's manly exploits preface it and his humble penitence follows it.

From this comparison, it is obvious that all three interpretations alter the plot structure of Genesis 38, although the manner and the extent differ. If we are sensitive to revised plot structures, we can more easily discern the different perspectives that distinctive religious communities bring to the biblical narrative. We can also better understand the central statements these communities express through biblical narrative, since revised narrative structure correlates with interpretive meaning. Comparative midrash would therefore do well to attend to the reconstruction of larger narrative configurations, since this locus reflects the interpretive meanings of biblical narrative.

Before we leave the discussion of narrative structure, it would be worthwhile to ask if there is actually any central core to Genesis 38. Is there any persistent configuration of narrative and thematic elements to which all three interpretations respond, or is the biblical narrative simply a repository of narrative raw material for later interpreters to mine at will? If meaning really emerges through the interaction between ancient text and later religious communities, one would expect the text itself to make important contributions to the production of meaning, not to remain inert and passive like clay for shaping by later readers. One candidate for this core would be the tension-filled relation between Judah and Tamar's sexual encounter, with all of its irregularities (including deception, prostitution, and incest) and its positive result in the birth of David's ancestor. Each one of the interpretations analyzed above wrestles with this tension and articulates a solution to it. *Genesis Rabba* keeps the biblical focus on the birth of the royal ancestor, but resolves some of the moral problems attending this birth (although it also indicates its awareness of the morally ambiguities in Genesis 38 through inclusion of interpretive motifs in contradiction to its overarching interpretation). The *Testament of Judah* takes the opposite approach. It highlights the morally offensive aspects of Genesis 38, and then completely severs the link between the events of the biblical narrative and the origins of the royal and messianic lineage. Instead, Judah's relations with Tamar become one of the means through which he and his descendants almost lose their status as Israel's kings. By contrast, *Targum Neofiti* reacts to the tension in the biblical narrative with a strategy of diversion. Leaving the morally ambiguous events of Genesis 38 and the story's positive outcome basically unaltered, the targum concentrates instead on developing Judah and Tamar as moral exemplars of the larger cultural ideal of "sanctification of the Name" in the narrative expansion. Perhaps every biblical narrative has a persistent core, to which later interpreters react. Comparison between different interpretations may therefore help identify the essential narrative and thematic structures of a biblical narrative. Thus, comparative midrash can also shed light on the dynamics of biblical narrative itself, as well as on its invested interpreters.

On the level of cultural factors that influence interpretive trajectories, the three interpretations of Genesis 38 analyzed in this study also show great diversity. Larger issues, literary patterns, and historical events in the wider cultural sphere shape the perceptions of readers of scripture and guide their directions of interpretation. Starting with the Hellenistic cultural sphere, it may be that the heroic pattern exemplified by Heracles influenced the development of the character of Judah in the *Testament of Judah*. In addition, other Hellenistic cultural trends may have contributed to the direction of interpretation in this work, including the widespread critique of physical strength as the defining criterion of ideal manhood in Graeco-Roman philosophical writings, the allegorical interpretation of legends concerning physical combat in terms of moral struggle against vices, and the employment of the figure of the king as a representative of ideal humanity in Cynic and Stoic philosophy. The two other interpretations bear marks of influence from larger discussions within the Jewish cultural context of Palestine. For example, the narrative expansion in *Targum Neofiti* reflects contemporary discussion about when it would be preferable to die rather than to violate ethical or religious principles, associated with the concept known as "sanctification of the Name," and it shows familiarity with the common employment of the narrative in Daniel 3 as an illustration of this concept. It also illustrates the rabbinic values of humility, consideration for another's reputation, repentance, and confession. *Genesis Rabba*, although from the same Palestinian cultural sphere, accentuates very different cultural currents. It emphasizes the theme of political and messianic leadership, in a historical period characterized by foreign rule. It idealizes the origins of Israel's king and messiah by depicting Judah and Tamar as worthy and pious royal ancestors and thus provides an alternate vision of reality within a period of occupation. *Genesis Rabba* therefore reflects historical and political realities as well as cultural and religious influences. These three interpretations attest to the distinctive cultural "horizons" from which some early Jewish readers perceived Genesis 38. Of particular interest is the fact that the diverse articulations evident in *Targum Neofiti* and *Genesis Rabba* emerged from the same basic cultural sphere of Palestinian Judaism. This fact demonstrates that even within one cultural sphere there is sufficient freedom to creatively assign a range of meanings to a single biblical narrative. In comparing interpretations and reflecting on the factors responsible for their differences, it is therefore important to look at the broader cultural contexts of exegesis.

Finally, comparison between exegetical treatments of biblical passages may be made on the level of the poetics of interpretation, or how interpreters implicitly argue for their understanding of the meaning of scripture through literary and rhetorical means. In the three examples studied here, the poetics of interpretation include the genres within which interpretation of Genesis 38 occurs, as well as the methods through which new meanings are integrated into the original biblical narrative. Through a variety of techniques, all three interpretive works claim authority for their very different articulations of the biblical narrative. *Genesis Rabba* accomplishes its interpretation of Genesis 38 through the means of anthological commentary. In this commentary, quotations of the biblical narrative are clearly demarcated from rabbinic comments about the text. This practice might appear to draw attention to the distinction between biblical narrative and later commentary and thus to highlight the innovative quality of rabbinic interpretation. In actuality, most interpretive comments on Genesis 38 in *Genesis Rabba* contain a reference to a specific detail of the Hebrew text, such as spelling, word choice, grammar, or connections with another biblical passage. These references integrate rabbinic interpretation with the particulars of the Hebrew text, implying that later exegetical motifs and traditions arose directly from scripture itself. The alternating quotation of scripture and rabbinic commentary in *Genesis Rabba* also tacitly ascribes to the latter an authority comparable to scripture. *Genesis Rabba* thus implicitly argues for the authority of the rabbinic sages to determine the significance of scripture, even if their various interpretations of individual lemmata conflict at times.

Genesis Rabba links its interpretation of Genesis 38 to the particular details of the Hebrew text more strongly than the other two works.

Of course, both *Targum Neofiti* and the *Testament of Judah* are written
in languages other than Hebrew, and this means that even where
links exist between inherited exegetical motifs and details in the biblical text, these links are obscured by the translation into Aramaic
and Greek. But translation into foreign languages is not the only
difference between *Genesis Rabba* and the other two works. These works
compensate for the loss of specific connections between exegetical
traditions and the Hebrew text by employing genres that incorporate
interpretation into the biblical narrative more directly than the commentary found in *Genesis Rabba* does. In *Targum Neofiti*, the genre of
expanded, paraphrastic translation includes a narrativization of lemmatic rabbinic exegesis. In the narrative expansion in *Tg.Neof.* Gen
38:25–26, biblical text and rabbinic commentary become one seamless whole. *Targum Neofiti* presents the narrative and thematic content, if not the precise details, of rabbinic interpretation without
demarcating it from the biblical text. Because the content of rabbinic
exegesis actually becomes incorporated into the biblical narrative, the
distinction between the two is obliterated. A similar conclusion may
be drawn from the *Testament of Judah*. Extra-biblical motifs appear
incorporated into the version of Genesis 38 running through the
testament genre of this work. In addition, the *Testament of Judah* presents its distinctive form of the narrative in Judah's own words. Since
Judah is one of the main characters of Genesis 38, the pseudepigraphal
aspect of the testament genre garners the authority of this biblical
figure in support of a reworked account of the biblical narrative.
Thus, the *Testament of Judah* makes a claim for the validity of its
interpretation of Genesis 38 through an implicit appeal to the status
of Jacob's son.

In the comparisons above between the *Testament of Judah, Targum
Neofiti,* and *Genesis Rabba,* differences rather than similarities predominate. Indeed, more than anything else these comparisons accomplish
the important purpose of highlighting each interpretation's distinctiveness on a number of levels. Recognition that three ancient Jewish
encounters with a single biblical narrative produced such dissimilar
results returns us full circle to the hermeneutic issues explicitly raised
in the introduction and first chapter of this book. The differences
between the interpretive treatments of Genesis 38 analyzed here
concretely illustrate the critical role of historically situated readers
for determining the religious meanings of a biblical narrative. The
interpreters responsible for the *Testament of Judah, Targum Neofiti,* and

Genesis Rabba emphasized certain episodes, themes, and points of contact between Genesis 38 and other biblical passages, while ignoring or rejecting other potentially productive features of this complex and ambiguous narrative. Their elaborations and clarifications therefore restricted and channeled the meaning of the biblical narrative in distinctive directions. Historical and cultural contexts predisposed these interpreters to focus on certain features of Genesis 38 and to perceive the central message of that narrative in particular ways. Also decisive were the distinctive hermeneutic strategies and received exegetical traditions that influenced the interpreters' understandings of the narrative. Each interpretation of Genesis 38 thus reveals at least as much about the community that produced it as it does about the biblical text itself. Finally, the striking differences between the treatments also stem from the very active nature of the interpreters' engagement with the biblical narrative, which included reshaping the narrative into forms capable of expressing the values and ideals of different types of ancient Judaism. One might apply the words of the astonished midwife to this type of interaction with the biblical text: "What a breach you have made for yourself!" The early Jewish interpreters responsible for the *Testament of Judah*, *Targum Neofiti*, and *Genesis Rabba* have indeed made breaches, or openings, into an ancient and somewhat puzzling narrative in order to interject much later values and religious ideals. And this is as it must be, if scripture is to retain its normative and vital function within living religious communities.

SELECTED BIBLIOGRAPHY

PRIMARY TEXTS

Buber, Solomon, ed. *'Aggadat Berešit*. Krakow: Y. Fisher, 1902.
—— ed. *Midraš Mišle*. Vilna: Romm, 1893.
—— ed. *Midraš Tanhuma*. Vilna: Romm, 1885.
Buffière, Félix, ed. *Héraclite, Allégories d'Homère*. Paris: Belles Lettres, 1962.
Charles, Robert Henry, ed. *The Greek Versions of the Testaments of the Twelve Patriarchs Edited from Nine Manuscripts Together with the Variants of the Armenian and Slavonic Versions and Some Hebrew Fragments*. Oxford: Oxford University Press, 1908; reprint, Hildesheim: Georg Olms Verlagsbuchhandlung, 1960.
Charlesworth, James H., ed. *The Old Testament Pseudepigrapha*. 2 vols. Garden City, NY: Doubleday, 1983–85.
Clark, E. G., ed. *Targum Pseudo-Jonathan of the Pentateuch: Text and Concordance*. Hoboken, NJ: Ktav Publishing House, 1984.
Díez Macho, Alejandro, ed. *Neophyti 1: Targum Palestinense MS de la Biblioteca Vaticana*. 6 vols. Madrid: Consejo Superior de Investigaciones Científicas, 1968–79.
Elliger, K., and W. Rudolph, eds. *Biblia Hebraica Stuttgartensia*. 2d ed. Stuttgart: Deutsche Bibel Gesellschaft, 1984.
Epstein, Isidore, ed. *The Babylonian Talmud*. 34 vols. London: Soncino Press, 1935–48.
Finkelstein, Louis, ed. *Sipre Debarim*. Berlin: Jüdischer Kulturbund in Deutschland, 1939; reprint, New York: Jewish Theological Seminary Press, 1969.
Freedman, H., and Maurice Simon, eds. *Midrash Rabbah*. 10 vols. London: Soncino Press, 1939.
Gaster, M., trans. *The Chronicles of Jerahmeel, or the Hebrew Bible Hisoriale*. London: Royal Asiatic Society, 1899; reprint, New York: Ktav Publishing House, 1971.
Jellinek, A., ed. בית המרש [The house of study]. 3d ed. 3 vols. Leipzig: Vollrath, 1853–77; reprint, Jerusalem: Wahrmann Books, 1967.
de Jonge, Marinus, ed. *The Testaments of the Twelve Patriarchs: A Critical Edition of the Greek Text*. Pseudepigrapha Veteris Testamenti Graece, vol. 1, 2. Leiden: E. J. Brill, 1978.
Kee, Howard Clark, trans. "Testaments of the Twelve Patriarchs." In vol. 1 of *The Old Testament Pseudepigrapha*, edited by James H. Charlesworth. Garden City, NY: Doubleday, 1983, 775–828.
Klein, Michael L., ed. *The Fragment Targums of the Pentateuch According to Their Extant Sources*. 2 vols. Rome: Biblical Institute Press, 1980.
—— ed. *Genizah Manuscripts of Palestinian Targums to the Pentateuch*. 2 vols. Cincinnati: Hebrew Union College Press, 1986.
Lauterbach, Jacob Z., ed. *Mekilta de Rabbi Ishmael*. 3 Vols. Philadelphia: Jewish Publication Society, 1933–35.
Liebermann, Saul, ed. *Midraš Debarim Rabba*. 2d ed. Jerusalem: Wahrmann Books, 1964.
Maher, Michael, trans. *Targum Pseudo-Jonathan: Genesis*. Vol. 1B of *The Aramaic Bible*. Collegeville, MN: Liturgical Press, 1992.
Malherbe, Abraham J., ed. *The Cynic Epistles: A Study Edition*. SBL Sources for Biblical Studies 12. Missoula, MT: Scholars Press, 1977.
Margulies, Mordecai, ed. *Midraš Haggadol*. Jerusalem: Rab Kook, 1947.
McNamara, Martin, trans. *Targum Neofiti 1: Genesis*. Vol. 1A of *The Aramaic Bible*. Collegeville, MN: Liturgical Press, 1992.
Midraš Rabba. Vilna: Romm, 1884–87.

Neusner, Jacob, trans. *Genesis Rabbah: The Judaic Commentary to the Book of Genesis: A New American Translation.* 3 vols. Brown Judaic Studies 106. Atlanta: Scholars Press, 1985.

Oates, Whitney J., ed. *The Stoic and Epicurean Philosophers: The Complete Extant Writings of Epicurus, Epictetus, Lucretius, [and] Marcus Aurelius.* New York: Random House, 1940.

Sokoloff, Michael, ed. *The Targum to Job from Qumran Cave XI.* Ramat Gan: Bar Ilan University, 1974.

—— ed. *The Geniza Fragments of Bereshit Rabba.* Jerusalem: Ben Zvi Printing Enterprises, 1982.

Sperber, Alexander, ed. *The Pentateuch According to Targum Onkelos.* Vol. 1 of *The Bible in Aramaic.* Leiden: E. J. Brill, 1959.

Theodor, J., and C. Albeck, eds. *Midraš Berešit Rabba.* 3 vols. Berlin: Defus Tsevi Hirsch Ittskavski, 1903–36; reprint, Jerusalem: Wahrmann Books, 1965.

Weiss, Isaac Hirsch, ed. *Sipra.* Vienna: J. Schlossberg, 1862.

SECONDARY LITERATURE

Albeck, C. מבוא לבראשית רבא [Introduction to *Genesis Rabba*]. In vol. 3 of *Midraš Berešit Rabba,* edited by J. Theodor and Albeck. Berlin: Defus Tsevi Hirsch Ittskavski, 1903–36; reprint, Jerusalem: Wahrmann Books, 1965, 1–138.

Albright, William F. "Historical and Mythical Elements in the Story of Joseph." *JBL* 37 (1918) 111–43.

Alexander, P. S. "The Rabbinic Lists of Forbidden Targumim." *JJS* 27 (1976) 177–91.

—— "The Targumim and the Rabbinic Rules for the Delivery of the Targum." VTSup 36 (1985) 14–28.

Alpers, Johann. *Hercules in bivio.* Göttingen: Dieterichium, 1912.

Alter, Robert. *The Art of Biblical Narrative.* New York: Basic Books, 1981.

Anderson, Janice Capel. "Mary's Difference: Gender and Patriarchy in the Birth Narratives." *JR* 67 (1987) 183–202.

Aptowitzer, V. "Asenath, the Wife of Joseph: A Haggadic Literary-Historical Study." *HUCA* 1 (1924) 239–306.

Arnand, Daniel. "La Prostitution sacrée en Mésopotamie, un mythe historique?" *Revue l'histoire des religions* 183 (1976) 111–15.

Astour, Michael C. "Tamar the Hierodule: An Essay in the Method of Vestigial Motifs." *JBL* 85 (1966) 185–96.

Auerbach, Erich. "Odysseus' Scar." In *Mimesis: The Representation of Reality in Western Literature,* translated by Willard R. Trask. Princeton: Princeton University Press, 1953, 3–23.

Baab, O. J. "Marriage." In vol. 3 of *The Interpreter's Dictionary of the Bible,* edited by G. A. Buttrick. Nashville: Abingdon Press, 1962, 278–87.

Bacher, Wilhelm. *Die Proëmien der alten jüdischen Homilie: Beitrag zur Geschichte des jüdischen Schriftauslegung und Homiletik.* Leipzig: J. C. Hinrichs, 1913.

Bal, Mieke. *Lethal Love: Feminist Literary Readings of Biblical Love Stories.* Bloomington: Indiana University Press, 1987.

Barr, James. "Which Language Did Jesus Speak? Some Remarks of a Semitist." *BJRL* 53 (1971) 9–29.

Barth, Lewis M. *An Analysis of Vatican 30.* Mongraphs of the Hebrew Union College 1. Cincinnati: Hebrew Union College Press, 1973.

Baskin, Judith R. "Rabbinic Reflections on the Barren Wife." *HTR* 82 (1989) 101–14.

Beattie, D. R. G. "The Book of Ruth as Evidence for Israelite Legal Practice." *VT* 24 (1974) 251–67.

Becker, Jürgen. *Untersuchungen zur Entstehungsgeschichte der Testamente der Zwölf Patriarchen.*

Arbeiten zur Geschichte des Antiken Judentums und des Urchristentums 8. Leiden: E. J. Brill, 1970.

Belkin, Samuel. "Levirate and Agnate Marriage in Rabbinic and Cognate Literature." *JQR* 60 (1970) 275–329.

Ben-Amos, Dan. "Themes, Forms, and Meaning: Critical Comments." In *Classical Hebrew Narrative*, edited by Robert C. Culley. Semeia 3. Missoula, MT: Scholars Press, 1975, 128–32.

Ben-Porat, Ziva. "Intertextuality, Rhetorical Intertextuality, Allusion, and Parody." *Ha-Sifrut* 34 (1985) 171–78.

Berlin, Adele. *Poetics and Interpretation of Biblical Narrative*. Sheffield: Almond Press, 1983.

Bersani, Leo, and Ulysse Dutoit. *The Forms of Violence: Narrative in Assyrian Art and Modern Culture*. New York: Schocken Books, 1985.

Bickerman, E. "The Date of the *Testaments of the Twelve Patriarchs*." *JBL* 69 (1950) 245–60.

Bird, Phyllis. "The Harlot as Heroine: Narrative Art and Social Presupposition in Three Old Testament Texts." In *Narrative Research on the Hebrew Bible*, edited by Miri Amihai, George W. Coats, and Anne M. Solomon. Semeia 46. Atlanta: Scholars Press, 1989, 119–39.

Blenkinsopp, Joseph. "Biographical Patterns in Biblical Narrative." *JSOT* 20 (1981) 27–46.

Bloch, Renée. "'Juda engendra Pharès et Zara de Thamar,' Matth. 1,3." In *Mélanges bibliques rédigés en l'honneur de André Robert*. Travaux de l'Institut Catholique de Paris 4. Paris: Bloud & Gay, 1956, 381–89.

—— "Note sur l'utilisation des fragments de la Geniza du Caire pour l'étude du Targum Palestinien." *Revue des études juives* 111–16 (1954–57) 5–35.

—— "Methodological Note for the Study of Rabbinic Literature." Translated by William Scott Green and William J. Sullivan. In *Approaches to Ancient Judaism: Theory and Practice*, edited by Green. Brown Judaic Studies 1. Missoula, MT: Scholars Press, 1978, 521–75.

Bloom, Harold. *The Anxiety of Influence: A Theory of Poetry*. Oxford: Oxford University Press, 1973.

—— "The Breaking of Form." In *De-Construction and Criticism*, edited by Bloom, Paul de Man, Jacques Derrida, Geoffrey H. Hartman, and J. Hillis Miller. New York: Continuum, 1990, 1–37.

Bos, Johanna W. H. "Out of the Shadows: Genesis 38; Judg 4:17–22; Ruth 3." In *Reasoning with the Foxes: Female Wit in a World of Male Power*, edited by J. Cheryl Exum and Bos. Semeia 42. Atlanta: Scholars Press, 1988, 40–49.

Bowker, John. *The Targums and Rabbinic Literature: An Introduction to Jewish Interpretations of Scripture*. Cambridge: Cambridge University Press, 1969.

Boyarin, Daniel. "Voices in the Text: Midrash and the Inner Tension of Biblical Narrative (Ex. 16)." *RB* 93 (1986) 581–97.

Braun, Martin. *History and Romance in Graeco-Oriental Literature*. Oxford: Basil Blackwell, 1938.

Bregman, M. "פתיחתאות מעגליות ופתיחתאות "זו היא שנאמרה ברוח הקודש" [Circular proems and proems beginning with the formula "this is what is said through the holy spirit"]. In מחקרים באגדה תרגומים ותפלות ישראל לזכר יוסף היינימן [Studies in aggada, targum, and Jewish liturgy, in memory of Joseph Heinemann], edited by E. Fleischer and J. J. Petuchowski. Jerusalem: Magnes Press; Cincinnati: Hebrew Union College Press, 1981, 34–51.

Brenner, Athalya. "Naomi and Ruth." *VT* 33 (1983) 385–97.

—— *The Israelite Woman: Social Role and Literary Type in Biblical Narrative*. Sheffield: JSOT Press, 1985.

—— "Female Social Behavior: Two Descriptive Patterns within the 'Birth of the Hero' Paradigm." *VT* 36 (1986) 257–73.

372   BIBLIOGRAPHY

—— אהבת רות: אשר היא טובה לך משבעה בנים [The love of Ruth: Who is better to
    you than seven sons]. Tel Aviv: Sifriat Poalim, 1988.
Brommer, Frank. *Heracles: The Twelve Labors of the Hero in Ancient Art and Literature.*
    Translated by Shirley J. Schwarz. New Rochelle, NY: Aristide D. Caratzas, 1968.
Brooks, Beatrice A. "Fertility Cult Functionaries in the Old Testament." *JBL* 60
    (1940) 227–53.
Brown, Francis, S. R. Driver, and Charles A. Briggs. *Hebrew and English Lexicon of the
    Old Testament.* Oxford: Clarendon Press, 1906; reprint, 1951.
Brown, Raymond E. *The Birth of the Messiah: A Commentary on the Infancy Narratives
    in the Gospels of Matthew and Luke.* The Anchor Bible Reference Library. New
    updated ed. New York: Doubleday, 1993.
Burrows, Millar. "The Ancient Oriental Background of Hebrew Levirate Marriage."
    BASOR 77 (1940) 2–15.
—— "Levirate Marriage in Israel." *JBL* 59 (1940) 23–33.
—— "The Marriage of Boaz and Ruth." *JBL* 59 (1940) 445–54.
Buttrick, G. A., ed. *The Interpreter's Dictionary of the Bible.* 5 vols. Nashville: Abingdon
    Press, 1962.
Callaway, Mary. *Sing O Barren One: A Study in Comparative Midrash.* SBL Dissertation
    Series 91. Atlanta: Scholars Press, 1986.
Carmichael, Calum. "Some Sayings in Genesis 49." *JBL* 88 (1969) 435–44.
—— *Law and Narrative in the Bible: The Evidence of the Deuteronomic Laws and the Decalogue.*
    Ithaca: Cornell University Press, 1985.
Carroll, Michael P. "Genesis Restructured." In *Anthropological Approaches to the Old
    Testament,* edited by Bernard Lang. Issues in Religion and Theology 8. Phila-
    delphia: Fortress Press; London: SPCK, 1985, 127–35.
Cassuto, Moses David. מעשה תמר ויהודה [The story of Tamar and Judah]. In ציונים:
    קובץ לזכרונו של י. נ. שמחוני [*Tsiyyunim*: Memorial volume for J. N. Simchoni],
    edited by J. Klatzkin. Berlin: Eshkol, 1928–29, 93–100.
Charles, Robert Henry. "Introduction." In *The Greek Versions of the Testaments of the
    Twelve Patriarchs Edited from Nine Manuscripts Together with the Variants of the Arme-
    nian and Slavonic Versions and Some Hebrew Fragments.* Oxford: Oxford University
    Press, 1908; reprint, Hildesheim: Georg Olms Verlagsbuchhandlung, 1960.
Childs, Brevard S. *Old Testament Theology in a Canonical Context.* Philadelphia: Fortress
    Press, 1986.
Clayton, Jay, and Eric Rothstein, eds. *Influence and Intertextuality in Literary History.*
    Madison: University of Wisconsin Press, 1991.
Coats, George W. "Widow's Rights: A Crux in the Structure of Genesis 38." *CBQ*
    34 (1972) 461–65.
—— "Redactional Unity in Genesis 37–50." *JBL* 93 (1974) 15–21.
Cohen, H. Hirsch. *The Drunkenness of Noah.* Judaic Series 4. University, AL: Univer-
    sity of Alabama Press, 1974.
Cohen, S. "Tamar." In vol. 4 of *The Interpreter's Dictionary of the Bible,* edited by G. A.
    Buttrick. Nashville: Abingdon Press, 1962, 515–16.
Collins, John J. "Testaments." In *Jewish Writings of the Second Temple Period: Apocrypha,
    Pseudepigrapha, Qumran Sectarian Writings, Philo, Josephus,* edited by Michael E. Stone.
    Assen: Van Gorcum; Philadelphia: Fortress Press, 1984, 325–55.
Culler, Jonathan. "Literary Competence." In *Reader-Response Criticism: From Formalism
    to Post-Structuralism,* edited by Jane P. Tompkins. Baltimore: Johns Hopkins Uni-
    versity Press, 1980, 101–17.
—— *The Pursuit of Signs: Semiotics, Literature, and Deconstruction.* Ithaca: Cornell Univer-
    sity Press, 1981.
Culley, Robert C. "Themes and Variations in Three Groups of Old Testament
    Narratives." In *Classical Hebrew Narrative,* edited by Culley. Semeia 3. Missoula,
    MT: Scholars Press, 1975, 3–11.
—— *Studies in the Structure of Hebrew Narrative.* Philadelphia: Fortress Press, 1976.

—— *Themes and Variations: A Study of Action in Biblical Narrative.* Atlanta: Scholars Press, 1992.

Daube, David. *Studies in Biblical Law.* Cambridge: Cambridge University Press, 1947.

—— "Consortium in Roman and Hebrew Law." *Juridical Review* 62 (1950) 71–91.

—— "Error and Ignorance as Excuses in Crime." In *Ancient Jewish Law: Three Inaugural Lectures.* Leiden: E. J. Brill, 1981, 48–69.

Davies, Eryl W. "Inheritance Rights and the Hebrew Levirate Marriage." *VT* 31 (1981) 138–44, 257–68.

le Déaut, Roger. "Aspects de l'intercession dans le Judaïsme ancien." *JSJ* 1 (1970) 35–57.

—— "The Current State of Targumic Studies." *BTB* 4 (1974) 3–32.

—— *Introduction à la littérature targumique.* Vol. 1. Rome: Instituto Biblico de Roma, 1966.

Delitzsch, Franz. *A New Commentary on Genesis.* Vol. 2. Translated by Sophia Taylor. Edinburgh: T. & T. Clark, 1894.

Díez Macho, Alejandro. "The Recently Discovered Palestinian Targum: Its Antiquity and Relationship with the Other Targums." VTSup 7 (1959) 222–45.

—— *El Targum: Introducción a las traducciones Arámicas de la Biblia.* Textos y estudios "Cardenal Cisneros," vol. 21. Madrid: Consejo Superior de Investigaciones Científicas, 1979.

Dion, Paul E. "Did Cultic Prostitution Fall into Oblivion during the Post-exilic Era? Some Evidence from Chronicles and the Septuagint." *CBQ* 43 (1981) 41–48.

Doniger, Wendy. "Sexual Masquerades in the Hebrew Bible: Rachel and Tamar." Loy H. Witherspoon Lectures in Religious Studies. University of North Carolina at Charlotte, March 21, 1990.

Driver, S. R. *The Book of Genesis.* 3d ed. Westminster Commentaries. London: Methuen and Co., 1904.

Droge, Arthur J., and James D. Tabor. *A Noble Death: Suicide and Martyrdom among Christians and Jews in Antiquity.* San Francisco: HarperSanFrancisco, 1992.

Dubois, Jean Daniel. "Joseph et la vertu dans le judaïsme hellénistique et le christianisme ancien." *Foi Vie* (1987) 25–33.

Dundes, Alan. "From Etic to Emic Units in the Structural Study of Folktales." *Journal of American Folklore* 75 (1962) 95–105.

Eagleton, Terry. *Literary Theory: An Introduction.* Minneapolis: University of Minnesota Press, 1983.

Eilberg-Schwartz, Howard. "Who's Kidding Whom?: A Serious Reading of Rabbinic Word Plays." *JAAR* 55 (1987) 765–88.

Emerton, J. A. "Some Problems in Genesis 38." *VT* 25 (1975) 338–61.

—— "An Examination of a Recent Structuralist Interpretation of Genesis 38." *VT* 26 (1976) 79–98.

—— "Judah and Tamar." *VT* 29 (1979) 403–15.

Eppel, Robert. *Le Piétisme juif dans les Testaments de Douze Patriarches.* Paris: Féliz Alcan, 1930.

Epstein, Louis M. *Marriage Laws in the Bible and the Talmud.* Cambridge, MA: Harvard University Press, 1942.

—— *Sex Laws and Customs in Judaism.* With an introduction by Ari Kiev. New York: Ktav Publishing House, 1948.

Faur, José. *Golden Doves with Silver Dots.* Bloomington: Indiana University Press, 1986.

Feeley-Harnik, Gillian. "Naomi and Ruth: Building Up the House of David." In *Text and Tradition: The Hebrew Bible and Folklore,* edited by Susan Niditch. SBL Semeia Studies. Atlanta: Scholars Press, 1990, 163–84.

Fisch, Harold. "Ruth and the Structure of Covenant History." *VT* 32 (1982) 425–37.

Fish, Stanley. "Interpreting the *Variorum.*" In *Reader-Response Criticism: From Formalism to Post-Structuralism,* edited by Jane P. Tompkins. Baltimore: Johns Hopkins University Press, 1980, 164–84.

—— *Is There a Text in This Class?: The Authority of Interpretive Communities.* Cambridge, MA: Harvard University Press, 1980.

Fishbane, Michael. *Biblical Interpretation in Ancient Israel.* Oxford: Clarendon Press, 1988.
——— *The Garments of Torah.* Bloomington: Indiana University Press, 1989.
Fontenrose, Joseph Eddy. *Python: A Study of Delphic Myth and Its Origins.* Berkeley: University of California Press, 1959.
Fraade, S. D. "Ascetical Aspects of Ancient Judaism." In *Jewish Spirituality from the Bible to the Middle Ages*, edited by A. Green. Vol. 13 of *World Spirituality.* New York: Crossroads, 1986, 253–88.
Friedman, Mordechai A. "Tamar, a Symbol of Life: The 'Killer Wife' Superstition in the Bible and Jewish Tradition." *Association for Jewish Studies Review* 15 (1990) 23–61.
Frymer-Kensky, Tikva. *In the Wake of the Goddesses: Women, Culture, and the Biblical Transformation of Pagan Myth.* New York: Free Press, 1992.
Fuchs, Esther. "Who Is Hiding the Truth? Deceptive Women and Biblical Androcentrism." In *Feminist Perspectives on Biblical Scholarship*, edited by Adela Yarbo Collins. Chico, CA: Scholars Press, 1985, 137–44.
——— "The Literary Characterization of Mothers and Sexual Politics in the Hebrew Bible." In *Narrative Research on the Hebrew Bible*, edited by Miri Amihai, George W. Coats, and Anne M. Solomon. Semeia 46. Atlanta: Scholars Press, 1989, 151–66.
Furman, Nelly. "His Story Versus Her Story: Male Genealogy and Female Strategy in the Jacob Cycle." In *Narrative Research on the Hebrew Bible*, edited by Miri Amihai, George W. Coats, and Anne M. Solomon. Semeia 46. Atlanta: Scholars Press, 1989, 141–49.
Gadamer, Hans-Georg. *Truth and Method.* 2d rev. ed. Translated by Joel Weinsheimer and Donald G. Marshall. New York: Continuum, 1993.
Galinsky, G. Karl. *The Herakles Theme: The Adaptations of the Hero in Literature from Homer to the Twentieth Century.* Oxford: Basil Blackwell, 1972.
Gantz, Timothy. *Early Greek Myth: A Guide to Literary and Artistic Sources.* Baltimore: Johns Hopkins University Press, 1993.
Gardiner, E. Norman. *Greek Athletic Sports and Festivals.* London: MacMillan, 1910.
Ginzberg, Louis. *The Legends of the Jews.* 7 vols. Philadelphia: Jewish Publication Society 1909–38; reprint, 1967–69.
Goldin, Judah. "The Youngest Son, or Where Does Genesis 38 Belong?" In *Studies in Midrash and Related Literature*, edited by Barry L. Eichler and Jeffrey H. Tigay. Philadelphia: Jewish Publication Society, 1988, 121–39.
Good, E. "The Blessing on Judah." *JBL* 82 (1963) 427–32.
Gow, A. S. F. *Theocritus: Edited with a Translation and Commentary.* 2 vols. Cambridge: Cambridge University Press, 1950.
Grözinger, K. E. "Prediger gottseliger Diesseitszuversicht." *FJB* 5 (1977) 42–64.
Gruenwald, Ithamar. קידוש השם: בירורו של מושג ["Sanctification of the Name:" Explanation of a concept]. *Molad* 24 (1967–68) 476–84.
Güdemann, M. "Joseph = Osiris." *Religionsgeschichtliche Studien.* Leipzig: O. Leiner, 1876, 26–40.
Gunkel, Herman. *The Legends of Genesis.* Translated by W. H. Carruth. With an introduction by William F. Albright. New York: Schocken Books, 1964.
Handelman, Susan. *The Slayers of Moses: The Emergence of Rabbinic Interpretation in Modern Literary Theory.* Albany: State University of New York Press, 1982.
Hartman, Geoffrey H., and Sanford Budick, eds. *Midrash and Literature.* New Haven: Yale University Press, 1986.
Hayes, C. E. "The Midrashic Career of the Confession of Judah (Genesis 38:26)." Parts 1 and 2. *VT* 45 (1995) 62–81, 174–87.
Heinemann, Joseph. הפתיחתות במדרשי האגדה: מקורן ותפקידן [The proems in aggadic midrashim: Their origin and function]. *WCJS* 4 (1965) 3–47, 174–87.
——— מבנהו וחלוקתו של מדרש בראשית רבה [The structure and divisions of *Genesis Rabba*]. *Bar Ilan* 9 (1971) 279–89.

—— אנדות ותולדותיהן: עיונים בהשתלשלותן של מסורות [Aggadic traditions and their development: Studies on the evolution of traditions]. Jerusalem: Keter Publishing House, 1974.

—— *Prayer in the Talmud: Forms and Patterns.* Studia Judaica 9. Berlin and New York: Walter de Gruyter, 1977.

Heller, Bernard. "Die Sage vom Sarge Josephs und der Bericht Benjamins von Tudela über Daniels schwebenden Sarg." *MGWJ* 70 (1926) 271–76.

Herr, Moshe David. "Genesis Rabbah." In vol. 7 of *Encyclopaedia Judaica.* Jerusalem: Keter Publishing House, 1971, 399–401.

Hillers, Delbert R. *Micah.* Hermeneia. Philadelphia: Fortress Press, 1984.

Hoffner, Harry A., Jr. "Incest, Sodomy, and Bestiality in the Ancient Near East." In *Orient and Occident: Essays Presented to Cyrus H. Gordon on the Occasion of His Sixty-Fifth Birthday,* edited by Hoffner. Alter Orient und Altes Testament 22. Kevelaer: Butzon & Bercker; Neukirchen-Vluyn: Neukirchener Verlag, 1973, 81–90.

Höistad, Ragnar. *Cynic Hero and Cynic King: Studies in the Cynic Conception of Man.* Uppsala: Karl Bloms Boktryckeri, 1948.

Hollander, Harm W. *Joseph as an Ethical Model in the Testaments of the Twelve Patriarchs.* Studia in Veteris Testamenti Pseudepigrapha, vol. 6. Leiden: E. J. Brill, 1981.

Hollander, Harm W., and Marinus de Jonge. *The Testaments of the Twelve Patriarchs: A Commentary.* Studia in Veteris Testamenti Pseudepigrapha, vol. 8. Leiden: E. J. Brill, 1985.

Horovitz, Jakob. "Osiris im Midrasch? Die haggadischen Überlieferungen über das Grab Josephs." In *Die Josephserzählung.* Frankfurt am Main: Kaufmann, 1921, 120–46.

Iser, Wolfgang. "The Reading Process: A Phenomenological Approach." In *The Implied Reader: Patterns of Communication in Prose Fiction from Bunyan to Beckett.* Baltimore: Johns Hopkins University Press, 1974, 274–94.

Jagendorf, Zvi. "'In the Morning, Behold It Was Leah:' Genesis and the Reversal of Sexual Knowledge." In *Biblical Patterns in Modern Literature,* edited by David H. Hirsch and Nehama Aschkenazy. Brown Judaic Studies 77. Chico, CA: Scholars Press, 1984, 51–60.

Jastrow, Marcus. *A Dictionary of the Targumim, the Talmud Babli and Yerushalmi, and the Midrashic Literature.* New York: Judaica Press, 1971.

Jeansonne, Sharon Pace. *The Women of Genesis: From Sarah to Potiphar's Wife.* Minneapolis: Fortress Press, 1990.

Johnson, Marshall D. *The Purpose of the Biblical Genealogies with Special Reference to the Setting of the Genealogies of Jesus.* 2d ed. Society for New Testament Studies Monograph Series 8. Cambridge: Cambridge University Press, 1988.

de Jonge, Henk Jan. "Die Patriarchentestamente von Roger Bacon bis Richard Simon." In *Studies on the Testaments of the Twelve Patriarchs: Text and Interpretation,* edited by Marinus de Jonge. Studia in Veteris Testamenti Pseudepigrapha, vol. 3. Leiden: E. J. Brill, 1975, 3–42.

de Jonge, Marinus. *The Testaments of the Twelve Patriarchs: A Study of Their Text, Composition, and Origin.* 2d ed. Assen: Van Gorcum, 1975.

—— "The Main Issues in the Study of the *Testaments of the Twelve Patriarchs.*" *NTS* 26 (1980) 508–24.

—— "The *Testaments of the Twelve Patriarchs:* Christian and Jewish: A Hundred Years after Fredrich Schnapp." *NedTTs* 39 (1985) 265–75.

—— "The *Testament of Levi* and 'Aramaic Levi,'" *RevQ* 13 (1988) 369–85.

Kee, Howard Clark. "The Ethical Dimensions of the *Testaments of the Twelve Patriarchs* as a Clue to Provenance." *NTS* 24 (1978) 259–70.

Keil, C. F., and F. Delitzsch. *The Pentateuch.* Vol. 1 of *Commentary on the Old Testament.* Translated by James Martin. Leipzig: Dörffling und Franke, 1862–72; reprint, Grand Rapids, MI: William B. Eerdmans, no date.

Keuls, Eva C. *The Reign of the Phallus: Sexual Politics in Ancient Athens.* New York: Harper & Row, 1985.

Klein, Michael L. "Associative and Complementary Translation in the Targumim." *Eretz Israel* 16 (H. M. Orlinsky vol., 1982) 134–40.

—— "Not to Be Translated in Public." *JJS* 39 (1988) 80–91.

Kugel, James. *In Potiphar's House: The Interpretive Life of Biblical Texts.* San Francisco: HarperSanFrancisco, 1990.

—— "The Story of Dinah in the 'Testament of Levi.'" *HTR* 85 (1992) 1–34.

LaCocque, André. *The Feminine Unconventional: Four Subversive Figures in Israel's Tradition.* Minneapolis: Fortress Press, 1990.

Langlement, F. "Israël et 'l'habitant du pays:' vocabulaire et formules d'Ex. 34:11–16." *RB* 76 (1969) 321–50, 481–507.

Leach, Edmund. "The Legitimacy of Solomon." In *Genesis as Myth and Other Essays.* London: Jonathan Cape, 1969, 25–83.

Lerner, Gerda. "The Origin of Prostitution in Ancient Mesopotamia." *Signs: Journal of Women in Culture and Society* 11 (1986) 236–54.

Levenson, Jon D. *The Death and Resurrection of the Beloved Son: The Transformation of Child Sacrifice in Judaism and Christianity.* New Haven: Yale University Press, 1993.

Levy, B. Barry. *Targum Neophyti 1: A Textual Study.* 2 vols. Studies in Judaism. London and Lanham, NY: University Press of America, 1986–87.

Lexicon Iconographicum Mythologiae Classicae. Vols. 4.1, 4.2, 5.1, and 5.2. Zürich and München: Artemis Verlag, 1988–90.

Liberman, Anatoly. Introduction to *Theory and History of Folklore,* by Vladimir Propp, edited by Liberman. Translated by Ariadna Y. Martin and Richard P. Martin. Theory and History of Literature 5. Minneapolis: University of Minnesota Press, 1984, ix–lxxi.

Malamat, Abraham. "King Lists of the Old Babylonian Period and Biblical Genealogies." *JAOS* 88 (1968) 163–73.

Mann, Jacob. *The Palestinian Triennial Cycle: Genesis and Exodus.* Vol. 1 of *The Bible as Read and Preached in the Old Synagogue.* Cincinnati: Mann Sonne Publication Committee, 1940; reprint, New York: Ktav Publishing House, 1971.

Mann, Thomas. *Joseph and His Brothers.* Translated by H. T. Lowe-Porter. New York: Knopf, 1948.

McNamara, Martin. *Targum and Testament: Aramaic Paraphrases of the Hebrew Bible: A Light on the New Testament.* Shannon, Ireland: Irish University Press, 1972.

—— "Targums." In supplementary vol. to *The Interpreter's Dictionary of the Bible,* edited by Keith Crim. Nashville: Abingdon Press, 1962, 856–61.

Milbank, John. *Theology and Social Theory Beyond Secular Reason.* Cambridge, MA: B. Blackwell, 1990.

Milne, Pamela J. "Folktales and Fairy Tales: An Evaluation of Two Proppian Analyses of Biblical Narratives." *JSOT* 34 (1986) 35–60.

—— *Vladimir Propp and the Study of Structure in Hebrew Biblical Narrative.* Bible and Literature Series 13. Sheffield: Almond Press, 1988.

Muilenberg, James. "Holiness." In vol. 2 of *The Interpreter's Dictionary of the Bible,* edited by G. A. Buttrick. Nashville: Abingdon Press, 1962, 617–18.

Murray, Gilbert. "Heracles the Best of Men." In *Greek Studies.* Oxford: Clarendon Press, 1946, 106–26.

Neufeld, Ephraim. *Ancient Hebrew Marriage Laws with Special References to General Semitic Laws and Customs.* London: Longmans, Green & Co., 1944.

Neusner, Jacob. *Messiah in Context: Israel's History and Destiny in Formative Judaism.* Philadelphia: Fortress Press, 1984.

—— *Comparative Midrash: The Plan and Program of "Genesis Rabbah" and "Leviticus Rabbah."* Brown Judaic Studies 111. Atlanta: Scholars Press, 1986.

—— "Toward a Theory of Comparison: The Case of Comparative Midrash." *Religion* 16 (1986) 269–303.

—— *Writing with Scripture: The Authority and Uses of the Hebrew Bible in the Torah of Formative Judaism.* Minneapolis: Fortress Press, 1989.

Nickelsburg, George, Jr., ed. *Studies on the Testament of Joseph.* SBL Septuagint and Cognate Studies 5. Missoula, MT: Scholars Press, 1975.

Niditch, Susan. "The Wronged Woman Righted: An Analysis of Genesis 38." *HTR* 72 (1972) 143–49.

—— *Underdogs and Tricksters: A Prelude to Biblical Folklore.* San Francisco: Harper & Row, 1987.

Noth, Martin. *Das System der zwölf Stamme Israels.* Beiträge zur Wissenschaft vom Alten und Neuen Testament 4, 1. Stuttgart: W. Kohlhammer, 1930.

Oden, Robert A. "Religious Identity and the Sacred Prostitution Accusation." In *The Bible without Theology: The Theological Tradition and Alternatives to It.* San Francisco: Harper & Row, 1987, 131–53.

Patai, Raphael. *Sex and Family in the Bible and the Middle East.* Garden City, NY: Doubleday, 1959.

Pavese, Carlo. "The New Heracles Poem of Pindar." *HSCP* 72 (1967) 47–88.

Perdue, Leo G. "The Death of the Sage and Moral Exhortation from Ancient Near Eastern Instructions to Graeco-Roman Paraenesis." In *Paraenesis: Act and Form,* edited by Perdue and John G. Gammie. Semeia 50. Atlanta: Scholars Press, 1990, 81–109.

Pfeiffer, Robert H. "A Non-Israelite Source of the Book of Genesis." *ZAW* 48 (1930) 66–73.

Pfitzner, Victor C. *Paul and the Agon Motif: Traditional Athletic Imagery in the Pauline Literature.* NovTSup 16. Leiden: E. J. Brill, 1967.

Phillips, Anthony. "Some Aspects of Family Law in Pre-Exilic Israel." *VT* 23 (1973) 349–61.

—— "The Book of Ruth—Deception and Shame." *JJS* 37 (1986) 1–17.

Philonenko, Marc. "Juda and Héraklès." *Revue d'histoire et de philosophie religieuses* 50 (1970) 61–62.

Plum, Karin Friis. "Genealogy as Theology." *SJOT* 11 (1989) 66–92.

Pritchard, James B., ed. *Ancient Near Eastern Texts Relating to the Old Testament.* 3d ed. with supplement. Princeton: Princeton University Press, 1969.

Propp, Vladimir. *Morphology of the Folktale.* Translated by Laurence Scott. 2d rev. ed. American Folklore Society Bibliographical and Special Series 9. Indiana University Research Center in Anthropology, Folklore, and Linguistics 10. Austin: University of Texas Press, 1988.

Rabin, Chaim. "Hittite Words in Hebrew." *Or* 32 (1963) 134–36.

von Rad, Gerhard. "The Joseph Narrative and Ancient Wisdom." In *The Problem of the Hexateuch and Other Essays,* translated by E. W. Trueman Dicken. Edinburgh and London: Oliver & Boyd, 1966, 292–300.

—— *Genesis: A Commentary.* Translated by John H. Marks. 9th rev. ed. Philadelphia: Westminster Press, 1972.

Rank, Otto. *The Myth of the Birth of the Hero: A Psychological Interpretation of Mythology.* Translated by F. Robbins and Smith Ely Jelliffe. New York: Robert Brunner, 1952.

Redford, Donald B. *A Study of the Biblical Story of Joseph (Genesis 37–50).* VTSup 20. Leiden: E. J. Brill, 1970.

Rosenberg, Joel. *King and Kin: Political Allegory in the Hebrew Bible.* Bloomington: Bloomington University Press, 1986.

Ruger, H. P. "Mit welchem Mass ihrmesst, wird euch gemessen werden." *ZNW* 60 (1969) 174–82.

Safrai, Samuel. קידוש השם בתורתם של התנאים ["Sanctification of the Name" in the teachings of the tannaim]. *Zion* 44 (1979) 28–42.

Sarna, Nahum M. *Understanding Genesis: The Heritage of Biblical Israel.* New York: Schocken Books, 1970.

Sasson, Jack M. *Ruth: A New Translation with a Philological Commentary and a Formalist-Folklorist Interpretation.* Baltimore: Johns Hopkins University Press, 1979.

Schäfer, P. "Die Peticha—ein Proömium?" *Kairos* 12 (1970) 216–19.

Schereschewsky, Ben Zion. "Mamzer." In vol. 11 of *Encyclopaedia Judaica.* Jerusalem: Keter Publishing House, 1971, 840–42.

Schmitt, G. *Ein indirektes Zeugnis der Makkabäerkämpfe: Testament Juda 3–7 und Parallelen.* Wiesbaden: L. Reichert, 1983.

Seeligman, I. L. "Lending, Pledge, and Interest in Biblical Law and Biblical Thought" (in Hebrew). In vol. 1 of *Studies in Bible and the Ancient Near East Presented to S. E. Loewenstamm on His Seventieth Birthday,* edited by Y. Avishur and J. Blau. Jerusalem: E. Rubinstein, 1978, 183–205.

Shinan, Avigdor. "The Angelology of the 'Palestinian' Targums on the Pentateuch." *Sefarad* 43 (1983) 181–97.

—— צלותהון ובעותהון: תפילותיהם של ראשונים בראי התרנומים לתורה [Their prayers and intercessions: Prayers of the ancestors in light of the targums to the Tora]. *Sinai* 78 (1975) 89–92.

Ska, Jean Louis. "L'Ironie de Tamar (Gen 38)." *ZAW* 100 (1988) 261–63.

Skinner, John. *A Critical and Exegetical Commentary on Genesis.* The International Critical Commentary. New York: Charles Scribner's Sons, 1910.

Slater, Philip E. *The Glory of Hera: Greek Mythology and the Greek Family.* Princeton: Princeton University Press, 1968.

Slingerland, H. Dixon. *The Testaments of the Twelve Patriarchs: A Critical History of Research.* SBL Monograph Series 21. Missoula, MT: Scholars Press, 1977.

—— "The Nature of *Nomos* (Law) within the *Testaments of the Twelve Patriarchs.*" *JBL* 105 (1986) 3–48.

—— "The *Testament of Joseph*: A Redactional Study." *JBL* 96 (1977) 507–16.

Speiser, E. A. *Genesis.* The Anchor Bible. New York: Doubleday, 1962.

Spiegel, Shalom. *The Last Trial, On the Legends and Lore of the Command to Abraham to Offer Isaac as a Sacrifice: The Akedah.* Translated by Judah Goldin. New York: Pantheon Books, 1967.

Steinberg, Naomi. "The Genealogical Framework of the Family Stories in Genesis." In *Narrative Research on the Hebrew Bible,* edited by Miri Amihai, George W. Coats, and Anne M. Solomon. Semeia 46. Atlanta: Scholars Press, 1989, 41–50.

Stern, David. "The Captive Woman: Hellenization, Rabbinic Judaism, and the Graeco-Roman Novel." Oral Presentation at the University of Chicago Divinity School, February 1994.

Sternberg, Meir. *The Poetics of Biblical Narrative: Ideological Literature and the Drama of Reading.* Indiana Studies in Biblical Literature. Bloomington: Indiana University Press, 1985.

Sturrock, John, ed. *Structuralism and Since.* Oxford: Oxford University Press, 1979.

Talmon, S., and Michael Fishbane. סוניות בסידורם של פרקי ספר יחזקאל [Aspects of the arrangement of passages in the book of Ezekiel]. *Tarbiz* 42 (1972–73) 27–41.

Theodor, J. "Die Midraschen zum Pentateuch u. der dreijährige pal. Cyclus." *MGWJ* 34–36 (1885–87).

—— "Bereshit Rabbah." In vol. 3 of *The Jewish Encyclopedia.* New York and London: Funk and Wagnalls, 1901–6, 62–65.

—— "Drei unbekannte Paraschas." In *Festschrift zum siebzigsten Geburtstage Jacob Guttmans.* Leipzig: G. Fock, 1915.

Thompson, Thomas, and Dorothy Thompson. "Some Legal Problems in the Book of Ruth." *VT* 8 (1968) 79–99.

Tigay, Jeffrey H. "An Empirical Basis for the Documentary Hypothesis." *JBL* 94 (1975) 329–42.

Tompkins, Jane P., ed. *Reader-Response Criticism: From Formalism to Post-Structuralism.* Baltimore: Johns Hopkins University Press, 1980.

van der Toorn, Karel. "Prostitution (Cultic)." In vol. 5 of *The Anchor Bible Dictionary,* edited by David Noel Freedman. New York: Doubleday, 1992, 510–13.

Travers, Herford R. *Talmud and Apocrypha: A Comparative Study of the Jewish Ethical Teaching in the Rabbinical and Non-Rabbinical Sources in the Early Centuries.* London: Soncino Press, 1933.

Urbach, Ephraim E. *The Sages: Their Concepts and Beliefs.* Translated by Israel Abrahams. Cambridge, MA: Harvard University Press, 1975; reprint, Jerusalem: Magnes Press, 1979.

VanderKam, James C. *Textual and Historical Studies in the Book of Jubilees.* Missoula, MT: Scholars Press, 1977.

Vawter, Bruce. *On Genesis: A New Reading.* Garden City, NY: Doubleday, 1977.

Vermès, Géza. *Scripture and Tradition in Judaism: Haggadic Studies.* 2d rev. ed. Leiden: E. J. Brill, 1973.

—— "Leviticus 18:21 in Ancient Jewish Bible Exegesis." In מחקרים באגדה תרגומים ותפלות ישראל לזכר יוסף היינימן [Studies in aggada, targum, and Jewish liturgy, in memory of Joseph Heinemann], edited by E. Fleischer and J. J. Petuchowski. Jerusalem: Magnes Press; Cincinnati: Hebrew Union College Press, 1981, 108–24.

Warnke, Georgia. *Gadamer: Hermeneutics, Tradition and Reason.* Stanford: Stanford University Press, 1987.

Westenholz, Joan Goodnick. "Tamar, Qĕdēšā, Qadištu, and Sacred Prostitution in Mesopotamia." *HTR* 82 (1989) 245–65.

Westermann, Claus. *Genesis 37–50.* Vol. 3 of *Genesis.* Biblisher Commentar Altes Testament. Neukirchen-Vluyn: Neukirchener Verlag, 1982.

The Westminster Study Edition of the Holy Bible. King James Version. Philadelphia: Westminster Press, 1948.

Williams, James G. "The Beautiful and the Barren: Conventions in Biblical Type Scenes." *JSOT* 17 (1980) 107–19.

Wilson, Robert R. *Genealogy and History in the Biblical World.* Yale Near Eastern Researches 7. New Haven: Yale University Press, 1977.

—— "The Old Testament Genealogies in Present Research." *JBL* 94 (1975) 169–89.

Wright, G. R. H. "The Positioning of Genesis 38." *ZAW* 94 (1982) 523–29.

Yamauchi, Edwin M. "Cultic Prostitution: A Case Study in Cultural Diffusion." In *Orient and Occident: Essays Presented to Cyrus H. Gordon on the Occasion of His Sixty-Fifth Birthday,* edited by Harry A. Hoffner. Alter Orient und Altes Testament 22. Kevelaer: Butzon & Bercker; Neukirchen-Vluyn: Neukirchener Verlag, 1973, 213–22.

York, Anthony D. "The Dating of Targumic Literature." *JSJ* 5 (1974) 49–62.

—— "The Targum in the Synagogue and in the School." *JSJ* 10 (1979) 74–86.

Zakovitch, Yair. על שלשה ועל ארבעה [Upon three and upon four]. Jerusalem: Makor, 1979.

Zimmermann, Frank. "The Births of Perez and Zerah." *JBL* 64 (1945) 377–78.

Zulay, Menahem, ed. פיוטי יניי [Liturgical poems of Yannai]. Berlin: Shoken, 1938.

Zunz, Leopold. *Die synagogale Poesie des Mittelalters.* Berlin: Julius Springer, 1855.

INDEX OF MODERN AUTHORS

INDEX OF BIBLICAL LITERATURE

HEBREW BIBLE

ANCIENT RECENSIONS AND VERSIONS

NEW TESTAMENT

INDEX OF ANCIENT LITERATURE

APOCRYPHA AND PSEUDEPIGRAPHA

398   INDEX OF ANCIENT LITERATURE

ANCIENT NEAR EASTERN SOURCES

CLASSICAL AUTHORS AND TEXTS

CHRISTIAN AUTHORS

SUPPLEMENTS

TO THE

JOURNAL FOR THE STUDY OF JUDAISM

Formerly Studia Post-Biblica

ISSN 1384-1261